critical race theory
critical suicide studies
critical whiteness
critique
Cuestionamos
curiosity
death practices
decolonial liberatory-based practices
deep organizing
dérive, the
drumming
embodied expression
embodied knowledge
emergent strategy
empathy
energy work
erasure, avoiding thereof
esoteric wisdom traditions
ethnodrama
etymology
existentialism
externalizing
failure
fat positivity
feminism
feminst ethics of care
fermentation
flâner
food sovereignty
forest bathing
fragments/fragmentation
freedom
generous systems
gift economies
Grace Lee Boggs
grief as nonlinear
group work
groups
harm reduction
healing circles
healing healers through the arts
healing justice
healing rituals
Hearing Voices Network
herbal justice
herbalism
holding space
humanness
humor
illders
improvisation
infinite blackness
intentional communities
interdisciplinary cataloging
intergenerational living
interspecies organizing
intuitive eating
justice-oriented counseling
land trusts
land, work, spirit, body
language justice
leaving well
liberatory education
life cycle, honoring the
liminality

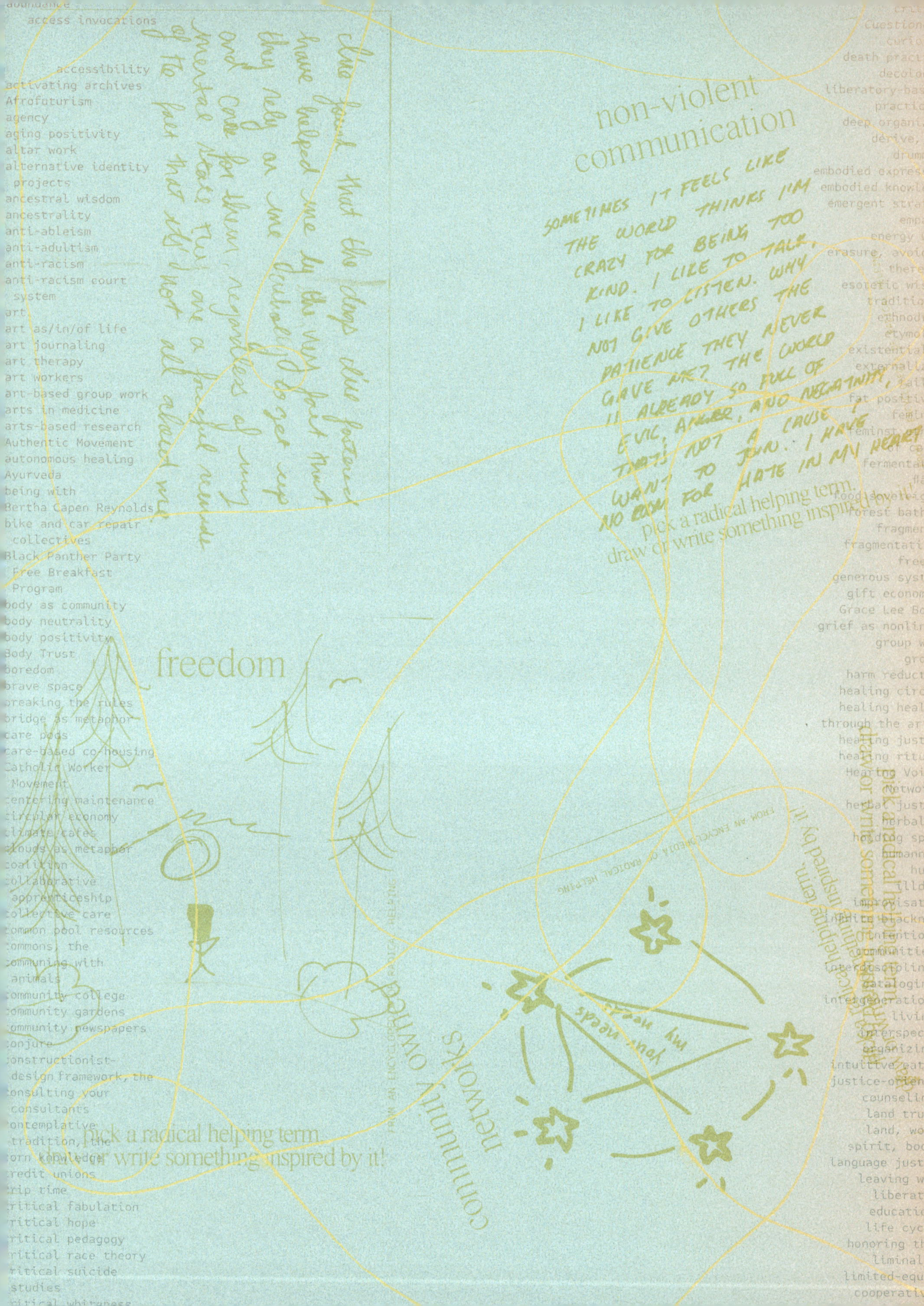
non-violent communication
SOMETIMES IT FEELS LIKE THE WORLD THINKS I'M CRAZY FOR BEING TOO KIND. I LIKE TO TALK, I LIKE TO LISTEN. WHY NOT GIVE OTHERS THE PATIENCE THEY NEVER GAVE ME? THE WORLD IS ALREADY SO FULL OF EVIL, ANGER, AND NEGATIVITY, THAT'S NOT A CAUSE I WANT TO JOIN. I HAVE NO ROOM FOR HATE IN MY HEART
pick a radical helping term. draw or write something inspired by it!
freedom
pick a radical helping term. draw or write something inspired by it!
community networks
your needs
my needs
FROM AN ENCYCLOPEDIA OF RADICAL HELPING
accessibility
activating archives
Afrofuturism
agency
aging positivity
altar work
alternative identity projects
ancestral wisdom
ancestrality
anti-ableism
anti-adultism
anti-racism
anti-racism court system
art
art as/in/of life
art journaling
art therapy
art workers
art-based group work
arts in medicine
arts-based research
Authentic Movement
autonomous healing
Ayurveda
being with
Bertha Capen Reynolds
bike and car repair collectives
Black Panther Party Free Breakfast Program
body as community
body neutrality
body positivity
Body Trust
boredom
brave space
breaking the rules
bridge as metaphor
care pods
care-based co-housing
Catholic Worker Movement
centering maintenance
circular economy
climate cafes
clouds as metaphor
coalition
collaborative apprenticeship
collective care
common pool resources
commons, the
communing with animals
community college
community gardens
community newspapers
conjure
constructionist-design framework, the
consulting your consultants
contemplative tradition, the
corn knowledge
credit unions
crip time
critical fabulation
critical hope
critical pedagogy
critical race theory
critical suicide studies
death practices
decolonial
liberatory-based practices
deep organizing
embodied expression
embodied knowledge
emergent strategy
empathy
erasure, avoiding thereof
esoteric wisdom traditions
ethnodrama
etymology
existentialism
externalizing
fat positivity
feminism
fermentation
forest bathing
fragments
fragmentation
freedom
generous systems
gift economies
Grace Lee Boggs
grief as nonlinear
group work
groups
harm reduction
healing circles
healing healers through the arts
healing justice
healing rituals
Hearing Voices Network
herbal justice
herbalism
holding space
humanness
humor
improvisation
infinite blackness
intentional communities
interdisciplinary cataloging
intergenerational living
interspecies organizing
intuitive eating
justice-oriented counseling
land trusts
land, work, spirit, body
language justice
leaving well
liberatory education
life cycle, honoring the
liminality
limited-equity cooperative

An Encyclopedia of Radical Helping

lingering
love
lunar cycle
magic school, the
mapping support
marginality (as a site of resistance)
marxist social work
membership theory in social work
mending
metaphor
mikveh
mobile libraries
movement lawyering
mutual aid
mycelia as metaphor
narradrama
narrative medicine
narrative therapy
nepantla/ nepantleras
nonviolent communication
ongoingness
peer counseling
peer-to-peer health network
person-situation perspective
perspective via faith
pleasure
poems/poetry
poetic meter
polarity work
post-oppositionality
postwork imaginaries
poverty-aware social work paradigm, the
power threat meaning (PTM) framework
pre(care)ity
prison abolition
professionalism without performance
progressive education
public benefits
public library, the
qigong
radical administration
radical care in the arts
radical childcare in movement spaces
radical inclusion
radical papermaking
radical presence
radical social work
Radical Therapist Journal, The
Rank and File Movement (RFM) in social work

reclaiming selfhood
recognition
redistribution
Reflecting on Justic
reflexivity
Reik
relational interviewing
relationality
resistance
resisting the parental loss narrative
resonance
respectful visiting
respite room
rest as resistance
revenge
revolutionary mothering
ritual
sanctuary
sandplay therapy
sauna
seed banking
sex positivity
shadow integration
Sick Woman Theory
slow textiles
slowness
social change ecosystem framework
social construction
social practice
social therapeutics
Social Welfare Action Alliance, the
solidarity
solidarity economy
somatic healing
songs/singing
sound healing
speculative design
spells
staying with the trouble
storytelling
street newspapers
strength perspective, the
sufficiency
sustaining movements
symbols
Taos Institute, the
tarot
temporary autonomous zones
Theatre of the Oppressed
theories of change
theosophy
therapeutic writing
togetherness
trans practices
transformative justice
traspatio
12-step programs
undercover anti-bullying teams
vigils
water
wildness
wintering as metaphor
wishes
witchery
yoga
zinemaking

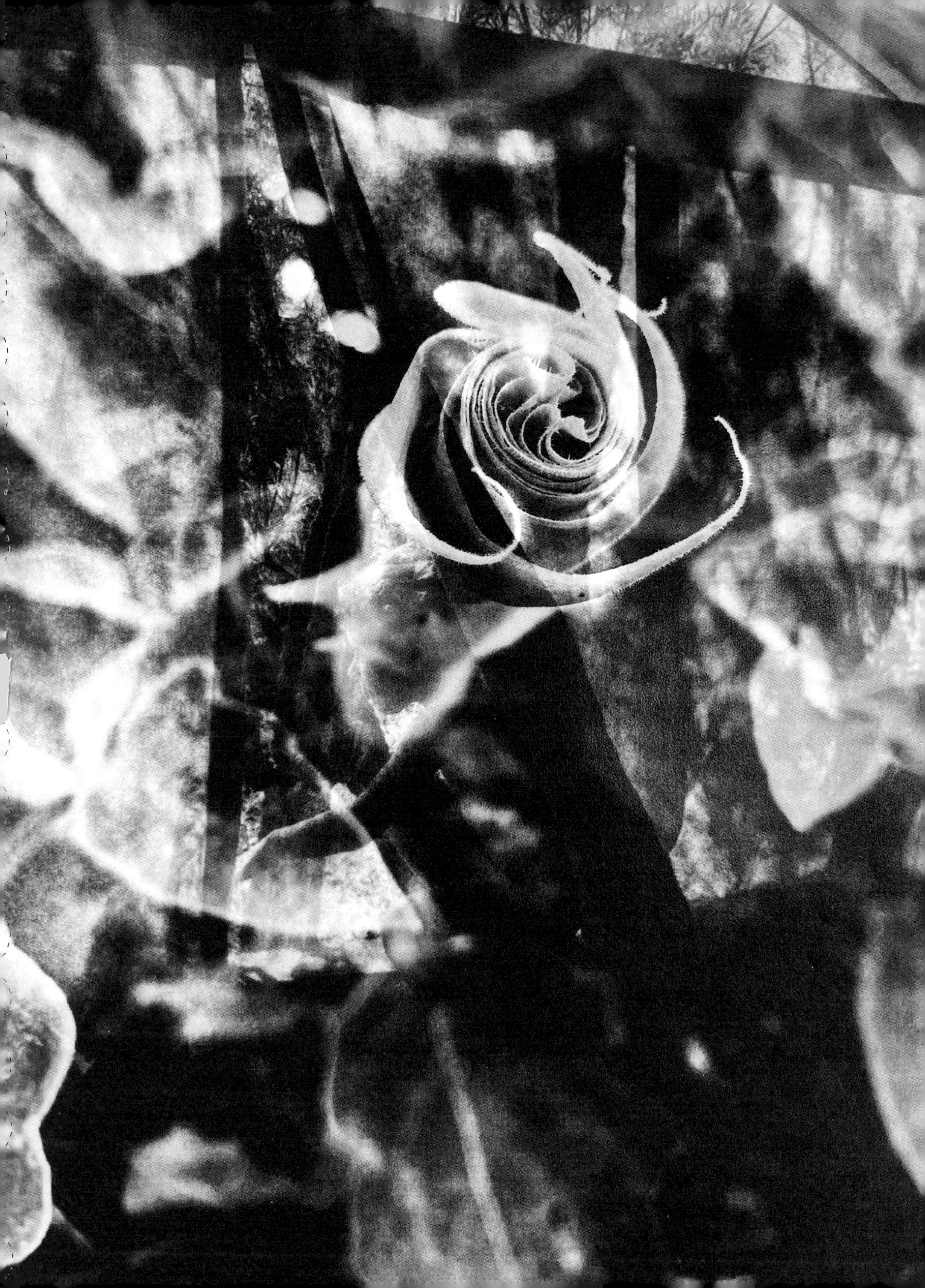

An Encyclopedia of Radical Helping

edited by
Erin Segal
Chris Hoff
Julie Cho

Table of Contents

Table of Contents

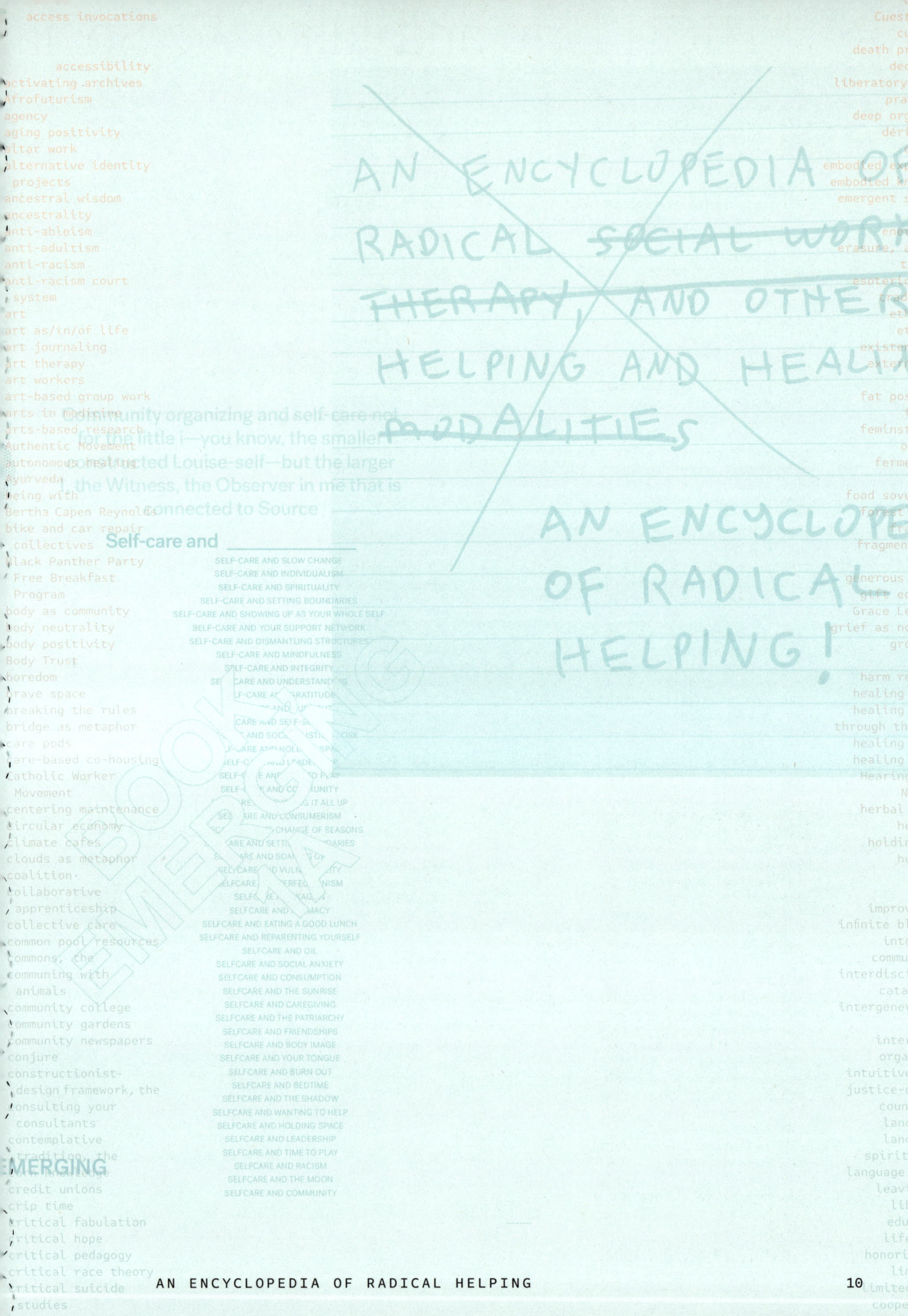
AN ENCYCLOPEDIA OF RADICAL SOCIAL WORK, THERAPY, AND OTHER HELPING AND HEALING MODALITIES
AN ENCYCLOPEDIA OF RADICAL HELPING!
Self-care and ______
SELF-CARE AND SLOW CHANGE
SELF-CARE AND INDIVIDUALISM
SELF-CARE AND SPIRITUALITY
SELF-CARE AND SETTING BOUNDARIES
SELF-CARE AND SHOWING UP AS YOUR WHOLE SELF
SELF-CARE AND YOUR SUPPORT NETWORK
SELF-CARE AND DISMANTLING STRUCTURES
SELF-CARE AND MINDFULNESS
SELFCARE AND EATING A GOOD LUNCH
SELFCARE AND REPARENTING YOURSELF
SELFCARE AND OIL
SELFCARE AND SOCIAL ANXIETY
SELFCARE AND CONSUMPTION
SELFCARE AND THE SUNRISE
SELFCARE AND CAREGIVING
SELFCARE AND THE PATRIARCHY
SELFCARE AND FRIENDSHIPS
SELFCARE AND BODY IMAGE
SELFCARE AND YOUR TONGUE
SELFCARE AND BURN OUT
SELFCARE AND BEDTIME
SELFCARE AND THE SHADOW
SELFCARE AND WANTING TO HELP
SELFCARE AND HOLDING SPACE
SELFCARE AND LEADERSHIP
SELFCARE AND TIME TO PLAY
SELFCARE AND RACISM
SELFCARE AND THE MOON
SELFCARE AND COMMUNITY
EMERGING
access invocations
accessibility
activating archives
Afrofuturism
agency
aging positivity
altar work
alternative identity projects
ancestral wisdom
ancestrality
anti-ableism
anti-adultism
anti-racism
anti-racism court system
art
art as/in/of life
art journaling
art therapy
art workers
art-based group work
arts in medicine
arts-based research
Authentic Movement
autonomous healing
ayurveda
being with
Bertha Capen Reynolds
bike and car repair collectives
Black Panther Party Free Breakfast Program
body as community
body neutrality
body positivity
Body Trust
boredom
brave space
breaking the rules
bridge as metaphor
care pods
care-based co-housing
Catholic Worker Movement
centering maintenance
circular economy
climate cafes
clouds as metaphor
coalition
collaborative apprenticeship
collective care
common pool resources
commons, the
communing with animals
community college
community gardens
community newspapers
conjure
constructionist-design framework, the
consulting your consultants
contemplative tradition, the
credit unions
crip time
critical fabulation
critical hope
critical pedagogy
critical race theory
critical suicide studies
critical whiteness

IN WHICH Erin and Julie, the Social Worker and the Graphic Designer Who Co-founded Thick Press, the Experimental Publishing Practice That Brings You This *Encyclopedia*, Address the Question,

"Why an Encyclopedia?"

INTRODUCTION

When people ask us how and why Thick Press ended up publishing *An Encyclopedia of Radical Helping*, we always begin by describing our fascination with the poetics of the index. Long lists of words and phrases have been an important feature of our work ever since we photocopied and distributed early iterations of *selfcarefully* (2019), by Gracy Obuchowicz, illustrated by Maria Habib, in the form of the very first title in our *book, emerging* series.

For the 2020 Printed Matter Virtual Art Book Fair, we organized our webpage around a poetic list of "findings" from our "inquiry into care," which is really just us reading and publishing books about care and trying to figure out together and with others what it all means.

We love these and other lists because they say very little but speak of so much; their poetry, we reckon, lies largely in the tension between economy and complexity.

Because we love lists and because we seek alternatives to medical-model (diagnose, treat) and neoliberal (efficiency, market logic) approaches to care, it made sense to create and populate a list of concepts and practices related to what, after conversations with our co-editor Chris Hoff, we came to describe as "radical helping."

Self-care and ____________

SELF-CARE AND SLOW CHANGE
SELF-CARE AND INDIVIDUALISM
SELF-CARE AND SPIRITUALITY
SELF-CARE AND SETTING BOUNDARIES
SELF-CARE AND SHOWING UP AS YOUR WHOLE SELF
SELF-CARE AND YOUR SUPPORT NETWORK
SELF-CARE AND DISMANTLING STRUCTURES
SELF-CARE AND MINDFULNESS
SELF-CARE AND INTEGRITY
SELFCARE AND EATING A GOOD LUNCH
SELFCARE AND REPARENTING YOURSELF
SELFCARE AND OIL
SELFCARE AND SOCIAL ANXIETY
SELFCARE AND CONSUMPTION
SELFCARE AND THE SUNRISE
SELFCARE AND CAREGIVING
SELFCARE AND THE PATRIARCHY
SELFCARE AND FRIENDSHIPS
SELFCARE AND BODY IMAGE
SELFCARE AND YOUR TONGUE
SELFCARE AND BURN OUT
SELFCARE AND BEDTIME
SELFCARE AND THE SHADOW
SELFCARE AND WANTING TO HELP
SELFCARE AND HOLDING SPACE
SELFCARE AND LEADERSHIP
SELFCARE AND TIME TO PLAY
SELFCARE AND RACISM
SELFCARE AND THE MOON
SELFCARE AND COMMUNITY

BOOK EMERGING

RGING

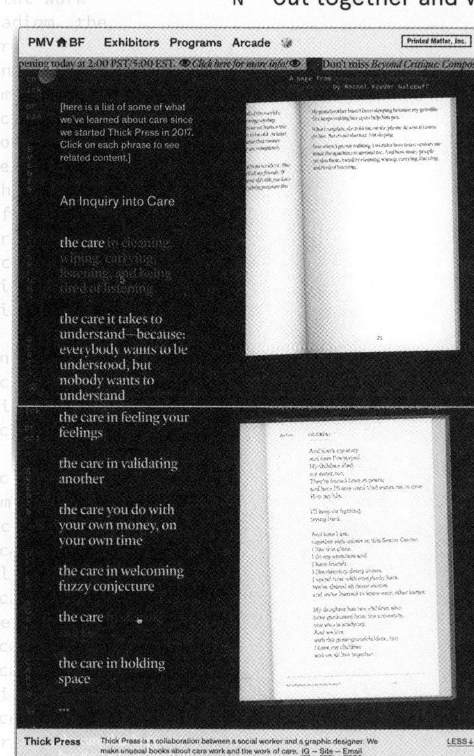

"Why an Encyclopedia?"

It felt important to us to create an encyclopedia that would be useful to radical helpers. As we explained in the Medium article that we circulated in order to elicit contributions, we wanted the book's

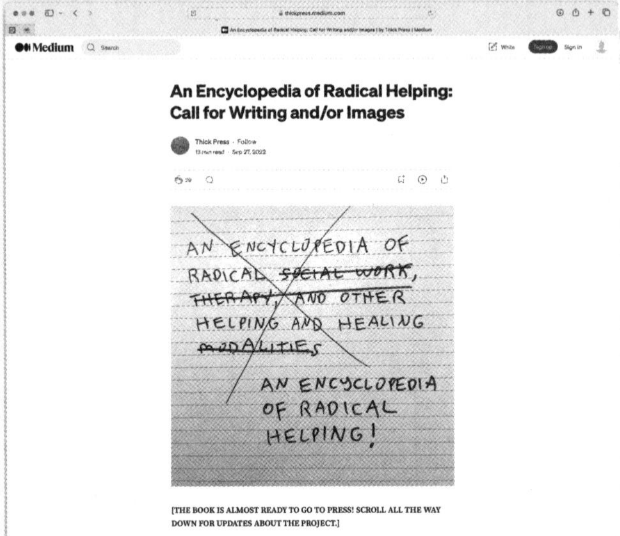

utility to lie not only in its content, but also in the way it playfully pushes against the encyclopedia, a medium that we associate with the impulse to reduce and present expert-vetted knowledge in taxonomical ways.

We decided that for our project, the "pushing against" would occur mostly via an inclusive, zine-like ethos: we would elicit all manner of writing and images from all manner of helpers and help-seekers, prioritizing process over product. Contributors might offer a definition of a concept, but that wasn't required; all we asked was that they somehow speak to the topic. We also decided to compile ideas and practices that don't often live together: high theory alongside the practical; art and creative nonfiction alongside academic writing; materialism alongside magick.

Partway into the project, we chatted with our old friend Elias Muhanna, who happens to be a scholar of encyclopedias, among other things. We learned that encyclopedias are old—like, one of the oldest known encyclopedias is from Roman times (and there are many younger, but still very old encyclopedias from the non-Western world). Some encyclopedias go deep, Elias explained; others go wide. Different encyclopedias use different methods to organize information. (All of this means that the Britannica-esque A–Z encyclopedias we picture when we hear the word "encylopedia" represent just a drop in the bucket.) When describing the people who compile encyclopedias, Elias used a word we had never heard before: "encyclopedist." We also learned that playful subversiveness is not just within the purview of contemporary literary types riffing on the encyclopedia; Elias shared with us the famous story of Diderot, whose Enlightenment-era encyclopedia hid critiques of religion in clever, ironic ways. For example, the cross-references for the work "anthropophagy" (which means cannibalism) sent readers to entries for "altar," "communion," and "Eucharist"!

I haven't been helped yet.

reclaiming selfhood

recognition
redistribution
Reflecting on Justice
reflexivity
Reiki
relational
interviewing
relationality
resistance
resisting the
parental loss
narrative
resonance
respectful visiting
respite rooms
rest as resistance
revenge
revolutionary
mothering
ritual
sanctuary
sandplay therapy
sauna
seed banking
sex positivity
shadow integration
Sick Woman Theory
slow textiles
slowness
social change
ecosystem framework
social construction
social practice
social therapeutics
Social Welfare Action
Alliance, the
solidarity
solidarity economy
somatic healing
songs/singing
sound healing
speculative design
spells
staying with the
trouble
storytelling
street newspaper
strengths
perspective, the
sufficiency
sustaining movement
symbol
Taos Institute, the
tarot
temporary autonomous
zones
Theatre of the
Oppressed
theories of change
theosophy
therapeutic writing
togetherness
trans practices
transformative
justice
traspatio
12-step programs
undercover anti-
bullying teams
vigil
water
wildness
wintering as metaphor
wishes
witchery
yoga
zinemaking

FEELING VERY ANXIOUS - THIS IS A LOT RIGHT NOW. THERE'S A LOT OF PEOPLE AND IT'S ALL QUITE LOUD - PEOPLE PUSH AND DON'T SAY SORRY. PEOPLE STAND AND HAVE CONVERSATIONS IN THE MIDDLE OF THE WALKWAYS. MY FRIENDS ARE EVERYWHERE, AND NO WHERE WHEN I NEED THEM. IT'S A LOT

pick a radical helping term,
draw or write something inspired by it!

FROM AN ENCYCLOPEDIA OF RADICAL HELPING

trans practices

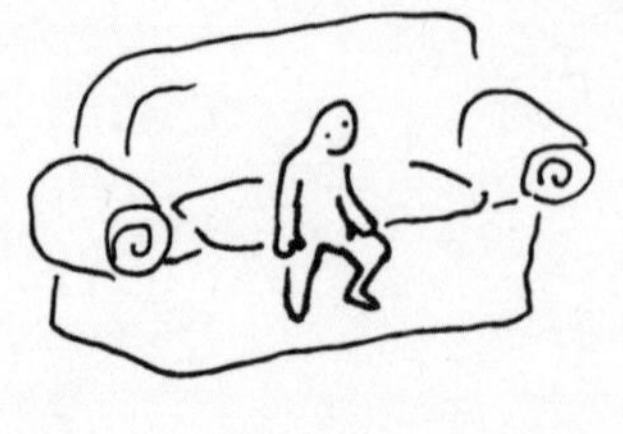

FROM AN ENCYCLOPEDIA OF RADICAL HELPING

pick a radical helping term,
draw or write something inspired by it!

anti-ableism

i had knee surgery for a genetic defect on my meniscus becoming disabled as an adult and experiencing the pity, the stares, the helpers, the oh oh let me look aungers, was an experience. it's still an experience. since i'm not visibly disabled any more, ppl get annoyed that I walk slow, aggressively hurry past me, get in my way and don't move. It's annoying. thank u to the ppl who help

FROM AN ENCYCLOPEDIA OF RADICAL HELPING

pick a radical helping term,
draw or write something inspired by it!

What helps is knowledge

Especially slowly working through Science

ancestral wisdom

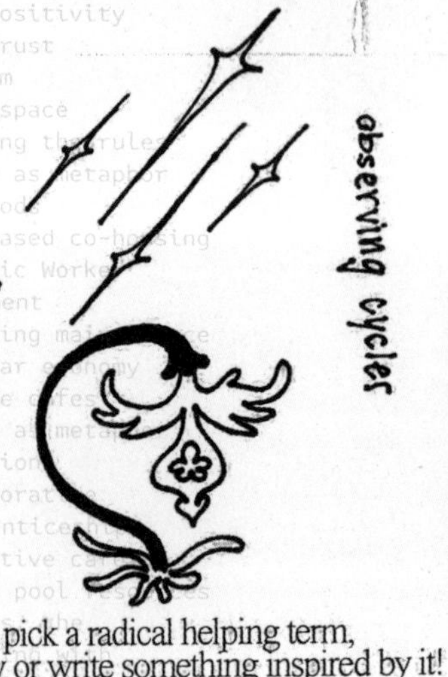

FROM AN ENCYCLOPEDIA OF RADICAL HELPING

pick a radical helping term,
draw or write something inspired by it!

togetherness

LAND BACK

FROM AN ENCYCLOPEDIA OF RADICAL HELPING

pick a radical helping term,
draw or write something inspired by it!

radical acceptance

AMOR
LOVE
rise UP
Break the chains

FROM AN ENCYCLOPEDIA OF RADICAL HELPING

pick a radical helping term,
draw or write something inspired by it!

wishes

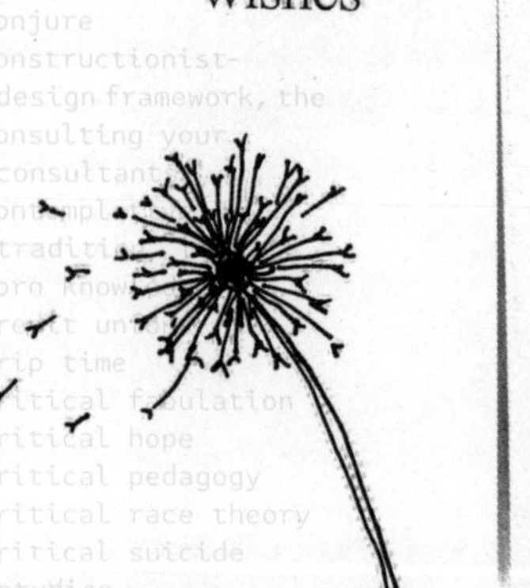

FROM AN ENCYCLOPEDIA OF RADICAL HELPING

Building a personal relationship with nature in a way that feels safe + unique to me. It has helped me navigate change + the struggles of living in the "Real World."

non-violent communication

SOMETIMES IT FEELS LIKE THE WORLD THINKS I'M CRAZY FOR BEING TOO KIND. I LIKE TO TALK, I LIKE TO LISTEN. WHY NOT GIVE OTHERS THE PATIENCE THEY NEVER GAVE ME? THE WORLD IS ALREADY SO FULL OF EVIL, ANGER, AND NEGATIVITY THAT'S NOT A CAUSE I WANT TO JOIN. I HAVE NO ROOM FOR HATE IN MY HE[ART]

pick a radical helping term,

reclaiming selfhood

Sharing folk knowledge of medicinal + local plants

• ALL THINGS SOMATIC. OVER THE LAST TWO YEARS I WAS IN A STATE OF CRISIS, WITH REGULAR PANIC ATTACKS, INTRUSIVE THOUGHTS, AND DISSOCIATION. ONE OF THE MAJOR WAYS I WAS ABLE TO FEEL BETTER WAS BOWLING WITH MY FRIENDS. A GROUP ACTIVITY WITH VERY LOW STAKES THAT IS MOSTLY SOCIAL, BUT ALSO CATHARTIC.

I believe in talking as medicine. Sometimes talking about my most extreme concerns have helped me to cope with them. Talking to friends a hundred times and while talking listening to what I say and how I am prefiguring the story. Listening to perspectives has helped me lately to check on mine, that own narrative.

art "is"

resistance

LIFE IS HARD. YOU ARE HERE, HAVE A SNACK!

(PIN)

FROM AN ENCYCLOPEDIA OF RADICAL HELPING

pick a radical helping term, draw or write something inspired by it!

I love YOU SO MUCH

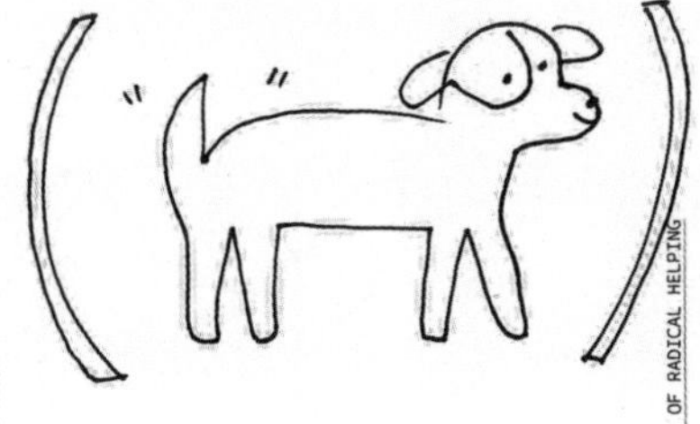

FROM AN ENCYCLOPEDIA OF RADICAL HELPING

pick a radical helping term, draw or write something inspired by it!

community owned networks

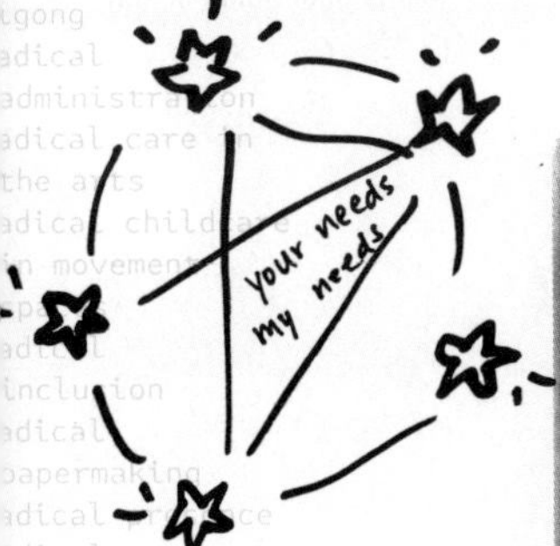

pick a radical helping term, draw or write something inspired by it!

FROM AN ENCYCLOPEDIA OF RADICAL HELPING

What has helped me @ least to concentrait on things is listening to pop music intromentally. I have ADHD so its very hard to focus which has made feel bad about myself.

being with

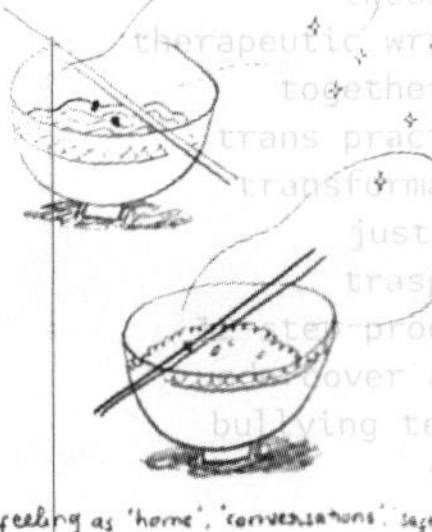

pick a radical helping term, draw or write something inspired by it!

Art therapy — ♡

mural making, involving physical movement

Anonymity

Half baked thought, but: It would be so much easier to use/access the public library if you didn't have to give your data away first. Paperwork & forms are not equally accessible to everyone, & not all people are comfortable + confident leaving copies of their personal information everywhere.

---

child life

drawing + painting, music, running wild, prayer, swinging, movies, ballet, reading, tea parties, crocheting

pick a radical helping term, draw or write something inspired by it!

FROM AN ENCYCLOPEDIA OF RADICAL HELPING

!! i don't pray bc i organize !!

i dont pray bc i organize
if you were me you'd do it too
bc i've seen victories on paper
that were losses in life
losses more than life
losses in a spirit for a liberated future

i don't want to lose you too.

everyday ill wonder how i can feed you
even if we aren't blood related
bc i know hunger from empty stomachs yearning for more
hungry for justice that lasts generations
infinite fighting chances for you here
and those who will come.

we are alive. living pictures of thee past.
of our ancestors carressing us w/ memories of there will be a tmrw.

we are tommorrow.

---

community bail funds

I CONTRIBUTED TO A BAIL FUND AT OCCUPY L.A. IN 2011. I DON'T KNOW IF THE FUNDS WE EVER USED. SO, I'M FOR IT.

—JOHN

FROM AN ENCYCLOPEDIA OF RADICAL HELPING

---

recognition

FROM AN ENCYCLOPEDIA OF RADICAL HELPING

I believe in talking as medicine. Sometimes talking about my most extreme concerns have helped me to cope with them.

Talking to friends a hundred times and while talking listening to what I say and how I am prefiguring the story.

Listening to perspectives has helped me lately to check on mine, that own narrative.

pick a radical helping term, or write something inspired by it!

---

community farms

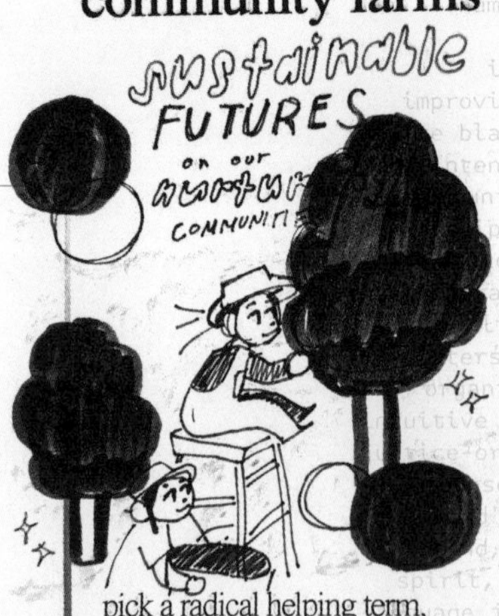

pick a radical helping term, draw or write something inspired by it!

FROM AN ENCYCLOPEDIA OF RADICAL HELPING

"Why an Encyclopedia?"

We left our conversation with Elias remembering that—beyond our intellectually derived itch to create something surprising and subversive within an existing medium, beyond our aesthetically oriented desire to become "encyclopedists"—this project is ultimately an earnest one, propelled by an impulse to gather together, share, and invite in

more,

more,

more,

of everything we've been learning about care and helping since we started Thick Press in 2017. For us, the format of an A–Z list organized by topic serves mostly as an arbitrary beginning, a scaffolding that encourages wandering and cross-referencing, which we hope offers space for

complexity
dreaming
failure
finding like-minded co-conspirators
healing
inspiration
knowledge-building
nuance
solace
worlds infused with love and freedom[1]
and more.

Just as the A–Z list offers structure, so does the book's design. The one-pica grid—which, old-school style, undergirds each page—turns

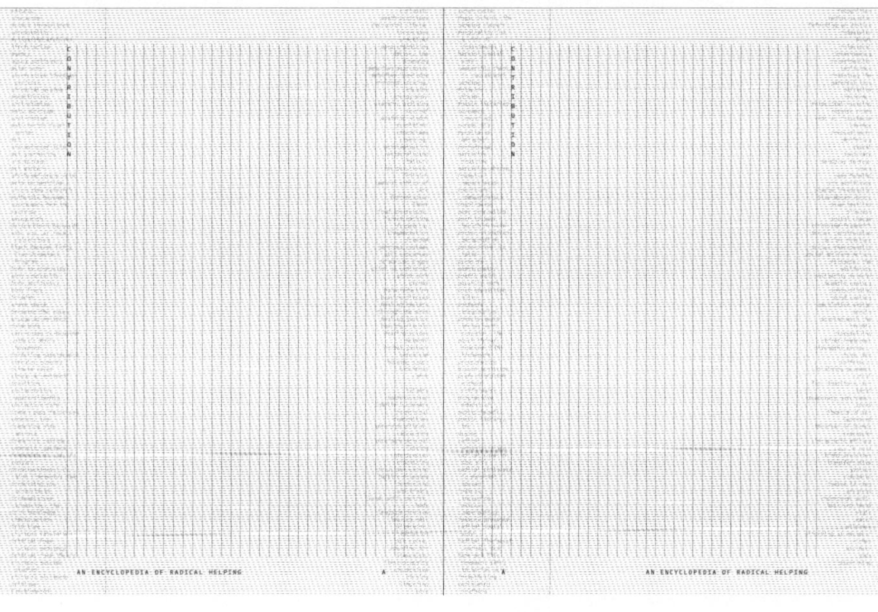

"Why an Encyclopedia?"

chaos into complexity, allowing for flexibility and expressiveness. The codex (by which we mean pages that are bound) unifies disparate forms, although, of course, unification is always soft and provisional.

Compositionism:

"...knowing that this has to be built from utterly heterogeneous parts that will never make a whole. But at best, a fragile, revisable, and diverse composite material."

BEYOND

(Here is a page from *Beyond Critique*, a *book, emerging* that we made in 2019 with Chris and his longtime collaborator, J. D'Arrigo. The quotation is from Bruno Latour.)[2]

It is our hope that *An Encyclopedia of Radical Helping*—which exists in terms of almost 250 marvelous multidisciplinary contributions; the process and people behind each one; and your experience of it all through the list, the grid, and the book itself—prefigures a world where multiple love- and freedom-enabling realities can coexist.

Huge and heartfelt gratitude to everybody who is making that world alongside and together with us.

—Erin and Julie
Washington, DC and
Los Angeles, CA
January 2024

1 We credit Robin D. G. Kelley for distilling what we, too, want into these two terms: freedom and love. See Kelley, *Freedom Dreams: The Black Radical Imagination*.

2 Latour, "An Attempt at a 'Compositionist Manifesto,'" p. 474.

IN WHICH Chris and Erin, a Family Therapist and a Social Worker, the Editors (Along with Julie) of This *Encyclopedia*, Address the Question, "Why Radical Helping?"

INTRODUCTION

In the summer of 2017, I [Chris] interviewed Dr. Scott Miller for my podcast, *The Radical Therapist*. He, with Mark Hubble, had just released their now seminal article, "How Psychotherapy Lost Its Magick: The Art of Healing in the Age of Science." In the article, Miller and Hubble detailed the finding that fewer people now turn to psychotherapy—33 percent fewer than 20 years ago, with most never returning after the first appointment. They also showed how, while people were turning away from traditional psychotherapy, the use of psychic services was growing annually by 3.4 percent. They explained how across all cultures, the history of healing has been infused with a sense of wonder and mystery that is now being lost to society's modernist tendencies—in particular, to the medical model and evidence-based practices. Even with the advancement of science-backed approaches, the "effectiveness" of psychologically informed treatments has not improved in more than 40 years. In their final analysis, they determined that "clinicians will have to embody what the majority plainly yearn for—a realm of possibilities for healing and change unbound by convention and traditional science."[1]

Fortunately, as the healing art of therapy was leaving magick behind, many helpers in the shadows and margins have continued to work with awe and wonder, bringing innovative practices to the work of helping. Most of these efforts are not new; indeed, some of the wellness philosophies and other helpful concepts described in this volume (e.g., Ayurveda, ancestrality, Reiki, drumming, herbalism, witchery, and many more) have been around for thousands of years. Many radical helpers and help-seekers whose work appears in this *Encyclopedia of Radical Helping* respectfully and lovingly apply those systems and concepts to contemporary life. Other contributors who see magick in drama, visual art, poetry, and storytelling organize their therapeutic practices around art-making or their artistic practices around collective healing and socially engaged meaning-making. Despite, or perhaps because of, the heartbreak involved in climate change, some contributors show us how finding meaning in nature and natural rhythms (e.g., harnessing the moon's power, embracing winter, communing with other species) can be both a precondition for human flourishing and a source of healing.

This *Encyclopedia* also describes many radical helping concepts that, even if they don't always feel magick-al, *do* stand in opposition to the neoliberal, medical-model logic that Miller and Hubble contrast with awe and wonder. Many non-medical-model approaches (particularly in social work, Erin's field) emphasize structural change, holism, group process, resistance to oppression, and/or material support via resource redistribution. *Encyclopedia* contributors who ally their work with movements for structural change often emphasize collectivity, mutuality, accessibility, and, increasingly, what it might mean to incorporate love, care, and healing (perhaps via magick-al means) into community organizing and consciousness-raising. With the advent of narrative and related postmodern therapies in the 1980s and 1990s, there has emerged a swath of helpers, often from family therapy (Chris's field), who focus on co-creating different futures with others rather than diagnosing and treating problems. Flowing through those and most other streams of radical

"Why Radical Helping?"

helping gathered in this *Encyclopedia* is the conviction that helpers must avoid controlling, disciplining, othering, and re-traumatizing the people we help. Related to this is the desire to erase social distance between "us" and "them," between those who "serve" and those who "receive." These articulations of helping stances are "radical" because they get at the "root" of care, before care became, as writer, cultural worker, and bodyworker Susan Raffo writes in this volume, "an institution… a responsibility without the assumption of connection."[2]

We realize that, in using the term "radical," we risk conflating the "radical" in "radical helping" with a specific US Leftist "radical" agenda. Aligning this *Encyclopedia* project with Leftist critiques of society is not inaccurate, per se. Many if not most of our collaborators would agree that 1) extractive, finance-based capitalism and heteropatriarchal racism are making us all sick; and 2) another world is indeed possible. But that doesn't mean that they/we all hold all the same feelings and interpretations, the same approach to how groups and institutions should handle issues of identity and speech, the same opinion about whether the carceral state should be reformed or overhauled, the same theory of individual healing and social change, and so on. One important example of diverging approaches: proponents of anarchism and mutual aid believe that government support staves off the revolution and creates stagnation, while other radical helpers advocate for a robust welfare state that redistributes wealth and generously supports care work (and perhaps also supports "impractical" labor like art-making). Are these two positions mutually exclusive? Is it possible to hold both—even if just for a moment—and see what emerges? It's not easy to sit with contradictory truths, but we believe it's an essential skill to cultivate.

An Encyclopedia of Radical Helping may be organized alphabetically, but there is nothing linear about the volume's content; it is more like a rhizome—a complex, interconnected network of ideas and practices that sprawls in all directions, defying traditional hierarchies and linear progressions. Like the underground rhizomes of plants, this polyphonic volume pre-consciously establishes connections and forges pathways that reach far and wide. It does not adhere to a single, predefined route, but instead encourages exploration and branching out into diverse territories. Do not let any contradictions found herein cause you to turn away. Contradiction is a pathway to deeper understanding, an invitation to explore the multiplicity of radical helping. It is on this winding path of contradictions that you may discover new perspectives, challenge your preconceptions, and ultimately uncover the richness of possibilities that lie at the heart of transformative helping and social change.

As you navigate its pages, letting the knowledge and experiences of radical helpers and help-seekers wash over you, perhaps following the cross-references signified by highlighted words on the edge of each page, you'll find that this *Encyclopedia* links you to diverse realms of thought, wisdom, and transformative practices, some of which have been nurtured and refined over generations. It is a living entity that invites you to weave your own threads into the fabric of radical helping, creating pathways to what might be possible in the expanding landscape of helping, healing, and transformation.

Each contribution in this *Encyclopedia* is an invitation to delve deeper into the magick of radical helping. Use the enormous reference list as a guide, allowing it to take you down unpredictable rabbit holes as you chart your unique course through the rich practices of helping. Whether you are a professional helper or somebody who volunteers their time to help others—and/or whether you yourself seek help—this rhizomatic guide to radical helping invites you to step into the project of enacting a world that supports healing and care, freedom and love.

—Chris and Erin
Los Angeles, CA and Washington, DC
January, 2024

1 Miller and Hubble, "How Psychotherapy Lost Its Magick: The Art of Healing in an Age of Science."

2 See Raffo, "On the Meaning of the Words We Are Using," 177.

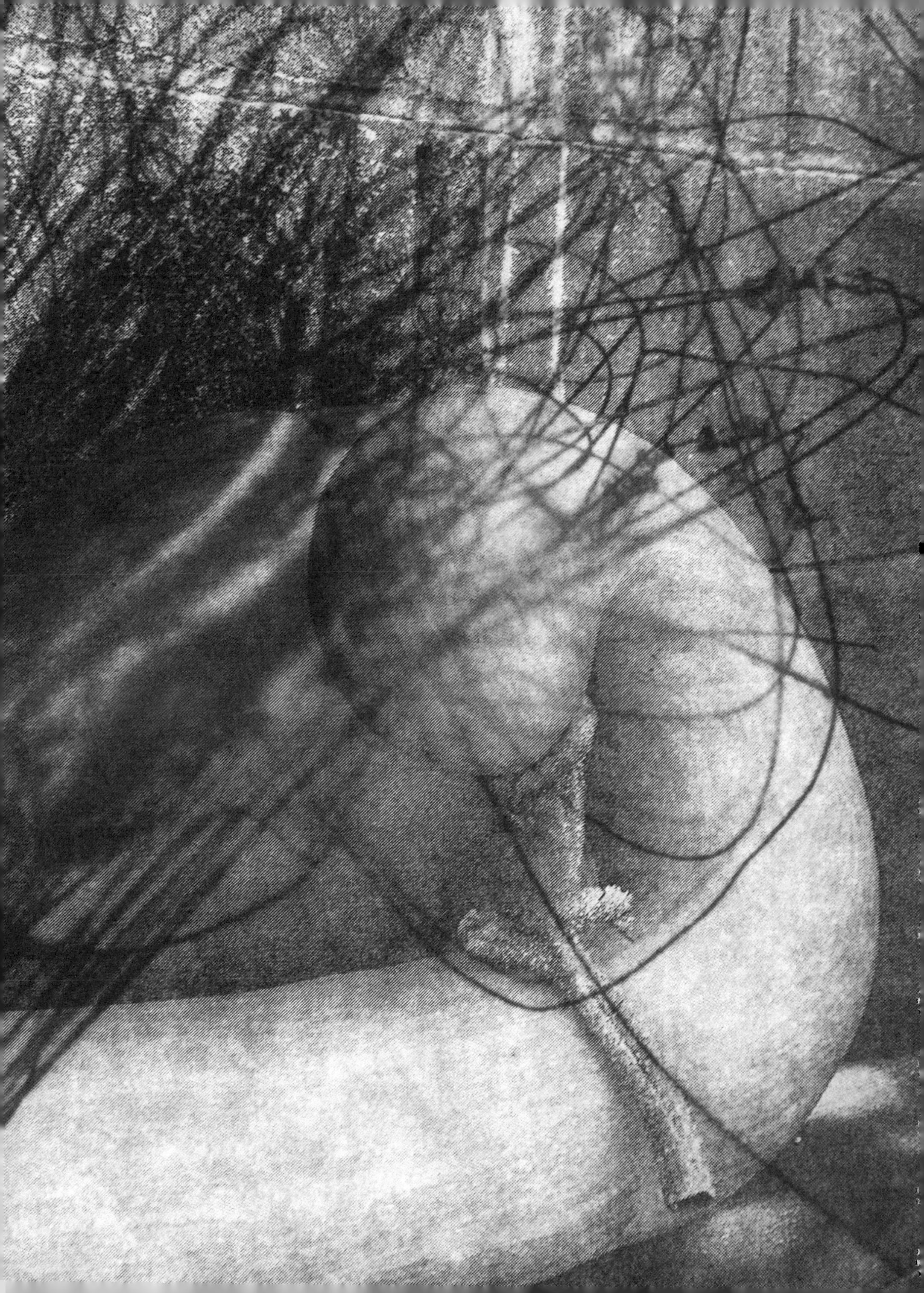

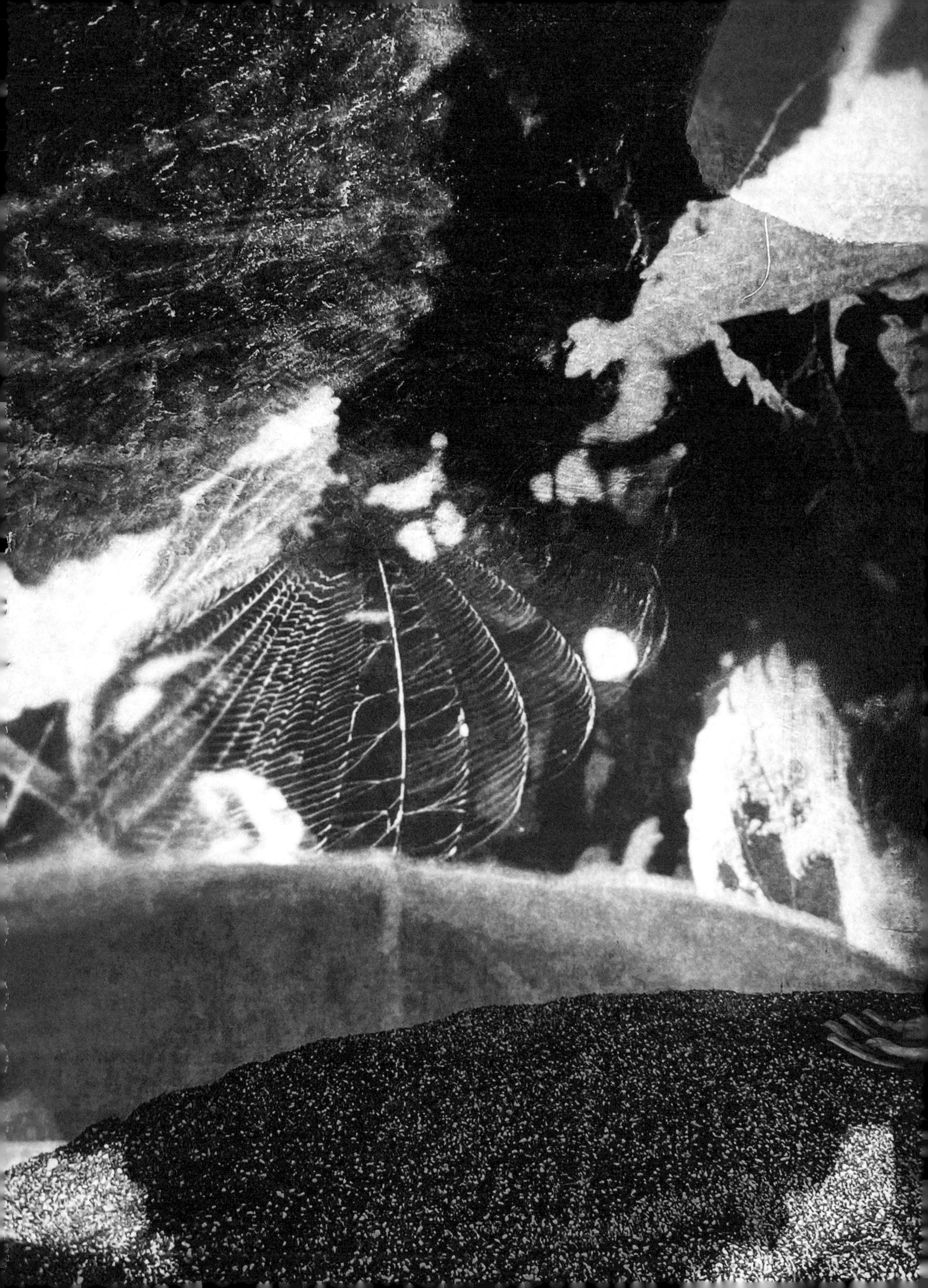

Encyclopedia Entries A–Z

ove
unar cycle
agic School, the
apping support
arginality
(as a site of
resistance)
arxist social
work
embership theory
in social work
ending
etaphor
ikveh
obile libraries
ovement
lawyering
utual aid
ycelia as
metaphor
arradrama
arrative
medicine
arrative therapy
epantla/
nepantleras
onviolent
communication
ngoingness
eer counseling
eer-to-peer
health network
erson-situation
perspective
erspective via
faith
leasure
oems/poetry
oetic meter
olarity work
ost-
oppositionality
ostwork
imaginaries
overty-aware
social work
paradigm, the
ower threat
meaning (PTM)
framework
re(care)ity
rison abolition
rofessionalism
without
performance
rogressive
education
ublic benefits
ublic library,
the
igong
adical
administration
adical care in
the arts
adical childcare
in movement
spaces
adical
inclusion
adical
papermaking
adical presence
adical
social work
*adical Therapist
Journal, The*
ank and File
Movement (RFM)

reclaiming selfhood
recognition
redistribution
Reflecting on Justice
reflexivity
Reiki
relational
interviewing
relationality
resistance
resisting the
parental loss
narrative
resonance
respectful visiting
respite rooms
rest as resistance
revenge
revolutionary
mothering
ritual
sanctuary
sandplay therapy
sauna
seed banking
sex positivity
shadow integration
Sick Woman Theory
slow textiles
slowness
social change
ecosystem framework
social construction
social practice
social therapeutics
Social Welfare Action
Alliance, the
solidarity
solidarity economy
somatic healing
songs/singing
sound healing
speculative design
spells
staying with the
trouble
storytelling
street newspaper
strengths
perspective, the
sufficiency
sustaining movement
symbol
Taos Institute, the
tarot
temporary autonomous
zones
Theatre of the
Oppressed
theories of change
theosophy
therapeutic writing
togetherness
trans practices
transformative
justice
traspatio
12-step programs
undercover anti-
bullying teams
vigil
water
wildness
wintering as metaphor
wishes
witchery
yoga
zinemaking

abundance

SEE: accessibility
activating archives
Afrofuturism
agency
aging positivity
altar work
alternative identity projects
ancestral wisdom
ancestrality
anti-ableism
anti-adultism
anti-racism
anti-racism court system
art
art as/in/of life
art journaling
art therapy
art workers
art-based group work
arts in medicine
arts-based research
Authentic Movement
autonomous healing
Ayurveda
being with
Bertha Capen Reynolds
bike and car repair collectives
Black Panther Party Free Breakfast Program
body as community
body neutrality
body positivity
Body Trust
boredom
brave space
breaking the rules
bridge as metaphor
care pods
care-based co-housing
Catholic Worker Movement
centering maintenance
circular economy
climate cafes
clouds as metaphor
coalition
collaborative apprenticeship
collective care
common pool resources
commons, the
communing with animals
community college
community gardens
community newspapers
conjure
constructionist-design framework, the
consulting your consultants
contemplative tradition, the
corn knowledge
credit unions
crip time
critical fabulation
critical hope
critical pedagogy
critical race theory
critical suicide studies
critical whiteness

CONTRIBUTION

exercises in abundance

YOU ARRIVE AT THIS PAGE, relatively close to the beginning of *An Encyclopedia of Radical Helping*. Hopefully, you feel comfortable and hydrated, ready to immerse yourself in alternative definitions. Before you begin reading this entry, is it time to take any meds? Do you need an extra pillow? Are you keeping cool/warm enough? Can you hear the waves rolling in the distance? Pause here if you need to get anything. There's no hurry.

~~~

Ready? Great, climb aboard and put on your life jacket. We'll begin our journey with a definition:

abundance (noun): a very large amount/more than enough of something
the state of having copious quantities of something

a brief etymological journey:

from Middle English *abundaunce* ~
from Old French *habundance* ~
from Latin *abundantia* (fullness, plenty)
~

from *abundō* (to overflow) ~
from ab- (from) + *undare* (surge, rise) ~
from *unda* (wave, billow)

On this micro voyage, consider:
How do I measure abundance?

Write your answer above whenever you desire (use a pencil, it may change). Some of the methods you may use to answer this question include speaking with your loved ones; eating a delicious meal; enjoying a form of art; looking out of the window; dreaming without limits, etc. If none of those seems to work, shouting at the sky is fine.

~~~

You wonder what the point of this exercise is. Perhaps at this point, you have an abundance of questions or apathy or disinterest or uncertainty or inspiration. The word returns to water and so will we.

Look. Ask your mind to drift. Journeys are transitory spaces. Absent time between here and there. Between the land you've come from and the land you're going there is only sea. See the waves tumbling over one another, breaking the shore's boundary in an overflow, surging towards the sides of the boat. The rush before a retreat that repeats. Hear the swelling and slapping against metal that, despite its weight, keeps afloat.

You've been told of patterns that predict subtle variations between now and then, a rise and a fall. How the moon's rope tugs, invisibly binding you to an unreachable place. Scientists measure gravitational slippage beneath plates. The captain listens for a wind whorling on the horizon and records wave speeds and frequency to find some rhythm pulsing in the vastness. You keep your eyes peeled for foaming crests.

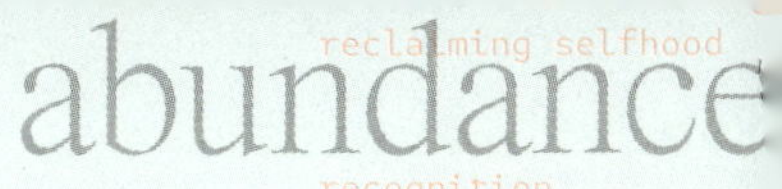

~~~

The noun *abundance* is often used in a positive sense, but you can't remember the last time you applied it to your life. It makes you think of nature: an abundance of water, greenery, and crops. It makes you think of capital: an abundance of wealth, property, and goods.

Before you reached the boat, the land you came from was a world where finite resources are carved up as profits soar, where bodies are codified and vilified into not-so-neat categories of This or That, where you are routinely told—by those who hoard abundance—that there is not enough. Instead, the measurement is abundance's opposite: scarcity. It sounds like Scare City. This noun is always used in a negative sense, and you can remember it applying to your life, your loved ones, and, in fact, every life.

Instead of a noun, you think of it as a verb. The doing word of a state that conjures up ghoulish migration policies, that cuts, cuts, cuts everything into smaller and smaller pieces, that prefers to balance the books than pay people fairly, that means your friends have to crowdfund for healthcare, that prides its vainglorious empire built on blood, that pushes families into foodbanks, that kills so many sick, mad, crip, disabled people year on year and then what? When does it stop?

You wonder how to balance scarcity (see its clouds lingering above the land?) with a drive to find abundance. That's why you got on the boat, right? As you were running to the jetty, frantically leaving voice notes before the signal cut out, trying to hold on to your loved ones' hands, cursing yourself for what you left behind, you saw it. On the horizon.

A glimmer of the possible not too far off. One that warmed your face before it was coated in clouds. Akin to a flower between pavement cracks. This life is shooting up in spite of. It's having enough and sharing it. It's making sure other people can continue, knowing reciprocation is an unwritten social contract. It's amassing Lucille Clifton's "collection of cares"[1] and sewing them into a city that can rewild over time. Can you see that city across the waves?

~~~

This entry is a way of unmaking and remaking abundance. A way of looking at language and the material and its usefulness. A game of how we could reframe meaning and make it into something useful that serves us all. It's a tongue-in-cheek experiment born out of failing to understand abundance.

Beyond its material definition, abundance feels like a mythic word. This attempt is, instead, an invitation for us to redefine what abundance could mean in a world on fire and how we can find it together. Think synonymously about how abundance can also be enough, joy, or contentment. Meaning is subjective, so we can bend it to fit.

You're almost at the end of the abundance entry and will have been wondering what, in your world, aligns with the original definition: a very large amount/more than enough of something. This isn't a trick question but an earnest proposition: invite abundance in. ➔

abundance

If you have some, there can be more. While it's easy to chalk up injustices, abundance is about what we have and do that outbalances them. In these seeds of possibility, remember Angela Davis saying, "Our work as activists is always to prepare the next generation. To create new terrains."[2] Growing a garden is a beautiful and radical act.[3] Tend to your patch and invite others in. Begin rewilding.

Abundance is the collection of herbs growing on your windowsill. When pain or fatigue is too great to sit up, you tilt your eyes to their shoots. Each hums with possibility. This one was/is a ________________ plant and this one a ________________. Their growth dances over your closing eyes and whispers: you are/have/can make/are part of enough. ❁

1 Clifton, "i am not done yet."

2 George, "Angela Davis Still Believes America Can Change."

3 Black Lodge Press, *Growing a Garden Is a Beautiful & Radical Act.*

BIO Jennifer Brough is a slow writer and workshop facilitator based in Nottingham, UK, who is currently working on her first poetry pamphlet, *Occult Pain*. Jennifer is also a co-founding member of resting up collective, an interdisciplinary sick group of artists that offers workshops on rest and creativity.

access invocations

SEE: relationality

CONTRIBUTION

Thick Press and Chris invited Margaret Price to contribute this text, found on the "Access Invocation" tab of her website, margaretprice.wordpress.com:

WHEN I GIVE PRESENTATIONS, I generally begin with an invocation on access. This invocation aims to present access as, in the words of Tanya Titchkosky, a "politics of wonder"—that is, something we can notice and question together, and something that will arise from the "interpretive relations" between our bodyminds. Because I am often asked to share my access invocation, I've created a page for it on this site, so that folks can adapt it for their own purposes. If you wish to cite it, I first used it (so far as I can remember) at the 2009 Society for Disability Studies Conference, as part of the plenary session "We Sing the Queer/Crip Electric: Disabled Writers Explore Presence Through Time, Space, and Memory." You can also just cite it from this website.

*

The image on the cover slide is _______. The title of this talk is _______.

As I begin, I want to recognize the space we're inhabiting together. [Describe some features of the space I notice—e.g. steps, lighting, presence of an interpreter or CART, crowdedness, air quality.] Please feel invited to use it in whatever way is accessible to you. For example, you may want to move around; stand up; lie down; put your feet up; go out and come back in; stim; engage with another person (for instance, by writing a note to a friend); tweet; take notes; or any other use of this space that feels right to you. Knitters, feel free to take out your work! If I was able to knit and deliver a talk at the same time, I'd be doing it.

Of course, it's not always possible to act on our access needs in any given moment. You might be in the middle of a crowded row of people; using a wheelchair or mobility device that's hemmed in by chairs; and you might inhabit a bodymind that doesn't feel safe moving around in public view. Access is not only a matter of taking care of *ourselves*. Insofar as it's possible, you might just want to take some time to notice the space you are inhabiting, and think about how your access is intersecting with others' as well.

I also want to recognize the cost and labor that have gone into making this space. Thank you, _________, for the labor of organizing this event, and thank you to ____ for generous sponsorship. Thank you to the people who have prepared this room, and who will clean it after I am gone, as well as to those who maintain its flooring and furniture, the light, the temperature, and the structure itself. Some of the things in this space—for example, the presence of CART—may not be familiar to you. Its presence is sometimes labeled as "expensive" or "an add-on," but in fact it is just as integral to an inclusive presentation as the presence of lights, air-quality systems, and sturdy flooring. And it costs a lot less than those items we no longer notice because they have come to seem "normal"—for instance, the abundant and well-maintained (though not gender-free) plumbing in this expensive university building.

Finally, I want to offer what's known in some communities as a trigger warning, or content warning. In this presentation, I will be discussing the issue of pain at length—including both physical and psychic pain—and at one point, I will describe what it's like to experience a psychotic break from my experience. Please feel invited to disengage from this talk in any way that feels right to you; please also feel invited to follow up with me later to discuss ways that you might engage with what I'm saying, but in a safer and lower-stakes setting. I am providing note cards if you'd like to jot any questions or notes to me; ______ will collect these before the Q&A begins. You are also welcome to email me. Please be aware that I might not be able to process questions after this talk well—

[This next part is just for presentations that have a PowerPoint and/or dedicated website. The dedicated website offered here as an example is one co-created with Aimi Hamraie, Melanie Yergeau, and Johnna Keller; hence the switch to "we."]

I'll be using a PowerPoint, which gives main ideas as I go along. I will describe all images as they appear. We've also created a space for Q&A here (https://sustainingaccess.wordpress.com). Our purpose is to try to take our time together and infuse it with crip time. Ellen Samuels, Alison Kafer, and Clare Mullaney have written powerfully on the notion of crip time, and in Alison's words, it is a way not just of expanding but of exploding time.[1] So our effort with this rudimentary web site is to add some additional dimensions, and an asynchronous time frame, into the spaces where we can potentially share ideas. We imagine this space as one that might be more accessible for those who prefer to communicate in writing rather than oral speech; or who can't be here physically, but have read a copy of one of our papers; or who simply think of an idea or a question after the fact. The nice thing about crip time is that it's not just for crips—or rather, it recognizes the ways that anyone, regardless of disability status, would benefit from a cripped form of space and time. ❁

1 Kafer, *Feminist, Queer, Crip*, 53.

B I O
Margaret Price is an associate professor at Ohio State University and the author of *Mad at School* (2011) and *Crip Spacetime* (2024).

accessibility
activating archives
afrofuturism
agency
aging positivity
altar work
alternative identity projects
ancestral wisdom
ancestrality
anti-ableism
anti-adultism
anti-racism
anti-racism court system
art
art as/in/of life
art journaling
art therapy
art workers
art-based group work
arts in medicine
arts-based research
Authentic Movement
autonomous healing
Ayurveda
being with
Bertha Capen Reynolds
bike and car repair collectives
Black Panther Party Free Breakfast Program
body as community
body neutrality
body positivity
Body Trust
boredom
brave space
breaking the rules
bridge as metaphor
care pods
care-based co-housing
Catholic Worker Movement
centering maintenance
circular economy
climate cafes
clouds as metaphor
coalition
collaborative apprenticeship
collective care
common pool resources
commons, the
communing with animals
community college
community gardens
community newspapers
conjure
constructionist-design framework, the
consulting your consultants
contemplative tradition, the
corn knowledge
credit unions
crip time
critical fabulation
critical hope
critical pedagogy
critical race theory
critical suicide studies
critical whiteness

critiqu
Cuestionamo
curiosit
death practice
decolonia
liberatory-based practices
deep organizin
dérive, th
drummin
embodied expressio
embodied knowledg
emergent strateg
empath
energy wor
erasure, avoidin thereof
esoteric wisdo traditions
ethnodram
etymolog
existentialis
externalizin
failur
fat positivit
feminis
feminst ethic of care
fermentatio
flâne
food sovereignt
forest bathin
fragments
fragmentation
freedo
generous system
gift economie
Grace Lee Bogg
grief as nonlinea
group wor
group
harm reductio
healing circle
healing healer through the arts
healing justic
healing ritual
Hearing Voice Network
herbal justic
herbalis
holding spac
humannes
humo
illder
improvisatio
infinite blacknes
intentiona communities
interdisciplinar cataloging
intergenerationa living
interspecie organizing
intuitive eatir
justice-oriente counseling
land trust
land, work spirit, body
language justic
leaving wel
liberator education
life cycle
honoring the liminalit
limited-equit cooperative

CONTRIBUTION

Access Suggestions for Public Events

WHAT MAKES AN EVENT ACCESSIBLE, and who is it accessible to? So many things determine who shows up for an event, and who isn't able to, including free time, money, childcare, transportation, interpreters, wheelchair access, fragrances, food options, and more.

This guide will help organizers think through ways to include a spectrum of people (with and without disabilities) in your public event. These suggestions are not comprehensive! They can prompt you to think through access barriers and how we can best disrupt them to create "liberated zones."

GENERAL GUIDANCE REGARDING ACCESS

ACCESS TAKES TIME AND COMMITMENT.
If you want your event to be accessible, think ahead! The longer in advance we consider these issues, the more likely we can address them. Remember that improving access is always a work in progress and we all have to start where we are!

WE LIVE IN A CAPITALIST, ABLEIST WORLD.
Unfortunately, access often comes with a price tag. People with disabilities should not be responsible for that cost. If you're an organization with a budget, notice what gets prioritized. Some access needs can be expensive, so create a plan to ask for financial support if needed, and find creative ways to make things work.

BE NON-DEFENSIVE WHEN RECEIVING FEEDBACK.
We often reinforce and replicate ableism, even when we are trying hard not to. Apologize, and work to find solutions. Defensiveness creates unnecessary barriers.

EVERYONE HAS ACCESS NEEDS, AND THEY CAN BE TALKED ABOUT WITHOUT SHAME.
Practicing speaking up about our own access needs increases the likelihood that our needs will be met.

ACCESS SUPPORT CAN BE SHARED.
Although some access needs, such as ASL interpretation, require specific skills and expertise, other forms of access support can be done collectively. This can look like tag-teaming note-taking or taking turns preparing plates of food.

DESIGNATE AN ACCESS COMMITTEE.
The larger the group of attendees, the more important this becomes, because it gets harder to meet everyone's needs as they emerge. Have designated volunteers who can trouble-shoot and find creative ways to respond to challenges that arise.

DON'T ISOLATE DISABLED PEOPLE FROM OUR FRIENDS AND COMMUNITIES.
If there is an accessible seating section, assume disabled people's friends will want to sit with us. If there is a shuttle to take disabled people from one place to another, assume we may be in a group, and there may be more than one wheelchair-user in the group. Don't let an access plan rely on the assumption that only one person will need an accommodation. If there is limited space, ask people to identify their party size ahead of time.

HAVE DISABLED PEOPLE ON THE ORGANIZING TEAM.
This makes accessibility a more organic process, identifying potential pitfalls early on, and shifting the idea that disabled people are only recipients of accommodation. ➔

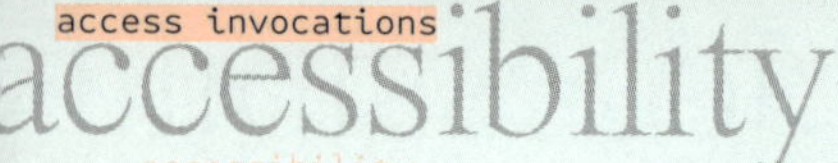

anti-ableism
crip time
language justice

REFLECT ON YOUR OWN ACCESS NEEDS.
Think about your own access needs and how they impact your experience of events. We can use our experiential knowledge as useful clues of what might be supportive for others.

HOLD COMPASSION FOR OURSELVES AND EVERYONE ELSE IN THE PROCESS.
Sometimes, even with the best planning, some access needs go unmet. A little humility goes a long way in addressing the frustration that ableism creates.

SPECIFIC ACCESS ITEMS TO CONSIDER INCLUDE

BEFORE THE EVENT:

- How are you promoting your event? Don't assume everyone is on social media or checks email. Text or call folks who might not see your posts or emails.
- Include access information with as many details as possible on any promotion, and invite folks to contact you with questions or additional needs.
- Ask folks to come to the event fragrance-free and provide instructions on how to do this.
- Ask people to stay home if they are sick, encourage masking, and ask for people to take rapid tests before attending the event.
- Use Arial or other plain, sans serif fonts, at least 14-point.
- Use high-contrast colors when layering text and background. If you're not sure if it's high-contrast, try viewing it as grayscale and see whether the text is still legible.
- Write image descriptions or alt-text for any visuals. If there is text in an image, include it in the image description so that screen readers can read it.

AT THE EVENT:

- Offer hybrid online/in-person options, with skilled tech people to manage livestreams or Zoom rooms, and plenty of staff or volunteers to respond to needs as they arise.
- Make sure it is clear how to get into the space, that pathways are unobstructed, and elevators are clearly marked.
- Provide seating, including sturdy chairs without arms.
- Provide lighting that is not overhead or fluorescent, and avoid flashing lights, including flash photography.
- Have folks provide visual descriptions of themselves before speaking, or hire audio describers to provide access for Blind and low-vision folks.
- Hire ASL interpreters, and provide them with materials ahead of time. If you can, work with teams of Deaf and hearing interpreters for increased language access.
- Provide interpreters for languages that you know will be used by people attending the event.
- Designate gender-neutral bathrooms to avoid anxiety or harm for trans and non-binary folks.
- Provide name tags for people to indicate their names and pronouns.
- Make sure the event space doesn't use air fresheners or scented cleaning products. Provide fragrance-free soap in the bathrooms and fragrance-free, non-toxic hand sanitizer. Set up HEPA filters to help clear fragrance and other particulates from the air. Create a fragrance-free seating area and make sure people know about it and keep it for folks who need it.

- If there is food, offer various options (gluten- and/or sugar-free, vegan, etc.), and post ingredients clearly for folks who have allergies or dietary restrictions.
- Hold awareness of "crip time," but also try to stick to a schedule, since many disabled folks have to plan their rides ahead of time.
- Designate a quiet space for folks who need a break from external stimulation.

For more detailed access suggestions, purchase Sins Invalid's disability justice primer at tinyurl.com/SinsShopping. ✿

BIO Sins Invalid is a Disability Justice–based performance project and movement building organization that centers Black, Brown, Queer, Trans, and Non-binary Disabled people's leadership and artistry. Founded in 2006 by Patty Berne and Leroy Moore, Sins Invalid continues to create work that articulates the wholeness and intrinsic worth of disabled people in the face of ableism, climate chaos, state violence, and other attacks on our bodily autonomy. www.sinsinvalid.org

activating archives

SEE: agency, ancestrality, brave space, critical fabulation, empath, harm reductio, herbalis, illder

CONTRIBUTION

GAINING PERSPECTIVE through "activating archives" has emerged as a critical facet of my socially engaged art practice. I'm drawn to processes and projects that surface difficult truths and liberatory possibilities held within the wrinkles and silences of historical materials. Rosine Association 2.0 (Rosine 2.0) is a model example of this method and its creative possibilities.

ROSINE 2.0

Initiated by Swarthmore College, Rosine 2.0 was organized as an interdisciplinary collective, which consisted of 20+ people including artists, harm reductionists, grassroots organizers and healers, archivists, and a core management team.[1] The papers of Mira Sharpless Townsend, a 19th-century Hicksite Quaker activist and co-founder of the Rosine Association, provided the initial historical inspiration.[2] The organization, founded in 1847, was run by women to help "fallen women" who engaged in sex work and substance use, faced physical abuse and exploitation, and experienced poverty and housing insecurity. In particular, two Rosine Association casebooks that chronicled the lives of 286 women penned by Townsend, and possibly others, provided the catalyst for present-day engagements.[3] Over two years (2021–2023), the Rosine 2.0 Collective grappled with historical legacies, envisioned collective futures, and cultivated radical empathy.

ORGANIZING PRINCIPLES

We grounded our creative work in the activation and analysis of historical materials and contemporary conditions to explore various facets of Philadelphia's history of care. The acquisition of the Townsend collection by the Friends Historical Library in 2019 resonated with the contemporary context of Philadelphia's struggle with the opioid and overdose epidemic. The impact of the Covid-19 pandemic and uprisings provoked by the deaths of George Floyd, Breonna Taylor, and the loss of many more Black lives also influenced the work. In developing Rosine 2.0, we encountered multiple ethical tensions:

Reconciling histories: While we wanted to reflect on the courage and commitments of Townsend and the other original Rosine managers (all privileged white women) in their context, we also recognized a need to transform these efforts to be part of present-day movements.

Honoring community expertise: Rosine 2.0 was determined to support community members in the preservation of their experiences. Prioritizing self-determination and demonstrating respect for the wisdom being shared was vital.

Addressing equity: We committed to working with women, trans-, and non-binary people whose lives are criminalized and subject to daily threats of violence. Each commission included compensation and decision-making structures to directly involve community collaborators.

Beyond acknowledging harm: Rosine 2.0 involved folks who have experienced persistent and systemic violence such as drug use–related harms, homelessness, incarceration, poverty, and criminalization of sex workers. We generated brave spaces[4] to break silences, foster self-determination, and build collective power. Community members' involvement was critical to building trusting relationships and catalyzing ideas for future, ongoing efforts.

Rosine 2.0's approach to activating archives prompted a departure from conventional historical exploration. Through engagement tied to care practices, we didn't observe history; we added untold stories and perspectives to an ongoing narrative bringing resources, capacity, and creative intensity to honor and refresh long-term efforts.

HOLDING MULTIPLE TRUTHS

"Taking inspiration but not direction from the Rosine Association, Rosine 2.0 explores how harm reduction and mutual aid reduce stigma and increase community health and social cohesion in marginalized communities."[5]

Rosine 2.0 formed interdisciplinary workgroups connecting artists and harm reductionists. In contrast to projects where an artist's individual practice defines the resulting work from the start, each team designed community-centered investigations. Ultimately, two new collectives emerged: Circle Keepers and Mad Ecologies. Their respective research-based processes led to art, events, and publications addressing harm reduction and collective care from diverse perspectives.

The Circle Keepers (Pamela Draper, Lilian Dunn, and Folami Irvine) brought together Philadelphia-based healers and helpers to support each other and share healing expertise. They gathered in green spaces across the city to convene healing circles. Each session began with sharing herbal libations to honor ancestors. Then, the circle moved into somatic practices, including silent nature walks and collective vocal toning. In response, Folami, Lillian, and Pamela, with artist/healer Misty Sol, created a Circle Keepers Deck featuring people, places, and naturally occurring plants found in the city. The cards and guidebook provided "special emphasis and reverence for networks of Black folk healing and Black women in Philadelphia who provide life-giving care to their communities."[6] Based on the group's desire to encourage others to utilize the practice, the deck functions as a conversation starter, a catalyst for play, and an invitation to inspire future Circles.

The Mad Ecologies collective (Nick Angelo, Raani Begum, Lulu Duffy-Tumasz, and Dont Rhine), organized listening sessions to reflect on recordings produced by community collaborators invited through Project SAFE.[7] Their sound investigation centered voices of unhoused community members involved in sex work and illicit drug use. The resulting text, "Philadelphia Principles,"[8] was co-written with a group of Philadelphians who shared a stake in reclaiming a radical core of harm reduction that can resist co-optation. This powerful and principled manifesto acknowledged harm reduction histories from the HIV/AIDS movement and writings released by Philadelphia-based collectives during the summer of 2020. It also identified shared struggles and beliefs to build cross-movement solidarities with labor and housing as well as environmental and disability justice.

CULTIVATING FUTURE HISTORIES

The companion publication, *Rosine 2.0: Futures and Histories of Collective Care*, provided multivocal points of entry into the Collective's analysis and process. Its form served as both a book and an archival container. Moreover, it aligns with the imperative of respecting the self-determination of Collective members and communities involved. The zines and other ephemera found in the front cover pocket were distributed independently through community networks, reflecting Rosine 2.0's commitment to supporting long-term organizing. Circulating these materials via community-collaborator distribution aligned with the imperative of respecting the self-determination of Collective members and communities involved.

Rosine 2.0's inclusive activation uplifted voices of care, sparked dialogue, and acknowledged the wisdom of lived experience. For example, *Nightshade Collective: Bound Together* resulted from a collaboration with Project SAFE's Nightshade sex worker collective and designer Elaine Lopez. *Bound Together* made space for Nightshade members to share their lives and experiences, told in their own words. The workshop and zine contrast and defy the perspectives shared in Townsend's Rosine casebook entries, which were framed and constrained by the narratives of respectability politics that defined the efforts of the original Rosine women.

Rosine 2.0 concluded in August 2023. The documentary evidence of the Collective's work forms the core of the Rosine 2.0 archive. Its legacy entrusts further insights to future researchers and readers, illuminating a path toward a more compassionate future.

YOUR TURN

How will your interpretations and intentions contribute to our collective future? There are many approaches to activating archives. Wherever the process begins, consider the following questions:

- From a radical helping context, whose lived experience must be centered? Why? [Take more time on this question.]
- Who else wants and needs to be engaged? Where are the tensions? Surface multiple truths!
- What form(s) will your work take—physical, digital, print, performative?
- What will you document and save? What must you let go of? Soon enough, your project will become an archive for future investigators, too! ❁

1 For more information, go to: www.rosine2.org.

2 The Mira Sharpless Townsend collection includes two Rosine Association casebooks, letters, journals, and commonplace books filled with journal entries, articles, and poems by Mira herself. For digitized materials go to: https://digitalcollections.tricolib.brynmawr.edu/collections/mira-sharpless-townsend-papers.

3 The handwriting in the casebooks is consistent with Mira's handwriting based on her letters, except in a few cases, which suggests some entries were written by other Rosine managers.

4 For an introduction to brave spaces and facilitation, read: Arao and Clemens, "From Safe Spaces to Brave Spaces."

5 Stakenas, Landes, and Price, *Rosine 2.0: Futures and Histories of Collective Care*, 7.

6 Circle Keepers, "Introduction."

7 Project SAFE is a grassroots, direct-service, and peer-based harm reduction organization. They organize with and provide women- and queer-centered services, focusing on community members living and working in the street economies in Kensington, Philadelphia. For more information: https://projectsafe.dreamhosters.com.

8 Mad Ecologies, *Philadelphia Principles: Radical Harm Reduction and the World We Want*. For more information: madecologies.com.

BIO Carol Stakenas commissions and produces public art, site-responsive exhibitions, and creative initiatives in service of strengthening social connections and building community power through socially engaged art and transdisciplinary alliances.

SEE: speculative design; wishes

CONTRIBUTION

Juniper Dreams

The world as we know it has come to an end and we must look for new places to live among the stars. Luckily, the Dream Incubator, a hyperbaric-healing-chamber-turned-rocket-ship, has been invented to transport black folks to freedom, powered by their own dreams of utopia. There are only 2 requirements to board this ship: 1) you must be able to dream up the world you wish to see and 2) you must travel lightly.

* * * *

JUNIPER ARRIVES at the chamber weigh-station with multiple bags attached to their person. Spirit heavy, back hunched, shoulders rounded, morale low. The only thing fueling them on what has felt like a never-ending trek across the scorched desert earth is daydreaming of a world where they can wiggle their toes on black sand beaches, where they can take naps in the serene mermaid coves that stay quietly tucked behind waterfalls.

Conductor: "I cannot allow you to board in your current state of being. Where we are going, you will never survive carrying this much stuff. You will break under the pressure."

Frustrated, frantic, and short of breath, Juniper asks, "Well, what am I supposed to do with it?"

Conductor: "You must find a way to rid yourself of the baggage."

"Don't you think I've tried that already?! No matter what I do, it somehow finds its way back to me. It's like I'm shackled to it forever…," Juni responds flustered, words trailing off in an air of defeat.

"I've tried throwing it away, but it showed up on my doorstep the next morning. I ran it over with my car. It didn't even make a dent. I even drenched it in liquor and set it on fire. Nothing works! It's indestructible!" At this point, anger and desperation ripped through Juni's words.

Conductor: "Breathe, my friend. Dream deeper. Dream Within," he says, gently resting his hand on his chest.

Juniper, annoyed and confused by the conductor's cryptic message, rolls her eyes and walks away in disappointment.

Too tired to fight this losing battle anymore today, Juni wanders until they find a soft place to lay their head.

Gazing up at the stars, Juniper asks her ancestors for help, requesting that they communicate to her through her dreams. The stars listened and just before dawn, whispered in her ears:

Let it out. Paint it. Scream it. Sing it.
Bury the rest. Wait for it to sprout.
Bring the seeds with you to your new world.

Under her ancestor's guidance, Juniper unburdened themselves little by little. The rolling red dunes lovingly absorbed the pain that radiated from their voice. What didn't come out in angry screams, messy paintings, or teary songs got buried deep in the sand.

Time passed by, but nothing grew in its place. Finally reaching the edges of their own limits, Juni surrendered. Falling to the ground, tears fell from their eyes. Those tears. Tears of healing and release began to grow life out of the ground. Cracked wide open, Juni floated upwards until she felt the softness of the clouds brush against her skin.

* * * *

It's Launch Day for the Dream Incubator. Juniper stands in line waiting anxiously for their turn.

Conductor: "Your bags are gone, but your spirit is still carrying too much."

A desperate Juniper bursts into tears at the thought of being left behind again. Ready to accept defeat, Juni turns to walk away when they feel a hand on their shoulder. Startled by a foreign yet familiar touch, she turns towards a warm and long overdue embrace.

"Here, let me take that for you." In that moment, the last bit of weight is lifted off their shoulders.

"You don't have to carry it alone."

The conductor smiles and shuts the door behind them. "Next stop, your wildest dreams!"

Juniper lets out a sigh and gazes into the

vastness of Space. Time seems to stand still. Stars dance outside their window. Juniper has never seen stars behave in such a still yet playful manner before. That is, until she realizes that she, too, is moving at the speed of light.

Juni smiles, whispers "thank you" to her ancestors on the other side of the window pane, and rests their head on another's shoulder. Eyes closed, Juniper allows herself to be whisked away by the dreams that carried her here.

* * * *

This is a story of transformation. Of healing oneself and the power of healing in community. We can't do it all on our own, but we have to start with ourselves. ❁

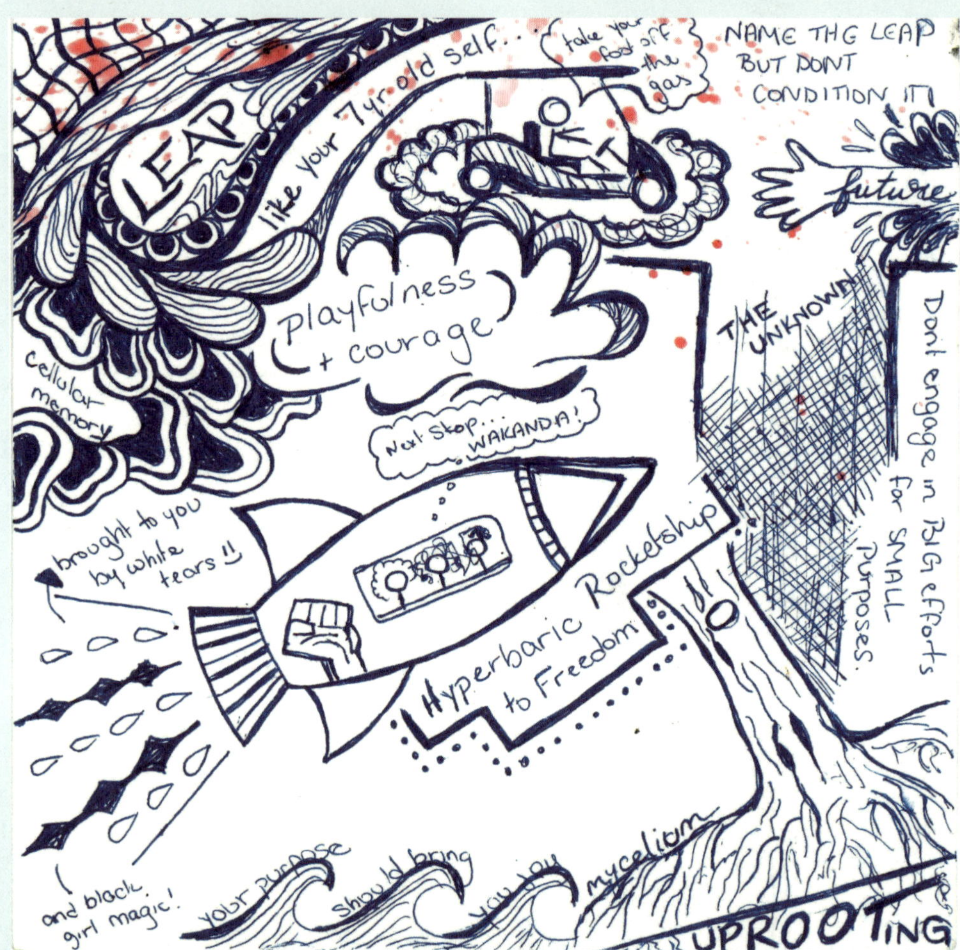

hyperbaric rocketship to freedom, pen and wax on paper.

B I O

Kassamira Carter-Howard is an artist, lover of sunflowers, and avid daydreamer creating bridges between worlds.

EDITORS' NOTE

"Afrofuturism" is a cultural and artistic movement that melds science fiction, history, fantasy, and the African diaspora to envision alternative futures rooted in Black experiences and traditions. It challenges the exclusion of Black voices from speculative genres, offering a lens through which to explore both the traumas of the past and the possibilities of the future. At its heart, Afrofuturism serves as both a critique of present-day realities and a celebration of the endless potential of Black imaginations. —CH

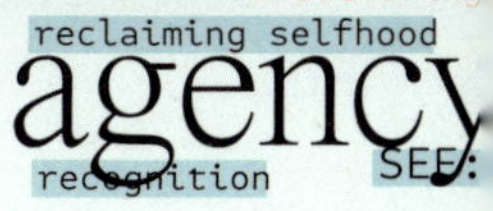

resistance
social construction
strengths perspective, the
trans practices

CONTRIBUTION

AGENCY AS A MYTH:

Dominant stories of singular, individual, human agency are intimately tied up to the post-Enlightenment idea of the "self" and have gained an atomising stronghold over our collective world. Consider the implications of this perspective, the limitations it imposes, and the alternative agentic stories it may overlook in the process. How might thinking about agency as a myth challenge these dominant narratives? How might reconfiguring agency as a myth open space for a more nuanced understanding of our intra-connectedness and collective responsibility in the (re)making of our world?

AGENCY AS A DANCE:

Imagine agency as a dance, a bodily enactment. Imagine it not as a singular, autonomous flow, but as movements that intertwine and harmonise with the rhythms and energies of those around us. How does embracing the idea of agency as a dance reimagine the foundations and potential of agentic action? How might it invite us to explore and reconfigure the dynamics of power, consent, and collectivity? In dance we not only intuit our motions with other collaborators, but we are able to grasp a new creative potential for other, for different. Always in motion, falling in and out of sync—and with *joy*!

AGENCY AS AN ECOLOGY:

The actions made available to us are a testament to the collective responsibility of all. To be in the world is to be *with* the world. We all co-constitute the universe and one another. Agency as an ecology accounts for the complex entanglements of intra-actions that play out—between humans, non-humans, dynamic processes and even inorganic matter. A multispecies web of motion. By reflecting on the idea of agency as an ecology, we are called to confront and challenge humanist visions of power and affect. Can we embrace agency in its transformative potential to foster sustainable relationships of reciprocity and nurture the interconnected web of agency for affirmational mutual futures? How might it invite us to recognise and account for non-human agentic power?

AGENCY AS A BRIDGE:

A web is a network of lines. Lines that connect from point to point, place to place, person to person. A line is a happening, a place of intra-play and coalescence. It is a bridge. If agency can be considered the power to act, then where does one acquire this power, and where does it go when acted upon? To imagine agency as a bridge is to account for the multidirectional flow of affect, action, and power. How might considering agency as a bridge support our commitment to the idea of intra-action? More than just an isolated act, but a give-and-take, an inhale and exhale. Does embracing agency as a bridge challenge the notion of agency as a singular one-way street, and invite us to explore how our actions can create stronger, more reciprocal bridges between persons and places and times? How can more and stronger bridges of mutuality support the dismantlement of oppressive one-way systems of power? ➔

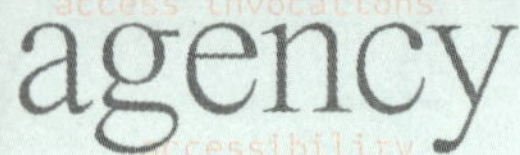

AGENCY AS A SEED:
The seed rests, biding its time, sitting in its own dormant potential. Imagine agency as a seed, waiting to be nurtured and cultivated. What might be the best environment to nurture and grow such a seed? To grow something of value and sustenance is to tend it with care, love, and intention. How might embracing agency as a seed challenge assumptions of agency as an innate, fixed, ready-made attribute? How might such reimaginings invite us to explore the ways in which we can actively foster agentic power within ourselves and others? What ingredients can we source to compost the most fertile soil?

AGENCY AS AN INVITATION:
To invite is to make a call, to request a presence. An invitation asks without expectation, something that is not involuntarily demanded of us, but a gentle drawing out. An invitation seeks us to exercise our own intention, asking us to actively embrace the call, and cultivate it. Here we find a space for active partnership. The invisibility of agency must end. Rather than a passive force that appears without warning, it can be reawakened as something we show up for. An invitation to step into full accountability for our power; to listen, learn, and shape our movements in the world. How might approaching agency as an invitation reinvigorate its transformative potential? Where, what, and who is it inviting us to? What might it be asking of us? How will you answer the call, and what will you be bringing with you? ❁

BIO Rae Turpin (she/her) is a community facilitator, artist, postgraduate practice-researcher, lover of nettles and all things urban wild.

aging positivity

SEE: ove, wildness

CONTRIBUTION

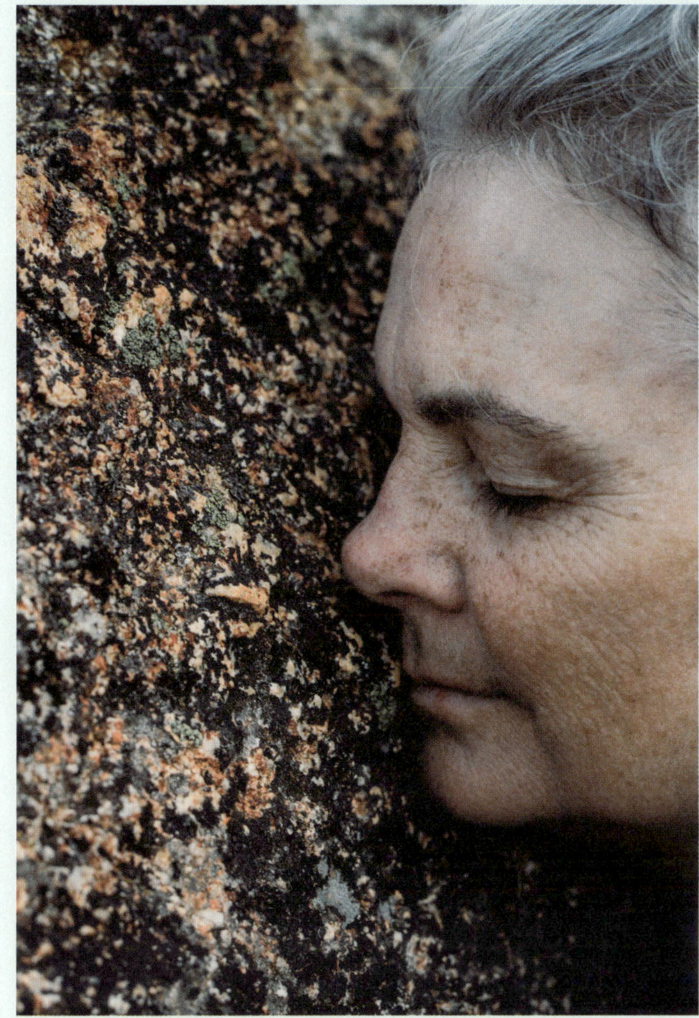

"Untitled," 2017, by Collin Morrow. Connie says, "I am in love with the textures and colors of granite, so making this photo with Collin helped me fall in love with my rough and colorful face!"

TO AGE WITH GRACE AND HUMOR or to fight the inevitable physical changes that come with middle and old age—this is a choice we must make daily if we are lucky enough to get to these life stages.

Nature is the force that keeps me from engaging in a war with my precious body. But each person's relationship with nature is as unique as the body they inherited from their particular line of ancestors. What inspires me may not resonate with you. In all offerings of "help," mine included, I recommend keeping an open mind in order to discover what works for you and what doesn't.

Spending time moving my body outdoors is my favorite self-care practice to enhance my health. Not only does it improve my health and increase my chances for longevity, it also brings me joy and feeds my soul. In my thirty-plus years of helping people positively connect with their bodies, I have observed the tremendous anxiety many individuals feel about trying to stay "healthy." I use quotation marks around the word because I can physically see the tightness that stems from fear as someone rejects the cookie or feels guilty if they eat it, if they miss a day at the gym or gain a few pounds over the winter. We all know that anxiety and stress lead to the opposite of health, so I am saddened when

aging positivity

death practice
ancestral wisdom
ancestrality
body positivity

I see people doing all they can to increase their chances of living a long life but hating the body they get when they succeed.

It takes courage to see our aging bodies as beautiful and valuable in a world that idolizes youthful appearance—a world where people and corporations make huge profits when we see ourselves as ugly and unworthy. More than 26 million people in the United States alone had some type of cosmetic surgery in 2022, an increase of 19 percent since 2019.[1]

I do not judge what others do with their bodies, and I absolutely understand the pressure that people, especially women, feel to look younger. As my wrinkles have deepened, my thighs turned lumpy, and my neck thickened and sagged, it's taken a whole lot of practice to see beauty in this changing body. But it's the choice I make every day because I refuse to let diet culture, the beauty industrial complex, or *anyone* dictate how I see myself.

This piece has been excerpted and adapted from Connie Sobczak's introduction to *Bodies of Nature, Nature of Bodies* (Thick Press, 2022), by Connie Sobczak and Collin Morrow. ❁

1 American Society of Plastic Surgeons, "American Society of Plastic Surgeons Reveals 2022's Most Sought-After Procedures."

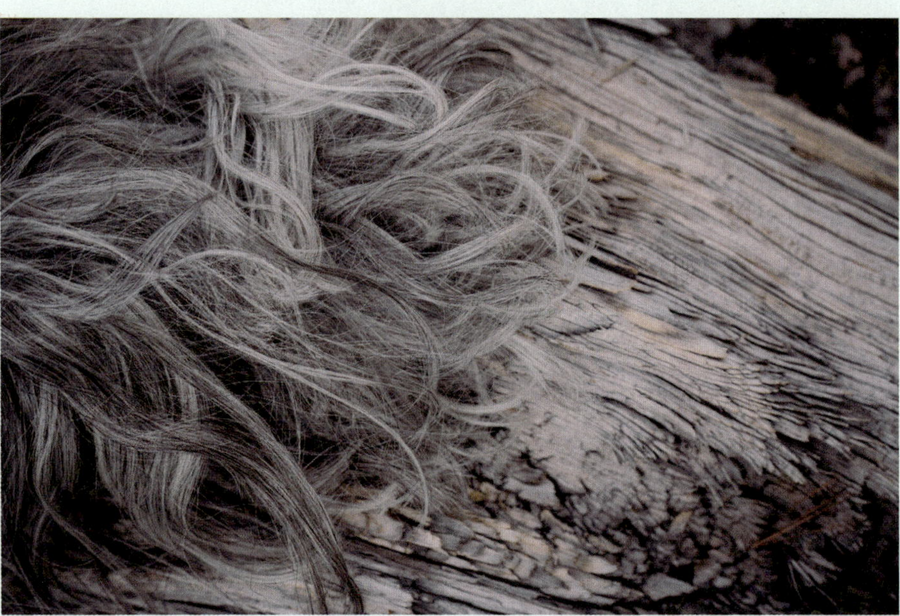

"Untitled," 2017, by Collin Morrow. Connie says, "My wild and curly gray hair seen against the backdrop of nature reminds me of the powerful line of free-spirited women who came before me!"

BIO Connie Sobczak (she/her) is the author of *Embody: Learning to Love Your Unique Body (and quiet that critical voice!)* and *Bodies of Nature/Nature of Bodies*, and Co-Founder and Executive Director of the nonprofit organization The Body Positive, as well as the leader of her new Wild Woman Within circles and host of "The Cooking, Eating, Healing Show" on YouTube.

altar work

SEE: ritual, sandplay therapy, water

CONTRIBUTION

AN ALTAR, an offering to them and to myself. We connect the senses, navigating a new level of intention and mindfulness—taste, touch, smell, sight, sound: each one to ground ourselves in the moment. I use the altar as a location for remembrance and reflection. For taste and smell I leave lost loved ones their favorite coffee on holidays; for sight, I leave collages I make from their photos: seeing them in futures I've created with their past. I play music for them, imagining the sound of their feet with mine, in a lifetime where we dance together again. Earth, fire, water, and air: elements I offer them in cups, candles, and in between cries. Connecting with my ancestors through altars as grounding work challenges western notions of healing. A healing that is learned through lineage, this altar a connection to myself and those who came before me. ❁

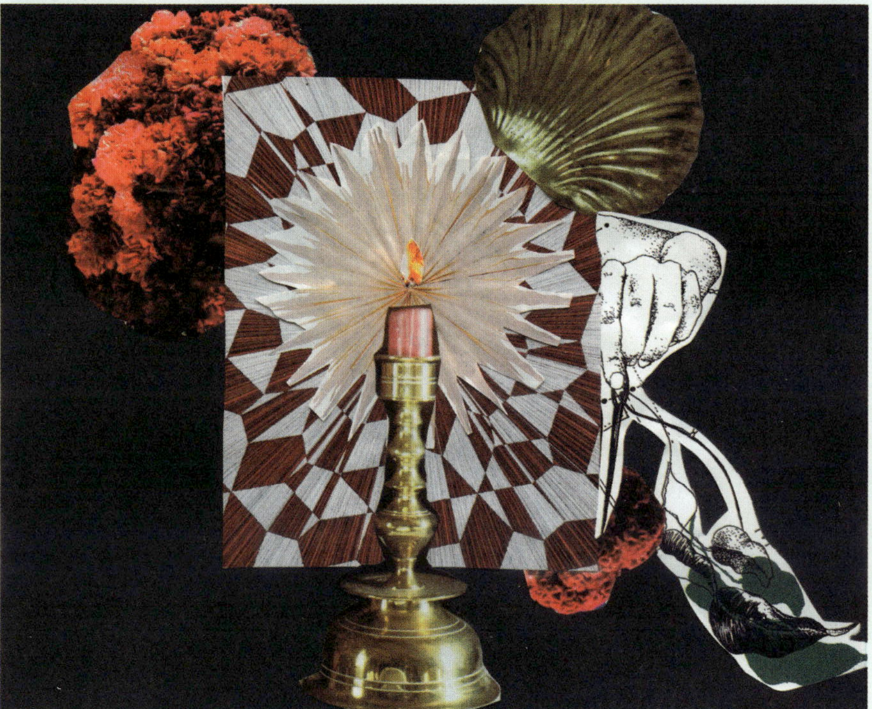

Ashley M. Lagrange, 2022, Mixed Media Hand-Cut Collage.

This collage was a visual altar created for my best friend's mother, April Sedall, who passed February of 2022. I made this hand-cut collage the week after her passing while I was facilitating an LGBTQA+ Grief Group. April battled lifelong cancer and utilized art, especially collage art, as a means of art therapy. This collage is meant to represent the craft that kept her going, which is a craft that has also kept me going.

BIO

Ashley M. Lagrange, M.Ed, LPC (They/Them) is a Queer Neurodivergent Fat Black DominicanAmerican Nonbinary Femme Therapist and Collage Artist born and based in NYC.

alternative identity projects

SEE: activating archives, agency, ancestrality, embodied knowledge, externalizing, failure, Grace Lee Boggs, group, illder

CONTRIBUTION

ALTERNATIVE IDENTITY PROJECTS[1] was proposed by Michael White, who pioneered narrative practices, as a way to reframe how we think about failure.

Failure is commonly understood as a problem that exists inside of us when we do not fit in, conform, or match up to expectations of productivity, success, confidence, strength, independence, and many other favoured ways of being that are asked of us in our culture. "Inadequate," "incapable," "falling short," and "left out" are a few of the ways in which people may describe this feeling of failure. In my conversations with people in therapy and community work, I have come to understand that sometimes, whole identities in themselves have represented a sense of failure for people who do not conform to heteronormativity, the gender binary, neurotypicality, Brahminism, and other normative ways of being.

The concept of alternative identity projects then compels us to ask: Could failure *not* be about inadequacy or falling short, but something else entirely? Could failure represent a person's refusal to live a life dictated by what's normative and favoured? Could failure open up a door to a precious knowing of a different life—"an alternative identity project"—that's home to what's most important and valuable to us? Is it possible that our so-called "failed identities" of being queer, trans, non-binary, disabled, people of colour, neurodivergent, and Dalit are in fact "successful expressions of resistance" and an audacious testimony to diversity? What would then become possible for us if we were to believe with all the stubbornness in our hearts that failure is not within us, but is a product of the unjust systems and norms around us? ❁

1 White, "Addressing Personal Failure."

BIO

Shweta Srinivasan, a narrative therapist and co-founder of TheMindClan.com, loves to nap, dance, walk by the beach, and sip on unlimited amounts of chai.

ancestral wisdom

SEE: narrative therapy; reclaiming selfhood; resistance; revolutionary mothering; strengths perspective, the; trans practices

CONTRIBUTION

What Is Your Legacy of Healing?

THE MORE TIME I SPEND with social justice advocates, the more I learn about the varied healing approaches of different communities. Many people I work with to build resilience recognize the need for some of the basic ideas—moving your body, getting sleep, connecting with people you love, finding ways to calm your nervous system—but when I ask about how healing is approached in their community, religious tradition, or cultural background, I often get a blank stare.

I encourage them to think about their ancestors and ask: Who were their healers in past generations? How did they operate? It's tempting to think that more modern approaches to healing are better, but what about the wisdom that comes from previous generations?

I would ask you to consider: Are you connected to those traditions? Do they bring you strength? Might they, if you learned more about them?

It is becoming increasingly clear that our current world disconnects us from others, which both isolates us and contributes to burnout. COVID made it worse, no doubt, but even before the pandemic we had begun living in increasing isolation. My guess is that if you connect at all to your healing traditions—either cultural or religious—you will find that those traditions encourage you to interact with other people.

Many religious traditions require a certain number of people in order for a congregational prayer to be recited or for a particular ritual to be performed. Many cultural and religious traditions include gathering a group of people to celebrate when a baby is born, or a couple marries, or to support people mourning a loss. The goal is to celebrate or mourn in community, not alone.

Will that by itself cure your burnout? I don't know. But I do know that learning from the wisdom of your ancestors and connecting to the people who care about you is an excellent first step to heal from burnout.

We each build resilience in ways that are unique to each of us as individuals; but let us not lose the collective power of the connections to others, and the collective wisdom from which we come.

Adapted from Beth Sperber Richie's blog, which can be found at www.FermataConsult/ideas ❁

BIO Beth Sperber Richie, psychologist, nonprofit consultant, and trauma specialist.

ancestrality

SEE:
activating archives
ancestral wisdom
embodied knowledg
Grace Lee Bogg
illder

CONTRIBUTION

They Whisper Me Through

I am the oldest daughter
of the oldest daughter
for at least seven generations

Drawn to
that of woman
my Lumbee people
my Appalachian hillbilly Celtic roots
& my Cuban ancestors

Held in the line
& dreaming forward
my daughters
& their children
& their children
& onward

We are each living & healing
in all directions.

Every grandmother
fertile bodyground

wombships of celestial memories & gestational waters
holding the egg-potentiality
sourcing our emergence

bloodroots
from which we each
are always & ever
dreamt forward

to remember ourselves
unfurl our blossoms
& reseed.

*

Listen! it's important, Momma said
whatever this Mystery is we are living must be

because there are *soooooo* many of them here to help us
giving such gentle care & attention   allowing glimpses of remembering   &
flashes of imagining
they wait patiently
as we come in & out of seeing & sensing
this "Yes" we opened into when our souls signed on
to follow our knowing   but no-telling feet
guided by their wise whispers   if we listen

I imagined Grandma Lilly would never die
her lithe little body would just keep shrinking smaller & smaller
condensing like her daddy's Jewel Ridge coal
until she was an eternal bright speck of light
a glowing spark of diamond & the lingering scent of smoke & Palmolive

her bones rest in the ground next to my grandfather outside of Baltimore
according to the tombstone, she hasn't died
I feel her so close to me & wonder

She was the first to show me to the studio & flow through my fingers
sending whole cloth flying out of closets
together, tearing all the fabrics
white curtains hand-sewn in newlywed days
lace tidbits & slipcovers from early nesting
balled twine from Spring labyrinths everything unraveling

Grandma Chat comes visiting too fine seamstress, she
they say, she could sew a perfect fit without a single measurement
Helen Schierbeck's favorite yellow suit
just one of the ways she knew the ways…

she leads through the belly, the tactile, the touch together, we feel
sewing without patterns connected to the veins
weaving & unweaving & reweaving
histories & hearts & minds

I tune to the line & they whisper me through
quietly they speak volumes.

*

RiverShe Queer Family Summer Sanctuary Invocation
(Capital Fringe Festival, Washington, DC 2023)

Let us ask our ancestors—*all* who have made this road by walking before us—to be here, today & always. As Chrystos[1] reminds us—we walk in the history of our people. Those of our blood & those of our belonging. Some whose names we know & many whose names only whisper in the mysteries. We invite all who have served us with their experience, wisdom, strength & their longing. We are their wildest dreams & we are grateful for their conjuring.

Let us call in those who have uplifted & enlivened us. Let us bring our minds together to honor their names & invite them to share our joy & our togetherness. Together, let us raise our hearts & call out their names with gratitude. Thank you to the grandmothers, grandfathers, aunties, uncles, mentors, writers, artists, sisters, brothers, healers & love warriors of all kinds for making the way to our today. I call some of the so many here & too, your calls & all unnamed into our collective breath. ➔

• Audre Lorde • James Baldwin • Gloria Anzaldúa • Fannie Lou Hamer • Ida B. Wells-Barnett •
(Breathe In)
• Pauli Murray • Paula Gunn Allen • Beth Brant • Pat Parker • Marsha P. Johnson •
(Breathe Out)
• Sylvia Rivera • Barbara Jordan • Essex Hemphill •
(Breathe In)
• Ma Rainey • Gladys Bentley • José Sarria • Stormé DeLarverie •
(Breathe Out)

& in the ways of those who have gathered in circles & have gathered me in circles so that I may remember who I am, let us honor the motherline—*all mothering in all forms* that carried us forward. I offer my motherline—& we gather your additions into our collective call—as prayer & medicine on behalf of all. May we listen & know that we are held, loved & adored.

• Cheryl Ann Oxendine • Lilly Virginia Young Oxendine • Cecilia Garcia Chavez •
(Breathe In)
• Mary Christian Young • Charity Oxendine Sampson • Evarista Rodriguez Diaz •
(Breathe Out)
• Maria Negrin Perez • Grandma Christian • Eliza Ellen Pruitt • Susie Jane Oxendine •
(Breathe In)
• Florence Oxendine • Maria Felicia Diaz Fleitas • Manuela de Paz Toledo • Louisa Smith •
(Breathe Out)
• Rachel Young • Charity Oxendine Jacobs • Mary Paul Dial Sampson • Mary Oxendine •
(Breathe In)
• Hilaria Fleitas • Josefa Corona • Antonia Toldeo Yanes • Josefa Leal Gonzalez • Mary Smith •
(Breathe Out)
• Eleanor (Nellie) Steele • Delilah (Eliza) Lowery • Edith Paul Dial • Nancy Carter Sampson •
(Breathe In)
• Abigail Oxendine • Christina Deskins • Nancy Pruitt • Elizabeth (Betsey) Locklear Lowery •
(Breathe Out)
• Elizabeth Revels Oxendine • Mary Lowery Dial • Milly Hammons Carter •
(Breathe In)
• Elvie Hammonds Sampson • Margaret Francisco Deskins • Sarah Ellen Hurt Pruitt •
(Breathe Out)
• Sarah Locklear Lowery • Mary Elizabeth Lowery Revels • Honor Erwin Lowery •
(Breathe In)
• Elsey Hammonds Sampson • Pussie Lowrie •
(Breathing Across The Motherline)

1 Chrystos is a Menominee, two-spirit writer & activist. Their poem, "I Walk in the History of My People" is included in the renowned feminist anthology, *This Bridge Called My Back: Writings By Radical Women of Color*, edited by Cherrie Moraga and Gloria Anzaldúa. (Kitchen Table Press, 1983.)

BIO Nicole Oxendine (she/her/hers) is an Indigenous Queer feminist artist & founder of RiverShe Collective Arts & mother guided by the love, whispers & stories of her Lumbee, Cuban & Celtic ancestors.

The Anti-Ableist Art Educators Manifesto

CONTRIBUTION

THE ANTI ABLEIST ART EDUCATORS MANIFESTO

@jtknoxroxs

1. **SHOW UP**
2. **ERADICATE ABLEISM**
3. **UPLIFT ACCEPTANCE**
4. **CREATE WITH AND NOT FOR**
5. **OUR DIFFERENCES SHOULD EMBOLDEN US**
6. **DISABILITY IS NOT A BAD WORD**
7. **VALUE ALL BODIES AND MINDS**
8. **ALLYSHIP IS SACRIFICE**
9. **OUR ART IS OUR SURVIVAL**

The anti ableist art educators manifesto / 1. Show up / 2. Eradicate ableism / 3. Uplift acceptance / 4. Create with and not for / 5. Our differences should embolden us / 6. Disability is not a bad word / 7. Value all bodies and minds / 8. Allyship is sacrifice / 9. Our art is our survival

The Anti-Ableist Art Educators Manifesto. By Jen White-Johnson, copyright 2023.

AS MY NEURODIVERGENT FRIEND AND EDUCATOR Lydia Z. Brown states: “Ableism is an entire way of thinking and doing that harms disabled people by treating some types of bodies and minds as valuable, worthy, and desirable, and others as undesirable and

ove
unar cycle
agic School, the
apping support
arginality
(as a site of
resistance)
arxist social
work
embership the
in social wo
ending
etaphor
ikveh
obile librar
ovement
lawyering
utual aid
ycelia as
metaphor
arradrama
arrative
medicine
arrative the
epantla/
nepantleras
onviolent
communicatio
ngoingness
eer counseli
eer-to-peer
health netwo
erson-situati
perspective
erspective vi
faith
leasure
oems/poetry
oetic meter
olarity work
ost-
oppositional
ostwork
imaginaries
overty-aware
social work
paradigm, th
ower threat
meaning (PTM
framework
re(care)ity
rison abolit
rofessionali
without
performance
rogressive
education
ublic benefit
ublic library
the
igong
adical
administrati
adical care
the arts
adical childr
in movement
spaces
adical
inclusion
adical
papermaking
adical presence
adical
social work
adical Therapist
Journal, The
ank and File
Movement (RFM)
in social work

re-authoring
reclaiming selfhood
recognition
redistribution
Reflecting on Justice
reflexivity
Reiki
relational
interviewing
relationality
resistance
resisting the
parental loss
narrative
resonance
respectful visiting
respite rooms
rest as resistance
revenge
revolutionary
mothering
ritual
sanctuary
sandplay therapy
sauna
seed banking
sex positivity
shadow integration
Sick Woman Theory
slow textiles
slowness
social change
ecosystem framework
social construction
social practice
social therapeutics
Social Welfare Action
Alliance, the
solidarity
solidarity economy
somatic healing
songs/singing
sound healing
speculative design
spells
staying with the
trouble
storytelling
street newspaper
strengths
perspective, the
sufficiency
sustaining movement
symbol
Taos Institute, the
tarot
temporary autonomous
zones
Theatre of the
Oppressed
theories of change
theosophy
therapeutic writing
togetherness
trans practices
transformative
justice
traspatio
12-step programs
undercover anti-
bullying teams
vigil
water
wildness
wintering as metaphor
wishes
witchery
yoga
zinemaking

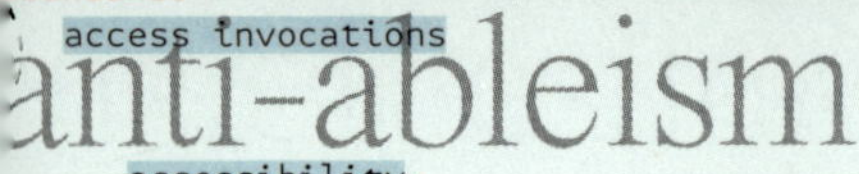

access invocations
accessibility
anti-adultism
anti-racism
crip time
language justice

unworthy. Ableism is embedded in legal, social, and political institutions, as well as in commonly accepted and unquestioned attitudes and assumptions."[1]

Recently I've transitioned from the grind of full-time teaching, and my career has taken a shift as I've begun prioritizing advocacy and activism work. As a disabled and neurodivergent mother, artist, and designer, I've noticed that internalized ableism occasionally creeps in, wanting to control and degrade my creativity. This Manifesto is meant to serve as a direct act of creative resistance, protest, and radical pedagogy designed to help the disabled and non-disabled community become more aware of how to uplift their disabled selves and their fellow disabled and neurodivergent students inside and outside the classroom.

In a recent interview published in truthout.org entitled "Ableism Enables All Forms of Inequity and Hampers All Liberation Efforts," abolitionist community lawyer, educator, and organizer Talila "TL" Lewis states that"[a]bleism has been used for generations to degrade, oppress, control and disappear disabled & nondisabled people alike."[2] TL also says, "Disability and ableism serve as the tie that holds oppressed communities together or the wedge that pits us against each other."[3]

The principles raised in The Anti-Ableist Art Educators Manifesto are meant to realize that art is connected to the survival of Black and Brown disabled communities. Anti-ableism and collective liberation stem from the understanding that we all have struggles that are deliberately and intimately connected, and that working together, through community, allows us to use the labor of love-justice to transform injustice. ❁

1 Autistic Hoya, "Autistic Hoya's Brief Abled Privilege Checklist."

2 Lewis, quoted in Yancy, "Ableism Enables All Forms of Inequity and Hampers All Liberation Efforts."

3 Lewis, quoted in Yancy, "Ableism Enables All Forms of Inequity and Hampers All Liberation Efforts."

BIO Jen White-Johnson, disabled & neurodivergent art and design educator and disability cultural activist; author of *KnoxRoxs* (Homie House Press, 2018).

SEE: ritual; undercover anti-bullying teams

CONTRIBUTION

Anti-adultism: Life in Recovery

If not for the unhealed hurts of adultism that we carry into adulthood, we would know how to stand up against injustice elegantly and thoughtfully… We must be hurt into going quiet and staying small as young people.
—Nanci E. Luna Jiménez[1]

EVERY ADULT is in recovery from childhood. Each one of us locates ourselves in some stage of change or awareness along this journeyed path. We simultaneously hold on to a piece of our own denial while moving forward in an ongoing state of mourning—of the opportunities denied to us, the dominance leveraged by adults that as children we had to live through, and the losses along the way that we had no control over. When I ask those in my care this question, "Who here is a former child in recovery?" I am greeted with initial silence. I watch tentative hands begin to raise themselves up, then more hands, nervous laughter, and finally a palpable release of energy, as we look around and really see each other not in our adult bodies, but as former children who shared this experience of adultism during our youth. There is relief in having it witnessed, spoken, and affirmed, even in rooms of relative strangers. We are not alone in knowing we have each survived childhood and its circumstances, beyond our control, inclusive of damages.

The word for this—adultism—reminds us what we are all recovering from. *Adultism*[2] is defined as the interpersonal and structural oppression of young people through the power wielded by adults in society, like other oppressive concentrations of power: for example, racism, classism, ableism, ethnocentrism, sexism, ageism, homo/trans/xenophobia, and other forms of structural oppression. It is ubiquitous, permeating the air we breathe in and out of our lungs, being absorbed into our bloodstreams, and filling every cell of our bodies. What makes adultism distinct from other "isms" is the way it encapsulates them, providing broad, inclusive cover to every method and system with which we marginalize and "other" each other. It is embodied in our ideas, sensations, and emotions, yet not comprehended with any reason or logic. Most adults have never heard the word adultism, though they are experts in it. By the time we reach adulthood, we have effectively internalized adultism, resulting in a shared mainstream culture of "bias" and "social addiction" towards adults and their beliefs, attitudes, and behaviors.[3] Adultism also primes us, providing what some call a "training ground" for oppression.[4] Adultist domination and childhood experiences of devaluation make us vulnerable to other oppressive beliefs, such as racism, classism, and queerphobia. It causes us to seek out hierarchy and authority over others, to place ourselves with the greatest access to power possible, and to distance ourselves from what we fear makes us vulnerable. We have absorbed the experience of being dominated and have learned dominance out of a need to survive. We learn to devalue others only when our own experience of self has been devalued.

Adultism includes and is not limited to rules of social inclusion or exclusion of children (curfews and bans on public streets and in private businesses; behavior-management strategies and punishment employed in social service agencies and institutions of learning by teachers and social workers; being arrested as young as preschool for misbehavior on school grounds); economic adultism (taxation on wages without voting rights); culturally and intergenerationally rooted forms of adultism (legalized corporal punishment in families; beliefs that youth are biological property of their families; the legal rights of adult caregivers to suppress or even force conversion of youth identity); and legal forms of adultism (being tried as an adult in courts of law; legal solitary confinement in carceral facilities for youth).[5] We also struggle with psychological adultism, as rampant as hazing—every adult has at some level internalized the belief that children are inferior, weak, incapable, and even ill-disposed, requiring them to be policed. Unschooling advocate and author John C. Holt reminds us, "To trust our children we must first learn to trust ourselves… and most of us were taught as children that we could not be trusted. And so we go on treating children as we ourselves were treated, calling this 'reality,' or saying bitterly, 'If I could put up with it, they can too.'"[6]

And so, throughout our childhood journey, despite our best hopes, our desire to conquer our fears, and our wishes to live authentically, our collective journey through adultism has occurred. So much of adult language, especially in spaces of solidarity, actually represents offerings to our younger selves. "Don't let anyone dim your light," we remind each other, centering agency and voice as best we can and calling for justice and community. "I *see* you and *hear* you," we say, honoring these simple sensory, relational gifts. So much work with adults necessitates the prioritization of healing the original-source wounds of childhood adultism and therefore requires a trauma-informed, shame-sensitive lens. Among the many hurts and harms emanating from childhood, we first and foremost carry with us a profound sense of loss of the young people we wished to be, the lives we could have lived, or the pain we had no choice but to feel—the residue of living in a world where adults dominated us and centered themselves, rather than stewarding our growth on our own terms.

And what of joy? How do we reconcile our desires to live, persist, survive, and thrive through our adultism journey with what is also incredibly beautiful about life? Although choosing our childhood was not possible, we do have considerable agency in how we heal. Author Gabor Maté states, "Trauma is not what happened to you, but what happens inside you as a result of what happened to you."[7] He reminds us to invest our healing energy into our forward momentum. We need to reclaim our sense of self, and know that we are more than our experiences alone. We can't change our childhoods nor undo our losses, trampled rights, and injustices. However, we can engage in a process of unlearning and relearning. Just as adults centered themselves as the authors of our childhoods, as recovering children we must center ourselves as the authors of our futures. We alone can re-narrate the meaning we make of what has happened to us and re-define our relationships to our bodies and to others as we grow into adulthood. Adult authenticity shines a light on a healing path from the shared childhood trauma of adultism. In moving forward as recovering adults, we have a unique opportunity to cultivate from our own self-empathy a commitment to justice for the next generation of children in our families, social circles, and broader society. In so doing, we invite in agency and power in new, creative ways.

Healing can start with us, giving ourselves permission to say that what happened to us was not our fault, nor deserved. From there it can radiate outward. We can receive other people—in various states of their own internalized adultism and healing journeys—who may argue that adultism is needed for kids' safety, or to prevent harm. We can access the care and empathy in ourselves to hear these kinds of statements as rooted in fear, not care, of children. Of ownership and rigidity, rather than mentorship and fluidity.

We tend to repeat what we don't repair. Therefore we must be attuned to the ways we may unconsciously or willingly engage adultism in moments of our own insecurities as adults, to give us something substantively stable to hold firmly, as a developmental marker of growth. Let's free ourselves from the oppression of our youth, in embracing our collective strengths as adults, and live the authentic life we always deserved.

> Your children are not your children.
> They are the sons and daughters of Life's longing for itself.
> They come through you but not from you.
> And though they are with you yet they belong not to you.
> …You are the bows from which your children as living arrows are sent forth.
> —Kahlil Gibran, *The Prophet* (1923)[8] ❁

1 Luna Jimenez Institute for Social Transformation, "Adultism: The Training Ground for All Other Oppression."

2 Freechild Institute for Youth Engagement, "Introduction to Adultism."

3 Freechild Institute for Youth Engagement, "Introduction to Adultism."

4 Luna Jimenez Institute, "Adultism: The Training Ground for All Other Oppression."

5 Krey, "Adults Just Don't Understand: Checking Out Our Everyday Adultism."

6 Holt, *How Children Learn*.

7 Maté, *The Myth of Normal: Trauma, Illness, and Healing in a Toxic Culture*.

8 Gibran, *The Prophet*.

BIO Shipra Parikh is a clinical social worker, educator, and community-based practitioner, trying her best to live free of adultism in all aspects of her life, especially in the relationships she holds closest.

anti-racism

SEE: anti-ableism, anti-racism court system, critical race theory, critical whiteness, freed, justice-oriented counseling

CONTRIBUTION

ANTIRACISM: practicing courage. And with it, making choices that support life.

"Oh, that wasn't my intention," a white leader might hastily respond when a colleague mentions that their comment felt harmful. But does that response foster accountability, or complicity in the status quo? Without accountability, where does the energy of the harm go?

"I'm ready to leave," a white protestor might say after being called out on their problematic behavior. But if they took a deep breath and a sip of water, could that call-out be metabolized as devotion to allyship? Could a willingness to practice following the leadership of people of color grow their trustworthiness and impact?

"That's below my pay grade," a white manager might think when their Asian director assigns them conference logistics work so their Black associate can facilitate a workshop. But do white people consider how it might foster repair to take on the menial, time-consuming tasks and give people of color space for creativity and leadership development?

"Just let it go," one might tell themself when critical questions come to mind about the integrity of their team's programming. But is it possible that courageous interrogation is an essential step on our way out of the racist status quo? By slowing down to consider alternatives, might we speed up the pursuit of equity?

"Between me and you..." a white employee might begin when telling their manager they contributed more to the project than their Black colleague. But are they aware of the possible repercussions of that message? Have they considered what it might be like for their Black colleague to live and work in an environment where nothing is shaped for their convenience or care?

"Why does it even matter?" a white person might ask their partner who has stated a boundary about not being in spaces where they are the only person of color. But what would it feel like for the partner of color to hear a simple "okay, I can respect that," even if their white partner has frustrations? Does the white partner have a community that can hold space for their feelings to be processed without emotional labor on the part of people of color?

"Capitalism is killing us," a white couple might existentially fret with each other. But have they considered building reparations budgets to redistribute their "disposable" income? Have they interrogated their place in a racialized economy that systematically reproduces a working class that can barely make ends meet? Do they feel what profiting off this economy might be doing to their humanity?

~~~

These are a few of the many, many moments where people who benefit from racial privilege can practice courage and anti-racism in our choices. They reflect patterns that I've noticed and tried to take responsibility for in myself. They may not be the questions that are most alive for you—especially if you hold identities that predispose you to harm in a racialized society—but I wonder what questions are most alive for you. Have you considered where you might make new choices, how you might show up differently in your interactions with other people and systems?

My experience has been that it's not about making choices that are "right" or "better" than how we're currently moving through life,
~~~

Reflecting on Justice
solidarity
theories of change

but discovering what makes us human, what connects us to the humanity of others. Getting as clear as possible on how racism distorts our shared humanity. Feeling on the deepest level what Fannie Lou Hamer said: "*Nobody's free until everybody's free.*" And then showing up to life with the courage to make choices that may not be easy or common, but that feel like the least violent choices we can make at that moment. Knowing that when our choices contrast with the racist status quo, we can move with greater dignity and integrity. When our choices actively oppose white supremacy culture, our humanity is more nourished and our presence on this planet supports life, moving us closer to the anti-racist, liberated culture we deserve. ❁

Alyssa Smaldino (she/her) is an anti-racism organizer, facilitator, and coach committed to discovering and practicing new ways of being that help us break free of dominant systems.

anti-racism court system

SEE: anti-racism, critical race theory, critical whiteness, freed[om], justice-orient[ed] counseling

CONTRIBUTION

An Anti-Racism Court System: A Road Map

THE DECISIONS THAT ARE MADE every day in courthouses across the country have a profound impact on the individuals, families, and businesses that make up our communities. However, race, privilege, and power continue to remain at the core of the legal system—a system that, as it currently stands, functions with daily instances of differential treatment and implicit bias.

To eliminate these influences from our systems, there must be an organizational shift towards judicial antiracism policymaking. It is an endeavor that requires an unwavering commitment to confront and address biases, systemic injustices, and historical inequalities that have shaped the framework of our court system.

In our vision of an antiracism court system, justice partners and community members work together to dismantle the structures that perpetuate inequity and build a roadmap towards a system that fosters true equality, fairness, and justice for all.

The journey to an antiracism court system begins.

Leadership of the court system **acknowledges** the issue of race and privilege as a barrier to a truly fair and equal justice system. They state their commitment to dismantling the current system for an antiracism court system. The call to action is inspiring; the court system is motivated to implement antiracism policies and procedures. Leadership's efforts are communicated externally; there is a public pronouncement of the new antiracism mission for the organization, and a challenge for change to justice partners with publicly stated goals and timelines. There is genuine collaboration and communication with communities in poverty, and communities of color. Those that are in proximity to the issues of racism are listened to and engaged with. Leadership begins to instill trust and confidence in a system that has long been feared and mistrusted.

Judicial officers and staff of the court **create opportunities for internal dialogue** to drill down into the barriers to fairness and equality within the workforce. This work is hard, often involving difficult—but necessary—conversations about race in the workplace. There is a continued education of the history of racism and its impact on Black, Hispanic, Asian, Indigenous, and other communities of color. These efforts of internal dialogue lead to a thorough review of all court policies and procedures through the lens of antiracism—a lens that is deliberate in identifying and meeting the needs of the workforce in their diversity and variety of experience. This review incorporates strategic and planned community engagement aimed at listening and educating the public regarding new processes, technologies, and available resources that the system is more equitable, fair, and just. The court system builds capacity from within its leadership to sustain this work to ensure that court users receive the intended benefits of an antiracism court system that meets the needs of the communities it serves.

Accountability measures to assess success and progress are part of day-to-day operations and are reviewed regularly by court leadership, court workforce, and system-involved communities. Success is a continuum of antiracism practices based on stated goals and milestones. Performance measures are used to inform policy decisions and accountability. There is a series of mechanisms in place to ensure compliance to antiracism policies and procedures. Court performance in timely disposition, quality representation, and access to justice is routinely evaluated by constructs such as race and gender. Court users are encouraged to share their perceptions of access and fairness of the courts, of how they were treated, and whether the court's process of making decisions seemed fair.

There is a transformation of the court system; it is a system of structures that advance fair and equal justice for all.

The journey to an antiracism court system begins again. ❁

BIOS

Melaine Malcolm is the Deputy Directory of the Department of Research and Planning, where she is responsible for the analysis and reporting of internal and external data ensuring access and accountability for a fair, just, and equitable legal system.

Judge Julie Bernard is an Associate Justice of the Massachusetts District Court, appointed to the bench in 2002; she has over 20 years of work experience in the court system and is committed to ensuring a fair, just, and equitable legal system.

Reflecting on Justice
solidarity
theories of change

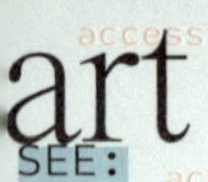

SEE:
art as/in/of life
art journaling
art therapy
art workers
art-based group work
arts in medicine
arts-based research
Authentic Movement
dérive, the
healing healers through the arts
improvisation

CONTRIBUTION

Art IS

AS A CHILD I was always creative, experimenting with materials, manipulating their properties, and sometimes destroying my parents' coffee table or yard tools in the name of art. I was called that "girl who can draw," the one who always oversaw the art portion of group projects, voted "most artistic" in my senior year of high school. Art was a daily pursuit; one I took to my undergraduate years majoring in fine art. There I learned that art had "rules." My creative expression was warped and molded into the output of a "good art student." I learned to differentiate between CRAFT and ART. I conformed my way of making to please my professors, always got A's on my work, and achieved the title "Outstanding Art Major" in my last year of college. I thrived, working to achieve a standard for my art, riding the highs of approval.

And when I graduated, it all disappeared.

I couldn't find my art anymore.

I lost my art for years.

Not for lack of trying, I dragged myself into trying and making art to come up with concepts and compositions.

To make a piece with meaning. Then I went to school to become an art therapist.

Art Therapy. In the program, I broke down my rules of what ART is, and ART and CRAFT became one again. I learned that art therapy has no rights or wrongs to art for my patients/clients… so why would I, an art therapist, put rules on my own art?

I dismantled my rules for ART and started to see that art was not only the visual depictions I created but was my way of thinking, my way of acting, and my intention. I started to see that my art was a line I made on paper, the way I arranged my desk; it was a picture I took of the sky on my way to school, it was the routine I created to make my cup of coffee, the process of baking something from scratch. Realizing *I was living my art*, my body and mind felt ALIVE again; I felt creatively free.

The only one who could tell me my art is art was ME. It is how I live, the process, the intention, and the feelings I experience when making something. ❁

ingering
ove
unar cycle
agic School, the
apping support
arginality
(as a site of
resistance)
arxist social
work
embership theory
in social work
ending
etaphor
ikveh
obile libraries
ovement
lawyering
utual aid
ycelia as
metaphor
arradrama
arrative
medicine
arrative therapy
epantla/
nepantleras
onviolent
communication
ngoingness
eer counseling
eer-to-peer
health network
erson-situation
perspective
erspective via
faith
leasure
oems/poetry
oetic meter
olarity work
ost-
oppositionality
ostwork
imaginaries
overty-aware
social work
paradigm, the
ower threat
meaning (PTM)
framework
re(care)ity
rison abolition
rofessionalism
without
performance
rogressive
education
ublic benefits
ublic library,
the
igong
adical
administration
adical care in
the arts
adical childcare
in movement
spaces
adical
inclusion
adical
papermaking
adical presence
adical
social work
adical Therapist
Journal, The
ank and File
Movement (RFM)
in social work

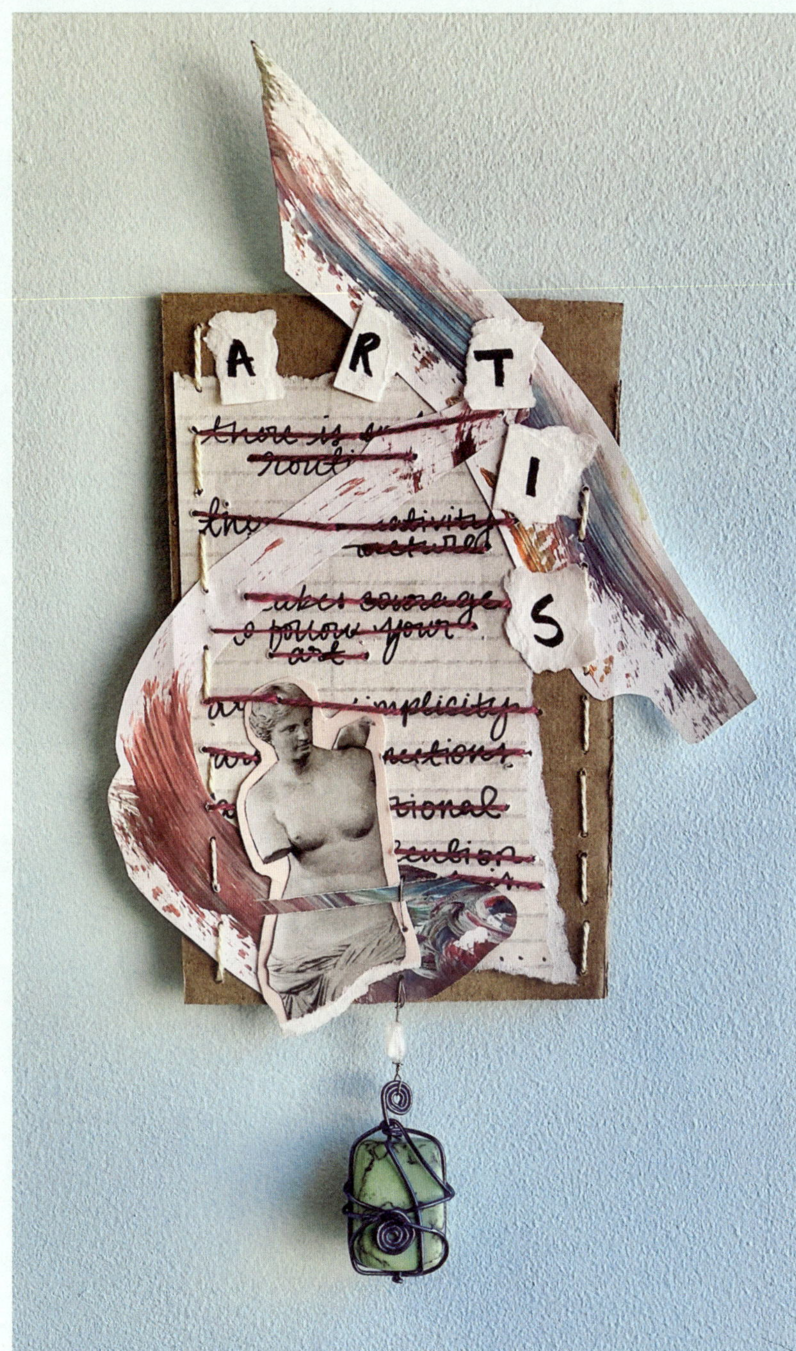

Sara Cantrell, Mixed Media, 2022.

B
I
O

Sara Cantrell, MA, ATR-P, LGPAT, LGPC, is an Art Therapist for a Pediatric Hematology/Oncology clinic at a Military Hospital who is passionate about using art to create space for voices to be heard, to learn more about oneself, to find opportunities for advocacy, and to foster community.

re-authoring
reclaiming selfhood
recognition
redistribution
Reflecting on Justice
reflexivity
Reiki
relational
interviewing
relationality
resistance
resisting the
parental loss
narrative
resonance
respectful visiting
respite rooms
rest as resistance
revenge
revolutionary
mothering
ritual
sanctuary
sandplay therapy
sauna
seed banking
sex positivity
shadow integration
Sick Woman Theory
slow textiles
slowness
social change
ecosystem framework
social construction
social practice
social therapeutics
Social Welfare Action
Alliance, the
solidarity
solidarity economy
somatic healing
songs/singing
sound healing
speculative design
spells
staying with the
trouble
storytelling
street newspapers
strengths
perspective, the
sufficiency
sustaining movements
symbols
Taos Institute, the
tarot
temporary autonomous
zones
Theatre of the
Oppressed
theories of change
theosophy
therapeutic writing
togetherness
trans practices
transformative
justice
traspatio
12-step programs
undercover anti-
bullying teams
vigil
water
wildness
wintering as metaphor
wishes
witchery
yoga

art as/in/of life

SEE: activating archives, Authentic Movement, body as community, care-based co-housing, centering maintenance, commons, the, community newspapers, death practice, dérive, th, embodied expressio, flâne, herbalis, interspecie organizing

CONTRIBUTION

STUBBORN AVANT-GARDE ARTIST ALLAN KAPROW, who makes lifeworks and writes about the blurring that occurs between art and life, inspired our thinking on this topic. Kaprow viewed art as a moral act and argued that art and life were "not simply co-mingled, [thus] the identity of each [was] uncertain."[1]

Taking inspiration from Marshall McLuhan, he argued that being called an artist and having your work considered art is simply a matter of expression, with the artist announcing it as art, and convincing others to believe it is art, given that "art is what you can get away with."[2]

We pose the question: Are you an artist? Kaprow argues that all artists can locate themselves among five modes of artistic engagement:

1. Work within recognizable art modes and present the work in recognized art contexts, e.g., paintings in galleries, poetry in poetry books, and music in concert halls.
2. Work in unrecognizable, i.e., non-art, modes but present the work in recognizable art contexts, e.g., a pizza parlour in a gallery or a telephone book sold as poetry.
3. Work in recognizable art modes but present the work in non-art contexts, e.g., a Rembrandt as an ironing board, a fugue in an air-conditioning duct, and a sonnet as a want ad.
4. Work in non-art modes and present the work as art in non-art contexts, e.g., perception tests in a psychology lab, anti-erosion terracing in the hills, typewriter repairing, and garbage collecting (with the proviso that the art world knows about it).
5. Work in non-art modes and non-art contexts but cease to call the work art, retaining instead the private consciousness that sometimes it may be art too, e.g., systems analysis, social work in a ghetto, hitchhiking, and thinking.[3]

We propose that, in art/as/in/of life, we, as artists/photographers/social workers, move back and forth between these modes.

We found Kaprow's idea that "ordinary life performed as art/non-art can change the everyday with metaphorical power"[4] informative for this contribution in which we used a series of Leanne's artworks as a visual metaphor and matched them to consumer definitions from *The MadQuarry Dictionary* to demonstrate the importance of language in social constructions of mental health. Thus, we created a pack of cards (for this entry) for use in therapy or teaching, or as readers deemed appropriate.

The title *MadQuarry Dictionary*[4] is a play on Australia's premier Macquarie Dictionary. It was the outcome of a consumer project intended as a radical critique of language use in mental health that fit our purposes, given that Leanne's felted artworks included a number of figures from her *Ship of Fools* and other medieval depictions of diversity. The "ship of fools" allegory originated from Book VI of Plato's *Republic*, about a ship with a dysfunctional crew. The allegory in this context is intended to represent the power of consumer language in reframing expert knowledge to undermine professional power. The cards offer metaphorical representations of mental health consumers' lived experiences of "ordinary life performed as art."

In this way, we attempt to highlight the absurdity of professional mental health perspectives and practices for mental health clients. Thus, our adapted definitions from *The MadQuarry Dictionary*—matched to Leanne's felt artworks—demonstrate the "metaphorical power" of art, that is, in this instance, the cards' ability to convey an alternative perspective on mental health and to open therapists' minds to their clients' lived experiences of professional interventions.

This entry serves as a partner to our entry on the strengths perspective and conveys a way to apply a strengths framework in understanding mental health that makes us question our taken-for-granted and received assumptions about mental illness. ❁

1 Kaprow, *Essays on the Blurring of Art and Life*, ed. Jeff Kelley, 82.

2 Kaprow, *Essays on the Blurring of Art and Life*, ed. Jeff Kelley, 103.

3 Kaprow, *Essays on the Blurring of Art and Life*, ed. Jeff Kelley, 175–176.

4 Our Consumer Place, *"The MadQuarry Dictionary: A Consumer's Guide to the Language of Mental Health."*

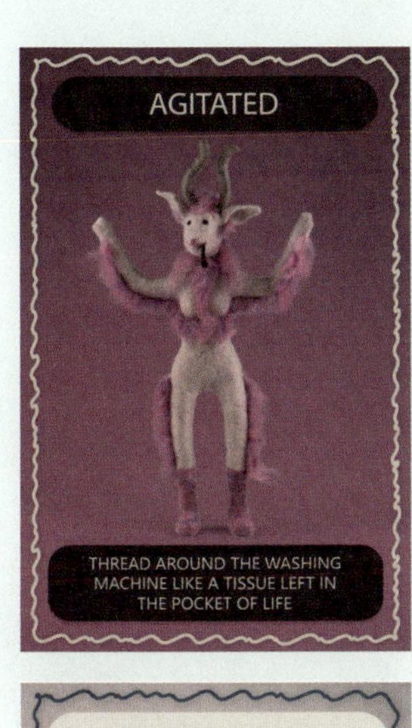
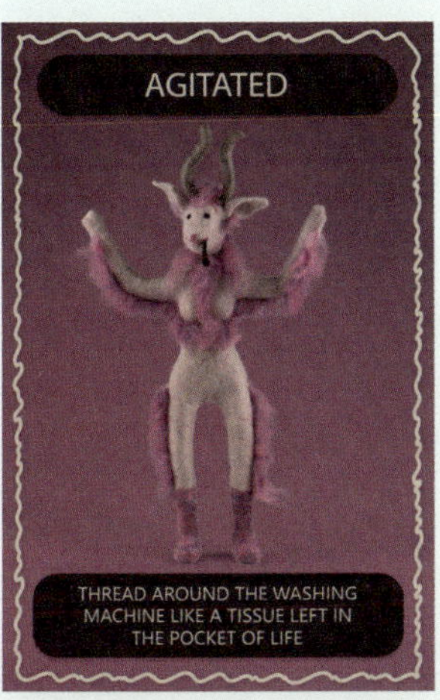

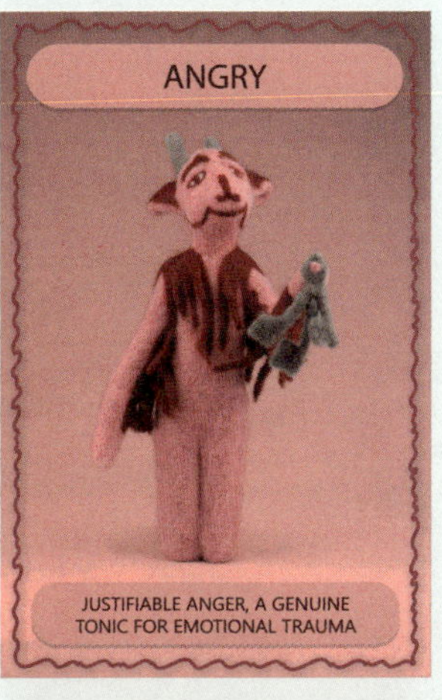

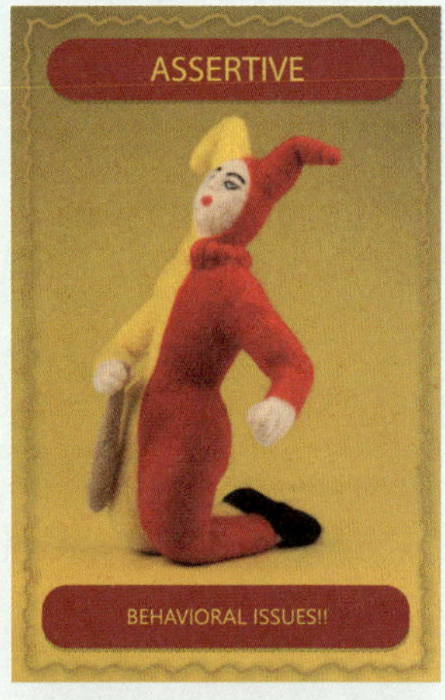

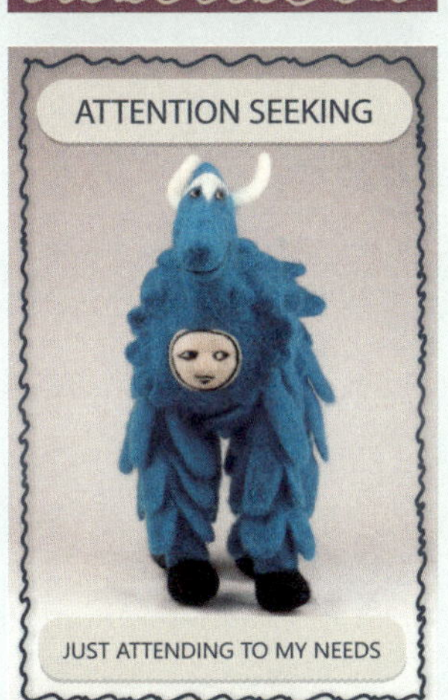
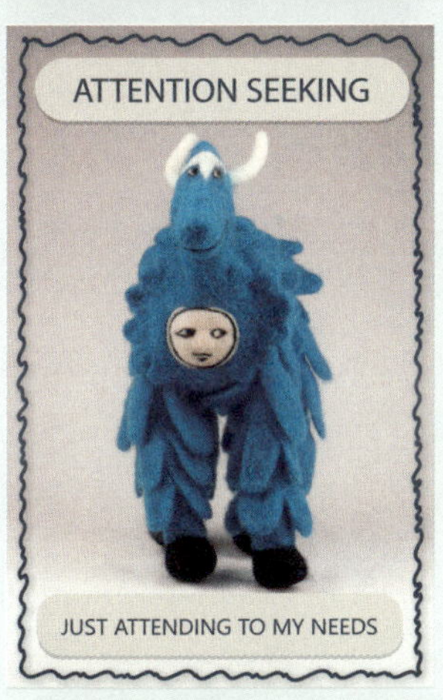

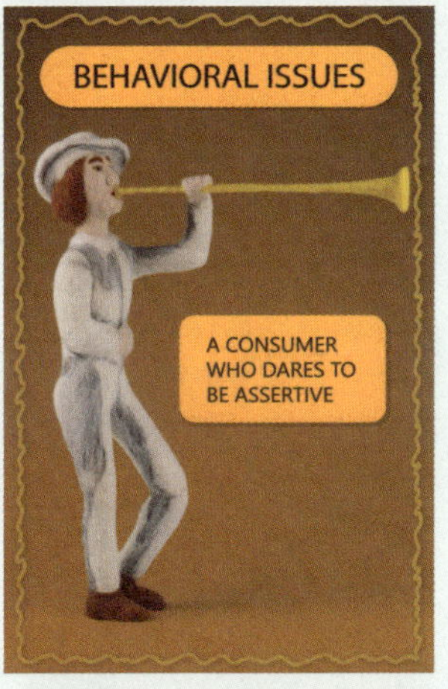

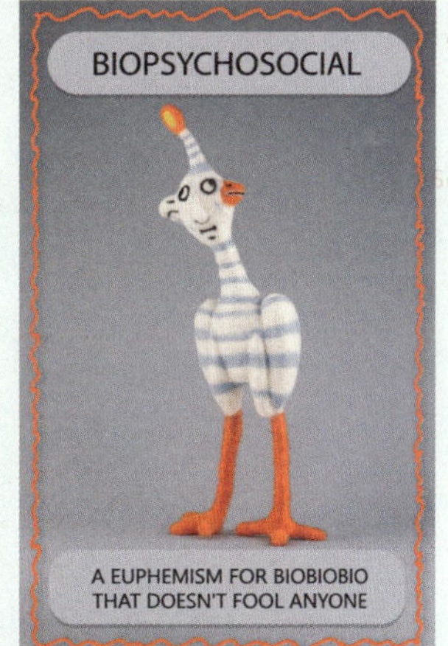

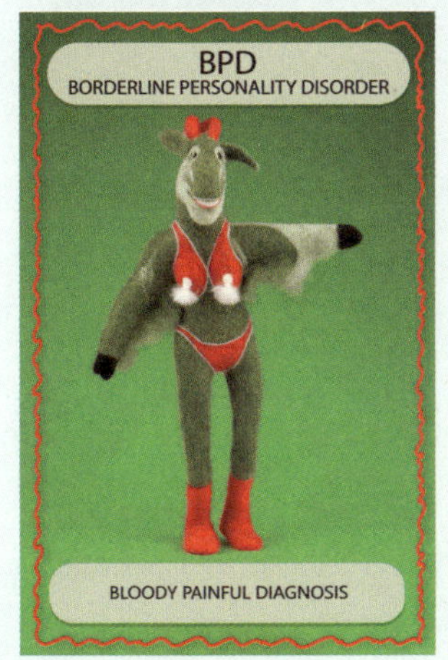
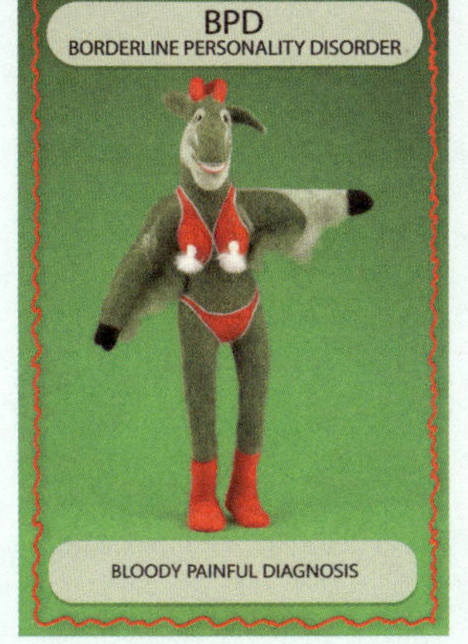

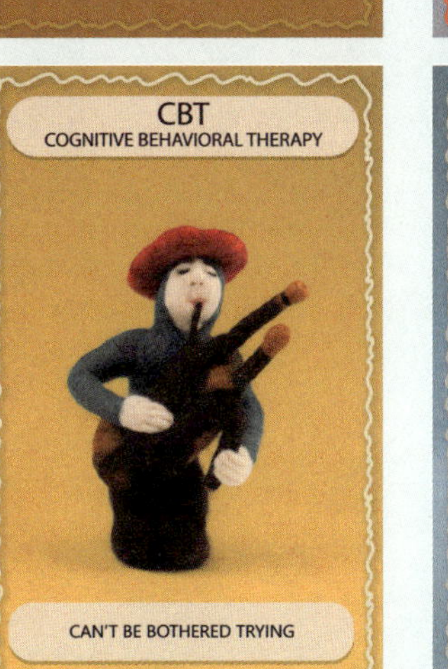

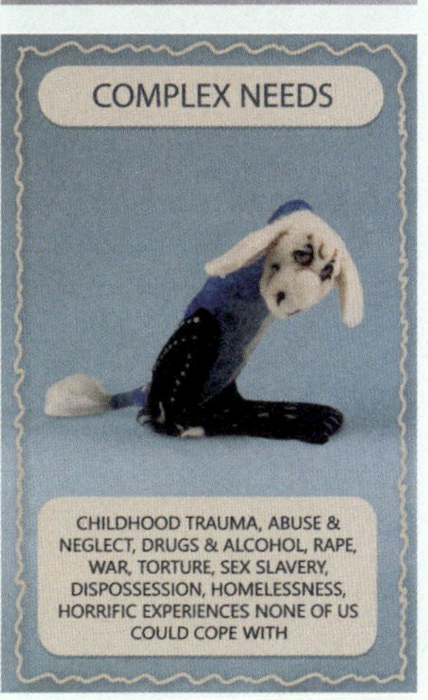

→

access invocations
accessibility
activating archives
Afrofuturism
agency
aging positivity
altar work
alternative identity projects
ancestral wisdom
ancestrality
anti-ableism
anti-adultism
anti-racism
anti-racism court system
art
art as/in/of life
art journaling
art therapy
art workers
arts-based group work
arts in medicine
arts-based research
Authentic Movement
autonomous healing
Ayurveda
being with
Bertha Capen Reynolds
bike and car repair collectives
Black Panther Party Free Breakfast Program
body as community
body neutrality
body positivity
Body Trust
boredom
brave space
breaking the rules
bridge as metaphor
care pods
care-based co-housing
Catholic Worker Movement
centering maintenance
circular economy
climate cafes
clouds as metaphor
coalition
collaborative apprenticeship
collective care
common pool resources
commons, the
communing with animals
community college
community gardens
community newspapers
conjure
constructionist-design framework, the
consulting your consultants
contemplative tradition, the
corn knowledge
credit unions
crip time
critical fabulation
critical hope
critical pedagogy
critical race theory
critical suicide studies
critical whiteness

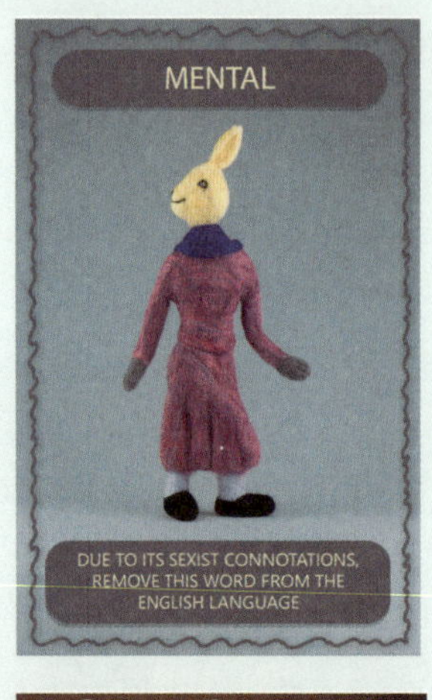

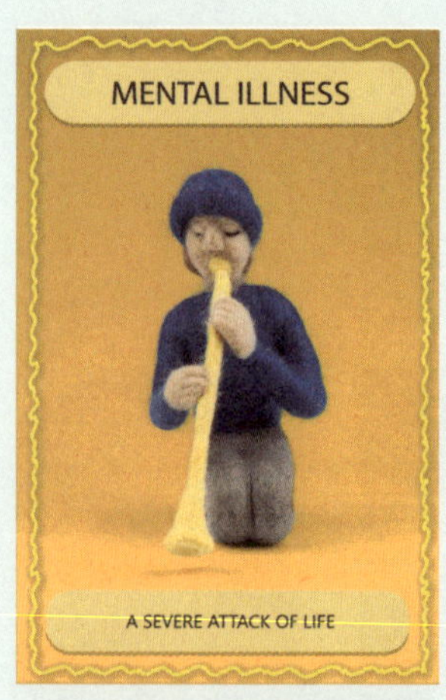

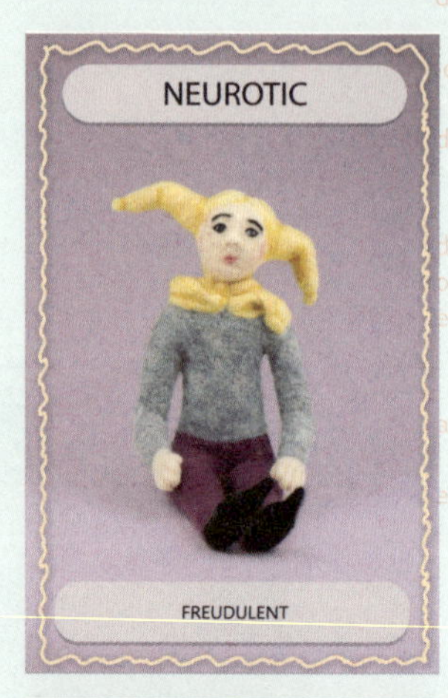

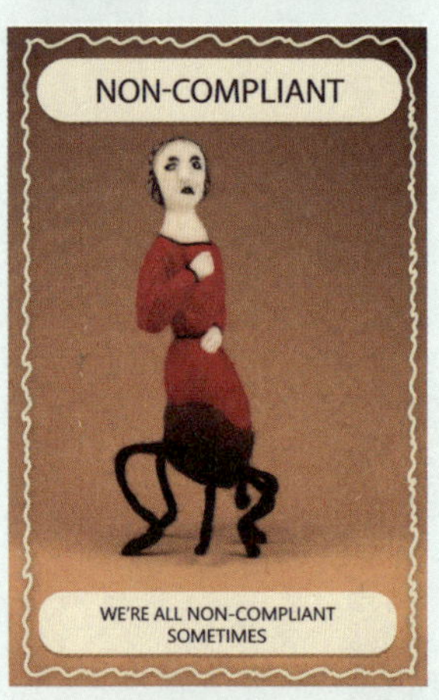

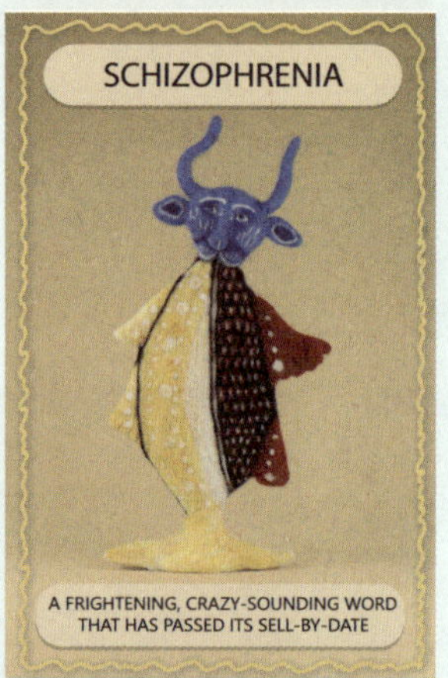

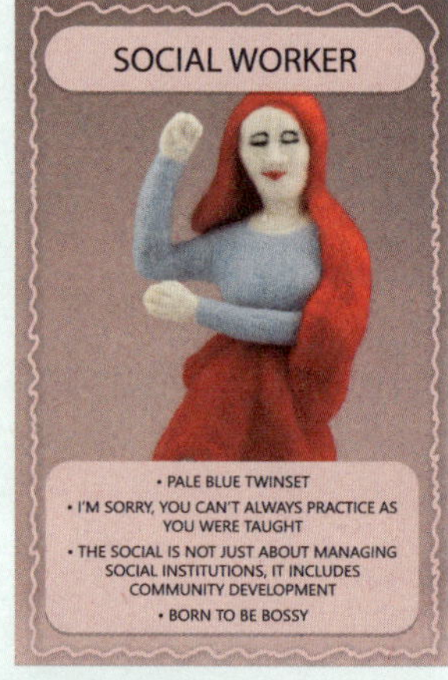

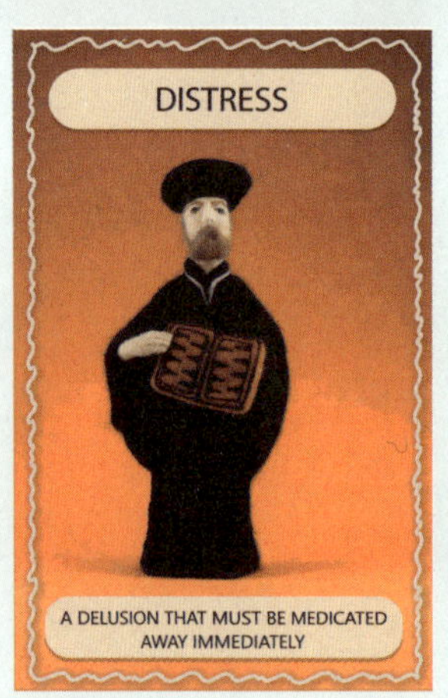

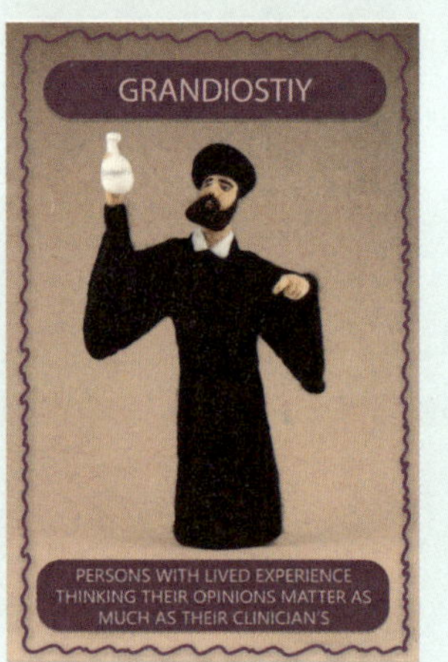

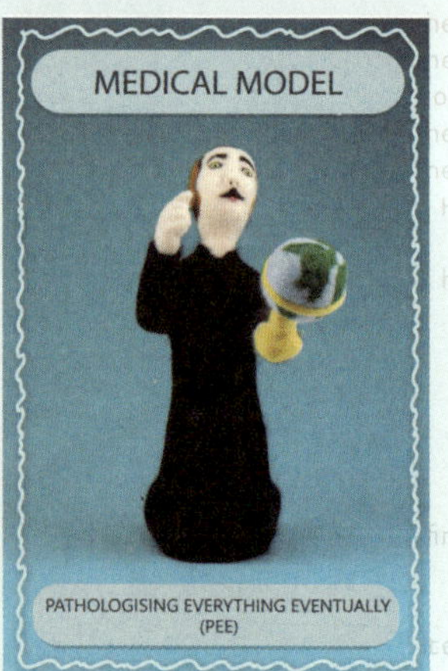

BIOS

Mel Gray (Professor Emeritus at the University of Newcastle, Australia)—photographer and social worker—has a longstanding interest in the art and science of social work practice—its relational-connective and evidence-based aspects that enhance its effectiveness.

Leanne Schubert (PhD)—artist and social worker—has an enduring interest in the relationship between social work and socially engaged art.

art journaling

SEE: poems/poetry; therapeutic writing

CONTRIBUTION

ART JOURNALING is the use of a blank journal of any kind to make personal artwork within, sometimes in conjunction with expressive writing or other sketches, often using mixed media. Any size or kind of paper you like will do; you can even turn a previously published, unwanted book into an "altered book" to use as your art journal. The benefit of art journaling is that it's your own sketchbook, intended for unfinished sketches. It is a place to work out new ideas, to start in the middle, to start upside down; it's a place of freedom, welcomed mistakes, self-expression, and unfettered creativity. Your art journal is a place that other people are not necessarily invited to look within, although you can certainly show off your journal artwork to others if you want to. Sometimes art journals are very private and are for your eyes only. An art journal is for your own musings, your notes, and your record of day-to-day life.

Art journaling is a practice you can come back to over time, and there are no rules regarding how often you use your journal or what marks you make there. It's more about the process than the final product—and words, colors, shapes, line, and forms are invited to mix and mingle there. When I feel confused or hurt or overwhelmed or joyful or loving or just full of thoughts, I go to my art journal and I let colors, shapes, and lines express my story. I've used pencils, markers, collage, words, stencils, fibers, stamps, stickers, quotes, scraps, print-making, pressed flowers, painting, watercolor, and a mix of all of these in my art journal!

My art journal is where I come home to myself. My art journal waits for me. It is not impatient. It's there for me when I want it and need it. My art journal is where I pray, sing, dance, explore—as an artist and a person and a human. My art journal is a place of radical healing. ❁

BIO

Gioia Chilton, PhD, ATR-BC, CSAC, is an artist, art therapist, researcher, and author who loves her family and art therapy community.

art therapy

SEE:
art
art as/in/of life
art journaling
art-based group work
arts in medicine
arts-based research
healing healer through the arts

CONTRIBUTION

ART THERAPY IS A FORM OF MENTAL HEALTH TREATMENT and community intervention that utilizes the creative process of artmaking. It can be provided in schools, hospitals, therapists' offices, or community centers to promote healing, process trauma, foster resilience, and improve cognitive and sensorimotor functioning. It is a way to build self-awareness and cultivate insight about what is going on in your life and in the lives of those around you.

Your art often knows more about you than you currently do; that's why artmaking is so powerful. The creative process and art may bring out your unconscious mind.

Let your artmaking inform you about who you are and what's there for you to notice. ❁

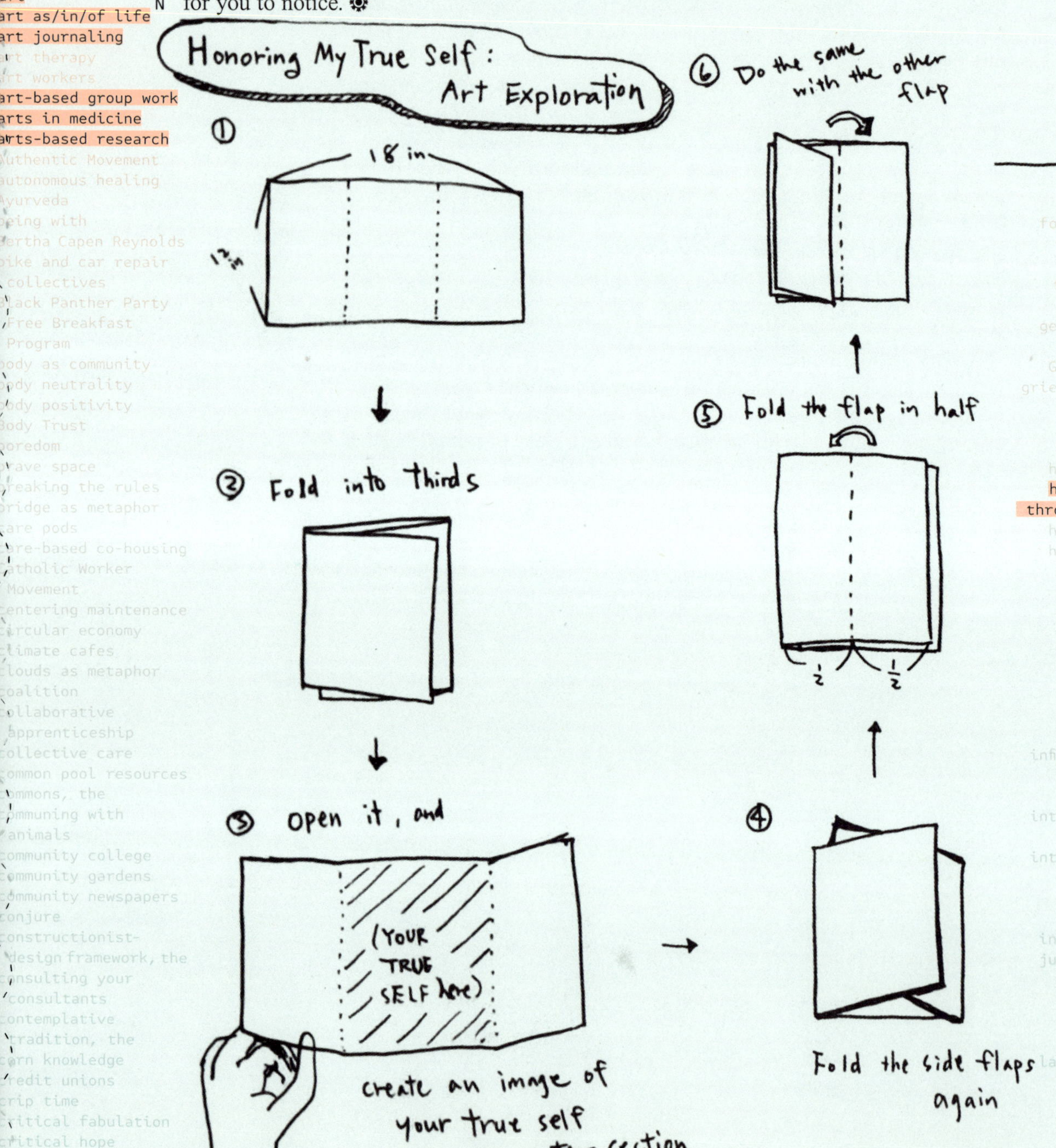

⑦ It looks something like this.

Now, create an image of the false self and its enviroment on the flaps (shaded section)

⑧ When you open, it looks like this:

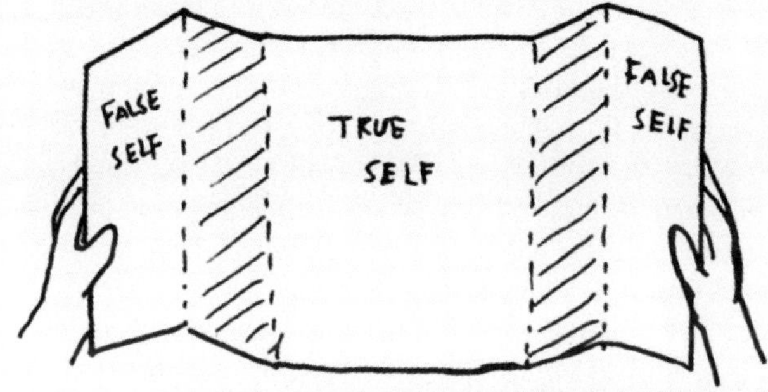

Now, let's fill in the sections between the true self and the false self (shaded sections).

- What creates the bridge between two selves?
- What is there now? And how is it working for you?
- What would you like to see/have there?

B Miki Nishida Goerdt, Artist/Art
I Therapist/Social Worker/Change
O Agent. mikigoerdt.com

art workers

CONTRIBUTION

Art Workers

QUESTIONS OF CLASS are as relevant now as they were during the French revolution, given that bourgeois representations still rule dominant aesthetics. For example: During the Weimar period in Germany, artists portrayed workers, but did not refer to themselves as workers, nor did they represent themselves as part of a working class. Up until today, the production of cultural goods is often regarded as an artful practice in itself, something sublime and removed from the pressure of everyday chores. This narrative mainly benefits the production of artistic goods, the artworks that in the art market are elevated from everyday objects, leading to the belief that therefore their production process must be sublime, too—and not merely as ordinary work. This forces many artists and curators into a double life, where they strictly divide their artist persona from their labor identity; in other cases, the "other" work of the artist and curator becomes a branding to their artistic and curatorial work, becomes therefore incorporated into the artistic and curatorial practice and has to follow its rules. Even though artistic and curatorial work has diversified in many ways, the stereotype of the sublime artists lingers on, while endless numbers of cultural workers continue existing in an invisibilized way in a non-unified, deregulated cultural field.

In the margins of dominant art worlds there are artists and other art workers coining new narratives of artistic labor that are far less removed from everyday life than their ascribed historic idols. Yet these modes of artistic labor are regarded as secondary. This implementation of inferiority is a direct consequence of Eurocentric dominance that has produced the sublime artist as a trope of capitalist idealism, of the self-sufficient, self-motivated, and self-exploitative individual. Indeed, this emergent artistic working class does not insist on their independence at all; they work collaboratively and in collectives, acknowledging their socio-ecological, socio-cultural, and socio-economic interdependence as well as the interconnectedness of infrastructural and organizational labor with art production.

For *AWC (Arts of the Working Class)*, when it comes to representation and self-representation of workers, and therefore of homeless people, we have to think of these as two different categories (SEE street newspapers). Interdependent labor has a problem with representation, because the given frames and infrastructures rarely allow for the less glamorous practices to unfold their potential. These practices rarely produce the kind of aesthetic surfaces in a short time that work well in the holy halls of art representation. You would, rather, find them in the art pedagogic basements, in the public program, or in the outreach projects of cultural institutions. The kind of art that works well in those holy places produces artists that are unable to unionize, not only because of their production schedules, but also their workers' identities would render their artworks less valuable. But the artists outside of this financial bubble of the other category begin to look for new forms of self-representation beyond the marketed self. While they gradually build up alternative infrastructures and support systems, they learn to rely on each other instead of competing. *AWC* seeks every opportunity to oppose with them competitive modes of living.

Thus, lived and often precarious utopias could serve as an inspiration to institution building and more generally to imagining new forms of social togetherness. *AWC* networks grow in the dark and maybe that is even the ideal way of emergence. Yet a wider audience rarely knows of these contemporary lived utopias. To summarize: While the artists of the Weimar Republic were looking for faces of workers, a larger audience had very little idea of the faces of today's cultural workers actively organizing in meaningful interactions and collaborations. In a time where imagery has diversified and visual trends only stay for short periods, the search for the face may be over, yet the question remains of how these practices and practitioners can become visible and recognizable. ✺

B I O

Arts of the Working Class is a multilingual street journal on poverty and wealth, art and society. It is published every two months and contains contributions by artists and thinkers from different fields and in different languages. Its terms are based upon the working class, meaning everyone, and it reports everything that belongs to everyone. Everyone who sells this street journal earns money directly. Vendors keep 100% of the sales. Every artist whose work is advertised designs with us its substance. AWC is published by Paul Sochacki and María Inés Plaza Lazo for the streets of the world.

art-based group work

SEE: art · art as/in/of life · art journaling · art therapy · arts in medicine · arts-based research · group work · healing healer through the arts

CONTRIBUTION

Liberation is always in part a storytelling process: breaking stories, breaking silences, making new stories. A free person tells her own story. A valued person lives in a society in which her story has a place. — Rebecca Solnit

A BLACK-AND-WHITE IMAGE of a pay phone hanging on the wall in an otherwise starkly empty hallway, seen from middle distance.

"I remember this photograph. It so captured the feeling of isolation."

"Isolation, yes, but also the desire to make contact. I can't recall if the client who made it was consciously thinking of these things or not, but then again, that's not how I take photographs either."

I am speaking with fellow art therapist, mentor, and former supervisor Jane Schulman, with whom I collaborated on a project some years ago, where we co-facilitated a group for people diagnosed with what was then called SPMI, or severe and persistent mental illness, at the urban board-and-care facility in which they lived. The folks in this group, many of whom experienced severe psychosis, had shared experiences of frequent hospitalizations, unstable housing and employment, houselessness, and incarceration.

Jane, a photographer, and I, a poet, recalled the group we created and co-led, in which we combined these two media. She taught the group members some basic techniques and approaches to photography and provided them with cameras in between our meetings, and I introduced them to some of the fundamental concepts of poetry and encouraged them to write poems about the images they created. At the end of the 8-week group, they all had portfolios of their work, and those who chose to do so participated in an arts-based focus group to share about their experiences in the project.

For years, Jane has continued to facilitate photography groups with people living with mental illness in board-and-care facilities. She explains, "After I have taught [the clients] some about photography, and they are given cameras to use, the prompt I give is simple. I ask them to make pictures that say something about themselves and their lives. And quite wonderfully they really do."

In the state of California, if you have mental illness, and additionally are subject to the systemic oppressions of poverty and racism, there is a good chance you may end up on the streets or in jail. Our county's jail system (the largest in the world) is also the largest mental health institution in the US, and of the more than 69,000 unhoused people in the county last year, 54 percent reported having a serious mental health condition. If you are "lucky," you may find yourself living in a board-and-care facility, usually places somewhat stark and spartan, where residents are given meals and a bed, and some assistance with daily living, such as hygiene and medication. Though far better for most than living on the streets, in these places there is a pervading sense of inertia, a feeling of being "in-between" one place and the next, without, for most, a strong sense of having somewhere else to go.

"People have a desire to be seen, to be known, to have who they are received and reflected back to them," observes Jane.

When I teach art therapy to undergraduates, I begin the class by showing the students an image of Neolithic cave art. You've probably seen this image or one similar: of hands, the fingers spread wide, layered over each other in outlines of white, red, and black across the surface of the rock. These hand stencils are found all over the world in caves dating from 40,000 to 13,000 BCE, and they are as legible and immediate to modern viewers as if they had been created yesterday. "What do you see when you look at this image?" I ask the students. Some of the answers I typically hear are: "A greeting." "A horror movie scene." "Reaching out." "Graffiti." "Like the people who made them wanted to record that they were there." There is something greatly moving in these hand images that I have come to understand as a sense of the artists' presence, that human impulse to leave a mark—to say, "I was here."

I am an art therapist because I believe that creating art is a deeply humanizing experience, and that at heart the work of a therapist lies in helping reacquaint people with their innate worthiness, purpose, belonging, and power. In a society that thrives on undermining our connection to the fullness of our humanity and relies on a hierarchical system of dehumanization to justify its harms, making art—especially for those who have been dehumanized—can be a radical act. It is no accident that when artworks created by prisoners at Guantánamo Bay made their way out of the prison and were exhibited publicly, the US government quickly shut the exhibit down, declaring all art created in the prison to be its property. It is an imperative that the subjects of state violence and repression be seen as less than human, or rendered invisible.

And so for the invisible to speak, putting something of themselves in an image or in words visible and legible to others may be the first and most radical act in the collective reimagining it will take to make the world anew. A world, to quote the writer and activist Rebecca Solnit, in which everyone's story "has a place." ❁

BIO Sarah Eggers is an art therapist, poet, and organizer living in the Los Angeles area.

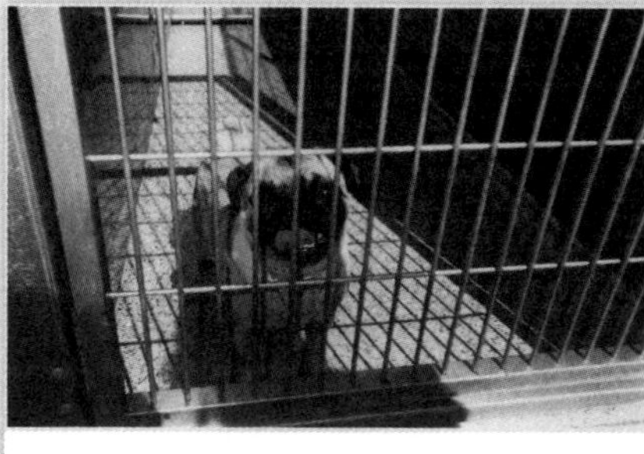

A Dog In A Shelter

**This picture makes me feel sad.
The dog is waiting to be adopted
and looks sad and hopeless.
She's wanting freedom,
but instead is trapped behind bars.**

I can relate to the dog.

Light

I took this self-portrait for fun, to see what it would look like.

The light comes out strong.

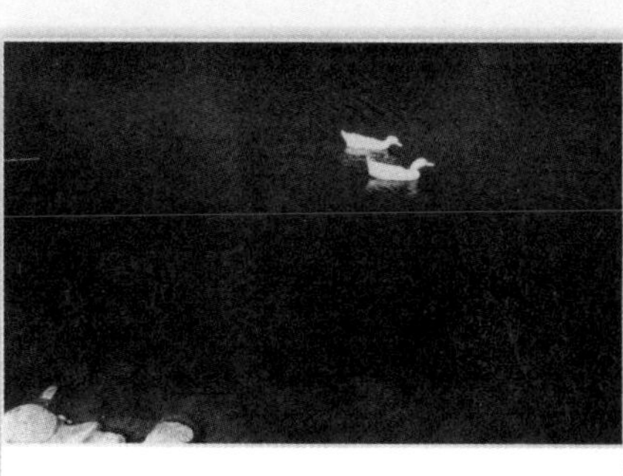

Love Partners

The ducks in the picture are partners.

Everyone needs a partner in life.

Images by anonymous participant in photography group, printed with permission.

SEE: art, art therapy, healing healers through the arts

CONTRIBUTION

Open Art Studio Collaboration: The Heart Grows through Art—Baylor Scott & White Health's Arts in Medicine Program

THE OPEN ART STUDIO at Baylor University Medical Center (Dallas, TX) is open to patients, patients' families, and staff. Individuals can drop by the Open Art Studio without an appointment and make art in the presence of an art therapist. Often the participants have been on complex medical journeys or are caregivers. The Open Art Studio is funded by the Baylor Scott & White Foundation.

The Open Art Studio participants decided to create a collaborative artwork. They were asked to think about what would represent the Open Art Studio community. The theme of growth resonated with the participants. Individuals were able to tie growth back to their experiences in the Open Art Studio. The imagery of a tree quickly became the focus, and *The Heart Grows through Art* was created.

The piece also needed to be thoughtfully designed to encourage participation from art studio regulars, as well as those who may drop in for a day or a few hours when visiting the hospital. When designing the tree, it was clear it needed to include lots of branches tangled together representing the unique personalities and talents of the Open Art Studio. Participants wanted a strong trunk and branches to represent the foundation of the Arts in Medicine program that started 7 years ago.

Participants shared examples of personal growth, such as greater confidence and consistency in developing their art practice, better ways of coping, feeling more grounded, and an improved mood. Many participants noted that their time in the Open Art Studio is their self-care.

The participants in our Open Art Studio find art to be healing and important to their day-to-day lives. Many of our artists found art therapy at Baylor University Medicine Center, leading them to discover that they, too, are artists. This has given them the confidence to continue to explore and develop their artist identity. ❁

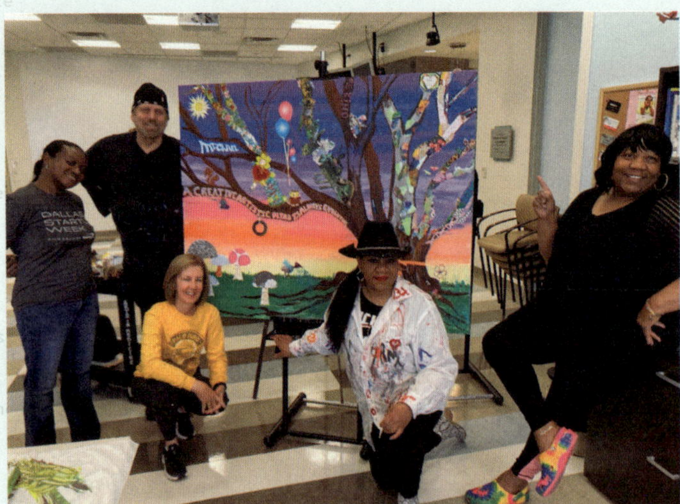

A few of our contributing artists (from left): Shani, Robert, Becky, Barbara, and Marilyn.

BIOS

Ashley Jones, MS, LPC, ATR-BC, studied art therapy at Florida State University and has worked in the Arts in Medicine program since it started 7 years ago.

Jennifer McSparron, MA, LPC, ATR, studied art therapy and counseling at Antioch University Seattle and has worked for Baylor Scott and White Health since November 2021.

Jessica Villegas, MPS, ATR-BC, LCAT, is a visual artist and studied art therapy at School of Visual Arts in NYC currently working at Baylor University Medical Center in Dallas, Texas.

love
lunar cycle
Magic School, the
mapping support
marginality
(as a site of
resistance)
Marxist social
work
membership theory
in social work
mending
metaphor
mikveh
mobile libraries
movement
lawyering
mutual aid
mycelia as
metaphor
narradrama
narrative
medicine
narrative therapy
nepantla/
nepantleras
nonviolent
communication
ongoingness
peer counseling
peer-to-peer
health network
person-situation
perspective
perspective via
faith
pleasure
poems/poetry
poetic meter
polarity work
post-
oppositionality
postwork
imaginaries
poverty-aware
social work
paradigm, the
power threat
meaning (PTM)
framework
pre(care)ity
prison abolition
professionalism
without
performance
progressive
education
public benefits
public library,
the
qigong
radical
administration
radical care in
the arts
radical childcare
in movement
spaces
radical
inclusion
radical
papermaking
radical presence
radical
social work
Radical Therapist
Journal, The
Rank and File
Movement (RFM)
in social work

re-authoring
reclaiming selfhood
recognition
redistribution
Reflecting on Justice
reflexivity
Reiki
relational
interviewing
relationality
resistance
resisting the
parental loss
narrative
resonance
respectful visiting
respite room
rest as resistance
revenge
revolutionary
mothering
ritual
sanctuary
sandplay therapy
sauna
seed banking
sex positivity
shadow integration
Sick Woman Theory
slow textiles
slowness
social change
ecosystem framework
social construction
social practice
social therapeutics
Social Welfare Action
Alliance, the
solidarity
solidarity economy
somatic healing
songs/singing
sound healing
speculative design
spells
staying with the
trouble
storytelling
street newspaper
strengths
perspective, the
sufficiency
sustaining movement
symbol
Taos Institute, the
tarot
temporary autonomous
zones
Theatre of the
Oppressed
theories of change
theosophy
therapeutic writing
togetherness
trans practices
transformative
justice
traspatio
12-step programs
undercover anti-
bullying teams
vigil
water
wildness
wintering as metaphor
wishes
witchery
yoga
zinemaking

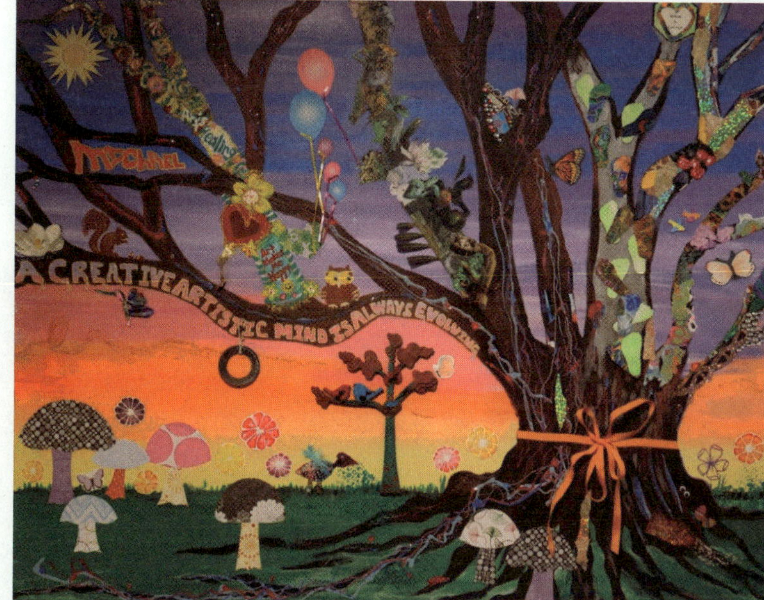

The Heart Grows through Art, Mixed Media Arts in Medicine Program, Open Art Studio 2023, 48 × 60 in.

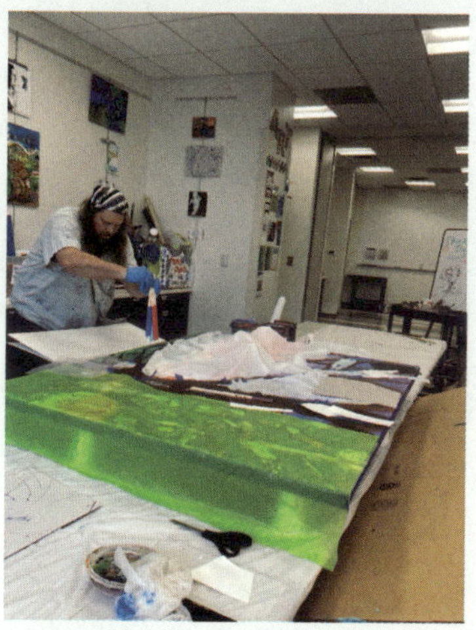

Artist Robert adding his original "triple-dipple" technique.

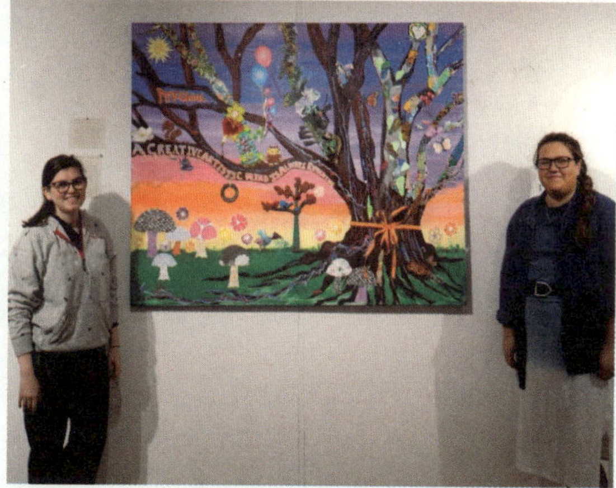

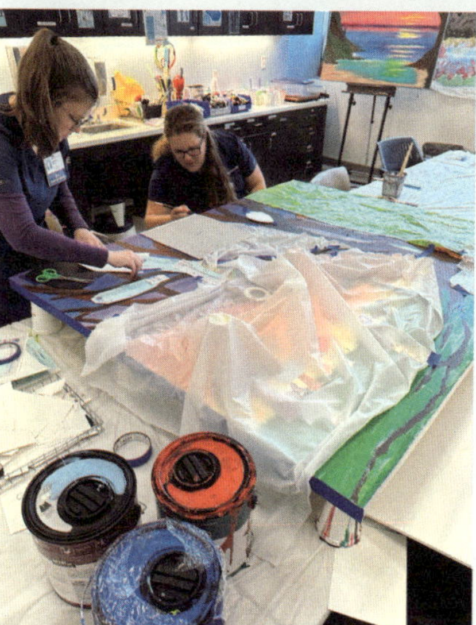

Top:
Art Therapists Ashley Jones and Jennifer McSparron.

Bottom:
Art Therapists Ashley Jones and Jennifer McSparron putting final touches on the community painting.

arts-based research

CONTRIBUTION

ARTS-BASED RESEARCH is a kind of research where the research is done not through analyzing interviews, or correlating numbers, but through doing artwork itself. It's good for exploring topics in health and social sciences and beyond to discover more about emotions, spirituality, ineffable aspects of human experience, and for developing new questions and insights about our existence. One cool thing about arts-based research is that the process and products are much more understandable than typical research, so it's more accessible to the general public. ❁

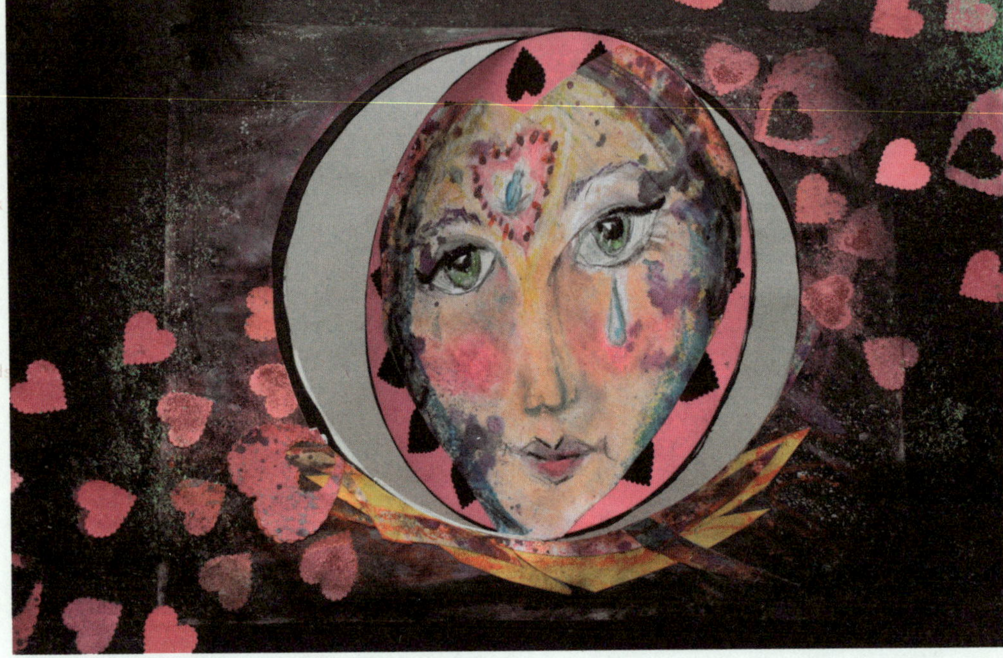

An example of response art from Gioia Chilton's 2014 dissertation, "An Arts-Based Study of the Dynamics of Expressing Positive Emotions within the Intersubjective Art-Making Process."

BIO

Gioia Chilton, PhD, ATR-BC, CSAC, is an artist, art therapist, researcher, and author who loves her family and art therapy community.

Authentic Movemen

SEE recognition, relationalit, social practice, trans practices

CONTRIBUTION

AS A DANCER, I first encountered the practice of Authentic Movement in workshops led by choreographers DD Dorvillier and Jennifer Monson working in New York City's downtown dance scene. The form was simple: two people pair up. One person is the mover; beginning in stillness, they close their eyes and move out of their internal instinct, with no need to perform or accomplish anything. The other person is the witness; they witness the mover and offer a supportive touch if the mover is about to run into a wall, etc. The relationship between the mover and witness is not prioritized; instead, the priority is the mover's psycho-somatic state.

I immediately loved it: it felt like the performative encounter distilled to its simplest form, and it reminded me why I felt most like myself while dancing. Somehow being witnessed offered me the safety to forget the witness entirely and go into an altered state of existence and movement. Only later did I research the form and come to discover it originated as a kind of movement therapy originally created by dancer Mary Starks Whitehouse.

Whitehouse studied with German expressionist choreographer Mary Wigman and later the queen of American modern dance, Martha Graham. She was also deeply invested in a private study of analytic psychology, especially Jungian psychology. Working in her studio in Los Angeles in the 1950s, she initially called the practice "movement in depth," emphasizing the aim to release culturally determined ways of moving and instead practice intuitive movement. This evolved into the practice of Authentic Movement described above. When asked what constitutes this purportedly "authentic" movement, Whitehouse responded,

> An authentic movement is in and of the Self at the moment it is done. Nothing is in it that is not inevitable, simple. When it is authentic, I can almost tell you what is coming next. When I see somebody move authentically, it is so real that it is undiluted by any pretense or any appearance or images. Often, it can be the movement of just one hand turning over, or it can be the whole body.[1]

Movement therapist Janet Adler elaborated on Whitehouse's practice after an intensive training with Whitehouse in 1969. It was Adler who coined the term "witness" for the role Whitehouse had previously called "observer" or teacher, which Adler took from the work of psychologist John Weir.[2] Adler explains the importance of this role in the practice of Authentic Movement:

> Though the mover's work, especially initially, is the primary focus of both the mover and the witness, the inner reality of the witness appears to be as vast, as complex, and as essential to the process as the inner world of the mover. With the movement of one as catalyst, the witness and the mover work together, over time, each refining her capacity to integrate her experience of formless material into form.[3]

Turning formlessness into form—what a stunning way to describe the alchemy of human relation, of being and being seen, of connecting with oneself and therefore others. ✺

1 Pallaro, editor. "An Approach to the Center: An Interview with Mary Whitehouse by Gilda Frantz."

2 Pallaro, editor. "Who Is the Witness? A Description of Authentic Movement by Janet Adler."

3 Pallaro, "Who Is the Witness?"

BIO elena rose light (they/them), choreographer, performer, writer.

autonomous healing

SEE: accessibility
access invocations
ctivating archives
frofuturism
gency
ging positivity
ltar work
lternative identity
projects
ncestral wisdom
ncestrality
nti-ableism
nti-adultism
nti-racism
nti-racism court
system
rt
rt as/in/of life
rt journaling
rt therapy
rt workers
rt-based group work
rts in medicine
rts-based research
uthentic Movement
utonomous healing
yurveda
eing with
ertha Capen Reynolds
ike and car repair
collectives
lack Panther Party
Free Breakfast
Program
ody as community
ody neutrality
ody positivity
ody Trust
oredom
rave space
reaking the rules
ridge as metaphor
care pods
care-based co-housing
Catholic Worker
Movement
centering maintenance
circular economy
climate cafes
clouds as metaphor
coalition
collaborative
apprenticeship
collective care
common pool resources
commons, the
communing with
animals
community college
community gardens
community newspapers
conjure
constructionist-
design framework, the
consulting your
consultants
contemplative
tradition, the
corn knowledge
credit unions
crip time
critical fabulation
critical hope
critical pedagogy
critical race theory
critical suicide
studies
critical whiteness

CONTRIBUTION

Autonomous Healing: Calling on The Unfuckwithables, Putamente Radicales

THE PLANET CONTINUES TO ENDURE the ravaging effects of the Covid pandemic. The Russia-Ukraine war and its global impact is now over a year. Iraq is still experiencing the repercussions of the US invasion 20 years ago. The death toll in Malawi surpassed 500 after the Tropical Cyclone Freddy this year. Civilian militias, the Village Defense Guards, are reviving in Kashmir—Muslim majority region—in response to seven Hindus' deaths motivated by anti-India sentiments.[1] The deaths of about 6,000 people in the Philippines in drug-related operations tied to the government's drugs war en 2016 are being investigated as crimes against humanity. El Amazonas is facing deforestation for the progress and development of the food and technology industries. Protests are at a peak in Paris, opposing president Macron's pension reform plan without a full vote in the Parliament. In Uganda, a country that already bans same-sex relationships, its Parliament just passed a bill that will further criminalize LGBTQIIA+ if it becomes law. Fracking in California continues to threaten animals, plants, air pollution, and water contamination. Valentina Trespalacios, a 21-year-old Colombian DJ, was strangled and her body thrown in a garbage container by her male partner, John Poulos, a White US citizen she met on a dating app. Poulos is currently incarcerated in Bogotá, facing charges for femicide.

As Western therapists,[2] we are called upon as responders to the huMan[3] impact of events like the ones above. Our response could be understood to be highly dependent on our consumption of tuition-based and licensing-driven English knowledge produced by the institutions of the Western suffering-market economy. To a large extent, such specialized knowledge assembles a fictional skin-bound huMan individual chopped from the earth and given an abstract mind and body, relational, internal-culpability, and triggering capabilities to be subjected to expert examination and assessment.

The constitution of a huMan individual keeps therapists in the dark from the complex colonial sociopolitical structures of fuckery, o de mierda, that make possible such an assemblage in the first place; and centers our focus instead on the identification of individual needs and the design of solutions. We are expected to heal the huMan-centric world, one huMan at a time, and maintain unchallenged the status quo of the suffering-market economy. Therefore, tuition-made therapists could be considered the material expression of Western modernity's thought. We translate colonial structures of war, ecocide, or femicide into an architectural design of a sovereign (dis)functional, guilty individual, fractured and separated from earth. Furthermore, we assemble an individual sufferer separate from and superior to the non-huMan, with privatized[4] behavioral, emotional, physiological, and cognitive features out of which we can produce needs that will sustain modernity's profitable, practice- or research-outcome-based therapeutic solutions with persuasive or marketable brands of change for consumption.

The hegemony of modernity/coloniality's logic[5] of helping, based on the production of global needs and solutions,[6] undoubtedly has benefited both tuition-made therapists and clients. Still, the prevalence of wars, ecocide, femicide, and exploitation in different forms of expression—huMan and non-huMan—calls for parallel options out of something other than the same

Cuestionamos
curiosity
death practices
decolonial
liberatory-based
practices
deep organizing
dérive, the
drumming
embodied expression
embodied knowledge
emergent strategy
empathy
energy work
erasure, avoiding
thereof
esoteric wisdom
traditions
ethnodrama
etymology
existentialism
externalizing
failure
fat positivity
feminism
feminst ethics
of care
fermentation
flâneur
food sovereignty
forest bathing
fragments
fragmentation
freedom
generous system
gift economie
Grace Lee Boggs
grief as nonlinear
group work
group
harm reduction
healing circle
healing healer
through the arts
healing justice
healing ritual
Hearing Voices
Network
herbal justice
herbalism
holding space
humanness
humor
illder
improvisation
infinite blackness
intentional
communities
interdisciplinary
cataloging
intergenerational
living
interspecies
organizing
intuitive eating
justice-oriented
counseling
land trust
land, work
spirit, body
language justice
leaving well
liberatory
education
life cycle
honoring the
liminality
limited-equity
cooperative
housing

dominant logic and market; and constituted out of the destitutions by Western therapy[7]. Thus, this is not a call for a new hegemony of therapy translated to apply across Colombia, France, Malawi, Russia, India, or the Philippines. Rather, it is a call for autonomous healing, putamente and radically different.

Autonomous healing means other than that performed by independent, self-sufficient individuals from our private therapy offices. Instead, it is communally governed[8] and nondependent, or non-governable by the structures of the current economy of suffering and its institutions (i.e., academic programs, accrediting organizations, licensing boards, publication houses, research labs, pharmaceutical companies); although possibly in dialogue with them, if at all. As I sense it, autonomous healing comes from the putamente radicales unfuckwithables.

Here, the unfuckwithables exist beyond ontological considerations. By this I mean that their existence is not within a renewed skin-bound being, with a privatized essence, and interior or exterior lives to aspire to and document in curricula vitae and social media, whose worthiness is based on salaries, degrees, licenses to heal, or publications. While they might exist with all these, that is beside the point for the unfuckwithables. Thus, if the question of the putamente unfuckwithables is not about their being, it is about what they do (heal and transform) and how they dwell (inter-communally in movement). That is, because the emphasis of being (ontology) fractures them from what they are not, as in the dualities of the human and not-human; therapists and clients; healers and sufferers. The emphasis on doing and dwelling instead connects them with what makes them and their existence—the communal, movement, and time.

The unfuckwithables are everywhere. They do and dwell plurally, like mycelium (different than the poststructuralist rhizome).[9] Mycelium are multicellular fungi assembled in time, collectively, and moving rapidly as an extensive and complex interconnected and interdependent network. They function underground and have the capacity to break down toxic substances and organic materials in digestible forms for reuse in the ecosystem as energy. Easily undetected by the human eye, this network is lifegiving. It acts as trees communicating among each other for water and mineral transportation. The mycelium attach to the roots as a large soaking sponge for trees to soak up all the nutrients that will maintain the ecosystem alive and healthy, and never depleted. Connected by mycelium, older and taller trees or trees growing under conditions of sunlight with roots in deeper soil communicate to each other, recognizing from the network the root tips of distress from trees in shady areas to favor them with nutrients that they can absorb.

Like mycelium, calling on the putamente unfuckwithables means calling on the communal by looking/sensing everywhere (beyond the therapy room), as that is where they are. As autonomous communal threads of healing, their connections are among various organisms that do not require huMan, professional or otherwise, features to organize their capacity to soak up and suck up healing energy from each other, when responding to the demands of shady fuckeries to keep the communal alive and never depleted. While professional degrees, therapeutic interventions, or innovative models of solution could factor in, what makes them putamente unfuckwithables rather is their relational capacidad de reception and sharing—not production y consumo. Putamente, they may function underground, undetected by Western eyes, breaking down structures of war, femicidio, ecocide, and exploitation, transforming toxicity into life-giving energy to sustain the earth's unchopped ecosystem. ❋ →

1 Al Jazeera, "Why India's revival of civil militias in Kashmir is raising fears."

2 Western therapists here mean decontextualized therapists with no history and no regard to positionality.

3 My spelling of "huMan" intends to convey that the Western notion of therapy is dependent on the particular notion of humanity that the Jamaican philosopher Sylvia Wynter (Wynter & McKittrick, 2015) critiques. For Wynter, while the West defines the human as a natural organism, its conception rather overrepresents the liberal, capitalist conception of pure, white, Man-as-human, whereby the white Man is the model for all human experience. Her decolonial project implies the generation of new modes of human life, as I intend to do here with the unfuckwithables.

4 Tichindeleanu, "The Struggle for Positive Peace and Pluriversality."

5 Mignolo, *The Politics of Decolonial Investigations*.

6 Escobar, *Autonomía y Diseño: La Realización de lo Comunal*.

7 Mignolo, *The Politics of Decolonial Investigations*.

8 Escobar, *Autonomía y Diseño*.

9 Escobar, *Autonomía y Diseño*.

BIO marcela polanco, descendent of the Muisca; nonconsensually racialized in the U.S. as heterosexual, brown, cis woman, and middle-class immigrant; domesticated in Westernized educational institutions in English (US) and Spanish (Colombia), hence active participant in the sustainability of eurocentric, capitalist, racist, and sexist systems of oppression.

I STARTED LEARNING about Ayurveda when I began studying yoga in my twenties and was always hungry to learn more about this 5,000-year-old science of self-care. In 2013, I signed up for an immersive Ayurvedic course, which helped me not only to learn about Ayurveda, but also to apply it to my life. I was amazed by how much more energized and grounded I felt when I was really practicing Ayurveda on a daily basis. I started a coaching program to help others apply Ayurvedic wisdom to their lives, and in 2019, I published *selfcarefully* (Thick Press), which focused on many Ayurvedic topics. In 2015 and 2017, I traveled with a group of my clients to Ayurveda Yoga Villa in Kerala, India, to experience the traditional Ayurvedic treatments I had read so much about. At that time, Dr. Jithin Namala was the doctor at the Ayurvedic center, but truly he was so much more than any Western idea of a doctor. He not only helped us to understand and treat the imbalances in our bodies, but also counseled us on our mental and spiritual well-being. His grandfather had also been an Ayurvedic practitioner and I felt this lineage of wisdom come through to us in his care. It was so unlike anything I'd experienced in the Western medical system!

As I prepare to rewrite sections of *selfcarefully* for republication in 2024, I wanted to interview Dr. Jithin. I was curious to get his perspective on how Ayurveda might help us face the immense issues of our time with a sense of integrity and well-being. I started the interview by asking him to describe Ayurveda from the beginning and was amazed by the richness his answer contained. —GO

DR. JITHIN: When I start speaking about Ayurveda, with the beginner, I start from the word Ayurveda itself. The word Ayurveda actually hides all the mysteries of Ayurveda. The word itself speaks a lot. Just the word Ayurveda for us is a philosophy. It is not just a medical science. It is not just a wellness practice. It's not a herbal medicine. It's a philosophy for life. Ayurveda means the science of life.

When I start talking about Ayurveda or giving lectures about Ayurveda, the basics, speaking to beginners, I start with the history, the beginning of Ayurveda. The word comes from Sanskrit, from the Vedic philosophy. It's a product of continuous research about all the aspects of life. Ayurveda is also a product from the Vedas. In the Veda where Ayurveda is originally from, it speaks a lot about life, spirituality, rituals, and such practices. Ayurveda comes from this, and the word itself means science of life. Reading between the lines, think about the mysteries this word hides. The first approach to Ayurveda should be: don't be skeptical, be open. It's a big, broad philosophy which speaks all—everything about life.

Always, Ayurveda is a theistic philosophy. The modern education is so materialistic; it has its own precise tools—measure, assess, data mine, analyze. It's very logic-based. It's very materialistic. When you try to assess the philosophy of Ayurveda using the tools of modern science, it's a bit difficult to understand and accept, because it's a science, but it has its own method of research, its own method of analysis, its own methods of finding the hypothesis. So you have to approach Ayurveda differently.

See, the very fundamental, basic ideology is a holistic science. It believes in the existence of body, mind, and spirit as a union in one unit; that's the human being. So you have to study it from the rules. Don't try to approach Ayurveda as a herbal medicine. When you approach Ayurveda as a herbal medicine, you try to understand how the herb works and what does the herb contain as the active principle inside, what's the chemical component of the herb. But the herb works not because it has this active component inside, or not that it has a particular chemical component inside. It also works for that reason. But at many times, the approach of Ayurveda is not for that reason. ➔

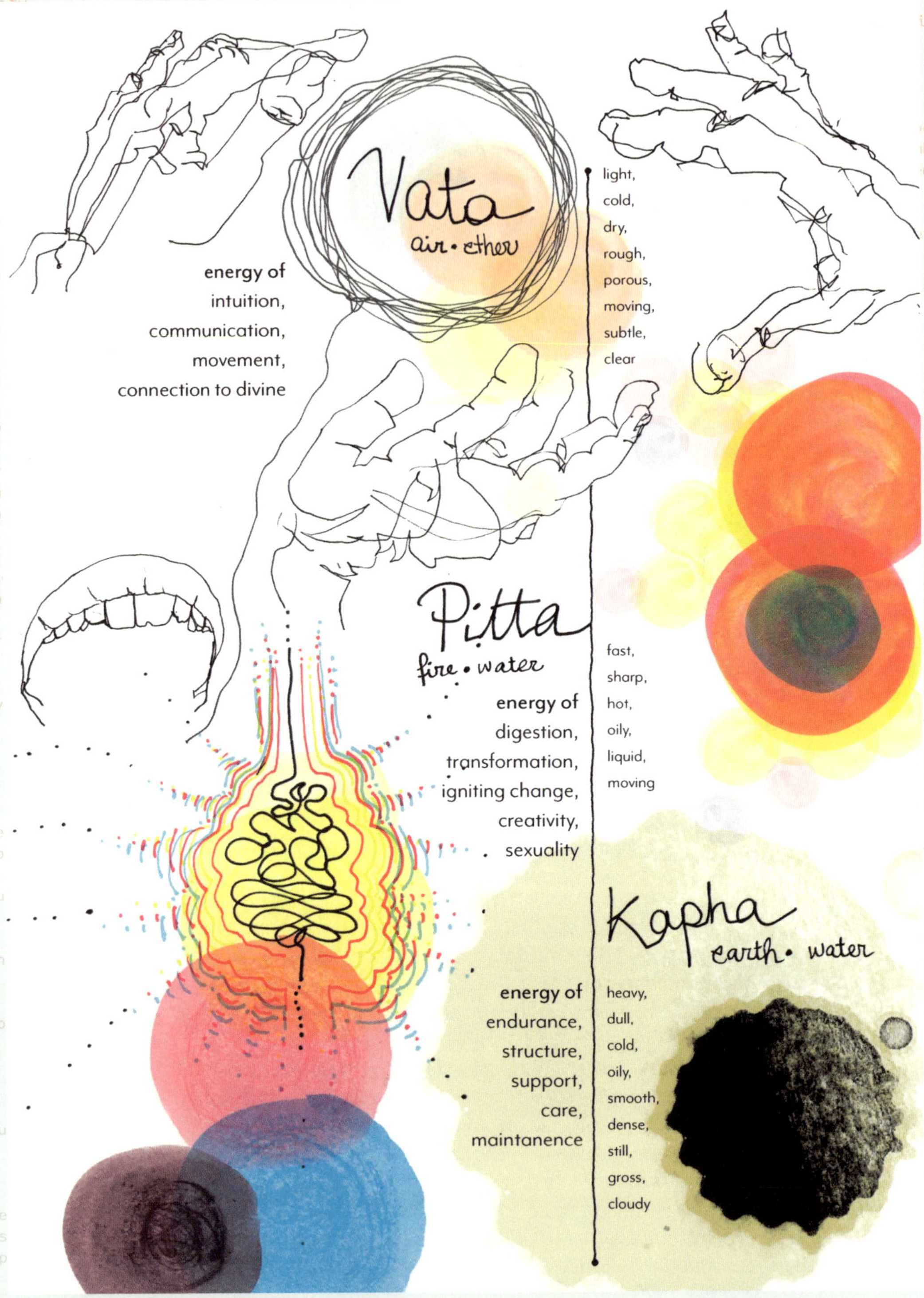

Ayurveda

Vata
air • ether

energy of
intuition,
communication,
movement,
connection to divine

light,
cold,
dry,
rough,
porous,
moving,
subtle,
clear

Pitta
fire • water

energy of
digestion,
transformation,
igniting change,
creativity,
sexuality

fast,
sharp,
hot,
oily,
liquid,
moving

Kapha
earth • water

energy of
endurance,
structure,
support,
care,
maintanence

heavy,
dull,
cold,
oily,
smooth,
dense,
still,
gross,
cloudy

Vata (air, ether): energy of intuition, communication, movement, connection to drive (light, cold, dry, rough, porous, moving, subtle, clear) / Pitta (fire, water): energy of digestion, transformation, igniting change, creativity, sexuality (fast, sharp, hot, oily, liquid, moving) / Kapha (earth, water): energy of endurance, structure, care, maintenance (heavy, dull, cold, oily, smooth, dense, still, gross, cloudy)

"The Energetics of the Doshas," Maria Habib and Gracy Obuchowicz.

That's why we consider the dosha, that's why we consider the doshas, that's why we consider the various fundamental factors.

We have to go back to the roots of Ayurveda. Ayurveda is basically a theistic philosophy. It believes in the existence of God. You cannot prove God, you cannot show God. You cannot materialistically understand or agree with the God, with the modern science. Nowhere when you study medicine, or when you study modern medicine or modern science, does it speak about God. But Ayurveda is a science that starts about God. See if you start reading any of the ancient texts of Ayurveda like the Ashtamga Hridayam Sutrasthana, which is considered the Bible of Ayurveda. It starts from the phrase:

> **रागादि रोगान् सततानुषक्तान् शेषकायप्रसृतानशेषान्औत्सुक्यमोहारतिदाञ्जघान**
> **यो अपूर्ववैध्याय नमो अस्तु तस्मै**
>
> **Salutation to The Unique and Rare Physician, who has destroyed, without any residue all the diseases like Raga (lust, anger, greed, arrogance, jealousy, selfishness, ego), which are constantly associated with the body, which is spread all over the body, giving rise to disease, delusion and restlessness.**
>
> ***This salutation is done to Lord Dhanwantari.***

That means the whole book starts from the phrase of bowing the head in front of the great physician—the God is referred to as the great physician. So it's a theistic philosophy. The theology is something you cannot explain with modern science tools. It's something you have to believe, which you cannot see. So when you start learning, you are forced to believe what you can't see. ❁

BIOS

Gracy Obuchowicz is a wellness facilitator who is passionate about secondhand fashion, day-to-day meal planning, and connecting the many dots between our personal self-care and collective liberation.

Dr. Jithin Paul Varghese Namala, Ayurveda consultant, Sagasfeld Ayurveda, and Yoga.

maria habib spends her days in her studio "DesignMa" with her two cats, designing, drawing, and gardening for food and medicine—all the while missing her home, Beirut, Lebanon.

being with

SEE: holding space, humanness

CONTRIBUTION

TOGETHERNESS EASES SUFFERING. Touch reduces physical and emotional pain, in the moment and in memory; simple presence of a loved one reduces suffering. While these have been demonstrated through positivist research[1], we know this intuitively as we seek out the comfort of our people when we are in pain.

Being with someone who is suffering gives them permission to focus on their pain: understanding the source of it, exploring the extent of it, learning to tolerate it, and deciding what to do about it. It puts boundaries around the suffering, giving it shape, and removes the terror of loneliness in facing the pain. *Being with* generates the conditions that make healing possible.

Anyone who is in a healing profession experiences this in the succor they provide on first contact, the palpable relief when a person sees that *someone is here to help*. While the newer clinician may then feel some obligation to *be helpful* in some explicit way, as if the relief is unearned or the expression of anticipation, the reality is that the provider has already provided some amount of comfort. Showing up is an act of love, *being with* is an act of love (SEE love). The stance of claiming to know another's pain without first having engaged with it, and thereby moving too quickly to intervention—rather than showing up and demonstrating a willingness to try (and fail) to understand—risks erasing key aspects of a person's experience and doing unintentional harm (SEE erasure, avoiding thereof).

The practice of *being with* involves putting aside one's own circumstances and preconceptions, focusing instead on trying to fully grasp the other's experience. It requires humility, an awareness that you will never be as expert on another's experience as they themselves are. It also requires a combination of the willingness to share in suffering and the capacity to stay afloat. *Being with* is capacious, in that it makes space for the fullness of the other person without hurrying, and it tethers the person to solid ground through the relationship rather than resulting in the suffering becoming infectious. ❁

1 Duschek et al., "Dispositional Empathy Is Associated with Experimental Pain Reduction During Provision of Social Support by Romantic Partners"; Sahi et al., "The Comfort in Touch: Immediate and Lasting Effects of Handholding on Emotional Pain."

BIO

Noriko Martinez works imperfectly as a radical helper by sitting with people, being curious, and loving the world.

Bertha Capen Reynolds

CONTRIBUTION

A Radical Prophet without Honor in Her Own Time

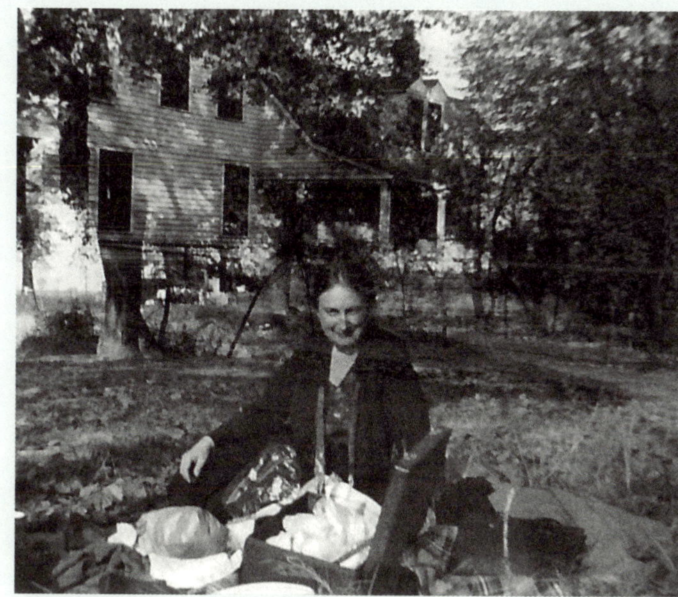

BERTHA CAPEN REYNOLDS (1885–1978) was a leading social work theorist and activist who integrated Freudian and Marxist concepts into both practice and educational frameworks. Although she had enormous influence on the profession, her radical views led to her marginalization until a new generation "rediscovered" her work a decade before her death in 1978.

As an undergraduate, Reynolds developed a class-consciousness that influenced her entire career. Although she did not self-identify as a feminist or play a leadership role in women's organizations, the independence and courage Reynolds displayed reflected changing ideas about women's roles in society. A white woman who grew up in a Methodist family in Western Massachusetts, after graduating from college she witnessed the social conditions affecting African Americans in the South through her work in Georgia. This experience had a strong influence on her future scholarship and political and social activism. She was a strong supporter of organized labor, particularly the multi-racial organizing of the Congress of Industrial Organizations (CIO), and the programs of the Communist and Socialist Parties during the 1930s and 1940s.

In the 1920s, Freudian psychology presented a radical challenge to prevailing theories of human behavior. For decades, Freud's ideas appealed to radical social workers because they stressed "client self-determination, clarity of agency function, and the importance of relationship."[1] Although Reynolds embraced many of the underlying concepts of Freudian psychology, she expressed concerns about the disease model at its core. She also noted how some social workers embraced Freudian ideas, not for their radical implications, but due to their unspoken fear that social revolution would occur if the façade of 1920s prosperity collapsed.

During the Great Depression, Reynolds became active in the Rank and File Movement among social workers, which addressed issues like the rise of fascism and racial repression in the South that mainstream professionals largely ignored. Always conscious of the impact of class differences, she

SEE: nonviolent communication, resonance, sustaining movements, togetherness, vigil criticized New Deal policies from a left-wing perspective and supported civil rights legislation, union organizing, and direct social action.[2] In the late 1930s, the newly created House Committee on Un-American Activities (HUAC) began to investigate "subversives" like Reynolds in the social work profession. Her affiliation with left-wing parties and organized labor led to her subsequent blacklisting. The anti-Communist purges of the McCarthy period further marginalized Reynolds as the social work field became increasingly conservative. Her important contributions were omitted from texts, and public officials blocked her from speaking at conferences. It was not until a new generation of activist social workers "rediscovered" her work in the late 1960s and 1970s that she regained her former prominence.

Reynolds's scholarship, teaching, and activism emphasized several key concepts. She believed that a nation's social welfare system should combine government-financed economic supports to meet basic human needs and psychosocial supports provided by social service agencies. She drew specific connections between anti-welfare and anti-labor attacks: "If public assistance could be destroyed, Labor would be forced to accept wages below subsistence levels, and without recourse. If protests of organized labor could be eliminated, public assistance itself could be reduced to legalized starvation under controls approximating slavery."[3]

Reynolds argued that if social work did not go beyond "offering palliatives to assuage the miseries of poverty and racism, [it] was destined to carry out the designs of the ruling class and victimize clients."[4] A natural corollary of this position was that social work needed to avoid "the path of exploitation and [adopt] a more radical vision of society."[5] Reynolds grasped the potential to synthesize the theories of Freud and Marx into a coherent radical practice framework that focused on both structural change and individual empowerment.[6] Decades before most of her colleagues, she criticized social work's uncritical embrace of the hierarchical medical model of practice and how unequal power dynamics influenced the social service setting. Instead, her proposed practice model focused on four key principles:[7]

1. The criterion of belonging;
2. The criterion of full adult status while receiving help;
3. The criterion of mutuality, that is having a recognized capacity to repay society at some time in some way; and
4. The criterion of having no strings attached to the receipt of assistance.

The egalitarian relationship this implied laid the foundation for what became critical social work theory and practice in the late 20th century.[8]

Similar themes shaped her ideas about social work education. Reynolds embraced "the themes of experiential learning, action and interaction, the study of man [sic] in nature, and the values of social responsibility."[9] Her teaching emphasized faith in science, the importance of experience, and the central role of a social vision to guide practice. She believed students needed to know the objective conditions that affected the people with whom they worked. She also recognized the importance of helping students overcome their fear of risk-taking and their resistance to acknowledging the power dynamics involved in practice.

Throughout her career, Reynolds believed that social work practice and education were inseparable from the process of social change. She consistently criticized the false dichotomy that existed in the profession between interventions to improve the distribution of vital resources and power and those designed to enhance people's quality of life. Social workers, she asserted, faced "a choice between contradictory forces in our society: those which are moving toward the welfare of the people… and those which destroy human life in preventable misery and war, and relieve poverty only grudgingly to keep the privileged position they hold."[10]

She questioned how social workers could rationalize practice with individuals in an environment of persistent poverty and growing human need[11] and pondered whether social workers would become agents of social control who doled out barely adequate resources to placate clients and thereby preserve the status quo. Instead, she envisioned a radical social work in the future that would "understand the dynamics of growth [and]… aid what is socially useful and try to inhibit forces that that are destructive to human well-being."[12]

These prophetic words have the potential to provide a roadmap for a more radical future. ❁

1 Schwartz, "Bertha Reynolds as Educator," 7.

2 Wenocur & Reisch, *From Charity to Enterprise: The Development of American Social Work in a Market Economy.*

3 Reynolds, *An Uncharted Journey*, 271.

4 Joseph, "The Bertha C. Reynolds Centennial Conference June 28–30, 1985: Taking Organizing Back to the People," 122.

5 Reisch, "Linking Client and Community: The Impact of Bertha Reynolds on Social Work," 63.

6 Reynolds, *Between Client and Community: A Study of Responsibility in Social Casework.*

7 Reynolds, *Social Work and Social Living: Explorations in Philosophy and Practice*, 33–52.

8 Reisch & Andrews, *The Road Not Taken: A History of Radical Social Work in the United States.*

9 Schwartz, 6.

10 Reynolds, Bertha Capen. Social Work and Social Living: Explorations in Philosophy and Practice, 6.

11 Reynolds, Bertha Capen. *An Uncharted Journey*, 17.

12 Reynolds, *Learning and Teaching in the Practice of Social Work*, 4.

BIO Michael Reisch is Distinguished Professor of Social Justice Emeritus, University of Maryland, Baltimore.

bike and car repair collectives

SEE: circular economy, common pool resources

CONTRIBUTION

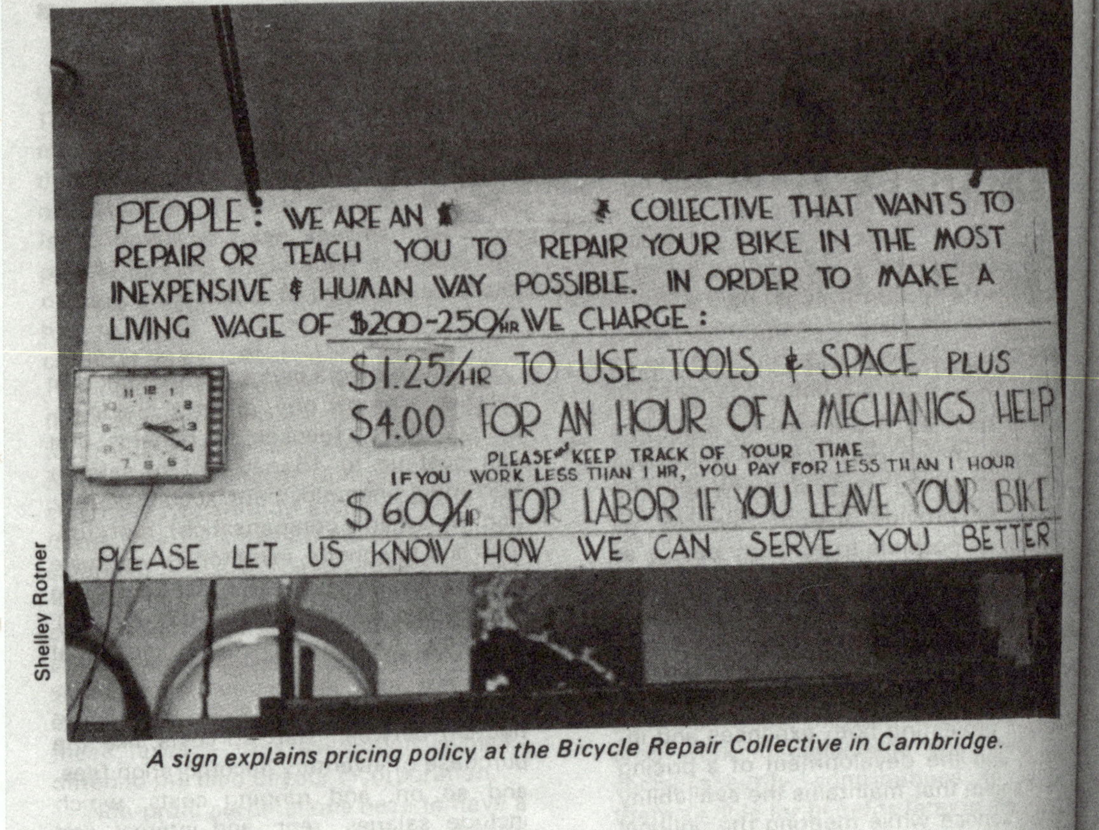

A sign explains pricing policy at the Bicycle Repair Collective in Cambridge.

From *No Bosses Here: A Manual on Working Collectively*, by Vocations for Social Change.

IN 1970s BOSTON, there were a number of collectively-run car and bike repair cooperatives that emphasized repair and education over profit.

The first was probably the Cambridge Cooperative Garage, which formed in 1970. The Garage encouraged people to watch and learn while staffers fixed their cars. Customers could become cooperative members for $10 plus a monthly fee. Members could use the Garage's space and tools to fix their cars, and they could buy parts at a steep discount.

The Lynn Auto Co-op and Hacker's Haven soon followed. Hacker's Haven (which counted future NPR *Car Talk* hosts Click and Clack as worker-owners) went the completely DIY route—offering space and tools for anyone to rent by the hour for a flat fee.

Like the Garage, the Lynn Auto Co-op offered parts at cost and a reasonable membership fee—and like Hacker's Haven, you could rent their space and tools by the hour. But they also introduced a few new ideas. First, you could pay a slightly higher hourly rate to get some staffers to help you fix your car. Or, if you wanted them to do everything, there was a third, higher price—which they guaranteed to be half of the going rate.

But repair cooperatives weren't just for cars—the Bicycle Repair Collective came next in 1972, borrowing ideas from these three garages and applying them to bikes. Hourly tool and space rental? Check. Slightly higher rate for them to help you? Check. And don't forget below-industry-standard prices if you wanted them to do it for you.

As you can imagine, these groups were motivated by pretty strong ideals. First, there was the customer angle. These groups aimed to cut down on consumerism, since you wouldn't need to buy as many things if you knew how to fix them. And since they emphasized repair rather than replacement, they helped cut down on waste—because you don't make as much trash if you don't throw broken things out. And then, by making things affordable and teaching people to do it themselves, these groups removed barriers for bike and car owners.

Second, there was the worker angle. These groups were set up as collectively run businesses, where all workers helped make decisions and shared in the profits—all of which was designed to fight workplace hierarchies and alienation. Everybody wins.

As the Bicycle Repair Collective explained in 1976, all of this added up to creating a new world—"working against profit, sexism, competition, and alienating ways of working. [We] want to do as much as possible to help people regain the power to control their own lives."[1]

Sadly, some of these experiments didn't last long—and predictably, money was one of the culprits. Hacker's Haven and Lynn both had trouble making rent, and were soon reborn as regular car garages.

The Cooperative Garage chased cheaper rents by moving further and further from the city, finally winding up in Watertown Square. But expenses were only part of the problem. The worker-owners became less enthusiastic about some parts of the experiment—and by 1976, they had dropped the cooperative membership plans and learning opportunities and shifted to a standard (though cheaper) repair model. Part of the problem here was the same 4 or 5 people ran the Garage the whole time—and as former member Barbara Taggart tells me, they got burned out trying to do it all. Pretty understandable. But even still, the Garage remained a collectively-run business until the early 80s.

The Bicycle Repair Collective was more fortunate. Maybe it was because there were more people involved (a number of worker-owners came and went over the years), but the business is still around today. Gone is the space rental and guaranteed super-low repair costs, but the Broadway Bicycle School (as it's now known) is still collectively run by worker-owners who teach classes and are glad to show you how to do it yourself.

And this generous spirit keeps adapting, recently giving birth to two affiliated collectives—the Somerville Bike Kitchen and the Dorchester Bike Kitchen—where volunteer bike technicians help you fix your bike at open shops a few nights a week (free, but donations gladly accepted). ❁

1 Brandow, McDonnell, and Vocations for Social Change, *No Bosses Here: A Manual on Working Collectively*, 99.

B I O
Tim Devin is an artist, writer, and proud self-publisher whose projects celebrate communities and the DIY spirit.

Black Panther Party Free Breakfast Program

CONTRIBUTION

1969, a Panther distributes drinks to children at St. Augustine's Episcopal Church (San Francisco), the site of the Party's first ever Free Breakfast Program.

TWENTY-SIX YEARS BEFORE THE UNITED STATES CENSUS Bureau began collecting well-being statistics on children, and 43 years before the Census included a question on food security, the Black Panther Party (BPP) started a free breakfast program aimed at school children. In 1967 in the United States of America, a Black family was two times more likely to fall under the "poverty level" than a white family. Despite the Great Migration—a pure collective effort to seek a better, more just future—Black Southerners were finding the same oppression, neglect, and violence in their new Northern and Western cities. This dissatisfaction prompted Huey P. Newton and Bobby Seale to create an organization wholly for the people. Rather than debate in ivory towers of academic institutions, the aim of the BPP was to educate and radicalize the Black proletariat, the people in the streets.

Though the Black Panther Party has come to be known for armed patrols and open carrying, this characterization is at best a disappointing oversimplification and at worst, a deliberate dehistoricization that prevents the BPP's more meaningful efforts from inspiring others. In fact, much of the Black Panther Party's actions centered around alternative community services. These acts of mutual aid, dubbed "survival programs" (also called "service to the people programs") consisted of a range of services operating at different capacities, depending on the needs and abilities of each BPP chapter and the communities they served. In total there were about 20[1] programs operating across the BPP's 45[2] chapters.[3] This included an employment program, medical research clinics, land banking, clothing and shoe donation, plumbing and repairs, and legal aid. The four defining programs of the Party, such that they were mandated by the Central (Oakland, CA) branch to be included in every chapter, were: liberation schools, free health services, police petition dissemination, and the Free Breakfast for Children Program. Each of these programs address the BPP's founding document, the "The Black Panther Party and Program." Written in October 1966, the ten-point program included the right to quality housing, a fair trial, clothing, food, and a life free of violence and harassment from police.

After the ten-point program was written in 1966 and before the first Breakfast Program's launch in 1969, the BPP focused much of its action on armed revolution.

Newton believed the imagery of armed Black men and women, which remains iconic to this day, would draw media attention and serve as a recruitment tool. The California State Assembly retaliated with the passage of the Mulford Act in 1967, which banned open carrying of guns in California and thwarted police patrols. BPP leadership then looked to more long-term actions to support Black liberation. Survival programs—of which the Free Breakfast for School Children Program was the first—were meant to provide the basic support that Black people lacked in a hostile country. With these supports, Black people could reach the consciousness necessary for armed revolution. Newton used the metaphor of a lifeboat to describe the programs in his autobiography *Revolutionary Suicide*: "A raft put into service during a disaster is not meant to change conditions but to help one get through a difficult time.... In themselves they do not change social conditions, but they are life-saving vehicles until social conditions change."[4]

The first BPP Free Breakfast for School Children Program (FBSCP) launched in January 1969 at St. Augustine's Church in Oakland, California. Though only eleven children attended the program's first day, 135 children were showing up for breakfast by the week's end. The FBSCP was launched in tandem with two other "survival" programs: The Black Panther Free Clinics and the Liberation Schools. The breakfast program launched after BPP community outreach, led by Bobby Seale, revealed a need from Oakland parents for support with morning childcare duties, particularly providing breakfast and helping children with their homework. Official BPP releases refer to *oppression hunger*. Thus, the FBSCP functioned as a corrective to the ways in which American racial capitalism kept Black people weak, tired, disengaged, and disadvantaged. According to academic research that arrived decades after the FBSCP and official Party publications, feeding children improved their school performance, while informal history lessons improved their sense of self and engagement in community.[5]

Just as armed self-defense was once a defining action and powerful recruiting tool for the party, so, too, were the FBSCP and other service programs. Soon after the Oakland program's success, FBSCP's became mandatory at every BPP chapter. By November 1969, fifteen chapters had breakfast programs. At its peak, the Party was serving 20,000 children a day across the United States.[6] Breakfast programs were open to children of any race and usually included escorts to and from the program site,

mutual aid
public benefits
solidarity
sustaining movements
theories of change

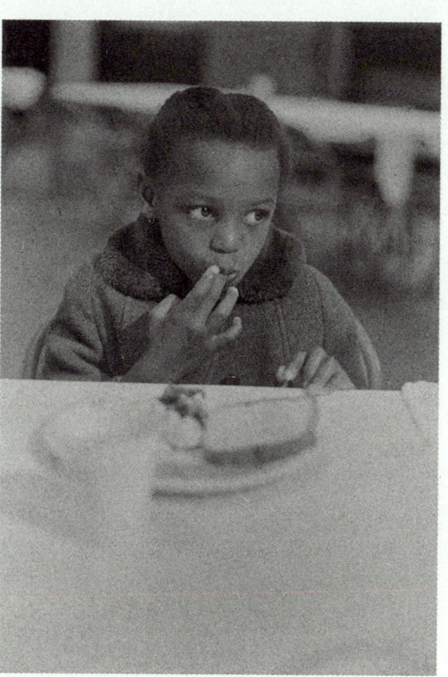

Black Panther Party Free Breakfast Program

a hot meal, help with homework, and Afrocentric teachings. Women streamed into the party and by the 1970s, more than half the BPP members were women. The Breakfast Program was volunteer based. Party members had mandatory duty, and much of the coordination, donation collection, and cooking were done by female members.

But, with every progressive action, there was often a repressive government response. The very same year that the FBSCP launched, the FBI set its sights on the BPP as part of its far-reaching counterintelligence program (COINTELPRO) under J. Edgar Hoover. Between 1968 and 1971, the FBI launched over 200 initiatives against the Black Panther Party in attempts to strip the party of money, personnel, credibility, and political will. The FBSCP was a main target of Hoover's as he feared its potential to attract a wider audience to the Panthers. Hoover, the FBI's director until 1972, explicitly recognized the political and organizing potential of the FBSCP; he described it as the "greatest threat" and the BPP's "best and most influential activity."[7]

The scale of violence and repression faced by the BPP at the hands of local police and the FBI can seem unfathomable now. Supplies and donations were often confiscated. In New York City, police officers would "drop in" on the Program in an attempt to intimidate children and party members; false information regarding the BPP's intentions and the safety of the food they served were disseminated by the FBI. In Chicago, cops damaged and urinated on donations on the FBSCP's very first day. Across the country there were mass arrests of influential organizers; and days after a fundraising rally to launch the Iowa Breakfast Program, the chapter was bombed.

*

I would argue that more than armed patrols, the FBSCP was a true example of an alternative future. Care and support were provided without a threshold of need like those of traditional government social supports; put simply, children were fed if they showed up. Their families were not scrutinized or stigmatized. This was the strength of the FBSCP—its holistic understanding of welfare, its connection of Black liberatory thought and action, its unyielding belief that simply providing and educating is all that is necessary to open oppressed people's eyes to their circumstance. ❁

1 This figure is taken from the Huey P. Newton Foundation document "The Black Panther Party: Service to the People Programs."

2 This figure is taken from Heynen (2005), "Bending the Bars of Empire from Every Ghetto for Survival: The Black Panther Party's Radical Antihunger Politics of Social Reproduction and Scale." See below for an elaboration on the nature of these statistics.

3 The BPP was an organization operated by young people; their records were not meticulous, thus some estimates may put the figure as lower or higher. N.D.B Connolly places the figure at 38 in his entry on the Party in the Encyclopedia of Chicago. http://www.encyclopedia.chicagohistory.org/pages/142.html.

4 Newton & Blake, *Revolutionary Suicide*, 322.

5 Chapman-Hilliard & Adams-Bass, "A Conceptual Framework for Utilizing Black History Knowledge as a Path to Psychological Liberation for Black Youth."

6 National Museum of African American History and Culture, "The Black Panther Party: Challenging Police and Promoting Social Change."

7 Quoted in *Power Hungry* by Suzanne Cope (2022).

BIO Lea Joseph is an aspiring urban planner with an interest in Black liberatory practices within the urban environment.

body as communit

SEE

CONTRIBUTION

WE WANTED TO SHARE a set of ideas we have found powerful and generative in our lives and practices. Through collaborative conversations, we have come to cherish the idea of the body as a whole community.[1] We relate to this community as an interconnected collective of members who are in relationship with one another, and with whom we are also in relationship with. Our hope in sharing these ideas is to invite others into conversation with their body and share some ways these concepts have helped us.

We want to begin this piece with a contribution from Hannia, who I (Fran) was in conversation with about a twenty-year-long hatred of her body, resulting in starving it, overfeeding it, and trying to make her brown skin as white as possible. Hannia described her body as her enemy, a status influenced by white supremacist, capitalist ideals of beauty, worthiness, and value in society. As she was telling me about this fraught relationship, I noticed her body rocking back and forth almost rhythmically. I became aware of my body being brought into a different rhythm. Although my head wanted to lead the conversation, I chose to let this rhythm guide us. I gently enquired what her body was trying to communicate or respond to through this movement. She looked surprised and told me she hadn't realised her body was doing this, but said it has always been her body's response when emotions are high. I asked what this movement in response to emotion represented. She replied that it's a sort of nurturing, caring, a calming… She said: I think I'd call it "mothering."

It was in this noticing of other expressions, movements, responses of her body that Hannia began connecting with ideas of her body as a community of interconnected members. She has shared an illustration of how she has connected with this community:

> Sometimes this is not an easy task and the different parts of my body conflict with each other—my eyes bring up the leaner body we have been admiring all day, my stomach wants to experience the nostalgic burst of flavour it has been craving since it first spied the chocolate bar on our kitchen counter, and my brain is already lamenting the work I have put in to drop the pounds to a healthier weight. I am starting to feel overwhelmed; everyone is speaking over each other and shouting angrily, so I close my eyes and ask my community how I can make sure everyone feels supported and what we might need to feel our best. After some searching, we agree that having a piece of chocolate would not harm our efforts or make our body sad as long as we had a nutritious meal before we had the chocolate bar. We prepare the meal lovingly, eat it slowly, and savour the delicious bar of chocolate afterwards. Everyone was happy with the arrangement, and we went to bed feeling full and glad.

Hannia shared: "I have a new friendship now, a loving and friendly one. I appreciate what members of my body need, what they do for me, and I talk to all different parts now depending on which part needs me."

For us this connects on many levels with how we have each taken up new relationships with our bodily community and what this has generated in our lives. We share an appreciation that we can consult these members and that they in turn may consult each other, that each member has a voice and wisdom. And each voice, wisdom, rhythm has a rich and storied history. The effect is a noticing of multitudes, beyond those loud, old familiar voices (such as the stomach shouting, the chest beating, mind whirring) toward a connection with the variety of responses held within us. New questions can emerge from this idea, questions that bring us into conversation instead of opposition, for example, "I asked chest what it was trying to let me know?" or "how might folded arms be offering comfort to jumpy stomach?"

We have noticed that when we allow space for members of the body to speak/feel/express, we transcend the linearity of a dominating mind and connect with timeless spaces and ancestral experiences. For example, an openness to how expressions of the body are connected to a long lineage of identity stories. When I (Fran) turned towards an unusual sensation in stomach recently and asked what it was expressing, I felt flooded with connections to ancestral experiences of persecution and survival. I felt connected with a strength and courage, which I allowed to guide my next rhythms.

In co-researching with the bodily community in this way, we are resisting some of the effects of individualised, neoliberal ideas that can have us relating to our body in totalising ways and as a limitless resource to be put to use. We notice increasing pressure from the "wellness" discourses to connect with our body, regulate it, and manage it, and we notice these creating more benchmarks to "fail" against and increasing pressure to keep the body well, productive, valuable. In visualising the body as a community, we are naturally drawn into practices of consent: "Which members are accompanying willingly today and which feel more hesitant? What might you, reluctant member, be expressing/needing?" We resist the urge to "push through" and force all bodily members to conform.

These ideas have weaved their way into many areas of our lives. We invite bodily members into consultations, supervisions, on our journeys through joys and hardships. For example, in writing this piece we asked other bodily members if they wanted to share or contribute, as our minds felt burdened and narrowed with discourses about "professional" writing. We asked, "What dominant discourses are pulled into mind?"; "Do any quieter members want to respond to these ideas?" Nadia noticed an opening, a softening in the jaw and shoulders; a widening and opening of chest. Fran described a softening of chest, a release, and an invitation to the mind to embrace more of the landscape.

In bringing the bodily community into our conversations, we have opened up a multitude of pathways and possibilities for connections—not only with ourselves, but with one another and those we are in conversation with.

Learn more about Fran, Nadia, and Hannah at atimeandspace.com.

1 Lee, "Our Bodies as Multi-Storied Communities: Ethics & Practices."

BIOS

Dr Fran Lassman, clinical psychologist and narrative practitioner, currently living and working in Portugal.

Dr Nadia Somers, clinical psychologist and narrative practitioner working in the NHS and private practice, in the UK.

Dr Hannah Stringer, clinical and community psychologist and narrative practitioner, working in London.

Hannia, who has been in therapeutic conversations with Fran.

body neutrality

THINK ABOUT the top of your right ear, the middle toe on your left foot, your right heel, or your left elbow.

What is the body part that you think about the least? Worry about the least?

What if that is how you felt about your entire body?

Body neutrality is about letting go of the impulse to label bodies as good or bad.

As beautiful or ugly.

Body neutrality says you don't have to love and celebrate your body.

You could just let go of the hatred and criticism.

What if you stopped putting any value judgment on your body?

What if society at large stopped putting any value judgment on bodies?

What if society at large stopped putting any value judgment on people based on their bodies?

Your worth as a person is not based on the appearance of your body.

Your worth as a person is not based on what your body can do.

What if you were kind to yourself regardless of how your body looks and feels? ❁

B Maya Druckmann (she/
I her) is a psychotherapist
O in Los Angeles.

body positivity

CONTRIBUTION

BODY POSITIVITY is a worldwide movement that entered public awareness on a large scale when social media became a substantial part of people's lives. My work with body positivity officially began in 1996, when I founded the nonprofit organization The Body Positive.

The organization started as a passion project stemming from my own struggles with an eating disorder in my teen years and the death of my sister, Stephanie, at the age of 36. Stephanie died from an autoimmune disease caused by faulty breast implants and malnutrition as a result of her 20-year eating disorder.

I was able to heal myself from bulimia at a time when there was very little knowledge about or support for people who struggled with eating disorders. I never even heard the word "bulimia" until I was nearly recovered. I feel lucky to have survived, because there was a point where I wasn't sure I wanted to.

In my healing process, I first had to decide if I wanted to live. After that decision was made, I knew that if I was going to live, it was going to be with a truly peaceful and free relationship with food, movement, and my appearance. I also knew I had to radically change my community. I left a four-year romantic relationship that was harmful to my self-worth, especially concerning my body, and created a new circle of friends who were free from what is now called diet culture.

I am grateful that recovery from my eating disorder was possible. I learned to nurture an inner strength that helped me realize my existence was precious and worth fighting for, but my life was changed forever. The suffering I experienced over my body radically shifted the course of my career and life purpose.

My daughter, Carmen, was 15 months old when Stephanie died. At that age, Carmen was wildly in love with her body. She was thrilled with her mastery of walking, and delighted in naming her body parts, especially her round tummy and belly button. Eating food was a nurturing and playful experience for Carmen. Her intuitive self knew exactly what her physical needs were, and she demanded to have those needs met. Carmen was—as most toddlers are—free to take pleasure in all aspects of her body.

Stephanie's death prompted me to question if it was possible to raise a child free from body hatred in a society so focused on image and physical perfection. Though long healed from my own problems with my body and self-image, I still worried that I would somehow cause Carmen to develop an eating disorder, or that societal messages would lure her into the traps that had caught me as a girl. It was then that I made the commitment to change the world for my daughter. Grandiose as that may sound, my fierce maternal instincts led me on an exploration of what that declaration truly meant. And that's when The Body Positive was born.

My desire for creating The Body Positive was to help people avoid the same painful road my sister and I—and so many of my friends—took that led to tremendous suffering and loss. In the nearly 30 years since its inception, The Body Positive and its licensed facilitators have liberated millions of people worldwide so they can listen to their bodies, learn from them, and thrive. The work interrupts the harmful consequences of negative body image: eating disorders, depression, anxiety, cutting, suicide, substance abuse, and relationship violence.

Although the world has not changed in many of the ways I'd hoped when I made my commitment to Carmen so many years ago, her world became unique from the moment The Body Positive was founded. She grew up free to love and respect her physical self, which meant she didn't experience the fear

SEE: body as community, body neutrality, Body Trust, fat positivity, feminism, intuitive eating (and in many cases hatred) most girls have of their growing, changing bodies. I didn't do this work alone; Carmen was immersed in a community of Body Positive individuals from the time she was four years old. She had as her role models people diverse in every way imaginable. Her babysitters were our teen peer leaders. She spent hours (probably more than she cared to!) standing by my side as I talked about my work to help people experience self-love and respect for their bodies.

Carmen is now grown and gone from home, and I see that the foundation she constructed growing up with The Body Positive serves her well. She is keenly aware of her physical needs and meets them as best she can. She is inoculated against the powerful influence of harmful messages about beauty and health. And, to my extreme delight, she uses her intuitive wisdom to guide not only her choices about physical self-care, but other life decisions as well.

My commitment to change the world for Carmen led to the creation of an organization where those who are ready to shift their beliefs about beauty, health, and identity in a positive direction are given the opportunity and resources to do so. I feel blessed to participate in the lives of so many courageous people who have chosen to defy the status quo by making peace with their bodies and taking ownership of their lives. I am grateful that my suffering over my own body and the pain I experienced from the loss of my sister weren't in vain; they provided me with work I truly love and a way to make sense of what happened in my life.

It is important to understand that everyone has their own unique journey with their body. Your journey to making peace with your body may be different from mine. To me, the goal of being "body positive" isn't about being positive at all times. It's about honoring that we are all worthy and valuable even with our struggles because we are here on this precious earth for a short ride, no matter how long we live. ❁

BIO

Connie Sobczak (she/her) is the author of *Embody: Learning to Love Your Unique Body (and quiet that critical voice!)* and *Bodies of Nature/Nature of Bodies*, and Co-Founder and Executive Director of the nonprofit organization The Body Positive, as well as the leader of her new Wild Woman Within circles and host of "The Cooking, Eating, Healing Show" on YouTube.

Body Trust

CONTRIBUTION

Body Trust Is a Birthright. Body Trust Is YOUR Birthright.

WE ARE NOT BORN INTO THIS WORLD fretting about the size of our bellies, butts, and thighs. Body shame is learned, so it can be unlearned. In fact, there's a lot more to unlearn than there is to learn on the path to Body Trust.

People are sovereign, thus bodies are sovereign. So many ways people learn to cope and survive in this world transmute that sovereignty. Body Trust believes that all coping is rooted in wisdom, and the ways you have coped have not been solely your invention or "fault." Bodies are assigned to hierarchy. Our relationships with our own bodies are impacted. We are encouraged to manage, control, discipline, and consider our bodies' needs and desires to be suspect. We, then, also become suspicious of ourselves.

Body Trust is a radically different way of relating to, occupying, and caring for our bodies in a culture that doesn't trust bodies. It challenges everything we have been taught to believe about food, bodies, weight, and health.

Body Trust is developing an analysis of what's come between you and being at home in your body.

Body Trust is a homecoming. It can help you get out of your head and back into your body.

Body Trust requires us to divest from diet culture, toxic fitness culture (a term coined by Ilya Parker), and social constructs of health and beauty.

Ultimately, Body Trust is a reclamation of self, body, voice, pleasure, food, movement, and more.

As a modality, Body Trust is a strength-based, trauma-informed, scientifically grounded framework that helps connect the dots between social justice and the work of healing. It was essentially created to address the predictable, repetitive pattern of dieting, disordered eating, and weight cycling fueled by shame, trauma, and body-based oppression.

Body Trust is greatly informed by liberatory frameworks and methodologies including Bobbie Harro's Cycle of Socialization and Cycle of Liberation, Barbara Love's Liberatory Consciousness, Desiree Adaway's Praxis of Liberation, as well as Niva Piran's Developmental Theory of Embodiment, Health at Every Size tenets, intuitive eating principles, shame resilience theory, motivational interviewing, self-compassion theory, relational cultural theory, mindfulness-based approaches, and post-modern therapeutic thought. Body Trust challenges pathology that has, at times, limited the breadth and depth of dialogue about disordered eating and body control to symptoms and their cessation. Body Trust is soma-psycho-social.

Body Trust is also made up of a community of providers who share in their commitment to address anti-fat bias in healthcare and helping settings and to improve care for people of all shapes and sizes. The Body Trust community shoulders each other in this effort, knowing that change will come through our collective effort and our presence as an evolving movement and social change ecosystem.

The narrative arc of Body Trust as a healing process is described in three phases: The Rupture, The Reckoning, and The Reclamation. This work often starts by understanding how we lost trust with our body, and then we reckon with the ways our relationship with our body has been ruptured by harmful ideas, constructs, and practices in our culture. The process of reclaiming trust with food, body, and self is not all that different from how we rebuild trust in any relationship in our life when trust is broken: through attunement and small, consistent acts over time, not conditional acts or large-scale gestures.[1]

We use the metaphor (and image below) of a tree working on establishing its roots to illustrate the ongoing and evolving process of reclaiming body trust. Working with the various concepts, ideas, tools, and practices in the tree is what helps people deepen their roots into body trust. ❁

1 Gottman, *The Science of Trust*.

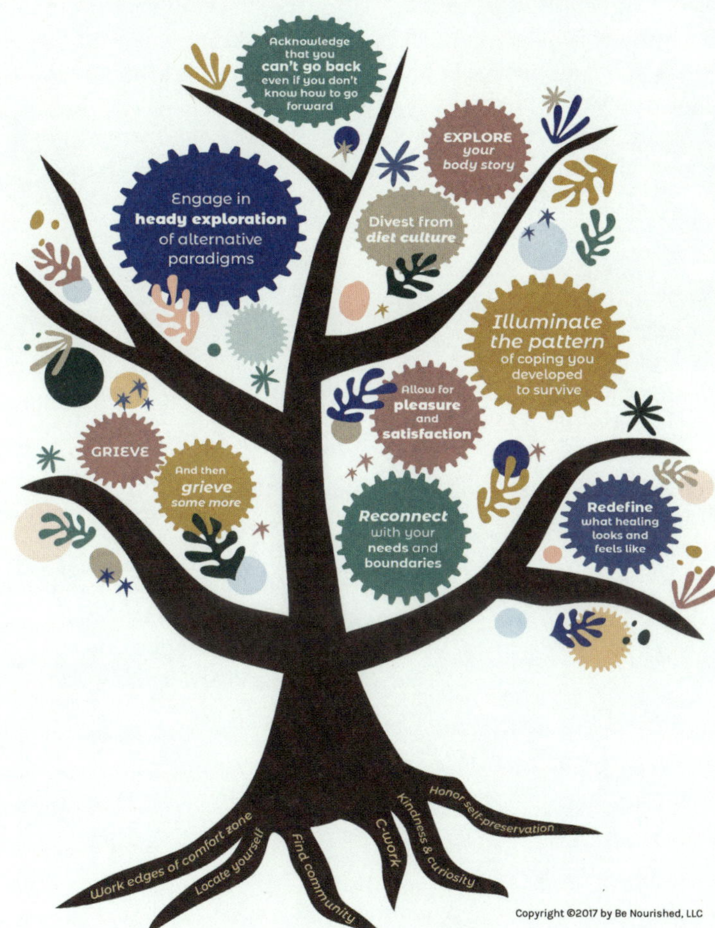

BIOS

Dana Sturtevant, MS, RD, is co-author of the book *Reclaiming Body Trust* and a registered dietitian whose work as a speaker, educator, and trainer focuses on humanizing health care, advancing health equity, and advocating for food and body sovereignty. https://centerforbodytrust.com/

Hilary Kinavey, MS, LPC, is a co-founder of the Center for Body Trust and co-author of *Reclaiming Body Trust*. She is a therapist, coach, and educator who focuses on culture change in healthcare settings and organization to reduce anti-fat bias.

boredom

SEE: agency; being with; erasure, avoiding thereof

CONTRIBUTION

BOREDOM IS MAGIC. Boredom makes things disappear. It makes the extraordinary appear ordinary. It directs your attention away without your even noticing; your brain slides off the surface of the boredom and moves on without realizing that it has missed something. Boredom is camouflage. Boredom is the bookshelf with a hidden door behind it, the pleat that hides the flash of color. It may also be the spoor of exactly that which you as the healer are hunting, because it hints at a secret that wants to stay hidden: To what end has something been cloaked in boredom? Is it too painful, too shameful, too insurmountable? Does it speak unspeakable truths? Seeing boringness as an *intentional act* of either the perceiver or the perceived makes it inherently interesting and worth tracking.

For a helper to bring sustained attention in spite of boredom is a heroic display of effortfulness and tending to an Other (SEE love). In an era where we are increasingly fed a steady diet of attention-getting tidbits, our capacity for self-directed attention atrophies. Attention is a precious use of our energy and time, and where we choose to expend it becomes the fabric of our lives. To engage with that which is boring is to reclaim agency over our own attention, willing into existence a fabric of our choosing rather than accepting that which is given.

An Other may be actively directing attention away by *being boring* (SEE erasure, avoiding thereof). Sustaining attention to that Other is radical as a way to try to truly know another, and radical to the Other in the experience of being worth effortful knowing, thereby recognizing oneself in the Other's gaze (SEE recognition). It is healing in itself, in its insistence on the value of the Other.

Boredom, then, is paradoxically intriguing, diagnostically useful, and a space of healing in itself. ❁

BIO

Noriko Martinez works imperfectly as a radical helper by sitting with people, being curious, and loving the world.

brave space

CONTRIBUTION

BRAVE SPACE IS A FRAMEWORK developed by Arao and Clemens[1] to support authentic engagement by diverse groups in educational activities focused on social justice, equity, and inclusion. Brave space is an alternative to the conventional goal of promoting safe space for learning activities about controversial and emotionally charged topics. As social justice educators, Arao and Clemens found that the language of "safe space" led their students to expect that learning activities would be comfortable and free of risk-taking and disagreement. These expectations were misaligned to the realities of social justice education, which often requires learners to explore difficult truths, be present with discomfort, and challenge one's own and others' viewpoints and perspectives.

Further, many students reported feeling "unsafe" when they experienced negative emotions such as guilt, shame, and sadness in the course of group-based learning about the privileges associated with their dominant group identities. Conversely, students with minoritized identities shared that talking about social injustice is never "safe" for them because it may be met with resistance and violence (e.g., physical, emotional, psychological, etc.), reopen wounds caused by oppressive systems and actions, and result in new traumatic experiences.

Brave space evolved as a means to acknowledge, account for, and help learners rise to these significant challenges. While it originated as a social justice education framework, it is also useful in other contexts wherein diverse groups of people need to practice vulnerability and engage in discourse about sensitive topics. There are many strategies that facilitators use to cultivate brave spaces. The following list is not comprehensive or prescriptive, but includes options from which to draw:

EXPLORE THE MEANINGS AND RELEVANCE OF BRAVERY. At the outset of a learning activity with a new group, state your goal of helping them to create a brave space for and with one another. Then, facilitate activities that engage them as thought partners in developing a shared understanding of what bravery means and why it might be needed in this context. State directly that social justice education often calls learners to step outside their comfort zones, which requires bravery. When time permits, provide opportunities for learners to reflect on moments in their lives when they have needed to be brave and what helped them to do so.

DEVELOP LEARNING COMMUNITY AGREEMENTS. Ask learners what they need from one another in order to create a brave space for and with each other. Make a running list of their responses in a format that all participants can access. Consider offering the following suggested group agreements if they are not put forward by the learners themselves.

> *Controversy with humanity*. This concept is drawn from the Social Change Model of Leadership Development, which advocates for controversy with civility as "a value whereby different views are expected and honored with a group commitment to understand the sources of disagreement and to work cooperatively toward common solutions."[2] Dr. Alejandro Covarrubias adapted this term to "controversy with humanity" in his brave space facilitation practice; this change addresses concerns about the word "civility," which is often used to discourage the expression of strong emotions (especially among people with minoritized identities) in social justice discourse.

> *Honor and make room for emotion*. Social justice learning is not purely intellectual; it's also an emotional exercise. Naming this reality helps learners to be more prepared to experience, hold space for, and explore their own and others' emotions. →

Own your intentions and your impacts. Learners may do or say things with neutral or positive intentions which nevertheless result in harm to others. In these situations, learners may focus primarily on clarifying their intentions, leaving impacted parties to attend on their own to the ways they were harmed. Asking learners to hold responsibility for both their intentions and their impacts helps to frame resolution of harms as a collective responsibility.

Challenge by choice. Acknowledge that learners make individual choices about whether and how much to challenge themselves to engage in educational activities. Invite learners to think critically about what prevents them from challenging themselves and consider what they might need in order to do so in the future. Such contemplation is especially important when the barrier to self-challenge is a reluctance to consider how one has participated in or received benefits from systems of oppression.

Respect. Respect is often asked for and readily agreed upon by learners without extended conversation. Help learners to explore the complexities of respect by asking questions such as "How is respect practiced in your communities?" and "What does it look like to challenge someone else's viewpoint in a respectful way?" The answers to these questions may surface different understandings of what constitutes respectful behavior, creating an opportunity for learners to further clarify their needs and wishes around respect.

No personal attacks. Like respect, this agreement is commonly suggested and accepted by learners even if they do not have a shared understanding of what constitutes a personal attack. Ask learners what distinguishes a personal attack from a critique of what someone has said or done, which may help learners to craft more thoughtful critiques and mitigate defensiveness when receiving critique.

PAY ATTENTION, SHARE YOUR OBSERVATIONS, AND ASK QUESTIONS.

Once learning community agreements have been established, support learners in practicing them by observing and offering feedback about the group's engagement. Rather than evaluate what you observe (e.g., "Some people are taking up too much airtime in this conversation and not allowing others to speak"), instead describe it (e.g., "I notice that some members of the group have done most of the speaking and others have spoken less or not at all"), and ask questions to engage the learners in making sense of it (e.g., "Are others noticing something similar? If so, what do we think that means?").

REVISIT AND REVISE COMMUNITY AGREEMENTS AS NEEDED.

Learners may become less conscious of their community agreements over time or need to revise them based on what they are learning about themselves, one another, and the subject matter. Periodically invite learners to review their agreements, assess how well they believe the group is honoring them, and offer ideas for adjusting or amending the agreements. ❁

1 Arao and Clemens, "From Safe Spaces to Brave Spaces" and "Confronting the Paradox of Safety in Social Justice Education."

2 Astin and Astin, *A Social Change Model of Leadership Development: Guidebook (Version III)*, 59.

BIO Dr. Brian Arao (he/him/his) is the President and Co-Founder of Brave Space Leadership, which offers coaching and consulting services focused on leadership development for diversity, equity, inclusion, social justice, and belonging.

SEE storytelling; strengths perspective, the; Theatre of the Oppressed

CONTRIBUTION

Conversational Hacks: Part 2

...CONTINUED FROM lingering

HACK 3: ASK "CLOSED QUESTIONS"

I've been out of graduate school for over 30 years and I hear from my students that they still learn something I heard in my training days: only ask "open questions." I'm here to give you permission to shoot this rule to Neptune.

The open/closed binary, like most binaries, ignores complexities and context. There are no purely "open" questions. The quintessential "open" question, *how are you feeling?*, isn't completely open: it points the responder to their feelings, not, for example, to their values, or to another person's perspective. Every question we ask has some degree of "closedness" to it because we imbue it with some meaning.

At times, questions that are more open can be overwhelming for some people. Offering questions that have a narrower focus provides discursive handholds to help prime people's storytelling pumps. These may be yes/no questions or limited-choice questions. Often, I offer an option of "or is it something else?" I find that this pump-priming often helps people find an entry point for a conversation they are interested in and ready to have.

THE HACK: *"Is this something you'd like to talk about? Do you think talking about it now will make the problem bigger, smaller, or different? Who would you be most likely to share this with after today—your teacher, coach, or someone else? Is the problem mad, scared, or something else now that you've told on it?"*

My intentions with this hack are to:

1. Ask answerable questions;
2. Respect the client (this is what meeting someone "where they're at" looks like);
3. Provide a focus if someone is overwhelmed;
4. Provide multiple options for possible conversations. ❁

BIO

Julie Tilsen lives on stolen Dakhóta land, the ancestral and contemporary homeland of the Dakhóta and Ojibwe Native Nations, which was obtained through violent acts of genocide, displacement, forced removal, and broken treaties.

EDITORS' NOTE

Thanks to Julie Tilsen for graciously agreeing to our playful suggestion to divide her very helpful essay, "Conversational Hacks," over two *Encyclopedia* entries. Please see "lingering" for the first part of the essay.
—ES & CH

bridge as metaphor

CONTRIBUTION

A BRIDGE IS A NATURAL OR HUMAN-MADE OBJECT that helps us overcome barriers in the landscape, to get from somewhere to another place. As a metaphor, it can symbolize a person's perception of their past, present, and future life. Art therapists have found making artwork about a bridge can be helpful to explore an individual's experience of transitions, perception of the environment around them, possible conflicts or barriers, problem-solving abilities, and future goals.

Try drawing a bridge and see if you don't learn something about where you want to go! Does your bridge remind you of the supports in your life that might help you move forward? Often a path or road is drawn as well to help illustrate the journey. ❁

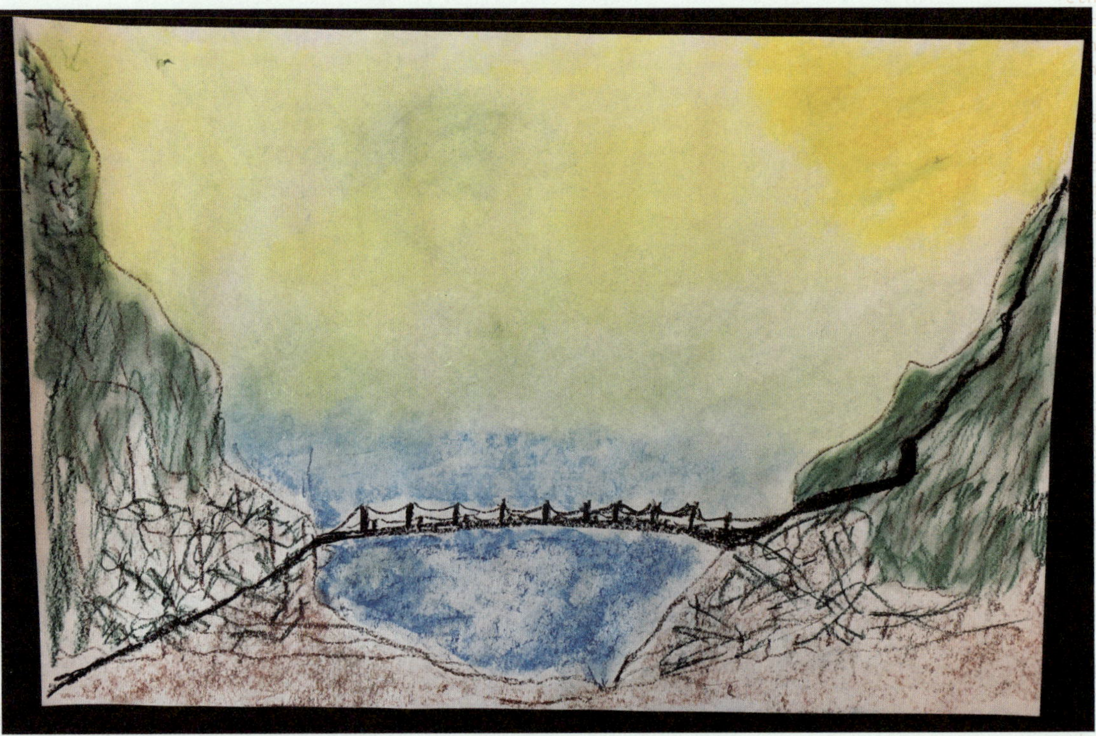

A "bridge with path" drawing by a participant in an art therapy session. Permission to reproduce was granted by the artist.

BIO

Gioia Chilton, PhD, ATR-BC, CSAC, is an artist, art therapist, researcher, and author who loves her family and art therapy community.

care pods

CONTRIBUTION

care pod (noun): an ad hoc group of two or more people with agreed-upon shared practices for the purpose of providing and receiving care to meet a specific need or desire

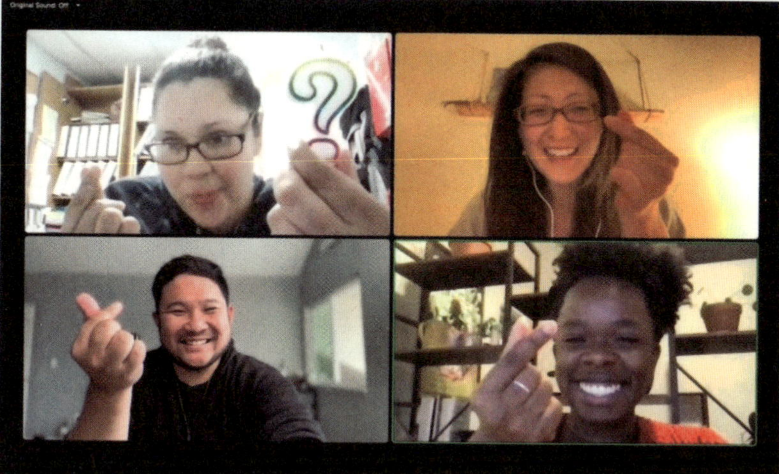

Screenshot of Sacred Heart celebrating one year of care-podding! Clockwise starting top left: Vanessa, Minna, Jasmine, and Anthony.

REMEMBER when the coronavirus quarantine sparked the notion of pods? It's as if our DNA-encoded wisdom about how to collectively survive suddenly got activated, and overnight, pods of all configurations mushroomed, both in-person and virtually. Due to the constraints of mandated quarantine, pods were usually small in number. Members agreed to provide support in its various forms, from staving off loneliness and isolation to providing physical care and childcare. While some pods functioned haphazardly, many pods were as conscious and considerate as possible, given the relentless stress we all experienced. Below are some examples of care pods from my own life, with hopes of inspiring richer and more meaningful ways of podding up.

*

March of 2020, I quickly found myself in a triad-pod with my two friends who I was out in public with before we were mandated to quarantine; the three of us met in 2015 in social work graduate school and became fast friends and neighbors within walking distance. Without much hesitation, we clung to each other out of fear of uncertainty and an anticipated need for connection—thus, the "Quaranteam" was born.

For over a year, we came up with agreements about how we would conduct ourselves during quarantine, always making space for modifications to mirror the constantly shifting safety guidelines and unpredictable coronavirus statistics; our shared social work values and skills came in really handy! While there were countless awkward, frustrating, and clumsy moments to work through, in the end, we achieved the purpose of our care pod—providing each other with company and support, while learning a great deal about tending to relationships during difficult times. Eventually, our care pod organically dissolved as we began to move more freely in public spaces. Looking back, I wish we'd invested as much care and intention into completing our time together as the Quaranteam as wc did in creating it, so as to honor it for all that it did for us.

In the midst of podding up as the Quaranteam, in October 2021, I signed up for a BIPOC Collective Care Pod, offered through wildseedsociety.com. This was a virtual space that provided guidance, tools, and structured opportunities to practice self-care and collective care as a way to decolonize from internalized oppression that disembodies us from ourselves and isolates us from one another. We practiced ways of reclaiming ancestral practices for communal care and nurturing our shared vision for collective liberation through experiences with our care pods. The pod I was assigned to was made up of four of us: Anthony, from San Jose; Jasmine, from Chicago; Vanessa, from Staten Island; and me, living in Baltimore at the time. We met biweekly for an hour over Zoom, adopting the care pod name of Sacred Heart to reflect the intentional and caring interactions that would outlast the BIPOC Collective Care Pod program.

Once we completed this collective experience, we decided to gather virtually every month. Today, our care pod has shifted into one that allows us to stay connected, with each of us checking in about what's on our hearts while receiving deep-listening and care. What was seeded as a care pod with shared intentions and values for co-cultivating liberatory practices now sustains our long-distance friendship.

The practice of creating care pods is not novel. Early human communities were communal, so our DNA is in fact encoded for collectivism! Our ancestors survived in communities for the advantage of shared resources, protection, mating, and caretaking. The coronavirus pandemic simply revealed our instincts to gather for survival, while also inviting us to be more mindful about how we gather. In fact, variations of care pods have always existed—from support groups, to coordinated care for loved ones, to group-chats. By framing these groups as "care pods," care, connection, and clear purpose are centered, while also being flexible with the proliferation of changes in the environment and the growing diversity of members' needs and desires.

Being clear about the purpose of a care pod will reveal its capacities and necessary actions to meet needs and desires. And the shifting and growing purpose will also invite us to evolve or complete the care pod or consider the need for other care pods.

So, how might one go about creating their own care pod? Below is a non-exhaustive list of guidelines. Feel free to amend this list, inspired by your own experiences of communal care (or lack thereof) and ancestral practices. Finally, be sure to make room for emergence, as everything we touch we change, and all that we change changes us.[1]

- Get clear on the purpose of the care pod.
- Stay open to change.
- Consider who will be a part of it. What is their role? What is their capacity?
- Consider the timeline. Then, stay open to how it may change. For example, I have a friend who created a care pod when her mother passed away. This year, on the anniversary of her mother's death, she found herself needing support, so she revived the care pod.
- How might ritual and ceremony be braided into care pod practices for gathering mindfully and tending to the container, one another, and yourself?
  - An example of a ritual may be having a routine way of opening and closing your time together.
  - An example of a ceremony is when Sacred Heart scheduled time to celebrate our one-year anniversary of gathering!

May we caringly pod up,
honoring the ways of our communal ancestors,
stirring this knowing that lives in our bones. ❁

1 Butler, *Parable of the Sower*, 13

BIO After resigning from 11 years as a heartbroken public school educator, 효영 HyoYoung Minna Kim is re-membering all of her multidimensional beingness while communing with Nature, riffing on rad-collaborations on humanizing ourselves, and missing her sweet pup-sibling, Mondu, who is living like a king on the east coast.

care-based co-housing

C O N T R I B U T I O N

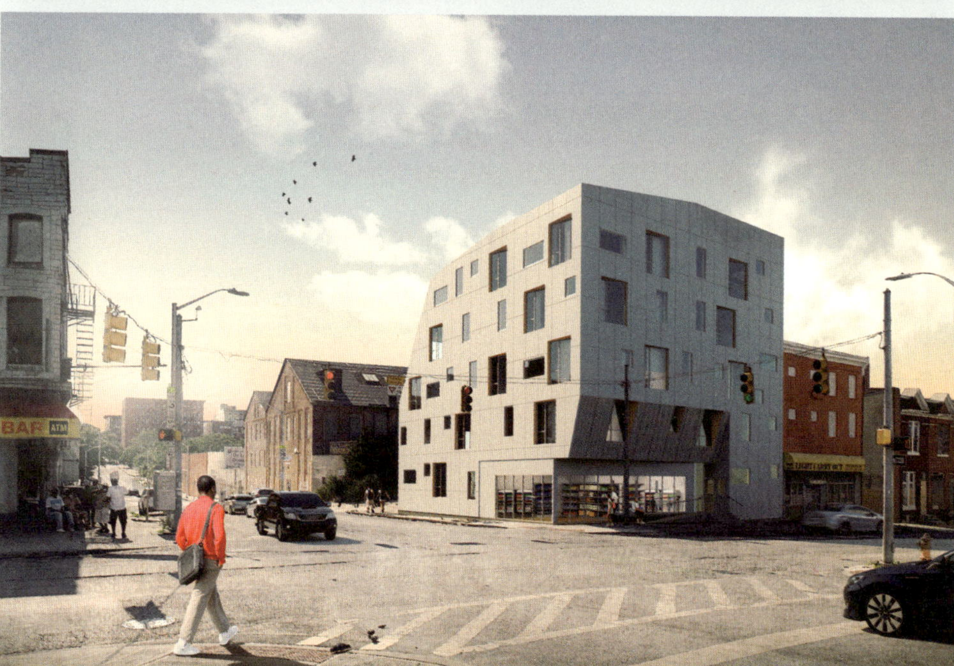

Designed by Rafi Segal A+U with collaborating artist Marisa Morán Jahn, Carehaus (carehaus.net) is the United States' first intergenerational care-based co-housing building. Carehaus is a simple yet innovative concept that combines stable housing, intergenerational care, social and arts integration, and neighborhood revitalization. The first location in central Baltimore features 21 units, housing 17 older adults and 4 caregivers with their families, a site manager, and a team of experts in nutrition, fitness, art, and wellness. Designed to address the United States' care and housing crisis, Carehaus's design and business structure is replicable and responds to each neighborhood's unique conditions. →

care-based co-housing

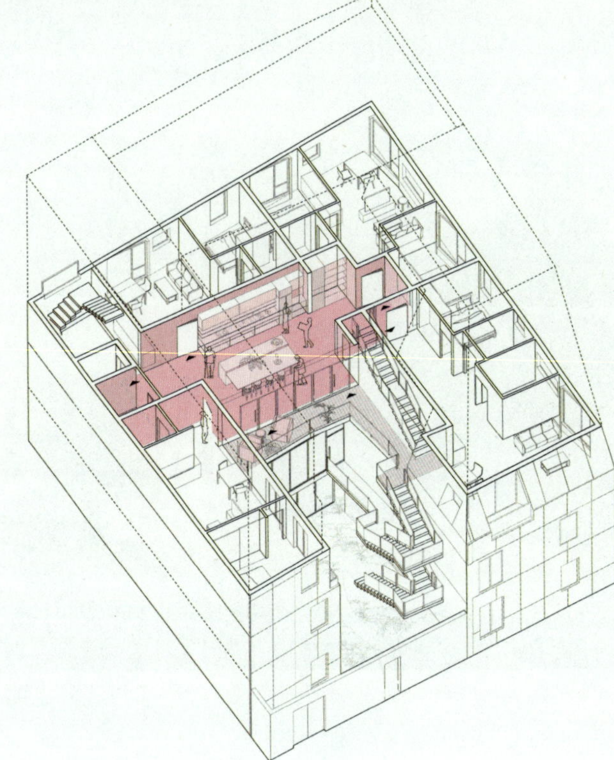

As seen on Carehaus' Baltimore's 3rd floor, residential units cluster around a shared kitchen space and an open terrace. A variety of single, double, and triple bedroom units accommodate residents' varying household sizes. The abundance of open shared space makes caregiving more efficient and safer: caregivers can take turns keeping an eye on those who need close monitoring or support each other in tasks.

Architecture: Rafi Segal A+U with collaborating artist Marisa Morán Jahn

BIOS

An architect and Associate Professor of Architecture and Urbanism at MIT, Rafi Segal's work involves design and research on an architectural, urban and regional scale with current focus on how emerging notions of collectivity can impact the design of buildings and cities. rafisegal.com @segal_rafi

An artist of Ecuadorian and Chinese descent, Marisa Morán Jahn's artwork "exemplifies the possibilities of art as social practice" (ArtForum) and explores "civic spaces and the radical art of play" (Chicago Tribune). She is the Director of Integrated Design at Parsons/The New School. marisajahn.com @marisa_jahn

EDITORS' NOTE

Care-based co-housing is a new housing model designed for older/disabled adults as well as caregivers and their families. All residents have their own private unit organized around communal spaces in which they can share activities, meals, and mutual support. By sharing resources in new ways, care-based co-housing promotes intergenerational social integration, affordability, good jobs, and reduced rent for caregivers, and sustainable neighborhood regeneration—all within buildings that fundamentally integrate art and design. These concepts build on insights learned from Carehaus, the United States' first intergenerational, care-based co-housing project, whose first location in Baltimore opens in 2025. Carehaus grew out of artist Marisa Morán Jahn's ongoing collaboration since 2010 with the National Domestic Workers Alliance and involves architect Rafi Segal and real estate developer Ernst Valery as co-founders. The building is designed by Segal in collaboration with Jahn; various caregivers, doctors, nurses, and local stakeholders have participated in co-design workshops. —ES and CH, in collaboration with MMJ and RS

SEE love; Marxist social work; perspective via faith; recognition; solidarity economy

CONTRIBUTION

Catholic Worker: Making It Easier to Be Good

Knitting is very conducive to thought. It is nice to knit a while, put down the needles, write a while, then take up the sock again.
—Dorothy Day

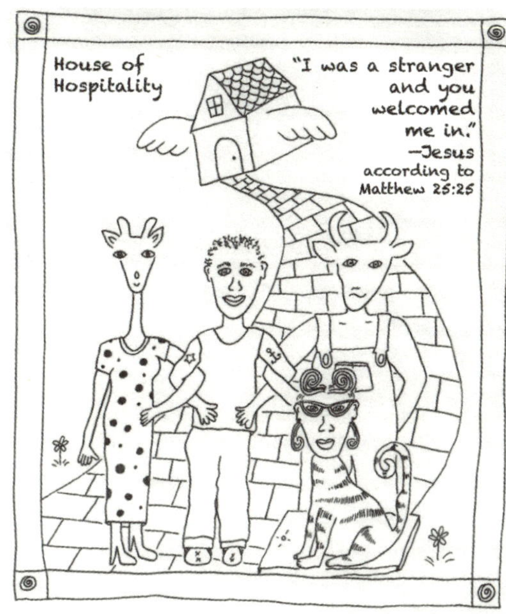

MY STEPFATHER, an excommunicated Catholic priest named John Duryea, introduced me to the Catholic Worker Movement when I was a kid, and later taught me more about Dorothy Day when I was a young, single mom and aspiring radical publisher. Dorothy had been a single mom, too, and started her movement with a radical newspaper—just like I wanted to do. In a world where Catholicism was increasingly associated with patriarchal control and abuse, my dad wanted to teach me about the more communitarian, red-diaper baby, love-centered, and socialist history of the admittedly flawed religion he'd dedicated his life to. He'd met Dorothy Day once, back in New York, and carried the inspiration with him all of his life, from his youth and adulthood within the institution of the church and through his later-life ongoing dedication to liberation theology outside of the church after he was excommunicated for marrying my mother.

The Catholic Worker Movement started with the *Catholic Worker* newspaper, created by Dorothy Day to advance pacificist Catholic social teaching.

Catholic Worker co-founder Dorothy Day said, "God meant things to be much easier than we have made them,"[1] and co-founder Peter Maurin wanted to build a society "where it is easier for people to be good."[2] With those humble, lofty goals in mind, the movement focused on economic equity and labor rights, political accountability, a morality of anti-oppression, demilitarization, and critique of capitalism.

The movement sees St. Thomas Aquinas's doctrine of the Common Good as a practical vision of society, where the good of each member is bound up with the good of the whole. The movement advocates a "green revolution"; a philosophy of "personalism," which centers the freedom and dignity of each person; and "a decentralized society" model that encourages experimentation with small-community living, cooperatives, and "any effort in which money can once more become merely a medium of exchange, and human beings are no longer commodities."[3]

Basically, it's radical politics meets Jesus Christ.

Founded in 1933, the Catholic Worker Movement is still doing its thing as a collection of autonomous communities of Catholics and their non-Catholic-identified pals who aim to "live in accordance with the justice and charity of Jesus Christ."[4]

The movement espouses nonviolence, taking seriously Mathew 5:9: "Blessed are the peacemakers, for they shall be called children of God."

The Houses of Hospitality, dedicated to serving the poor, remain central to their philosophy in practice. More than 200 local Catholic Worker communities across the U.S. provide social services and go about the work of social justice in their own ways.

They are also big on manual labor and voluntary poverty. As Dorothy Day said, "The mystery of poverty is that by sharing in it, making ourselves poor in giving to others, we increase our knowledge and belief in love."[5]

My whole childhood, our phone number and address were listed in the local phone book as a church, and folks would knock on our large, Mission-style front door day and night looking for food, for shelter, for spiritual counseling. My stepdad, while sometimes grumpy about this calling, would always answer.

He was surely more a disciple of Dorothy Day and Peter Maurin than he was of any institutional Catholicism. When I asked if he thought his idol, Dorothy, should become an official saint, he said, "No! She would hate that!" But I'll admit that sometimes, especially back when I was more often hungry and in need of shelter, I prayed to Mama Dorothy and she did deliver miracles in the form of radical community. ❁

1 Catholic Worker Movement, "The Aims and Means of the Catholic Worker."

2 Catholic Worker Movement.

3 Catholic Worker Movement.

4 Catholic Worker Movement.

5 Catholic Worker Movement.

BIO Ariel Gore is an author with the Feminist Press.

SEE

CONTRIBUTION

DEAR ERIN, JULIE, AND CHRIS,
I am writing to you from late August in Berlin, where we are nearing the end of summer 2023, and the last few mornings have been chilly with gray clouds pillowing the sky.

At the end of last spring, when it was also slightly chilly but luckily sunny, my friend Sarah asked if anyone wanted to join her community garden plot. I responded with a big "YES!" and then shortly after found myself in a Telegram group with multiple gardeners, where we picked a date to prepare the plot. Many joined in this joyous opening ceremony. The light on that day was an orangey-blue and we tilled until the evening. I remember someone commenting that with the amount of people involved, even if only a few remained throughout the summer to help, the garden would still have more than enough people to maintain it.

The maintainers!

This fellow gardener vocalized what I had imagined for myself. While others naturally stepped into the "planting" role, I assessed that my contribution would be to walk over after long home-office days to water and to tend—especially because I live so close. Also, for the last few years my artistic research practice has examined which work is deemed as unproductive and unprotected labor; unfortunately, many maintenance and service roles fall under this category. Given this focus, I've been trying to find ways to move out of the research space and more actively put my values into practice. I want to challenge myself—and all of you—to embody the values of maintenance for the spaces and communities we care for.

Therefore, I used the garden space as a personal invitation to center maintenance. By doing so, I could step into the role of a maintainer and embody stewardship for this communal garden.

*

Erin, Julie, and Chris:
Can you recall a time when your current or previous role was to maintain rather than to direct or to follow?

Many projects start out in good faith, and over time the energy and spirit of their beginnings wanes. Although it's important to recognize that things naturally end, it is fruitful to collectively reflect on the times where we wished for a project, space, collaboration, promise, or plant—yes a plant!—to last.

Enacting maintenance routines can be a beautiful practice, especially when centering implementation in community infrastructure; in radically centering maintenance, we can collectively confront the capitalist conventions that keep it invisible and overlooked.

Yes, maintenance is repetitive; but it can be recontextualized as the most valuable role.

In addition to the community gardening project, I'd like to tell you all about the other projects I am part of in Berlin:

I am a member of an artist collective called Offline, which is currently tucked away on the ground floor of an Altbau in Schillerkiez, Neukölln. The first Thursday of every month, we host a KüfA dinner, and while the people who carry out the duties are ever-shifting, the maintenance guideline is fixed: "Each dinner should have two opening [and] cooking volunteers and two cleanup volunteers." Attendees are, of course, welcome to help with setup and cleaning, but the volunteers "make sure that work has been done." ➔

centering maintenance

My friends Meg, Santiago, and I are cooking for an upcoming KüfA.[1] We've informed the group chat—and Sarrita, who is the main contact for the dinners, has asked: *Who will help clean?* While cleanup roles are harder to fill, there is an understanding that a KüfA dinner cannot fully proceed if cleanup roles are not filled. It is especially important to highlight that Offline's maintenance-centering relies on asking the collective for volunteers, and so far the group very readily responds to help. This routine repeats itself every month.

In another embodiment of maintenance-centering, I co-facilitate a Feminism(s) Reading Circle, also known as the F(S)RC, with my friend and collaborator Emily at her studio space in Schöneberg. Our RSVP email asks for someone to arrive half an hour early to help us set up before the others arrive. After the reading circle is finished, all participants collectively *reset*, or rearrange, the space again back to how we found it. Maintenance here shifts from one person to the entire group at the end of the evening.

There are plenty of other ways that centering maintenance occurs. Looking outside of my Berlin circle, centering maintenance can look like established, ancestral knowledge, such as a *prescribed burn*—an indigenous maintenance-centering land practice, which was previously outlawed in the US as well as in parts of Australia. In a cultural burning, fire is used as a spiritual tool to "cultivate the biodiverse, sustainable growth that makes landscapes more resilient."[2] By burning the land in a controlled way, this practice restores the earth in order to ensure its strength for upcoming seasons. How devastating that this restorative practice was not only ignored as a sensible fire management strategy but also criminalized by European settler colonizers! The violence is felt on multiple levels: towards communities who have culturally centered the maintenance of their lands, and to future generations whose land is now screaming, burning uncontrollably. By not centering maintenance and the various forms it can take, what other indigenous and cultural traditions are we ignoring and preventing? What larger, more dangerous problems are we allowing to persist when we do not maintain?

From learning from indigenous land practices to cleaning the dishes in a communal space, centering maintenance is a radical concept to move beyond the theoretical and into the embodied. It is a way to radically help ensure the future. You have to *do it* as a way to close the current chapter and ensure the continuity and longevity of what you care for.

*

My partner and I did indeed frequently tend the garden after work and on early morning weekend walks. However, our maintenance work was not done in isolation. Another couple who lives even closer to the plot watered often, too; and throughout the summer, other gardeners joined our group to maintain as well. Additionally, it rained a lot this summer so Mother Nature joined in our rotation of maintainers.

I am grateful for the garden's lesson to center maintenance in my life. With winter coming, the larger garden collective is planning an end-of-season cleanup, and my fellow gardeners want to plant winter garlic.

It's what I love most about being in the maintainer role: doing the maintenance work ensures that the next iteration will happen. Spring will return. And until warmer seasons arrive, many cycles of maintenance will occur: KüfA dinners will be planned and cooked for; more readings will take place; we'll wash the dishes and then return them to their shelves; we'll fold the chairs and then sweep the floor; we'll keep at these small and large maintenance tasks knowing that our earth will turn again. And again. And again.

Maintaining happiness,
Stephanie ❁

Some Maintenance Tips for Radical Helping

- Have a core member of your group detail what the maintenance guideline is for the event/project/space/etc.
- Announce when you will do the maintenance task, and likewise, announce in person or in the group chat when it has been finished.
- Reflect on whether that person has been doing the task multiple times in a row.
- Use a shared platform to communicate the desire to help through a maintenance task or role.
- Very important: thank the person(s) who carried out the maintenance task! Recognition goes a very long way. <3

1 KüfA is the shortened form of the German "Küche für Alle" which translates to "a kitchen for all." At Offline, we host a minimum of two monthly KüfA dinners: one for the public, including casual presentations of community-led projects, and a second for the "disassembly" group who meet to discuss what tasks, actions, or ideas should be addressed for the space.

2 Schelenz, "How the Indigenous Practice of 'Good Fire' Can Help Our Forests Thrive."

BIO Stephanie Marie Cedeño (she/her) is a first-generation Panamanian-U.S. American designer, artist, writer, and educator oscillating between applied and experimental contexts.

EDITORS' NOTE One of the earliest texts we read as part of Thick Press's "ongoing inquiry into care" was Mierle Laderman Ukeles's "Manifesto for Maintenance Art 1969!—Proposal for an Exhibition of 'Care,'" which sets up two opposing structures: "development" ("pure individual creation; the new; change; progress, advance, excitement, flight or fleeing") and "maintenance" ("keep the dust off the pure individual creation; preserve the new; sustain the change...")[1] We found this binary useful, albeit incomplete. While emailing with Stephanie about her proposed idea, Ukeles's work informed our suggestion to file this contribution under "centering maintenance." —ES & JC

1 Ukeles, "Manifesto for Maintenance Art 1969!—Proposal for an Exhibition 'Care,'" 210

circular economy

SEE: bike and car repair collectives; centering maintenance; fermentation

CONTRIBUTION

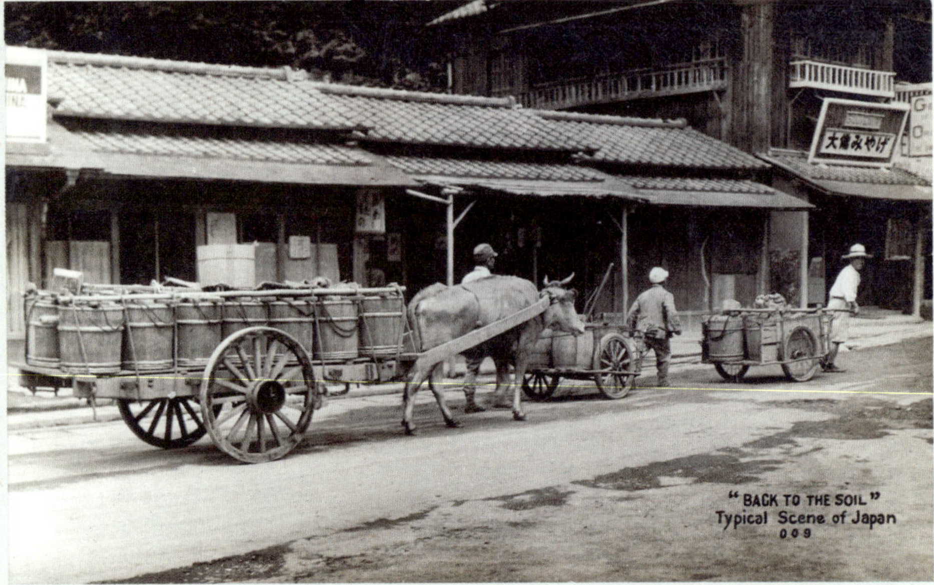

Night soil collection in urban Japan for return to rural farmers to use as fertilizer, 1944. Photographer unknown.

THE CONCEPT OF A CIRCULAR ECONOMY (CE) is based on a biological model: it produces with planned cycles of birth, life, death, and decomposition that provide nutrients for subsequent births of products. There is not one CE, but rather a multiplicity of them, some taking organic life cycles as a reference, and some, such as with circular agriculture, actually being biological. The "economy" in CE should be understood in terms of its Greek origin in *oikonomía*: the management of the home or household. What is the boundary of this home? Today, the financialized idea of economy is often distant from such a nurturing site. Indeed, a CE counters a linear economy narrowly focused on financial profit, indifferent to how that profit may result from negative environmental impacts left out of any accounting. A linear economy pursues a production and consumption sequence of take-make-dispose, while a CE is instead a regenerative economy. Byproducts that may typically be considered waste and pollution are channeled into other products or systems. Helping environmental restoration, preservation of resources, and reduction of carbon emissions are some possible benefits of the approach.

The circular economy concept is expressed by the "3Rs" of reduce, reuse, recycle, as well as the idea of "cradle-to-cradle" manufacturing, the opposite of a linear "cradle-to-grave" model.[1] A related concept, "extended producer responsibility," is where manufacturers include end-of-life costs in their products' prices, thereby enabling return and material recovery from products that otherwise would be waste. While CE is often discussed in terms of manufacturing products with life-cycle concepts, the scope of potential CE practice is vast: it ranges from goods to food production, raw materials, infrastructure, services, buildings, spaces, knowledge, and skills.

A CE is about environmental inputs and outputs, and hence about metabolism. Though metabolism is a term that originates in biology to describe the feedback between an organism and its environment, its meaning was broadened by Karl Marx to encapsulate both social and biological interactions. An example stemming from Marx shows what a healthy CE can be. He famously describes "an irreparable rift" in the "social metabolism" between rural farmers and the city dwellers consuming their produce, since nutrients from city dwellers' sewage resulting from the farmer's food was not returned to the countryside to become fertilizer.[2] In London, it was instead dumped in the River Thames. By the nineteenth century, this had led to terrible pollution of the river and the proliferation of water-borne diseases. Such a rupture of social-biological relations—what has become known as a "metabolic rift"—is what CEs aim to repair.[3] Opposite this rift in England, it's notable that Japan practiced the careful collection of human sewage in its cities into the 1960s.[4] This "night soil," some varieties of which were more prized than others depending on the diets of different urban neighborhoods, was then returned to rural farmers to be transformed into fertilizer, to grow fresh crops for sale back in the city. This circular practice led to a far higher level of urban sanitation and a longer life expectancy in nineteenth-century Tokyo than in London at the time.[5]

Pre-fossil fuel societies based on less processed, less complicated, and remotely-made products have often been circular.[6] In contrast, now in the fossil-fuel driven Anthropocene, CEs are often hypothetical rather than actual. There is a danger of the idea acting as greenwash, enabling further destructive growth. As a case in point, it's estimated that only 5 to 6% of all plastics in the United States are in fact recycled as of 2021.[7] But plastic manufacturers welcome the perception of a circular, sustainable use of their products, when in fact the corporations and swamped sanitation departments rarely pay for the recycling processes.

A typical pro-growth corporate and governmental policy ideal is that CEs will "decouple" growth from resource consumption—meaning that traditional capitalist notions of growth can simply continue with the implementation of proper reuse and recycling.[8] However, as analysts have observed, the yearly quantity of new production in many areas increases at a rate far outstripping the rate at which existing products reach the end of their service lives and become available to harvest.[9] As such, the objective of "reduce" may be the most important if difficult of the three Rs to achieve. A post-growth or degrowth practice of reduction is likely the only way circularity truly makes a wide impact. The CE concept is therefore what has been called a "contested paradigm," in tension between growth and degrowth, and between what's technically possible and socially performed.[10]

The definition of growth in capitalist society—one detached from growth in health, well-being, and knowledge, for example—is, like the typical idea of economy, extremely limited in its reduction to financial growth. It may as a result be more helpful to pursue a circular society rather than a circular economy, with "society" emphasizing shared cultural objectives taking us beyond the monetary.[11] ❁

1 While the exact origin of the 3Rs as a slogan is unclear, it seems to have started to be common in the US context in the 1970s, with the appearance of Earth Day and the formation of the Environmental Protection Agency. It has since become an explicit policy objective for various organizations and governments. For cradle-to-cradle versus cradle-to-grave, this concept has been popularized by the work of architect William McDonough and chemist Michael Braungart. See McDonough and Braungart, *Cradle to Cradle: Remaking the Way We Make Things*.

2 Marx quoted in John Bellamy Foster, *Marx's Ecology: Materialism and Nature*, 155. Foster discusses Marx's example of urban sewage on page 163.

3 "Metabolic rift" is John Bellamy Foster's deft rephrasing of Marx's thinking. See Foster, *Marx's Ecology*, 155.

4 See Sorensen, *The Making of Urban Japan: Cities and Planning from Edo to the Twenty-First Century*, 41.

➔

5 See Hanley, *Everyday Things in Premodern Japan: The Hidden Legacy of Material Culture*, 2.

6 It should be noted that such societies were also not reliant on petroleum-based fertilizers, now globally ubiquitous.

7 See Greenpeace, "Circular Claims Fall Flat Again: 2022 Update," 3.

8 This widespread corporate and governmental embrace of the idea is noted in Friant, Salomone, and Vermeulen, "A Typology of Circular Economy Discourses: Navigating the Diverse Visions of a Contested Paradigm," 1.

9 See for example De Decker, "How Circular is the Circular Economy?"

10 See Friant, et al., "A Typology of Circular Economy Discourses," 1.

11 It should be noted that the Japanese Ministry of the Environment uses the phrase "Sound Material-Cycle Society" to describe Japan's circular ambitions. See Ministry of the Environment, "The World in Transition and Japan's Efforts to Establish a Sound Material-Cycle Society."

BIO

Casey Mack, an architect, is the founder of Popular Architecture and the author of *Digesting Metabolism: Artificial Land in Japan 1954–2202* (Hatje Cantz, 2022).

CONTRIBUTION

A Container for Staying with the Trouble

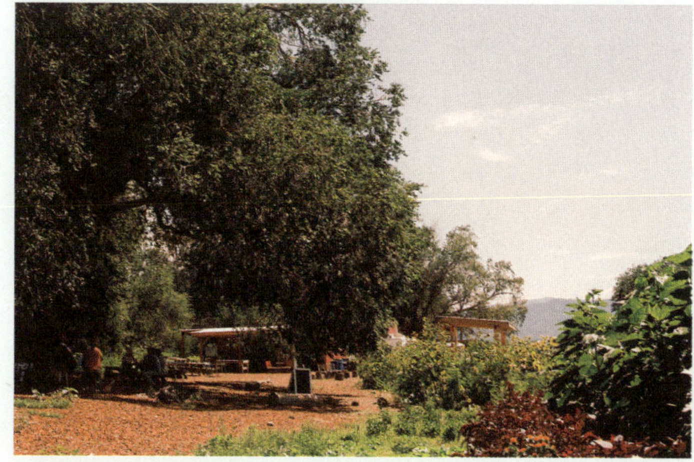

9.1.22. WE GATHER under a mighty cottonwood on a late summer day at Reunity Resources, a regenerative two-acre urban farm, soil, and compost yard in the heart of Santa Fe, New Mexico. Ten of us situate ourselves around a large picnic table in the early evening hours, grateful to receive shade from the deciduous poplar above. It feels fitting to be held by the shadow of this tree, a species in our high desert ecosystem threatened by the climate crisis, which has prompted our gathering.

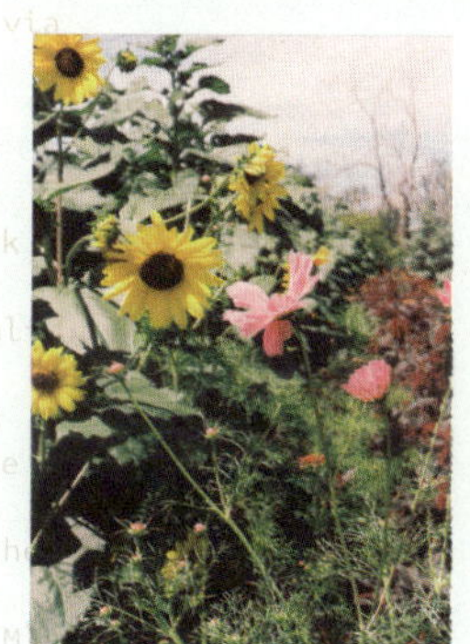

As pollinators populate the garden below, our cafe begins. I acknowledge the Tewa and Tanos people as the original inhabitants and stewards of the land, then share a brief history of climate cafes, a concept originally created by the Climate Psychology Alliance to create "*informal, open, respectful, and confidential spaces to safely share emotional responses and reactions related to the climate crisis.*"[1] Climate cafes are a place to pause from the hum of daily life and to be **with the feelings of this time, rather than do anything.**

I share my intent for facilitation: *to cultivate a space for the community to connect and reflect on the climate crisis together*. I explain that after the 2022 Calf Canyon/Hermit's Peak Fire, the largest and most destructive wildfire in the history of New Mexico, my heart ached for a place to communally process grief. After this sharing I pause, acknowledging the breath change in our circle. Although we do not yet know each other's names, we all relate to the heartbreak present in the mention of wildfires.

As our container continues to form, I share my identity as a queer artist and art therapist. I name my past experience of feeling paralyzed by climate grief in 2019, which led me into climate justice work. After expanding upon my experience, I review community agreements in an effort to hold our emotional explorations.

The group is invited to breathe together, creating a web of interconnectedness through the pathway of shared air. Three rounds of sharing proceed, following the CPA outline of a climate cafe: sharing, discussion, and contemplation.

In the first round, everyone is invited to gaze into a basket of items I have set forth on the table in front of us, choosing an object. This object creates a pathway for orientation and symbolizes the notion of a *hyperobject*, a term coined by ecophilosopher Timothy Morton to describe concepts that contain a massive distribution amid time and space to transcend spatiotemporal specificity, such as global warming. Hyperobjects speak to the immense structural forces all around us, even inside us, of which we only grasp a facet rather than being able to engage with their totality.[2] →

death practices

grief as nonlinear
group work
groups

holding space

collective care

communing with animals

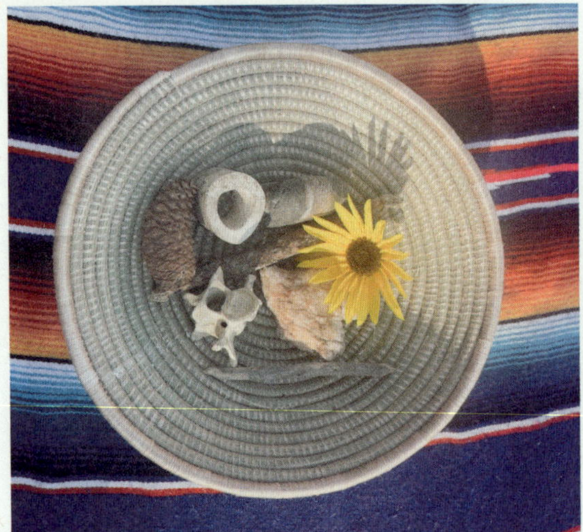

After choosing an object, everyone is invited to share their name and pronouns, something about themselves, their relationship to the climate crisis, their intention for gathering, and any connection to the object they have chosen to hold from the basket of items. The group is diverse in age and background, ranging from a retired climate activist to a current ER doctor in the process of recovering from the strains of the pandemic. While varied in identity, each individual shares a love for the land.

To close the round, we breathe together again as the cottonwood branches dance above our heads in a gentle breeze. We then proceed into the second round of conversation. I invite folks to share any thoughts, feelings, reflections, or words in response to introductions. Connections spark within the group, and moments of laughter fill the air. We dance between complexities and then feel a weight emerge at the mention of grief, of loss.

As the dialogue finds a natural resting place, I return us to breath and pose a question to guide our third, and final, round of conversation: *What has been your experience and connection, along with impact, to the recent fires in New Mexico?* Silence seeps through the air as we acknowledge the palpable grief ushered forth with the mention of wildfire. Someone begins, modeling vulnerability, which ripples outward among the group. I notice the dialogue change, turning toward action. Folks strategize ways of moving forward, pathways toward "fixing" current local climate issues. The notion of privilege is brought into the conversation, as one member states: "*To have solar panels on your home, you need to own your home, which is an immense privilege. To buy an electric car, you need the funds to do so, another privilege. 'Going Green' requires access to money; not everyone has that.*"

Checking the time, I notice we are nearing the end of our gathering and I gently invite the group to co-regulate through breath. I name the shift from feeling into thinking, reminding everyone of the intent for the cafe to be a reflective container of *holding* and *being*.

"*There are places for action, in our activist work, and we are here to be together in our feelings*," I say.

Again, we return to our breath, to our bodies. I offer gratitude for the land and to all who chose to show up. "*In doing so, you have said YES to yourself and your community. This is no small gesture*," I say. Folks are invited to write their emails down on a piece of paper as a way to stay in touch. Conversations continue with newfound connections as the sun sets to the gentle hum of insects in the fields below. I wonder to myself what they think of our gathering, and smile as I embark on my journey home. ❁

1 Climate Psychology Alliance, www.climatepsychology.us.

2 Morton, *Hyperobjects: Philosophy and Ecology after the End of the World.*

BIO Chelsea Call, MA, LPCC, ATR (she/her/they/them) is a queer artist, art therapist, and interspecies ally whose work is informed by the wisdom of her ancestors, queer identity, and connection to more-than-human kin.

clouds as metaphor

SEE

CONTRIBUTION

FROM ARISTOPHANES' 4TH CENTURY BCE play *The Clouds* to the present, clouds are strewn throughout the arts and philosophy. It has been suggested clouds might be the most useful metaphor of all time. Clouds have given rise over the centuries to many metaphors, images, philosophical speculations, poems, novels, plays, photographs, paintings, and wonderings. Recently "the cloud" has become the accepted shorthand for electronic data storage. By the Renaissance clouds were a metaphor for what is perpetually in a process of change, of becoming something else, that things could be otherwise. Since 2005 the Cloud Appreciation Society has sent a cloud-related image and quote to its worldwide members every morning. Renaissance scholar Rachel Eisendrath asks, "Why do animals not look at clouds?"[1] She proposes that humans have a psychic need for clouds. Clouds as metaphors can lead us to places where Enlightenment reason is weakened, even disabled, replaced by fabrics of feelings that call for us to attend.

Poets have written magnificent poems featuring clouds; Baudelaire writes "those whose desires assume the shape of mist or cloud"[2] and Coleridge "O! it is pleasant, with a heart at ease/Just after sunset, or by moonlight skies/To make the shifting clouds be what you please."[3] In Shelley's poem *The Cloud*, he uses the transformation of an "earthbound" drop of water to a larger mass in the sky, a cloud, as a metaphor for human change from despair to hope. Contemporary poet Carolyn Forche writes, "Souls have their own world. They are the descendants of clouds."[4] In classical music there is the remarkable opera in the clouds, *Light*, by Karlheinz Stockhausen, performed in helicopters.

Many playwrights have incorporated clouds in various ways. August Strindberg thought that clouds contain many meanings and clouds find their way into his *A Dream Play*. Tennessee Williams's *Something Cloudy, Something Clear* is an autobiographical play dealing with unrequited gay love. In 1977 Samuel Beckett wrote a short play, *…but the clouds*, taking his title from a line in a poem by Yeats. For Beckett as for Yeats, decay is a central motif seeing life as a walking shadow, presenting us with the evanescence of existence—isolation and loss. Clouds for Beckett were metaphors for the wispy, insubstantial, ethereal nature of existence, creating an atmosphere of melancholia.

Philosophers and theologians have been fascinated by clouds. Karl Popper's "clocks and clouds" metaphor describes the two ends of the spectrum of predictability in social science with clouds representing the disorderly and irregular, and clocks representing the predictable and rational. Ludwig Wittgenstein writes, "You can't *build* clouds. And that's why the future you dream of never comes true."[5] In a 14th-century anonymous mystical text "The Cloud of Unknowing," God is enveloped in darkness, "a cloud of unknowing"[6] that can only be reached, revealed, and understood through feeling and love, not through knowledge.

Among the many visual artists who prominently include clouds are English Romantic landscape artist John Constable and contemporary sculptor Anish Kapoor. From 1820–1822 Constable painted remarkable cloud studies where he depicted the moods of the sky through the emotion and drama of clouds. Kapoor's large sculpture *Cloud Gate* in Chicago's Millennium Park was in evidence during Obama's victory speech in 2008. Novelist David Mitchell in *Cloud Atlas* metaphorically juxtaposes the two words of the title that stand in an ambivalent relation to one another. Clouds are ephemeral, fleeting, not fixed; Atlas in Greek mythology is the god of endurance, permanence, eternity. Metaphorically as the novel unfolds through six interconnected stories separated by large swaths of time, clouds represent disparate people connecting with intertwining fates and how our humanness drifts across time like clouds across the sky.

Clouds are often associated with the imagination and for William Blake "we are all imagination."[7] For Romantic artists, the creative imagination is the best source of knowledge. It is for this reason that on the ceiling of the New York Public Library's Rose Reading Room is a painting of beautiful clouds, there to stir the imagination of readers.

Social work (and other helping professions) is a practice where the imagination has the paramount informing power to shape what we do. The imagination gives us profound indications into the interior lives and experiences of other people and helps us to see them as fully human, to understand diversity, irony, uncertainty, and ambiguity.

Clouds say much about our lives and work:

- Clouds provide experiences of wonder, amazement, and drifting astonishment—for the philosopher Wittgenstein, astonishment is a form of thinking.
- Clouds are contexts, not codes—a context is fluid, changeable, unfinalizable, opening us to creative significance.
- Clouds are non-historical.
- Clouds are constantly in motion, changing the mood of the day; metaphors for the fragility of moments.
- Clouds as unruly strangers.
- Clouds as metaphors for uncertainty and unknowing.
- Clouds are fractals, non-linear, un-mappable, and cannot be measured—why do we think we can measure humans?
- Do clouds assist in communication between earth and sky?
- Can we think of clouds as anti-Cartesian, challenging order and measurement?
- Clouds as metaphors for fluid identities, metamorphoses, transformations, sensations, emotions.
- Clouds form and reform in arbitrary positions, remind us of chance, chaos, divisions, magnifications, playfulness, and madness.
- Clouds as metaphors of escape; part of the sea escapes into the sky and may not return for a long time.
- Clouds as metaphors for wandering, discovery, and journeys.
- Clouds as metaphors for instability—rain, lightening, snow, hail, wind.
- Clouds as metaphors for blur, without borders, vague, subtle, unfixed, spontaneous, unsettled, fuzzy; as Beckett writes, "haze is our sole certitude."[8]

The time has come, as the Walrus said, to think of many things, one of which is to look at social work as metaphorically atmospheric, as a cloud painting that might at times be composed of pure mist and gold. ❁

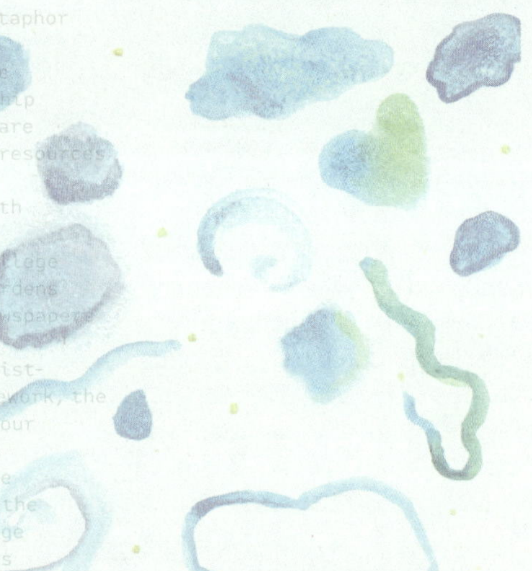

1 Eisendrath, *Gallery of Clouds*, 135.

2 Baudelaire, *Flowers of Evil*, 189.

3 Coleridge, *Poetical Works*, 435.

4 Carolyn Forché, *In the Lateness of the World: Poems*, 12.

5 Wittgenstein, *Culture and Value*, 41.

6 Anonymous, *The Cloud of Unknowing*.

7 Frye, *Fearful Symmetry: A Study of William Blake*, 30.

8 Samuel Beckett, *Nohow On: Three Novels*, 78.

B Allan Irving, social work
I educator, a dweller amidst
O the fragments and chaos.

SEE resonance; revolutionary mothering; sanctuary; solidarity; togetherness

CONTRIBUTION

one final dance; in loving destruction; the coalition emerges

I HAVEN'T YET LEARNED to attune my attention, *my attention*, toward my body's multiple rhythms, the cuts that might open, or the sudden pulls of loss, or the gaps that allow my awareness to keep looking ahead. *But you*, in the blur of *our* practice, have picked up on the gravity, *those gravities* yet to be materialized, unspoken, unheard. And the space of appearance within what is unknown, the possibilities of it, the ground it offers, the horizon it draws out, or maybe it doesn't, not just yet. *How is it that you knew?* Offering gently words you crafted; placing them in my hands to remold and undo and detangle this shell, *that one I dwell in*. Not out of help, nor service, nor guilt. In this action of crossing over, in *loving destruction*, in commitment and with care, toward the building of a place where we can be, as our interwoven and yet contained selves, in fullness, for that space of being only rises of an *us*.

The coalition emerges here: in our convergence of not knowing, beyond the language, not exactly this or that, it's in *here*! In this space of presence; in the practice of it. *Because we are merely practicing*.

We are practicing acknowledgement. We are practicing the bearing. We are practicing out loud, in public and with the monsters underneath the bed, we are practicing to fail, to dig deep into the openings, to cultivate all those stories we *thought we knew so well*. We practice at coalition, at the living and breathing thing, at the relations which might harm us, and so often they do. As metastatic, as poison. Arriving at the surface after years of deep dispersal. Practice. Practicing to dissipate. Practicing for the joy of it. Practicing while knowing well the dangers and the stakes. That this might not work. That we might lose each other. That the absences will never be quite the same. That in losing you, I lose myself. And yet, that's also what makes this so worth the while.

Whoever said *this practice* had no stakes?

Help assumes that my power has been taken, that I, unlike you, am uniquely dependent. Of course we *know* that is a falsity, but we don't always practice as such. We might practice out of goodness and that might get us somewhere for a while. But our coalitions will only ever emerge; in unabashed upheaval, an unwillingness, an attitude. *Goodness won't cut it here*. Coalition comes of rage and heartache, forged for years under the ground. It comes of necessity. Of the urgency to be and feel. And it boils between an *us*, finally, dancing at the warehouse party. The crowd is small enough to feel like family. Big enough to feel packed. We know all the DJs. They play all our favorite songs. *Here*, we are present. One final dance before the world shuts down. Before sickness arrives. Before we do as we always have. Moving through uncertainty.

Coalition isn't spectacle. It's not something we can point at. We aren't always made aware of its arrival. As mundane as it is sacred. It will also dissolve back.

We were strangers turned kin; as honest as grief; and maybe back again.

So where does the coalition emerge? ❁

BIO Kimi Hanauer is an artist, media-based organizer, collective member of Press Press, and steward of the Center for Liberatory Practice & Poetry.

collaborative apprenticeship

CONTRIBUTION

FRANK, SRUTI, AND VALE are friends and students in a craft department at an art school.

Frank has an interview for a job but was asked to keep sanding his bookshelf by his professor; he has to choose between preparing for his next gig and finishing his final art piece.
Sruti shares a few different supports that they can offer Frank as he wraps his semester, ranging from practice interviewing to sanding. Frank reflects, and asks Sruti to finish his bookshelf so he can attend his interview.
After his interview, Frank tells Sruti what excites him about this job, and they explore Frank's dreams outside of school together.

Vale is hydro-dipping metal pieces for a chair she's making; the chair will look like a floral tablecloth her family used, in Venezuela and in Miami.
Sruti offers to help Vale with the metal handling process and asks if they can also talk about their collective memories and reflections on diasporic art and craft traditions while working on the chair.
Vale takes Sruti up on their offer, and they spend four hours building together.

Sruti is trying to figure out how specific skills in craft and construction developed in a highly capitalist educational environment relate to cultural movements against capitalism. Frank, Vale, and others in the craft department welcome Sruti into collaboration and build a communal practice of exchange and reflection to model what life will look like for artists who choose to exist outside a PRODUCTion exclusive economy. ❁

BIO

Sruti Suryanarayanan is a Tamizh American craftsperson and writer who helps build tools to help people collaboratively question extractive economies.

collective care

SEE
peer-to-peer health network
radical care in the arts
solidarity economy
12-step programs

CONTRIBUTION

CASSIE: I love this Vikki Reynolds video you showed me called "Resisting Burnout with Justice-Doing Part 1: Collective Care & Ethical Pain."[1] She contests the politically neutral framing of "burnout" amongst community workers providing services to unhoused people in downtown Vancouver. At one point in the video, she says, *Don't worry, I won't make you touch your toes or go to your happy place or anything*. She may be the first person who could describe what collective care is to me in a way I could feel.

The context she describes is very different from the situations that you and I inhabit right now—she is talking to people doing social work in an opioid epidemic that is also riddled with inadequate housing, racist police violence and an environmental crisis. We are living in Berlin, where we are engaged with projects such as The Holographic School of Social Medicine and in various community support work. And we are certainly surrounded by addiction, inadequate housing, racist police and an environmental crisis, though we are not frontline workers in it. Frontline social work, as the kind of waged work she describes, can never truly transform the unjust systems it is situated within: *We are in structures that are oppressive and we are staying alive and our hearts are broken and that is a hard task.* But she goes on to ask, *How are we treating each other collectively?*

Collective care implies that the people who give care are cared for, and that there is no one who is just a heroic caregiver and no one who is just a broken patient. In the social work context, Reynolds says this means that we have to allow each other to take breaks, eat lunch, and leave on time. *If you are the person who is managing, and you don't take breaks or eat, we are teaching others to do that. Heroic posturing teaches people the wrong thing.*

She encourages social workers providing frontline care to check in on each other—the implication being that if they don't do that for each other, no one else will. There is not a system of care in place to make sure that the people who put themselves at risk for others are themselves cared for. This is a worldwide mechanic that seems to go unquestioned—that we continue to extract energy and resources from people who are already depleted. The remedy for this is not the kind of self-care that Reynolds jokes about—touching your toes and going to your happy place. Only when the people around us are okay will we be truly okay.

It's not a secret that the whole of society is held together by reproductive labor, domestic labor, and social work. And it is not a surprise that these things are undervalued or that this work is largely done in invisibilized ways by feminized and/or racialized people. I see The Hologram[2] as an opportunity to challenge these extractivist capitalist mechanics around care. When I invite three people to care for me, I support each of those people in setting up their own holograms. It is a special moment outside of an emergency context, when we can feel what it is like to ask for help, but also what it's like to ensure that caregivers are cared for.

There's a much deeper form of collective mutuality in this practice compared to an exchange which replicates a capitalist transaction—I'll only give you (an individual) something if you give me (another individual) something back that's of equivalent value. When we practise asking for help and supporting the people we ask to receive help or care, we are beginning to set a new pattern in our brains and in our collective habits. I think this is how we remake the world: through changing collective habits. When care is provided from conditions of abundance rather than depletion, I have seen it produce energy for both the caregiver and receiver.

Sarah, do you agree that when care produces energy in this way, it is a kind of magic created by humans?

SARAH: I do! And I also think that the opposite is true—that when care is devalued and extracted in ways that are non-consensual, it creates a huge amount of destructive energy. I thought about my family of origin here as a kind of inverse Hologram: it was one person (my mother) providing care for three other people—my disabled father, my grandmother with Alzheimer's, and me as a child. My father had been in the army his whole life before he retired and he carried over the colonial and patriarchal underpinnings of that institution into the institution of the nuclear family.

My mother worked constantly when I was a child—I'm not sure I have any memories of her where she was not exhausted, both emotionally and physically. Yet I'm not sure that anyone in my family would have described the huge burden of caregiving that fell on her as work. It was just normal stuff that housewives do. To acknowledge that she performed important work would have been to acknowledge that my father relied on others to meet his needs. He could never have accepted this kind of vulnerability. So he took care more than he received it—as an entitlement under an extractivist hierarchy rather than freely given labour offered in a system of collective mutuality.

If the nuclear family is often a closed unit where caregiving falls disproportionately on one person who is not sufficiently cared for, The Hologram is the opposite of this: a series of interdependent units connected by the understanding that we all need to receive care from other people and that all caregivers must be cared for.

It doesn't really feel possible to say how my family would have been different if it had functioned around this understanding. It feels about as possible as trying to imagine what it would have been like if we'd lived on the moon when I was growing up. But when I practise The Hologram now, it does feel like a kind of liberatory magic—a proof that collective care practices can show us the best in each other. How would we be changed collectively if we all practised giving and receiving care in ways that are not transactional and extractive? ❁

1 Reynolds, "Resisting Burnout with Justice-Doing Part 1: Collective Care and Ethical Pain."

2 The Hologram is a peer-to-peer network for non-expert healthcare. One person, the "Hologram," invites three people that they trust to meet on a regular basis to focus on their physical, mental, and social health. Over time, this group reflects a multifaceted image of the central person—like a hologram. For more, see "peer-to-peer health networks."

BIOS

Cassie Thornton is an artist and activist who makes a "safe space" for the unknown, for disobedience, and for unanticipated collectivity. She is also the author of a book that was secretly written with all her friends and published by Pluto Press: *The Hologram: Feminist, Peer-to-Peer Health for a Post-Pandemic Future.*

Sarah Adelaide is a counsellor, lawyer, and somatic sex educator practicing in Berlin. They help people to analyse power, author liberatory stories about themselves and find pleasure in their bodies.

common pool resources

SEE solidarity economy, sufficiency

CONTRIBUTION

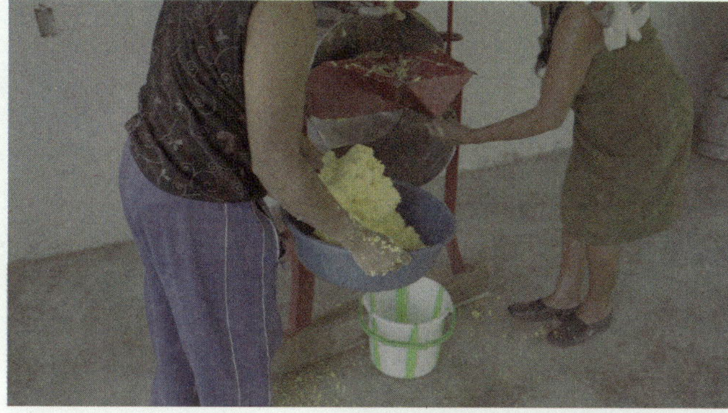

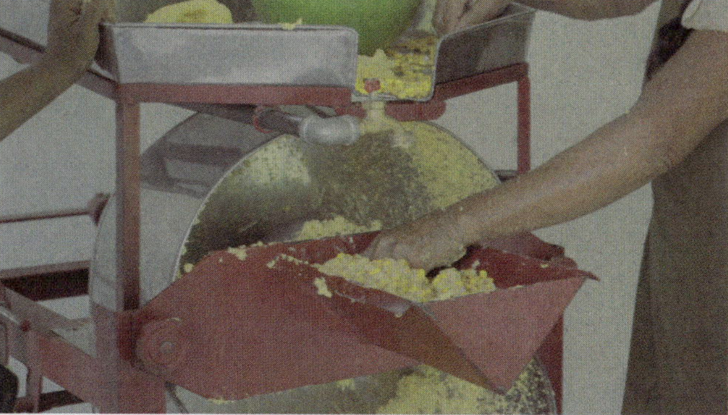

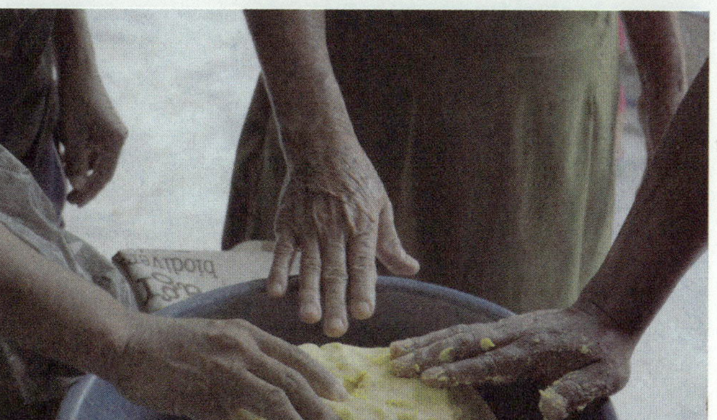

Doña Mary Carmen and her mom, Doña Magdalena, using the community's corn mill to make masa. Video stills courtesy of Andrea Macias-Yañez, 2021.

BIO

Andrea Macias-Yañez is an artist researcher based in Berlin, Germany, working with video and writing to enact forms of environmental remembering, to reveal situated pasts as they exist in the present.

commons, the

SEE:

CONTRIBUTOR'S NOTE

"THE COMMONS" represents the concept of natural and cultural resources that are available to anyone in a community. The term was popularized by the essay "Tragedy of the Commons," in which human ecologist Garrett Hardin warns readers of the dangers of shared resources through the example of a large field used for grazing livestock.[1] He describes the field going bare from overuse while the grass behind fences thrives, as community members' self-interest leads them to only care about preserving the land which they consider fully theirs. Economists such as Elinor Ostrom have since studied real life "commons," like fisheries and irrigation institutions, to find out how successful examples avoid this "tragedy." She found that "the commons" can work when continually invested community members choose (and hold each other to) adaptable systems with boundaries and conflict-resolution systems based on the unique factors of their people and land.[2]

This poem explores the (perhaps initially uncomfortable) process of going from a world of private ownership to one of collective ownership. It might take a generation to move past the systems that have kept our needs scarce enough to be profitable, creating true abundance through indigenous practices that treat nature like a collaborator. It might take another generation to truly trust that our needs will continue to be met.—MSM

CONTRIBUTION

Act 1: Tragedy
When the fences first fall
Sheep worry for weeks that the grass will be smaller again tomorrow
They eat for future hunger
And leave the fields bare

Unending questions no longer decided by blood and sweat:
What do we grow, if not the seeds that sell?
How should we divide work, if not by power?
Are our needs really so scarce?

Act 2: Comedy
Did only grass ever grow here?
Today it is chaos of abundance
Layers of life
Children and grape-heavy vines climbing trees
If colonizers came again, they might again fail to recognize the human intelligence of it all
Not knowing work that doesn't produce in neat rows
Deep in our DNA we remember our place in every cycle
A gift from nature like every other
A gift we share like any other

We rest while we watch our needs regenerate
The things we used to ask nature for
One can take too much of
It was easier than the easiest of victories in a zero-sum game
We are animals
Fruits want to be eaten
We want each other to survive ❁

1 Hardin, "Tragedy of the Commons."

2 Ostrom, *Governing the Commons.*

BIO

Mia Stone-Molloy (she/her) is a labor organizer and poet with a bachelor's degree in Economics and Political Science from Brown University and a passion for the connection between personal and societal healing.

communing with animals

CONTRIBUTION

communing with animals, noun,
[kuh-myoon-ing with an-uh-muhls]

The simple pleasure of noticing and being in the presence of other animals as a means to explore our inner knowing of ourselves and the world around us.

MY BEST FRIEND IS A HUMMINGBIRD WHO SHARES IN THE SWEETNESS OF LIFE.

She zooms by my window each morning, her chest feathers glinting against the misty fog.

She flits and floats, skimming the trees looking for the juiciest of treats.

She dances in the rainbow-speckled shower when I water the plants.

Chirping her blessings at me for the impromptu bath.

She ascends with ease, chirping her little song, content in her role as nectar gatherer.

MY SQUIRREL NEIGHBORS ARE TEACHING THEIR KIDS THE ROPES.

What's safe? What's dangerous? Showing their squirrel kits how to live in the world.

They have learned the art of scrambling up the telephone poles.

Watching the little balls of fluff with a still-growing tail testing out their limits.

Their parents show them how to walk under the wires to evade the hawks.

Now the squirrel kits are free to roam and test out their newfound freedom.

A COMMUNITY OF BISON LIVE AMONG THE REDWOODS IN MY CITY'S PARK.

"Good morning, bison!" I cycle past in my spandex gear made in the Philippines.

They sit together in the paddock on the hill sharing in their communal meal.

The sheer size of them. Their thick brown coats nestled along the hill.

I yearn for their freedom. A valley filled with bison as far as the eye can see.

Their tails switch against the early fog, aching for the plains their ancestors once roamed.

THE ANIMALS AROUND US ARE REMINDERS OF OUR CONNECTION TO THE EARTH.

We build our tall, vast concrete cities and sit in our dinosaur-powered steel boxes to keep nature out, but we are nature.

Nature never left us.

And we never left nature. ➔

communing with animals

As much as our societies try to hide our reality, we are just like the birds, squirrels, and bison that live among us. We may commute to our day jobs, do the laundry, and transport ourselves through the sky on jet planes, but we are still of the animal kingdom.

We have a role just as other animals and plants serve our ecosystems.

COMMUNING WITH OUR FRIENDS BRINGS US BACK TO OURSELVES.

No matter where in the world, there is always nature to find. Even cities have birds in the sky and little critters on the ground. This healing practice is accessible no matter where you call home. Nature and the creatures around us can be a powerful tool for us to reconnect with ourselves.

A daily practice I adopted early in the pandemic was noticing the animals around me in the morning. I began to take walks through my neighborhood park. I noticed the squirrel's patterns, how different birds behaved, and how animals interacted with the human world. It allowed me to immerse myself and settle into a state of curiosity and calm before moving into the hectic world of corporate life in America.

In the human world, our role is to work, produce, buy, and go, go, go to maintain unsustainable growth. Instead, the animal kingdom asks for us to settle, notice, and live aligned with the earth. That means giving our bodies what they need, especially when that is rest. We can live more in balance when we notice what is around us.

STRENGTHENING OUR PRACTICES OF NOTICING BUILDS RESILIENCE.

Take a few moments out of your day. Start with as little as 5 minutes, or 30 minutes if you can spare it. Go outside or go to a window where animals are more present. My favorite places are parks or lakes, but it can be any spot you can find on your lunch break, walking the dog, or daydreaming in class.

Once you're there, just simply notice. Be curious about what you see. Watch how the world moves in front of you. Do you see birds in the sky, critters on the ground, or maybe signs of some nighttime activity? It is not about interacting with wild animals but noticing and feeling more connected to the beings around us. To remind ourselves that there is so much more beyond the human world despite its constant demands for our attention.

When we notice what is around us, we can also better connect with ourselves and notice what's inside. Feeling more connected to the animals can help us feel more care toward ourselves as we move through the human world. ❁

BIO Sam Chavez is a writer, strategist, curious human, and founder of Roots of Change Agency, which empowers activists and organizations to cultivate social change through storytelling.

community college

SEE redistribution

CONTRIBUTION

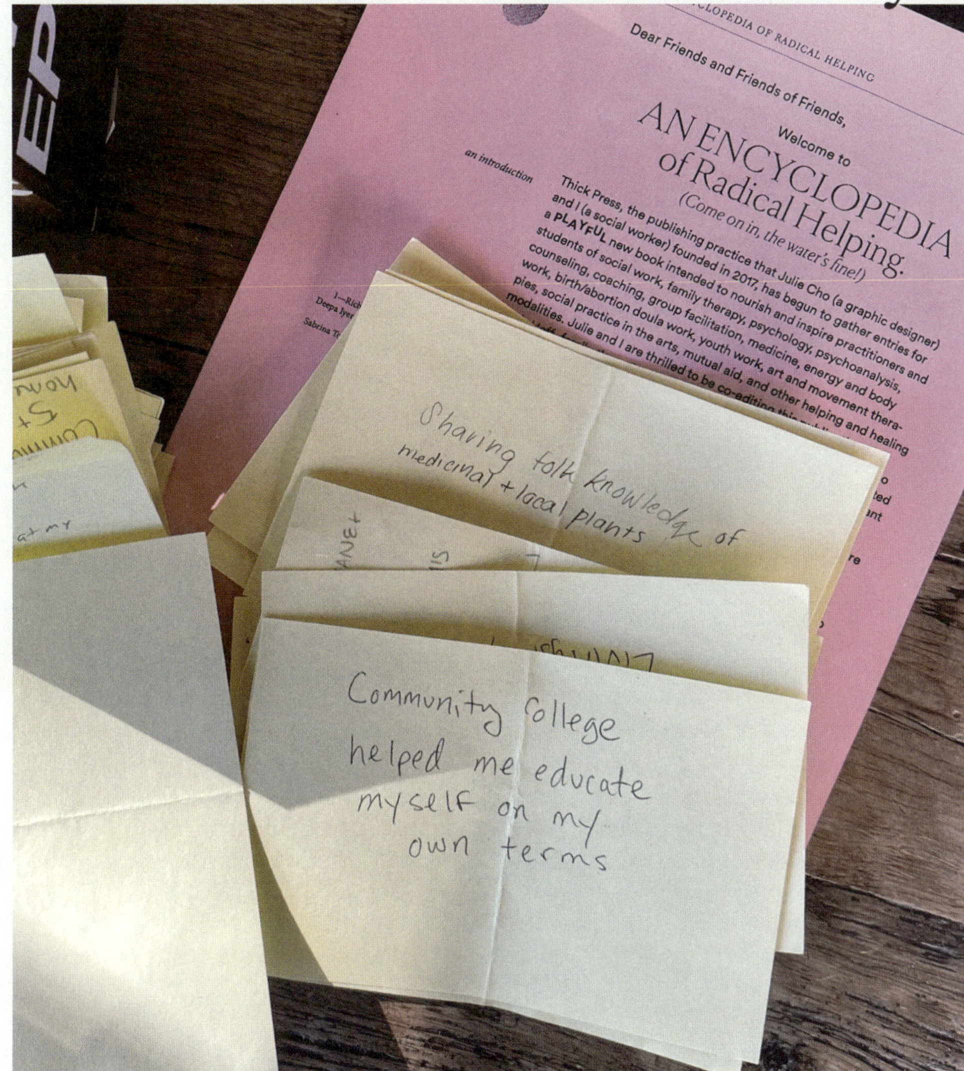

Anonymously scribed notecards collected at Printed Matter's 2022 New York Art Book Fair.

EDITORS' NOTE

This contribution (and this idea for a topic) arrived in the form of a notecard responding to the prompt we offered at the Printed Matter 2022 New York Art Book Fair ("What beyond the Western medical model has helped you?") As a product of community college myself, I also found much freedom in community college to try on different identities of who I might be or what I might do. Community college allowed me the room and freedom to craft my own schedule based on my interests and curiosities, and to experiment with a variety of subjects including poetry, creative writing, art, and eventually psychology. All without the pressure or constraints of a more traditional four-year university.—CH

community gardens

CONTRIBUTION

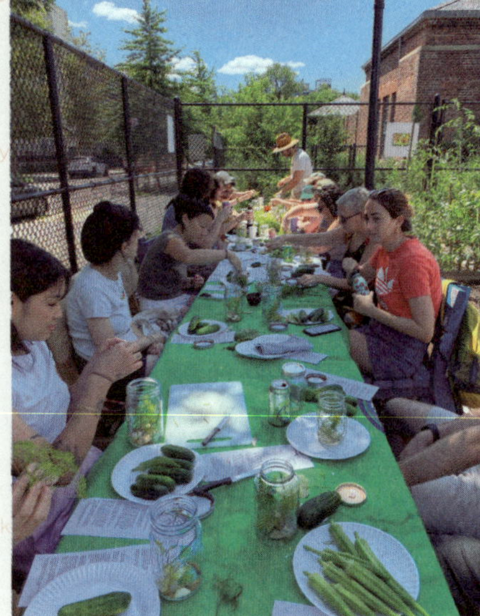

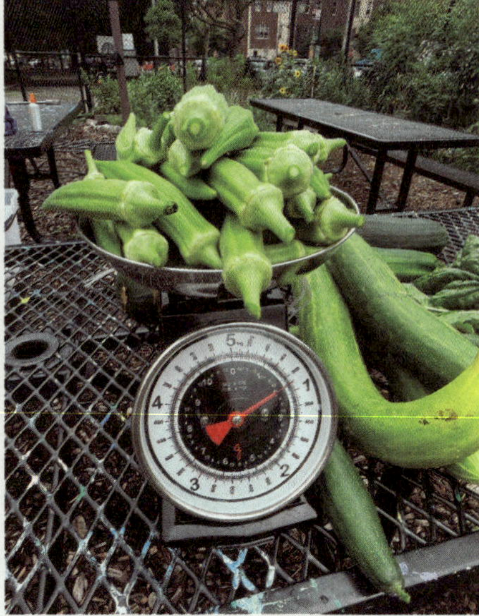

My Mother's Pickles - pickling workshop, hosted by Amy Pekal, one of the many educational events at the McCarren Demo Garden.

IN AN URBAN LANDSCAPE, community gardens present the opportunity to decenter the human from the muck of humanness and place us in participation with the living world. In the garden, nothing makes itself without others; it becomes a site to bring mutual relationships into being. It is a zone of collaboration human to human, human to plant, plant to critter, and a plethora of other combinations beyond these humble imaginings. Therefore, the practices of care that percolate within a community garden continually ask: What does it mean to be in relationship with more-than-human worlds? For us stewards, the McCarren Demo Garden activates and encourages volunteers to perform the worlds we want to see.

Situated in Williamsburg, Brooklyn, the McCarren Demo Garden is a partnership with Grow NYC and North Brooklyn (NBK) Mutual Aid. The garden is stewarded by volunteers. Together, we learn about environmental sustainability, ecosystems, and urban gardening. At the core of the community garden is the practice of growing organic food for two NBK community fridges. Each year we receive organic seedling donations from local nurseries and we cultivate the vegetables and herbs. A few times a week, we harvest, log, weigh, and deliver the produce to the local community fridges. In 2022 and 2023 we harvested over 750 pounds of food during each growing season.

Alongside the practice of cultivation, the garden is also a space to host educational workshops that range from seed saving, pickling, the circular economy, family harvest days, planting days, and pumpkin carving, among dozens more, including a panel discussion about the Catholic nun who fought for environmental justice in Greenpoint. These workshops, facilitated by members of our local community, help us to gain a better understanding of our neighborhood's history and ongoing fight toward the creation of hyper-local climate-just worlds.

The maintenance work in the garden is the type of labor that brings neighbors together. In our first year gardening together, we learned how to prune tomatoes, how to keep powdery mildew from spreading across the crops, how to attract pollinators, and how to water the garden so that the roots soaked up the water in a drought-ridden summer. There was still much to

SEE: ancestral wisdom, altering maintenance, circular economy, common pool resources, fermentation, food sovereignty, herbal justice, herbalism learn as the growing season came to an end, but I held on to the new knowledge gained through practice for a climate-just future.

In the situated reality of North Brooklyn, accessibility to plant-people relationships is something we must seek out and commit to repeatedly. What is special about this garden is there is no real expectation; you come to do good work, meet like-minded people, and build community from the ground up. It's a host to so many ecologies, relations, and opportunities for ongoing learning. As we grow more familiar with what surrounds us, we become more invested in the interdependent relationships between plants and people. By engaging with lively matter in the act of growing food, we also acknowledge the complexity of nature's systems and the dedication needed to cultivate symbiotic relationships to bring climate-just worlds into being.

The garden is a space of learning and community stewardship that is year-round, dynamic, and accessible to every age group. By engendering care and maintenance as foundations of the community garden, we commit to a practice of radical help. The physical act of just digging into the earth heals and restores our relationship to the living world. By delivering the food we grow to the community fridges, we extend our help beyond the garden's fence. The work of NBK Mutual Aid at the McCarren Demo Garden is radical and omni-directional—where help is carried from the plants to us, from us to the plants, from the garden to the community, and from the community back to the garden. It helps us know our neighbors; it helps us know our local businesses; it helps us know why we call North Brooklyn home. ❁

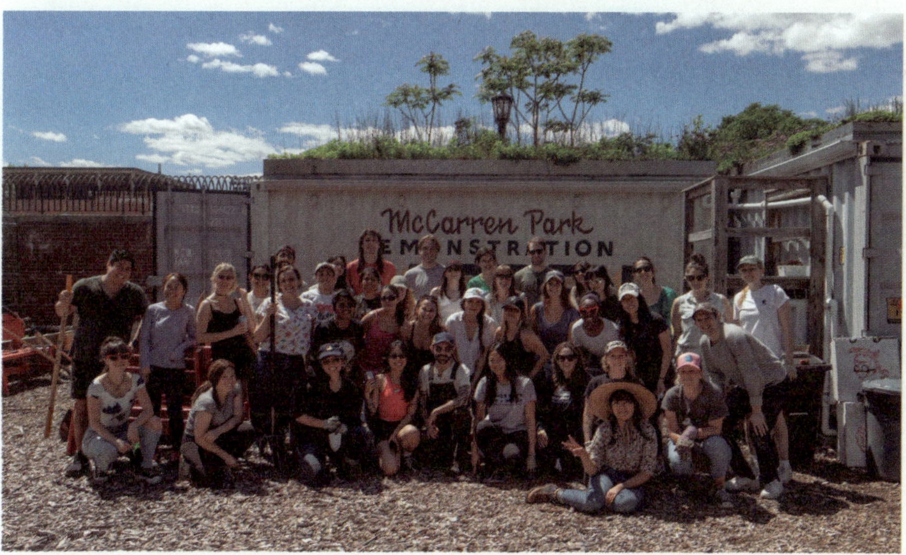

B I O

Amy Pekal is an artist and researcher; she examines climate breakdown as an ecological and ethical urgency and remains dedicated to living as Naturecultures.

community newspapers

SEE: activating archives; art as/in/of life

CONTRIBUTION

AS A CHILD, I took newspapers for granted. There they were, everywhere. Rubber-banded each morning on the front steps. Scattered across the kitchen table, stained with coffee and milk. Stacked in the recycling bin. The Sunday funnies, the only section in color. Hats folded from the front page. Fires started with the sports section. Christmas ornaments wrapped in the advertising inserts. Newspapers: there they were.

Now, they are not so easy to find. Countless local papers have been gobbled up by national conglomerates with syndicated stories, forced to go online-only, or shut down completely.

In northern coastal California, we are lucky that there are a few robust community newspapers left. There's the *Point Reyes Light*, serving West Marin county from Muir Beach to Tomales; the family-run weekly is the connective social tissue for a constellation of dispersed, unincorporated rural villages. There's the *Independent Coast Observer*, a weekly serving the Mendocino-Sonoma ("Mendonoma") coast from Jenner to Elk; its long-time publisher took over from his mother, who founded the paper in 1969 from her kitchen table. In an effort to remain sustainable into the future, the ICO recently became a nonprofit and will now be known as the *Independent Coast Observer Community Newspaper*. They achieved their new 501(c)(3) designation by following a playbook[1] created by *The Salt Lake Tribune*, which in 2019 became the first legacy paper in the US to successfully transition into a nonprofit model.

And then there's the *Bolinas Hearsay News*, a gem in the rough, an anomaly, a "can't believe it still exists" community newspaper. The *Hearsay* has been published three times per week since its founding in 1974. Yes, you read that correctly. It is edited, printed, and distributed by a rotating, ragtag collective of whoever is available, and it's a central feature of a tight-knit community that is known for its boisterous togetherness. The *Hearsay* was Nextdoor before Nextdoor existed. I have helped with the paper since 2017, less frequently now that I live out of town. During the height of the pandemic lockdown, we kept the *Hearsay* printing, and for some elders in town, it was their primary way to stay connected to friends and neighbors. Some people in town live without the internet, and so the paper copies in stock at the liquor store, grocery store, natural food store, bar, and hardware store were a lifeline.

Local newspapers are an incredibly powerful form of community media. They have the power to connect, inform, and include. While I am guilty of romanticizing their heyday, it's undeniable that there's something very potent in imagining a vast network of children facilitating daily delivery to the front door, and an entire community all turning the same pages at their respective breakfast tables. When else does that happen? Not often in this digital age.

I was a visiting artist for many years, working as a guest in host communities that were not my own. I worked to observe, engage, and translate the unique senses of place and identity that I found in these communities. I wanted to facilitate collective expression, encourage the joy of togetherness, and embrace the complexity of people and place. I visited the rural desert town of Green River, Utah, annually for five years, creating projects with the people who lived there. The first was *The Green River Newspaper*. My collaborator Sarah Baugh and I guided middle- and high-school students (and some adults) to create a newspaper for their town. We'd been inspired by the archives in the basement of the town's river history museum, deep and rich troves of community publications dating back a hundred years.

It's often difficult to gauge the "success" of a co-creative community project, but sometimes you just know. *The Green River Newspaper* was a success, full stop. Everywhere we went, for years after—the grocery store, the post office, the restaurant at the truck stop—people asked us, "Are you the newspaper girls?"

and complimented the project. The release party was the most well-attended community art event that our host organization had ever had. I tell you this not to sing our own praises but to sing the praises of the newspaper format.

The artist Corbin LaMont is the editor of *The Changing Times*, a roving community newspaper project that completed fourteen issues in fourteen different locations, over the course of three years. (The first twelve issues were created in twelve months!) Though the contributors and content shifted each time, the goal was the same: to illuminate the things that connect us all, and to celebrate connection and togetherness across time and space. From Tokyo, to the rolling lentil fields of Eastern Washington, to a pastoral San Juan Island, to Ciudad de México, *The Changing Times* achieved a difficult thing: creating artifacts of local place and community while creating expansive webs of connection across the globe.

There are certainly power imbalances within journalism, and ample opportunities for abuses both ethical and political. But on a good day, a newspaper is a vehicle for inclusion and participation. At its best, a local newspaper is a co-created snapshot of a time and a place. Each of its components—sections, articles, columns, captions, images, advertisements, classifieds, letters to the editor—is an opportunity for a community member to participate, and for a reader to glimpse a thread of the social fabric. A local paper can be an arena for debate, a container for conflict, and a tool for resolution, helping a community define its values and see itself reflected back.

Print newspapers may have had their heyday, but I choose to believe that means the medium is ripe for reimagining. ❁

Reference/Credits

The Green River Newspaper, 2013. Core collaborator: Sarah Baugh. Hosted by Epicenter, sponsored by the City of Green River.

The Changing Times, a project by Corbin LaMont/Office of Virtue. 2017–2018.

Bolinas Hearsay News, since 1974.

Point Reyes Light (formerly *The Baywood Press*), since 1948. Owners Tess Elliot and David Briggs.

Independent Coast Observer, since 1969.

1 *The Salt Lake Tribune*, "Nonprofit Playbook: A National Model for Sustaining Local Journalism."

BIO Nicole Lavelle is an artist, writer, and designer whose work addresses place, identity, and community.

conjure

SEE: ancestral wisdom; ancestrality; death practices; herbalism

CONTRIBUTION

CONJURE is the funkiest folk tradition this side of the rock called Earth. Also known by its colloquial name, "hoodoo," conjure is a distinctly African-American supernatural belief system with accompanying practices that protect and project.

Originating in kidnapped West Africans' forced migration to Turtle Island, conjure is the resulting blended set of ancestor-reverent and animist understandings of how the world works, informed and inspired by both the Indigenous Peoples whose homelands they now shared and environs new to them.

Conjuring includes bone/playing card/candle/Bible divination, ring shouts, and other call-n-response and ecstatic rituals, protection prayers, midwifery techniques, cemetery and dead rituals, an herbalist tradition called "rootwork," and much more. Conjure does not inhabit a canon as much as contain similar practices that have variations based on regions (which are related to slave port cultures).

These practices are often known by multi-generation Black Americans and/or southerners by reputation. On a scale of fear of Black diaspora spiritual traditions, conjure is somewhere in the middle. It is arguably *less feared in the U.S.* than its Caribbean siblings, Santería and Vodou; however, it is certainly *more feared* in the U.S. than its colonial-era Christian charismatic traditions (which adopted similar practices as conjure, and simply added their divine justifications for the genocidal system of chattel slavery). Indeed, conjure is both the everyday acts of spiritual defiance against the daily terrorism of enslavement and the eclectic remix and creation of new practices by enslaved/free Blacks and those around them to survive and make meaning of their conditions.

The Great Conjure Revival began in the 2010s when millennials and Generation Zers (re)discovered the tradition at a time when huge numbers of African Americans were seeking ancestral reconnection and/or spiritual systems outside too many corrupted churches, mosques, and other institutional religions. Long live the spirit of conjure!

BIO

Richael Faithful is a Black trans-southern multi/interdisciplinary healer, culture worker, and attorney.

constructionist-design framework, the

SEE social construction; songs/singing; speculative design; spells; wishes

CONTRIBUTION

The Constructionist-Design Framework: Research as Future-Forming

THE CONSTRUCTIONIST-DESIGN RESEARCH FRAMEWORK highlights the interconnectedness of ourselves and the ecosystem as we create knowledge. It is an invitation to see how nature, people, and our environments are related and shape our reality. This framework embraces research as participatory and world-making and researcher as a change agent producing knowledge while changing the system. The researcher here is not the neutral and objective subject discovering reality, but an agent who explores the multiplicity of perspectives, celebrating diversity, and transcending dichotomies.

In traditional research, we are most commonly invited to see our research environment and people as stable and uniform—and with that, the aim is to find single solutions and fix problems. The constructionist-design framework subverts and transcends single answers, liberating the researcher from the constraints of the so-called realism. By combining the philosophy of social construction with the attributes and principles of design thinking, a future-forming framework offers a dynamic research path focusing on co-creating novel results and unfolding new worlds.

This framework joins the research movement of forming futures through inquiry. This movement emphasizes the shift from investigating the world as it is to creating the world we would like to see.

UNDERSTANDING THE PHILOSOPHICAL PERSPECTIVE: SOCIAL CONSTRUCTION

First, let's understand the philosophy behind it. The focus of social construction is on meaning-making. Constructionists assume that meaning is created when people interact. Social construction also acknowledges that the meaning is never stable; it is constantly changing and framing culture and history, generating local situatedness realities. Social construction invites us to take a closer look at what people do together in local contexts, since this is where knowledge (meaning) is produced. The interest here is on exploring the polyphony of voices and perspectives that play a role in shaping and framing the meaning of issues we confront in our community.

In the context of research, social constructionism takes knowledge as a co-construction by people in their relationships. By questioning what we take to be true, real, or good, social constructionist research creates openings for the co-creation of new futures.

UNDERSTANDING THE PRACTICAL APPROACH: DESIGN THINKING

Now let's understand design thinking. Design thinking has been growing as a creative and innovative way of working with various formats to tackle more complex problems. It creates and nurtures a life-centric approach, always focused on being useful to the people involved. It's also context-related, encouraging a sensitivity to what the locality is asking for. Collaboration is at the center of this approach, offering creative tools to encourage the expansion of perspectives and meaning-making. Design thinking engages with co-creation where a diverse group of participants come together to generate different possibilities.

THE FRAMEWORK

The constructionist-design research framework proposes a path through four phases, combining social construction with design thinking. The first phase is about understanding and co-creating a topic; appreciative inquiry is a major influence here. After exploring your topic, you are ready for the second phase, which is about framing and reframing, zooming in and out, and designing a powerful inquiry question that is directly connected to the demands of the context studied. The third phase is about data generation and data meaning-making. Here, the creative tools of design thinking are very helpful. The fourth phase is about experimenting with the initial findings, prototyping what is possible to enact.

This framework can support researchers in attending to important points in the unfolding process of conducting research; it also assists practitioners working with complex systems, supportive in articulating who to involve, what to do, and how to do it, while simultaneously avoiding the fallacy that there is "one right way." It also calls attention to working formats that promote participation, co-creation, and the emergence of preferable futures.

RADICAL SUBVERSION OF THE ROLE OF RESEARCH: UNFOLDING NEW WORLDS

If knowledge is co-created in relationship, in context, and in history, this approach to research invites not only an understanding of this creation, but also a recreation of new forms of knowledge—and with that, new worlds unfold.

When we understand meanings and actions as constructions—that is, by-products of participants' engagements with each other and their environment—then we acknowledge research as a process of change, not just as the production of knowledge. Research here has the power of radical help as it taps into the collective intelligence of the people involved, focusing on what a context needs in order to transform present difficult situations into more promising ones.

The constructionist-design research framework invites researchers to become practitioner-researchers. This is a radical subversion of the role of research: people together, co-creating their place, space, and society, unfolding new worlds.

If you want to dive deeper into this framework, this is the book: *Design Thinking and Social Construction. A Practical Guide to Innovation in Research*, by Celiane Camargo-Borges and Sheila McNamee.

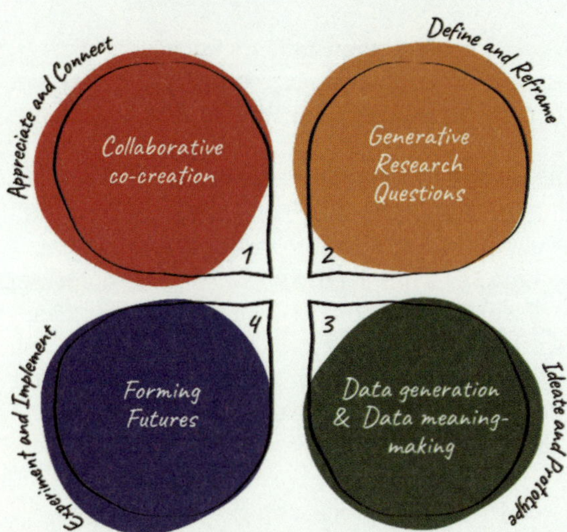

BIO Celiane Camargo-Borges, PhD, is a psychologist and a facilitator of dialogic processes. She is faculty at Breda University of Applied Sciences, The Netherlands, and a board member of the Taos Institute, USA.

consulting your consultants

CONTRIBUTION

THE PRACTICE OF CONSULTING YOUR CONSULTANTS is a narrative practice, discussed in the book *Playful Approaches to Serious Problems*,[1] in which people are positioned as experts on their own experience and radically consulted as to their knowledge. This alternative knowledge can be circulated to wider audiences (with permission) to benefit others. In this way, therapy becomes a "two-way process" that benefits the therapist and others they may encounter who are grappling with similar difficulties. White & Epston term this as "a sense of fair exchange,"[2] and this aims to redress the balance between practitioner and individual and family.

Children especially are often conceptualised as recipients of knowledge rather than contributors. Marston, Epston, and Johnson suggest narrative processes such as consulting your consultants serve to "flatten hierarchies" of knowledge between "expert" adults and children. They suggest it is the practitioner's role to bring children's knowledge to the fore and treat them not only as valuable but as "invaluable."[3] Narrative practices situate children's knowledge as noteworthy and identify this as a community achievement. That is, in sharing this valuable knowledge with others, the child becomes increasingly legitimised and their sense of agency is increased.

Consulting your consultants is part of the re-authoring process in narrative therapy—that is, "thickening" and giving richness to subjugated stories of people's lives and, in doing this, increasing their visibility. Stories are seen as constitutive in that they shape future experience, not merely offering an interpretive lens to understand the past. In identifying the "active ingredients" of their mastery of their difficulties, we assist children in telling new stories that can become preferred ways to live their lives.

In their book *Playful Approaches to Serious Problems*, Freeman et al. document many ways this can be done. The approaches have been used with a variety of difficulties described in the literature.

- "Communities of concern": In these, the expertise of people facing difficulties is circulated and available to communities of people struggling with the same problem, e.g., Anti Anorexia League,[4] The League against Upsets after Divorce or Family Change,[5] and the Deconstructing Addictions League.[6] These are often added to as more people share their experiences.
- Handbooks: These offer a discrete body of knowledge on a person or group's way of actively resisting the influence of the problem in their lives. The concept of handbooks has been applied to areas such as child sexual abuse,[7] fears and phobias,[8] and losing a loved one to suicide.[9]
- Co-research: This is a way of collaborating and inviting people of various cultures and backgrounds to interpret and study their own lives. In this way, the researcher and participants become partners.[10] Co-research has joined researchers and participants[11] together in the face of respiratory disease,[12] anorexia,[13] dystrophic emolysis bulosa,[14] researching people's experience of narrative therapy and the contribution they bring to the therapeutic process,[15] and the effects of certain questions in these processes.[16]
- Rite of passage: This method uses narrative questions to celebrate the transition from master's students to graduating family therapists to honour change in identity status to a preferred one.[17]
- Multiple family-group interventions: These target school non-attending children and their families in Hong Kong.[18]

Consulting your consultants practices seek to enrich and develop preferred identities to give people a foundation for action to approach challenges that may present in their lives, strengthen a person or a group's relationship to their "insider knowledge" in reclaiming their lives from problems, and pass on that specialist "insider knowledge" to link lives and therefore decrease alienation.

Adapted with permission from Lindsey's 2016 publication, "Lessons Hard Won: An Introduction to the Theory and Applications of Consulting Your Consultants'" in *Context: The Magazine for Family Therapy and Systemic Practice*. ❁

1 Freeman, Epston, and Lobovits, *Playful Approaches to Serious Problems*.

2 White and Epston, cited in Fox, "Using Therapeutic Documents: A review," 33.

3 White and Epston, cited in Fox, "Using Therapeutic Documents: A review," 33.

4 Epston, "The History of the Archives of Resistance: Anti-Anorexia/Anti-Bulimia—Narrative Approaches."

5 Hampson, "The League against Upsets after Divorce or Family Change."

6 Anthony, "Narrative Maps of Practice: Proposals for the Deconstructing Addictions League."

7 Hillier, *The Outrageous Adventures and How They Turned Sad Beginnings into Happy Endings*.

8 Hampson, *Jake and the Weather Scare: A Booklet for Health Professionals Working with Children with Fears*.

9 Sather and Newman, "Holding Our Heads Up: Sharing Stories Not Stigma after Losing a Loved One to Suicide."

10 Dulwich Centre, "Narrative Therapy and Research."

11 Epston, "Co-research: The Making of an Alternative Knowledge."

12 Epston, "Co-research."

13 Epston, "Co-research."

14 Epston, "Co-research."

15 Redstone, "Researching People's Experience of Narrative Therapy: Acknowledging the Contribution of the 'Client' to What Works in Counselling Conversations."

16 Morgan, Epston, and White, cited in Dulwich Centre, "Narrative Therapy and Research."

17 Keiley and Piercy, "The 'Consulting Your Consultants Interview': A Final Narrative Conversation with Graduating Family Therapy Masters' Students."

18 Lau, "A Multiple-Family Group with Youngsters Who Refuse to Attend School: Learning and Implications for School-Based Family Counseling."

BIO

Dr. Lindsey Hampson is a clinical psychologist, systemic family practitioner, and UKASFP accredited Solution Focused Practitioner who works for the National Health Service (NHS) within specialist child and adolescent services.

contemplative tradition, the

CONTRIBUTION

Rewilding Sensation

ABOUT 10 MONTHS after my second child was born, I found myself experiencing a storm of intensity in the middle of a sports store. It was familiar and unsettling—a tangled mess of thought, sensation, and emotion. My interpretation of this moment, and myself, was that I wasn't OK.

This small cluster of "storms" started when I let a stranger with a beer hold my baby. Usually relaxed, I suddenly had a sinking sensation that he might run off with her. A couple of hours later as I drove over the High Level bridge, like I'd done a thousand times, I panicked while she was in the back seat. Bewildered, I said *wtf* out loud. I rushed to distract myself—turning up the radio. *What's going on? There must be something wrong.*

These questions, heavy with self-criticism, cost me a night of sleep—only intensifying my sensations. As I felt them meander, spear, and throb—I gave them intimidating names. Panic. Anxiety. Post-partum. Because of this naming, I visited my doctor, who offered me Ativan. *No thank you*, I said. Taking it would be evidence that something was wrong. That I was wrong. That I couldn't handle the basics: my mind, my body, my baby.

But I had the basics, down—didn't I? I've done this baby thing before. I lead a team and support a minister. I've got paid maternity leave and a supportive partner. Nothing fazes him, even my sleepless nights.

In the middle of one of these "micro-storms" back in that sports store—I remembered a teaching: *The Welcoming Prayer*.[1] As I stood next to the Nalgene bottles, I closed my eyes and whispered it.

STEP 1

Invitation: *Bring mindful awareness to the sensations you're experiencing in your body. Stay with them. Watch them shift, move, dance, dissolve, meander.*

I stayed in that moment. Felt the shooting discomfort in my throat. Watched my mind jump to "*see, see that's it, that's panic. Why the fuck are you panicking, there's literally nothing going on.*"

Drop that thought.
Return to sensation.
Shit! The thought's back.
Drop the thought, return to sensation.
What's happening between the fibers of your muscles, tendons, and skin?

As I breathed, I could feel my sensations moving, all on their own. I watched them like a snake in the grass. Moving slowly at first and then gone. Only skin-dust behind.

Sensations traveling. Migrating. Moving. Dissolving.

STEP 2

Invitation: *Once the sensation begins to subside, shift, or dissolve in intensity, "Welcome"*[2] *what you're experiencing (yes, give it a name).*

I began to breathe more easily. I had somehow managed to stay with sensation and I watched it release its grip.

Welcome, fear, I said, my hands now at my side. Relaxed.

As I welcomed what "was," the intensity of my sensations folded back onto itself—like a sea anemone gently pulling its tentacles into a soft belly.

Nothing to do, nothing to do.
Welcome just this. Fear. ➔

SEE
poems/poetry
somatic healing
spells
wildness

contemplative tradition, the

Fear of my interpretations. Fear of my body.
Breath returning.
STEP 3

Invitation: *After you've welcomed your experience, say "I let go of my desire for security, affection, control, and embrace this moment as it is."*[3]

My ego craves security, affection, love, and control. All necessary and healthy foundations of a strong Self.

Yet I was attached to an identity as a Super-mom who's always in control and never undone. My collection of micro-storms threatened this. And so I raced to re-establish order. I resisted sensations that electrified (made them wrong). I tried to "control" them through distraction (turn up the radio). Find a root cause (it must be the sleep). All this "control" to "manage" the sensations made me feel worse.

So in that water-bottle aisle, I practiced the third and final step.
I said, "I let go of my desire for control"
I let go of my desire to control this body.
I let go of resisting my sensations.

With that final whisper to myself, compassion flowed in. My storm of intensity didn't have to be different.

None of it felt intimidating anymore.

*

This wasn't the first time I'd practiced *The Welcoming Prayer*. It's hard as f*k to do this in the wilds of a heightened sympathetic nervous system.

But my incantation to the fiery storm dissolved the distance I tried to maintain from my immediate experience.

My sensations, I realized, were not like sedimentary rock. They're dynamic.

Watching them and allowing them free movement liberated their naming and became just what was happening.

Sensation was no longer calcified or threatening.

During those months, I practiced in many ordinary moments. In the passport line, at the community theater, breastfeeding my daughter. With practice, my interpretation folded gently back into itself, allowing a wider intelligence.

1 The Welcoming Prayer, taken from mystical, contemplative tradition, was popularized by Thomas Keating, and developed by founding member of Contemplative Outreach, Mary Mrozowski. See contemplativeoutreach.org/welcoming-prayer-method/

2 Contemplative Outreach, "Welcoming Prayer."

3 Contemplative Outreach.

contemplative tradition, the

A rewilding incantation:

Rewild your sensations.

Untangle them from the grips of language and naming.
Undo the braid of categorical conception.

Allow them to quiver like the tall green grass.
Thunder like a bolt of sky fire.
Ripple like hot skin under a lover's touch.
Contract like a viper whose den is under threat.
Sit like cold stone, four feet under mountain snow.
Unfurl like wind, passing through an open sail.
Let them be free to pierce, strike, pulse, and soften.

None of them needs naming to be real.
Animate your body with a wild life force that
demands your closest attention.
Your fiercest compassion.

When you do, everything is
right
just as it is.

BIO

Jennifer England, curator + host of transformational experiences, wilderness adventurer, writer and host of the *Tension of Emergence* podcast.

EDITORS' NOTE

In this evocative narrative, Jennifer takes us on an introspective journey rooted in "contemplative traditions." Inspired by contemplative practices from various wisdom traditions, Jennifer draws on the practice of "The Welcoming Prayer," attributed to Father Thomas Keating, to help navigate life's storms. Her vulnerability and the application of mindfulness, self-compassion, and letting go draw from the rich history of contemplative teachings, demonstrating how historical wisdom can guide us through modern challenges. —CH & ES

corn knowledge

CONTRIBUTION

I ONCE BROUGHT BACK MAÍZ CRIOLLO from a community in the state of Chiapas to Berlin, Germany. Historically the indigenous populations of the southern region of Mexico are known to be the original producers of corn, or rather maíz. To cultivate maíz requires a knowledge that encompasses aspects like the preparation of soil, detecting the incoming rain season, or knowing when to fertilize. These details describe the customs that are increasingly forgotten and consequently reappropriated by agribusiness. To know maíz in today's Mexico also depends on the region and its own grasp of tradition. A curious gardener friend planted the Chiapaneco maíz and months later several two-meter stalks grew. Air roots extended from the bottom, seeking the ground soil in order to stabilize themselves. The thin leaves began to curl in preparation to hold a husk, but instead what grew were bundles of wispy grass. This grass was blueish-green, a cousin to wheat in appearance. No corn bloomed. When I asked my aunt, a farmer, her first intuition was that the maíz criollo probably felt the unknown soil, weather, and geography. What may have occurred is that the seed retracted to an early evolutionary phase, as a teosinte, the wild ancestor grass that was domesticated to become corn. Whether or not this is what truly happened, it is a reminder of the kernel's ability to access its 10,000-year-old genetic, indigenous memory.

For many present-day indigenous and campesino communities, milpa is the most common method for growing maíz. It's a cultural intercropping system of corn, beans, and squash; the latter two can be swapped out for fava beans, chiles, tomatoes, and up to 100 other seeds. The family or community of cultivators decide through conversation which seeds suit the season. The milpa also showcases the social infrastructure, which uses tools of assembly and accord when discussing which crops to include. Sometimes milpa colloquially means solely corn. In the community where I collected the maíz criollo, they harvest red, white, purple, and yellow corn that is transformed into tortillas, tascalate, pinole, tostadas, and pozol. When noon arrives it's routine to drink pozol, providing the calories and energy needed for a day's work. It's a drink made with fermented masa that is diluted with water, sweetened with sugar, and served with ice. Others like to drink an unsweetened version while chewing on salted chiles in between sips. In Chiapas these transformations continue to delicately exist even as food culture is homogenized. In an attempt to continue the know-hows of corn knowledge, here's a recipe for my family's favorite version of pozol:

Cacao Pozol

1.5 liters of water
2 cinnamon sticks
150g of toasted cacao, ground
200g fermented masa (corn dough)
100g of sugar

1. Toast the cacao on a medium fire until the cacao becomes darker in color. Take out and peel the cacao with your hands and put aside.
2. In a processor, mix the cacao and cinnamon.
3. Add the cacao and cinnamon and mix into the masa with your hands until the masa has a brown color.
4. Place the cacao masa into a large bowl and add the water bit by bit, dissolving it into the water with your hands.
5. Once it's been diluted, add ice and sugar to sweeten. Place pozol mixture in a jug and pour into a glass. Shake your glass occasionally so that the grains don't build up at the bottom. Enjoy! ❁

BIO Andrea Macias-Yañez is an artist researcher based in Berlin, Germany, working with video and writing to enact forms of environmental remembering, to reveal situated pasts as they exist in the present.

credit unions

SEE
solidarity economy
sufficiency
temporary autonomous zones
wildness

CONTRIBUTION

A CREDIT UNION is a cooperative financial institution—a group of people invested in each other. They are often already connected through their jobs, churches, social groups, or neighborhoods, so they are motivated to make sure the credit union is benefiting the community as a whole. A member can keep their money there and earn interest on it as well as take out loans in a variety of forms, from a mortgage to a credit card.

Credit unions are great examples of how economics can be made compatible with radical values. Both a bank and a credit union are designed to allow people to save without the money staying stagnant in their accounts, helping no one. A dollar that's moving is much more valuable than one that stays in the same place—it adds value to the life of each person it touches. With every trade people choose to make, both sides end up with more of what they want. When creating more value for the community is the primary goal of a financial institution, unlike the profit-oriented goals of banks, the concept of lending out community members' savings becomes a powerful tool for abundance.

Credit unions provide these financial opportunities to neighborhoods while allowing their members to participate in structural change in their day-to-day life. By keeping their money in credit unions instead of banks, community members redirect funds from the capitalist investments favored by banks, which make their money by taking from the environment and underpaying workers, to investments in their neighbors. This is real power being exchanged.[1]

There are some aspects of credit unions that we need to be cautious of while we transition away from capitalism and white supremacy. If there are strict restrictions on who can join, credit unions risk emphasizing class differences by giving wealthier communities access to a much larger pool of resources. Those put at a historical disadvantage probably have less saved, meaning their credit unions have less money to invest in community members. Part of managing this risk will mean maintaining "neutrality" as a credit union, not preferring the interests of savers or borrowers. This means that there will be fewer incentives to be exclusive about who can join.[2]

There are also good reasons to be suspicious of money in general (for example, it can be hoarded). Institutions like credit unions demonstrate one benefit of keeping a currency, but a currency isn't necessary to use collaboration to create more value for everyone. Maybe one day we will engage in a gift economy, or another way of managing scarcity without money, as many historical societies did. In that case, the concept of credit unions can transform into a new kind of space—one where people meet to exchange resources, find collaborators, and fulfill each other's dreams. ❁

1 Pavlovskaya, et al., "The Place of Common Bond: Can Credit Unions Make Place for Solidarity Economy?"

2 McKillop et al., "Cooperative Financial Institutions: A Review of the Literature."

BIO

Mia Stone-Molloy (she/her) is a labor organizer and poet with a bachelor's degree in Economics and Political Science from Brown University and a passion for the connection between personal and societal healing.

crip time

SEE: accessibility, activating archives

EDITORS' NOTE

"Crip time" is a phrase sometimes used within and among groups of disabled people when they refer to time. In *Feminist, Queer, Crip*, feminist and disability studies scholar Alison Kafer offered this often-cited summary: "Rather than bend disabled bodies and minds to meet the clock, crip time bends the clock to meet disabled bodies and minds."[1] The bold resistance to ableism that we see in Kafer's words is typical of invocations of crip time, which has become something of a liberatory concept. Some disabled authors, like Ellen Samuels in "Six Ways of Looking at Crip Time," invite readers to think about some of the less "appealing" aspects of crip time. Olivia's *Encyclopedia* contribution, with its exquisite attention to the everyday details that make a life, does the same, finding meaning in experiences like patience and hope. —ES

1 Kafer, *Feminist, Queer, Crip*, 27.

CONTRIBUTION

WHEN I GET AN EMAIL from an online magazine asking if I would be interested in writing a 2,500-word essay for $280, I immediately think about the $300 I just spent at the vet and my bank balance of $500. I think about how, for years, I dreamt of being approached for commissions rather than having to send pitches—something I eventually stopped doing because it made me feel like I was trying to prove my worth, my value, my voice. So, I smile and send a screenshot of the email to my boyfriend captioned: '!!'. Am I finally a *writer*?

A few minutes later, I realize I don't actually have much to say on the topic they want me to write about. It is a topic I discuss almost daily, out of frustration and survival, but not something I want to have to make a shape out of, nor sit with the terrible facts and rework the words until it says what I mean to say. Do I know what I mean to say?

I spiral into thoughts of having a deadline, forcing myself to write, forcing myself to think, to sit up at my desk. How I will have to write boring words first, before the meaningful ones. It will become a process—a thing—with a timeline, an end result. I panic because my body has a history of not adhering.

I say yes to the commission because I feel I cannot say no. A month later, after being unable to sit down even once to attempt to write, I email an apologetic withdrawal.

//

There are many days of my body being unable to do more than witness, and many where my body cannot even do that. I stay between the sheets, foggy and pounding. Time becomes a river and it is still from the shore, but roaring in the current.

I am too sick to write every day, too sick to have any type of routine other than the routine of being sick. Most days I don't know how to make time for anything else and wonder when I will write again. Writing, and the brain it requires, slips away with such ease. I used to think this was writer's block, but now I realize it's just writing with illness.

Yes, weeks have passed without any new words, but it feels unfair to consider these weeks as time when I have not been able to track it, feel it, be in it.

//

Today, there is a window. My brain is whispering permission into itself. But first I must take my dog out and I must eat, and after that, who knows what will be possible. I might be back in bed in an hour or I might be clicking these keys with fury.

The crip of this time points to something like patience.

//

After our walk, I unlace my boots and strip my layers, my temperature dysregulation the worst thing about coming back inside on Maine's coldest days. I pour myself another cup of coffee and a bowl of cereal I don't really want.

I sit in my chair.

I send an email.

Half an hour ago I was on the edge of my seat sitting tall and now my neck is pushing into my chest and my shoulders are hunched. I am falling forward. I am going to abandon this piece and lie down on the couch. I have to preserve some energy so that I can dust the snow off my car and shovel the driveway later. Crip time teases you this way, sliding the clock in and out from underneath you.

//

Five days later, I am revisiting. Could not read more than two pages of my book because my mind was writing. I fold open the computer and read these ramblings. I scroll up to find the spots to revise or replace,

but just as I get there,
my body rings its bell of fatigue. Only a few minutes ago I was sure that my body was in the right place. And again,

it is not. I retreat to my bed after writing this interlude of sorts.

//

Eight days later, no writing. So tired. I am angry, and side-eye my illness with taunt.

What would I sacrifice to be able to read and write as much as I truly want?

//

Five months later. I have been writing but in ways I cannot document, or even remember. It comes in bursts and then I surrender.

//

One year later. I work on things, but nothing ever gets finished. I see that there is something valuable in this kind of un-promise, the sliding clock. I used to value completion, wanting everything to be *good* and *worthy* and *publishable*. Now I value my body and the way it feathers its way through the current.

I am alive in my crip time, holding out a hand, waiting. ❁

BIO Olivia Spring is the founder and editor of *SICK* magazine and writes about illness and disability from her home in Maine, beside her dog Black Bean.

critical fabulation

SEE speculative desig
therapeutic writin

CONTRIBUTION

If it is no longer sufficient to expose the scandal, then how might it be possible to generate a different set of descriptions from this archive? To imagine what could have been? To envision a free state *from this order of statements*?[1] —Saidiya Hartman

HARTMAN'S THEORY AND PRACTICE of critical fabulation grapples with yawning gaps and silences found in the historical record. Her method interweaves archival research with critical theory and fictional narrative. In "Venus in Two Acts," the essay in which she introduces the term, Hartman confronts the challenges and ethical issues that shape racialized and stigmatized histories. She moves beyond damage-centered research and analysis to potential and possibility.

Hartman's radical approach troubles a relationship with the gaps that someone discovers and the temptation to fill them in. She writes, "As a writer committed to telling stories, I have endeavored to represent the lives of the nameless and forgotten, to reckon with loss, and to respect the limits of what cannot be known."[2] Acknowledging losses and limits is a necessary part of the process when opening to future realities. ✺

1 Hartman, "Venus in Two Acts," 7.

2 Hartman, "Venus in Two Acts," 4.

BIO

Carol Stakenas commissions and produces public art, site-responsive exhibitions, and creative initiatives in service of strengthening social connections and building community power through socially engaged art and transdisciplinary alliances.

critical hope

CONTRIBUTION

"Critical thinking without hope is cynicism. Hope without critical thinking is naïveté. ...But evil only prevails when we mistake it for the norm. There is so much goodness in the world—all we have to do is remind one another of it, show up for it, and refuse to leave."[1] —Maria Popova

LEARNING TO HOLD criticality and hope is a constant and tenuous balance in my own personal journey. I often find myself leaning towards cynicism if I'm not cautious. There's no glamour or fame in community stewardship and the work is often tedious and undervalued by societal systems at large.

"Perhaps, however, the moral of the story (and the hope of the world) lies in what one demands, not of others, but of oneself."[2]—James Baldwin

Critical hope is not only an individual aspiration, but should be a shared communal vision as we are all interdependent. Having people and a community around you that can remind you that what the news and greater society are saying is not the only reality that is possible is vital to having critical hope. When a community has a shared vision, we can build and share a better future for everyone.

"Hope begins in the dark, the stubborn hope that if you show up and try to do the right thing, the dawn will come. You wait and watch and work: you don't give up."[3]—Anne Lamott

In the age of information, it's easier now than ever to believe that our individual actions and having hope are futile, especially in the wake of systemic injustice, climate change, and late capitalism's aftereffects. But these are all valid reasons why critical hope is so necessary.

1 Popova, "Hope, Cynicism, and the Stories We Tell Ourselves."

2 Baldwin, *No Name in the Streets*, 10.

3 Lamott, *Bird by Bird: Some Instructions on Writing and Life*, 26.

BIO Camille Nibungco is a designer and ambient musician.

EDITOR'S NOTE

The concept of "critical hope" captures the delicate balance between optimism and thoughtful analysis in our complex world. As Camille astutely points out, critical thinking devoid of hope can lead to cynicism, while hope without critical thinking can result in naïveté. This thoughtful reflection underscores the importance of cultivating both qualities, especially in our turbulent times. Critical hope is not merely an individual pursuit but a shared vision, an acknowledgment that we are all interconnected and that collective action is essential for progress. —CH

critical pedagogy

CONTRIBUTION

I INVITE YOU to think of a moment, recent or not, in which you felt nourished.
first, focus on how this moment manifested in your body.
pause here
to allow the memory—or the dream, for not all of us have felt nourished—to unfurl.

if you feel stuck, consider the opening of
a tender bloom or fingertips, prospecting underwater only to find a lost ring, an iridescent pebble.
can you reach a moment that feels like this?

now, how does this remembering, honouring, or anticipation feel?

is it a buzzing behind your knees?
is it maybe heat around the tongue, the vibration of words you finally feel you can express?
perhaps it is something completely different.

it's no coincidence that these are also erotic moments.

nourishing involves meeting a body in its need. body, in this context, includes nerves, synapses, heart, and dreams. nourishing involves supporting and caring for the survival of all of these parts, as well as their appetites. herein lies intent-ful desire—often instinctual—before it is known and possibly communicated.

now, what was—what would be—the setting for your nourishing?
 a surface of blanket, table, or land where food and stories are shared?
 a song on the dance floor
  on the bus
 in a library, pulling piles to the floor
 a classroom where you learned of kindreds for the first time
 a morsel of food that brings you home

Writing on and about pedagogy usually centres the classroom, but it can and should and does unfold everywhere—especially in contexts wherein those in power censor curriculum. Settings for pedagogical discussion must acknowledge what happens in "classrooms" in an expanded sense because pedagogy predates classrooms. It unfolds in kitchens, bedrooms, forests, and oceans.

keep your moment of nourishment in your mind: this is what critical pedagogy is.

a feeling as well as an approach to teaching and learning
an authenticity, a perception/understanding/application of consciousness.

sometimes this transpires with words in conversation with peers and facilitators[1]
other times, in gesture in relation to land or ancestral knowledge[2]
always in energy and position[3]

In chapter two of his book *Pedagogy of the Oppressed*, the late Brazilian educator Paulo Freire lays out fundamental aspects of using conversation as a tool for not only engaging with new knowledge, but developing a subjective, aware position as a contributing member of community/ies.

Oppression silences communities, and Freire was committed to teaching and learning methods that supported every individual's ability to critically perceive the world and their place in it via conversation with those around them. This cannot happen if educational systems operate according to what he called a "banking" model. In this model, students, employees, or citizens are empty vessels that become full via the deposits of a teacher or structure. What they receive is in accordance with a dominant narration. A designed curriculum. Freire stipulates this alienates pupils and detaches them from "the totality that engendered them and could give them significance."[4] Not only is this a form of knowledge-oppression, but it can be a coercive, violent training. Lee Maracle writes of Residential Schools in the history of what is currently "Canada," pointing out their role as "ideological processing plants… turning out young people who cannot produce the means to sustain themselves."[5]

Freire stipulates that critical pedagogy involves students and teachers in partnership: all developing consciousness and mutual awareness; all with knowledge; all invested in an authentication of thinking, which is then acted upon, in the world. The result is a grouping of "teacher-student" with "students-teachers" who are exercising a method of dialogical learning from one another's perspectives on a common problem or topic. This model encourages demythologisation of reality, self-reflection, deepened consciousness, mutual recognition, and informed action.[6] **critical pedagogy nourishes rather than fills.**

Indigenous epistemologies and pedagogy, explains writer, musician, and scholar Leanne Betasamosake Simpson, also centre relationships and holistic perspectives. She offers descriptors for what it feels like to be "immersed in a nest of Nishnaabeg" intelligence: observation from plant and animal teachers; embodiment and conceptual thought; application of learning to the self; creativity; patience; sharing; love and trust. Simpson shares the story of Kwezens, a Nishnaabeg child, who "comes to know" maple sugar through watching and learning from a squirrel and telling her mother and Elders, who then work together to harvest and process the tree sap.[7] Anti-colonial curricula are distinct from critical pedagogy, but they are mutually expansive in their meaning-making.

Critical pedagogy cannot be generalised across settings, nor betwixt experiences. Re-centring relationships to place, land, community, and problem-posing are so important in anti-colonial, decolonial, and critical pedagogies alike. That said, they can be kindred: between Freire's critical pedagogy and Maracle's rematriation, Simpson's coming into knowing, for example, is the subsequent emancipation of individuals within community. When critical or relational, pedagogy cannot be exploited for "success" or domination. Rather, it enables actualising authentic means and needs.[8] bell hooks refers to this as well, and she also calls it love.[9] ❁

1 Freire, *Pedagogy of the Oppressed*, 71.

2 Lee Maracle (Stó:lō) was a writer, poet, singer, mother, and academic from the unceded territories of the Skwxwú7mesh (Squamish) and Səlilwətaɬ (Tsleil-Waututh) Nations. If new to her work, I suggest *My Conversations with Canadians* (2017), which starts around a table, in a kitchen.

3 bell hooks's writings on pedagogy link her well-known theories on race, gender, and sexuality. See: *Teaching to Transgress: Education as the Practice of Freedom* (1994)

4 Freire, *Pedagogy*, 71.

5 Maracle, "Education," in *I Am Woman: A Native Perspective of Sociology and Feminism*, 88–92, 88

6 Freire, *Pedagogy*, 80, 90. Freire argues this method centres the social aspect of knowledge.

7 Simpson, "Land as pedagogy," 6, 7.

8 Maracle "Education," 89–90.

9 hooks often cross-references her text *All About Love: New Visions* in her essays on pedagogy. See "To Love Again," in *Teaching Critical Thinking: Practical Wisdom*, 159–164.

BIO maya rae oppenheimer (she/her) works with, through, from, and around paper: she makes it, writes with it, reads from it and sometimes dreams about it. okstamppress.ca

critical race theory

SEE
movement lawyering
radical social work
Reflecting on Justice
social construction
theories of change
transformative justice

CONTRIBUTION

CRITICAL RACE THEORY (CRT) is a branch of critical postmodern theory (CPT) that analyzes oppressive aspects of society as part of an attempt to create societal and individual transformation. Major tenets CRT derived from CPT are included below. Each branch of CPT views oppression through a unique lens; for example, while CRT focuses on racial oppression, neo-Marxism focuses on class segregation, feminist theory focuses on gender oppression, and queer theory focuses on oppression based on sexual orientation and/or gender identity.

CRT emerged in the U.S. in the 1980s out of the Critical Legal Studies Movement, led by legal scholars including Derrick Bell. It examined how racial oppression is at the heart of many U.S. legal institutions and remains there to benefit the powerful in society. As a result, anti-discrimination laws in the U.S. are often ineffective because they are insufficient to overcome the pervasive effects of structural racism and white supremacy. Since around 2015, CRT has drawn criticism in the mainstream media and from politicians on the grounds that it promotes and is founded on false truths regarding the reality of race in U.S. society. As a result, the teaching of CRT has been banned from some states' educational institutions.

Major tenets of CRT derived from CPT include:

SOCIAL CONSTRUCTION. This concept purports that reality is socially constructed in a manner that creates preferred universal conceptions of what should be done and what is considered normal or ideal human behavior. CRT emphasizes how race is a product of social construction rather than biology. An example of how social construction influences perception is the acceptance of binary thinking and categories, in which concepts or groups are divided into mutually exclusive categories, such as White/Black, and meanings are attached to each category.

CONTEXT. History, socioeconomic realities, and immediate situations influence people's behavior. This tenet rejects the essentialist tendency to regard individuals and groups as possessing inherent, unchanging characteristics rooted in biology or a self-contained culture that explains their status. At the heart of the emphasis on context is the idea that culture is dynamic, not static. In CRT, the implication is that race permeates all aspects of social life, and race-based ideology (i.e., white supremacy) is threaded throughout society.

INTERSECTIONALITY. In addition to recognizing the dynamic qualities of culture, the concept of intersectionality posits that it is also important to acknowledge the range of cultural influences that affect people. That is, each person has multiple intersecting dimensions and cannot be defined in terms of one demographic variable. Therefore, instead of viewing race, class, gender, sexuality, ethnicity, religion, nationality, age, ability, and other identifying variables as isolated features of social organization, it analyzes them as mutually constructed components that shape and are, in turn, shaped by individuals' experiences.

POSITIONALITY. A corollary to the notion of intersectionality is that people's social position (e.g., race, class, gender, religion, age) influences their construction of reality and the ways they interpret other people's constructions and behaviors. Standpoint theory, from which this concept emerges, further argues that the location of an individual or group in the context of hierarchical power relationships produces common challenges for individuals similarly located. These shared challenges foster similar perspectives on history and current reality that are essential for taking collective action to alter that reality. A related concept is subjectivity, that each person lives their own truth. In CRT, this concept can be challenged due to the reality of racism in our society.

COLLECTIVITY. Because of diverse, multiple influences, individuals are not isolated and do not act alone. They are affected by and have an impact on their communities. Often, this concept is expressed through the emergence of collective consciousness about a group's social situation, the acceptance of a common paradigm or interpretive framework to explain social phenomena, or the development of oppositional knowledge that defends an oppressed group's interests and fosters the group's self-definition and self-determination. Together, these can produce a counternarrative to the prevailing master narrative, which often serves to perpetuate dominant-subordinate relationships.

AGENCY. As a result of the emergence of these counternarratives, even people in desperate situations can possess a self-defining and self-determining will that enables them to maintain some sense of control over their lives. This concept is consistent with an empowerment perspective and a strengths-based approach to practice. Locating the voice of the marginalized and ensuring that it is heard is an essential component of CRT.

HISTORICITY. An important prerequisite for the implementation of agency is the growth of people's awareness of their place and role in history, and affirmation of their ability to produce change over time. This concept is particularly valuable to consider in today's complex and rapidly changing environment and as part of CRT's commitment to social justice. ❁

BIO

Jayshree S. Jani, PhD, LCSW-C, is an Associate Professor of Social Work at the University of Maryland, Baltimore County, and practices clinical social work in Maryland and Washington, DC.

CONTRIBUTOR'S NOTE

To learn more about Critical Theory and CRT, see Malcolm Payne's book: *Modern Social Work Theory*, and Robert Adams, Lena Dominelli, and Malcolm Payne's edited book, *Social Work: Themes, Issues, and Critical Debates*. –JJ

critical suicide studies

SEE: narrative therapy, reflexivity, solidarity

CRITICAL SUICIDE STUDIES ("CritSui") is an evolving site of transdisciplinary scholarship, practice, and activism. It has emerged in response to some of the perceived shortcomings of mainstream suicidology, which has historically tended to draw on narrow, positivist research methodologies and individualistic, biomedical, and pathologizing frameworks for understanding and responding to suicide.

CritSui seeks to mobilize a range of critical and creative frameworks for "thinking" suicide, including intersectional, critical, queer, feminist, critical disability, anti-racist, decolonial, arts-based, and Indigenous methodologies. CritSui takes power, language, context, and knowledge into account and challenges dominant and thin mental illness narratives for explaining suicide. It recognizes that individual experiences of distress and suffering can often be understood as responses to deeply unjust, inequitable, structurally violent histories and current contexts. CritSui calls for the inclusion of more diverse voices and perspectives, including persons with lived experience of suicide, in the generation of knowledge about suicide and our responses to it.

CritSui also welcomes critical questions about "prevention" as an unqualified good and recognizes the potential for harm to be done in the name of helping. CritSui is guided by an explicit set of ethics and politics that invites professional helpers to go beyond individual risk assessment and the categorization and monitoring of risk to provide responses and questions that center curiosity, empathy, reflexivity, compassion, respect, justice, and openness. CritSui is also committed to working in solidarity across academic, therapeutic, practice, and activist communities to support the conditions that will create worlds worth living in for all.

For more information about CritSui go to criticalsuicidology.net.

Jennifer White, professor, writer, co-editor of *Critical Suicidology: Transforming Suicide Research and Prevention for the 21st Century* (UBC Press, 2016).

critical whiteness

SEE: anti-racism, critical pedagogy, critical race theory, curiosity, decolonial liberatory-based practices, embodied knowledge, healing circle

CONTRIBUTION

WHITENESS HISTORICALLY is synonymous with comfort, entitlement, knowingness, and oppressive power. Critical whiteness then wants to edge toward discomfort, humility, divestment, and the unknown. I feel this discomfort in the writing below, as I write from my white subjectivity and my personal relationship to critical whiteness. I do not purport to define this concept with finitude or certainty. Instead I offer this as an attempt, a beginning, an opening for dialogue and practice.

In an adaption to the forward of their book, *The Racial Imaginary*, published on Lithub, Claudia Rankine and Beth Loffreda write, "…we do think white people in America tend to suffer an anxiety (and many have written of this): they know that they are white but they must not know what they know. They know that they are white, but they cannot know that such a thing has social meaning; they know that they are white, but they must not know that their whiteness accrues power. They must not call it whiteness for to do so would be to acknowledge its force."[1]

Per Rankine and Loffreda, white people stay in the delusion of neutrality. We tend to imagine ourselves outside of Foucault's metrics of biopower.[2] But what if it were possible to acknowledge whiteness, to know the social meaning, power, and force of this racial privilege? This is my understanding of critical whiteness: an oxymoron, in which it is possible to "acknowledge the force" of whiteness while still avoiding the reification of that power. In my experience, embodying critical whiteness as a white person in social and political space feels contradictory, confusing, sometimes even abject. It's an unstable, improvisational dance of social and personal critique, in the vein of the meme created by @malefragility pictured below.

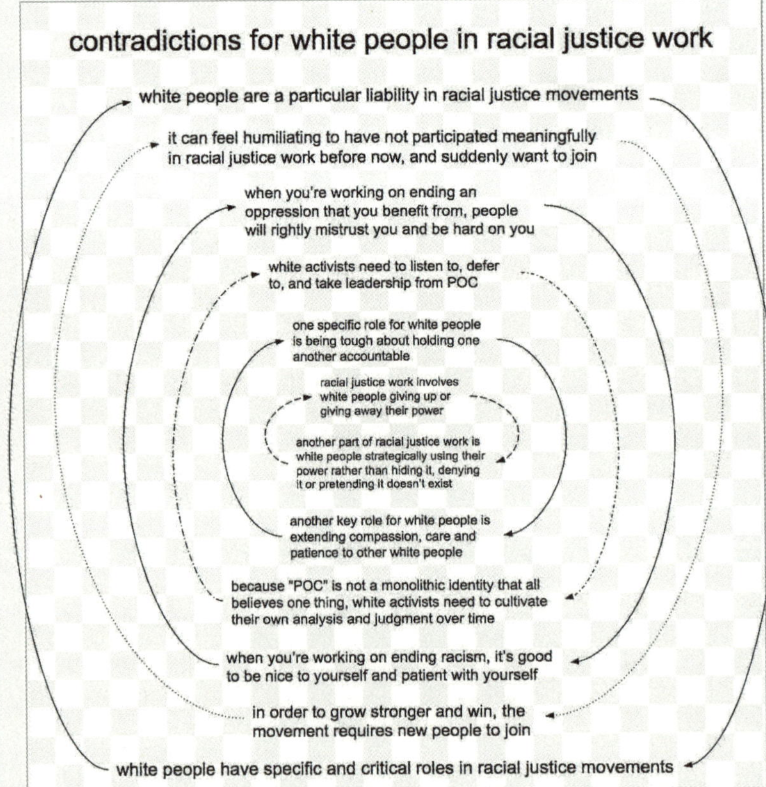

hannah baer

The phrase "critical whiteness" is most often used within the context of critical whiteness *studies*, an interdisciplinary academic practice aiming to "home in and dissect whiteness as a distinct power formation within the structures of race, racism, and white supremacy that rose with and sustained colonialism, and today forms an essential part of coloniality."[3] This practice originates in the work of Black and indigenous thinkers (see: James Baldwin, Franz Fanon, Gloria Anzaldúa, Audre Lorde, W.E.B. Du Bois, Édouard Glissant), and continues in the work of Saidiya Hartman, Rankine, Christina Sharpe, and others, all of whom bring into light the white supremacist, colonial world order that has sought to eradicate the "other." While it is near impossible to consider whiteness without discussions of anti-Blackness, critical whiteness also identifies the ability of whiteness to shape-shift and gather power in relation to various racialized bodies beyond the Black/white binary.

As a white person, and as a practitioner of dance and movement, I am personally drawn to understandings of critical whiteness that frame it as an antiracist practice and mode of embodiment. I have sought out practical strategies for how to deal with the complex web of complicity outlined by Rankine and Loffreda. Racialized healer and psychotherapist Resmaa Menakem's notion of somatic abolitionism is one such framework, in which "through repetition, you collectively build resilience, discernment, and the ability to tolerate discomfort that comes with confronting the brutality of race."[4] I also look to Prentis Hemphill's Embodiment Institute for practical tools as well as the work of Layla F. Saad, especially her *Me and White Supremacy* handbook. All of these practitioners provide tangible strategies for noticing the ways white supremacy culture shows up in our social lives and embodied experiences—effectively, they offer practices of critical whiteness.

The practical labor of critical whiteness has historically fallen on those who do not benefit from the privileges of whiteness—in short, anyone who is not white tends to already practice critical whiteness. White people, meanwhile, have the privilege of being uncritical: through inaction, we can reify the anti-Black, white supremacist world order that our bodies tend to uphold. Because of the inertia of uncritical whiteness, white people today have a greater responsibility to critical whiteness as an embodied political praxis. We must acknowledge the power of our whiteness in order to dismantle it. ❁

1 Rankine and Loffreda, "On Whiteness and the Racial Imaginary."

2 Foucault, *The History of Sexuality*, Vol. 1.

3 Hunter and van der Westhuizen, "Preface."

4 Menakem, "What Somatic Abolitionism Is."

BIO elena rose light (they/them), choreographer, performer, writer.

critique

SEE: critical hope

EDITORS' NOTE

When we compiled the list of topics for this *Encyclopedia*, it was important to us that every single topic live in a realm beyond "critique." This is because it has been our experience that critique and its applications often invite incurious, "gotcha" ways of interacting, crowding out possibilities for transformation. That said, we think it's important to recognize that going beyond critique is only possible because critique exists! "Critique"—which we think of as assessing the current state of affairs and naming injustice—can be an act of love, an act of care. This is what we see in the work of my social work colleague Akin, who sometimes publishes poetry in academic journals. —ES

CONTRIBUTION

The Socioeconomic Life of Water

ABSTRACT: IN THE NEO-LIBERAL ERA where transnational corporations drive the agenda of globalization, privatization, and deregulation, there is increasing inequality in the world perpetuated by the socioeconomic policies of many nation-states. This agenda has negative repercussions for the provision of social welfare for the poor and working poor in many countries. This poem attempts to grapple with how the corporatist, capitalist business model and the so-called Protestant work ethic impact many individuals at the micro level of their existence, interactions, and well-being. It also calls for critical reflection regarding how our world is deliberately arranged.

For the poor who are "deserving"
If they're hungry, we'll give them cake.
Cake:
That's what we produce —
From English Washington
to French Ottawa and
Spanish Mexico City
The notorious Triangle of Free Trade
Who said, "axis of evil"?

For their thirst they can drink coke
Coke for Coca-Cola
We already privatized water
And punished those who in Bolivia
Collected strands of rain in buckets
You can shower with coke if you want,
Water is way too precious to cleanse your dirt
Water is way too precious to cleanse you of dirt
Or have you considered Blood?
They say "the blood" can make you whiter than snow

The poor
The poor you'll always have with you
Globalized
Far beyond your state confines
They are the world

We are the world, too

Let's see what trickles down
That you might struggle with the dogs for

Let's see what trickles down
From the Good Samaritan

Let's see what trickles down
to Lazarus after his first death

The poor you always have with you.
But why?
    We can give them just enough,
    That they may pant as the deer after water
    Like almonds pant in California
    For water from the Stock Exchange

What kind of world are we building? ❁

BIO Akin Taiwo is an Associate Professor of Social Work at King's University College at Western University, London, Ontario, Canada

Cuestionamos

SEE: Bertha Capen Reynolds; critical pedagogy; critique

CONTRIBUTION

IN 1971, a group of Leftist psychoanalysts based in Argentina and Uruguay contributed clinical essays to the first volume of *Cuestionamos* (We Question), an edited collection compiled by Austrian exile Marie Langer. Since the mid-1960s, Uruguay and Argentina had oscillated between military and civilian rule, culminating in coups d'état in 1973 and 1976, respectively, followed by a period of coordinated military dictatorships across the Southern Cone. For the authors of *Cuestionamos*, this violent political climate demanded not only a rethinking of classical Freudian theory, but also the development of new clinical techniques attentive to the civic and subjective conditions of state terror.

The collection's title—"we question"—establishes the authors' interrogatory method of casting doubt on the institutional hierarchies and training procedures governing psychoanalytic practice, as well as orthodox clinical tenets that kept political reality outside the purview of psychoanalytic thought. *Cuestionamos* contributors took particular aim at the principle of analytic neutrality, which, according to the Argentine Psychoanalytic Association (APA), included political neutrality. Several authors complained that neutrality severed the consulting room from social reality and set impossible standards for the analyst's political objectivity, falsely implying that analyst and analysand could escape the ideological conditions of the world around them. Neutrality, they argued, was itself an ideological position in support of the status quo.

Cuestionamos advocated for psychoanalysis as a form of consciousness-raising and vernacularized psychoanalysis in the language of Latin American movement politics, laying the theoretical and practical groundwork for what the authors called "psychoanalytic praxis":[1] a mission to develop "all the possibilities of applying psychoanalysis in the struggle for a new society and for the creation of the new man."[2] Such a project would not only expand the patient's transformational potential, but it would also enable clinicians to continue performing an analytic function amidst social and political upheaval without denying the impact of that upheaval on the consulting room.

Cuestionamos emerged out of a series of institutional ruptures transforming the Argentine psychoanalytic profession when it was published (first in 1971, with a second volume in 1973). This process began in 1969 at the International Psychoanalytic Association's (IPA) official meeting in Rome, where a splinter group of European Leftist analysts, still reeling from the events of May 1968, convened to discuss their grievances against the IPA's hierarchy and training structure, as well as the limited socioeconomic scope of its bourgeois constituency. The group wrote its own "International Platform" (Plataforma) of institutional demands, spurring the development of local Plataforma groups in Switzerland, Italy, Austria, and Argentina, where Armando Bauleo and Hernán Kesselman, both analysts trained by Marie Langer, founded a national branch they called Documento. Documento targeted the institutional practices of the APA, initially collaborating with several senior members like Emilio Rodrigué and Eduardo Pavlovsky in an effort to reform the association. Many Argentine members eventually broke from the IPA and APA, forming their own governing bodies and training institute (the Centro de Docencia e Investigación, CDI) alongside reformist psychiatrists in the Argentine Federation of Psychiatrists (FAP).

Cuestionamos describes and responds to clinical challenges unique to the extreme political violence that fractured contemporary civic life in the 1960s to 1980s, but it also challenges long-standing assumptions that psychoanalysis is unable or unwilling to engage with social, political reality. Highlighting the importance of historical specificity in psychoanalytic thought and practice, Langer argues, "psychoanalytic interpretation can complement our sociological and political comprehension, but it loses meaning if we issue it in isolation instead of locating it within a social structure which Marx made intelligible for us."[3] *Cuestionamos* serves as a reminder that, for all its reliance on universal principles of human subjectivity, psychoanalysis has always been a diasporic practice shaped by the worldly contingencies of political upheaval and exile. The extent to which psychoanalysis acknowledges and confronts those contingencies can inform the degree of cultural relevance it maintains as a therapeutic practice. ❁

1 Communist psychoanalyst José Bleger coined the term "psychoanalytic praxis" in 1969 (See "Theory and Practice in Psychoanalysis: Psychoanalytic Praxis" in *The International Journal of Psychoanalysis*, 2012). Though Bleger was part of the organized Left, he never split from the APA, and was something of a celebrity lecturer at the University of Buenos Aires during this period.

2 Langer, "Prólogo," 20–21. Translated by the author.

3 Langer, "Prólogo," 20.

BIO Rachel Greenspan holds a PhD in Literature and is a psychoanalyst practicing in New York.

curiosity

C O N T R I B U T I O N

ANY HELPING must come from a place of loving and wanting to know more, of knowing that I don't know, of approaching the divine in the other (SEE love). I must be actively, intentionally, effortfully, deliberately *curious*. Isn't it curious that when I say one should be curious, I could be advocating *wanting to know more* or I could be advocating *being odd*? Is it odd to want to know more? But helping without curiosity becomes control—trying to flatten, normalize, or reduce the other into something decidedly not-curious. It is shaving away parts of the other (SEE erasure, avoiding thereof) in order to re-form the other into a knowable, finite thing that fits easily into patterns of interacting.

Curiosity is the antimatter of boredom (SEE boredom), that which cancels it out; but curiosity is also an active choice. If I know everything already, if I can predict everything already, then there is no hope. There is no point in being curious. And when I am the person-to-be-known, if the other is not curious about me, then I am unable to speak to the other person, because I am not actually there. An avatar of me, a caricature of me, a compressed version of me, is all that is getting through. On the other hand, when the other person is curious to know more of my complexity, then I can embark on the expansive process of revealing myself to a receptive other (SEE being with). And often that process is not just a revelation to the other but a revelation to myself, as I come to know myself in the context of a new connection and can be curious about myself as well. ❂

B I O

Noriko Martinez works imperfectly as a radical helper by sitting with people, being curious, and loving the world.

death practices

CONTRIBUTION

Ultimology

IN OUR READING GROUP on the traditions of the Irish wake, a number of people described practices of placing the body of the deceased on a table, a ledge, a kitchen counter. Any provisional surface that would allow the body to stay, to rest in the home, visible. The body stays close and the living people, relations, family and friends, stay awake. For three days or so visitors come and go, but watch is kept consistent; someone always keeps the body company. For as long as the physical body remains intact, those who are living attend, are present. Games, drinks, food, repetition of words, chanting, and other activities, all are ways to keep those living people attentive, to maintain a waking state. Collectively, the body is paid attention to, its condition of death witnessed. This is a mode of accompaniment, both to the body of the dead and between the living present.

I've been gathering knowledge around the ways we react to death over the past years as part of artistic research that explores how to establish a concept called Ultimology, or the study of endings. This project, a collaboration with curator Kate Strain, began in 2016 as the *Department of Ultimology*.[1] Sited in our former university, Trinity College Dublin in Ireland, we propose that there should be a cross-disciplinary subject for the study of things that are at risk, obsolete, waning, no longer in use.

Our interest was provoked by the slide library, a room of mounted negative photographs which, due to the availability of images on the internet, had become a relic rather than the active site of knowledge production it was during our studies a decade before we began this project. Kate and I were very fond of the slide library. Once the sole space we went to seek out an image of a painting or building, we wondered what had happened to equivalents of this resource across the university, and how these changes had altered the study of other disciplines.

We began our project through interviews with different specialists across the campus, asking "What is ending in your field? What is already lost?" We asked these questions as the Department of Ultimology, and in doing so we declared this entity into being.

A retiring glass blower in the Chemistry department, canonical texts in the study of English literature, the lone scholar, the concept of a "soul." These were some "endings" we encountered. We went on to organize events—a "purge" where researchers could nominate aspects of their work they thought should be Ultimological, a conference and a series of clinics.

As this practice continued, I noticed a fuzzy interaction in the words we used to describe what we were looking at. When we spoke about endings we would sometimes describe our non-human subjects as "dead or dying." Could the closure of a workshop on a university campus be described as a "death"? What could we learn from the ways people treat the death of human beings, to inform the development of Ultimology? These questions led me to initiate a reading group on the subject of death and dying. Alongside an online group, each month we would discuss materials that explored this subject from as wide a range of geographies and contexts as possible.

I noticed in this group that the nature of the discussion engendered a certain atmosphere; speaking of death made for uniquely vulnerable and intimate conversations. People had personal experiences to share, often noting that they had never spoken to anyone about the stories they expressed.

As I attempted to document this atmosphere of vulnerability and experience, and support an atmosphere of care for participants, I went on to establish an embroidery circle with people to discuss personal memories of traditions around death and dying. Sewing offered scope to hold these conversations while engaged in an activity, while also preserving the fullness of our experiences in a shared document, a tablecloth imbued with things said and unsaid. Participants in a sewing circle could always stop speaking, or look away, with the hand work of embroidery as an alternative occupation. ➔

The types of practices shared in the reading group and sewing circle were subjective, experiential, and had often been passed through generations without explanation. A number of people described how they assimilated what to do when mourning a death from someone older than them, not through explicit instruction, but through paying attention, being present, witnessing, and settling into the environment. One participant described the specific fruit cake her family in Belgium made when a person died, another spoke to me about her family in Pakistan and the nuance of the type of conversation you could have around a death, how you ought to keep the conversation going, but not speak too much, and only about certain subjects.

Tim Ingold, writing on education, emphasizes the importance of paying attention as a practice of care, and makes a distinction between knowledge and wisdom: “To know is to have things accounted for, explained away or embedded in context so they no longer trouble us; to be wise is to bring things back into the fullness of presence, to pay attention, and to care. Knowing is rational and intellectual; wisdom relational and affective.”[2]

To “bring things back into the fullness of presence,” as Ingold describes, is our intention as we develop Ultimology into a concept, a method, or practice for education. One which acknowledges absences and pays attention to them.

Vinciane Despret, an author, philosopher, and anthropologist, writes in her book *Our Grateful Dead: Stories of Those Left Behind* about certain specific contexts into which the dead are more likely to feel comfortable, and to make their presence known to the living. In both the original French of her writing and in English, she refers to these contexts as “milieu,” and tracks their occurrence across moments in time. For them to make themselves known, she writes, it “requires the dead to be situated, in a very concrete fashion: that they be assigned a location from which ‘they can finish what they were made to do’; that a place has been *made* for them. Then there are more things needed: care, attention, activities, a milieu that, if not conducive or welcoming, is at least not too hostile.”[3]

Despret gestures towards hospitable, caring, and attentive conditions in which the dead may co-exist with the living. In the practice of Ultimology we are not seeking to preserve the endings we encounter, or to accelerate them. We are interested in generating a type of milieu as Despret describes, an environment in which to co-exist with and pay attention to the passings that might otherwise go unnoticed. We are interested in the potential of this type of milieu as a site of education. We see this as a form of radical helping, informed by the ancestral and nebulous knowledge of mourning that we continue to gather, that continues to inform our activities. ❁

1 The term Ultimology was one we heard from writer and linguist Ross Perlin. Ross set up the Endangered Language Alliance in New York City and speculated that there should be an umbrella term for the study of all things endangered.

2 Ingold, “On Not Knowing and Paying Attention: How to Walk in a Possible World.”

3 Despret, *Our Grateful Dead: Stories of Those Left Behind*.

BIO Fiona Hallinan is an artist, researcher, filmmaker, and, alongside Kate Strain, co-founder of the Department of Ultimology, a practice for the study of endings.

EDITORS' NOTE We learned about Fiona Halliman and Kate Strain's work on ultimology through Thick Press's 2019 publication, *Stages: On Dying, Working, and Feeling*, by Rachel Kauder Nalebuff. We decided to file their contribution (penned by Fiona) under “death practices,” which we think of as the practice of intentionally engaging with death and dying in order to live a richer, more examined life and enact a society that prioritizes end-of-life care and dignity.
—ES & JC

existentialism
grief as nonlinear
life cycle, honoring the liminality

decolonial liberatory-based practices

SEE Reflecting on Justice, solidarity, transformative justice

CONTRIBUTION

Decolonization, which sets out to change the order of the world, is, obviously, a program of complete disorder. But it cannot come as a result of magical practices, nor of a natural shock, nor of a friendly understanding. Decolonization, as we know, is a historical process: that is to say that it cannot be understood, it cannot become intelligible nor clear to itself except in the exact measure that we can discern the movements which give it historical form and content. —Franz Fanon

COLONIALITY MATRIX OF POWER

The control of history, knowledge, health, and justice are features of the colonial matrix of power, or coloniality.[1] Groups that have greater social, economic, and political power in any given society create and control the representation of different social identity groups. In general, individuals who belong to underrepresented, marginalized, or oppressed social identity groups are ascribed to the category of "other."

Quijano describes coloniality as manifesting in at least three interconnected and interdependent forms:

- systems of hierarchies: racial division and classification as the organizing principle of white supremacy
- systems of knowledge: privileging of Western or Eurocentric forms of knowledge as universal and objective
- societal systems: reinforcing hierarchies through construction of the state and specific institutions to regulate, segregate, and diminish decolonizing systems of healing and lived experiences[2]

Examples of these hierarchies and categorizations are visible in the many ways that our lives are compartmentalized into silos. Capitalism is most certainly a crucible of this hierarchical system. The silos of the social services and the prison-industrial complexes, physicians and big pharma, corporate agriculture, and education are shaped by a principle of prioritizing corporate profits at the cost of human lives. The academic disciplines that produce professionals to populate the silos are cordoned off from one another's scholarship, and professionals in mental health or health are bifurcated as advocates or clinicians, academics, or activists. The list is endless and constitutes a powerful capitulation to the hierarchies established by coloniality. These hierarchies are directly contiguous with the formation of families and communities, with emotional bonding being but one factor in the analysis and health and well-being of families and communities. →

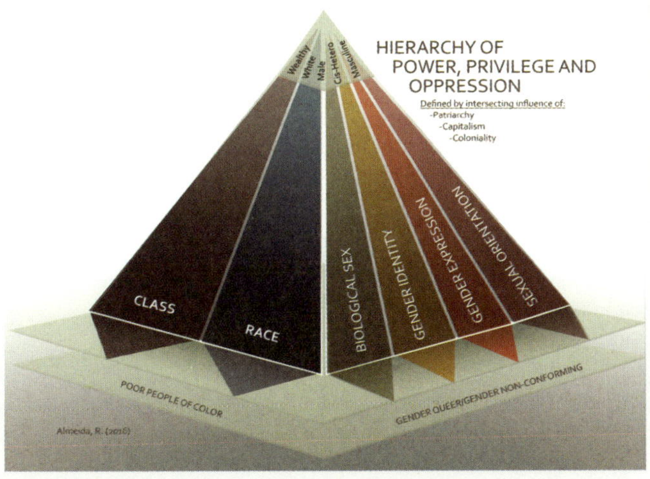

"Hierarchy of Power, Privilege, and Oppression,"[8] by Rhea Almeida, 2016.

decolonial liberatory-based practices

INTERSECTIONALITY

Like the concepts of world feminism and queer theory, the concept of intersectionality originated from Black and Chicana feminist theory.[3] Intersectionality holds that classifications such as gender, race, class, and other signifiers of identity cannot be examined in isolation from one another. They interact and intersect in the lives of individuals and their families, societies, and social systems, and they are mutually constitutive. Analyses of systemic power, privilege, oppression, and social location/standpoint yield critical insights.[4]

Unfortunately, the nuanced concept of intersectionality as deployed in academia and professional journals has been appropriated and commoditized in common parlance, skewing and limiting its impact. Intersectionality decodes the "colonial matrix of power" and creates a foundation for decolonizing and liberation praxis.

Multiple identities coexist and complicate the ways in which we typically think of class, race, gender, and sexuality in isolation. Intersectionality reflects the complexity and fluidity of lived experiences along multiple trajectories of hierarchies and overcomes the challenge of compartmentalizing the pillars of privilege, domination, and oppression.

The historic usage of diversity and inclusion trainings, as well as implicit bias trainings, have proven to cognitively change a few individuals, but most leave the unbrokered power of the colonial institution intact. Instead of focusing on diversity and inclusion within institutions, the process of liberation is better served by interrogating institutional structures, norms, and values using a Black liberation and gender equity scaffolding.

LIBERATION PRAXIS

Liberatory healing practices have distinct foundational strategies that draw from knowledge across academic disciplines to disrupt and dismantle the residue of colonial structures. These structures affect clients, practitioners, and students who engage in teaching and learning contexts in search of healing for themselves and their communities.[5]

Although individuals, families, and communities will experience varying emotions based on their own lived experiences and embodiment of the varying social identities constructed by society, building collective critical consciousness creates a platform for liberation.[6] Gathering knowledge that structural forces exist and control all levels of social, economic, and political interaction provides clients with what Mignolo refers to as strategies of epistemic disobedience.[7]

Healing circles utilize a form of liberatory practice in which participants disengage from the western colonialist construction of individualism. These heterogenous helping communities bring together members of families who seek healing, clients at the end of their healing trajectory, and a team of therapists that includes interns. By welcoming each participant—in all of their intersectional complexity—and naming the systems that impede the empowerment and liberation of ALL individuals, healing circles work together to encourage resistance to the norms that maintain hierarchies of power, privilege, and oppression. Healing circles thus form a shared repository within which participants redefine problems from a decolonial perspective. Together, they render liberatory solutions for healing as their pursuit of shared power takes shape and voice.

Strategies of liberatory healing through decolonizing include:

- Naming structures of dominance in pursuit of transparency
- Redrawing the boundaries of inclusion
- Disrupting the hierarchical categories of coloniality around racialization, class, gender, sexual identity, etc.
- Desegregating healing spaces

access invocations
accessibility
ctivating archives
frofuturism
gency
ging positivity
ltar work
lternative identity projects
ncestral wisdom
ncestrality
nti-ableism
nti-adultism
nti-racism
nti-racism court system
rt
rt as/in/of life
rt journaling
rt therapy
rt workers
rt-based group work
rts in medicine
rts-based research
uthentic Movement
utonomous healing
yurveda
eing with
ertha Capen Reynolds
ike and car repair collectives
lack Panther Party Free Breakfast Program
ody as community
ody neutrality
ody positivity
ody Trust
oredom
rave space
reaking the rules
ridge as metaphor
are pods
are-based co-housing
atholic Worker Movement
entering maintenance
ircular economy
limate cafes
louds as metaphor
oalition
ollaborative apprenticeship
ollective care
ommon pool resources
ommons, the
ommuning with animals
ommunity college
ommunity gardens
ommunity newspapers
onjure
onstructionist-design framework, the
onsulting your consultants
ontemplative tradition, the
orn knowledge
redit unions
rip time
ritical fabulation
ritical hope
ritical pedagogy
ritical race theory
ritical suicide studies
ritical whiteness

critique
Cuestionamos
curiosity
death practices
decolonial liberatory-based practices
deep organizing
dérive, the
drumming
embodied expression
embodied knowledge
emergent strategy
empathy
energy work
erasure, avoiding thereof
esoteric wisdom traditions
ethnodrama
etymology
existentialism
externalizing
failure
fat positivity
feminism
feminst ethics of care
fermentation
flâner
food sovereignty
forest bathing
fragments/fragmentation
freedom
generous systems
gift economies
Grace Lee Boggs
grief as nonlinear
group work
groups
harm reduction
healing circles
healing healers through the arts
healing justice
healing rituals
Hearing Voices Network
herbal justice
herbalism
holding space
humanness
humor
illders
improvisation
infinite blackness
intentional communities
interdisciplinary cataloging
intergenerational living
interspecies organizing
intuitive eating
justice-oriented counseling
land trusts
land, work, spirit, body
language justice
leaving well
liberatory education
life cycle, honoring the
liminality
limited-equity cooperative housing

- Disposing of the script of coloniality
- Affirming and developing knowledge and practices from border spaces across disciplines and geographic localities
- Sharing social and political capital to create a pathway toward economic capital

CONCLUSION

No clear roadmap exists to guide the process of decolonizing and the pursuit of liberation. Frequently the early stages of decolonizing yield chaos. Such dissolution is a necessary and vital precursor to fully dismantling the power of entrenched colonialist systems and creating new structures and institutions designed to uphold the liberation of all. ❁

1 Mignolo, "Geopolitics of Sensing and Knowing: On (De)Coloniality, Border Thinking and Epistemic Disobedience"; Quijano, "Coloniality and modernity/rationality."

2 Quijano, "Coloniality of Power and Eurocentrism in Latin America."

3 Anzaldúa, *Borderlands/La Frontera: The New Mestiza* (1st and 2nd eds.); Collins, *Black Feminist Thought: Knowledge, Consciousness, and the Politics of Empowerment*; Collins, *Black Sexual Politics: African Americans, Gender, and the New Racism*; Collins, "Foreword: Emerging intersections—Building knowledge and transforming institutions"; Crenshaw, "Mapping the Margins: Intersectionality, Identity Politics, and Violence Against Women of Color."

4 Harding, "How Standpoint Methodology Informs Philosophy of Social Science"; Hankivsky and Cormier, *Intersectionality and Public Policy: Some Lessons from Existing Models*.

5 Almeida, Melendez, and Paez, "Liberation-based healing."

6 Du Bois, *The Souls of Black Folk*; Freire, *Pedagogy of Hope: Reliving Pedagogy of the Oppressed*; Almeida, "Creating collectives of liberation"; Almeida, Parker, and Dolan-Delvecchio, *Transformative Family Therapy: Just Families in a Just Society*.

7 Mignolo, "Epistemic Disobedience, Independent Thought and Decolonial Freedom."

8 Almeida, "Hierarchy of Power, Privilege, and Oppression" graphic.

BIO

Rhea V. Almeida, MS, PhD, LCSW, founder of the Institute for Family Services, is a practitioner of Liberatory Healing Practices, a decolonial therapeutic approach. Dr. Almeida is the author of numerous journal articles and four books.

deep organizing

SEE: Black Panther Party Free Breakfast Program; freedom; healing justice; land, work, spirit, body

CONTRIBUTOR'S NOTE

Deep organizing is a model of community organizing theorized by K. Wayne Yang and Jane McAlevey and practiced by a variety of movement leaders and organizations, such as the Black Panthers (although not called "deep organizing" at the time, their use of survival programs to address the needs for the community they were mobilizing meets the criteria), and union organizers. Deep organizing seeks to create a nurturing and sustaining movement that transcends specific times and problems. It instead focuses on creating a functional space for the marginalized themselves to thrive and bring to the struggle what they can. Principles include prioritizing participants' current well-being as necessary for change, nurturing their complex personhood and conflicting desires, and appreciatively recognizing their differences. —MSM

CONTRIBUTION

The revolution is a pot and perpetual flame
You will find yourself at the door with more in your pockets than you knew you had
– roots and seeds
– hands to stir
– the warmth you radiate
Everything in between flows from the tap

The revolution is a discussion had on a full stomach
You will find yourself at the table with more knowledge than you knew others cared to hear
– proof of human goodness written in the names of those you love
– well-earned doubts from a lifetime peppered with consequence
– every makeshift way you have made your impossible world work
Everything actionable can be done in the morning

The revolution is a home and a hammer and its holder
We share it with ancestors and our children's children as much as each other
With the love we layered in
It will last long after freedom loses its novelty ❁

BIO

Mia Stone-Molloy (she/her) is a labor organizer and poet with a bachelor's degree in Economics and Political Science from Brown University and a passion for the connection between personal and societal healing.

dérive, the

TO LIVE IN THE CONTEMPORARY WORLD can be a disorienting experience. Chaos, even. We are pulled along in ever-changing spaces and happenings in the contemporary everyday, risking the loss of our own groundings and roots. But what happens when we surrender to this flighty mode of existence? What form can this take, and what creative potential can it unleash?

In the mid-twentieth century, the *dérive* emerged as a notable concept-practice within the Situationist International art movement—a collective of artists and theorists, in which Guy Debord[1] was a notable figure. Debord conceived of the dérive as a means of comprehending the rapidly transforming urbanisms of the modern city. Tied closely with other practices of psychogeography, which seek to explore the feelings and affects arising from one's surroundings, Debord's dérive emphasised the creative potentials arising from "drifting" through the myriad ambiances of place. In its definition as a practice of drifting, Debord sought to open up a method of moving with the flows of ever-changing orientations, and intuiting pathways through divergent *inner* and *outer* spaces.

In my practice, the dérive is an invitation to get lost in order to get found, to deliberately lose myself in the happenings beyond my door as a means of discovering how I am situated amongst the continuous emergences of the world. It is a practice that not only invites a disruptive break of routine, challenging narratives about always having to *do*, but also initiates a taking up space and entering into relation with other persons and events without the weight of expectation. To follow my own inclinations—a colour, direction, a sign, a sound—through shared places of communion is to re-affirm pleasure in the flows of simply being in, of, and *with* the world. It is a welcome reattunement to the beauty of the proximate and the mundane, particularly in times where lived experience feels oversaturated with the propulsion of contemporary demands.

In the material flows of the inner-outer worlds, such practices are welcome teachers in the state of flux. More than just a chance meeting with the fissures of the urban character, to enter into a dérive is to embrace the ever-flowing weaves of life. As one moves through a space, one is always in entry as much as one is in exit. We submit ourselves to the wave of relational happenings in the universe around us, aware of ourselves and others continually coming and going. In the pavement passing beneath my feet, my body rhythmatising to and from the melodies of place, I lean in to my own nomadic nature—not a static being but a fluid *becoming*, with the capacity of ebb and flow, capture and release. The dérive is a practice to ground us in our vital unrootedness, an invitation to step into creative dialogue with(in) the world's fluid relationalities.

DÉRIVE RECIPES

One can dérive alone, or one can dérive in relation with others; arrangements in small groups of two or three others, or even a canine companion, can facilitate an altogether different experience where intra-actions and zigzagging dialogues can formulate altogether different impressions. These recipes are written, and should be read, as starting points only. They are invitations for you to begin attuning with the inner and outer landscapes of your own world, letting yourself be drawn to and from all your encounters. →

RECIPE 1: LEAN IN TO THE UNFAMILIAR. Set out to follow your own road less travelled. At each juncture, commit to following the path with which you have never or least regularly convened. See where it takes you.

RECIPE 2: FOLLOW A THREAD. Find a point of sensory interest to help direct your dérive. It could be a colour, a shape, a texture, an architectural feature. Observe where it takes you, and how it appears and reverberates in various forms throughout your explorations.

RECIPE 3: 360 DEGREES. Leave your front door. Pick a number between 10 and 360. Use this number as an angular degree to direct your walk. Head out in a straight line as directed by your angle of choice.

RECIPE 4: FOLLOW YOUR SHADOW. Best set-off time before midday, and if possible allow a full day to let the changing orientations of your shadow be your guide. ❁

1 Debord, "Theory of the Dérive"

BIO Rae Turpin (she/her) is a community facilitator, artist, postgraduate practice-researcher, lover of nettles and all things urban wild.

drumming

SEE
resonance
somatic healing
songs/singing
sound healing

CONTRIBUTION

DRUMMING IS AN ANCIENT TRADITION (found almost everywhere on Planet Earth, and likely also on the hype planet Uranus that rotates on its side) which involves the contact of hand, stick, bone, or mallet on the surface for a body-swaying groove. Drumming fundamentally makes you move. To strike a surface without a groove is just called "hitting a thing." Drummers come in all kinds; drums come in all shapes; drum methods come in all types; and yet, we know a drumbeat when we hear it. Ultimately the sound of drums invokes and evokes, whether through soul-stirring syncopations or technical harmonies. Drumming is our percussive heartbeat—the instrument that ensures we are alive. ❁

BIO

Richael Faithful is a Black trans-southern multi/interdisciplinary healer, culture worker, and attorney.

embodied expression

CONTRIBUTION

THE ENOUGH PORTRAIT PHOTO series is a collaboration between artist Anne Wolf, photographer Lisa Levine, and participants who wish to convey a personal embodied gesture of ENOUGH. Each participant reflected on and wrote their thoughts about ENOUGH, then chose how to locate and mark the word directly on their body.

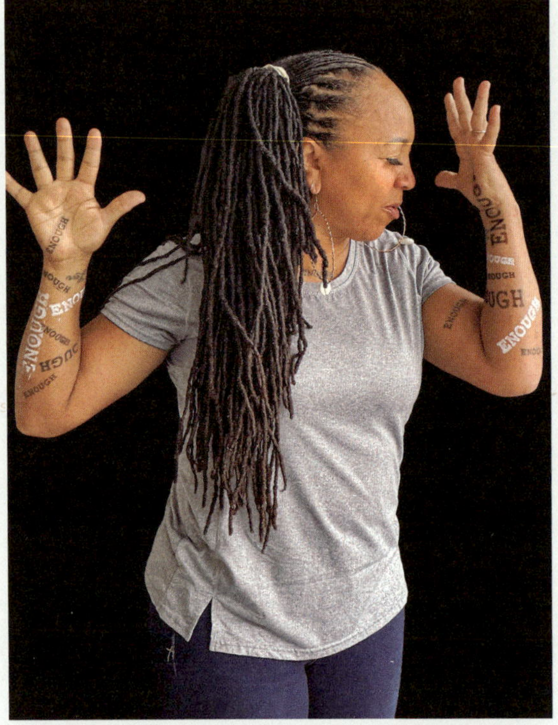

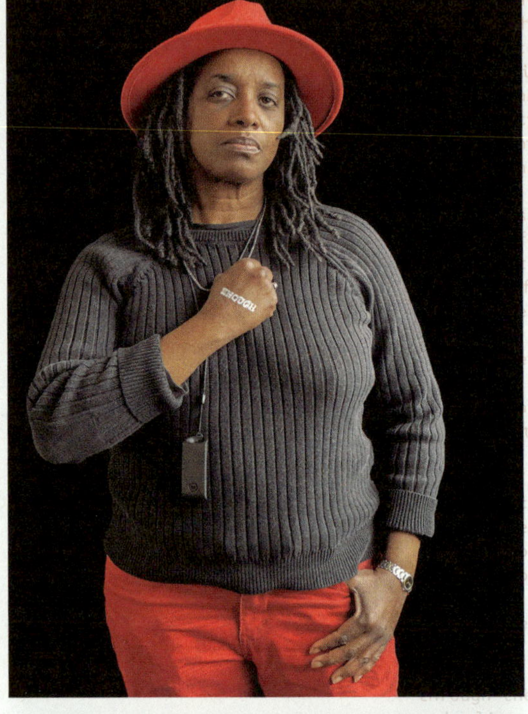

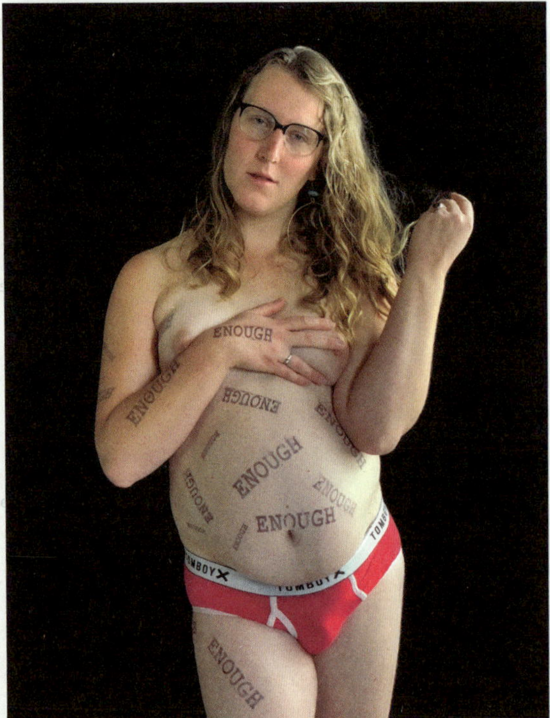

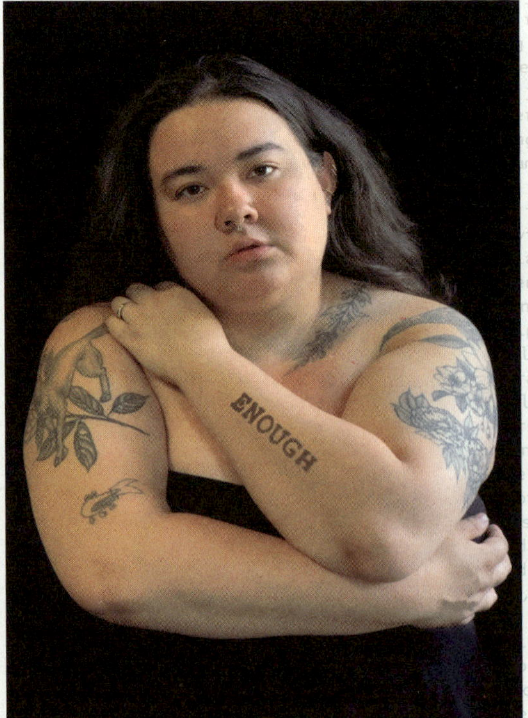

SEE:
access invocations
accessibility
activating archives
afrofuturism
agency
aging positivity
altar work
alternative identity projects
ancestral wisdom
ancestrality
anti-ableism
anti-adultism
anti-racism
anti-racism court system
art
art as/in/of life
art journaling
art therapy
art workers
art-based group work
arts in medicine
arts-based research
Authentic Movement
authentic movement
Ayurveda
being with
Bertha Capen Reynolds
bike and car repair collectives
Black Panther Party Free Breakfast Program
body as community
body neutrality
body positivity
Body Trust
boredom
brave space
breaking the rules
bridge as metaphor
care pods
care-based co-housing
Catholic Worker Movement
centering maintenance
circular economy
climate cafes
clouds as metaphor
coalition
collaborative apprenticeship
collective care
common pool resources
commons, the
communing with animals
community college
community gardens
community newspapers
conjure
constructionist-design framework, the
consulting your consultants
contemplative tradition, the
corn knowledge
credit unions
crip time
critical fabulation
critical hope
critical pedagogy
critical race theory
critical suicide studies
critical whiteness
Cuestionamos
curiosity
death practices
decolonial
liberatory-based practices
deep organizing
dérive, the
drumming
embodied expression
embodied knowledge
emergent strategy
empathy

embodied expression

The resulting portraits reveal the body as a site that holds stories which have been unspoken, ignored, unaddressed, unconsidered. This somatic exploration becomes a means of healing an old wound or violation, a message of boundaries and protection, or a means of sanctifying one's own sense of abundance. ❁

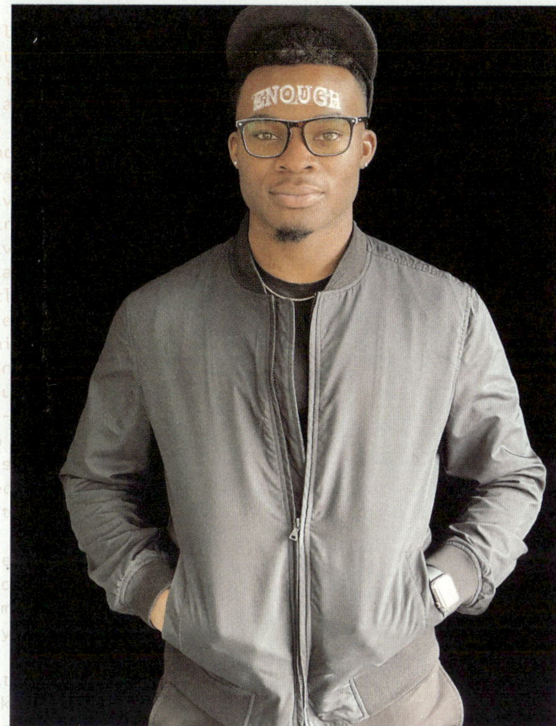

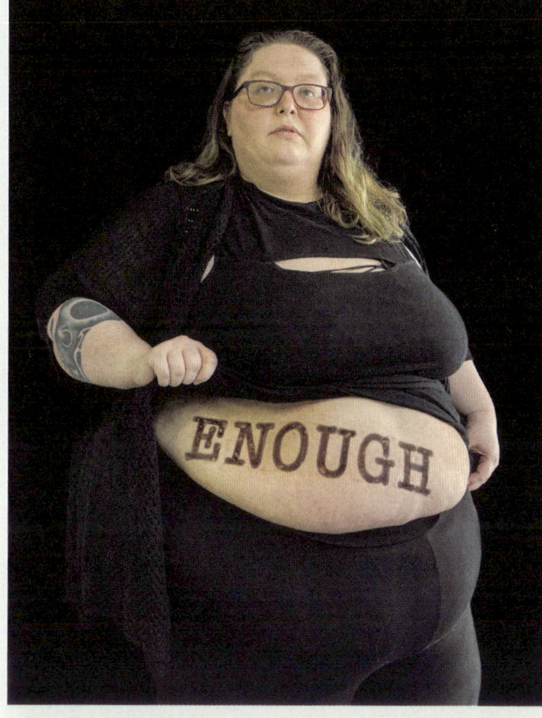

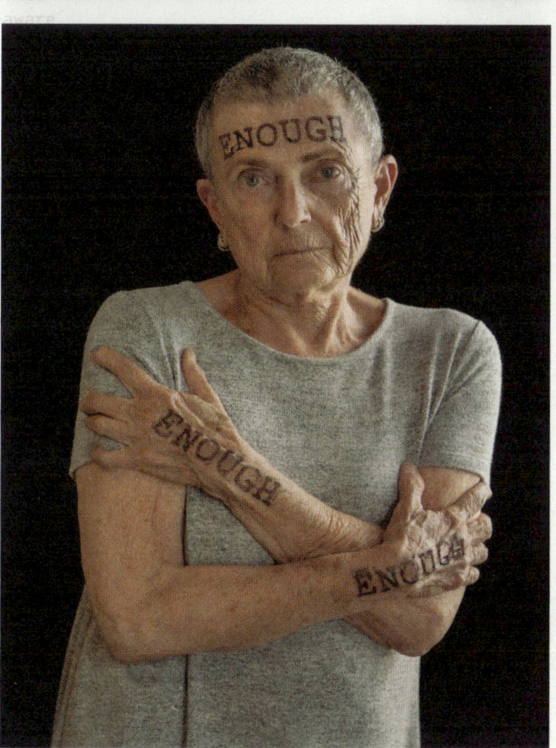

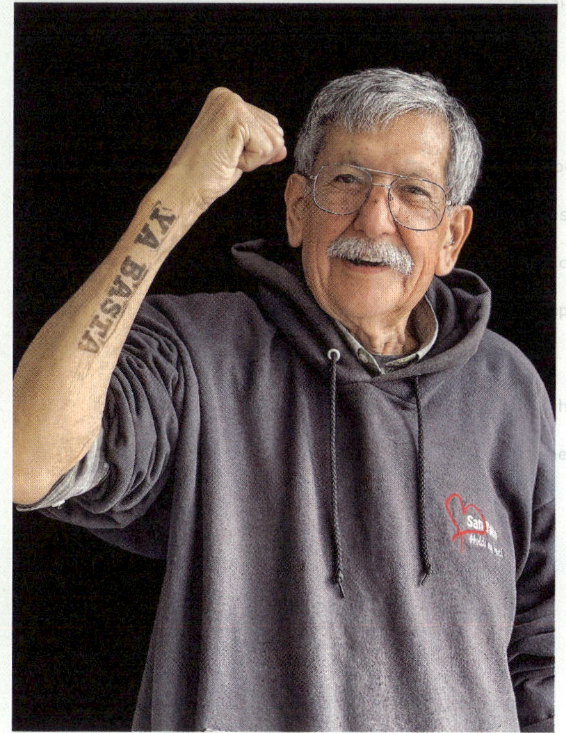

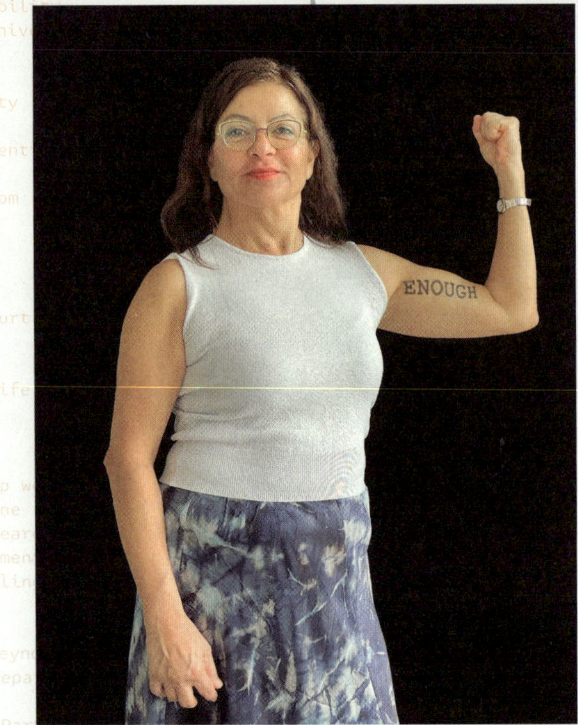

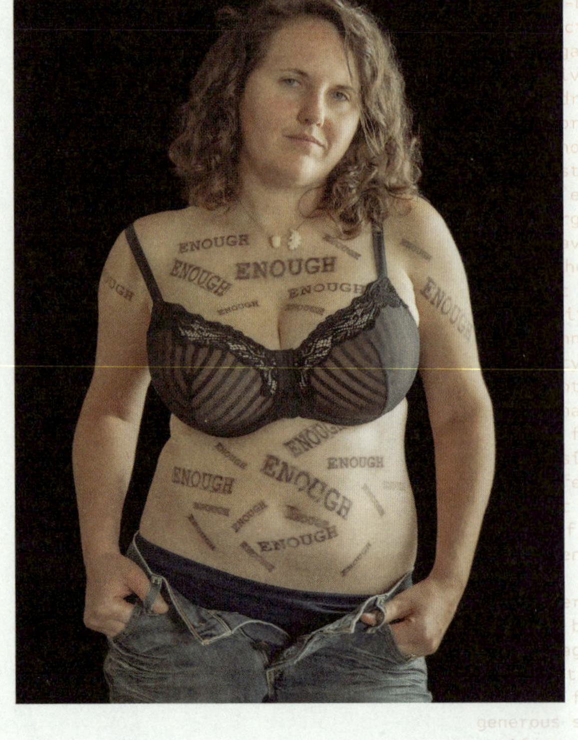

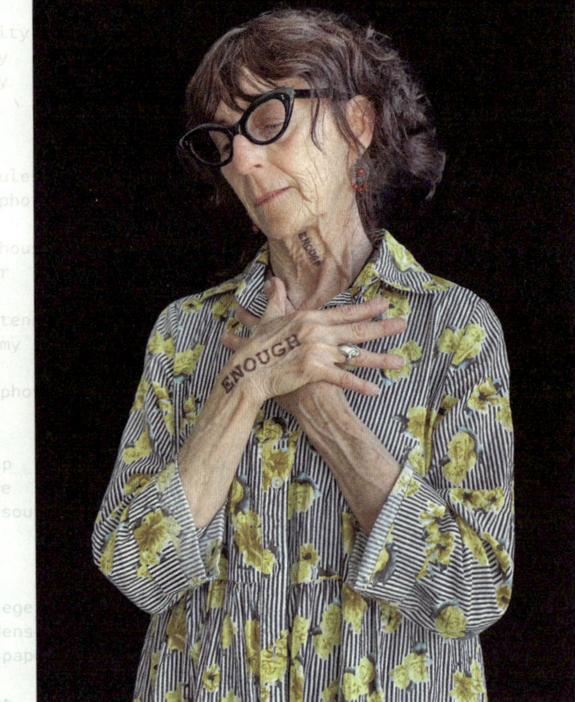

B I O S

Anne Wolf is a sculptor and educator who is committed to the idea that art can be a catalyst for healing, growth, and transformation.

Lisa Levine is a photographic artist and educator who has a deep interest in creating commissioned public art that intimately engages viewers while transcending the confines of museums and traditional art venues.

embodied knowledge

SEE mikveh, Reiki, rest as resistance, sauna, somatic healing, trans practices, yoga

CONTRIBUTION

SOMATIC BODYWORK is a technique in which a practitioner supports a client through touch, breath work, rocking, and stretching to make contact with the life force energy that moves through the client's body. Through intuitive and energetic listening, the practitioner supports the client in bringing attention to the places their body holds constrictions built up from lived or inherited experiences and encourages them towards release. The experience can bring attention to sensation and move energy so that individuals can open to new possibilities.

As a somatic bodyworker, it is important to me to be in a practice of receiving the care I offer clients as consistently as possible. Bodywork is a place to weave intuitive wisdom, ritual, and traditional medicine. The more I receive bodywork myself, the more open, connected, and purposeful I can be in supporting my clients.

This poem tells the story of my experience receiving somatic bodywork in November of 2022.

This bodywork session took place in the midst of a lot of life transitions. Prior to the session, I set the intention to hold myself with love and to allow what wanted to move through me to move through me. I requested support from my ancestral guides to lead me to the message I needed to help me make sense of what I was moving through in my healing journey. The messages I received were: *we got you, let go*; *stop reaching, receive*; and *remember the beauty, too*. Our bodies know complexity and have the capacity to self-heal. I often think about what might be possible if more of us had access to the supportive techniques that bring us back to this knowledge. So often I focus on the pain and trauma that is at my back. This session invited me to know the softness and beauty that lives there, too. →

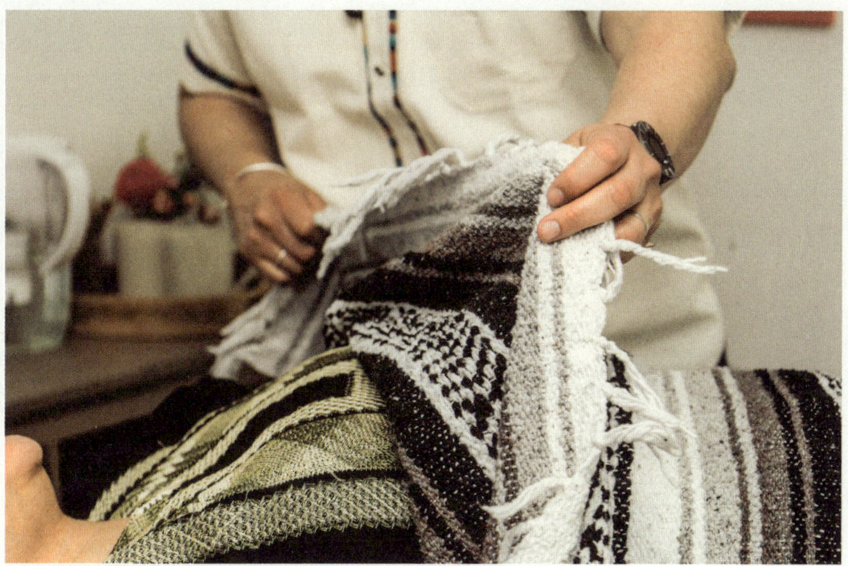

Image of René offering bodywork to a client in their office in San Leandro, CA, in April 2023. Photo was taken by Dorean Raye of Dorean Raye Photography based in Oakland, CA.

embodied knowledge

ancestral wisdom
ancestrality
energy work

the familiar twinge
by rené benavides

a light creak
table shifts
my vulnerability on display

i feel for grandmother earth

contact made
tight breathing
my body is constricting

i sense how old this energy is

the familiar twinge
behind my shoulder blades
the terror passed through generations

a commitment made
my work to do
to turn and face the past

i know how to let go

arching back
kicking feet
salty tears
release

i have been here before

settling
body
lowering
breath
a softness in my cheeks

the twinge
relaxing

i know this place

i remember my beauty too

BIO René Benavides, MSW, PPSC, ICF-ACC (they, she) is a facilitator, somatic coach, and bodyworker who lives and works on Ohlone land in San Leandro, California.

C
O
N
T
R
I
B
U
T
I
O
N

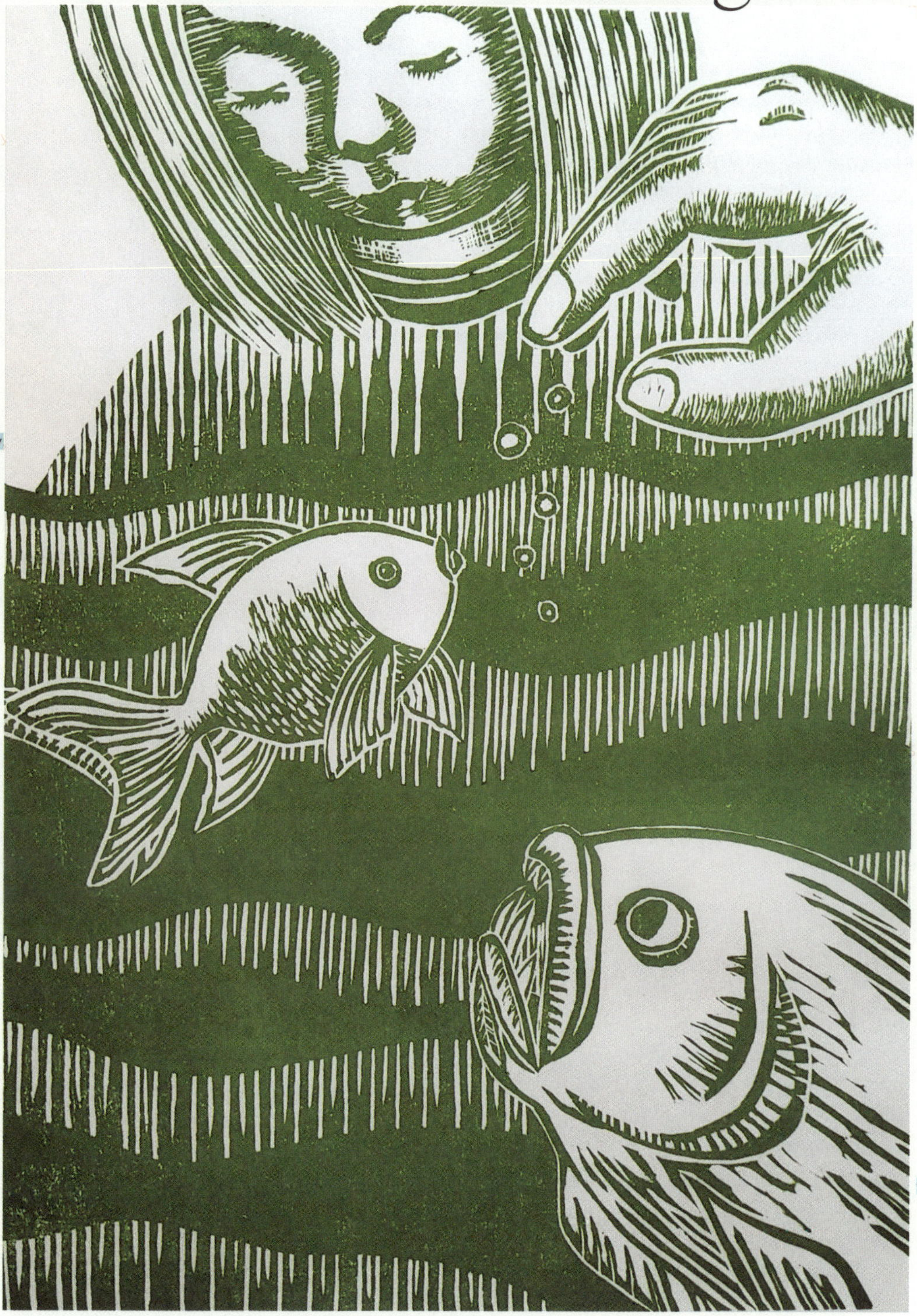

What you pay attention to grows, per *Emergent Strategy*.[1] What you feed becomes bigger. What are you planning to feed today?

→

emergent strategy

EDITOR'S NOTE

"Emergent strategy" was developed by group facilitator, organizer, and author adrienne maree brown. Largely inspired by the work of science fiction writer Octavia Butler, among others—for example, Grace Lee Boggs—as well as by metaphors from the natural world, emergent strategy is an approach to collective and personal action. Throughout *Emergent Strategy: Shaping Change, Shaping Worlds*, brown relies on Nick Obolensky's definition: "Emergence is the way complex systems and patterns arise out of a multiplicity of relatively simple interactions."[2] Emergent strategy is organized around core principles related to fractals, relationships, abundance, trust, attention, and more. Many thanks to Miki for contributing this woodcut, which illustrates the principle, "What you pay attention to grows."[3] —ES

1 brown, *Emergent Strategy*, 42.

2 Obolensky, *Complex Adaptive Leadership: Embracing Paradox and Uncertainty*, quoted in *Emergent Strategy*, p. 13.

3 brown, *Emergent Strategy*, 42.

BIO

Miki Nishida Goerdt,
Artist/Art Therapist/Social Worker/Change Agent
mikigoerdt.com

CONTRIBUTION

Empathy (Not to Confuse with "Empath, Being an"), or a Six-Month Journey to an Empathetic Encyclopedia Definition of Empathy

WHEN I STARTED TALKING about this text, people were saying, "This is so you, you're so empathetic." The more I heard this sentence, the more I felt blocked around actually writing about it. This was in March 2023. What did that mean about the word and about me?
And also…
am I writing about *empathy*?
am I writing about me?
am I writing about *empathy* through writing about me?
can anyone else relate to this?

I am writing this text from a clinic that faces a lake with a Las Vegas–like fountain in its middle, queerly colored every night and with a moon rising just behind the shoreline.see side note #1 I am here for three weeks and I have more than enough time to think about myself… *and empathy*. Therefore, the way of understanding what *empathy* means—although, when do we ever fully know the meaning of our words? maybe we start with acknowledging their power first—goes along with understanding myself better, with moving towards being in my body and being in right relationship with given self, others, and what surrounds me. These three constitute a triangle, not surprisingly. Nothing more and nothing less and that's already a lot. see side note #2 Let's take this triangulation apart. ➔

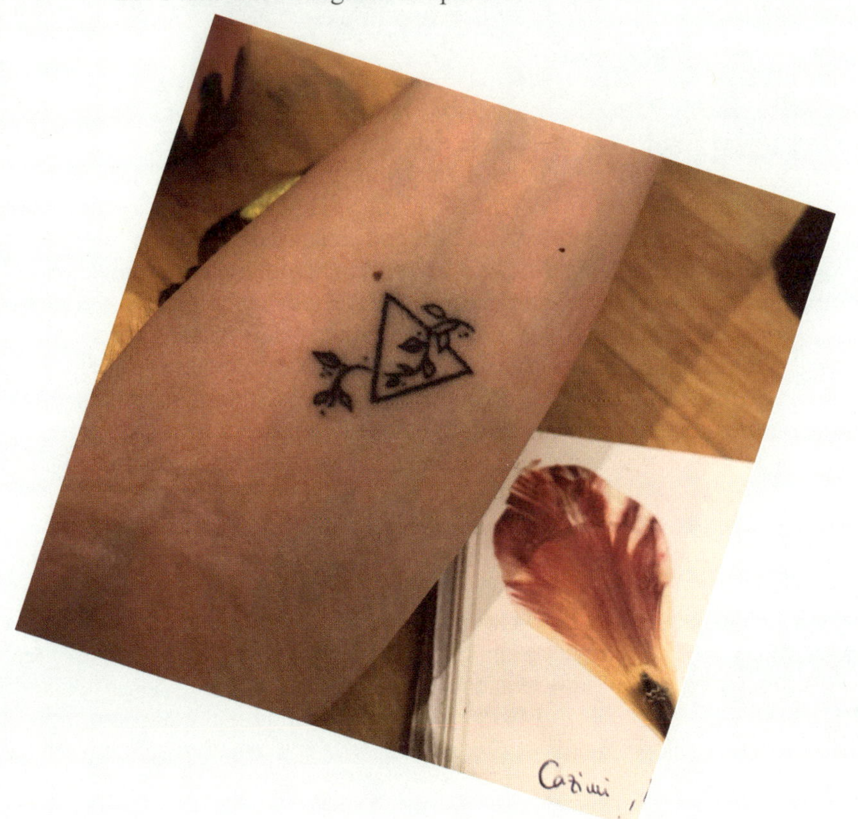

empathy

Someone who I am learning to love deeply at the moment told me that *empathy* is a cultivation. *Empathy*, like trust, like love, is something that happens actively; it is relational practice, it is about co-regulation and it is about the flow between (all kinds of human and non-human) bodies. **see side note #3**

side note #1 ~ this text is written in the shadow phase of the last super full moon of the year, end of September 2023.

side note #2 ~ I am writing this while on a rehabilitation journey for a spinal condition called scoliosis, learning to have empathy towards my spine and her ripple effects.

side note #3 ~ I am a Cancer sun and rising, the moon is my planet, and while she was full and flowing I listened to Renee Sill's "embodied astrology." This is inspired by their readings.

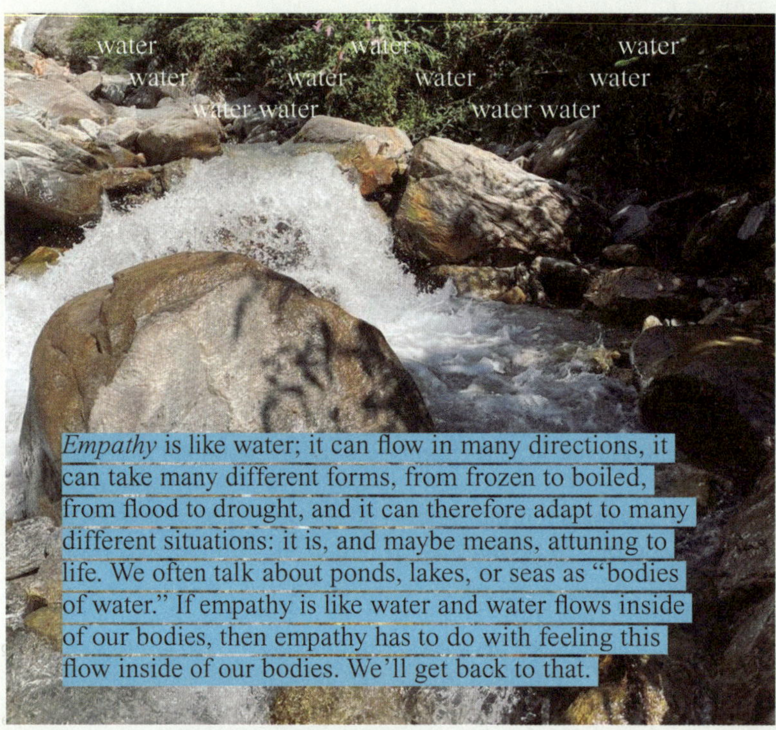

Empathy is like water; it can flow in many directions, it can take many different forms, from frozen to boiled, from flood to drought, and it can therefore adapt to many different situations: it is, and maybe means, attuning to life. We often talk about ponds, lakes, or seas as "bodies of water." If empathy is like water and water flows inside of our bodies, then empathy has to do with feeling this flow inside of our bodies. We'll get back to that.

In German, *empathy* translates to Einfühlung: literally meaning feeling into (and we Cancers know how fast we feel into and out of our own boundaries). Maryam Hasnaa writes that "empathy means practicing energetic hygiene by not absorbing or taking on other people's energy."[1] This is probably my biggest learning curve as a fully grown Cancerian being: Who am I and of how many multitudes am I made? I often wonder how that works. Where do I end and where does the other (not only human) start? I've thought about this the last few days, hearing doctors talk about my spine, its canyons and curves, where it pushes on which organ and what that will mean 20 years from now. I panicked; I totally lost my body and projected my whole being into the future, completely losing sense of the present moment and therefore my body.

Earlier we mentioned water as a metaphor for empathy; its bodily feeling inside of us: the waves between ourselves, the outside and our environment. We are sensing the flow of our emotions as part of what we can call a somatic, meaning physical, practice of embodiment. *Empathy* then is an active embodied practice, rooted in being present with myself, being in my body and sensing what is happening in that compost heap. A compost, like the cosmos, is harmonically organized chaos, constantly digesting the old to grow something new.

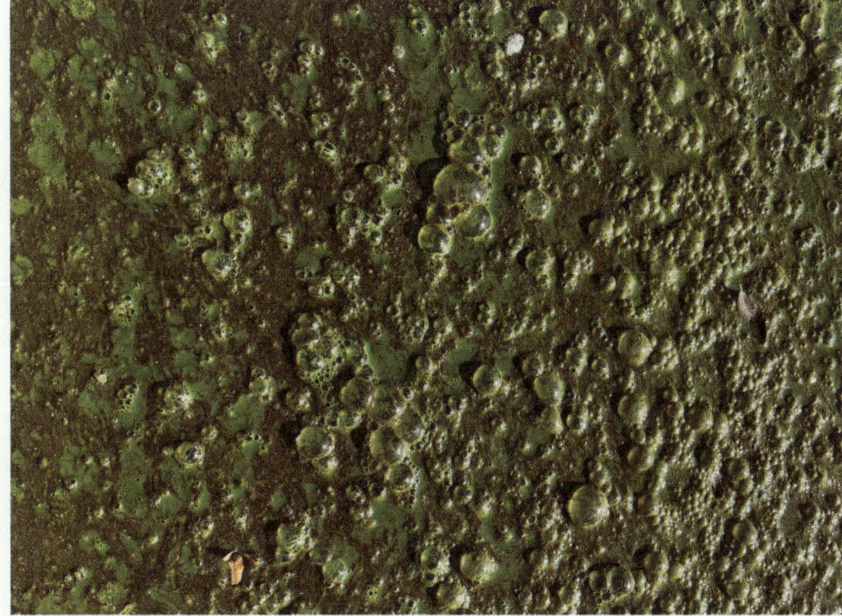

For parts of the shapeshifting work I do, within an anticapitalist health autonomy project called The Hologram, we invented a position called "social glue." I am the glue, relating to everyone and weaving nets. I got lost in this ocean very quickly, because I lost myself between too many relationships, old ones and new ones. But the more I talked about it, the more I realized that I did not always practice being in grounded relationship with those around me, within or outside of that social web, and therefore in grounded relationship with myself. Do we actually let others be who they are or do we want to change each other? How do we take part in relationships and what is our role in them? And this goes for any kind of relationship, from friends to lovers to (all possible kinds of) family, to trees, ducks, and bacteria.

During the last years of work I/we realized that with these relationships comes something else: the response-ability of differentiating myself from others. Or maybe I should say, these relationships come with listening to others while not merging with them.
Empathy then seems to be practicing embodied listening at any moment of relating to that triangle we live in. Again: ourselves, others, and the world around us.

More than a character trait for sensitive humans, *empathy* is authentic presence. It's a skill that everyone can grow, like a tree growing roots. From here, feel how far down through our center we can reach. ❁

1 Hasnaa, Maryam, "Energetic Hygiene."

BIO florence freitag is a Berlin-based artist, body- and land-tending net-weaver, compostist practitioner & community organizer inspired by collective gardens as forms of social medicine.

energy work

SEE: agency, ayurveda, drumming, forest bathing, humanness

CONTRIBUTION

SO, YOU KNOW when someone is walking behind you and you notice that they're there even if you're not hearing them move or hearing their breathing or anything else?

So, that's essentially energy you see, it's a bunch of molecules in vibration—yes; and it's really more than that!

It's like a force that you feel, like when you have instant chemistry with someone, it's not the feeling itself but the thing between you both…

And that thing, called energy, can be summoned or directed like when you call a dog. And like human-dog relationships, you can call nicer and clearer and with more confidence than the next human.

And what's really neat is that if you practice enough times, you're able to "work" energy in a way that is like dancing. You are leading the energy to do certain things that can facilitate the other person feeling content, joyful, balanced, serene, part of a vibe or a big release, whatever they need to feel at that moment to be more fully within their human experience.

So, when we say energy worker, we mean someone who is aware of that more-than-molecules force; someone who feels that force with the lightning-like clarity of instant chemistry; someone who is trained to call on that energy as easily as one calls a dog; in an exchange that is similar to a suave mambo dance (guided by conga drums; SEE drumming for more) that makes onlookers and dance partners swoon in what it creates. That's energy work—a kind of intentional magic that is much easier to experience than to read about. ❁

BIO

Richael Faithful is a Black trans-southern multi/interdisciplinary healer, culture worker, and attorney.

erasure, avoiding thereof

SEE reclaiming selfhood
recognition

CONTRIBUTION

EVERY PERSON HOLDS INFINITE COMPLEXITY and is constantly changing over time. As with the proverbial river that cannot be stepped in twice, I cannot encounter the same person twice. Trying to understand and fully know the complexity of another person at one point in time is not possible; multiply that by the fact that the person and I are both changing continuously, such that each time we meet it is meeting anew. To imagine that I know another person fully is to erase everything I don't know, to reduce a person to a simulacrum. It erases curiosity in encountering another person, and it prevents me from fully being with another person, because I can only ever be with the picture of the person rather than the whole person. What does helping look like that does not erase the unknown and unknowable?

How can I interact with that which I see without forgetting that the unseen exists? It seems unlikely I will ever see the far side of the moon, even though I know it is there. The surface of the side I see—its texture, its smells, the sparsest of atmospheres—I likely will never know either, and can only guess at. I can appreciate the beauty of a waxing crescent moon that defies nighttime stereotypes by hanging around in daylight, and still understand how little I know of it; I can luxuriate in the thickness of an ongoing relationship in which I love the process of forever meeting another person (SEE being with).

Erasing complexity is a violence to the other person but it is also an imprisonment of oneself: I would be trapping myself in a world devoid of color, in a world in which there are limits and finitude. It would also reduce the relationship of care into one of coercion, where the only help offered is the one that requires erasure of self as the price of entry. ❁

BIO

Noriko Martinez works imperfectly as a radical helper by sitting with people, being curious, and loving the world.

esoteric wisdom traditions

ESOTERIC WISDOM TRADITIONS (from the Greek *esoterikos*, of an inner circle; from the Proto-Germanic *wisadomaz*, knowledgeable judgment; from the Latin *traditio*, a handing over), systems of passing along authoritative insight within restricted groups of initiates. Esotericism is a loose and debated umbrella term for a wide assortment of religious, mystical, and philosophical ideas and their related movements, mainly in "Western" societies, generally emphasizing hidden knowledge and an enchanted worldview.

As an academic field of scholarship, Western esotericism encompasses the study of alchemy, magic, secret societies, theosophy, and mysticism, among other topics. Some cosmological systems and tendencies described as esoteric include Gnosticism, Hermeticism, Pythagoreanism, Neoplatonism, and Kabbalah. These are often considered within, adjacent to, or in conversation with religions historically present in Europe, Northern Africa, and Western Asia during the last two millennia, such as Christianity, Islam, Judaism, and varieties of paganism (ethnic religions). Although the concept is predominantly understood as particular to the "West," some have sought to consider "non-Western" systems, such as Hinduism and Buddhism, in a more global application of esotericism.

Esoteric traditions are characterized by an occult sensibility concerning the discovery and teaching of hidden Truth—a notion that, regardless of appearances, reality is a singular, unified totality. Beyond their belief in hidden Truth, esotericists incorporate hiddenness as a method of arrangement and practice in the form of secrecy. In group organization, this can appear as a secret society or merely a closed, private circle of members. In teaching, through writing or oral culture, the principle of secrecy generates linguistic complexity, opacity, and allegory. Esoteric writing implements particular techniques to ensure only readers who learn to "read between the lines" will grasp the true meaning of the text. As an intentional strategy of intra-cultural transmission, esotericism might respond to conditions of persecution, especially when "hidden Truth" is potentially subversive of a dominant social order. On the other hand, esotericism functions exclusively, limiting its conveyance to a spiritual elite. As such, esotericism possesses properties that both uphold authority and challenge authority, lending it equally to orthodox and heterodox systems.

Access to esoteric wisdom is bequeathed by initiation into a circle through mystical revelation, or the alteration of one's state of consciousness. This may involve rigorous study, meditation, hallucinogenic experiences, and other rituals. "Wisdom" here indicates the ability to "see"—the initiate is "awakened" to a hidden Truth, revealing greater depth or meaning in what was formerly observed only superficially. Wisdom can thus connote expertise and authority in its proximity to Truth, particularly due to its "elevated" or "deep" understanding of reality in contrast to common knowledge.

Ancient esoteric circles that had a profound impact on future developments can be found around the Eastern Mediterranean. The Eleusinian Mysteries, secret rites of transformation following the goddesses Demeter and Persephone, possibly played a significant role in Athenian life during the first millennium BCE. They are notable among other mystery cults (*mysteria*), from which the term *mysticism* derives. The seeds of esotericism are also visible in the figure of Pythagoras, who sought hidden universality in numerology and mathematics. So too is an esoteric ontology expressed by Parmenides, arguably the originator of metaphysics, who rejected sensory experience as illusory and posited thought as the sole means by which Truth could be known. These systems of philosophy, science, and religion would influence Plato, who advanced the concept of the Monad, the Absolute, or the One, representing the original (Supreme) Being or the totality of the cosmos. The view that abstract objects exist—objects beyond space and time, beyond the physical and mental—is a central principle of Platonism, forming the mystical core and logic of virtually all "Western" intellectual systems after Plato.

esoteric wisdom traditions

The first millennium CE saw a parallel emergence of several movements around the Eastern Mediterranean typically referred to as esoteric. They are notable for their syncretic character, mixing discrete schools of thought into a single totalizing system. Among these are the Gnostics, an assortment of Jewish and Christian groups (such as the Sethians and Valentinians) who viewed the material world as evil or illusory, striving for unity with a True, hidden God. Another is Neoplatonism, formulated by Plotinus, which similarly sought Oneness but opposed the Gnostic (Sethian) disdain for materiality, instead affirming its goodness. The exceedingly syncretic Hermeticism, based on the teachings of the legendary Hermes Trismegistus, also appears in this period, putting forward a proto-pantheistic view of the One as encompassing all things. While each system can be described distinctly, there was much cross-pollination, stemming from their common intellectual lineage and contemporaneous exchange of knowledge.

These systems have continued to inform esotericism in the many centuries since, sometimes in contention, and sometimes in reconciliation. Gnostic concepts remained widespread and provocative, crossing the breadth of Eurasia via religions such as Manichaeism and in negative form through Catholic campaigns against "Gnostic" heresies (such as the Albigensian Crusade). Neoplatonic inspiration is prevalent in the writings of significant theologians, representing the major religions of the Mediterranean and beyond, from Augustine (Christianity) and al-Farabi (Islam) to Avicenna (Islam), Maimonides (Judaism), and Meister Eckhart (Christianity). Hermeticism endured in spiritual movements like Rosicrucianism and the works of Giordano Bruno, Jakob Böhme, Isaac Newton, and G. W. F. Hegel, among others, paving the way for modern philosophy and science. Organizations of Freemasonry would further Hermetic thought in recent centuries, with many social radicals and revolutionaries counting among its membership. New religious movements in the late 19th and early 20th centuries borrowed heavily from esotericism, key examples being Helena Blavatsky's Theosophy and Rudolph Steiner's Anthroposophy. Carl Jung's interest in esotericism (especially Gnosticism) even contributed to his development of analytical psychology. Syncretic tendencies in esoteric circles eventually generated perennialism, or the view that all religious systems share the same single metaphysical Truth. Along with the prominent author Aldous Huxley, this philosophy was propounded by the Traditionalist School, originating with René Guénon, whose esotericism remains relevant for contemporary reactionaries. Many esoteric concepts would ultimately coagulate in the eclectic New Age movement, generally concerned with individual, inward illumination. ❁

CONTRIBUTOR'S NOTE

This entry was informed by my ongoing studies of religion and esotericism, with Judaism as my nexus of interest. Along with various encyclopedic articles, video lectures, and formal coursework, several authors have been vital for my understanding of the topic. One of the best brief overviews of Western esotericism is Erica Lagalisse's *Occult Features of Anarchism*, although preference is given to its influence on modern Leftism. A more ambiguous yet energetic description of some esoteric and "heretical" movements can be found in *The Ecology of Freedom* by Murray Bookchin; the chapter titled "The Legacy of Freedom" pulls from the work of Hans Jonas, specifically on Gnosticism, and explains the revolutionary and reactionary tendencies of such ideas. Gershom Scholem, who effectively initiated the field of scholarship on Jewish mysticism, makes a similar point about messianism in *The Messianic Idea in Judaism*, and he remains a recurrent point of departure for me. I also think in tandem with Leo

esoteric wisdom traditions

Strauss's concept of "esoteric writing" and James C. Scott's concept of "hidden transcript," the latter of which I found helpfully considered in *Nahmanides in Medieval Catalonia* by Nina Caputo. Of the figures cited in the entry, Parmenides, Augustine, and Maimonides are especially of interest to me. Maimonides's *The Guide for the Perplexed* is itself generally known as a rather esoteric text, but it equally encourages readers to learn how to analyze a text closely. I can attribute a good amount of my broader understanding of esotericism to the highly accessible YouTube channels of Justin Sledge (*Esoterica*) and Filip Holm (*Let's Talk Religion*). I've solidified my statements through my own ethnographic observations drawn from engagements with self-described mystics, *ba'al teshuvot*, and other contemporary strains of reactionary thought.—ZW

B Zach Whitworth hails from
I the Umpqua Valley of the
O Pacific Northwest.

ethnodrama

SEE narradrama, Theatre of the Oppressed

CONTRIBUTION

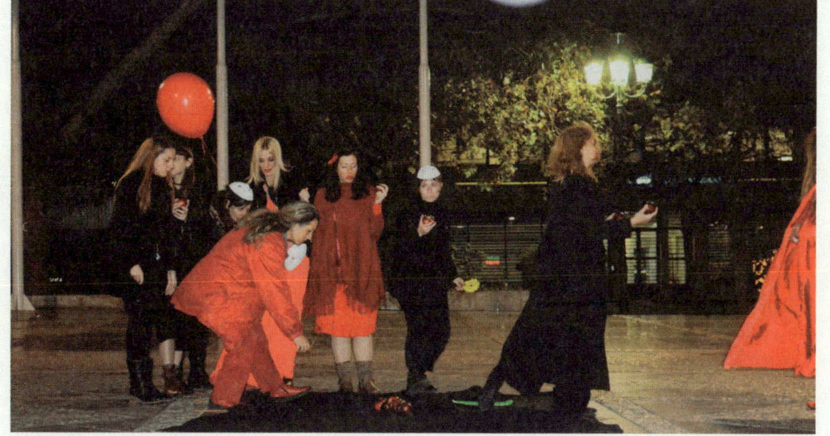

Liminals, 2016. “If we all fall in love, the state will collapse.” An ethnodrama inspired by the drama-therapy process and a message on a wall of the city of Athens during the economic crisis. Photo: Christos Tsakas.

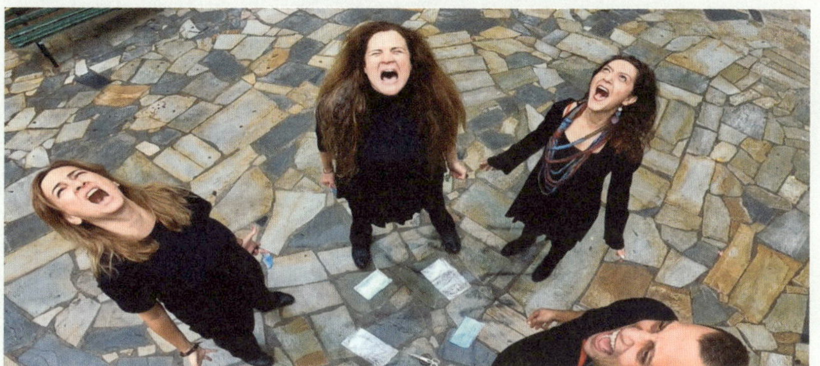

Liminals, 2020. “A healing message to humanity from Athens.” Ethnodrama in different countries, organized by Dimitra Stavrou, with the aim of amplifying the voice of Nemonte Nenquimo.[5] Drone photo: Dimitra Stavrou.

ETHNODRAMA IS A CRITICAL FORM of artistic representation that blurs humanities and social science with arts. “Ethnodrama,” a compound term drawn from “ethnography” and “drama,” is a hybrid, artistic form resulting from ethnographic research. The term “ethnodrama” was coined in 1982 by the anthropologist Viktor Turner, who introduced the concept originally in an academic/educational context. Jim Mienczakowski, in Australia, introduced ethnodrama into a mental health institution at the beginning of the ’90s as a form of “theatre of reality.” He used this method in his work with alcohol-dependent patients. He combined the Bakhtinian idea of “dialogic interactions”[1] and the philosophy of the “Theatre of the Oppressed” of Augusto Boal[2] to create a critical embodied ethnography. In the same period, the theatre artist Johnny Saldaña introduced ethnodrama in theatre with the play “Street Rat,”[3] where the script resulted from the field notes of the ethnographic work of Suzan and Macklin Finley on homeless youth in New Orleans.

Mienczakowski described the three phases of an ethnodrama: a) ethnographic research and data collection, b) scripting, and c) performance. The performers of an ethnodrama might perform either their own life stories as ethnographies (autoethnography), or the ethnographer performs the information he collected from others. Ethnodrama might be a method in different fields aiming to produce a change (psychotherapy, education, activism). The work of Mienczakowski inspired the drama therapist Stephen Snow, who works with ethnodrama in his drama-therapy clinical practice and research, thus forming the new drama therapy model of ethnodramatherapy. Other drama therapists who have been working with ethnodrama in the USA, Canada, and Europe during the last two decades include Nisha Sadjnani, Renée Emunah, Suzana Pendzik, Armand Volkas, Ornela Kapetani, and Dimitra Stavrou. In these drama-therapy practices, ethnodrama gets different forms, which span from self-ethnographic or self-revelatory performances (Emunah, Pendzik, Volkas) to ethnodramas where the "patient" becomes the ethnographer of others (Snow, Sadjani, Stavrou), aiming to restore new connections with otherness and the community.

Ethnodrama changes the status of the person asking for support and therapy from the role of "patient" to the role of "investigator." The interpretation of the collected information for the creation of a script is a critical part of the process. The performance needs further creative work with the transformation of the field notes to scenes through metaphor and symbolization, adding the aesthetic elements of the play. The spectators/witnesses might differ in ethnodramatic interventions, depending each time on the context and the purpose. As Marsh and Davis[4] have written, ethnodrama is one of the many analytical methods that aim to create and give space for alternative voices and ways to see the world and might call for action. It introduces a new situation, different from the dominant narrative, which is able to transform the ideological content. Ethnodrama in psychotherapy, and in all its forms, is a powerful, critical method because it focuses on social factors, such as history, culture, and the social positionality of the individual. In this sense, mental health is not considered to be an individual clinical case that stigmatizes the person; but the trauma can be seen in its connection with psychosocial and historical factors and also as a result of power relations and social injustice. ❁

1 Bakhtin, *The Dialogic Imagination*.

2 Boal, *Theatre of the Oppressed*.

3 Saldaña, "Street Rat: An ethnodrama."

4 Marsh, "Ethnodrama and Ethnotheatre."

5 Nenquimo, "This Is My Message to the Western World—Your Civilization Is Killing Life on Earth."

B I O Dimitra Stavrou is a Licensed Psychologist, Social Anthropologist (MSc.), Drama Therapist, and environmental activist from Greece working internationally.

CONTRIBUTION

On the Meaning of the Words We Are Using

WORDS ARE STORIES. Each one carries the history of the people who lived and evolved its meaning. When we are raised in a language, we are raised along with the histories behind those words. This is true even if we are the first generation to speak this language, even if the people who evolved this language forced our families to speak it.

The oldest root of the word "care" is "to call out, to scream." Words like lament and grief carry the same root as the word "care." It's a word where most of its history is entwined with grief, with sorrow and this sense of keeping close watch, attending to… This root of "care" is so much more physical than thinking of care as an institution, as a responsibility without the assumption of connection. I remember what it is like to be on bed watch as someone is very ill or about to die. I know the feeling of sitting there, attending to the rise and fall of each breath, the shifting color of skin, the small signs of temperature change and awareness. Our oldest selves knew of care as companionship, the attention of someone outside ourselves.

Doing the work of radical help means listening for what histories are carried in the words we most usually use: care, crisis. Each word carries stories, some that support the radicalness of our help and others that get in the way. I listen to these words and remember a time when care was always slow, not the kind of pace provided by modern pharmaceuticals and medical technologies. When care was about trying and waiting… Trying and waiting… and feeling the grief and sorrow as you see the contraction of a beloved's aliveness, knowing that they could rise back up or fall further down into being gone. We care. Deeply.

And then the word became a strategy more than a state of being, and out of this came some practices that have saved those I love, those you love, possibly you yourself… And other practices that focus more on the goal and far less on the companionship of staying close to someone, feeling their impact on our lives, and watching and remembering their breath.

The history of "crisis" is the opposite of the history of "care." In the present times, "crisis" is an activation word, the nervous system arc-ing up, eyes and face and back of the neck circling at attention, looking to identify what needs to be stopped, attended to. It's a word that assumes a response before thought, before the consciousness of choice. It's an overused word, one that falls like sharp thuds across headlines and out of the mouths of newscasters. This happens by design: hear the word crisis and up you go, imagine prairie dogs upright, fast and twitchy, looking all around. It's a money-making word.

Not every moment that might be painful, uncertain, or hard demands the gathering of your kin, your attention. A call of crisis should not mean stop what you are doing and act, but instead, in its oldest ways, the word asks for a pause. In most situations, even when violence is present, there is still the space for three breaths; for an inhale and an exhale.

The oldest meaning of "crisis" is this: to decide, to distinguish, to sift, to sieve. It is what that person does who sits at the bedside, as they notice changes in coloring, breath, and sound. *Is this it?* they ask. They assess, they discern, they sift. *Is there something else we should do? Is there more information here that might help us to know our next step?* There is a kind of trust in this old way, something that is missing from how we use the word "crisis" today. After all, when we pause and look around, assess, sift through the information, there is the possibility, always, that something might come out of this moment that is positive, that is restful, that means getting to the other side. There are histories embedded in this change, in moving from assess to act right now. ➔

etymology

"Radical" is one of those simple ancient words that hasn't traveled quite as far from its beginning times as other words. It just means "root." It just means the place of origin, not at the first beginning place but what happens right after, where life first reaches for its own nourishment and grounding before lifting up to something bigger and wider. This is how our bodies are wired, how our communities are wired, when other things don't get in the way. When the heart supports oxygenated blood moving back into the body—ready to feed each cell, each organ, each moment of life—the first thing it does is branch out with an artery that feeds itself. Not self-care that is separate from the whole, but putting on the heart's own oxygen mask first before turning towards the care, the remembering, of others. Radical is a word of connection between the beginning place and the prayer of possibility.

And then there is the word "help." This word's oldest root means something like "to love," but this word "love" is not about a tender glance or the feeling of a parent for a child. This word, this old, old word, is rooted in the meaning of being free; of not being in bondage. It is a word that, at its core, remembers the difference between care given freely and care that is forced. It is a word that emerges from memories of enslavement, old Roman and Norse enslavement, when those who spoke the language that became English were held in bondage, thousands of years ago.

It is no wonder that in order to care, to remember, to show up with the intensity of our grief and sorrow as well as our capacity for joy, we have to assess, to discern, to wonder about what is happening in front of us right now, what is needed, what is not needed, rather than rush in with ideas and cures and approaches that cut us off from our own roots, our self-oxygenation, while rushing in with histories of bondage held in our hands and voices, even though some part of us believes that we are doing what is needed, what is best for the person in front of us. Without the full consent. Without the dignity of being fully free.

—

All stories about histories are theories, suppositions that people make based on putting together fragments and looking for throughlines across time. All theories are poetry, designed to evoke and create wonder as much as to establish concrete fact. The places I look at for understanding the histories of words include the *Oxford English Dictionary*, etymonline.com, etymologeek.com, etym.org, and etymologynerd.com. ❁

B I O
Susan Raffo lives on Dakota land in Minneapolis, Minnesota. A writer, cultural worker, and bodyworker, she is the author of *Liberated to the Bone*.

SEE narrative therapy
nepantla/ nepantleras

CONTRIBUTION

The field of Chicana Existentialism does not officially exist yet… The idea of a Chicano Existentialism is not new, but it is anemic and phallocentric.
—Mariana Alessandri[1]

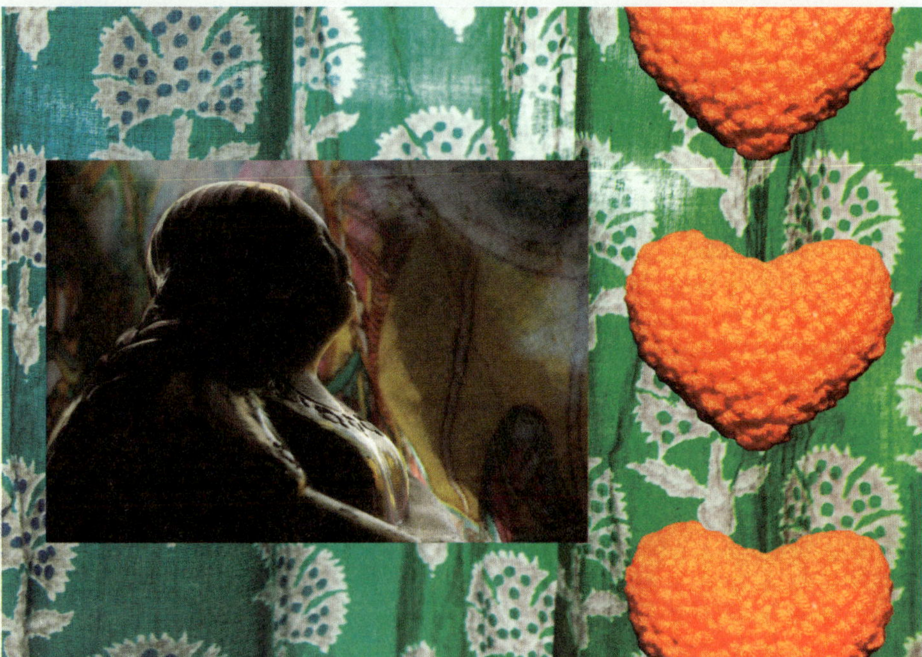

Coatlicue: Nepantlera Existencial © 2023 Coatlicue Sierra Rose.

EXISTENTIALISM IS A LOT OF THINGS, but pessimistic, it is not. In a 1963 interview, Black queer existential writer, activist, and playwright James Baldwin said, "I can't be a pessimist because I am alive. To be a pessimist means that you have agreed that human life is an academic matter,"[2] and mainstream academic discourses have a way of minimizing, depoliticizing, marginalizing, and silencing those who engage in this "philosophical practice that is premised upon concerns of freedom, anguish, responsibility, embodied agency, sociality, and liberation."[3] Existential angst is (among other things) a dizzying experience of radical empathy[4] in the face of abject aloneness, and the philosophical analysis this angst spurs creates cognitive dissonance that demands action. Whether that action results in action for liberation or for oppression depends on whether you lean more toward honesty or denial.

I knew for sure that I was an existentialist when I was reading autobiographical works by people of color with vitiligo, the autoimmune pigmentary condition I've had since my preteen years. Vitiligo starts small but can eventually devour every last melanocyte in your body in an unpredictable lifelong feeding frenzy. Sometimes it goes dormant for years before emerging from hibernation, hungry as a bear. Other times, it fucks off completely. There's no rhyme or reason and no way of knowing what it'll be like for you. The discovery of your first white spot, especially for people of color like me, can be alarming, frightening, anxiety-provoking, and dizzying. Existential philosophers describe this as the onset of an existential crisis. Jean-Paul Sartre called it anguish and nausea; Kierkegaard called it dread. But I've always related more fully to *La Reina* Gloria Anzaldúa's description of *el arrebato*, the kind of rupture that brings on *un choque*'s[5] cultural collision and dislocation, along with the whole family of emotions that hang with despair in her depressive

Coatlicue state that follows before psychosocial reintegration and community action are possible.

In time, I came to realize that my little voids in pigmentation were actually quite full, holding within them an unknowable future of life in a body displaying anything from a mottled pattern of reverse freckling to complete depigmentation. Autobiographers who came before me described waking up to find that their invasive new whiteness had colonized their face and hands, like splashes of white paint, or that their hair had turned suddenly platinum. I identified hard with their sudden and sustained deep sadness, anxiety, self-loathing, indignation, and anger. Queen Anzaldúa described this experience as *el susto*, the stunning aftershock of *el arrebato*.

As a Chicana with the kind of internalized *vergüenza* that growing up in an isolated environment of southern evangelical Christian white supremacy can create, I was confronted with the existential crisis of turning involuntarily white while navigating generational poverty, my developing identity, teen parenthood, and the mid-'90s neoliberal policy changes that shredded what was left of the U.S. social safety net for my generation onward.

Throughout her works, Anzaldúa spoke to the power of literacy, language, and the writing process as we experience lifelong cycles of rupture, shock, disintegration, and psychosocial integration. In a 1963 interview for *Life* magazine entitled "The Doom and Glory of Knowing Who You Are," Baldwin testifies to the strength of this medicinal practice:

> You think your pain and your heartbreak are unprecedented in the history of the world, but then you read. It was Dostoevsky and Dickens who taught me that the things that tormented me most were the very things that connected me with all the people who were alive, or who ever had been alive. Only if we face these open wounds in ourselves can we understand them in other people.[6]

I've always kept my library card right next to my electronic benefit transfer (EBT) cards. Feeding my soul by way of my mind has always taken the same precedence as hunger satiation. There have been countless times in my life that I've felt that, without books to help me make sense of it all through the experiences of others, what's the point of keeping my body alive? Countless hours at the public library with my mother and sister throughout my childhood taught me the deep and abiding truth of Baldwin's words.

Many years after my initial vitiligo diagnosis, I lived on South Padre Island while working at the University of Texas Rio Grande Valley. By this point, almost 100% of my pigment was gone and I'd developed a severe sun allergy, making my choice to live on an incessantly sunny tropical island questionable to some. Late one night, my teenaged daughter and one of her best friends frantically shook me from sleep and led me to the Gulf side of the island on foot. As my groggy brain began to shift the deserted beach scene into focus, I saw a vast, shimmering bioluminescence sparkling in the tide beneath the inky, star-strewn sky. During the day, this delicate blue glitter had been bleached out completely beneath the Texas sun's unrelenting onslaught. "Were the color white not historically claimed by light-skinned people who put dark-skinned people beneath them, it might be the clear choice for the color of depression—an overbearing whiteness that drives out all color."[7] Chicana existentialism resists this sun-blasted whitewash, awakening us to moonlit sands, ancient constellations, and a surf teeming with sparkling life. ❁

1 Alessandri, "Three Existentialist Readings of Gloria Anzaldúa's Borderlands/La Frontera," 121.

2 Baldwin and Perspectives, "The Negro and the American Promise," James Baldwin Interview.

3 Gordon, *Existence in Black: An Anthology of Black Existential Philosophy* (as cited in Alessandri, *"Three Existentialist Readings of Gloria Anzaldúa's Borderlands/La Frontera"*), 120.

4 Givens, *Radical Empathy: Finding a Path to Bridging Racial Divides.*

5 Anzaldúa, *Borderlands/La Frontera: The New Mestiza.*

6 Howard, "Doom and Glory of Knowing Who You Are," 89.

7 Alessandri, *Night Vision: Seeing Ourselves through Dark Moods*, 115.

B I O

Dr. Coatlicue S. Rose is a proud queer Xicanx healer, researcher, and policy nerd.

externalizing

SEE: agency, alternative identity projects, body neutrality, curiosity

CONTRIBUTION

THE MATTERING

Trauma. Empowerment. What do they mean? What do they mean to a therapist? What do they mean to a family in the face of violence? What do they mean to a family in the face of desire for connection?

During my training as a family therapist intern, I was disquieted by my therapeutic efforts to explore these questions. In turn, I initiated a curious, collaborative, and externalizing conversation to co-create meaning related to trauma and empowerment. Here, I will highlight the emergence of a new and different way to talk about, think about, and visualize dominant discourses around trauma and empowerment, through an externalizing conversation about "orbiting" and "bubbles." I want to acknowledge the tenacity and authenticity of the family I worked with, the fierce support and encouragement from my supervisor (now colleague). They have influenced my practice and me to bravely take risks, not letting important new ideas burn out, but instead remaining guiding stars in the sky.

THE JOURNEY

I met the Marvel family (all names and details are changed to protect the confidentiality of each family member), comprised of Sonia (mom), her 3 children, and 3 cats. Sonia is a single mother, with sole custody of her kids, whose father no longer has contact with them. Sonia shared that they moved to Calgary for her children to receive specialized mental health and school supports. I came to understand that a lot of the struggles they faced were due to the family's collective experience of trauma from domestic violence. The Marvel family came to therapy to help improve their relationships with each other.

My work focused on supporting healing interpersonal patterns through various strategies to empower mom and co-create ideas for connection.[1] During the first 11 sessions, I used trauma-informed tenets of safety, trust, choice, collaboration, and empowerment to anchor the work around a solid therapeutic alliance. I focused on Sonia's capabilities, values, expertise, and efforts through ongoing validation and identification of strengths in these areas. I also included reflecting teams to join me in this effort.

For example, we deconstructed the idea that "professional supports are better than personal supports." We discussed which supports were helpful or not, as an empowering strategy to offer her the opportunity to exert her expertise as a mother and validate family as a legitimate support. We brought forth the voice of her father and his pride and encouragement of Sonia, qualities about herself that are important to her and allow her to be a good mother. We externalized the impact of the experienced trauma, and how that gets in the way of her relationship with her son Danny. I shared the strengths I heard and noticed with Sonia throughout. To enhance a strengths perspective for Sonia I offered a therapeutic letter after the session.

THE GUIDE

Sonia often shared that it was hard for her to recognize her own strengths, noting that she was a different person since her violent relationship. During the 12th session Sonia shared with me that we said "all these nice things about her," but she couldn't believe them to be true for herself. I experienced a sense of disquiet leading up to this moment. I wondered how my strengths-based helping was not really helping. I decided in that moment to try to name my disquiet by acknowledging the barrier she shared. I asked Sonia if perhaps what she was experiencing was like a "bubble" surrounding her, preventing her from taking in these "nice comments." Sonia took up this metaphor and further noted that it was like these messages were "orbiting" around her. We continued to build on this metaphor of how she acknowledged the existence of her abilities but struggled to accept them to be true and a part of herself.

I then asked questions about who else on her team offered "orbiting" messages, and what they were. I noticed that it seemed easier for her to name and identify her strengths "from afar," so to speak. At the end of the session, when I asked what a next step would be, she shared, for the first time, that maybe she wanted to see that she was doing "all that she can" and to see her children were doing better and still learning and growing. I then left her with an invitation to notice: When the messages are orbiting, are they near or far? Do they ever stick to the bubble for a while or a little? What difference might it make to take the orbits in a little closer?

So, what did I learn? Listening for strengths and offering clients feedback of their strengths may not be sufficient in empowering someone to accept their own capabilities and improvements. The externalizing intervention emerged—one that was more deeply attuned to Sonia's experience, while co-creating new meanings of both trauma and empowerment.

A Clinical Guide

Orbiting strengths; moving beyond noticing and naming. Attending to the bubble

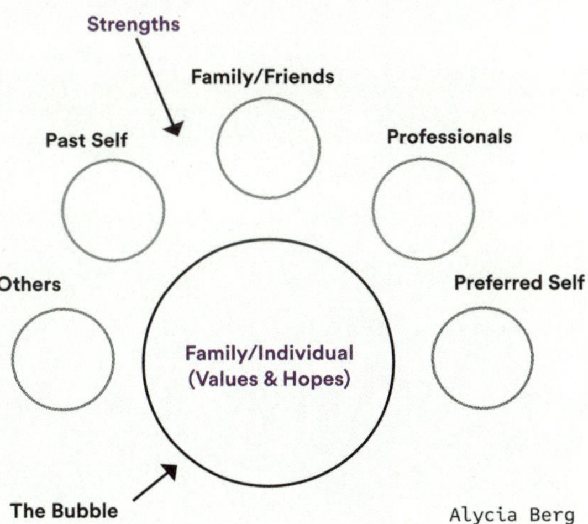

Alycia Berg

THE AFTERMATH: EXTERNALIZING FOR A COMMUNITY

Since this time, I have continued to use this diagram with individuals in my current public mental health practice. I credit the collaborative experience each time, so clients know there is a community of experiences like theirs. Individuals continue to resonate, in the same way Sonia did. For some it has evoked deep emotional responses. It seems to open the door to a new conversation, one that balances strengths/empowerment with barriers/trauma in an external, visual, validating, expansive, creative, and relational way.

I have wondered about further refinement to enhance the intervention as a phased approach. Perhaps the phases in the therapeutic process could be orbiting phase, bubble phase, embodying phase, and agency phase. I also have wondered about how values and hopes can and do remain at the heart

love
lunar cycle
Magic School, the
mapping support
marginality (as a site of resistance)
Marxist social work
membership theory in social work
mending
metaphor
mikveh
mobile libraries
movement lawyering
mutual aid
mycelia as metaphor
narradrama
narrative medicine
narrative therapy
nepantla/nepantleras
nonviolent communication
ongoingness
peer counseling
peer-to-peer health network
person-situation perspective
perspective via faith
pleasure
poems/poetry
poetic meter
polarity work
post-oppositionality
postwork imaginaries
poverty-aware social work paradigm, the
power threat meaning (PTM) framework
pre(care)ity
prison abolition
professionalism without performance
progressive education
public benefits
public library, the
Qigong
radical administration
radical care in the arts
radical childcare in movement spaces
radical inclusion
radical papermaking
radical presence
radical social work
Radical Therapist Journal, The
Rank and File Movement (RFM) in social work

reclaiming selfhood
recognition
redistribution
Reflecting on Justic
reflexivit
Reik
relationa
interviewing
relationalit
resistanc
resisting th
parental loss
narrative
resonanc
respectful visitir
respite room
rest as resistanc
reveng
revolutionar
mothering
ritua
sanctuar
sandplay therap
saur
seed bankir
sex positivit
shadow integratic
Sick Woman Theor
slow textile
slownes
social chang
ecosystem framework
social constructic
social practic
social therapeutic
Social Welfare Actic
Alliance, the
solidarit
solidarity econom
somatic healir
songs/singir
sound healir
speculative desic
spell
staying with th
trouble
storytellir
street newspape
strength
perspective, the
sufficienc
sustaining movemen
symbc
Taos Institute, th
tarc
temporary autonomou
zones
Theatre of th
Oppressed
theories of chanc
theosopl
therapeutic writir
togethernes
trans practice
transformativ
justice
traspati
12-step program
undercover anti
bullying teams
vigi
wate
wildnes
wintering as metaphc
wishe
witcher
yo
zinemakir

of a person, despite the orbiting experience of their own strengths. Perhaps this is a map towards weaving in existing and new ideas to radically help, with new externalizing visuals, new language, and new understanding around the complexities of people's lives. ❁

1 Tomm et al., *Patterns in Interpersonal Interactions: Inviting Relational Understandings for Therapeutic Change.*

BIO Alycia Berg (she/her) is a lifelong learner, social worker, and practicing therapist who strives to facilitate conversations that matter for people to co-create preferred pathways for healing & wellness in the context of their lives, families, communities, cultures, histories, and worlds.

EDITORS' NOTE In this piece, Alycia offers an application of "externalizing" that reveals its transformative power in the therapeutic process. At its core, externalizing language gives space so matters of identity can be negotiated rather than taken for granted. This perspective shift can lead to profound change, offering restored agency in the lives of those who seek our help. The nuance of this approach is rooted in narrative therapy and allows for the deconstruction of oppressive stories and the co-construction of alternative narratives that access preferences and hopes and dreams. —CH

CONTRIBUTION

~~FAALURE~~ *(autocorrect)* *FAILURE*

IF WE GO TO THE ROOT, several of our planet's ancient languages describe failure as a *stumbling*— *skhalate* in Sanskrit, *škarwidan* in Middle Persian, *sxalem* in Armenian.[1]

We are a hypersocial species, and feeling like a failure as a human can feel like a very personal end-times moment. It certainly does to me. We are tested regularly throughout our lives against the norms and standards of our time that seem utterly arbitrary from a wider, deeper perspective like, say, the life of a mountain or an island or a dragon. I've failed at so many things and then cursed myself for the failing itself. Blaming myself for not being the things I am "supposed" to be. Blaming myself, essentially, for being myself.

I have failed, continue to fail, at beauty, at fashion, at heterosexuality, at not hating myself. I have repeatedly failed the mysterious Body Mass Index, I regularly fail at being a woman, an adult, a child. I fail daily at being an animal in a body—even though this is one of my favourite things to be. I fail at being the successful, confident brand that will win me the money I need to survive. I have failed maths exams and so many tests I didn't even know I was taking—I have failed to have the right accent, the appropriate clothes, the correct haircut, the right music taste. I have failed to attract the people I wanted to attract. I have failed at knowing how to talk at parties, I have failed at being a friend, lover, family member, I have failed to love and to believe. I am a most exuberant failed Catholic.

I have failed so many times at writing this piece. I failed to meet multiple deadlines that the editors generously offered—I don't even know if they will include this in the publication, that's how late I am.

But if I can pause between my shallow, anxious breaths, and take in a deep long one, let it out through my hips to the floor, I see it is not the failure that makes us ill. It's the stories we digest about failure, the lies we've been told about failure; it's how we feel about failure. We associate failure with a not-enough-ness or a not-successful-ness judged largely by capitalist, white, patriarchal measures, by tests and exams that test and examine us, by standards made up in R&D rooms of marketing and advertising companies, engineered to spill over to our peers and to people who know us only through a small bright screen.

***

In *The Queer Art of Failure*, Jack Halberstam asks, "What kind of rewards can failure offer us?"[2]

One is the stumbling. As toddlers we learn how to walk by stumbling, falling, sitting down unexpectedly midstride or tumbling forward on toes to reach the place where we can hold on to something. We keep stumbling and mistake-making and we are (largely) loved for it. Faces smile, hands clap, arms stretch towards us. As adults if we trip, we laugh at ourselves and feel foolish, even if no one else sees us. Why are we so embarrassed by stumbling, tripping, falling? We learned that once you've grown up mistakes are bad, stumbling is stupid, and failure is a sin. ➔

The story of failure hangs heavy and old in the recovering Catholic in me. The original failure to be perfect, failure as sin. The Fall from all graces. But that is not my story. That fall is different from stumbling and forgets all that happens in the falling. The moments before we hit the ground. The possibility of never hitting the ground.

When we stumble, an obstacle throws us off balance, trips us up, sets us to falling. We learn what it means to fall and how to catch ourselves. When we stumble, often someone comes to help keep us upright. Other times we have to do it for ourselves. Still again are the times we splat on the ground with nothing to break our fall.

Stumbling into being.

***

Some of the most painful times in my life were internal crises deeply rooted in the oldest stories of not-good-enough-ness, not-straight-enough-ness and not gender-conforming-enough-ness, not to mention not being-happy-enough-ness. I spent many years—whole decades!—failing at being myself. I slashed off desires, needs, selves at an alarming rate, and was confused to see myself increasingly empty, going about the world part dead, like an uninhabited shell.

I didn't understand that my failures (in the given understanding of success under neoliberal capitalism—consumption, accumulation, growth as status) were some of the most interesting, brilliant parts of me, of the community and of the creatures and landscape around me. Failure to succeed here is not negative—it's what makes us beautiful unique creative magical strong connected.

Being with the stumbling, though, is the healing; welcoming the gorgeous failures within you; letting yourself stumble, fall even, knowing that this is what it means to be human. Here we will find healing and help; here we will catch ourselves off-balance, foolish, laughing and loving. We will catch someone else's eye as we trip and wink and grin. We will shout bravo and genuinely clap when we see someone stumble on the street. We will keep stumbling. We will reach out arms to ourselves and each other. We will see differently.

The stumbling moment of failure is so rich with possibility; we do not grow or heal without it. Healing is relational, so let us fail to be individuals. Let us fail to be right all the time. Let us call home all the lost, exiled parts of ourselves, let us re-member. Let us stumble into ever deepening relationships, hoping to continually make mistakes, striving to fail more lovingly each time. Knowing that most times the mistake itself—our failure—is the growth and the discovery, is us loving ourselves, is the fabric that holds us all together. ❁

1 etymonline.com.

2 Halberstam, *The Queer Art of Failure*, 3.

BIO Fid Thompson is a queer writer, gardener, artist, friend, and f/allower, in love with all the languages this world has to offer.

fat positivity

SEE: somatic healing

CONTRIBUTION

Healing from Internalized Anti-Fat Bias

I'D LIKE TO BEGIN my entry with some background information to be sure that you understand the context and reasoning for what I'll offer to you at the end. After more than ten years supporting fat people to heal their relationships with their bodies as a fat yoga teacher, wellness coach, group facilitator, and now yoga therapist, I've noticed some trends, both through my own journey of healing and in those I work with. Living in the world as a fat person is a traumatizing experience, but many fat people don't realize that this is the case. We are routinely gaslighted by medical and wellness professionals, friends, and family, while also receiving incessant subtle and overt messages from the media about the wrongness of our bodies and, as an extension, the wrongness of ourselves.

Many people believe that fat folks are fat either because they don't know how to care for themselves or they don't care about their health. As a result, many thin people give fat people truly harmful advice that is misguided and often unsolicited. This advice is rooted in their own assumptions about fat people, not in the reality of the person's life or experiences. When repeated over and over again (as is often the case), the experience of hearing this advice results in fat people coming to believe negative things about themselves that are not true.

For example, many of my clients express to me that they believe they are lazy, and that they do little to nothing in the way of self-care. They blame themselves for their physical and emotional suffering and believe that if they could just get it together, they would exercise more, eat less, be thin(ner), and as a result, feel immeasurably better in every way. They have internalized the false rhetoric fed to them by society that says that being fat is a moral failing and a punishment of sorts, and that it directly leads to a huge number of health issues.

In reality, most of these clients of mine have actually been working incredibly hard their entire lives to 1) cope with the feelings of inadequacy and defectiveness they've internalized because of the messages we *all* receive about fat people and the way people treat them, and 2) do everything in their power to become thin. Most of them do a great deal to take care of themselves, but they don't recognize it because what they're doing hasn't resulted in weight loss.

So with all of that in mind, here's what I do with my fat clients:

If they haven't already, I help them to recognize that they have likely internalized the anti-fat bias that has been directed toward them. This can be a long-term process that often requires education through books and podcasts (see resource list below). I guide them toward understanding that the best thing they can do for their health and well-being is to begin to see themselves in a new, positive way.

I point out how resilient their body is. Through all the restrictive diets and punishing exercise and harsh judgments, their body has persevered and carried them forward. I guide them toward beginning to see their body with eyes of love and compassion, rather than eyes of judgment and disdain. I point out how and why they are worthy of love and compassion.

I always give them choice when it comes to movement. I remove hierarchy from movement options and guide them to choose the options that they think would feel best in the moment. I encourage them to gently experiment, supporting them in discovering that movement can be pleasurable and gentle, rather than a painful, exhausting punishment.

I help them cultivate gratitude for the ways their body has protected them, fought for them, and helped them experience joy and pleasure. I tell them that fatness is not wrong or a mistake or a disease. →

I ask them if they can find delight in the softness, power, and comfort that their body provides.

I invite them to find their reflection in the round moon, the curve of a wave, the plumpness of the very best fruits, helping them to see that they belong here, among the other wonders of nature.

I support them as they begin to forge this different way of relating to and thinking about their bodies—celebrating the victories and growth and normalizing the struggles and pain. I help them to see that all people have struggles, their pain is not their fault, and intentional weight loss is never the quick fix that it's made out to be. ❁

Resource list

Podcasts:

- *Maintenance Phase*
- *Food Psych*
- *She's All Fat*

Blog:

- *Dances With Fat*

Movie:

- *Fattitude*

Books:

- *What We Don't Talk about When We Talk about Fat* by Aubrey Gordon
- *The Body Is Not an Apology* by Sonya Renee Taylor
- *Things No One Will Tell Fat Girls: A Handbook for Unapologetic Living* by Jes Baker
- *Fearing the Black Body: The Racial Origins of Fat Phobia* by Sabrina Strings

Other Resources:

- Association for Size Diversity and Health
- HAES health sheets (haeshealthsheets.com)

BIO Naomi Finkelstein (she/her) is a fat yoga therapist (C-IAYT), health and well-being coach, and Be Body Positive facilitator who is passionate about helping people heal from diet culture and develop a loving and nurturing relationship with their precious bodies.

body as community
body neutrality
body positivity
Body Trust
embodied knowledge
intuitive eating

SEE: reclaiming selfhood; recognition; redistribution; Reflecting on Justice; reflexivity; Reiki; relational interviewing; relationality; resistance; resisting the parental loss narrative; resonance; respectful visiting; respite rooms; rest as resistance; revenge; revolutionary mothering; ritual; sanctuary; sandplay therapy; sauna; seed banking; sex positivity; shadow integration; Sick Woman Theory; slow textiles; slowness; social change ecosystem framework; social construction; social practice; social therapeutics; Social Welfare Action Alliance, the; solidarity; solidarity economy; somatic healing; songs/singing; sound healing; speculative design; spells; staying with the trouble; storytelling; street newspapers; strengths perspective, the; sufficiency; sustaining movements; symbol; Taos Institute, the; tarot; temporary autonomous zones; Theatre of the Oppressed; theories of change; theosophy; therapeutic writing; togetherness; trans practices; transformative justice; traspatio; 12-step programs; undercover anti-bullying teams; vigil; water; wildness; wintering as metaphor; wishes; witchery; yoga; zinemaking

CONTRIBUTION

Just *Girls: Weathering the Patriarchal Storm*

"HUMAARE SAMAAJ MEIN LADKI HONA HI GUNAAH HAI" (being a girl is a crime in our society)—these words by fourteen-year-old Rhea echoed the sentiments of countless young women growing up in a society where there are widespread daily accounts of gender-based violence. Where girls are killed even before they are born because they bring "*baddua*" (curse), where the mother of a child with a disability is blamed for bringing "*badkismat*" (bad luck) into the family, and where girls who challenge patriarchy are seen as "*badchalan*" (characterless). Where every step away from society's warped idea of morality is shamed, stigmatised, and, at times, even banished.

We are trained into self-surveillance from an early age so as to jump through culturally sanctioned hoops. This indoctrination is dangerous because it's invisible to us. It's like the air we breathe day in and day out, in our homes, schools, movies, literature, advertisements, news, and not to forget, on social media.

Therefore, it isn't a surprise that mental health struggles in girls have skyrocketed, propelled by the pandemic. It's convenient to blame them with the refrain "girls these days!" rather than look at the cultural context that breeds this dangerous self-surveillance. Convenient labels like depression, anxiety, eating disorders, self-harm, and addictions are a reflection of harm being done to women. In my decades of work as a therapist, I have never seen such intensity of self-doubt, self-hatred, and sense of failure among women as I'm seeing now. Where the internalised judgements of not measuring up to society's standards of beauty, worthiness, and goodness rob them of a sense of agency, purpose, and connection.

It shows how significant it becomes for us to be accountable as a collective rather than seeing "measuring up" as an individual responsibility. It would also be absurd to assume that women are passive recipients of hardships. Resistance has taken shape as social movements led by women on a larger scale in India, such as *Justice for Nirbhaya*, *Narmada Bachao Andolan*, the *Shaheen Bagh protest*, the *Chipko movement*, *Irom Sharmila*, *Mothers of Manipur*, and the recent women wrestlers' protests, all of which have shaken the cobwebs of our male-dominated society.

For example, Rhea had been referred to me for "anger management" after she stood up to her school's male principal when he asked her to take her male classmate's offensive comments about her body as a compliment. He added that she had invited it upon herself by keeping the top two buttons of the school T-shirt open. The next day, all the girls (and some boys) in the class turned up to school with the top buttons open! When I asked Rhea what she would call this act, she said with a smile, "*Dar ka button kholna*" (unbuttoning fear)! A big salute to micro-acts of reclamation of justice and solidarity.

JUST GIRLS

A typical social response is to dismiss girls as "just *girls*." As if they don't matter, their voices can be silenced. Thus, through a play of words and a little punning, in our organisation we call this initiative "*Just* Girls," a solidarity of women coming together for justice—to externalise what has been internalised, to politicise what has been personalised, and to visibilise the invisibilised.

We use the metaphor of a **Courage** journey to explain and keep track of our work together. It has helped us to navigate our challenges as well as "just steps" that have supported young women to flip the gaze on patriarchy and have a sense of agency, reclaim their preferred identity, and foster solidarity.

Maybe you would like to try it out too? (Irrespective of your gender, race, religion, etc.)

Charting our territory—What are the recent challenges/storms (big or small) that you've had to face in life? What name would you give them? ➔

agency
body positivity
collective care
critical suicide studies
feminist ethic of care
life cycle, honoring the

On the stepping stones—What are tiny, little, or big things that you do every day, despite the presence of these storms, that sustain you and keep you going?

Using the compass—What are the values and beliefs that make you stand strong and carry on?

Resistance Torch—What names would you give to the big storms in your culture in terms of societal pressure? How do people end up internalising these storms and questioning their worth? How does it push them into isolating themselves, comparing themselves with others, and totalising their worth? What are the small ways in which you have lit your Resistance Torch to stand up to the "patriarchal storm"?

Along with the tribe—Who are the people who introduced you to these skills of survival or are aware that these things are important to you? If someone was to get to know you over months and years, what would they learn to appreciate about you?

Gifts to fellow travellers—What hopes do you have of contributing to your community or tribe? What small or big steps are you taking to support others in their journey of life?

Enduring adversity and finding our North Star—What stopped you from seeing yourself as a victim but more as a survivor/a fighter/a courage traveller? What would you call this skill that is able to endure and withstand all the storms?

As a young woman once remarked, "We are trees with deep roots, storms may try to destroy us, but if we stand together as a forest and have strong roots, nothing can bring us down."

Mental health struggles in women conceal issues of social injustice. We cannot be complicit in reproducing the misogynistic culture. *Just* Girls is as a micro-social movement that started in the therapy spaces and has started creating tiny ripples. It has invited conversations on collectivising **Courage** experiences so that the problems are not seen as personal failing, but as issues of social justice where people can come together to cross-pollinate their insider knowledge and skills of living through letters, documents, poems, and songs.

Acknowledgement to all the young women who are on this *Courage* journey.
To know more about the Just Girls collective
childrenfirstindia.com/narrative-collective-india/just-girls/

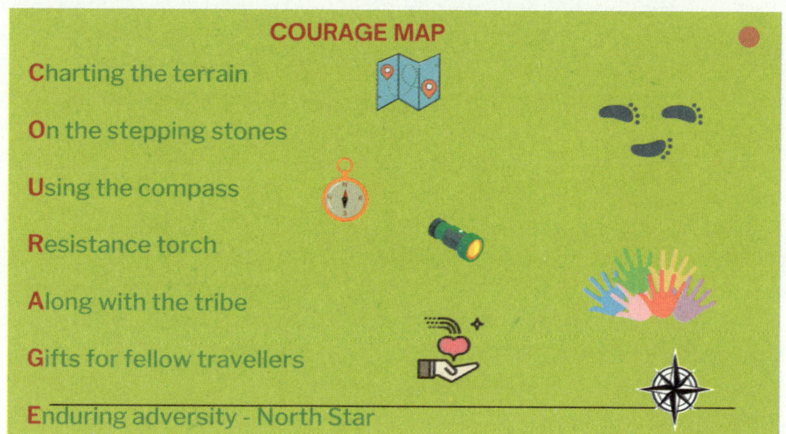

BIO Shelja Sen is a narrative therapist, writer, co-founder of Children First, and international faculty at Dulwich Centre, Adelaide.

feminist ethics of care

SEE: rest as resistance, slow textiles, slowness, traspatio

CONTRIBUTION

Sloppy Stitching as an Embodiment of Feminist Ethics of Care

FEMINIST ETHICS OF CARE developed in the late twentieth century as an alternative to established moral theories, such as Kantian ethics and utilitarianism, amidst a revolutionary surge in the validation of women's experience as part of a feminist movement.[1] From its beginnings as a critique of liberal individualism prevalent in the dominant moral theories that regard persons as independent rather than relational,[2] care has evolved as a conceptualisation and set of practices that challenge neoliberal capitalism's ability to address the current existential crises in forms of environmental deterioration and social inequalities.[3] One of the most widely cited definitions of the "ethics of care" is that by Joan Tronto and Berenice Fisher:

> On the most general level, we suggest that caring be viewed as a species activity that includes everything that we do to maintain, continue and repair our "world" so that we can live in it as well as possible. That world includes our bodies, ourselves, and our environment, all of which we seek to interweave in a complex, life-sustaining web.[4]

Jacqueline Millner, leader of the *CARE Network*, a group of Australian feminist artists and researchers, observes that imagining alternatives to prominent economic structures and practices is particularly advantageous to artists, many of whom are working in neoliberal societies. The network (and associated *Care Project*) exemplifies this advantage by generating new knowledge through research that employs care as a strategy and a platform for art practice.[6]

My practice-based PhD project applies a theoretical framework of care to position the creative work it is generating. The project is interested in crafting a holistic feminist strategy that encompasses three interrelated forms of care, including: care for the environment; care for the familial and cultural histories of women's reproductive labour and textile-based work; and self-care. As such, the project aims to embody and extend a feminist ethics of care as both "value and practice,"[7] utilising it as a framework for a practice that proposes an antidote to neoliberal structures of production and consumption.[8]

The key hypothesis of my research is that by focusing upon the historical relationship between women and needlework, an alternative approach to stitching can be employed to protest patriarchal regimes and represent a form of action, thereby asserting a feminist ethics of care. My project proposes a specific methodology of stitching that subverts textile's normative move towards perfection in craft histories. It does so by affirming a process of *sloppy stitching* as an integrated concept and practice functioning as a counter-technique which embodies the project's material and ethical concerns. This idiosyncratic methodology (as *sloppy* implies carelessness) simultaneously communicates rejection of skill associated with a patriarchal context of production in which women historically learned and practiced embroidery and reclaims needlework as a resilient and relevant feminist practice. ❁

abundance
access invocations
accessibility
activating archives
Afrofuturism
agency
aging positivity
altar work
alternative identity projects
ancestral wisdom
ancestrality
anti-ableism
anti-adultism
anti-racism
anti-racism court system
art
art as/in/of life
art journaling
art therapy
art workers
art-based group work
arts in medicine
arts-based research
Authentic Movement
autonomous healing
Ayurveda
being with
Bertha Capen Reynolds
bike and car repair collectives
Black Panther Party Free Breakfast Program
body as community
body neutrality
body positivity
Body Trust
boredom
brave space
breaking the rules
bridge as metaphor
care pods
care-based co-housing
Catholic Worker Movement
centering maintenance
circular economy
climate cafes
clouds as metaphor
coalition
collaborative apprenticeship
collective care
common pool resources
commons, the
communing with animals
community college
community gardens
community newspapers
conjure
constructionist-design framework, the
consulting your consultants
contemplative tradition, the
corn knowledge
credit unions
crip time
critical fabulation
critical hope
critical pedagogy
critical race theory
critical suicide studies
critical whiteness

Remediation III, 2022, Turmeric and beetroot dye, bra lace and thread on recycled shirt, 58 x 37 cm.

1 Held, *The Ethics of Care*, 23.

2 Held, *The Ethics of Care*, 13.

3 Millner and Coombs, *Care Ethics and Art*, 1.

4 Tronto and Fisher, “Toward a Feminist Theory of Caring,” 61.

5 Millner and Moore, *Contemporary Art and Feminism*, 163–164.

6 Millner and Moore, *Contemporary Art and Feminism*.

7 Held, *The Ethics of Care*, 9.

8 Millner and Moore, *Contemporary Art and Feminism*.

BIO Monika Cvitanovic is an artist and a PhD candidate (UNSW, Australia) who uses stitching as a feminist strategy of care encompassing both her lineage of textile-based practices and textiles in circulation.

femini
intergenerational living

fermentation

SEE: solidarity

CONTRIBUTION

'FERMENTATION' IS...

sour acid raw bacteria poland family home deli
sharing 'same but different' stinks perseverance Korea
Iran commercialised hip viewpoint farmers fields
trans*formation bubbly foamy garlic dill salt
no vinegar ongoing tradition 'the longer the better' crunchy
'better together' juicy cond -iment /-om migration jar boil
steamed upside down disinfected green lid struggle
soil aunties zupa ogórkowa patience mis/understood cozy
classic yellow

...when I think about:

summers spent in the polish countryside. cozily tucked in between golden fields of rye and oat. sitting in the shade to escape the dry heat. empty jars, lining the concrete yard floor. they had been disinfected with hot and steamy water in a giant metal pot. aunty H gave us plenty of *ogórki gruntowe* from her farm, grandpa's place of birth. then, he would fetch garlic, dill, and horse-radish from the weekly market in the town twenty kilometers from our village. mum and dad and aunty W sat on plastic chairs—their hands thoroughly washed to prevent mold spores from spreading—stuffing the jars in front of them with the aromatics. placed neatly at the bottom of the jars. leaving as little space as possible between the bundle of dill and the stinking root vegetables. then the small and slightly thorny gherkins came atop. under the wary eye of grandpa, the last ingredients were administered: a heaping spoon of salt, and boiling water poured directly from the kettle to the jars' rims. no vinegar but time to be patient and wait, as the jars rested upside-down.

i guess, the story could end here. leaving you with a good feeling of my sentimental *and* useful recipe to make polish-style dill pickles. but to me the dill pickle is far more than a condiment. more than cucumbers soaked in sour, fizzy brine. it is a metaphor for rural temporalities, a sharing economy, being severed from our ancestral soil, and the perseverance of immigrants.

i grew up in germany, the country which used to kidnap my ancestors to work on nazi fields. for me, as a child of polish and irani immigrant parents, the dill pickle was integral to maintaining my identity within these hostile lands. one and the same pickle jar could be used to make my mum's *zupa ogórkowa* and my dad's *salade shirazi*. now on Turtle Island, i buy similar ones at the kosher jewish deli where the pickles chill in a huge bucket. honestly, i'm mesmerized by how the dill pickle unites the many different geographies which i call home.

apart from the dill pickle, fermentation also reminds me of bitchin' with my [w]asian friends about hipsters making money out of cultures they once apprehended. calling out their white silence, when anti-asian hate is sweeping through the world, but non-Koreans make money out of selling their overpriced, yet spiceless and toned-down appropriation of kimchi in organic supermarkets across gentrified neighborhoods.

the dill pickle is inherently about solidarity; an interspecies group effort! a testimony that we as humans are inherently symbiotic. when we put those firm and crunchy gherkins into the jar, we aren't doing the labour of fermentation. we rely on anaerobic *lactobacillus* bacteria, who were living their best

lives on the gherkin's skins until they got trapped in our jars. without air, these fighters don't give up, starting to eat away at the gherkin's natural sugars and pooping out lactic acid. in return, making our jars sour and fizzy. [fun fact, lactic acid is also what makes our muscles feel 'sore'].

ok, back to my recipe: two weeks have passed since my family's afternoon spent pickling. the lid makes a hefty *plop* sound, as we open the first jar. while bubbles rush to the surface, grandpa examines the fruit of our labour, pierces into the jar with a clean fork. [yupp, mold can still spoil the jar, so be care_ful!] grandpa gives me the first pickle, my teeth cut through it, the once crunchy gherkin remains whole on the outside yet is bloated inside now. brine bursts in my mouth, as i suck the juices out of the pickle. i swallow the first bite in delight and declare: *są dobre*! [they taste good!]. our interspecies solidarity continues, as the *lactobacillus* bacteria now reside in my gut. in return for being fed, they shall make my gut healthier until one day, we shall finally return to the soil together, next to where my aunty picked the cucumbers and my grandchildren shall as well.

and with a jar full of pickle brine,
i cheer to this,
na zdrowie, به سلامتی, לחיים!

BIO princex naveed is a polish/irani/jewish artist (performance, installation, poetry) and humanities scholar.

body as community
community gardens
dérive, t
interspecies organizing

SEE: respectful visiting

CONTRIBUTION

flâner, verb, [flâ·ne·r]

To stroll around the streets. Derived from the French word, flâneur (noun), meaning an idle man-about-town.

I AM LUCKY TO LIVE IN A PART OF THE WORLD that is filled with stunning beauty. Flowers blooming, squirrels burrowing in the succulents, rocky terrain next to a super bloom along the hillside, and the ocean booming in the distance.

I've learned that whenever I feel stuck, going outside with a sense of curiosity helps. I bundle up, placing my hoodie over my head to protect myself from the gusty fog. Headphones in. Escaping from the sounds of traffic. I usually start out a little frustrated. Maybe I'm impatient and thinking how stupid this is and how cold I am. Sometimes it takes longer for my shaky legs to make it one block. After a while, my anxious energy dissipates down my legs carrying me up and down the hills. I begin noticing things around me. Signs scribbled by kids hanging in a house's window, a nautical mailbox that I'd never noticed, the new bloom appearing on my favorite tree. I let my body carry me at the pace it needs, to the places it wants to go. I allow myself, for this walk, the simple pleasures of being completely lost and found at the same time.

Experiencing the world around me helps me to ground myself. I feel more connected with the human experience. It helps give me perspective. While the idea of "nature bathing" has become more common and I am a huge proponent of communing with animals (SEE communing with animals), there are benefits to wandering even if you don't have nature nearby. It's possible to get many of the same benefits by giving yourself permission to wander no matter where you are. I recently discovered a word that describes this exact experience. *Flâner* is the French saying for wandering aimlessly through a city.

The beauty of this word is that you are not lost, but intentionally exploring and being curious about your surroundings. I might run into a neighbor and give them a good morning wave, help hold open the door so a delivery man can more easily bring in packages, or watch a shop clerk greet their customers.

While it can be difficult to take time away in our hyper-productive world, I've found giving yourself space can turn out to be a huge time-saver. If a 30-minute walk can kick-start my inspiration, then I've saved time I would have wasted writing and rewriting drivel.

The more I've leaned into social justice work, the more I've learned the importance of connection and community in my life. These flâner moments allow me to feel more connected with real people (*not faceless internet users*), which grows my connection with myself. As a collective, we become better grounded into the present so we can best show up for ourselves and others. I've found my best work comes when I am connected to myself. ❁

BIO Sam Chavez is a writer, strategist, curious human, and founder of Roots of Change Agency, which empowers activists and organizations to cultivate social change through storytelling.

SEE: ancestral wisdom
circular economy
community gardens
life cycle, honoring the

CONTRIBUTION

Togetherness Is Like Dough: A Meditation on Food, June Jordan, and Togetherness as a Method

LIVING IS NOT AN ATOMIZED ACT. Instead, living is an act that requires us to be masters of prepositions, always moving toward and against, among and besides, and inside and around each other.[1] Our baseline way of being is what I'll call an uninterrupted togetherness—a fact perhaps brought into relief most by eating.

An exercise of the imagination: Envision an apple on your dining table, anticipating your first bite, and consider all the hands it had to touch before landing in yours. At some point, that apple was grown, harvested, processed, and packaged before you selected and purchased the fruit from, let's say, a supermarket. When the apple satiates your appetite, maybe you compost what's left, toss the carcass in a trash bin, or enact a more inventive way of handling the remains. Regardless, it's irrefutable that your apple is an assemblage of countless people's time, labor, and expertise, from farmers to drivers to cashiers to scientists to sanitation workers. And let's not forget the linchpin role of the more-than-human world at every turn.

Everything we eat originates in a matrix of food systems; our food systems originate from a togetherness that is the cell-deep connective tissue between all Earthlings. However, it is not a togetherness that reliably administers variations of care, such as empathy, equity, and tenderness. Thinking alongside professor and author Christina Sharpe, who has written about beauty as a *method* for incubating new ways of being, we might consider how matters of what we feed ourselves and each other help us understand that togetherness is also a method that can invite a multiplicity of ends.[2] A particular June Jordan poem feels useful here.

In Jordan's "Focus in Real Time," a deceptively mundane bowl of rice is more than fare for delighting in the company of others, shorthand for affection, or "just" sustenance. It disguises a ledger of violences, including those that compose the substrate of food systems in the United States. Early in the poem, a series of interrogations have us consider all the relationships—seen and unperceived, tangible and immaterial, in our timeline and haunting us from others—that pulsate beneath the meal's seemingly static surface, that make the meal possible:

Who grew these grains
Who owned the land
Who harvested the crop
Who converted these soft particles to money
Who kept the cash
Who shipped the consequences of the cash
Who else was going to eat the rice
Who else was going to convert the rice to cash[3]

Jordan suggests that though togetherness was inherent to making the rice, it is a togetherness rife with brutality's many faces. Urgently, she calls us to bear witness to and remember farm worker

exploitation and histories of enslavement (*Who grew these grains, Who harvested the crop*), legacies of land theft and desecration (*Who owned the land*), inadequate compensation for the arduous task of feeding (*Who kept the cash*), and asymmetrical access to nourishing food (*Who else was going to eat the rice*). The rice's mundanity dissolves into a pool of perversities. Jordan's food lens reminds us that no form of togetherness is a ready-made gesture toward transformation, love, or repair. Togethernesses that are transforming, loving, and repairing are like dough, in that we must forge and shape them with intention, especially to reorient it all: our power dynamics, community formations, and the values that mobilize us. Togethernesses that are transforming, loving, and repairing charge us with obliterating unworkable arrangements adopted from an unworkable present.

A togetherness builds the bedrock for a specific architecture for living; a togetherness is rehearsal for a particular reality. The architectures and realities we end up with depend on us. As the pandemic continues to demonstrate, there are moving, sweet togethernesses, like those that surface when performing domestic rituals with a loved one. And some togethernesses establish cruel communions. Police officers agglutinating like cancer cells to dispense terror in our streets come to mind. Somewhere in the middle, just-are togethernesses unfurl, such as when teenagers transform parking lots into living rooms. In our pursuit of more moving, sweet togethernesses, especially those that will help invoke the counter-worlds we have reached for across lifetimes, food, again, is instructive. More specifically, the framework of food sovereignty can be a compass.

Food sovereignty aims to make real a togetherness in our food systems anchored in "the people's right to determine their own agricultural and food policies;"[4] its vision provides a method for being together in ways that revere the beyond-human realm and dislodge systems predicated on power hoarding, ungovernable growth, and unprejudicial extermination. More particularly, food sovereignty as technology offers togetherness tenets that yield new, emboldening answers to familiar questions: *Who grew these grains* (our community, which owns the means of production and uses local and ancestral methods that don't undermine the value of our more-than-human relations), *Who harvested the crop* (our beloved food providers, who are at the center of all decision-making related to our food production), *Who owned the land* (we have removed the land from the enclosure of privatization, remembering it as our kin), *Who kept the cash* (we decommodify food, ensuring it is always accessible and not a tool for profit-making), *Who else was going to eat the rice* (we know food is a "basic" need, not a private good that creates illusions of food scarcity or deservingness). Food sovereignty aims to collapse the "right-now" in favor of a "could-be" only possible through carefully orchestrated relationalities.

A togetherness within food sovereignty is localized seed banking, the reclamation of the agricultural know-how of generations past, and neighbor-fueled pantries. Food sovereignty graces us with a togetherness ethic rooted in trust, mutualism, horizontal power, regeneration, abundance, and intergenerational intimacy. And it is an ethic within a broader constellation of maps toward being

solidarity
sufficiency
temporary autonomous zones
togetherness

together, better. Ethics for crafting moving, sweet togethernesses are everywhere, including beyond our plates. They are in clouds, among vegetal life, in our dreamscapes, all begging us to ask: Where in my togethernesses are there opportunities to challenge the status quo, with whom and what can I erect better togethernesses, and what togethernesses are most needed right now? ❁

1 Boyer, *A Handbook of Disappointed Fate*, 67–69.

2 Sharpe, "Beauty Is a Method."

3 "Focus in Real Time," from *Directed by Desire: The Complete Poems of June Jordan*, Copper Canyon Press © Christopher D. Meyer, 2007. Reprinted by permission of the Frances Goldin Literary Agency.

4 McMichael, "Food Sovereignty, Social Reproduction, and the Agrarian Question."

BIO Amirio Freeman, writer and interviewer who explores the relationship between humans and our more-than-human kin, creator of *The Down to Earth Deck* (Loam, 2022).

ancestral wisdom
bridge as metaphor
communing with animals
dérive, th
energy wor

forest bathing

SEE: pleasure, respectful visiting, ritual, somatic healing, sound healing, wildness

CONTRIBUTION

ALICE: I first heard of “forest bathing” from my grandmother, who lived for most of her adult life in Kaohsiung, a city that has suffered from poor air due to its own urban development as well as the drift of pollutants from neighboring industrial regions. She loved going for walks and claimed that her favorite ones were those taken on visits to see my family in New York when I was a child. There were many walking paths through dense woods near our home at that time. During these walks, she always had a serene smile on her face while breathing slowly, deeply, fully: this was her forest bath.

KAREN: My paternal grandparents grew up in Japanese-Taiwan. When I was a child, they would visit us, and every morning they took walks outside. Sometimes I would join them. My feet never gained mileage until I moved to New York City. Life as a pedestrian connected my physical and emotional spaces. Walking home from work, walking my dogs, walking with nowhere to go: my mind would clear through the overflow of senses. Over a decade ago, I traded the urban cacophony for the loneliness of the suburbs. The same route, past the same homes, on the same streets, is somehow always different. On my walks, I listen to the wind, the crows, little chickadees and juncos, muffled traffic, barking dogs, sometimes frogs. There is refuge in ritual. I only learned of the term “forest bath” a few years ago. This allowed me to give a feeling a name. ❁

BIOS

Karen Hsu is a middle-aged mother, middle child, and one-third of the design studio Omnivore.

Alice Chung is a designer, educator, wife, mother, learner, and one-third of the design studio Omnivore.

EDITORS' NOTE

The concept and term “forest bathing,” known in Japanese as *shinrin-yoku*, developed in Japan in the 1980s as an antidote to the stresses of daily life and has since been studied by researchers around the world. The practice involves retreating into the forest (“bathing”), sometimes with a guide who leads various activities that engage the five senses. In this brief conversation, Alice and Karen (Julie Cho's studio partners) remind us that many people practice forest bathing without realizing that their actions connect to a codified therapeutic activity. —ES

fragments/fragmentation

SEE: clouds as metaphor, existentialism, liminality

CONTRIBUTION

The beauty of the world which is so soon to perish, has two edges, one of laughter, one of anguish, cutting the heart asunder. —Virginia Woolf

A fragment must as a miniature work of art be entirely isolated from the surrounding world and perfect in itself like a hedgehog. —Friedrich Schlegel

POSTMODERN WRITER DONALD BARTHELME has one of his characters utter the line "fragments are the only forms I trust."[1] Often when one is trying to make sense of one's life, it only comes to one in fragments, not in a totality. We are a mosaic of fragments. One of the founders of 19th-century Romanticism, the poet/philosopher Friedrich Schlegel, the first philosopher of the fragmentary, remarked, "My whole self is a system of fragments." His friend Novalis felt similarly: "My nature consists of moments."[3] Art historian Linda Nochlin argues that the fragment is a metaphor of modernity.[3] Two key literary examples are Coleridge's poem "Kubla Khan" and T. S. Eliot's poem "The Waste Land." Coleridge tells us that while he was composing it in 1797 he was interrupted by a caller, and when he returned to finish the poem he couldn't remember how it was to continue and as a result it remained a fragment.[4] Towards the end of Eliot's poem is the line "these fragments I have shored against my ruins" as the poem is constructed from fragments.[5] A literary work can be exceedingly long yet still a fragment, as is the case with Marcel Proust's massive novel, *In Search of Lost Time* (1913–27), which brings us to a realization that sublime happiness and a sense of wholeness can stem from the accumulation of mere fragments of existence, even the most banal—the taste of a madeleine, the sound of a clinking spoon, the unevenness of two paving stones.[6]

Postmodernists generally argue against totality, with philosopher Jean-Francois Lyotard declaring, "Let us wage a war on totality… let us activate the differences."[7] What postmodernists argue for is difference, the fragmentary, pluralism, and heterogeneity. Lyotard drew inspiration from the cultural theorist Theodor Adorno, who envisaged the fragment as that part of a totality which resists totality.[8]A writer of fragments, E. M. Cioran's fragments are themselves so shattered that they often seem to be no more than a particle, a speck of dust, or thought decayed.[9] Fragmentary writing is an instance of what Deleuze and Guattari call "nomad art": moving away from the fixed, from definitions, concepts, or any kind of conventional preoccupations.[10] This reverberates with Friedrich Schlegel's preferred mode of philosophy, valuing the fragment over logic and systematic thought, which he called "philosophical grotesques."[11] Two contemporary philosophers see the fragment as encompassing "an essential incompletion" where there is always an endless deferral without a definitive resolution of elements or events.[12]

One of the most important philosophical works of the 20th century, Ludwig Wittgenstein's *Philosophical Investigations* (1953) is "a dramatic text of fragments, in which elegy, expressing a sense of lost or never quite fully realizable human possibilities, is blended with quest romance, expressing a sense of movement toward these possibilities…"[13] A connection can be made between philosophical fragments and irony as undecidability resisting doctrine, dogmatism, and frigid rationalism.[14] Wittgenstein writes of the improvisations that fragments allow, attempting to move us away from interpretation and the certainty of knowledge, welcoming instead uninterrupted ambiguity and the dismantling of boundaries that give the imagination freedom to roam.[15]

In visual art there are many examples of fragments—a particularly compelling one is the installation "Cold Dark Matter: An Exploded View," 1991 (image on internet) by Cornelia Parker. She created it by exploding her garden shed and then constructed the work from the resulting fragments. Wholes become fragments and then something entirely new.[16]Artists Cindy Sherman and Robert Mapplethorpe often fragment the body in their work so that we are confronted with the body in pieces,

as happens in the way medicine views the body. The new is a jumble of fragments, what the writer Elena Ferrante called *Frantumaglia*. In classical music we can look to the recent composition for viola and orchestra by Cassandra Miller titled "I cannot love without trembling," assembled from fragments—a Maria Callas recording, an American Baptist hymn, birdsong, and others. The title of her score comes from philosopher and mystic Simone Weil, "Human existence is so fragile a thing and exposed to such dangers that I cannot love without trembling." Music critic Alex Ross advises that "this is music that reminds us how to cry."[17] From a postmodern perspective these examples tell us that in a world of fragments there is no Logos, no metanarrative that gathers the pieces other than the artist.

We might consider fragments to be irrepressible forces of dispersion, proliferation, and multiplicity, showing the resistance of fragments to all forms of fixed identity and inevitability, a world beyond all conventional limits. The fragments within that make up our being so often combine to create an inner chaos that erupts to hurt and betray others; perhaps, then, the most we can expect is a world of imperfection, impermanence, and uncertainty.

With the three atomic explosions that occurred in 1945, the world splintered and fragmented forever. ❁

1 Daugherty, *Hiding Man: A Biography of Donald Barthelme*, 359.

2 Wulf, *Magnificent Rebels: The First Romantics and the Invention of the Self*, 159.

3 Nochlin, *The Body in Pieces: The Fragment as a Metaphor of Modernity*, (1994).

4 Hart, *Postmodernism*, 68.

5 Hollis, *The Waste Land: A Biography of a Poem*, 519.

6 Tronzo, *The Fragment: An Incomplete History*, 19.

7 Lyotard, *The Postmodern Condition: A Report on Knowledge*, 82.

8 Adorno, *Aesthetic Theory*, 45.

9 See for example Cioran, *A Short History of Decay*.

10 Deleuze and Guattari, *A Thousand Plateaus: Capitalism and Schizophrenia*, 492–500.

11 Schlegel, *Philosophical Fragments*, 27.

12 Lacoue-Labarthe and Nancy, *The Literary Absolute: The Theory of Literature in German Romanticism*, 42.

13 Eldridge, *Leading a Human Life: Wittgenstein, Intentionality, and Romanticism*, 10.

14 Eldridge, *Leading a Human Life*, 83.

15 Varley-Winter, *Reading Fragments and Fragmentation in Modernist Literature*, 174–75.

16 Tronzo, *The Fragment: An Incomplete History*, 93–94.

17 Ross, "De Minimis," 71.

B Allan Irving, social work
I educator, a dweller amidst the
O fragments and chaos.

freedom

SEE: coalition; infinite blackness; land, work, spirit, body; liberatory education

CONTRIBUTION

FREEDOM (from the Proto-Indo-European *prī*-, to love; + d^{h}*óh*$_{1}$*mos*, thing put or placed), the agency to develop abilities and potentialities through volition. It connotes consciousness attained and grown through struggle against obstacles, according with the spontaneity of nature. As an ethical demand, it emerges from an organic feeling of duty toward maximizing capability to the greatest extent possible, pushing the expansion and evolution of life. ❁

BIO

Zach Whitworth hails from the Umpqua Valley of the Pacific Northwest.

EDITORS' NOTE

We used to consider "freedom" an individualistic word, perhaps even antithetical to care, until, as part of Thick Press's "ongoing inquiry into care," we read two books that helped us see otherwise: Maggie Nelson's *On Freedom: Four Songs of Care and Constraint* and Robin D. G. Kelley's *Freedom Dreams: The Black Radical Imagination*. Those texts inspired us to include freedom in the list of *Encyclopedia* terms; thanks to Zach for this elegant, flexible definition of freedom. —ES & JC

SEE: mutual aid, postwork imaginaries, prison abolition, revolutionary mothering, sanctuary, solidarity economy, temporary autonomous zones, wildness, zinemaking

CONTRIBUTION

Stories from the Global Free Store for the Hawai'i Triennial 2022

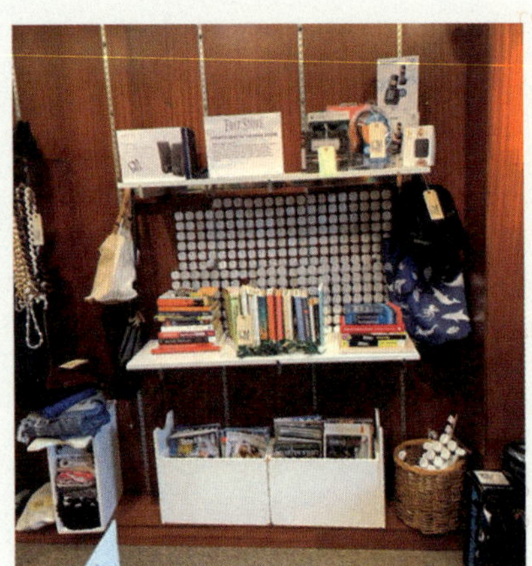

Athena Robles and Anna Stein, Double A Projects. *Global Free Store*, 2009/2022, public art project, dimensions variable.

IT'S NOON AS WE OPEN THE DOORS to the Free Store located on Level 2 at the Royal Hawaiian Center. We look out over the Tiffany jewelry store below us and across the way to the Hermès boutique. Donations in the form of goods contributed to the installation are reviewed, tagged, and placed with care on display for free shopping.

This is the second installment of Free Store and we can't help but notice similarities to our first one years ago in Lower Manhattan.

Once word got out about our project in New York, we received special deliveries of contributed goods, including boxes of editioned t-shirts from artist Andres Serrano's studio. These appeared randomly at our door one day after Mr. Serrano heard about us in the news. This time, we received unexpectedly a large UPS delivery of bottled water from Waiākea. We were told it was donated to our public project as a gesture to give back to the community.

As before, our shopkeeper neighbors visited us nearly every day, this time not only to shop, but also to bring us flowers and treats (thanks, Esther!).

When shoppers enter, we ask them to take what they think they need or can really use and to check out at the counter. After hearing this, shoppers often pause to reflect and share their insights. We hear many thoughts on what people need and why, as well as their ideas on the Free Store as a non-commercial work in a commercial context.

Some feedback we heard included:

- "It's a dream come true for those who really need it."
- "Having this store—it's almost unAmerican!"
- "This is something so needed at this time. Can't you stay?"
- "I don't need anything. But I want to open a Free Store like this when I return home."

Some were also more self-conscious in the Free Store, telling us they felt "ashamed" or "I'm so embarrassed!" to shop for free. Others would

take out their wallets either out of habit or because they were unsure if there was a catch.

However, there was no hesitation from our repeat customers, many who returned with items once they saw how the process of participating worked. This happened with both locals and tourists, as well as families and individuals. Other participants chose not to shop and only to give items that they carefully selected from home.

Some of our regulars were people who lived nearby and were coming to find items to furnish their apartments. Thanks to a story on KHON2 with Kamaka Pili, who interviewed us, some came by bus for particular items seen on the broadcast, such as a rice cooker.

At times it felt more like a community center, where information on various constituents was shared. One woman who works with the unhoused told us they have a constant need for shorts or pants for men, never shirts. It seems tops come in abundance in donations, but bottoms are harder to come by.

Fellow artists supplied many handmade and one-of-a-kind items to the store, like one who brought a block-printed t-shirt originally made from a line that sold at HoMA. The stories of what people chose to give seemed as important as the stories of what they chose to take.

A favorite story of ours is when one man found a book on music theory at the store. He had been trying to take a class online on the subject recently and had given up. He felt it was a sign that we happened to have a copy of *Music Theory for Dummies*, and he gladly took it home. At the end of each day, we closed up and looked forward to the many more encounters the installation we created would bring by connecting people to items, ideas, and each other.

This piece was written on the occasion of the Hawai'i Triennial 2022.

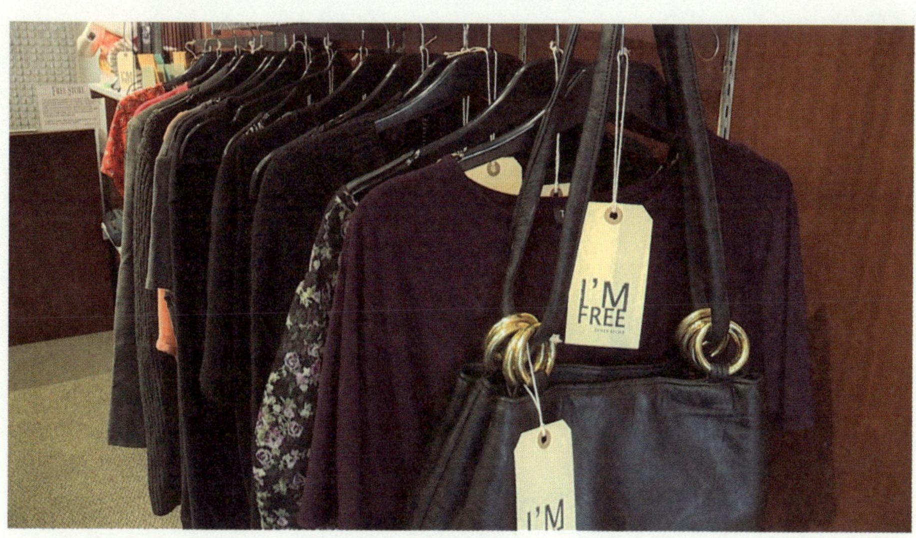

Athena Robles and Anna Stein, Double A Projects. *Global Free Store*, 2009/2022, public art project, dimensions variable.

collective care
common pool resources
deep organizi
emergent strate
gift economie
land trust

generous systems

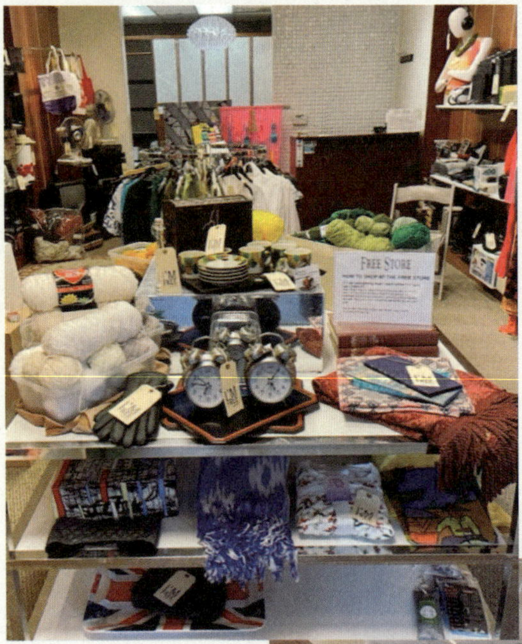

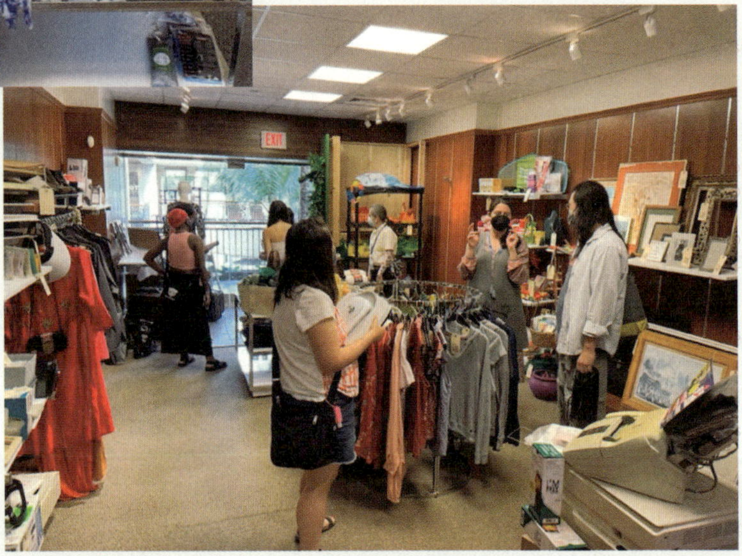

CONTRIBUTORS' NOTE

Alternative and generous systems such as bartering and free exchange have long been used in times of financial hardship. Artists, in particular, who are familiar with having to be creative to make ends meet, have functioned on generous systems, especially artist-to-artist. *Global Free Store* aims to broaden this circle of trust and exchange by including the general public. *Global Free Store*, 2009 was a non-commercial pop-up shop in Manhattan's Financial District that operated on a free exchange system. For two months, *Global Free Store* became a hub for locals and tourists who shopped and discussed ideas generated by the project, such as generosity, a gift economy, and mutual exchange. For Hawai'i Triennial 2022, the artists presented the project again in a storefront in the Royal Hawaiian Center in Honolulu. —AR & AS

BIOS

Artists Athena Robles and Anna Stein make public interactive projects that explore concepts of generosity, exchange, and audience engagement, employing "social experiment" strategies that act as tools for community building.

gift economies

SEE: collective care; generous systems; land trust

CONTRIBUTION

IN DISCUSSING GIFT ECONOMIES, I want to share some new truths I've learned in my readings, specifically from *The Gift: Imagination and the Erotic Life of Property* by Lewis Hyde. Coincidentally, this was lent to me by a friend with whom I have spent the summer exchanging small treasures. They found it in one of those tiny free libraries on the side of the road; common, it seems, in New England communities. But we'll return to this later.

First, the gift—this has been defined in some circles as "a present for which an equivalent return is always expected."[1] The return need not be to the gifting party, but a key truth is that "*the gift must always move*."[2]

Giving gifts establishes relationships in a way that purchasing commodities doesn't, which separates it from something like a barter economy. In a gift economy, for example: tonight, I make you dinner (we chat), tomorrow you give me a book that reminds you of our conversation.

Or alternatively—tonight, I make you dinner (we chat), tomorrow you make a painting based off our conversation and give it to another friend, then all three of us have a conversation about the painting. If we were just bartering, I might have given you the ingredients to make your own dinner in exchange for a book on a topic I will use to further my ambitions.

Maybe I don't want to buy everything on Amazon; maybe I want to wait for my friend to build me a stool from scratch so that when someone visits me at home, I can point to it excitedly and tell them the origin story. Maybe I don't want to go to a bookstore; maybe I want to peer in curiously through the window of the free library down the street, where I can learn what interests my neighbors. Buying something outright requires me to part with some integral piece of me I cannot yet name.

Unlike gifting, buying and selling require a certain distance between parties. To negotiate prices or broker deals means disregarding personal circumstance in favor of a bigger picture, which often entails profit for some at the expense of others. Sympathetic appeals are ineffective in the marketplace—you can't get a discount or a perk for emotional distress. You might get a gift, though.

The practice of gifting lends itself to traditions of making and relational maintenance that modern economies seem to want to erase. I think the best gift I have ever received was a little tieback top my housemate made me one afternoon, using leftover fabric from a dress that my mother sent me. I don't think my housemate thought much of it when she made it, but I think it solidified for me that I was welcome somewhere. It makes me smile to wear it.

Gifting is an act of restoration. It speaks to communal memory. When I give a gift, I remember my place in the world. When I get a gift, I remember I am seen. The gift economy suggests that we are not, in fact, alone. The gift moves and we all grow wealthier for it. ❁

1 Hyde, *The Gift: Imagination and the Erotic Life of Property*, 3.

2 Hyde, 4.

BIO Deborah Tsogbe is a designer focused on knowing and creating for grief, memory, and comfort.

Grace Lee Boggs

SEE:
revolutionary mothering
solidarity economy
sustaining movement
temporary autonomous zones

CONTRIBUTION

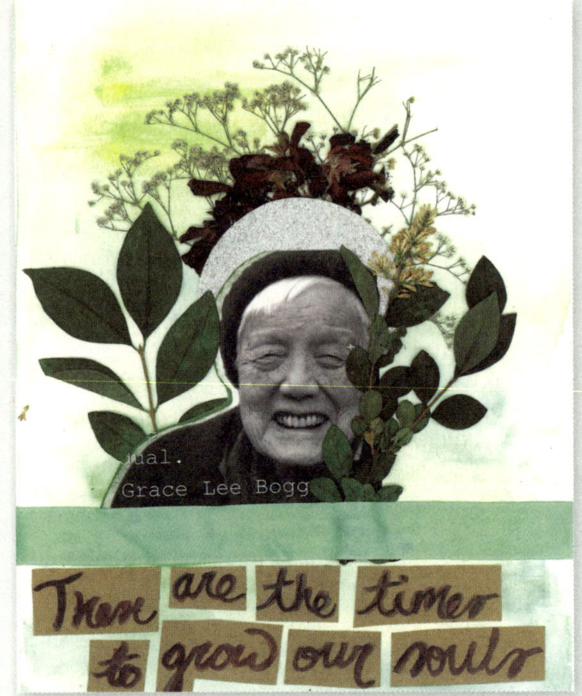

INTRODUCTION BY WAY OF DREAMING

I met Grace the day after she died.

There I was, in the middle of the death of one dream and the beginning of another. It was the last year of college and the first year of another kind of school. Since I was a little girl, I had grown up dreaming of being someone powerful. I wanted to give grand speeches on marble staircases. I wanted people to listen. I wanted to be a "first."

I was just beginning to realize that to be a "first" meant you would be the only one. I was just beginning to realize that being the first one allowed into institutions of domination and discipline was no great achievement. Places designed to hoard power would change me long before I changed them. You could look new, but you were unlikely to usher in new ways of being.

I was beginning to discover the weight of my difference, the history of those who shared my face, my loves, my ideas. I initially saw in Grace a difference that on the surface matched my own. Chinese American. Woman.

But when I listened to her speak—

Revolution is evolution towards something much grander in terms of what it means to be a human being.[1]

I wanted to be part of that grandeur. I knew that her difference was only the beginning of my connection—not just to her person but more importantly to the visions she spent her life articulating.

THESE ARE THE TIMES TO GROW OUR SOULS[2]

Born in 1915 in Providence, Rhode Island, Grace Lee Boggs was a Chinese-US American activist, revolutionary, and philosopher who lived until 2015. Throughout her 100 years, she was involved with a variety of racial, economic, and environmental justice movements, many of the great humanizing movements of the 20th century. Alongside her husband, James "Jimmy" Boggs, she settled in Detroit and remained committed to that city until the end of life. She saw Detroit as a city from which radical post-industrial imagination was growing. In response to a student asking her about burnout, she said:

Grace Lee Boggs

> I stayed involved because I've stayed in one place for the last 55 years. I think it's because I grew to love Detroit and to feel responsible for Detroit that I was able to grow. And trying one thing after another and trying to learn from everything that I try. That's the only way. The illusion of a quick answer leads to burnout.[3]

Throughout her life, she was constantly learning, growing, evolving, and changing. In a documentary about her life, she reflected:

> On the one hand, I have endured. And on the other hand, I have changed. I can remember swearing when I was young that I would not change because if I changed, I would betray the revolution. And as I've grown older, I've understood that I should change and changing is really more honorable than not changing.[4]

In a time when political optimism and revolutionary hope seem scarce, her emphasis on the need to constantly evolve one's ideas of revolution to meet the challenges of the current political moment spoke to the young organizer in me. There I was, fresh out of undergraduate in 2016, full of ideas of the power of community organizing but ill equipped to face the political realities of the moment. In moments of deep disappointment and frustration, Grace and Jimmy's questions to young people like me resonated deeply: *What time is it on the clock of the world?*[5] *What would it mean to grow our souls? How do we use our imaginations to create a new world, while grappling with the deeply felt material cruelties of the one we are currently living in?*

In a conversation with Immanuel Wallerstein, Grace provided her own answer to the question *what time is it on the clock of the world*?

> To be at that time on the clock of the universe when we can make that huge change from "othering" other people to feeling that they are part of us and we are part of them—that's a wonderful opportunity. It's a wonderful time to be alive.[6]

1 Boggs, *American Revolutionary: The Evolution of Grace Lee Boggs.*

2 Boggs and Kurashige, *The Next American Revolution: Sustainable Activism for the Twenty-First Century.*

3 *Boggs, American Revolutionary: The Evolution of Grace Lee Boggs.*

4 *Boggs, American Revolutionary: The Evolution of Grace Lee Boggs.*

5 Boggs and Boggs, *Revolution and Evolution in the Twentieth Century.*

6 Boggs, *Conversation between Grace Lee Boggs and Immanuel Wallerstein.*

A POEM ON POLITICAL IMAGINATION:

We carry within us
The histories of who we are
The broken structures
Embedded into our daily lives

In a sense
There is no escape
There is no real refuge
Because we are a part of existence
We cannot be apart from it

There is a profound responsibility
To being alive
While we are of this world
We do not have to accept
The governance of it
As much as we are made
From past stuffs
We also carry the seeds of the future
We are almost always
Creating it

We carry the way the world is
But we are also capable of
changing it

In this contradiction lies
If not liberation
At least
Something different
Something new

Grace said:

We do not get to choose the times
we live in
But we do get to choose who we
want to be
And we do get to choose
How we want to think

The time has come for a new dream

Resource list

Books:

- James and Grace Lee Boggs, *Revolution and Evolution in the Twentieth Century*.
- Grace Lee Boggs, *Living for Change: An Autobiography*.
- Grace Lee Boggs with Scott Kurashige, *The Next American Revolution: Sustainable Activism for the Twenty-First Century*.
- Stephen Ward, *In Love and Struggle: The Revolutionary Lives of James and Grace Lee Boggs*.

Documentaries and Recordings:

- *American Revolutionary: The Evolution of Grace Lee Boggs* directed by Grace Lee
- *Conversation between Grace Lee Boggs and Immanuel Wallerstein*: youtube.com/watch?v=2CSE0PlsyVk
- *Conversation between Grace Lee Boggs and Angela Davis*: youtube.com/watch?v=h9IsJwE0B1c

Some organizations in the lineage of the Boggses:

- The James and Grace Lee Boggs Center to Nurture Community Leadership, boggscenter.org/
- The James and Grace Lee Boggs School, boggsschool.org/
- Visionary Organizing Lab, visionarylab.org/
- Feedom Freedom Growers, youtube.com/watch?v=OGmOqUrVGVE (documentary about this community organization)

BIO Lily Luo is a scholar, poet, and visual artist who is currently working on a dissertation about the revolutionary legacy of Grace Lee Boggs and the power of radical pedagogy.

grief as nonlinear

CONTRIBUTION

i believe *grief* has no timeline, so don't rush me.

denise shanté brown

devoted to remembering it all without forgetting the person we're shedding into.

all of my parts tell me that grief is an ongoing invitation for our sorrows to be softly woven into our days as we learn how to live the next cycles of our lives without the people and experiences we love.

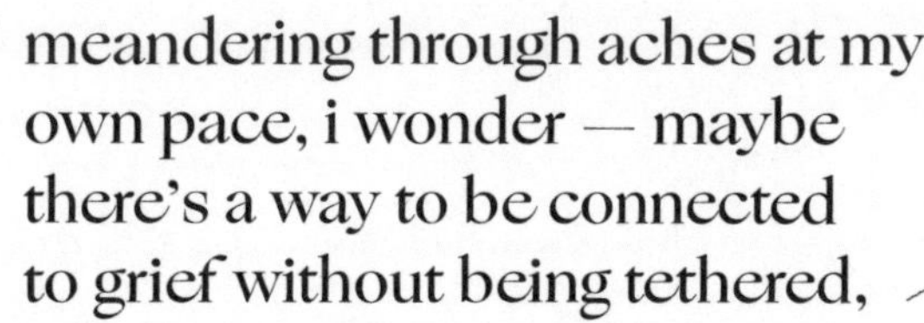

meandering through aches at my own pace, i wonder — maybe there's a way to be connected to grief without being tethered,

invitation: as you read this piece and follow the lingering lines, notice what sensations, memories, and possibilities are

because that's what grief does —
it changes us. and with the slowness to
be felt, it creates new shapes out of
everything we've ever lost.

fully in touch with each
shattering heartbreak without
drowning our essence in despair,

what if we let grief's (re)creation
process move through its series
of unraveling moments?

what if we allowed its beauty and
terror to take however long it needed
to sculpt us into another form?

there, we may find that grief is also a
timeless ceremony waiting to witness
with us, build with us, live with us.

present or long to be present. breathe with relief.
name what can be your soothing balm through the transitions.

B I O Denise Shanté Brown, multidimensional designer creating moments where we dream and design felt futures for care, intimacy and liberation.

group work

SEE: art-based group work, brave spaces, care pods, decolonizing liberatory-based practices, emergent strategy, group, healing circles

CONTRIBUTION

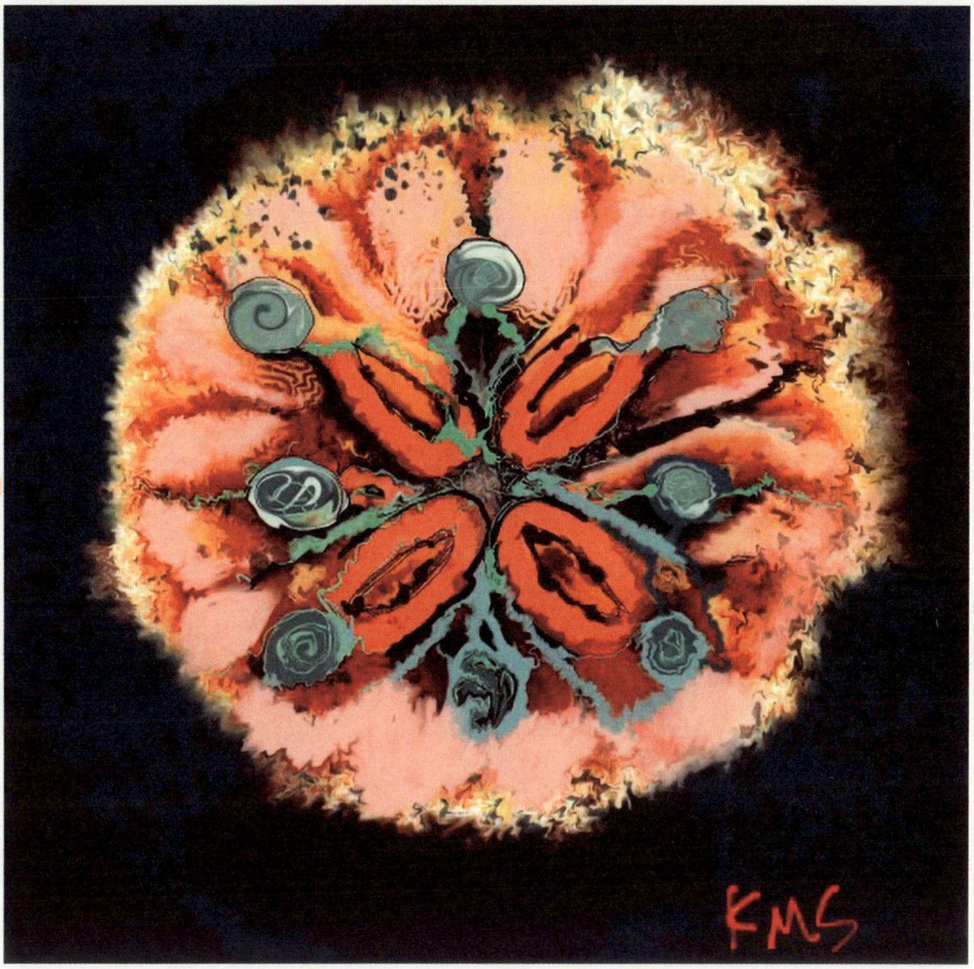

Melting into Collective Healing, 2023, Kirk Shepard, LPC CGP.

CONTRIBUTOR'S NOTE

In the realm of group work, conflicts are met not with retribution, but with courageous conversations and compassionate resolutions. Group work cultivates a space where accountability becomes a shared responsibility, and healing becomes a collective endeavor. In my experiences both as a participant and facilitator of group work, I have felt a shift toward contextual understanding over individual pathology. Group work challenges the individualistic and medicalized paradigm of neoliberal mental health discourse by encouraging participants to move beyond the limitations of the diagnose-treat model, fostering resilience, solidarity, and a shared sense of purpose in the pursuit of mental health and liberation. —KS

BIO

Kirk is a commitment to curiosity, shared wisdom, and inspiration. Kirk is a group facilitator, supervisor, educator and trainer who shares strategies and experiences that support relational and collective growth.

SEE: Reflecting on Justice; social therapeutics; 12-step programs; nonviolent communication

EDITORS' NOTE

Group work, wherein group facilitators attend to boundaries and harness the power of group dynamics, is a fundamental modality of social work and other helping professions. But what about groups—like 12-step groups, book clubs, and other informal groups—that lack a facilitator? Paula and Lisa suggest that those groups, too, have transformative potential. —ES

CONTRIBUTION

Communal Non-Therapy.

STEP 1: Notice a shared problem. For us, it was that post-pandemic, all the women in our practices seemed burned out, exhausted, stressed, isolated, sad, and overwhelmed.

STEP 2: Consider a therapy group. As therapists do.

STEP 3: Decide that a therapy group is expensive and a big time commitment and could, possibly, contribute to the overwhelm. Also, so many boundaries kind of contribute to more isolation, and not less. Consider, perhaps, that all of our stress is connected to our being brainwashed by capitalism to live in a desperately separate way when humans are meant to live in communal villages.

STEP 4: Decide to be less… therapisty. Preferably over a meal. With some fries and a shake. Wonder, is this allowed? Decide, why the hell not? AA does it, why can't we?

STEP 5: Form a Village. Of whatever kind you want. For us it was a female-identifying, monthly, donation-based Village inviting women to come together, vent, bond, rant, cry, do some journaling, laugh, share, and relax. Oh, and snack. Definitely have snacks.

STEP 6: Do some light marketing. Instagram. Facebook. Email lists. Whatever suits your fancy. Invite folks from your practice, or invite the general community. Whatever feels right for you. If you invite folks from your practice, you can work out the boundary stuff beforehand. You're a good therapist. You can shift a bit, be flexible, make it work. (Is this rigid boundary stuff too patriarchal, anyway? You can wonder and discuss this over more snacks. You will feel a little bad. Like you are breaking a therapy law for even asking the question. Bacon can help you process this. Maybe pancakes. Mmmm, pancakes.)

STEP 7: Perhaps before we form the Village, remember that we, too, are burned out, exhausted, stressed, isolated, sad, and overwhelmed. We are allowed to create something that heals us, too. Challenging the patriarchy is challenging the belief that we must be in service to others at all times. The shared problem is shared by us as well. Radically, what if there were help that also helped the healer? It's a bit radical, is it not, to consider receiving help while creating a group or an experience, a Village, per se, we hope will help others? Perhaps we can both heal and be healed, and that is just fine? ➔

STEP 8: Develop some Ground Rules to set the frame. But let yourself really think about them, and not just follow "therapy standard convention." Keep the idea of a Village in mind. What feels "Villagy"? Think outside the White, male, patriarchal therapy box a bit. Perhaps over some cake. Write rules that feel right to you and will foster the community you want to foster. If you find yourself thinking only in terms of Freudian rules, have some more cake. Think some more.

STEP 9: Come up with a bit of an intro prompt. An inspiring exercise. Something to give folks something to bounce off of. An icebreaker, but low-key. Perhaps a meditation, a poem, a story. Low-key for you to plan and for folks to do. It's relaxing, after all. We are not trying to add to the overwhelm. For anyone.

STEP 10: Do the ice-breaker thing. Then open the floor. See what you've created! For us, we accidentally created an AA-like support group for women coping with late-stage capitalism! What will your Village create? ❂

BIOS

Paula D. Atkinson is a queer therapist/healer/witch from California; she's a body justice professor, an artist, and a writer of pieces about fat phobia, faith, & feminism. pauladatkinson.com

Lisa Kays received her clinical social work licenses by passing the racist, ableist ASWB licensure exam and can be found @theimprovisationaltherapist trying to find and bring amusement, a little bit of justice, and some healing to herself and others.

harm reduction

SEE: solidarity, strength perspective, the, 12-step program, perspective via faith

EDITOR'S NOTE

"Harm reduction" is a pragmatic and compassionate approach to addressing various health and social issues, such as substance mis-use. It centers on minimizing the negative consequences of substance mis-use rather than focusing solely on abstinence. This approach acknowledges the complexities of human behavior and the fact that individuals may not be ready or able to completely stop certain activities. Instead, it aims to provide support, education, and resources to reduce the harms associated with these behaviors, ultimately improving the health and well-being of individuals and communities. Harm reduction programs and policies prioritize safety, dignity, and harm minimization, offering a vital alternative to punitive approaches and fostering a more inclusive and empathetic society. —CH

CONTRIBUTOR'S NOTE

This entry on harm reduction came together from a series of roundtable conversations facilitated by Carmen Ostrander at the Psychedelic Psychotherapy Forum in Nanaimo, British Columbia, in 2022. The gathering was intended to promote interdisciplinary discussion in an area that's moving very fast, and making a number of assumptions—like, that we all mean the same thing when we refer to ethics and ethical practice. There were First Nation elders, therapists, doctors, social workers, nurses, students and psychiatrists present. My attempt to slow down and tease out the idea of ethics invited people to participate in different ways. Deep listeners doodled on large sheets of paper, some wrote messages to the next round of folks due to sit at the table, some captured words and ideas that jumped out, and I had a go at making a rescued word poem out the parts I was able to capture. It's clear to me ethics are opportunities to put into practice things we really care about, and that some of us care about very different things—which is great, as long as we have space to make these cares and positions visible to the people we work with. —CO

CONTRIBUTION NOTES

- Facilitating the safest possible space for substance use.
- Asking ourselves, "How can I take help keep you safe, alive, and well?"
- Taking responsibility for our own communities' challenges and liberatory practices.
- Doing the best we can with what we have now.
- Sharing what we know based on people's experience and centering community knowledge.
- Understanding we do this best when we genuinely love and care for the people we work with.
- Practitioners are also at risk of harm (of the moral injury kind) when the system they work within doesn't allow them to respond or care for people in line with their values.
- Harm reduction = solidarity.
- "HR is the actions done by an oppressive system in an attempt to decrease the harms of that system, which most significantly affect the marginalized and less advantaged within the system, but is often erroneously framed as acting to protect marginalized individuals from harming themselves." ➔

harm reduction

RESCUED WORD POEM

"I Don't Know"

Distrust in institutions
Information we listen to
Isolation
Poisoned drug supply
Courting colonialism
People lost
Realism and practicality
People's experiences count
Solidarity
Longing
Over promising
Speed kills

Don't give up on me
On you
Nuance
Harm versus risk
Lived experience honoured
Unfolding
Slippery slope
Caring
Trust yourself
Be you more than anyone else
Uncovering complexities
Opportunities
Fun
Otherwise what's the point?

We're all human
All compelled
To change State
What you want
See you, hear you
Honest suffering
I'm worried you will die

Collective healing
What do you need?
Love first
Big respect

BIO

Carmen Ostrander is a community-centered therapist based in Canada, but not from there, providing Narrative, Expressive Arts & Substance Assisted Therapy as Square Peg Therapy.

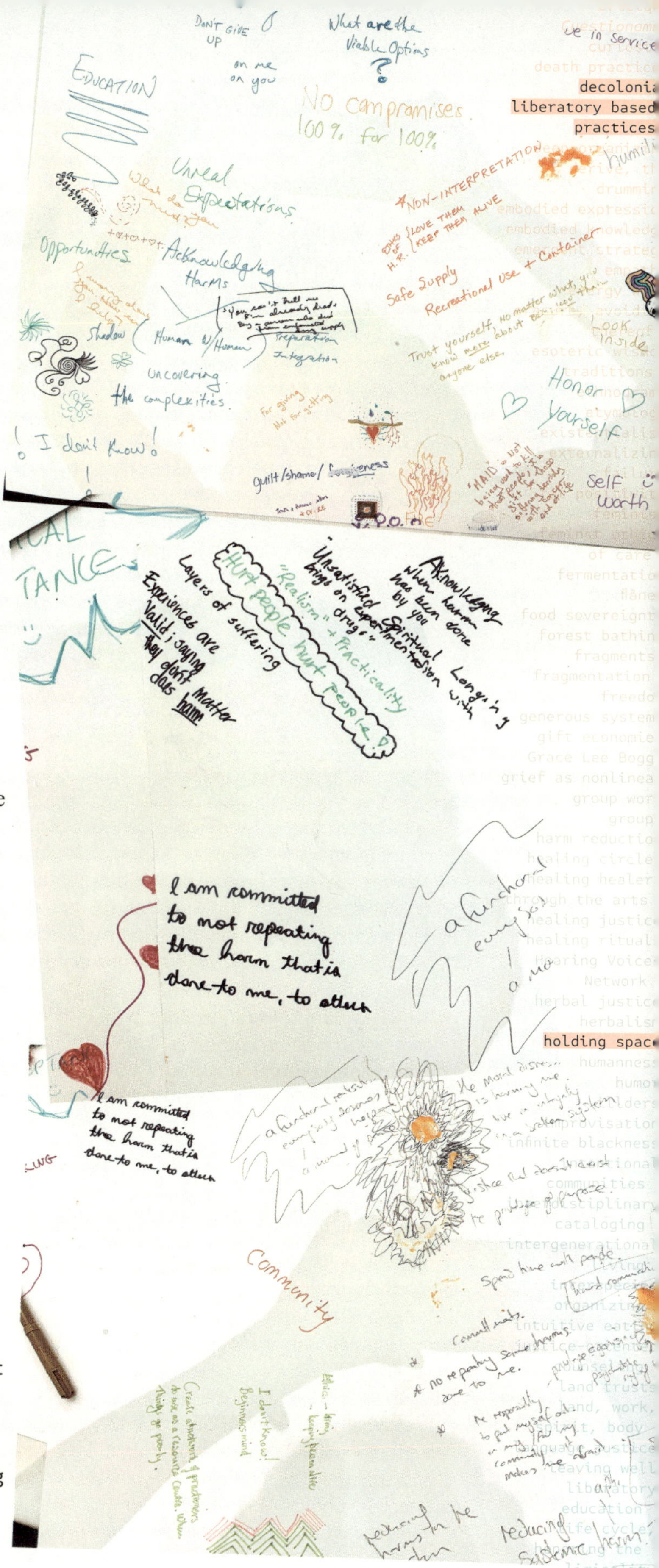

healing circles

SEE: Reflecting on Justice; solidarity; movement lawyering

CONTRIBUTION

Silence from and about the subject was the order of the day. Some of the silences were broken, and some were maintained by authors who lived with and within the policing strategies. What I am interested in are the strategies for breaking it.
—Toni Morrison

ONE OF THE MOST powerful weapons of the colonial matrix of power is hiding crimes against indigenous and enslaved peoples. These harms reverberate through generations, social groups, and families through the complicity of institutions—the colonial matrix of power—that reinforce hierarchies, thus tethering those experiencing oppression to the sickness of a conquering society.

Healing circles offer an antidote. These heterogenous helping communities comprise members of families who seek healing, clients at the end of their healing trajectory, and a team of therapists that includes interns. Healing circles provide a context in which participants—in all of their multi-dimensional, intersectional complexity—collectively engage one another's experiences, as well as prompts from popular culture, including film and music. Working together, participants discuss, analyze, and reflect on the challenges of living within and traversing intersecting and compartmentalized worlds within the colonial matrix of power. In the process, they expand the borders of their own lived experiences and explore those subaltern spaces of liberation and wounding.

Through healing circles, participants collectively embrace and encourage resistance to norms that maintain hierarchies of power, privilege, and oppression. Such communities embody epistemic disobedience through their challenges to the rules and norms of the status quo.[1]

Gathering and curating knowledge about the lived experiences of those who reside at the intersection of the colonial wound is essential to creating pathways for emancipation and liberation. No one person has a single identity. A person might be gay, Latino, Chinese-American, disabled, cis-gender male, and middle class. Another might be female, African-American, and poor. Or white, cis-gender, elderly, disabled, and poor; able-bodied and poor; middle class and disabled; female, trans, and wealthy; Christian, Jewish, Muslim, Buddhist, or Hindu.

The intersecting aspects of a person's identity create paths that manifest differently in the context of various contiguous life-affirming and disruptive contexts. Each aspect of our identities is concurrently located in multiple spaces, creating an *intersectional* experience with embedded aspects of advantage, disadvantage, and nuance. Intersectionality offers possibilities to decolonize the political and institutional aspects of social location and standpoints of people in their lived experiences in multiple contexts.[2] In the corridors of imparting knowledge, consideration of social location and standpoint must include the various and intersecting identities imposed and embraced by various people.

Additionally, identities come with privileges, advantages, disadvantages, and varying levels of power; some are mutable, while others are not. Those seeking freedom through liberatory healing must grapple with the challenge of acknowledging not only the ways that their own identities make them vulnerable to oppression (as, for example, middle-class white women face oppression by middle-class white men), but also the ways that their identities grant privilege (the white women's movement forgets the plight of women who have been multiply marginalized, including women of color, women in poverty, lesbians, trans women, and people with expansive and fluid gender and sexual identities). To be effective, professionals, students, and activists alike must keep the entire matrix of power, privilege, and oppression—coloniality—centered within the landscape of freedom conversations and liberatory strategies for healing. ➔

Healing circles redefine and expand the therapeutic context and invite community healers and activists to engage in the circle of healing. These circles should contain a cross-section of people of diverse backgrounds—social classes, race, culture, religion, gender identities, expressions, and sexual orientations—who are seeking therapy for a variety of problems. If you practice in a community where there is little or no diversity, then introduce it through film, popular media, and literary writings. Homogenous spaces can always be interrupted, allowing for the introduction of expanded experiences and knowledge. Healing circles illustrate a decolonial path that disrupts the western psychological project of coloniality.

Paying attention to the larger context of organizing variables—as they operate both in the public sphere and within individual and familial spaces—is key to healing. Liberatory healing disavows simplistic notions of cognitive pain, dressed as symptoms, without a contextual analysis of that pain situated in histories of coloniality. Legacies of colonialism, coloniality, racism, homophobia, sexism, and religiosity ought to be centered in healing endeavors. Other nuances of marked advantage and disadvantage as in physicality, age, undocumented status, and numerous other such markers all add to the complexity of this mapping. Consider the ways in which an intersectional perspective highlights the exclusionary nature of certain initiatives meant to "even the playing field," such as affirmative action. People with multiple identities can be excluded because such efforts focus on only one oppressed identity, rendering other identities invisible.

This broader approach diverges radically from seeing the solitary (rugged) individual—or even families—as isolated, self-sustaining systems. A commitment to intersectionality and decolonization pushes therapists to think more broadly about how we can empower clients to make liberatory and transformative change in their lives. Such change extends beyond the boundaries of the individual and the family to alter hierarchies of power, privilege, and oppression.

Our lifelong connections to our multiple identity groups profoundly shape the attitudes, feelings, and behaviors we bring to each personal encounter. Therefore, we each face the challenge of identifying how our particular community connections bring with them privileges we take for granted and prejudices we've been indoctrinated into embracing. Accepting this marks the beginning of the journey toward critical consciousness, whose rewards include an increased awareness of the social, economic, and political forces driving interpersonal behavior, a more self-assured understanding of personal accountability, and a lifetime of more satisfying relationships. ❁

1 Mignolo, "Geopolitics of Sensing and Knowing: On (De)Coloniality, Border Thinking, and Epistemic Disobedience"; Almeida, *Expansions of Feminist Family Theory through Diversity*; Almeida, "Creating Collectives of Liberation"; Almeida, Dolan-Delvecchio, and Parker, *Transformative Family Therapy: Just Families in a Just Society*; Almeida, Melendez, and Paéz, "Liberation-Based Healing."

2 Harding, "How Standpoint Methodology Informs Philosophy of Social Science."

BIO Rhea V. Almeida, MS, PhD, LCSW, founder of the Institute for Family Services, is a practitioner of Liberatory Healing Practices, a decolonial therapeutic approach. Dr. Almeida is the author of numerous journal articles and four books.

healing healers through the arts

SEE:

CONTRIBUTION

HALF OF ALL PHYSICIANS, and even more physicians-in-training, are burnt-out, which leads to depression, poor communication, lower empathy with patients, and ultimately suboptimal patient care.[1] This has sparked initiatives to improve wellness for physicians at the institutional and individual levels. In fact, the Accreditation Council for Graduate Medical Education requires that training programs address the psychological, emotional, and physical well-being of trainees as they are critical components in the development of the competent, caring, and resilient physician.[2] Art has been shown to improve health and well-being by improving coping strategies, lowering stress, and improving empathy. The World Health Organization recommends supporting the inclusion of arts and humanities education within the training of health-care professionals.[3] Including art in medical education has shown improvement in empathy and resilience.[4] Thus, as the program director for the pediatric hematology/oncology (PHO) fellowship at Children's Hospital Los Angeles (CHLA), along with my colleagues, I aimed to improve wellness, empathy, and a sense of belonging in our trainees with an innovative art in medicine curriculum.

Using Kern's model of curricular development, we designed the art in medicine curriculum for PHO fellows and expanded the program to many different pediatric subspecialty divisions' fellows at CHLA after a successful pilot. We included twelve art activities, one per month, over the course of our academic year. These activities were designed based on the results of a survey that assessed which art modalities were most meaningful to the trainees. We also examined the trainees' attitudes regarding art in their daily lives and the relationship between art and medicine. Our trainees identified painting/visual arts, photography, cooking/baking, and music as their most meaningful art forms, but stated they do not often have time to enjoy these activities during their busy training years. The art activities were held during their scheduled noon-hour lecture time, occasionally in the evenings, and during their annual fellowship retreat.

Favorite activities have included "Create a Collaborative Playlist" in which all trainees bring a song that they listen to when they are happy and one when they are sad, play a clip of each song, and then share with the group why they chose that song. Another popular activity was a guided drum circle that took place outside on the hospital helipad. We have completed arts and crafts such as painting pumpkins and decorating stockings, sweaters, and ornaments. Additionally, we have held instructor-led cooking, painting, and pottery-making classes and created collaborative photo collages over time as well as a cookbook of faculty and trainees' favorite recipes. At the end of each activity, we debrief with the following questions: "How did this activity make you feel?" and "How will this activity affect your ability to care for your patients?"

All trainees enjoyed the activities, and the vast majority said that they gained something from participation—including new bonds with colleagues, the ability to express their feelings openly, time to focus on wellness, a mental break during the day with time for personal reflection, relaxation and stress relief, inspiration to create art at home and to participate in more art-based activities, and an opportunity to learn about the hidden artistic talents of their colleagues. With regard to patient care, participants reported that they now encourage families and patients to participate in art activities, they have increased morale and creativity while working on the ward, they are more patient and relaxed at work, they have increased empathy for their patients and colleagues, and they notice improved observational skills and connections with patients and families.

Adding creative elements into a stressful workplace allows participants to stop and take time for self-expression and bonding, and is largely inexpensive and feasible for groups of many sizes. The key is to have a budget that addresses

wellness and to allow a dedicated time and space for activities to occur. The curriculum can be modified to fit the needs of its participants and content can be added using artistic talents of colleagues. Incorporating art activities into your workplace, medical training program, and daily life can have a positive impact on well-being, bonding, and empathy. ❁

1 Dyrbye et al., "Burnout among U.S. Medical Students, Residents, and Early Career Physicians Relative to the General U.S. Population"; Shanafelt et al., "Burnout and Satisfaction with Work-Life Balance among US Physicians Relative to the General US Population."

2 ACGME Program Requirements for Graduate Medical Education in Pediatrics.

3 Fancourt and Finn, "What Is the Evidence on the Role of the Arts in Improving Health and Well-Being? A Scoping Review."

4 Zazulak et al., "The Art of Medicine: Arts-Based Training in Observation and Mindfulness for Fostering the Empathic Response in Medical Residents"; Orr et al., "The Fostering Resilience through Art in Medical Education (FRAME) Workshop: A Partnership with the Philadelphia Museum of Art."

BIOS

Jamie Stokke, MD, is a pediatric hematology/oncology physician with a passion for medical education including creating innovative ways to promote wellness for physicians and other healthcare providers.

Rachel Gallant, MD, MS, is a pediatric hematology-oncology physician with a desire to improve trainee well-being and promote art and humanities in medical education.

Cassandra Wang, MD, is a pediatric hematology-oncology fellow committed to fostering trainee wellness through creative approaches at the intersection of art and medicine.

healing justice

SEE: mutual aid, sustaining movement, transformative justice

CONTRIBUTION

THE WORKING-CLASS, queer and trans, Black, Indigenous, and other organizers, healers, and artists of color in the southeastern US who developed healing justice in a group, named Kindred: Southern Healing Justice Collective,[1] would be the first to tell you that healing justice has deep roots, even an origin story, that is traced to community members' deaths and rapid response to the human-made disaster of Hurricane Katrina.

They would tell you that healing justice is definitely not a movement—it's a framework that seeks to integrate healing into social justice movements, and that healing justice is a movement-building effort, not another movement altogether.

They would tell you that healing justice is centered on a critique of the medical industrial complex, and if your analysis isn't informed by reproductive justice, disability justice, environmental justice, harm reduction, and transformative justice movements, you are missing critical political education.

They would tell you that healing justice has always been part of liberation struggle particular to specific places and contexts. They would explain that their articulation is not about creating a singular or definitive authority; rather, they don't want healing justice to be appropriated, commodified, and stripped down to lifeless parts.

They would tell you that over the last ten years, as healing justice has popularized, that efforts to co-opt it have been resisted, and one of those efforts to reclaim healing justice has entailed those who were there and their comrades/mentees/students writing their own stories; among those efforts is *Healing Justice Lineages: Dreaming at the Crossroads of Liberation, Collective Care, and Safety* by Cara Page and Erica Woodland.

They would remind you that healing justice is a living set of practices, in which they iterate a working definition of healing justice every few years as our collective practice sharpens our understanding of what this work is.

They—including Cara Page, who was there, and Erica Woodland, a friend/comrade/mentee of Cara's and co-author of the aforementioned book—would tell you that the Healing Justice Lineages book tour was a perfect opportunity to workshop their working definition and map healing justice strategies at each city they visited.

In a former church renovated as a community center on October 18, 2023, they—being Cara and Erica—would articulate healing justice as seeking "*to intervene on generational trauma to build collective power towards resistance*."

Alongside Cara and Erica in a stained-glass encased room, inside a former church renovated as a community center in mid-October 2023, these folks sat next to each other as healing justice practitioners:

ancestral healers who held sacred space for organizers;

grief workers who showed up at sites of violence and mediated community conflicts in the most systematically deprived neighborhoods in the city;

radical social workers who were challenging therapy industries to be more responsive and accessible to those who needed support the most;

mental health policy advocates pushing for more humane psychiatric policies and protocols;

culture workers who are excavating lost stories and archiving our work so the powers-that-be couldn't lie on them later;

accessibility
Black Panther Party Free Breakfast Program
deep organizi
embodied knowled
emergent strate
freedo
Grace Lee Bogg
harm reductio

among others who were intervening in creative and visionary ways tending to generational trauma and building collective power;

and some of them who held evolving roles over time and multiple roles at the same time.

Because they—we—were there. And we can tell our own stories.

Because, as Nikki Giovanni wrote in "Quilting the Black-Eyed Pea," "It's a life-seeking thing."[2] ❁

1 Kindred, kindredsouthernhjcollective.org.

2 Giovanni, *Quilting the Black-Eyed Pea (We're Going to Mars)*.

BIO Richael Faithful is a Black trans-southern multi/interdisciplinary healer, culture worker, and attorney.

SEE: ritual, spells

CONTRIBUTION

Abortion Healing Ritual

PREPARATION

Gather these simple materials: Paper and pen or pencil, candle, stone, feather, bowl of water, a drawing or image of a spiral, salt water (or fresh-water with salt added), a dropper or cloth, "gifts" (such as a photo, flower, bracelet, toy, etc.).

Each person, draw a picture or write a letter to the spirit of the baby who was aborted. You may simply tell the baby, "I love you, goodbye," or anything else you would like to tell or say to them.

CLEANSING WITH SALT WATER

Close your eyes and invite into your awareness the spirit of the baby involved in the abortion. Hold the salt water: "This water from [ORIGIN] is a little bit salty, like tears, ocean water, and the amniotic fluid in the womb." Dab some on each person's eyes, heart, and hands: "May our eyes find love, May our heart feel love. May our hands share love."

CASTING THE CIRCLE

Say aloud the names of any ancestors, spiritual guides, deities, divine beings, or presences whom you wish to invite to the ritual.

Build your altar. Place candle on the South of the altar: "Spirits of fire, please inspire us with passion and will to move through this transformation with power and integrity."

Place feather on the East of the altar: "Spirits of air, please keep our mind focused on the work of this ritual and our intentions clear as we move through it into our lives beyond."

Place stone on the North of the altar: "Spirits of earth, please strengthen us to carry the power of this ritual. Ground us in the knowledge that both death and life are sacred to the Goddess."

Place bowl of water on the West of the altar: "Spirits of water, please open our hearts to humility; let our emotions flow through us easily and honestly."

Place an image of a spiral in the Center of the altar: "Spirits of matrix, the sacred center, please open our spirits to the magic of this ritual and our intuition to feel our oneness with all things."

"The circle is cast. We are between worlds. And what happens between worlds, changes all the worlds."

SETTING FREE

Singing a song or circling the altar (counterclockwise, the female direction) raises energy to prepare for the heart of the ritual.

Each person, place your letter on the altar or read it.

"Spirits who did not enter this world, we see your beauty, and we love you."

Place your gift on the altar. If you choose, say aloud the baby's name or the name you have chosen for them, and feel their spirit as they accept your gift. "Spirits who did not enter this world, we love you, we honor you, and we set you free."

Tell the baby in your heart goodbye, thank you, and that it will always be a part of your family.

A nice time to sing or move together. For our ritual, a child chose "Happy Birthday." →

OPENING THE CIRCLE

When the ritual feels complete:

"Spirits of the center, of matrix, thank you for being with us today. Thank you for the power of ritual.

Spirits of the west, of water, thank you for being with us today. Thank you for opening our hearts to our feelings.

Spirits of the north, the earth, thank you for being with us today. Thank you for making us strong to hold this transformation.

Spirits of east, the air, thank you for being with us today. Thank you for giving us clarity to focus on our goal.

Spirits of fire, thank you for being with us today. Thank you for the passion for transformation."

Say thank you and goodbye to any ancestors or spirits you invited to be here—feel free to use their names—then say: "The circle is open, but unbroken. Merry meet, and merry part, and merry meet again." ❁

CONTRIBUTOR'S NOTE

This ritual can be done alone or with any or all members of the family or community affected by your abortion—the people that the baby might have known. I developed it for myself and my family when I felt depressed after an abortion. For me the healing effects were immediate, complete, and lasting: in the twenty years since the ritual, I have felt only peaceful, calm, and grateful about my abortion. The ritual can be done any time after your abortion, even years later.—AF

BIO

Annie Finch is author of *The Poetry Witch Little Book of Spells* and the founder of Poetry Witch Ritual Theater and PoetryWitchCommunity.org.

Hearing Voices Network

SEE: mutual aid; strengths perspective, the

EDITORS' NOTE

"The Hearing Voices Network" (HVN) groups are peer-led spaces for people who hear voices and have thoughts, visions, olfactory, tactile, and other experiences that are considered to be outside conventional norms. HVN groups offer a non-pathologizing space for members to come together to share their experiences, offer support, and gain camaraderie. HVN groups exist on an international level with groups in many countries around the world. There are companion groups for friends and family members of voice hearers as well. It is essential to recognize that voice hearing is a diverse and deeply personal experience that transcends diagnostic boundaries. We extend our gratitude to Kelly (see next page), who has generously shared her lived experiences. —CH & ES

→

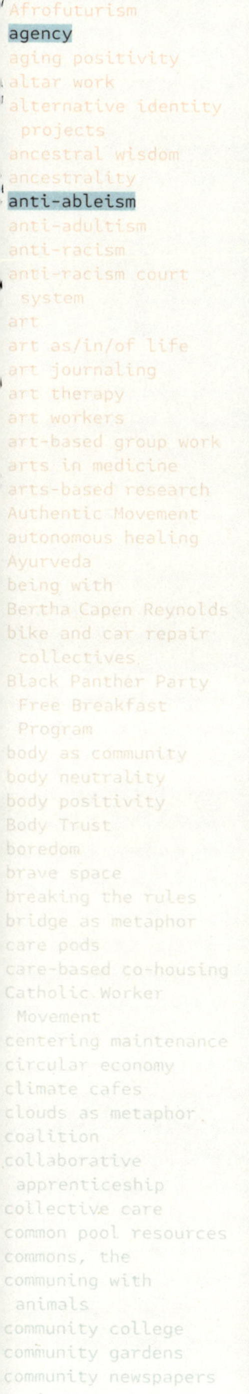

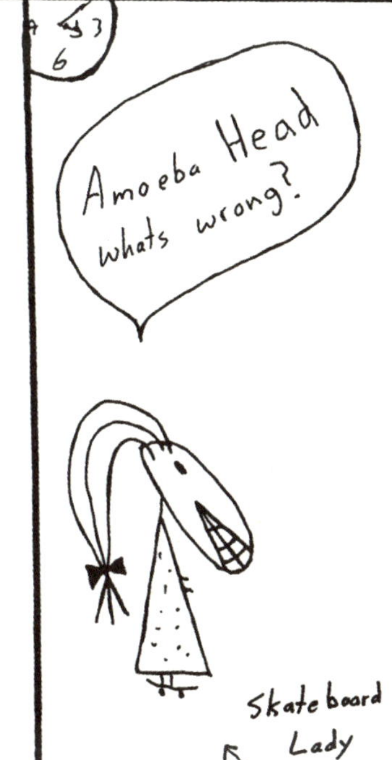

"lived experience, mutual aid," paper and ink, 2023

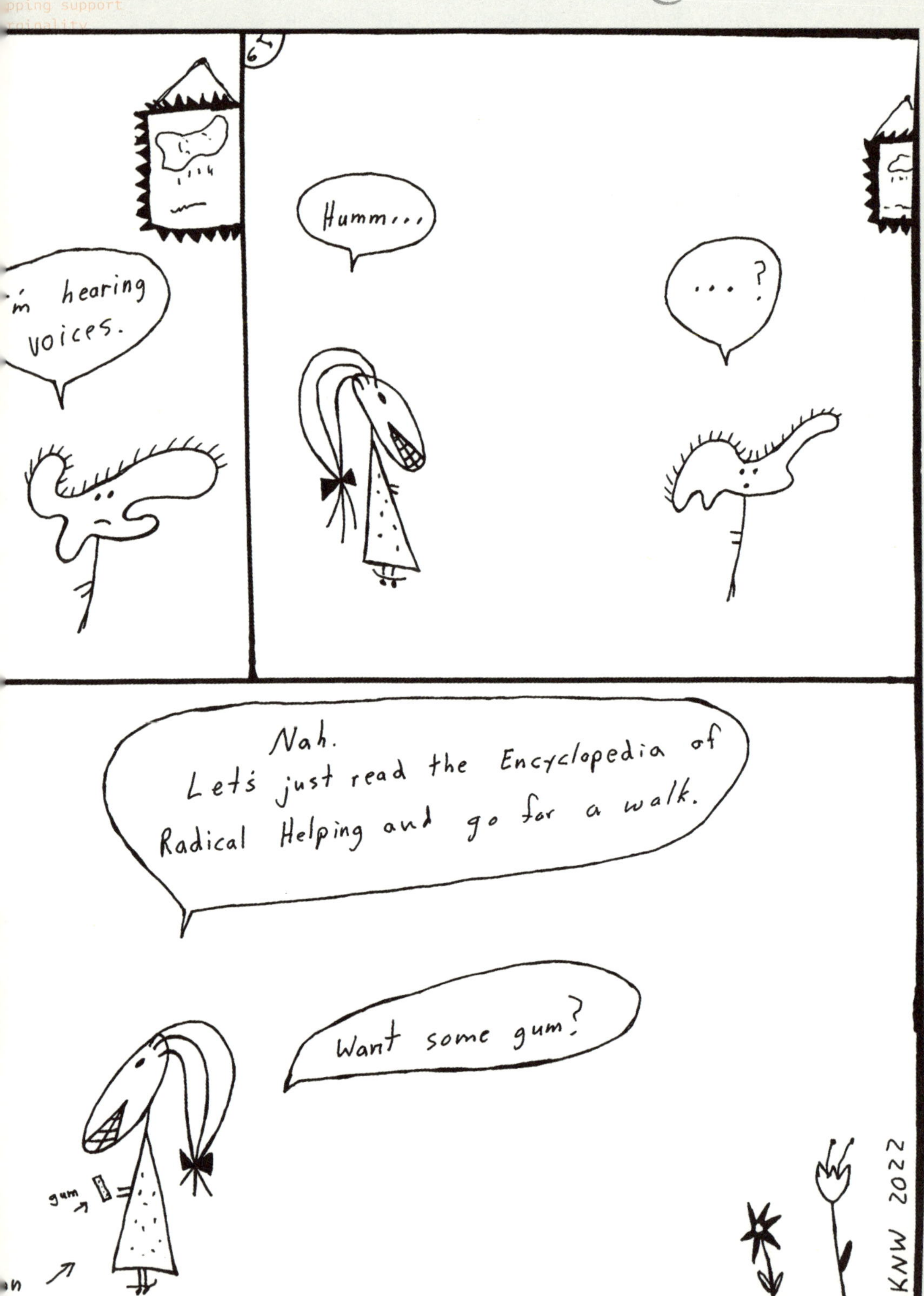

BIO Kelly Waterman is a psych survivor and lives in Minneapolis, MN.

reclaiming selfhood
recognition
redistribution
Reflecting on Justice
reflexivity
Reiki
relational interviewing
relationality
resistance
resisting the parental loss narrative
resonance
respectful visiting
respite rooms
rest as resistance
revenge
revolutionary mothering
ritual
sanctuary
sandplay therapy
sauna
seed banking
sex positivity
shadow integration
Sick Woman Theory
slow textiles
slowness
social change ecosystem framework
social construction
social practice
social therapeutics
Social Welfare Action Alliance, the
solidarity
solidarity economy
somatic healing
songs/singing
sound healing
speculative design
spells
staying with the trouble
storytelling
street newspaper
strengths perspective, the
sufficiency
sustaining movement
symbol
Taos Institute, the
tarot
temporary autonomous zones
Theatre of the Oppressed
theories of change
theosophy
therapeutic writing
togetherness
trans practices
transformative justice
traspatio
12-step programs
undercover anti-bullying teams
vigil
water
wildness
wintering as metaphor
wishes
witchery
yoga
zinemaking

herbal justice

SEE: Black Panther Party Free Breakfast Program
herbal
community gard
generous syst

CONTRIBUTION

FOR THE PAST TWO YEARS, Herban Cura has been offering a mutual aid initiative called Plants to the People, which we founded in the summer of 2022. The main mission of Plants to the People is to make herbs and plants more accessible to low-income, BIPOC, and immigrant communities. We distribute fresh and dried, locally grown, organic herbs at no cost to the general public. We set up our distribution events in publicly accessible spaces, most frequently in community parks and along sidewalks in residential neighborhoods. Our Plants to the People offering has also extended to concert venues in partnership with Reyna Tropical.

The locations of our distributions are chosen primarily to accommodate working-class people of color—those who have been here for generations, as well as first-generation immigrants and their families. Over the past two years we have distributed more than 2,000 plant bundles in New York City, Chicago, Detroit, Los Angeles, Washington, DC, and North Carolina. Once a month we drive down from the Mahicantuck (Hudson) Valley with a car packed to the brim with freshly harvested herbs. Some of the herbs we distribute are tulsi, epazote, plantain, sage, thyme, basil, lemon balm, purslane, mint, lemon verbena, lemon grass, shiso, and mugwort. At each Plants to the People alongside the fresh plants, we offer 5-point auricular acupuncture for wellness, stress reduction, and detox. We give thanks to the efforts of Mutulu Shakur for the work in making auricular acupuncture available as an effective and accessible detox protocol.

Every Plants to the People event is an opportunity for all of us to exchange lived experience and wisdom of how we and our lineage have turned to plants for healing. Plants to the People emerges from a long lineage of people taking care of people. We re-member the work and care of generations of beloved aunties, abuelas, nonnas, seed keepers, healers, the Black Panthers, the Young Lords, and the Indigenous People of the earth. Plants to the People is here to celebrate and uphold this lineage by sharing opportunities for reconnection and healing in community. As we spend time with the plants together, they help nurture in us an embodied sense of belonging: to the earth, to ourselves, and to the diverse communities we are a part of.

HERBAN CURA'S MISSION STATEMENT

Herban Cura is a healing justice–centered herb and ecology school, bridging ancestral and living wisdom to urban contexts. We offer opportunities to learn about the histories that have severed us from the land, while creating learning opportunities that restore our diasporic memory and cultural lifeways. We do this through in-person and online classes, growing herbs, seed saving, creating herbal remedies, redistributing herbs to low-income BIPOC communities in urban contexts, and building networks between knowledge keepers to amplify their stories. We see this remembering of embodied, land-based lifeways as an essential piece in our movement and social justice work. ❁

BIOS

Herban Cura is a healing justice–centered herb and ecology school, bridging ancestral and living wisdom to urban contexts.

Antonia is a Chilean-American clinical herbalist, gardener, educator, community organizer, and founder.

SEE:
mutual aid
perspective (via faith)
somatic healing
traspati

CONTRIBUTION

Herbalism for the Social Body

"The body is itself a kind of place—not a solid object but a terrain through which things pass, and in which they sometimes settle and sediment." [David Abram] To wonder why some things settle in some bodies and not in others is to begin to ask questions about power, injustice, and inequity, questions that are bound in modern medicine with questions of colonialism. —Raj Patel and Rupa Marya

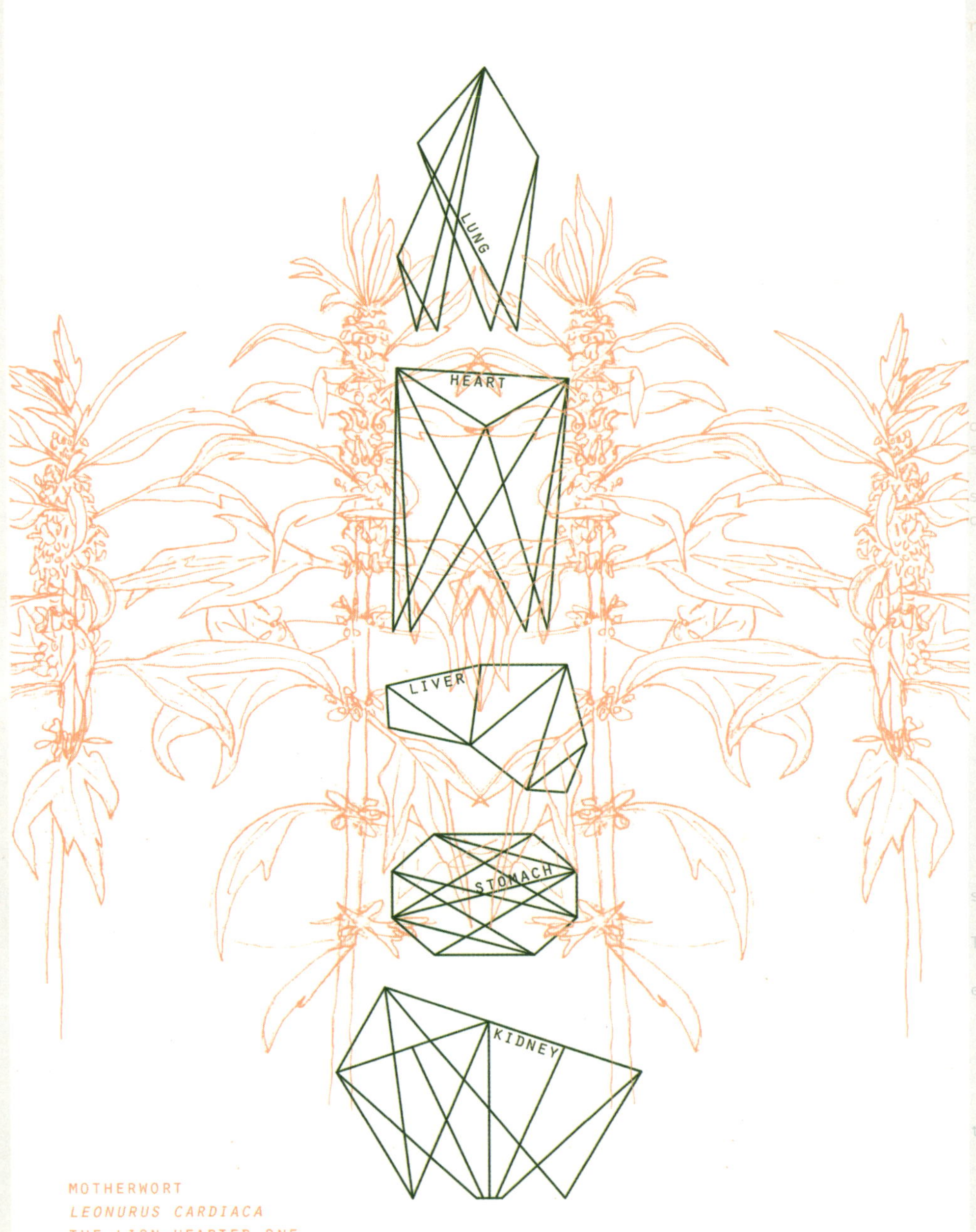

MOTHERWORT
LEONURUS CARDIACA
THE LION-HEARTED ONE

GARDEN AS BODY AND BODY AS GARDEN

The Social-Body Apothecary works with the body as garden and the garden as body. We combine intercultural plant knowledge with bodywork, weaving together many different sources, streams of information, and experiential knowledge of all participants to create space for questions around systemic violence, resilience, and regeneration. Through this process, medicinal encounters take place that address the social body.

The body that is emerging is not strictly anatomical. It is mixed, hybrid, queer, monstrous, relocated, decentralized, a multiple being that defies norms.

This is a project that entails various practices that reflect on oppressive systems and contribute to building practices of solidarity and community.

- We do so by collectively designing and constructing dwellings/shelters based on organ centers and bodily systems.
- We begin with the question: What is hurting? Walking through the garden, we meet plants that can be allies or companions for these ailments, addressing the personal, social, and political dimensions of those pains. As we make herbal medicines collectively, we exchange stories of oppression, practices of healing, and plant knowledge.
- We invite engagement with plants as teachers and allies, formulating questions as emergent strategies, by reading them not just for their extracted components but by meeting their complex situatedness in specific geopolitical ecologies.

The first incarnation of this project took place in a former garden school in Berlin, Germany (Campus Dammweg), that was closed and overgrown, then temporarily revived as a social center for art, ecology, and cultural practices, dedicated to the local neighbors coming from post-migration backgrounds.

WHAT IS THE SOCIAL BODY?

The apothecary that we are proposing invites regeneration of the social body by restoring the personal body, valuing the knowledge and resources stored in our bodies and lands. Making medicine together is a decolonial practice of resistance against structural violence. By building community we can understand the connections between symptoms that appear in individualized bodies as indications of what might be rooted in systemic injustices. Through coming together, exchanges and conversations arise, revealing how the experiences we often feel alone with are personal and political, shared and different.

WHAT ARE MEDICINAL PROCESSES? HOW CAN WE LEARN FROM THESE ABOUT PROCESSES OF SOLIDARITY, ALLYSHIP, AND ADVOCACY?

All the plants are always many. They are beings of complexity, rife with contradictions, extending across spectrums, their qualities speaking in subtle nuances beyond the scope of binaries, moving in the dynamics along spectrums. These plants support multiple aspects and systems within the body and socio-ecological context simultaneously. The point is not to divide and isolate them or utilize them as easy fixes, but to see how this multiplicity indicates that there are many ways to aid or support the social body from different perspectives. Rather than offering cures, promises, or solutions, the plants work to address what is needed through medicinal dialogue. We value dynamic engagement with these plants as healers, teachers, collaborators, and allies, asking how we might be in reciprocity with them.

Taking prompts from the plant known as Motherwort or *Leonurus cardiaca* (the lion-hearted one) in allyship with the human organ of the heart:

Motherwort has bold, lacerated leaves that organize themselves rhythmically around a firm, almost prickly stem. Even their purple flowers are slightly

furry. Motherwort has the capacity to find rhythm. It helps regulate heart palpitations back into a steady rhythm. When the heart reacts with fluttering or irregularities from stress, panic, exhaustion, or anxiety in times of crisis or ongoing conditions of oppressions, Motherwort can become an ally to steady and to soothe. This plant has been offered to people with a uterus to regulate menstruation, induce abortion or birth, and aid recovery after childbirth. It speaks to the rhythmical organs, which are the lungs, the heart, and the uterus, enhancing both the movement of coming together and letting go. These seemingly opposite qualities are what let the rhythm and flow reappear. Although they are part of the mint family, their taste is bitter, astringent. Astringency, like the string that can draw together or open more loosely, creates tension in the tissues; the tone gets changed. Embryologically, the mouth developed over the heart. Maybe that is how we learned to speak from the heart, and as we do so, we may reflect with what tone we speak and how we speak up, with, or for what we believe in.

The heart is a pump that cares for the margins and the marginalized. It is connected to the tongue, a willful anatomy that articulates the sensitivities felt by the heart.

Our dwelling-sculpture of the heart is a multi-tiered space with positions of multiple perspectives. One can of course sit in solitude there, but as a social space it allows for several people to come together while facing different directions, integrating outlooks and circulating those within the heart space. So, negotiation is needed amongst those co-existing within that heart, shifting positions, and trying out each other's perspectives.

EMERGING QUESTIONS OR PROMPTS:

What is the heart of the social body in your experience?
What could processes/practices of the heart include?
How can we navigate regulation and dysregulation of the heart?
What are the connections between the heart and mental health?
What are the rhythms we want to sync with?
How do we learn to pulse within the tensions we are experiencing?
How can we find connections in coming together and letting go?
How can we do this collectively on different tempos and scales, allowing ourselves to find shared rhythms and polyrhythms when monotone rhythms of normativity try to dominate? ❁

BIO

Social-Body Apothecary, currently based in Berlin, Germany, has been initiated by Siegmar Zacharias (Romania/Germany), Kitti Zsiga (Hungary), and Shelley Etkin (USA/Israel-Palestine) in collaboration with Lili Birk Waehneldt (Germany) and Paule Potulski (Poland/Germany), and local neighbourhood community with post-migration backgrounds including Syria, Iran, Kurdistan, Afghanistan, and Turkey. The geographies grow as more people need to take refuge, and thus contribute to the social body.

holding space

SEE: Ayurveda, being with, humanness

CONTRIBUTION

selfcare and

Holding space

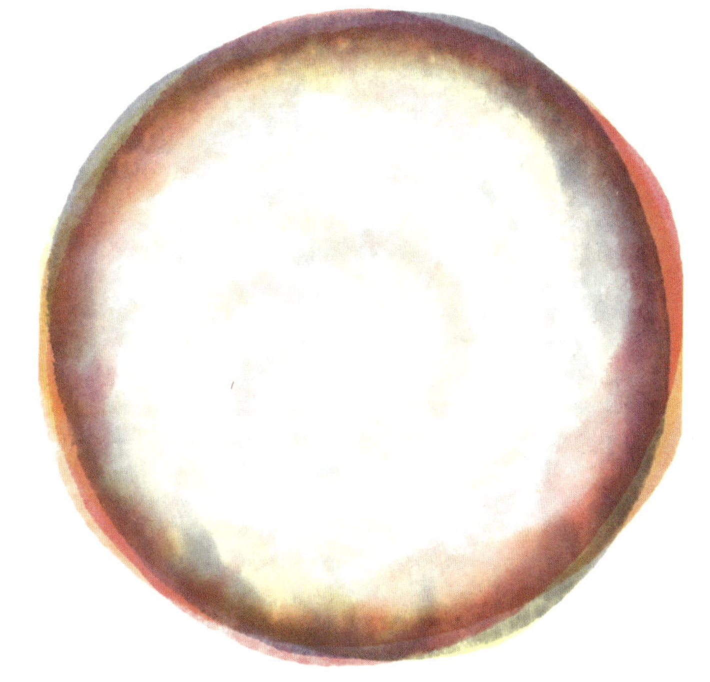

A spread from *selfcarefully*, written by Gracy Obuchowicz, designed and illustrated by Maria Habib (Thick Press, 2019).

holding space

Over the past few years, I've increasingly heard the phrase "holding space" to describe the act of supporting another's healing. Holding space—simply giving another person your time and attention while she figures out her own situation—feels so passive that it might be confused with doing nothing. And yet when I experience another person holding space for me during a difficult moment, I find it powerful and effective.

When someone holds space for me, rather than telling me what I should do or any other form of actively trying to help me, it feels like a sign of their faith that I can figure out my way forward. I feel their support in the background, reminding me that I am not alone. This support gives me the strength I need to keep working with the hard parts of change.

My approach to working with clients is mostly about just holding space. Of course, I give some basic self-care guidelines, usually founded on Ayurveda. Then, I ask them how they feel, encourage them to experiment, and remind them to trust their growth through the ups and downs of the process. Mostly, I have full faith that my clients will figure it out, because over and over, they do. To me, this feels like a very feminine way to help others.

I wonder what it would be like for us as a culture to hold space for ourselves right now. Rather than shouting over each other about the "right" way, what if we could step back, stay quiet, and trust our own process? My sense is that a little less effort could go a long way. It might help us gain the self-awareness to really grow up as a world.

BIOS

Gracy Obuchowicz is a wellness facilitator who is passionate about secondhand fashion, day-to-day meal planning, and connecting the many dots between our personal self-care and collective liberation.

maria habib spends her days in her studio "DesignMa" with her two cats, designing, drawing, and gardening for food and medicine—all the while missing her home, Beirut, Lebanon.

humanness

SEE: being with, holding space

CONTRIBUTION

FORGET HELPING. Such a radical concept. Trying to help or thinking you know how to be helpful can get in the way, as can expertise and good intentions. It can even make things worse. Instead of *helping*, think *humanness*: How can we put humanness back in our work?

We live in a world swirling in exasperation and hopelessness, a world filled with violent injustices, vanishing resources, conflicting ideologies, persisting poverty, blaming others, and exalting expertise.

Often people do not want the help *we think we know they need*. People, individually and collectively, around the world demand and fight to have a voice. They want to have input, to participate in creating solutions, policies, and laws that affect their lives. They know better what help and services they need than well-meaning professionals who are not walking in their shoes and who are often perceived as not understanding their unique situations.

Think about the last time you had a conversation with someone who was feeling hopeless. Often, we naturally try to point out the positive and good in their lives. Our well-intentioned support or advice frequently does the opposite. They feel worse, because to them we do not understand. In my experience, I have learned that having a sense the helper understands is monumental. A brief example is brought to my mind as the war in Ukraine rages on.

A colleague and I were invited by an NGO to consult with an agency in a country destroyed by war. What was left were desperately grieving women, because most men had been killed and their bodies were unidentifiably buried in mass graves. We were asked to support the women who staffed the agency, who themselves had experienced and were overwhelmed by the same tragedies as the women they wanted to help. We optimistically walked into the room, eager to know them and learn about their work. Our curiosities were met with blank stares or expressions of their exhaustion and feelings of hopelessness. Nothing we said seemed to engage the women, nor elicit any sense of confidence or competence, much less hope, but rather the opposite. Frustrated, we took a break to ponder the situation and our naivete. We realized our earnestly wanting to learn about their work was privileging our voice, excluding and silencing theirs.

We returned and thanked them for letting us know how hopeless they felt the situation was. Of course, how could they possibly help and instill hope in the aftermath of the war and its destruction of their country and families when they were traumatized and victimized themselves, like the women they were tasked to help.

Taking a 180-degree turn, we abandoned our original plan and asked them to tell us more about their hopelessness and the despondent situation. As foreigners from a peaceful country, we could not imagine such annihilation of human lives. It was as if those still alive seemed dead, or death would have been better than what they were left with. Painful and almost unbelievable stories about their own experiences slowly began to spill out. The atmosphere was heavy and filled with hopelessness. We next asked them to continue sharing with us and each other in two smaller groupings. We each joined a group. One group stayed on the theme of the hopelessness and futility of their efforts. A woman continued with her story about the horror and tragedy she and her children experienced as they awaited the return of the father who never came. They knew he was killed, and she struggled to maintain her composure while daily trying to comfort the children. I asked the storyteller to tell me about her husband, the children's father. She continued to talk, smiling with tears streaming down her face. Others slowly joined in to talk about their lost loved ones.

The other group drifted to the theme of escaping. I wondered, where would they escape to? A woman immediately responded, "to the sea." Slowly all seemed to resonate with this idea, and eagerly talked about going to the seashore and what they would do there.

Soon, all staff in each group was spontaneously talking. Heaviness, with a touch of lightness, now filled the air. My colleague and I did not talk except to offer a brief comment or question. We were *listening and trying to understand from their sense-making as best we could*. Realizing we were beyond the designated end time, we apologized, thanked them, and said we looked forward to meeting with them the next day.

The next morning, they were chatting with each other as we entered the room. The atmosphere did not feel as despondent and hopeless as it did the previous day, for them or for us. We learned that some of the women had stayed after that session and continued sharing. They said this was something they had not previously done for fear of emotions, hopelessness, and vulnerability becoming overwhelmingly unbearable. They had so much more they wanted to tell each other about their lives and their lost dreams and future hopes.

We entered the first day thinking we knew what they needed. Their responses to us quickly invited us to retreat. They sensitized us to respond to them, not to who we thought they were. As social psychologist and philosopher John Shotter[1] suggests, it's knowing how to participate within a situation rather than from outside it, knowing how to listen and respond, that honors and respects the humanness of all of us. ❂

1 Shotter, "Methods for Practitioners in Inquiring into 'the Stuff' of Everyday Life and Its Continuous Co-emergent Development."

BIO Harlene Anderson, therapist, consultant, trainer, and author.

nonviolent communication
radical presence
resonance
sustaining movements
togetherness
vigil

humor

SEE: accessibility

CONTRIBUTION

MOST OF US AGREE that words aren't neutral, and that labels are sticky. I think about the blurry space between naming things into being and awareness and pathologising them. In that little bit of wiggle room is the potential for some pot-stirring humour that asks you to imagine a world where "normal" is decentered and diversity (neuro or otherwise) is preferred, recognized, and strongly encouraged. ❁

BIO Carmen Ostrander is a community-centered therapist based in Canada, but not from there, providing Narrative, Expressive Arts & Substance Assisted Therapy as Square Peg Therapy.

Neurotypical Syndrome:

a neurobiological disorder characterized by preoccupation with social concerns, delusions of superiority, and obsession with conformity.

A sign created by Carmen hangs in two offices that she has inhabited. She found the cobbled-together text on the internet.

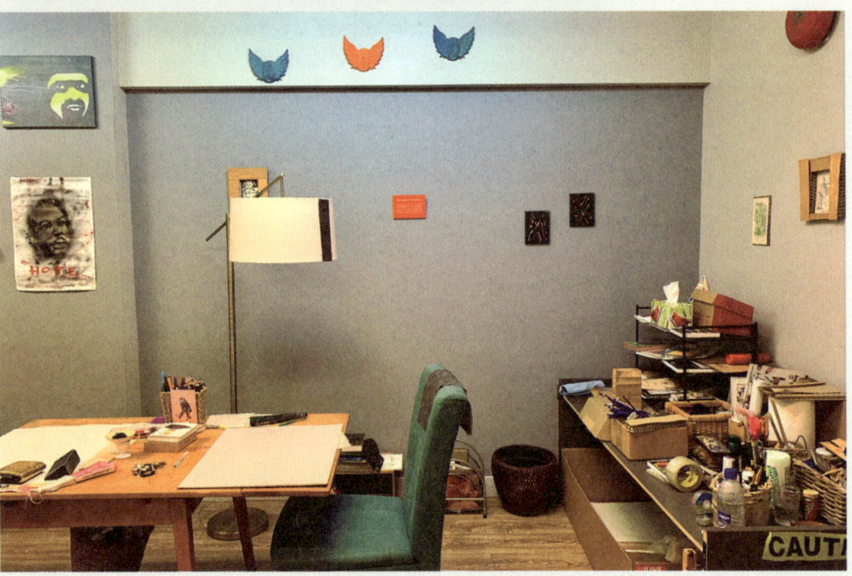

CONTRIBUTION

JD DAVIDS JOINED the direct-action AIDS activist organization ACT UP Philadelphia in his early twenties, becoming a treatment activist under veteran Kiyoshi Kuromiya's tutelage. Three decades later, Davids is himself an "illder," a term he coined, continuing to do crucial work in health advocacy with and for multiply-marginalized people.[1] In a recent piece linking HIV/AIDS and long-Covid activism, Davids remembers a training Kuromiya conducted about advocating for people in the hospital. Kuromiya taught that "when someone's in the hospital and they need clean sheets, you just go and you find them the sheets," Davids writes. Kuromiya urged his trainees to "always relate with compassion and practicality to both the hospital staff and the patient in the room [because] they're all on the team, and they all are to be treated as if they're in it together, with common cause."[2] Rather than strictly delineating medical caregivers, patients, and friends/visitors, in Kuromiya's model, care circulates among them. Compassion and practicality course through sheets, hands, beds, and bodies, connecting people as his mentorship did for succeeding generations of activists.

During Kuromiya's last days in Pennsylvania Hospital, May 1–10, 2000, a rotating group of friends and comrades kept a vigil in his hospital room. On loose-leaf paper in at least 5 different hands, they record the experience in a range of genres: part medical chart, part meeting minutes, part living memorial of Kuromiya's thoughts, feelings, and trademark humor. They do what needs to be done, carrying forward Kuromiya's own teaching on hospital care. With compassion and practicality, they name the nurses and doctors, occasionally questioning their interventions or advocating for alternatives, as they massage his feet, laugh with him, or help him back into the bed.

There are so many meaningful aspects of this remarkable document. I'm interested, for instance, in the way the note-takers almost compulsively mark time, night into morning, 6:45 and then 7:15, 2:55 and then 3:20. These intervals keep the medically mediated pace of the pumps of Demerol and the taking of vitals, but they also mark people's comings and goings, or the length of Kiyoshi's sleep, when he vomited blood, sighed, or spoke. At a certain point over the course of the 53-page document, timestamps become a convention of its newly minted genre: new writers continuing the tradition of their forebears. As the days and pages advance, we get less talking and more touching:

> 5/5
> 3 p.m. Most excellent foot massage by Heshy and Lise. Patient was kvelling.
>
> 5/7
> Bartlett 10:30 I arrived and Mrs. K is giving Kiyoshi a gentle hand massage—he is fast asleep. Seems to be sleeping well now. ➔

5[00] Horace, Heshi, Judith, Chris, Jane, Jackie, Julie, Erme
David A., Scott, Jeff, Charlie, Larry Kobnat

Gary, Helen & Jason from AZ. stopped by

- declined breathing txt
- Jeff brought a rose
- pressing Demerol button q 15 min.
- cold compress on his head

5[50] 67/42

Ripped from a legal pad, a piece of white paper with light blue lines, a pink margin, and blue handwriting reads: 5:00 Horace, Heshi, Judith, Chris, Jane, Jackie, Julie, Erme, David A., Scott, Jeff, Charlie, Larry Kobnat // Gary, Helen & Jason from AZ stopped by// -declined breathing txt/-Jeff brought a rose/-pressing Demerol button q 15 min./-cold compress on his head//5:50 67/42.

JD Davids papers, John J. Wilcox, Jr. LGBT Archives, William Way LGBT Community Center, Philadelphia, PA.

And then, simply, gathering. The final page of the hospital log is mostly a catalog of names:

> Horace, Heshi, Judith, Chris, Jane, Jackie, Julie, Erme, David A., Scott, Jeff, Charlie, Larry Kobnat…Gary, Helen and Jason.

Kiyoshi died surrounded by the community he helped to create, progeny, next of kin: someone bringing a rose, another holding a cold compress to his head. ❁

1 Davids, "The Cranky Queer's Guide to Chronic Illness."

2 Davids and Khanna, "Such a Powerful Love: Disabled and Chronically Ill People and Our Long Fight for Justice," 237.

BIO Libbie Rifkin teaches English and Disability Studies at Georgetown University, with a particular focus on the poetics of care and a commitment to mentoring for social justice.

improvisation

SEE: ethnodrama, failure, humor

CONTRIBUTION

SO OFTEN PERFORMED AND GATEKEPT BY MEN, improvisation was actually birthed by a woman. It was birthed by a mother, Viola Spolin, seeking to foster communication among Chicago's immigrant children in The Settlement Houses.

Look it up. It's true.

Improvisation is ours. All of ours. And it was birthed in social work, not for entertainment and laughs, but for connection and communication.

That is easy to forget these days, when it is taught as a means to entertain an audience, not to heal a self or connect a community.

What a loss.

Let us regain it.

A recipe for improvisation as radical healing—whether you are doing improv games, or just being a regular therapist or community social worker, or just, well, being in any setting, really, as any healer—is to teach and model this:

- Whenever possible, privilege play over knowing for sure.
- Privilege the real over the funny, authenticity over entertaining. (Entertaining = pleasing, indulging, appeasing… do you see it now?)
- Eliminate but. Use only "and." Ever. Try it, you'll see.
- Accept one another's realities. Don't deny. When difficult, use "if." If this, then what? If you experience X, then what? If you see X, then what? I do not have to see it the same way to validate the impact. This is how we heal racial harm, and couples' strife, too—if we can stick with it and feel the pain in it, instead of denying, deflecting, dismissing, minimizing. We are saved so much work when we need not argue the other's reality, but can accept it with an "and…?" Hard work. But worth it.
- Privilege collaboration over individual striving. What is done together, with others, in community, can and should always be valued and recognized over figuring it out yourself. Individual striving is easy. It is not vulnerable. It is not messy or painful. The doing together, the asking for help, the co-creating of reality, that is the shame-buster, the way to heal the Superwoman, the isolated, bullied child, the scapegoat, the perfect one who "never needed much." It is also, by the way, the way out of White Supremacy culturally.
- Applaud mistakes. Literally. Clap. Send "Congratulations!" cards, with glitter, when someone screws up, when they are swimming in shame. For they have taken a risk, done something wild, entered the unknown and found out something about flying before they fell. How brave. How marvelous. It's weird, at first, to high-five a fuck-up, but then it's healing. It obliterates those perfectionistic neurons, starves them of food. The improvisers clap when someone messes up in a game. We cheer failure. Because it means you did something. Anything. You moved. This is the cure for stuckness, for depression, for stagnancy, for staying the same. Create energy and enthusiasm for movement of any kind. You'll be surprised at how suddenly no one can sit still anymore.

They will itch to improvise their path toward the light. ✺

BIO

Lisa Kays received her clinical social work licenses by passing the racist, ableist ASWB licensure exam and can be found @theimprovisationaltherapist trying to find and bring amusement, a little bit of justice, and some healing to herself and others.

DECODE THE SECRET MESSAGE

11
6
9
3
13
4
12
5

5
14

12
8
1
2
7
10

Hint:

That sacred space from which all life emanates

1 2 3 4 5 6 7

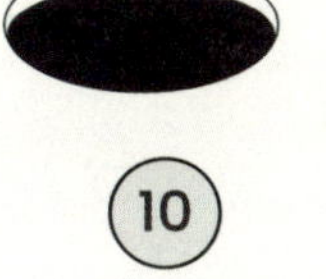
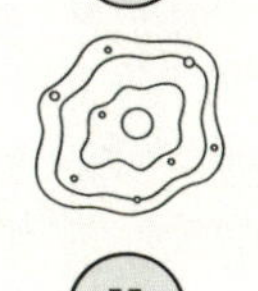
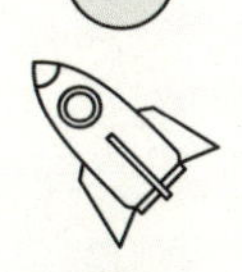
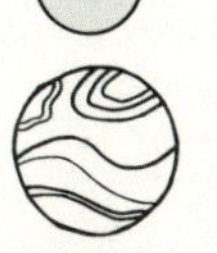
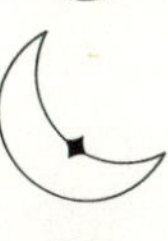
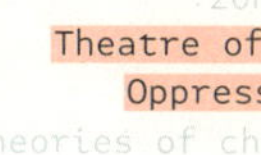

8 9 10 11 12 13 14

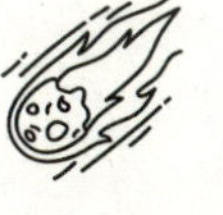
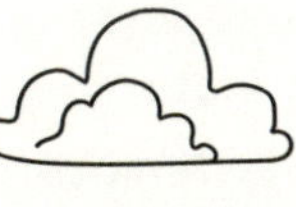

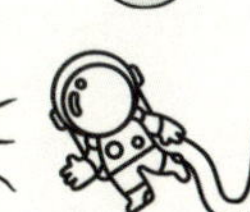
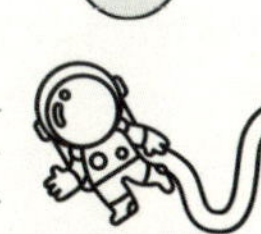

Secret Message: ______________________________

→

nfinite blackness

CONTRIBUTOR'S NOTE

While there is no singular definition for the term "infinite blackness," this author understands it as a recognition of the unending darkness of the cosmos which house all life and non-life, matter and non-matter. blackness is everywhere all the time; from the months spent in the belly of the one who birthed us to the moment of our final breath. darkness has for so long been equated with evil, and i want us to continuously challenge the white supremacist roots of that notion, which has found its way into every aspect of our consciousness. darkness can provide protection from a piercing hot sun, and solace from racing thoughts (think sensory deprivation tanks). Many a seed that has grown into a beautiful flower or delicious fruit first found life in darkness, and so too can you. —OA

BIO

Onyịnye smiles while bathing in the sunlight of life // ọchị na anwụ.

intentional communities

SEE temporary autonomous zones, togetherness

CONTRIBUTION

INTENTIONAL COMMUNITIES (from the Latin *intendere*, stretching out; from the Latin *communitatem*, shared by all brought together), societies comprised of members living together on a voluntary basis, sharing certain moral aims and collectively formulating agreements of organization. They are generally distinguished from the mainstream societies in which they exist and are often framed as experiments in striving for a more ideal way of life. Intentional communities center on common moral visions, both exemplifying alternative social arrangements and providing practical residential and co-working environments for their members.

A participant in an intentional community can be referred to as a *communitarian*, denoting an emphasis on communal living and labor. Although the terms *communitarianism* and *communism* have both historically been used to describe the ideological impetus of intentional communities, *communitarianism* encompasses them on the whole, while *communism* is a more particular philosophy of economic arrangement. The related term *commune*, referring to a residential group (such as a municipality or cooperative), can overlap with intentional communities, and the two terms are often invoked as descriptors interchangeably. However, an intentional community is specifically a free association of persons in which membership is voluntary. In this sense, intentional communities share history with the cooperative movement.

The moral character of intentional communities is tied to their voluntary organization centered on shared values rather than by circumstance. Usually, these values are framed in opposition to the mainstream societies from which the community emerges. They have variously featured negative desires for the abolition of the family, slavery, or bureaucracy as well as positive desires for a scientific, spiritual, vegetarian, or democratic society, to name a few. While many communities maintain personal diversity among their membership, some have been built upon principles of social exclusion on the basis of sex and ethnicity, ranging from separatism to supremacism. A community's structure might be egalitarian or hierarchical.

The *intentional* aspect tends to place emphasis on agreement or an explicit social contract—the foundational principles and systems of an intentional community must be agreed upon by its members, and newcomers later on are expected to accept the community agreements in order to join. This is meant to clarify both the requirements and benefits of life in the community for all members. For example, members may be asked to perform some amount of labor for the upkeep of the community, in turn affording them housing, food, and even health care. Labor includes daily chores, but certain models entail working in the community's agricultural or fabrication business. As an intentional community is a voluntary association, a member can choose to leave freely, forfeiting their obligations and benefits. Depending on the moral foundations of the community, they may potentially be barred from rejoining. On the other hand, some intentional communities allow for transitory membership, with persons coming and going, and they are only expected to follow community guidelines while in residence.

Many intentional communities are grounded in religion, often with highly ascetic ideals. This can appear as "simple living," with members eschewing certain "pleasures" associated with mainstream society or the material world itself. A prominent form is the monastery, which features in some religions as a site for intensive ritual practice. In Europe, urban versions of the monastery—convents and *beguinages*—developed around the 13th century. In the ancient Mediterranean, a major example of intentional communities can also be found in the Pythagorean circles of southern Italy. It is from this legacy that intentional communities have come to be frequently conflated with cults in the popular imagination.

In recent centuries, intentional communities have been associated with utopianism, especially "utopian socialism," a broad assortment of alternative societies that emerged during the late 18th and early 19th centuries in the wake of major revolutionary upheavals (e.g., the French Revolution). Prominent utopian socialists include

Charles Fourier, Robert Owen, and Henri de Saint-Simon. The United States in particular became a center for such intentional communities during the 19th century, with a significant number of projects influenced by utopian socialists. New Harmony, Brook Farm, the North American Phalanx, and the Northampton Association of Education and Industry feature among the plethora of individual communities, and groups such as the Icarians and Am Olam established multiple communities around the country. Although some were organized on a secular basis, many also centered on Christian millenarianism, such as the Oneida Community and the Shakers, while other Christian communities like those of the Hutterites have older origins in the Anabaptist movement. The longevity of these communities ranged greatly—for example, the Oneida Community in New York lasted for three decades before dissolving and converting to a joint-stock company, while the Fruitlands commune in Massachusetts operated for only seven months.

By the end of the 19th Century, new agrarian communes increasingly followed anarchistic ideas, such as those of the Russian author Leo Tolstoy, who advocated an ascetic, non-urban, and pacifistic lifestyle, and American author Henry David Thoreau, whose environmentalism, abolitionism, and individualism proved highly informative for modern countercultural movements. Some grew out of socialist labor groups as well as the "single-tax" economic proposals of Henry George. More communities appeared beyond the American East Coast and Midwest, including New Odessa, Altruria, and the Home Colony along the West Coast.

A "back-to-the-land" tendency—a broad trend of interest in ruralism, autonomy, and autarky—continued to be a core tenet of communities founded during the 20th century. Countercultural movements like the Beat Generation and New Age carried it into the postwar period, variously combining the earlier sentiments with orientalism, psychology, and new forms of mysticism. Druid Heights, The Farm, and Twin Oaks came out of this wave in the latter half of the 20th century, the last of which still operates today alongside fellow members of the Federation of Egalitarian Communes. By the 1970s, ecology and feminism proved to be crucial principles for many communitarian projects, with some of the most prominent contemporary intentional communities including "Ecovillages," such as Earthaven, and "Womyn's Land," such as the Oregon Women's Land Trust. ❁

BIO

Zach Whitworth hails from the Umpqua Valley of the Pacific Northwest.

CONTRIBUTOR'S NOTE

My own historical scholarship is focused on the community of New Odessa and its ideological context in the late 19th century. Due to the limitations of space in this publication, I've restricted the scope of description here mainly to the 19th and 20th centuries in the United States, which I have the most familiarity with. While most of the projects I mention are agrarian, this is not to suggest intentional communities are inherently agrarian or rural. In fact, many are notably industrial and urban. Among the listed authors and communities, I would especially recommend to anyone interested in this subject the writings of Robert Owen—*A New View of Society and Other Writings* is a great collection to start with. To get a broader understanding of intentional communities in the United States, a fine entry point is *Two Hundred Years of American Communes* by Yaacov Oved.

interdisciplinary cataloging

CONTRIBUTION

(INTERDISCIPLINARY CATALOGING AS AN APPROACH FOR SELF-SOOTHING): an action, part of the noun, part of the reflective practice. For example, I label my love for you endlessly. To complete a list of items, typically one in alphabetical or other systematic order, by way of emotion, medium, or pursuit: ∎ a list of all the books or resources in your personal library. ∎ a publication containing details and often photographs of memory you can't escape esp. one produced by a friend, a teacher, a lover, or some neighboring stranger. ∎ a descriptive list of works of art in an exhibition or collection that has given you a reason to survive. (For reference, watch American movie (c. 1999) and write down the name of the jeans the director is wearing. Go buy them). v. (-logs, -logged, -log·ing; also -logues, -logued, -logu·ing) [tr.] Now make a systematic list of (items of the same type or material or feeling or color). ∎ enter (an item) in such a list. ∎ list (similar situations, qualities, or events) in a sort of succession: the result is a catalog of your own existence. What's startling about living? Do you collect perfumes because your mother had them? If so, why are they all half empty? We describe what we avoid feeling. We list what we cannot make of. Now you've got it, a catalog for your own truth. You were brave for that, and I'm proud of you. ❁

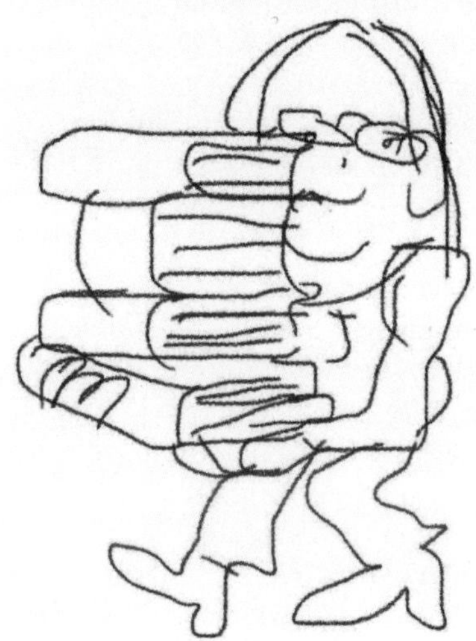

BIO

Jessie McCarty, cataloger and poet, author of *The Bovine Huff* (Track and Field Studios, 2021).

CONTRIBUTOR'S NOTE

Catalogs are a wonderful way to sort out emotions. Labels become fragmented modes of journaling. When visiting the *Field Guide to Photography and Media* exhibition at the Art Institute of Chicago, I noticed a flash image of a tiny ram. He was stuck in a branch, his eyes staring down past the lens. I catalog this under the terms (claustrophobia) and (jealousy), as I wish I were the one who took it. A man looks toward me, saying the ram looks afraid. I took a photo of the piece with my iPhone. It is as if I was moving in a circle. I log the day under (present tense), as in, I am living in the moment. —JM

ntergenerational living

CONTRIBUTION

Generations of Love

MY ABUELITAS ALWAYS BLOOM beautifully in my memory, even though I can count on one hand the number of exchanges I had with them. Sadly, we were 3,300 miles too far apart from each other to develop a deeply rooted relationship. And so, what I do know about these women comes mainly from the tales others tell.

Stories about my foremothers revolve around their no-nonsense, can-do attitudes. These were women accustomed to making a lot from little, and unapologetic in their acquisition of knowledge. Like my bisabuelita known for her love of reading. Although widespread interest and access to books was not common in 1920s rural Mexico, she always devoured words. When there wasn't a book in sight, bisabuela read the piece of newspaper hastily wrapped around her most recent purchase from the butcher. After every word on the page was consumed, she used the sheet as toilet paper. Her go-to motto: read everything, reuse everything.

I grasp tightly to these memories. Without them, the distance between California and the heartland of Mexico would have completely erased my abuelitas, and their world, from my emotional landscape.

Perhaps because I only had stories instead of doting abuelitas to hold on to, I desperately wanted something different for my children. I wanted them, and me, to be surrounded by love and family. I wished for maternal sages by our side, to guide us and smile at our existence.

Yet, when my firstborn arrived, the nuclear family felt so natural. After decades in California without elders close at hand, I instinctively mothered in the stereotypical American way: in isolation. I did almost everything by myself, without much help at all. When my hair started falling out in clumps, I knew serious change was required. The bald spots had left my failed parenting experiment and postpartum depression utterly exposed, impossible to ignore.

Motherhood forced me to reimagine what kind of family structure I needed in order to flourish. And what my children ultimately required in order to thrive, too. My growing baby bump—my second child—made the situation even more urgent. Help was essential. Every day. Multiple times a day. I craved connection and emotional safety. I dreamed of around-the-clock community. The comfort and security of a family blanket seemed the only possible salve.

I was aching for an intergenerational home. The confines of parenting at home, alone all day, proved unsustainable and lacked the kind of layered complexity necessary to sustain myself. Certain that the companionship of another generation would alleviate my circumstances, I invited mamá to move in with us. To join our family on a daily basis.

Still, I was terrified. What would it mean to live with my mother at this stage of life? How would we navigate child rearing and personal space? Without examples around, I couldn't imagine how a residence with three generations would function, though I was curious to find out firsthand. In Mexico, I had plenty of extended family members who inhabited multigenerational abodes. But could this arrangement work within the borders of a more individualistic country where historically the cultural and religious undertones were so unlike what existed in Mexico?

Answers to these complex questions were scarce.

She moved in anyway.

I wasn't sure what our weeks would look like, but in the broken moments of early motherhood, it didn't matter. Anything was better than trying to manage alone. Fortunately, for me and my growing family, mom agreed to unpack her bags and stay a while.

At first, our parenting instincts diverged gigantically. I tried to nurse my kids on demand, practiced attachment parenting, and subscribed to a "no tears" sleep solution. She advocated for letting kids cry and not carrying them too much, lest they become "spoiled." We argued, often.

Slowly, we developed a delicate dance between dependence and independence, between sought-after advice and well-intentioned but meddlesome interjections. We took turns drawing boundaries. Then, we watched as those lines were obliterated and began anew.

Despite it all, we thrived.

The kids have learned how to process and simultaneously hold two distinct, often contradictory, understandings of the world. They benefit enormously from our family's integration. Fluidly maneuvering between contemporary Los Angeles customs and Abuelita's Mexican traditions is the norm for my children. Her insights also allow them to locate their realities within a larger rainbow of family and human experiences. All this, while being surrounded by unabating affection.

Amá, in many ways, gets to relive her parenting years with the patience and presence of mind that only time and distance can bring. She did it once, but now she gets to enjoy the journey more. The delight of being around children, getting their hugs and kisses, is frequently hers without the direct responsibility of parenting. Meanwhile, our company acts as a shield against the loneliness that often afflicts people in her age group. To be valued and cherished undoubtedly helps mom continue to blossom.

Close proximity has further strengthened my relationship with mamí. Our interactions are robust and multilayered in ways that were once unimaginable. I can now see her not just as my mother, but as a woman, a grandmother, and an independent individual. We laugh, we fight, we reflect, and we try to make the most of our moments together. Time has created a depth to our bond, gradually mending some of our differences. Every day we get a chance to connect as women, friends, and housemates.

By living together, we are doing more than merely redefining static mother-daughter roles. We are wholeheartedly embracing a way of functioning strongly rooted in our Latinx heritage. Existing under the same roof is an act of reclaiming and affirming cultural knowledge. Our family practice is a quiet but powerful revolution against the lonesome child-rearing convention currently dominating the United States.

Over the years, I have learned that creating an intergenerational home did not mean I had failed as a parent. The isolating custom of nuclear households simply did not work for me. My hope is that my children will flower with the help of their abuelita's love and eventually come to interpret their multigenerational upbringing as an invitation to embrace ancestral cultural understandings that work for them.

And herein lies the beauty of intergenerational living. ✱

BIO Norma Fabian Newton is an Indigenous Latina writer, speaker, and Latinx storytelling advocate.

nterspecies organizing

EE: imate cafes, mmuning with animals, dérive, the, groups, improvisation

CONTRIBUTION

LARPing for Bountiful Biodiversity Born of Interspecies Political Action

IN 2019 a planetary health check revealed over a million species on Earth at risk of extinction because of human action.[1] Treating the location of our gallery in Finsbury Park, London, as a microcosm of the whole imperiled Earth, we co-devised a 5-year series of exploratory LARPs (live-action role-play events). A LARP is a game of collective make-believe where people adopt new characters and interact with each other in a fictional setting. There are no lines to recite, only improvisation in response to fictitious events.[2] We hoped to use the power of play, with park communities, to rediscover and renew our relationship with nature.

This constellation of LARPs, which went under the heading of *The Treaty of Finsbury Park 2025*, sought to stimulate action towards socially and ecologically sustainable futures—for instance, by scaffolding people's imaginations, providing equitable spaces for exploration, and building new networks and capacities.[3] And in doing all this, catalyse the blooming of a bountiful biodiversity born of interspecies political action.

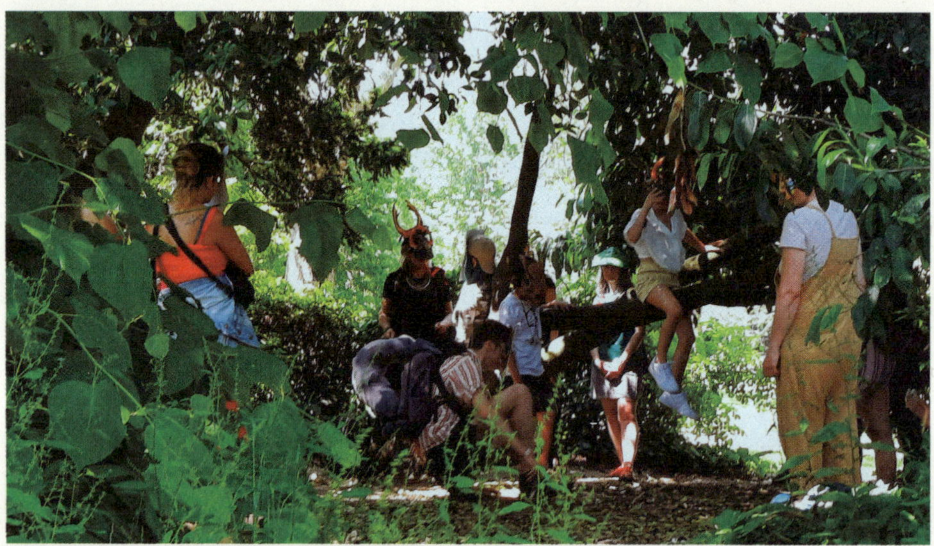

The Interspecies Festival hosted by Furtherfield took place on three scorching days in June 2023 in Finsbury Park, North London. The first activity took place in the trees of the Old Forest, where each species explored their different senses. Image courtesy of Furtherfield.

Starting in 2020, this collaborative project[4] depicts the dawning of interspecies democracy. It's a new era of equal rights for all living beings, where all species come together to organise and shape the environments and cultures they inhabit in Finsbury Park. The immersive fiction is played from more-than-human perspectives; people participate in a ritual supported by the *Sentience Dial*, a new technology which allows them to tune in to all flora and fauna, and supports communication between all living entities.

Meanwhile, in the "real world," local and global struggles intersect. Like many urban parks, Finsbury Park is fraught with environmental issues—from noxious gases and traffic noises to governance struggles and financial sustainability.[5] On the ground, a furious battle rages with the local council about the care of this crucial public amenity. Civil servants once spoke with pride about biodiversity action planning as part of a commitment to make Haringey London's "Greenest Borough."[6] Now, after fifteen years of Tory "austerity" policies, the park has become an asset for exploitation; an income-generating venue for corporate hire. The park must pay for its own upkeep. The onslaught of massive commercial festivals takes its toll on local human and non-human communities alike. Field habitats are devastated by soil compaction and churn caused by huge vehicles, multi-tonne stages, five-metre-high steel perimeters, and tens of thousands of stampeding party-people. The pollution and noise are unbearable for local people, and this year the cacophony drove fifteen different species of nesting songbirds from their homes in the ancient trees.

In our LARPs, players were matched with one of seven Mentor Species of the park and were supported through costume, scenarios, and ceremony to spend games inside the mind and body of their Mentor Species—with their human self as witness to all that occurs. This multi-species citizenry rises up and finds its political voice through a story in three episodes:

- In 2020–22, people played *The Interspecies Assembly Games* to plan the *Interspecies Festival of Finsbury Park 2023*—an event to celebrate the drawing up of a treaty of interspecies cooperation.
- At *The Interspecies Festival of Finsbury Park in 2023* all the species of the park were invited to join the summer festival. Festival activities devised by players of the Interspecies Assemblies included: the multisensory mystery tour; the interspecies daycare and spa; the multispecies choir; and the zero-waste feast (or pass-the-poo-parcel). Activities culminated in a procession to the Gallery with placards and songs, after which we returned to our human selves, where we discussed our new perspective and proposals for a new treaty for equal rights for all species with everyone, sharing their priorities and feelings.
- By 2025 a treaty of interspecies cooperation will go on display at Furtherfield Gallery along with festival highlights and an invitation to ALL park users to pledge their support to bountiful biodiversity in Finsbury Park.

Scientists can be sniffy about anthropomorphisation, as it can “lead to inaccurate understanding of biological processes in the natural world,”[7] and misinterpretations of the actions and agency of other beings. However it is also a way for humans to build empathy beyond our own species. It is therefore perhaps a crucial technique for exploring new subjectivities and so resisting the unquestioning presentation of non-humans simply as resources for extraction. Besides, rather than anthropomorphisation, we were promoting other-species-isation.

A crisis of imagination leaves us unable to conceive of political and economic systems of organisation that do not contribute to further threats to the earth and all its life forms. Human populations and governments have responded to impending climate collapse for decades with denial and inaction. Interspecies LARPing supports group-driven, place-based discovery by allowing people to feel differently. In Professor Ann Light’s words: “Not only to feel different but to feel relationships that are not ubiquitously available at present.”[8]

We have learned through this project that by acting as other species in carefully crafted scenarios such as interspecies festivals or multi-species assemblies, people:

- Start to perceive new dimensions of social and material reality beyond the limits of human sense perception,
- Build new empathy pathways to other life forms, and
- Connect with nature’s webs of life in new ways.

By treating life forms as resources to be managed and exploited for profit, rather than lived with and learned from, humans are condemned to lonely self-destruction. If colonial systems of dominance and control over living beings—human and non-human—continue, we all face an apocalypse.[9] Biodiversity is crucial in

ritua
Theatre of th Oppressed
togethernes

mitigating the effects of climate change. As cities now hold some of the world's greatest biodiversity, we can't help but wonder if they also hold the greatest potential for positive impact. It's time to spark new ways of being, feeling, and acting together locally, nationally, transnationally…[10]

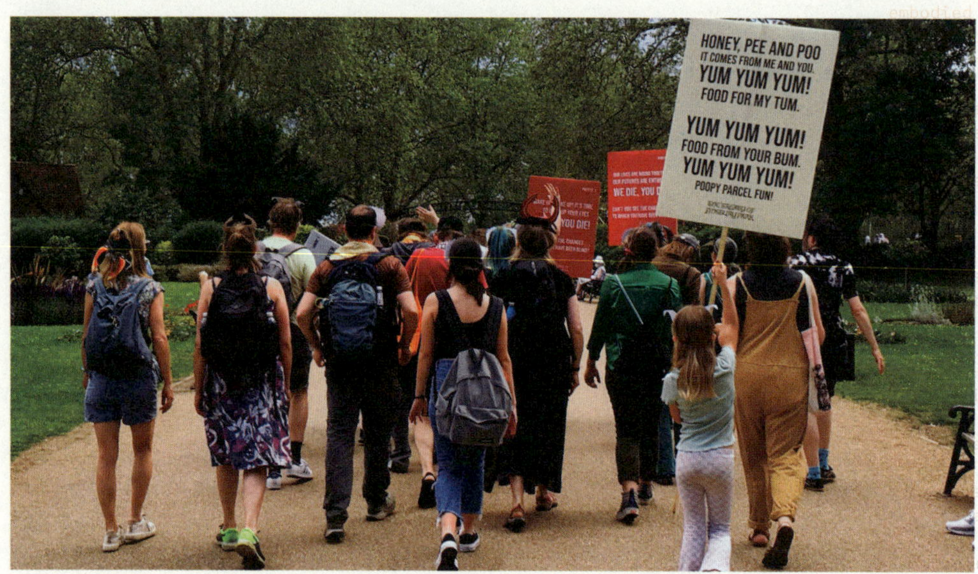

The Interspecies Festival of Finsbury Park, 2023, by Furtherfield. Image courtesy of Furtherfield.

1 IPBES, "The Global Assessment Report on Biodiversity and Ecosystem Services."

2 LARPs exist on a spectrum. At one end sit historically detailed, play-by-play battle re-enactments. At the other end are the immersive, improvised, future-fiction or fantasy, art performances of Nordic LARP. Treaty is made in the Nordic LARP tradition.

3 creatures-eu.org/about/

4 *The Treaty of Finsbury Park 2025* is based on an initial concept by Ruth Catlow and Cade Diem (New Design Congress) and co-authored by Ruth Catlow and Charlotte Frost (Furtherfield) with Bea Xu and Max Dovey, originally as part of the European research collaboration, CreaTures, Creative Practices for Transformational Futures.

5 Furtherfield, *The Treaty of Finsbury Park*.

6 Haringey Council, *Biodiversity Plan*.

7 Milman, "Anthropomorphism: How Much Humans and Animals Share Is Still Contested."

8 Light, *In Dialogue with the More-Than-Human: Affective Prefiguration in Encounters with Others*.

9 Diehm and Catlow, concept paper for *The Treaty of Finsbury Park 2025*.

10 Furtherfield, *The Treaty of Finsbury Park*.

BIOS

Ruth Catlow is an artist, curator, writer, and Co-Director of Furtherfield.

Charlotte Frost is Co-Director of Furtherfield, a creative sector strategist, consultant, & digital specialist; a talent developer, coach & integrative therapist; an obsessive self-expressive, a writer, educator & a feminist!

EDITORS' NOTE

"Intuitive eating," which has certainly been "invented" or "discovered" by many people in many contexts, is often associated with the work of Evelyn Tribole and Elyse Resch, whose book, *Intuitive Eating*, first published in 1995, invites readers to reject diet culture and health-related fearmongering and pay attention instead to their bodies' emotional, instinctual, and rational cues. Joni's evocative poem offers a glimpse into the experience of intuitive eating. —ES

CONTRIBUTION

💔*intuitive eating with a broken heart*💔

intuitive eating

with a broken heart

red cherries
pineapples

during a thunder storm

a weird mix of anxiety

shoulders

my

off

lifting

the accumulation of five-years'-worth
of
emotional
sediment

on

to chest

my

just above my stomach,

sits
Yet a sunken feeling still →

, not quite on my lungs.

the weather seems to weep for me
light(e)ning strikes and thunder-cracks
parsing out the complicated insides

but magnifying it,
turning into another sensuous shadow

intoxicating
eight thousand
eight hundred
eighty eight times

green onion pork chops
garlic broccoli
salted egg stir fried shrimp

some times I want to try
to slide
the whole world into my mouth.

imagine

how up thewalls

itpushing of

wouldagainst my

feel, esophagus

some times I want to sip on a

ody neutrality
ody positivity
ody Trust
fat positivity

intuitive eating

black hole

when I don't feel like eating anything at all

it might bring back my appetite

sucking
every
atom
out
of
me
into

its
vortex

⚙

B
I
O

🔮Snack Witch Joni Cheung🍡
is a wicked ✨ #magicalgirl who
eats art and makes snacks
across Turtle Island: Follow
her edible adventures
@snackwitch or snackwitch.ca/

SEE: ancestrality, anti-racism, commons, the, critical pedagogy, critical race theory, decolonial liberatory-based practices, generous systems, limited equity cooperative housing

CONTRIBUTION

Prospect.

PROSPECT COUNSELLING + TRAINING is a POC-led counselling practice dedicated to providing accessible and exceptional counselling to BIPOC communities while disrupting the capitalist values currently upholding standard clinical training programs. Rather than building wealth for practice owners, proceeds from provided services support further training, thereby enhancing the services offered while funding projects for collective healing within the community.

We were chatting away about life, its goings-on, and our frustrations with training folx within an institutional setting, when we came to the topic of liberation. We shared our hopes to engage in spaces where there's already a buy-in into the ethics and radical politics that inform our work. Not having spaces where the messiness of dreaming up and creating liberatory practices felt like a lost opportunity that cost too much. What are we leaving on the table when we only engage in institutionalized training and educational practices? What change could we spark if we created a space for therapists-to-be to build their practice on a more radical foundation?

For several years, Bhupie had envisioned a community-oriented learning space where students and practicing counsellors can come together to learn/unlearn together in a way that also serves the community in more radically useful ways. Abby's excitement and passion for the idea propelled it forward. From there, we began to co-create what it would look like on a practical level and how it may evolve in the future. Putting boots to the ground, we collectively made Prospect what it is today.

We're just figuring things out as we go, but we are thrilled to continue having creative, tough, and fiercely radical conversations with each other and the community as we do our part in moving towards collective liberation. Connect with us at prospectcounselling.ca.

With care, Bhupie + Abby

We are uninvited settlers, occupying the stolen, unceded, ancestral territories of the xʷməθkʷəy̓əm (Musqueam), Skwxwú7mesh (Squamish), Səl̓ílwətaʔ/Selilwitulh (Tsleil-Waututh), and S'ólh Téméxw (Stó:lō) peoples. Our relationship with these lands dictates our commitment to understanding the ongoing impacts of colonization and decolonizing our practices in and out of the counselling room. ❂

BIOS

Abby Chow, therapist, writer, and co-conspirator for more radical projects like Reflecting on Justice, Prospect Counselling + Venturous Counselling.

Bhupie Dulay, therapist, supervisor, dreamer.

land trusts

SEE
reveng
solidarity
solidarity economy
togetherness

CONTRIBUTION

TECHNICALLY, land trusts are legal entities used to manage land, often for conservation, development, or investment purposes. The most common forms are conservation land trusts created to prevent development on family land so that families can continue to live on the land or serve environmental goals like animal repopulation. These kinds of land trusts can be owned by a nonprofit and are attractive costwise because they're eligible for tax deductions.

What's really interesting is that over the last couple of decades there's been an increase in what are called community land trusts. Community Land Trusts (CLTs) are legal vehicles that allow nonprofits to hold land on behalf of a place-based community for the benefit of community assets. From its inception, CLTs served as long-term stewards for affordable housing. Recently however, CLTs and land trusts more generally have been used by historically marginalized groups (Black, Indigenous, and Migrant) to reclaim and protect land of which they were original or generational stewards; gain access to land that is otherwise made systematically unavailable; and/or bring land back into the Commons for communal benefit instead of private interests. Used in this way, land trusts have become a creative strategy for new or returning farmers, land workers, and land stewards to collectivize resources and support a broader set of mutual communal needs.

Given the colonial and violent history of property law in the United States/Turtle Island, land trusts are part of a broader set of strategies designed to repossess stolen land, resist maneuvers to take land, and extend collective land ownership among often exploited land workers. See this 2019 NPR story as an example:

npr.org/2019/10/03/766706906/5-decades-later-communities-land-trust-still-helps-black-farmers.

BIO

Richael Faithful is a Black trans-southern multi/interdisciplinary healer, culture worker, and attorney.

and, work, spirit, body

SEE: accessibility, ancestrality, centering maintenance, collective care, decolonial liberatory-based practices, deep organizing, embodied knowledge, erasure, avoiding thereof, group work, healing justice

CONTRIBUTION

THE SUBTITLE of a powerful tool developed as part of Southerners on New Ground (SONG) Organizing School in the early 2000s, which served both as a map for understanding what was happening at the moment and the foundation for political analysis for systemic change. Land / Work / Spirit / Body are the four dimensions in the "temperature check" part of the analysis. The guiding questions included:

- What is happening in our communities around work right now? Who has work? Who does not? What kind of work do people have?
- What is happening in our communities around bodies right now? How are our bodies doing? What do we need?
- What is happening in our communities around land right now? Who has control of land? Who can/is using land to grow food and live on, etc.?
- What is happening in our communities around Spirit right now? How are our spirits?

The answers to these guiding questions and other stories that emerged led to a discussion about how capitalism, governance, finance, and social control shaped our gender and sexual realities.

For many younger queers, including the author of this encyclopedia entry, this activity was transformational. Many people in the room expressed that this was the first time in their activism they were ever asked about relationships to dimensions of ourselves. What's more, the mapping of our *relationships* to Land / Work / Spirit / Body didn't occur only through words—they were through drawings or other visual representations that included us in the art. There was a feeling of, and through, our relationships rather than an intellectualization about our relationships; that is, we were a part of these relationships, not separate from them. And for some folks, including the author of this entry, it was the first time as an organizer ever being asked about land, body, and spirit. Intersectional Community Mapping was much deeper than Power Mapping, and a stark contrast to more patriarchal, militaristic organizing schools that prioritized understanding others' power, and systems that we had to control.

The tool is still on the internet! Try it out.

southernersonnewground.org/wp-content/uploads/2019/10/SONG-The-Intersectional-Community-Map-Land-Body-Work-Spirit1.pdf.

BIO

Richael Faithful is a Black trans-southern multi/interdisciplinary healer, culture worker, and attorney.

language justice

SEE recognition resistanc solidarit somatic healin sustaining movemen

CONTRIBUTION

Thick Press and Chris invited Margo and Vero to contribute the following text, which they often read aloud before providing Spanish interpretation at various events.

WE WILL BE practicing language justice in this space by providing Spanish interpretation [and closed captioning in English]. At its core, language justice is the right we each have to communicate in the language in which we feel most powerful. We recognize the limitations of our practice, as today we are only providing Spanish interpretation [and closed captioning in English] and there may be other languages and language access needs represented on this call.

We recognize that language is a place of connection, but also a place of trauma.

We recognize the fact that the cities where we live and work are in indigenous lands, and that colonization has erased thousands of languages.

We recognize the loss of languages due to slavery, and the fact that today many of us do not speak the language of our ancestors.

Language justice is rooted in a history of resistance by communities and peoples whose voices have been silenced for generations, and to practice language justice is to focus on decolonization and a healing approach to language.

Practicing language justice is everyone's responsibility. As such, we ask that you do your part by speaking slowly and clearly, keeping in mind that Spanish is 30% longer than English.

If you are on the Spanish line, you might be surprised to hear some words ending in an "e" that usually end in an "a" or an "o." This is not a mistake, but part of our commitment to gender justice by using inclusive language. ❁

BIOS

Margo de Torres and Vero González are a Puerto Rican mother-daughter language justice team known as ¡Wepa Translations!

eaving well

SEE: death practices, deep organizing, group work, holding space, life cycle honoring the

CONTRIBUTION

LEAVING WELL is the art and practice of leaving a thing, with intention and purpose… and when possible, joy.

Often used by those who live outside of their passport country, whether due to a military or mission-based posting, or due to a job relocation or for any other reason, leaving well in that circumstance offers a beautiful way of commemorating the place you've called home, as you prepare for a new city, a new town, a new base.

Leaving well is also a term utilized in situations of hospice care or in the final days of life during the process of dying. The exercise of leaving well is an opportunity for those left behind and the person processing their own death to navigate through emotions and memories, and to say goodbye in meaningful ways.

Leaving well is also incredibly important in the workplace, or community-based projects, grassroots organizing, caregiving, mutual aid, volunteerism, etc. Reclaiming our individual power to exit and navigate transitions in those spaces allows us to begin normalizing these types of necessary endings. It offers opportunities to better process the grief and loss that can come from changes in our careers and impact-based activities.

Leaving is inevitable.

So if it's true for all of us, that we will one day leave our workplace, our jobs, our gigs—why do we avoid intentionally planning the way we leave?

For leaders inside social impact organizations, we might think that building a beautiful culture around "leaving well" might make people leave faster. In personal/life situations, we avoid endings because we hope that our situation is fixable, or because we are scared of the future.

We often fail to realize that the related stress levels that accompany prolonged staying are higher than those related to leaving. Sometimes we assume that conflict or drama will accompany decisions around leaving. But what if being intentional about instituting and embodying a culture of leaving well actually allowed us to meet our organizational and personal goals in even better and faster ways?

I believe that we avoid prioritizing endings and leaving in a healthy way because we have never been taught how to navigate this leaving well.

Over the last ten years of working in the realm of organizational health, I have witnessed numerous transitions of executive leaders and CEOs. While much attention is often placed on the selection and onboarding of new leaders, the process of departing leaders leaving with grace and leaving behind a positive legacy is equally critical—and I argue that it is actually more important than the hire ever will be. The end is just the beginning.

Imagine if organizations normalized these work endings, rather than focusing on them as a negative! Imagine if organizations prioritized individual resources and support to implement leaving well each and every time a new opportunity knocked. ❁

BIO

Naomi Hattaway is an affordable housing and workplace transitions consultant whose love language is accountability, tattoos, and great playlists.

love
lunar cycle
Magic School, the
mapping support
marginality (as a site of resistance)
Marxist social work
membership theory in social work
mending
metaphor
mikveh
mobile libraries
movement lawyering
mutual aid
mycelia as metaphor
narradrama
narrative medicine
narrative therapy
nepantla/nepantleras
nonviolent communication
ongoingness
peer counseling
peer-to-peer health network
person-situation perspective
perspective via faith
pleasure
poems/poetry
poetic meter
polarity work
post-oppositionality
postwork imaginaries
poverty-aware social work paradigm, the
power threat meaning (PTM) framework
pre(care)ity
prison abolition
professionalism without performance
progressive education
public benefits
public library, the
qigong
radical administration
radical care in the arts
radical childcare in movement spaces
radical inclusion
radical papermaking
radical presence
radical social work
Radical Therapist Journal, The
Rank and File Movement (RFM) in social work

CONTRIBUTION

Gardens, Not Prisons

In our current climate, school is a prison and authenticity is a crime

Energising, creative, fulfilling, changing, liberating -

Profit driven, potluck, rigid, compliance driven, hierarchical, structured, institutional, set curriculum and outcomes

The free-flowing river of expectation is quickly dammed by reality

We need to centre accessibility in our ways of doing and being in classrooms

BUT... We're stuck in a system of standardisation where teaching is the same no matter how learners engage

"You're not perfect the way you are" - Osaka Punch

"You stay soft, get beaten. Only natural to harden up" - Mitski

Where your worth as a human being is based upon your ability to produce (unless you're rich!) and expertise is centered in those who access power and privilege

LOOKS LIKE: debt, privilege, ableist, unclear expectations, classist, hetero-normative, racist, patriarchal, power dynamics

"How can the world want me to change? They're the ones that stay the same. They can't see me, but I'm still here" - John Rzeznik

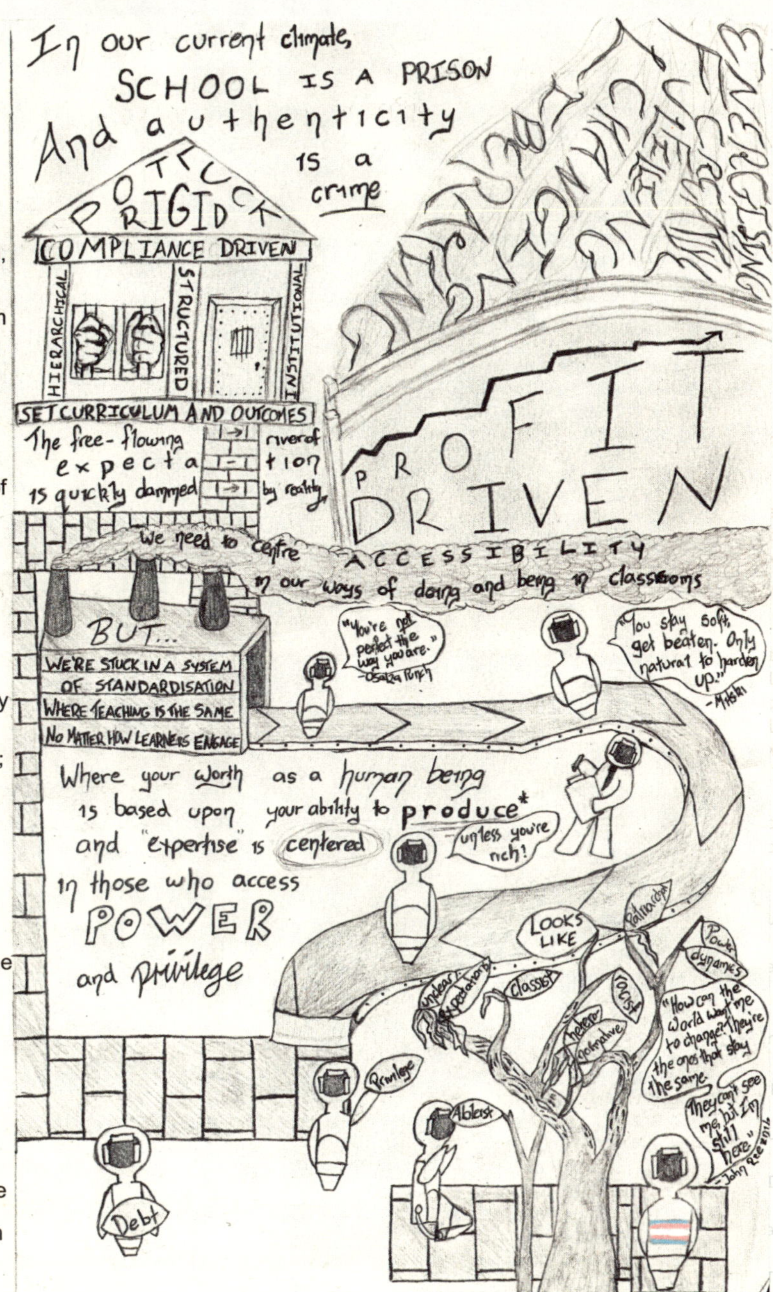

reclaiming selfhood
recognition
redistribution
Reflecting on Justice
reflexivity
Reik
relational interviewing
relationality
resistance
resisting the parental loss narrative
resonance
respite room
as resistance
revenge
revolutionary mothering
ritual
sanctuary
sauna
seed banking
sex positivity
slow textiles
slowness
social change
solidarity
songs/singing
sound healing
spells
storytelling
strengths
sufficiency
symbol
tarot
Theatre of the Oppressed
theories of change
theosophy
therapeutic writing
togetherness
trans practices
transformative justice
traspatio
12-step programs
undercover anti-bullying teams
vigil
water
wildness
wintering as metaphor
wishes
witchery
yoga
zinemaking

→

Ableism - its roots run so deep, buried within the soil of white supremacy

FEELS LIKE: guilt, sacrifice, thoughts feel like mush :(, brain needs dopamine, it hurts, I want to achieve, I'm doing my best, unfair

“We have to constantly critique imperialist white supremacist patriarchal culture because it is normalised by mass media and rendered unproblematic” - bell hooks

“To alienate humans from their own decision making is to turn them into objects” - Paulo Friere

Trying to alter our neurotypes to behave the same, learn the same, think the same. It's an act of violence

“The kids are not alright” - P!nk, 2022

“The kids aren't alright” - The Offspring, 1998

We need to deconstruct our thinking of learning spaces. Relationships are fundamental to our learning systems - we are wired to learn and grow in community

“It is in collectivities that we find reservoirs of hope and optimism” - Angela Davis

Mentorship should be an equal exchange. It shouldn't matter where inspiration comes from

SOUNDS LIKE: listening to marginalised communities, follow the dopamine, collaboration, curiosity, trust, warmth, agency enthusiasm, patience

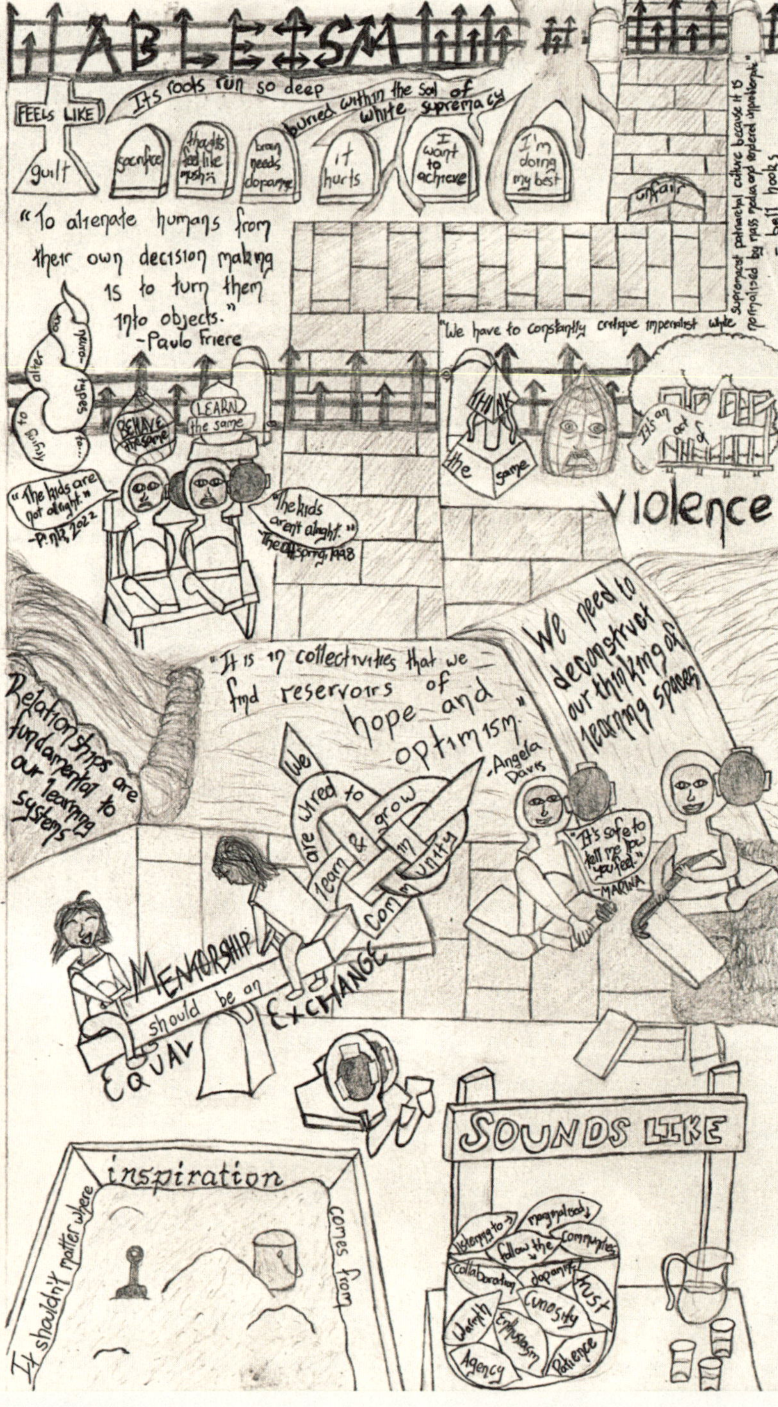

Our communities as a whole grow stronger when our most vulnerable are supported

(Like the curb cut effect - Google it!)

When we recognise behaviour as communicating unmet needs, we can remove this culture of shame and create spaces where learners can truly engage

Understanding can't be cemented in perfection

The world needs diversity to thrive

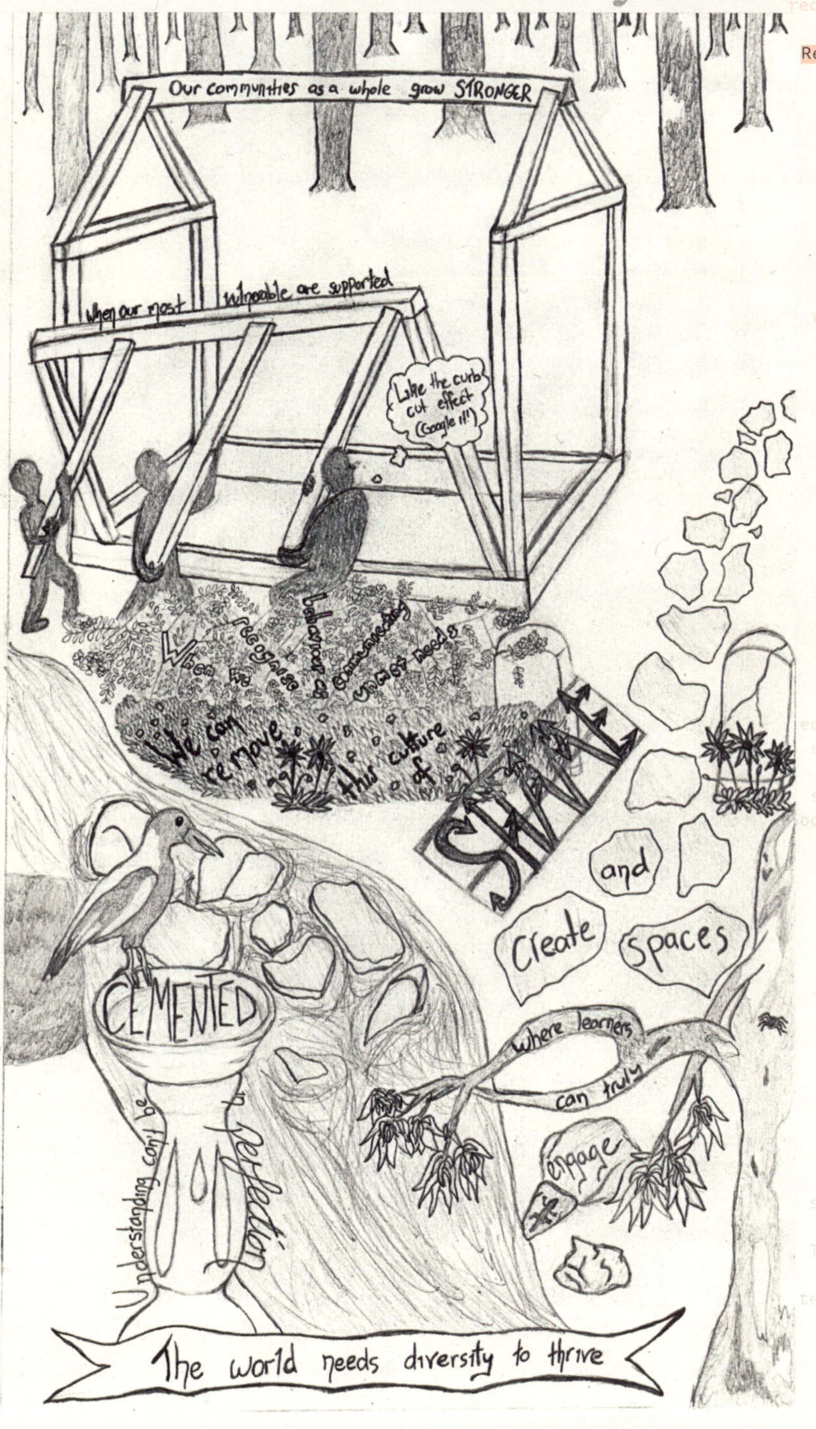

BIOS

K.C. is an educator and activist living in Naarm.

Owen Smith is an educator living on Bunurong Country.

ife cycle, honoring the

EE: death practices, etymology, feminism, leaving well

CONTRIBUTION

I LISTEN TO SYMPTOMS OF ILLNESS and descriptions of pain, discomfort, disorientation. People's bodies contract and shrink from illness. Mine swells and changes with life. I'm offered seats people rise from, or space at the end of the bed where feet move to accommodate me. Holy, sacred spaces acknowledging we are all experiencing our own bodies at the same time, in this institutional space. Doctors tell family members they can expect someone to die within weeks, days, hours. I readjust my aching hips in the waiting room chairs and feel the baby flip. Your loved one is leaving (to where?), mine is soon due to arrive (from where?). We are both afraid and expectant, uncertain what to do with our love.

The woman with abdominal cancer is doubled over in pain, her face pressed against the guardrails of the bed. As I tiptoe in to meet her for the first time, in the very first, secret days of my pregnancy, I whisper "hello." She opens her eyes, takes me in, and a radiant smile fills her face—"Oh! You are going to have a baby!" she proclaims. What do we do with our observations of each other? This work creates time and space for connection, witnessing of one another. I see her pain, and somehow through that pain, she sees me with clairvoyance. We are strangers, yet united in our corporeal experiences.

A mother sits at her son's hospice bedside as the waning city sunlight streams into the room. Her sadness is palpable. In the doorway I offer a quiet greeting, my swollen belly arriving before the rest of me. "You shouldn't be here!" she chides. "It's not good for a baby to be around this sadness." She looks angry and disapproving of me. Should I not be here? Is the sadness catching? Will the baby be predisposed to darkness or loss because of this "exposure"? From her seat, I wonder about the universe of feelings she is experiencing I cannot yet grasp. I linger in the room, I don't know how to connect with her. The chasm between us feels uncrossable. She looks out the window until I leave. I wish I had been able to acknowledge this out loud, to soften the space between us, not to let my anxious reverence for her motherhood quiet my clinical mind. As I breathe in the hallway outside her son's room, I ponder how to be in this work, in my body, as I feel impending motherhood changing me.

Family members of patients touch my belly; one elderly woman offers a "good luck pat," which feels more like a slap. Her husband has died and we are sending each other off, out of the hospital, back to the rest of our lives where her family has shrunk and mine has just begun to grow. We have orbited a space where she has reminisced about a life she shared with a man who slips away from her, and we have talked about how she will take her first steps forward, without him. As I make offerings to her, she does the same to me. We are each venturing into new territory.

I finally stop resisting talking about my big belly, if my feet ache, if I think it is right to be around death. I feel deeply connected to the cyclical rhythms of life, to witness beginnings and endings happening in our soft animal bodies. I offer my words and my silence, I honor the acts of love I see as we care for one another. I wonder how patients and families receive our presence, guidance, offerings. Are we making their journey better, lighter, more comfortable or meaningful? Is that why we are here? How do we witness their experiences of their bodies? Are we helping them prepare? What do we need at the beginning, or the end, as we stand (or sit) with compassion in the reverence of our transitions? Do we heal in the witnessing of our own bodies relative to others? And if we find connection and meaning in this witnessing, how do we share it at our most tender intersections?

life cycle, honoring the

SEE
membership theory in social work
person-situation perspective
reflexivity
relationality

Who sees who first?
I walk into a sterile room that belonged to someone else yesterday, to see you.
You have been stripped of your real clothes, the fabrics of your choosing that cover your body, that could tell me something about you
I walk in wearing my clothes, in my body, but it is assumed that you are not to notice, not to comment, our meeting is about you they say
It is often assumed that my job is to see you, to learn and hold your story, with an attention that resides somewhere other than myself, my body, my experience
I think this is how we protect ourselves, protect from the feeling of being so touched by someone else's suffering, that it changes us
Protected from the reality that there are just some things we cannot change, some pains that will not go away, some injuries to the heart and spirit that forever modify how the world works
In order to be with another in that kind of space, you, I, have to be there, in the room, feeling this body, tending to the places in ourselves that come alive and activated and scared and tender, through another's story
You do see me though
You comment on my pregnant belly, it's definitely a boy you say
Have I eaten dates? It's good for pregnancy you say
How am I feeling, do I have other children, how can I do this work as a parent you say
I am in the room, you want to talk about it, about me, you want me to exist outside this place, for you
This tide is turning, has always been turned in some places
I'm learning, there is little helping, there is little service, if one side is blank, if it's "not allowed to be about me, too, as a professional helper"
This thinking, this posturing, assumes separation, assumes one directional healing, assumes professionalism means not having a feeling experience in front of another who is impacting you
You need to know I am affected by you, I want you to know that you matter enough that your story lands someone in me, and changes me
I let the conversations about my pending baby go on, every time I see you
What a relief, relief from your own story that you do not want to tell again
I share, it is hard to be in the hospital pregnant, it hasn't been easy
Your eyes gaze upon me so tenderly, a moment of caring in my direction. ❁

BIOS

Meagan Lyon Leimena is a social worker, mother, and neighbor working towards a healthier and more equitable South.

Bridget Sumser is a social worker, mother, and friend who practices at the intersection of illness, living, and dying.

EDITORS' NOTE

When Bridget and Meagan shared their emergent essay with us, we struggled to figure out where in this *Encyclopedia* we should file it: Was it about bodies and embodiment? Bodies in flux? Reflexivity? Conscious use of self in hospice work? Of course, their thought-provoking piece is about all that and more, so we settled on a topic that gestures at the importance of infusing clinical practice (among other things) with wonder and respect for the "life cycle." —ES

liminality

SEE: clouds as metaphor, existentialism, failure

CONTRIBUTION

LIMINAL COMES FROM the Latin word *limen*, meaning threshold. Liminal space can be understood as territories of life where we are in between what was and what is not quite yet.

Entries into liminal space can happen in two primary ways. From a place of personal agency, meaning we chose to enter some form of change in our lives. This looks like actively pursuing a new job or career change, moving to a new city or country, or entering a new relationship. More often liminality is imposed on us. This happens in job loss and layoffs, divorce or break-up, or death of a loved one. There is no escaping the disruptive and destabilizing experience of liminality in our lives. These in-between places of waiting and uncertainty are everywhere and inevitable.

Unfortunately, many of us do not do uncertainty well. We are always in the struggle of manufacturing control in a world when, if listened to, our inner knowing understands there is none to be found. In my role as a therapist, I have come to see my job as not so much helping folks manage pathologies, but rather helping folks lean in to and move through uncertainty. I no longer view myself as a "therapist." I prefer the title of Liminal Space Tour Guide.

When goals, new intentions, or personal development projects ultimately don't come to fruition, I don't fault the many hopeful folks for their attempts at goals, new intentions, and personal development projects. I know how hard real change is. Not meeting the career goal, not starting the new business, the relapse, all of which gets characterized as self-sabotage, are not personal failings, but rather a turning back to what is known and familiar in the face of liminal space, or uncertainty.

In a world that is losing many of its rites of passage, I think it's important to acknowledge markers of potential transformation and change. We are being called to build a new world, a new way of being with each other. But we are losing the skills needed for the job. Here is where an understanding of the journey toward changes and transformation can steady us for the small and large sacrifices and *patience* that real change requires.

Regardless of whether it is voluntary or imposed, separation and entry into liminal space will often start with the experience of failure. We live in a culture now that doesn't understand the fruits of failure. If we are to make any significant changes in our lives, communities, or world, we need to make friends with failure. No deep change can happen without the experience of failure. If the fear of failure is keeping you from doing the hard thing you want to do, or know you need to do, I get it. Risking failure requires us to take some uncomfortable countercultural positions. Risking failure will require us to abandon aspirations of perfection in our own and others' eyes. Risking failure will require us to trust in our abilities, wisdom, and sense of worth, rather than outsource these things to others. And risking failure will require us to be okay with failing.

We need a new understanding of failure. Failure should be regarded as a signpost of doing, effort, and courage. In his book *The Queer Art of Failure*, Jack Halberstam writes that: "Under certain circumstances failing, losing, forgetting, unmaking, undoing, unbecoming, not knowing may in fact offer more creative, more cooperative, more surprising ways of being in the world."[1]

I couldn't agree more.

So, what is it you need to separate from in the coming months or year? Is it a job or a relationship? Is it old ways of being or old identities? What sort of separation do you see on the horizon that may be imposed on you? How do you want to meet the impending changes? With a death grip on the way it used to be? Or with a free fall into the liminal? ❁

1 Halberstam, *The Queer of Art of Failure*, 2–3.

BIO

Chris Hoff, PhD, LMFT, is the Founder and Executive Director of California Family Institute and a Liminal Space Tour Guide.

lingering
love
lunar cycle
Magic School, th
mapping support
marginality
(as a site of
resistance)
Marxist social
work
membership theory
in social work
mending
metaphor
mikveh
mobile libraries
movement
lawyering
mutual aid
mycelia as
metaphor
narradrama
narrative
medicine
narrative therapy
nepantla/
nepantleras
nonviolent
communication
ongoingness
peer counseling
peer-to-peer
health network
person-situation
perspective
perspective via
faith
pleasure
poems/poetry
poetic meter
polarity work
post-
oppositionality
postwork
imaginaries
poverty-aware
social work
paradigm, the
power threat
meaning (PTM)
framework
pre(care)ity
prison abolition
professionalism
without
performance
progressive
education
public benefits
public library,
the
Qigong
radical
administration
radical care in
the arts
radical childcare
in movement
spaces
radical
inclusion
radical
papermaking
radical presence
radical
social work
Radical Therapist
Journal, The
Rank and File
Movement (RFM)
in social work

limited-equity cooperative housing

SEE

CONTRIBUTION

New York City limited-equity cooperative projects, *30 Years of Amalgamated Cooperative Housing, 1927–1957* (New York: James Peter Warbasse Memorial Library, 1958).

CONFLICT BETWEEN USE VALUE AND EXCHANGE value is at the center of the housing crisis. Market-rate housing is a for-profit commodity, valued for its appreciation in cost at the time of sale or rental, rather than as a widely affordable place used for living a high-quality life. On the other hand, affordable rental housing created for tenants unable to pay market rate doesn't allow for the creation of equity.[1]

Housing in limited-equity cooperatives (LECs) offers a middle way between these two conditions. A concept used for multifamily housing, LECs offer affordability while also allowing the creation of equity for their residents. An unlimited future profit upon sale is traded for a lower purchase price, mortgage, and maintenance fee. Through a limited percentage of profit at resale as well as paying down their mortgage, residents can gain equity while also preserving affordability.[2]

While market-rate cooperatives exist, affordability is typically a main goal for them, with today's co-op principles originating with the Rochdale Society of Equitable Pioneers in 1844 in England. An organization of weavers, the Rochdale Pioneers were a response to industrialization's negative impact on skilled labor's livelihood. Their principles, used with some interpretations, are still in use for co-ops ranging from groceries to housing and other functions. Revised in 1966 by the International Co-operative Alliance, Rochdale's six principles are:

1. Open, voluntary membership
2. Democratic governance
3. Limited return on equity to promote affordability
4. Surplus or profit belongs to members
5. Education of members and the public in cooperative principles
6. Cooperation between cooperatives[3]

To address some of these principles in the context of housing, "democratic governance" takes the form of an elected board composed of residents. While residents own shares in the overall co-op property, their individual

reclaiming selfhood
recognition
redistribution
Reflecting on Justic
reflexivit
Reik
relationa
interviewing
relationalit
resistanc
resisting t
parental loss
narrative
resonanc
respectful visitin
respite room
rest as resistanc
reveng
revolutionar
mothering
ritua
sanctuar
sandplay therap
saun
seed bankin
sex positivit
shadow integratio
Sick Woman Theor
slow textile
slownes
social chang
ecosystem framework
social constructio
social practic
social therapeutic
Social Welfare Actio
Alliance, the
solidarit
solidarity econom
somatic healin
songs/singin
sound healin
speculative desig
spell
staying with th
trouble
storytellin
street newspape
strength
perspective, the
sufficienc
sustaining movemen
symbo
Taos Institute, th
taro
temporary autonomou
zones
Theatre of th
Oppressed
theories of chang
theosoph
therapeutic writin
togethernes
trans practice
transformativ
justice
traspati
12-step progran
undercover anti
bullying teams
vigi
wate
wildnes
wintering as metapho
wishe
witcher
yog
zinemakir

apartments are leased from the co-op. Regardless of how many shares a resident-shareholder owns, each apartment has only one vote in the election of the board or in other co-op affairs.[4] A major appeal of the model is that resident control allows for collective decisions to create various kinds of shared amenities, improvements, and organizations, as well as introduce changes in policies and finances. It can also allow for the creation of apartments for different forms of households not catered to by the market.[5]

"Limited return on equity to promote affordability" is controlled by resale formulas determined by each co-op, with the need for affordability set by income restrictions for applicants. In addition to the typically small percentage of profit conveyed to the shareholder at the time they sell their apartment, once sold, LECs also typically collect a specified flip tax paid into the co-op's shared reserve fund—"profit belongs to members." This fund is separate from one used for cyclical maintenance created from monthly fees. With the co-op's profits reinvested in itself and local businesses rather than into global speculation, LECs promote what can be called "circular flows."[6]

Speaking broadly to the principles of "education of members" and "cooperation between cooperatives," residents in an LEC are required to use their home as their primary residence, not as a sublet or pied-à-terre. This requirement underlines the commitment to building local community through various forms of direct participation by residents, such as through the board, committees, leading projects, etc.

Despite the shared principles, cooperatives are quite varied in their specifics. While related rental co-ops exist elsewhere, notably in Europe, the capital of LECs is New York City.[7] But even within New York, LECs vary a lot, from serving more middle- to lower-income residents, and from being in purpose-built buildings to converted existing ones.

At the start of the twentieth century in New York, trade unions lent funds for construction and mortgages for co-ops housing their members.[8] An early and important example of this is the Amalgamated Cooperative Apartment House, built in the Bronx in 1927 for members of the garment workers' union. Abraham Kazan, the president of the Amalgamated Clothing Workers Credit Union who led the Bronx project, initiated multiple major LEC developments throughout New York City after World War II. These range from the Hillman Housing Corporation (1950) on the Lower East Side, to Rochdale Village (1963) in Queens, to Co-op City (1973) also in the Bronx and the largest LEC in the world, with 15,372 units. While built with tight budgets, these projects delivered durable and well-considered designs with ample outdoor space.[9]

In 1955, LECs in New York got a new infusion of support through the passage of the Mitchell-Lama legislation. This government program, which helped Kazan's ventures, provided developers with tax abatements, low-interest mortgages in exchange for limits on their profit, and the ability to withdraw from the limited-equity structure and go market-rate after twenty to thirty-five years. Around 105,000 Mitchell-Lama apartments have been built in more than 226 buildings.[10]

A different type of LEC program started in the early 1980s, with the city's Housing Development Fund Corporation (HFDC) law. This program was aimed at low-income renters looking to be cooperative owners, taking over derelict private properties purchased by the city. The city offered tax abatements to HFDC co-ops, and the Urban Homesteading Assistance Board (UHAB), a non-profit founded in 1973, provided financial, technical, and organizational support for renovations and co-op formations. UHAB continues to help today with HFDC co-op projects.

New York's LECs are an impressive contribution to affordability and resident control throughout the city's fabric, but they're also under threat. The pressure to enter the speculative market is immense, and has frequently broken down the commitment to long-term affordability and stable, supportive community. How can the limited-equity model best be sustained and reinvigorated?[11] ⚙

1 The definition of equity in this context is the difference between the value of an owner-occupied apartment and its outstanding mortgage, hence what a resident stands to gain if the apartment is sold.

2 The allowable percentage of profit can vary from co-op to co-op.

3 See Wikipedia, "Rochdale Principles." Note that the International Cooperative Alliance has since made another revision of the principles, in 1995. While much the same, they speak less directly to limited equity in phrasing. For comparison, see "Cooperative Principles," ica.coop/en/whats-co-op/en/whats-co-op/co-operative-identity-values-principles.

4 Share quantities vary depending on apartment size.

5 While not LECs per se, examples of cooperative housing in Germany, Switzerland, and Spain show the rapport between co-ops and non-standardized apartments designed for a spectrum of household types and lifestyles. For coverage of such innovative co-ops in Zurich, see Dominique Boudet, *New Housing in Zurich: Typologies for a Changing Society*. In the American LEC context, this diversification is for future investigation.

6 See Delz, Hehl, and Ventura, *Housing the Co-op: A Micro-political Manifesto*, 25.

7 See *New Housing in Zurich*.

8 Dagen, Bloom, and Lasner, *Affordable Housing in New York*, 42.

9 The main architect for Kazan's developments was Herman Jessor, who was involved with more than 40,000 units of cooperative housing over his lifetime.

10 The Mitchell-Lama program was not exclusively for LECs, as it also significantly delivered rental units.

11 In May of 2022, New York congressman Jamaal Bowman introduced the Affordable CO-OP Act. With CO-OP an acronym for "Collective Opportunities for Owning Property," the act aims to promote anew the development of limited-equity housing cooperatives. As of 2023, it remains under review for further action.

BIO Casey Mack, an architect, is the founder of Popular Architecture and the author of *Digesting Metabolism: Artificial Land in Japan 1954–2202* (Hatje Cantz, 2022).

lingering
love
lunar cycle
Magic School, the
mapping support
marginality (as a site of resistance)
Marxist social work
membership theory in social work
mending
metaphor
mikveh
mobile libraries
movement lawyering
mutual aid
mycelia as metaphor
narradrama
narrative medicine
narrative therapy
nepantla/nepantleras
nonviolent communication
ongoingness
peer counseling
peer-to-peer health network
person-situation perspective
perspective via faith
pleasure
poems/poetry
poetic meter
polarity work
post-oppositionality
postwork imaginaries
poverty-aware social work paradigm, the
power threat meaning (PTM) framework
pre(care)ity
prison abolition
professionalism without performance
progressive education
public benefits
public library, the
Qigong
radical administration
radical care in the arts
radical childcare in movement spaces
radical inclusion
radical papermaking
radical presence
radical social work
Radical Therapist Journal, The
Rank and File Movement (RFM) in social work

reclaiming selfhood
recognition
redistribution
Reflecting on Justic
reflexivit
Reik
relationa
interviewing
relationalit
resistanc
resisting th
parental loss
narrative
resonanc
respectful visitin
respite room
rest as resistanc
reveng
revolutionar
mothering
ritua
sanctuar
sandplay therap
saun
seed bankin
sex positivit
shadow integratio
Sick Woman Theor
slow textile
slownes
social chang
ecosystem framework
social constructio
social practic
social therapeutic
Social Welfare Actio
Alliance, the
solidarit
solidarity econom
somatic healin
songs/singin
sound healin
speculative desig
spell
staying with th
trouble
storytellin
street newspape
strength
perspective, the
sufficienc
sustaining movemen
symbo
Taos Institute, th
taro
temporary autonomou
zones
Theatre of th
Oppressed
theories of chang
theosoph
therapeutic writin
togetherness
trans practice
transformativ
justice
traspati
12-step program
undercover anti
bullying teams
vigi
wate
wildnes
wintering as metapho
wishe
witcher
yog
zinemakin

Conversational Hacks: Part 1

I OFFER THREE CONVERSATIONAL HACKS[1] that I find useful in my efforts to: 1. center people's knowledges, values, and aspirations; 2. foster generativity and meaning-making; and 3. encourage a responsive, creative, situated practice, one free from the constraints of a paint-by-numbers approach to therapeutic conversations.

These hacks also stand in resistance to the reductive and facile ways (thanks, TikTok!) we have collectively come to talk about our experiences of distress and how to respond to them. When considering your use of these hacks, keep these points in mind:

- Keep them responsive to and situated in the relationship: always reflect the language and vibe of the client and the conversation you're having.
- One example is one example, not a template.
- Each hack uses a sample problem for the purposes of illustrating the hack.
- There are always multiple possible conversational pathways to take in a conversation; the hacks here are neither prescriptive nor exclusive of other possible responses in any given dialogical moment.

I think of the first two hacks as elaborations on what Michael White calls *lingering* or *loitering*, or on Harlene Anderson's mantra, *slow down to hurry up*. The third hack is about breaking a common "rule" therapists have been taught forever.

HACK 1: "If you didn't have that word..."

The language of diagnosis and psychopathology used to be the rarified language of the psy industries. Today we can't escape it. It's the language people use to describe not only the distress they're experiencing, but also their identities. People don't just "have" ADHD, for example, they *are* ADHD. There's also the omnipresent diagnostic-adjacent language such as "triggered," "dysregulated," "executive functioning," and "trauma-response." These are just a few ways that therapy-speak has jumped the guardrails from professional contexts to casual conversations with the person next to you in the grocery checkout (thanks, TikTok!).

One assumption I hold is that people have much richer, contextualized, and experience-near ways of describing themselves and their experiences... they just need to be asked about them.

The Hack: *"I really want to understand the distress you're experiencing and I don't want to assume I know what* you *mean for* you *when you say you're 'dysregulated.' If you had never heard that word before, how would you describe what's happening or making trouble for you?"*

My intentions with this hack are to:

1. Interrupt what likely has become a story the person has told over and over to the point it's on autopilot. Pausing creates space for reflection and makes way for a more personalized version of their experience.
2. Center their ways of understanding and storying their experience; de-center decontextualized, universalizing, professionalized understandings, which assume pathology.
3. Invite a more experience-near and richer contextualized description.
4. Resist recruitment into medicalized and pathologizing constructions of identity.

***

HACK 2: "What will this make possible...?"

This hack is about leveraging an important opportunity for cultivating richer meaning and generating more complex and nuanced preferred stories. When people name a new development, or a change they've made (or would like to make), I often will take the time to understand the significance of the new development. I'm interested in connecting the new and preferred outcome to other relationships or aspects of the person(s)'s life that may not be directly or explicitly central to the change.

The Hack: *"When you're no longer captured by Imposter Syndrome, what do you anticipate will become possible? What will that make possible, not only in your work, but in other aspects of your life?"*

If it's a change that has already happened, adjust the question appropriately. For example: *"Now that you know Imposter Syndrome is a fraud and that you have an authentic claim to Confidence in your art, what's that making possible for you in other aspects of your life?"*

My intentions with this hack are to:

1. Construct change as more than a discrete, isolated "goal," one which is storied and has implications for multiple domains of life.
2. Invite generativity, further meaning making, and thickening of preferred stories by connecting change to values, intentions, aspirations, knowledges, and practices.
3. Discursively connect stories across past, present, and future temporalities.
4. In the case of a desired (but yet-to-be-realized) change, linger in the imaginary and aspirational, inviting detailed descriptions of life after this change emerges.

***

...CONTINUED UNDER breaking the rules ✺

1 SEE breaking the rules for the third hack.

2 Again, SEE breaking the rules.

BIO

Julie Tilsen lives on stolen Dakhóta land, the ancestral and contemporary homeland of the Dakhóta and Ojibwe Native Nations, which was obtained through violent acts of genocide, displacement, forced removal, and broken treaties.

EDITORS' NOTE

Thanks to Julie Tilsen for graciously agreeing to our playful suggestion to divide her very helpful essay, "Conversational Hacks," over two *Encyclopedia* entries. Please see "breaking the rules" for the second part of the essay.
—ES & CH

ove

SEE:
access invocations
accessibility
tivating archives
frofuturism
gency
ging positivity
tar work
lternative identity projects
ncestral wisdom
ncestrality
nti-ableism
nti-adultism
nti-racism
nti-racism court system
rt
rt as/in/of life
rt journaling
rt therapy
rt workers
rt-based group work
rts in medicine
rts-based research
uthentic Movement
utonomous healing
yurveda
eing with
ertha Capen Reynolds
ike and car repair collectives
lack Panther Party Free Breakfast Program
ody as community
ody neutrality
ody positivity
ody Trust
oredom
rave space
reaking the rules
ridge as metaphor
are pods
are-based co-housing
atholic Worker Movement
entering maintenance
ircular economy
limate cafes
louds as metaphor
oalition
ollaborative apprenticeship
ollective care
ommon pool resources
ommons, the
ommuning with animals
ommunity college
ommunity gardens
ommunity newspapers
onjure
onstructionist-design framework, the
onsulting your consultants
ontemplative tradition, the
orn knowledge
redit unions
rip time
ritical fabulation
ritical hope
ritical pedagogy
ritical race theory
ritical suicide studies
ritical whiteness

CONTRIBUTION

WHAT CAN BE SAID OF LOVE? Choosing, effortfully and insistently, deliberately and consistently (SEE boredom and curiosity); showing up and attending to another (SEE being with); wanting for that person a flourishing, a self-realization, a never-ending unfolding; doing all of this based on continually trying to know and without erasing (SEE erasure, avoiding thereof), and without needing anything to unfold in any particular way: at its least, love does this.

But love is also justice, because you cannot love another without wanting justice for another. And there is no justice for one person unless there is justice for all people, and so you cannot love another without wanting justice for the world. And if you want justice for the world, then you must love the world, and so you cannot help but be forever seeking to be better at loving. When you encounter a person, just as there is an unknowable complexity that you must yet try to know (SEE recognition), there is also an unachievable justice that you must yet try to achieve. Insisting on continuing to try, even in the face of that impossibility, is also love. ❁

BIO

Noriko Martinez works imperfectly as a radical helper by sitting with people, being curious, and loving the world.

Cuestionamos
curiosity
death practices
decolonial liberatory-based practices
deep organizing
dérive, the
drumming
embodied expression
embodied knowledge
emergent strategy
empathy
energy work
erasure, avoiding thereof
esoteric wisdom traditions
ethnodrama
etymology
existentialism
externalizing
failure
fat positivity
feminism
feminist ethics of care
fermentation
flâneur
food sovereignty
forest bathing
fragments/fragmentation
freedom
generous systems
gift economies
Grace Lee Boggs
grief as nonlinear
group work
groups
harm reduction
healing circles
healing healers through the arts
healing justice
healing rituals
Hearing Voices Network
herbal justice
herbalism
holding space
humanness
humor
idlers
improvisation
infinite blackness
intentional communities
interdisciplinary cataloging
intergenerational living
interspecies organizing
intuitive eating
justice-oriented counseling
land trusts
land, work, spirit, body
language justice
leaving well
liberatory education
life cycle, honoring the
liminality
limited-equity cooperative housing

lunar cycle

SEE recognition, Reflecting on Justice, ongoingness, solidarity, wintering as metaphor

CONTRIBUTION

LIKE US, THE MOON IS ALWAYS CHANGING. Within that change, there are cycles with rhythm worth tuning into. She reminds us that when we attune to our inner depths, tend to emotional needs, cultivate intuition, we might more easily, and certainly more wisely, navigate. The moon, like us, is also always, always whole. Its fullness is just one side of that wholeness. Even in the hard work of reflection, the moon takes breaks, respite, bathes us and itself in sweet darkness. Any point in the cycle can be considered a beginning (and an ending). Situating ourselves within the lunar cycle and being with a story of cosmic time can help us feel connected to something bigger, more real, and more enduring than calendar time. Lunacy isn't linear.

Commonly, though, the new moon, this moment of respite from the work of reflecting and light, is considered the beginning of our lunar months. During this time of darkness, newness, and possibility, the sun and moon are aligned, thus we might align with our deeper purpose as well. This fecundity is potent for planting seeds, making wishes, setting intentions, saying prayers, invoking our most creative imaginations with art animating what we are most needing in the days to come.

As the moon waxes (is increasingly illuminated), a week or so in we can gaze upward and witness a half moon, also known as the first quarter moon. We are one-fourth of our way through the cosmic cycle of ever-shifting consistencies. This is when the sun and moon are in a creative tension with each other. These times are for the work of giving the dreams we've envisioned more shape. It's about taking action, a time in which effort and attention are asked of us and propel us forward, spiraling toward greater fullness.

These perfect orbs take another week to dance into their biggest brightness. The brilliance of these cosmic luminaries radiates through the darkest places. In most depictions of the moon (especially in film and TV), we see her full. This is where the drama of living reaches crescendo, so that makes some sense, but it's useful to remember in heightened moments that the moon has other shapes. We tell stories of increased lunacy at this apex. Embracing the wildness of the ride is more fun. The tides are at their highest and lowest during full (and new) moons. These waves in their extremes tug at our own emotional tides, reconnecting us with mystery and magic. The sun is as far away from the moon as it gets during these times of fullness, reminding us of the oceanic vastness of space (and time). The tension there can be even more felt than the quarter moons because these planetary bodies are facing each other in full revelatory radiance, seeing each other eye to eye, mirroring. Whether we're drawn into deeper intimacy or fighting with our reflection, paying attention helps.

The full moon wanes (moonlight appears to be lessening), and about a week later, the second quarter moon of this pattern appears. The sun and moon are again perpendicular to one another and we are called to the effort of integration and closure. Instead of beginning, we are wrapping up, coming to whatever completion can happen in a 29.5-day revolution, trusting that this cycle will enliven our beings again and again, willingly letting go. Rather than neglecting the power of endings, the way so many of us have been enculturated, this waning reminds us that for us to save seeds, a bloom must wither; for us to be nourished, we must concede to compost.

BIO

Stella Lawless aka the Good Enough Witch was born on Halloween, received their first tarot deck at age 11, and adores sharing the meaning and mystery of the cosmos through ritual, readings, and astrological counselling.

Magic School, The

EE: gency; lternative identity projects; nti-ableism; nti-adultism; ody as community; consulting your consultants; externalizing

CONTRIBUTION

I WORK WITH CHILDREN AND YOUNG PEOPLE who often struggle to attend school, whether that be due to moral injury, neurodivergence, or a combination of factors. I have developed a therapeutic practice that I call The Magic School. It is largely based on the work of Belgian therapist Sabine Vermeire. Sabine, in her article "What If...I Were a King?"[1] invites children to imagine if they were king or queen what laws or rules they would establish. In this way she aims to connect with important values, wishes, and principles of the child. This child is invited to take up agency in relation to their difficulties, as an expert in their own lives, rather than being enveloped in a "victim" identity. In Sabine's original paper, the child becomes king or queen, and she, their loyal subject. Sabine describes how this change of position permits children to speak, think, and ask certain things as an authority on their own knowledge. It allows children to speak *to* the trauma without speaking *about* the trauma, giving them a safe place to stand.

In Western society, we expect children to learn and attend school in a specific way. If their abilities or preferences fall outside our societal norm, we pathologize them using mental ill health or developmental constructs. We focus our attentions on specialist schools, "othering" them or stepping into narratives about "noncompliance" or "lacking motivation," which can further disenfranchise young people from the educational setting. We may even search them for weapons or limit their whereabouts if we become captured by narratives about them being "risky" or that they are "trouble."

In The Magic School I invite children to imagine a magic school where limitations do not exist and everything is exactly how they would want it to be. We might write up a fantasy timetable, classroom setting and size, classmates, a fantasy staff list (some staff at Hogwarts have appeared here as well as YouTubers), a fantasy floor plan, and a menu for the dinner hall. We might create the school rules and draw pictures of the uniform (or lack thereof). Maybe there are additional services the school provides like a worker to look after parents or younger siblings whilst the child is at school. The Magic school could be adapted to The Magic Workplace, The Magic College, The Magic Street, or The Magic Community.

Often young people who have experienced moral injury or experience neurodivergence can struggle to generate ideas, so it may be that we have some prompts on cards or Post-it notes such as "Would your teachers be relatives? Famous people? Past teachers you liked?" From here, we can connect to themes that may be important to the young person and therefore enable them to return to an educational setting. We can help workers around them introduce some of these ideas, showing that workers are listening and prepared to enter the child's world.

For example, one young man whose identity featured neurodivergence wanted the school staffed by YouTubers who were funny and playful. Playfulness was a theme we could take forward and make recommendations around. Playfulness allowed this young man to feel safe. He had not always felt that way and often felt misunderstood and rejected. He also wanted the uniform to be fleecy hoodies to suit his sensory needs. Another young man wanted no lessons and just to meet up with his friends. This allowed us to wonder not only about the power of connection for this young man, but also the potential impact and effects of missing so much school that it was impossible to keep up, so, in his mind, lessons just had to go completely!

The Magic School is a therapeutic practice that offers multiple possibilities for everyday use in face-to-face work, consultation, and supervision. We often dissuade people from dreaming when we say, "Let's be realistic." I wonder about the possibilities of being unrealistic in our therapeutic practice. ❁

1 Vermeire, "What If...I Were a King?: Playing with Roles and Positions in Narrative Conversations with Children Who Have Experienced Trauma."

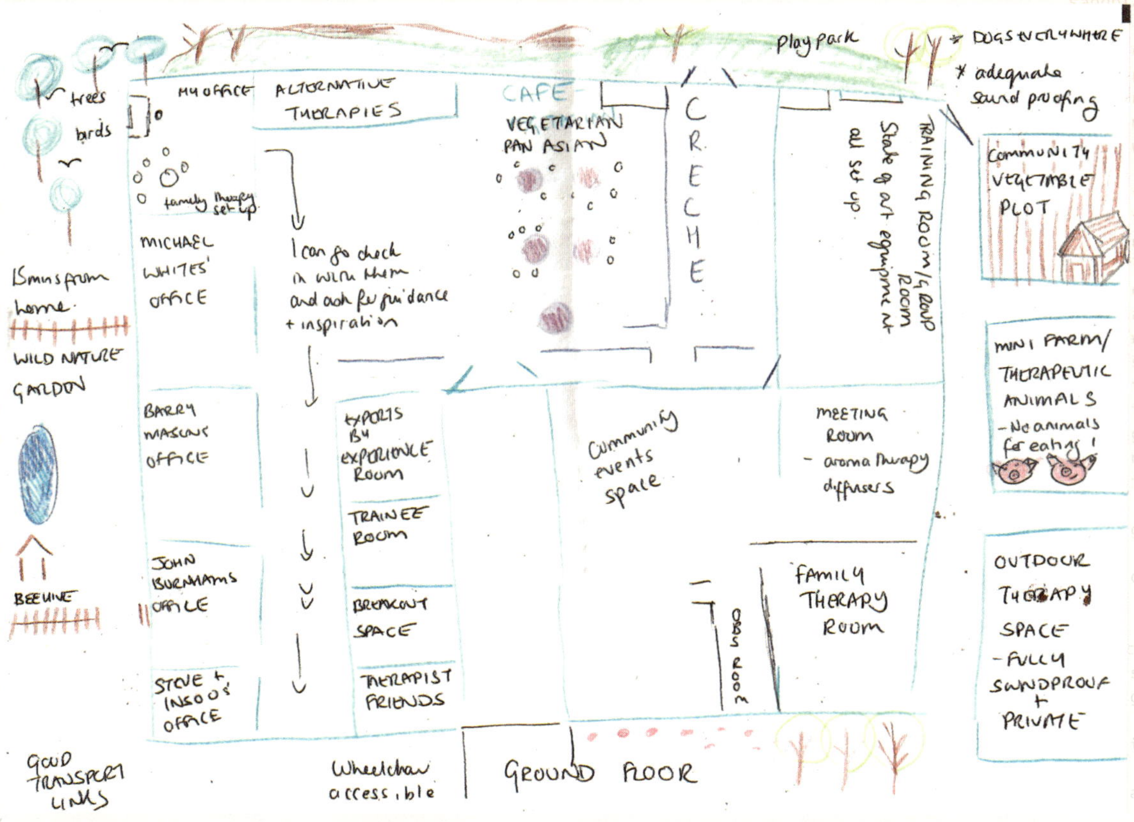

A magic workplace of one mental health worker.

BIO Dr. Lindsey Hampson is a clinical psychologist, systemic family practitioner, and UKASFP accredited Solution Focused Practitioner who works for the National Health Service (NHS) within specialist child and adolescent services.

mapping support

SEE: life cycle honoring the

CONTRIBUTION

The Fluid Socially Constructed Genogram

CONSTRUCTING, RECONSTRUCTING, deconstructing, and co-constructing our lives is a fluid endeavor that may require a fluid and ongoing visual representation of supports. Traditional genograms are a family tree of sorts, fashioned together with boxes, circles, and lines (and many other symbols) defining a visual representation of relational, behavioral, or medical patterns across generations. The traditional version assumes one knows their biological family. It lacks space for the emotional connections we make in our everyday relationships. The socially constructed genogram (SCG)[1] is made up of the "family" that an individual chooses for themselves. The SCG places the individual in the middle and their social supports in relative spaces around them, depending on how close or distant they consider the relationship. The SCG is fluid in nature. And with a few office supplies we can give the exercise life in a way that matches the intent. It requires two to three colors of Post-its, a pen, and poster board.

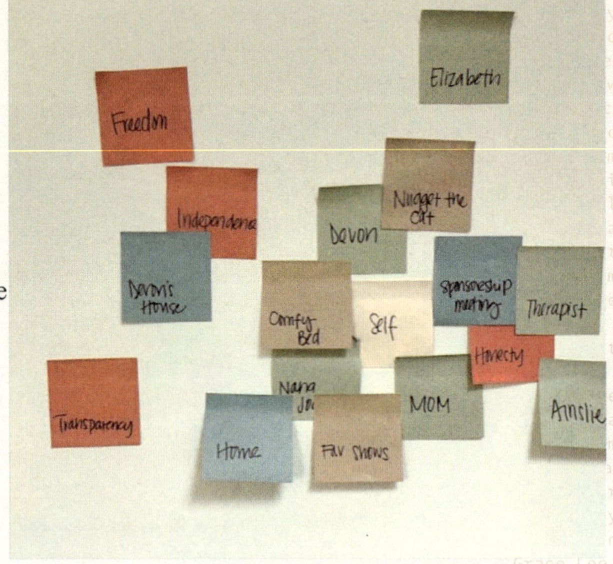

Using Post-its to add fluidity to the socially constructed genogram, today (green = people; blue = places; red = values; brown = things).

One color of Post-its for what we traditionally call the "family," the individual's choice of people, places, and things they consider "family." These can be blood-related members, kinships, friendships, deceased loved ones, pets, etc. The first Post-it will be the individual constructing the SCG, with their name written on the paper. It will be placed directly in the center of what you can imagine looking like a bull's-eye target on the poster board. Next, the individual will write one supportive figure per Post-it and place the Post-its relative to the emotional connection they feel. The closer to the center, the closer the "family" member. One might find a lot of supportive figures equally close to them in nature, whether close or more distant (this may result in a bunch of Post-its in the same area); in this case, the Post-its may overlap without issue.

Another color of Post-it can be used for preferences regarding emotional connections. What are this individual's preferences for themselves? If the desired closeness or relationships are different than what's on the poster board, that can be indicated, written on another color, and placed in the desired space of the genogram.

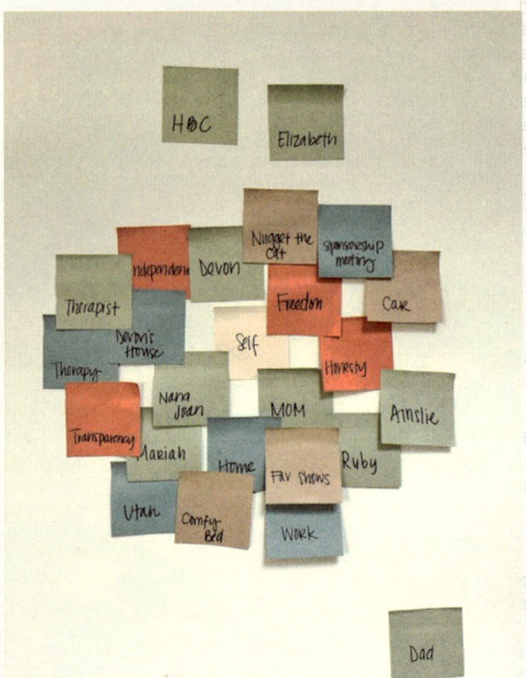

Using Post-its to add fluidity to the socially constructed genogram, 3 years ago (green = people; blue = places; red = values; brown = things).

Using different color Post-its can enhance creativity by organizing ideas in a visual way. The individual can write categories of supportive figures on different colors. For example, friendships on one color, culture on another, activity on another, etc. Utilizing color threads may give rise to the multi-dimensional nature of our lives.

The purpose of using Post-its is to allow for movement. Over time relationships change, as will our socially constructed genogram. The ease of moving the figures on the poster board normalizes the ebb and flow of connection and the natural changes in our stories.

Be curious and have fun! ❁

1 Duvall & Béres, *Innovations in Narrative Therapy: Connecting Practice, Training, and Research.*

BIO Heather Black-Coyne, curious, happy, lover of people, therapist, adjunct professor, and passionate substance use disorder provider.

EDITORS' NOTE In social work and family therapy, there is a long tradition of using graphic tools to map out the broader social, emotional, and structural ties and/or supports that shape an individual's life. In social work, the eco-map invites students and practitioners to "think systems"[1]; in family therapy, the genogram brings multiple generations of family members into the room.[2] The more recently developed socially constructed genogram expands the scope of the genogram to include social connections.[3] Heather's contribution expands upon the socially constructed genogram's focus on fluidity by describing how she incorporates Post-its into her mapping. —ES & CH

1 Hartman, *Diagrammatic Assessment of Family Relationships.*

2 McGoldrick, *Genograms in Family Assessment.*

3 Duvall and Béres, *Innovations in Narrative Therapy.*

marginality (as a site of resistance)

SEE: coalition, liminality

C O N T R I B U T I O N

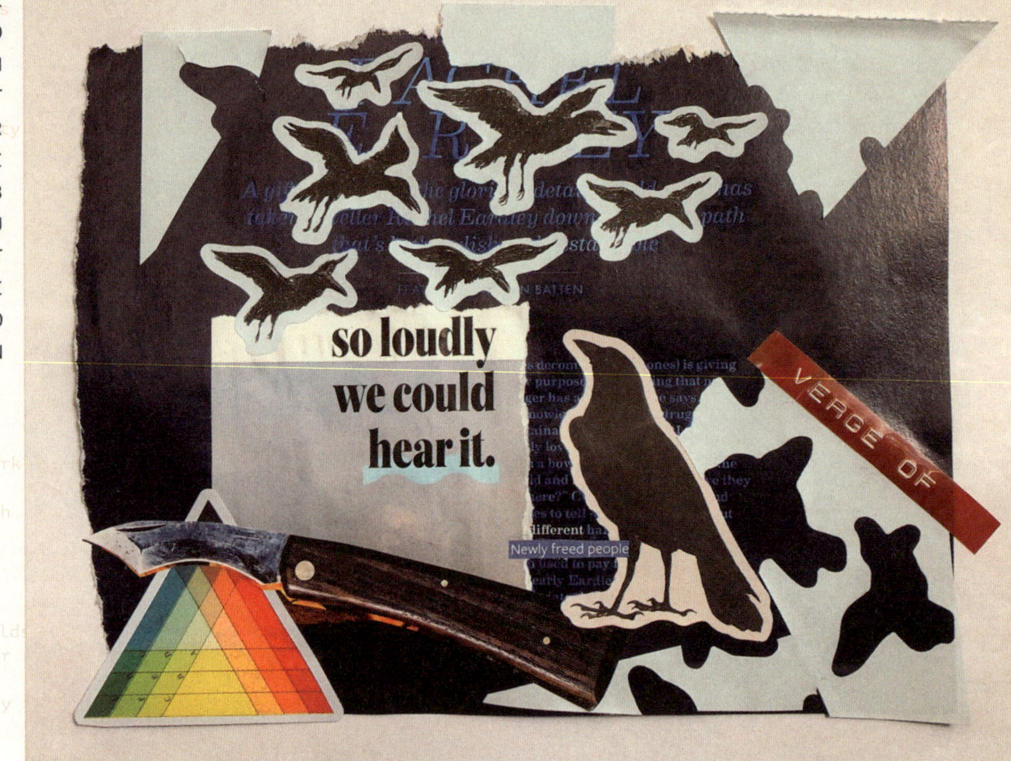

Mixed-media collage, 2023.

B I O

Tanya Paperny is a writer, editor, translator, artist, and community builder in Washington, DC—learn more at tpaperny.com.

E D I T O R ' S
N O T E

This term is from bell hooks's essay "Marginality as a Site of Resistance," another text from Thick Press's "ongoing inquiry into care" reading list. —ES & JC

Marxist social wor

CONTRIBUTION

POVERTY IS A CORE ASPECT OF SOCIAL INJUSTICE and human misery that confronts social workers and other human service helpers. Poverty is particularly acute in the "least developed" nations in the global South that have been affected by the historical legacies of colonialism, slavery, and the ruthless extraction of natural resource wealth. But poverty and economic precarity also affect large numbers of people in wealthy industrialized countries, even though these nations have more than enough aggregate wealth to ensure a decent material standard of living for all.

Why is this so? Karl Marx and Friedrich Engels addressed these questions almost two hundred years ago. Their ideas—and the work of generations of scholars and activists who have followed in their footsteps—can help us to understand the crises of the present moment. Marxist thinking can help us to formulate strategies for social justice in the face of an economy that is profoundly unequal and exploitative, politics that undermine human dignity and freedom, and the environmental emergency that is threatening us with extinction of human and other forms of life.

Marx and Engels pinpointed the revolutionary nature of capitalism as it developed in the late 18th and early 19th centuries. They described clearly how modern industry and global finance ruthlessly exploited wage labour to amass wealth for a few, while at the same time turning the meeting of human needs and the fulfillment of human desires into exclusively market transactions. Various forms of domination and oppression—of women, racialized groups, those with different abilities, and gender diverse persons, among others—can be best understood in the context of a global capitalist order based on the exploitation of human labour and the natural world.

There is a widespread misconception that "Marxism" should be equated with police state terror in the former Soviet Union, especially when it was ruled by Joseph Stalin for almost three decades until 1953. In fact, Marxist theory and political practice have remarkably varied forms and are full of debates and diverse views.

One of the fields in which Marxist thinking has been influential is social work. The model of *radical social work* that emerged in the 1970s was directly derived from Marxist insights of the New Left era that began in the latter half of the 1960s. This approach in social work was mapped out by writers such as Bailey & Brake[1] and Corrigan & Leonard.[2] This Marxist perspective has had multiple and pervasive influences on later critical models of social work practice—including those that are feminist,[3] structural,[4] and anti-oppressive.[5]

Social workers who are left-leaning social critics and reformers can be found throughout the history of the profession—and they have often paid a heavy personal and professional price for their activism. Two outstanding examples of Marxist-influenced social workers are Bertha Capen Reynolds in the United States and Bessie Touzel[6] in Canada.

A key Marxist insight into social work is that the profession is caught in a fundamentally contradictory position. On one hand social workers deal with the "casualties" of capitalism, which is an economic system that keeps wages low, makes workers expendable, and concentrates wealth and power in the hands of the bourgeoisie (as Marx labelled those who control the economy). Social work can be seen as managing capitalism's bad outcomes such as poverty and related social problems, keeping workers labour-market-ready and obedient to their bosses, and heading off discontent or even revolutionary tendencies among the working class. In these ways, so the argument goes, social work plays a key role in legitimating and supporting the capitalist system. ➔

EE: rtha Capen Reynolds Cuestionamos feminism

On the other hand, social work is a profession and an academic discipline that defends human dignity and the right of all not just to survive but thrive in circumstances of freedom and economic security. Social workers must play a role in working towards an equitable economic system, a democratic political order, social justice, and a sustainable biosphere. Social workers can contribute towards achieving these goals in many different ways—by advocating for economically marginalized workers and their families, by organizing communities against the ravages of large corporations, and by working within (and sometimes against) governments to ensure policies that will tame and transform capitalism.

In the present moment, as we face economic turmoil and ecological disaster, Marxist-feminist thinkers such as Nancy Fraser[7] and Kathi Weeks[8] have much to offer social workers with their radical critiques of capitalist production, patriarchal social reproduction, and the role of the state in maintaining these processes. These thinkers point to the need to transform waged work, unpaid care work, and the commodification of human relationships so that we can challenge and transcend capitalism. Such change is required if we are to end gender-related oppression, racism, colonialism, xenophobia, and other forms of social violence. In this struggle, groups such as the Social Work Action Network in Britain and the Social Welfare Action Alliance in the United States can serve as models for how radical social work can play its role in building economic and social justice in an ecologically sustainable world that is a home for all species, human and otherwise. ❁

1 Bailey & Brake, *Radical Social Work.*

2 Corrigan & Leonard, *Work Practice under Capitalism: A Marxist Approach.*

3 E.g., Dominelli & McLeod, *Feminist Social Work.*

4 E.g., Mullaly & Dupré, *The New Structural Social Work: Ideology, Theory, and Practice* [4th ed.].

5 E.g., Baines, *Anti-Oppressive Practice: Roots, Theories, Tensions.*

6 See Johnstone, "'Don't Take the Social Out of Social Work': The Social Work Career of Bessie Touzel (1904–1997)."

7 See youtube.com/watch?v=PNeAvN5eZ0A.

8 See WFHB, "The Strange Life of Work: Kathi Weeks."

BIO James Mulvale (MSW, PhD, RSW) is a Professor in the Faculty of Social Work at the University of Manitoba.

membership theory in social wor

CONTRIBUTION

Membership Theory in Social Work: The Time Is Now

MOST SOCIAL WORK THEORIES that explain human behavior have a dual focus: the individual and the environment in which the individual is situated, labeled person-in-environment. This dual focus dichotomizes the internal (the person) and the external (the environment) by presenting them as two constructs rather than "a single, unified reality."[1] Falck argues that this conceptualization limits our ability to broaden our understanding of the complexity of the human condition.[2] Another dual focus of social work is the conflict between micro and macro social work. This second dual focus is found in social work education, practice, and the professional identity of social workers. In education and practice, the dichotomization has divided social work practice into working with individuals, families, and groups (micro) or working toward social change at the neighborhood, community, and society levels (macro). The person-in-environment and the micro-macro dualities obscure the true purpose of social work: to improve the human condition.

As our understanding of the human condition has changed over the years, we learned about and continue to work to incorporate new concepts and constructs that have added to the complexity of the human condition, such as intersectionality, social determinants of health, and the role discrimination has on individuals. All of these additional constructs impact health and **b**io**p**sycho**s**ocial**s**piritual**s**exual**c**ultural (BPSSSC) outcomes. I submit that using the lens of **membership** will lead social work to build a stronger understanding of the human condition and develop interventions that attend to all the parts and pieces of individuals.

Membership theory, a relational social work theory, was developed by Hans S. Falck in the 1980s. He found that the prevailing social work theories supporting the dual foci were inadequate in understanding and explaining the human condition. He contended that we must start with the premise that humans are social beings, and their interactions with others (e.g., people, organizations, and institutions) influence their beliefs, behaviors, and motivations.[3]

Membership theory holds that social workers have several functions with the person, group, or organization they work with. The first is that the social worker is a member based on their relationship with those they work with. Second, social workers do activities *with* members; they do not do activities *to* members. This distinction is important as it emphasizes the client or patient member's goals, values, and beliefs, not what the social worker thinks is best for the member. Third, social work provides "professional aid in the management of membership."[4] In other words, the social worker offers aid through activities intended to support how those they work with get along with those they are in relationship with.[5]

Some core concepts of the membership theory are that each person is a member of multiple groups of people connected in various way, the social (rather than individualistic) nature of self-determination, and the principles of constant connectedness (connection is needed to survive) and conditional accessibility (flexibility of connectedness). Another underlying concept is that how a member experiences their memberships will influence them during an interaction and beyond.[6] →

membership theory in social work

Viewing each person as a social being and a member of multiple groups is conceptualized at three levels: primary, secondary, and tertiary. The levels are determined based on the extent of the BPSSSC closeness and the type of interactions. The further away members are from each other, the less attention is paid to the feelings, behaviors, perceptions, and motivations of another member, called affective intimacy;[7] the closer they are, the more attention is paid, and thus more affective intimacy. The fewer face-to-face interactions between members, the fewer personal connections, resulting in impersonal decision making; thus, the decision-making members are much less likely to take the other members, who will be influenced by the decision, into account.[8] (SEE TABLE 1.)

The primary group comprises members who interact face-to-face, including video and audio interactions, and the relationships are affectively intimate, such as the family of origin, families of choice, and close friends.[9] The secondary groups include face-to-face interactions, but the relationships do not include affective intimacy. Examples of this level include co-workers, church members, and neighbors, to name a few. Finally, tertiary group members do not interact directly, and relationships are as nonintimate as they come. Tertiary groups include race, culture, citizenship, and political parties, to name a few.[10]

In membership theory, self-determination has been transformed into social self-determination: to recognize that a member's decisions affect other members. The traditional view of self-determination is based on the concept of individualism, which membership theory does not accept as a feasible strategy for understanding the human condition.[11] Viewing a person as a social being implies that any decision they make affects those they are in relationship with. An example is when a member decides not to continue treatment for a condition, disease, or disorder, the decision impacts their life and the lives of other group members. When social workers use the construct of social self-determination, they are allowing the opportunity for those they are working with to explore how their decision can influence others. Thus, discussing the impact their decisions may have on their primary and secondary group members, rather than waiting to see how they react, could minimize or improve these relationships.

The principle of constant connectedness proposes that connections are vital to survival and that connectedness is not a matter of choice but a matter of necessity. The principle of conditional accessibility highlights the flexibility of constant connectedness, as each member can choose to allow or disallow another member to influence them or not.[12] These two principles are similar to how semi-permeable cells function in our bodies. First, all cells are linked to every other cell in one's body, like constant connectedness. Second, the function of cells is to move oxygen, nutrients, and molecules to organs. The blood-brain barrier, like conditional accessibility, allows the cells that nourish and support a healthy brain to move through the barrier while those that are toxic to the brain are blocked. This barrier selects what it allows in and what it does not. The semi-permeability of membership is when one selects what members they want to interact with, need to be in a relationship with, those they can tolerate for a short period, and those they do not want to interact with. Thus, conditional accessibility does not reverse the continued connections but can limit the influence these connections have on a member.

I believe that now is the time to learn and implement membership theory as the theoretical foundation of our work. Doing this would benefit the social work profession, as it makes the role of social work more understandable to those who ask for or accept help from us, those we work with on interdisciplinary teams, and those who pay our salaries. It is also time to bring the membership theory into our research, as it would help frame intersectionality and social determinants of health into our understanding of their influence on health and BPSSSC outcomes. Finally, including this theory in social work education could change the profession's perception of micro and macro practice, from suggesting that one area is better than the other to an inclusive perception which acknowledges the strengths of integrating the expertise across the micro-macro continuum to understand better, explain, and intervene at all levels to improve the human condition. ❂

1 Carlton, *Illustrations of Health Social Work Practice*, 3.

2 Falck, *Social Work: The Membership Perspective*.

3 Carlton, *Illustrations of Health Social Work Practice*; Falck, "What is central in social work?"; Falck, *Social Work: The Membership Perspective*; Falck, "Investigations of membership theory in social work."

4 Falck, *Social Work: The Membership Perspective*, 56.

5 Falck, *Social Work: The Membership Perspective*.

6 Carlton, *Illustrations of Health Social Work Practice*; Falck, *Social Work: The Membership Perspective*.

7 Carlton, Falck, and Berkman, "The use of theoretical constructs and research data to establish a base for clinical social work in health settings."

8 e.g., policymaking; Carlton, *Illustrations of Health Social Work Practice*; Falck, *Social Work: The Membership Perspective*.

9 Carlton, *Clinical Social Work in Health Settings*; Falck, *Social Work: The Membership Perspective*.

10 Falck, *Social Work: The Membership Perspective*.

11 Falck, *Social Work: The Membership Perspective*; Falck, "Social Work and the New Integrative Hospital."

12 Carlton, Carlton, *Illustrations of Health Social Work Practice*; Falck, *Social Work: The Membership Perspective; Falck*, "Social Work and the New Integrative Hospital."

Table 1: Group levels by types of interaction and closeness

Group Level	Interactions	Intimacy	Impact of decisions (includes how it influences members)
Primary	Face-to-face	Affective intimacy	Most often
Secondary	Face-to-face	No affective intimacy	Less often
Tertiary	No face-to-face	Nonintimate	Not at all

BIO

Karlynn BrintzenhofeSzoc, PhD, MSW, FAOSW, is a Professor and the Dr. Renato LaRocca Endowed Chair in Oncology in Social Work at the Kent School of Social Work and Family Science at the University of Louisville, in Louisville, KY.

mending

SEE: centering maintenance, circular economy

CONTRIBUTION

WHEN WE MEND OUR CLOTHES, we are participating in a process that is naturally happening all around us—it *is* us. Our bodies mend when injured or sick, the spider mends her web, the clearcut forest reseeds with pioneer plants. We can tap into this ancient, body-felt knowledge for how to repair. Using our hands and ingenuity, we restore a garment to usefulness in the same ancient, ingrained gesture.

Mending is a meditative practice, a literal and figurative act of healing. When our hands are busy, our anxious minds begin to unfurl and relax. The antsy reflex to check the news is soothed. Fixing a sweater today is enough, this moment is enough.

And yet, such a small, personal gesture is such a radical act in our consumerist culture filled with factory-made things! When we mend, we upend the near-ubiquitous disposability mindset that defines our times. We affirm our belief in the worthiness of all things, our belief in healing. With each mend, we choose gratitude over irreverence, and we become more and more resilient. ❁

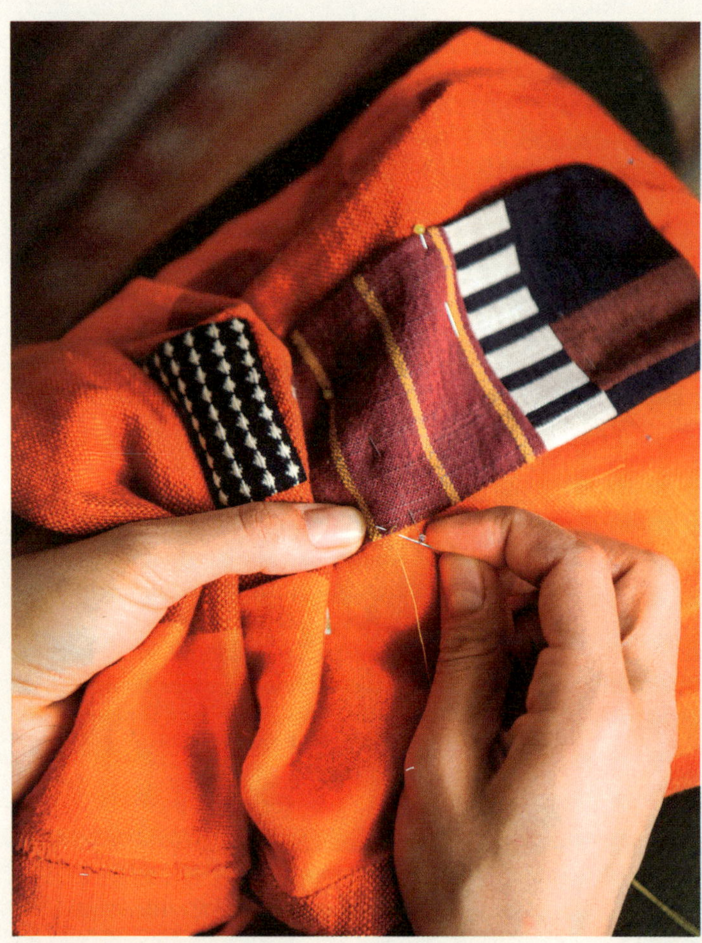
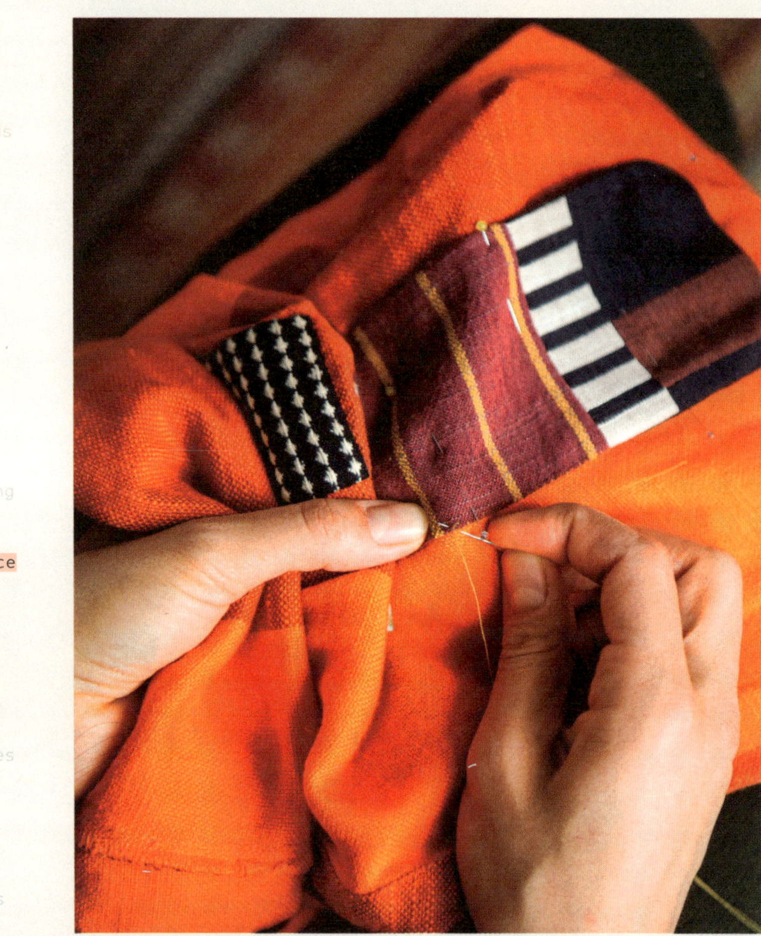

Nina Montenegro's hands mend an Ace & Jig garment.

BIO

Nina and Sonya Montenegro are sisters, as well as mothers, illustrators, printmakers, and dreamers, collaborating as The Far Woods (thefarwoods.com) for the past ten years.

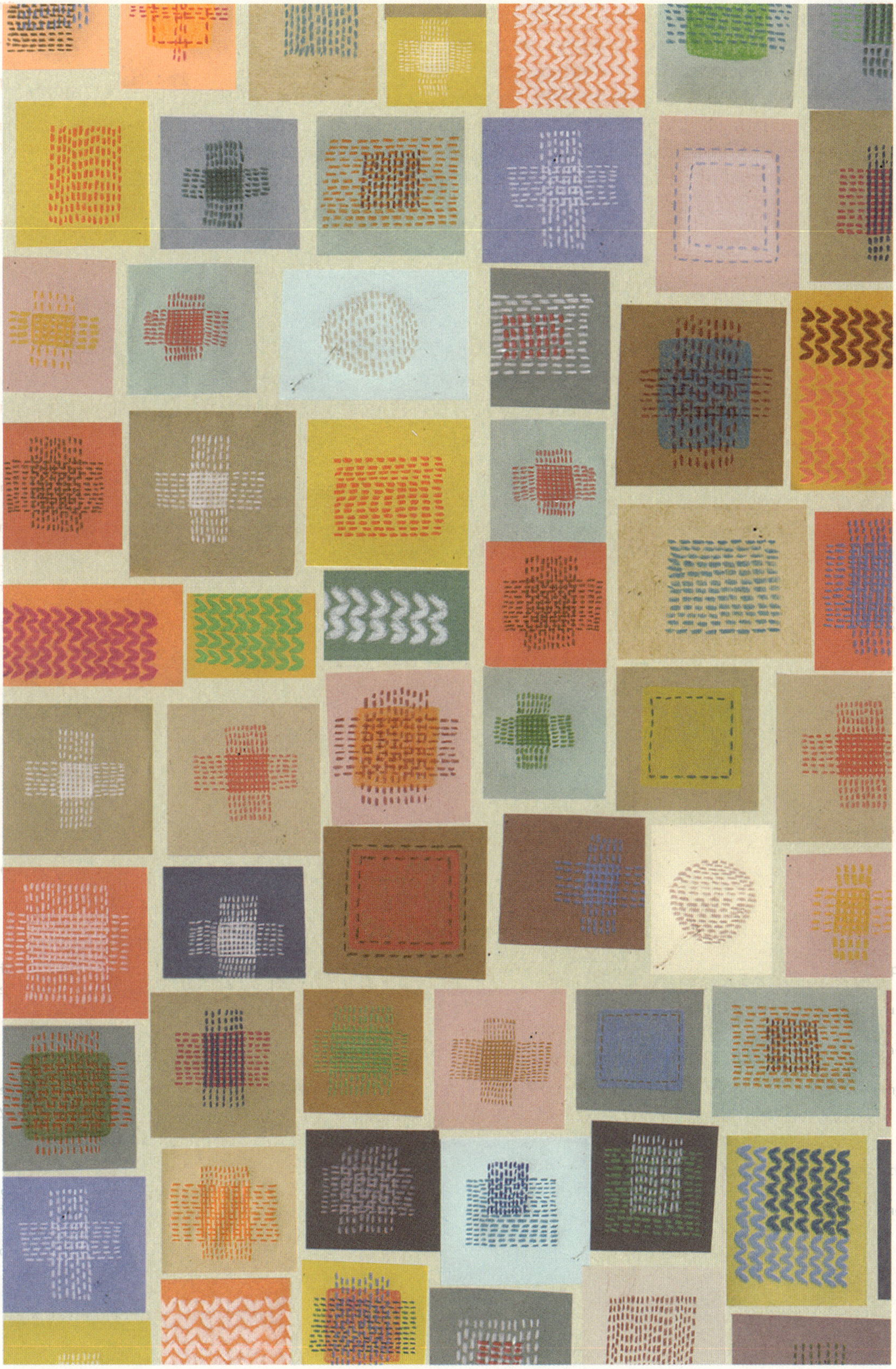

Colorful patches and mends by Sonya and Nina Montenegro, The Far Woods.

metaphor

SEE:

ncestral wisdom
ncestrality
rt therapy
ridge as metaphor
loud as metaphor
grief as nonlinear
life cycle, honoring the liminality

CONTRIBUTION

METAPHORS link symbols together to convey our experience to ourselves and others. Metaphorical and symbolic communication can be particularly useful to help us communicate complex experiences, ideas, emotions, or feelings as we express and explore what it's like to be human. Metaphors create an analogy between two ideas to communicate powerfully. For example: "Her hug was like a thousand cups of hot chocolate." ❁

BIO

Gioia Chilton, PhD, ATR-BC, CSAC, is an artist, art therapist, researcher, and author who loves her family and art therapy community.

lingering
love
lunar cycle
Magic School, the
mapping support
marginality
(as a site of
resistance)
Marxist social
work
membership theory
in social work
mending
metaphor
mikveh
mobile libraries
movement
lawyering
mutual aid
mycelia as
metaphor
narradrama
narrative
medicine
narrative therapy
nepantla/
nepantleras
nonviolent
communication
ongoingness
peer counseling
peer-to-peer
health network
person-situation
perspective
perspective via
faith
pleasure
poems/poetry
poetic meter
polarity work
post-
oppositionality
postwork
imaginaries
poverty-aware
social work
paradigm, the
power threat
meaning (PTM)
framework
pre(care)ity
prison abolition
professionalism
without
performance
progressive
education
public benefits
public library,
the
Qigong
radical
administration
radical care in
the arts
radical childcare
in movement
spaces
radical
inclusion
radical
papermaking
radical presence
radical
social work
*Radical Therapist
Journal, The*
Rank and File
Movement (RFM)
in social work

mikveh

SEE
mycelia as metaphor
poems/poetry
saur
storytellir
symbo
therapeutic writir
12-step program
wate
wintering as metapho

C O N T R I B U T I O N

THE MIKVEH is a spring- or rainwater-fed bath that is part of millennia-old Jewish traditions for purification. Most often the mikveh is used by more observant Jews as purification before the sabbath or after the menstrual cycle. It is also used as part of the conversion process into Judaism. Like many moderately observant Jews, I spent most of my life not surrounded by people who used the mikveh regularly. In a sense it felt a bit oppressive and sexist—like saying a normal part of your being, your menstrual cycle, made you "dirty" and in need of cleansing.

Alongside this critique of the tradition, there's been a resurgence in the use of the mikveh for non-traditional purposes. This is where I came across the concept and began to look at it differently. I was finishing nine months of chemotherapy for gestational cancer (that is cancer caused by pregnancy), and within the same period my mother had passed away. I wanted to find a way to mark finishing my treatment and ending this horrible phase of my life. My rabbi suggested that I give the mikveh a try.

Going to the mikveh is like rebirth. You enter a spa-like facility, shower, clip and clean under your fingernails, and remove all jewelry. There should be no barrier between you and the purifying waters, not even germs or dead skin. You then enter a room with a small pool into which you descend via stairs. Prior to entering the pool you may say some prayers with your rabbi or the attendant and then you submerge completely. I was unprepared for how intense it would be. As you submerge, you are not supposed to touch the walls or the floor of the pool, so it is as if you are in utero. I dunked down and held my legs up to my chest and immediately felt a deep connection to my mother and everything I'd lost in the last year. I felt washed of some of the deep sadness that had become my cloak. I sobbed alone in a pool as I held myself in the warm, pure water. I emerged both lighter and supported by community and history, by millions of women who had performed the same ritual all the way back 2,000 years ago. I felt stronger and ready to weather the emotions of the year of mourning and healing ahead of me.

Like many things in religion, but in Judaism in particular, you take the things that work for you and leave behind the rest. The mikveh is one of those traditions that many have left behind, but if you take from it what works for you, it can be a beautiful and healing addition to your life. Cultures all over the world have bathing traditions, some connected to faith, most not. Even without the connection to a formal religious tradition, these bathing traditions are meaningful, and often quite spiritual. The mikveh, like many of these traditions, is a beautiful example of the connection between physical cleansing and ritual purification. ❁

B I O Marianna Sachse is a mother, maker, and entrepreneur.

reclaiming selfhoo
recognition
redistribution
Reflecting on Justi
reflexivi
Rei
relation
interviewing
relationali
resistan
resisting t
parental loss
narrative
resonan
respectful visiti
respite roo
rest as resistan
reven
revolutiona
mothering
ritu
sanctua
sandplay thera
saur
seed banki
sex positivi
shadow integrati
Sick Woman Theo
slow textil
slownes
social chan
ecosystem framewor
social constructi
social practic
social therapeutic
Social Welfare Actio
Alliance, the
solidarit
solidarity econo
somatic heali
songs/singi
sound heali
speculative desig
spell
staying with th
trouble
storytellir
street newspape
strength
perspective, the
sufficienc
sustaining movemer
symbo
Taos Institute, th
taro
temporary autonomou
zones
Theatre of th
Oppressed
theories of chang
theosoph
therapeutic writir
togethernes
trans practice
transformativ
justice
traspati
12-step program
undercover anti
bullying teams
vigi
wate
wildnes
wintering as metapho
wishe
witcher
yog
zinemakin

mobile libraries

EE: generous systems

CONTRIBUTION

Mobile libraries are a tool for bringing the power of print to the people. In the face of book bans targeting life-affirming texts that explore issues of identity and intersectionality, mobile libraries can help us recenter vital works from underrepresented voices. When we set up a library wherever our community is—from the parking lot of a grocery store to the side yard nestled next to the neighborhood garden—we make it easeful and accessible for those we care about to connect to stories that can inform, inspire, and heal. ❁

—Kate Weiner, Loam

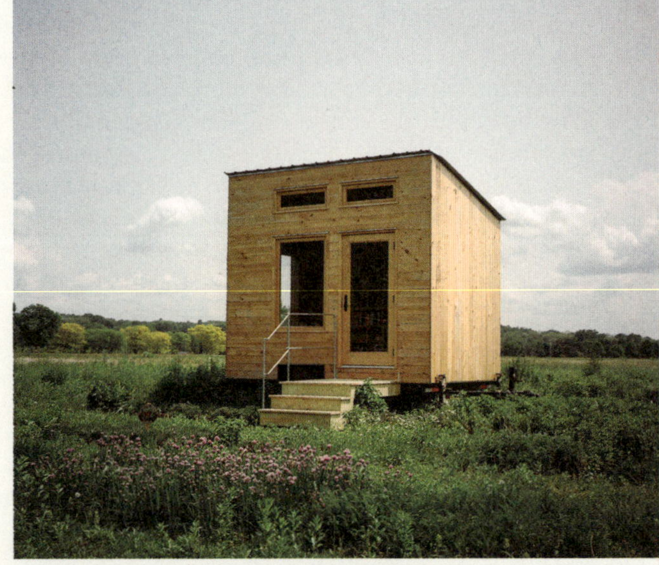

The Loam Library at an herb garden in the Hudson Valley.

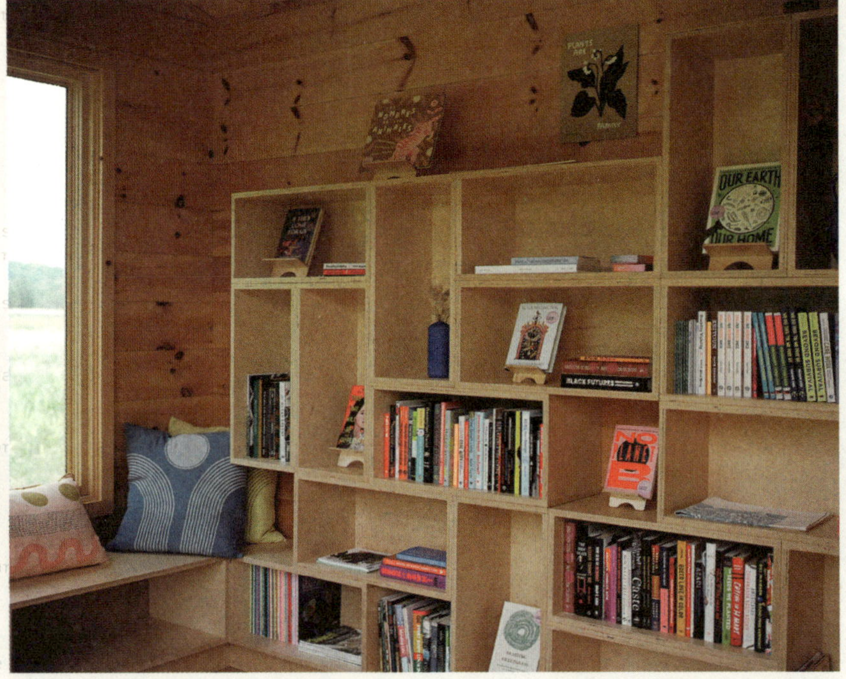

Bookshelves brimming with inspiring reads on climate change, social justice, and community care.

BIO

Loam is a community-powered publishing project. As the publishing branch of Weaving Earth—a nonprofit organization dedicated to relational education for action at the confluence of environmental, social, and personal systems change—we tell stories of interrelationship, belonging, dignity, and respect.

CONTRIBUTION

Two Ballads

"Voices at the Intersection: A Tribute to Kimberlé Crenshaw" (collaboration between Jules Rochielle and ChatGPT)

Suggested Chord Progressions:

Verse: Em - C - G - D
Chorus: G - D - Em - C - G - D - Em
Bridge: Bm - G - D - A

(VERSE 1)

In the fight for justice, a voice emerged so clear,
Kimberlé Crenshaw, a beacon we must hear,
For her wisdom tells us how identity and power entwine,
Through intersectionality, the truth we'll find.[1]

(CHORUS)

In the intersections we stand, our voices raised.[2]
The most vulnerable we'll defend, through the haze.[3]
No more cracks to fall through, we will unite.[4]
For a world where race and gender, together, fight.

(VERSE 2)

As we walk the path to change, let's not forget,
The need to intertwine, the battles we've met,
Feminism and antiracism, we must combine,
Against racism and patriarchy, together, we'll climb.[5]

(BRIDGE)

For too long we've been divided, our struggles apart,
But now we'll join our forces, a united heart,
In this world of unity, no one left behind,
A future of equality, together we'll find.

→

"The Ballad of Michelle Alexander: A Collaborative Musical Celebration of Social Justice and Reform" (collaboration between Jules Rochielle and ChatGPT)

Potential Chord Progressions:

Verse: C - G - Am - F
Chorus: G - Am - F - C
Bridge: Dm - F - G - Am

(VERSE 1)
In a land where freedom rings, yet shadows cast,
A history of pain, a legacy that lasts,
From a voice that speaks truth, Michelle Alexander rose,
To unveil the New Jim Crow, a story to be told.

(CHORUS)
Oh, we've birthed a new racial caste, can't you see?[6]
In this age of colorblindness, we're not free.[7]
We must rise and break these chains, redesign.[8]
For true justice to prevail, we must unite.

(VERSE 2)
Though the times have changed, and laws have been rewritten,
Explicit race no more, but the truth remains hidden.[9]
Discrimination thrives, exclusion wears a new face,
In this era of colorblindness, we must embrace.

(BRIDGE)
In the shadows of the past, we find our present truth,
A caste system redesigned, a battle to unloose,
Together we must stand, for justice to prevail,
A brighter future we'll demand, a new story to unveil.

1 Crenshaw, "Demarginalizing the Intersection of Race and Sex," 142.

2 Crenshaw, "Demarginalizing the Intersection of Race and Sex," 142.

3 Crenshaw, "Why Intersectionality Can't Wait."

4 Crenshaw, "Why Intersectionality Can't Wait."

5 Crenshaw, "Mapping the Margins," 1255.

6 Alexander, *The New Jim Crow*, 33.

7 Alexander, *The New Jim Crow*, 47.

8 Alexander, *The New Jim Crow*, 52

9 Alexander, *The New Jim Crow*, 47

BIO
Jules Rochielle Sievert is an artist, educator and organizer.

mutual aid

SEE Reflecting on Justice

mycelia as metaphor
ongoingness
postwork imaginaries

CONTRIBUTION

MUTUAL AID IS A SET OF ETHOS AND TACTICS[1] that facilitates the sharing of resources within a group or community, with the aim of meeting needs without imposing any requirements or expectations on the recipients. In the process of obtaining these needs, mutual aid projects aim to establish a shared understanding of why the systems in place fail to meet these needs in the first place.[2] The function of solidarity in mutual aid operates as an infrastructural tool for building a shared politics while ensuring collective survival. To provide a few examples, mutual aid can include actions such as preparing and distributing food, building trust with neighbors, offering emotional support, assisting with childcare, establishing ride-share networks, and participating in political education.

"We can do it together RIGHT NOW!"[3] This call to action is often heard among proponents of mutual aid, emphasizing the urgency of taking action through cooperative agency for systemic transformation processes. Mere survival is not the ultimate goal. It is a means to achieve abundance by also dismantling the ways we have learned to relate to one another under the logic of a racist, patriarchal, and planetarily destructive capitalist system. In the words of Mariam Kaba, "We have to actually help people survive if we're going to then get to the point where we can be fighting together for the things we want to create the world that we want to live in."[4]

HISTORICAL BACKGROUND

Mutual aid, as a concept and practice, does not stem from a particular location or history.[5] More than just a political ideology, it is embodied in abolitionist practices rooted in radical Black tradition and indigenous knowledge. It aids oppressed groups such as migrant communities, disabled communities, and LGBTQ+ communities, whose needs are often unmet. The practice may also go unnamed or be described differently. For example, in diasporic communities, mutual aid efforts can manifest as neighborhood support circles or solidarity networks without being labeled "mutual aid." In the zine *History of Mutual Aid Networks*, Mutual Aid Medford and Somerville (MAMAS) provides examples, from the *sociedades mutualistas* in Texas in the early twentieth century to the Young Lords takeover of Lincoln Hospital in the 1970s.[6] These examples demonstrate that there can be a response to address immediate, acute crises like natural disasters[7] as well as long-term, systemic crises like state-sanctioned anti-Black violence.

Although mutual aid is not associated with a particular historical event or place, it has been conceptualized and explained by thinkers such as Russian anarchist geographer Peter Kropotkin. In 1902, he published his book *Mutual Aid: A Factor of Evolution*. To provide brief context on the conceptualization of the term mutual aid, the phrase "survival of the fittest" was coined in 1852 by Herbert Spencer to describe human history, which was then taken up by Darwin seven years later when he published *The Origin of Species*. These ideas were later embraced by advocates of market liberalism, as well as defenders of European genocide and colonialism. Kropotkin's counterargument disputed the belief that prosperity is solely determined by an individual's innate fitness, whether human or non-human. He argued that "in the long run the practice of solidarity proves much more advantageous to the species than the development of individuals endowed with predatory inclinations."[8]

The late David Graeber, an American anthropologist and anarchist activist, suggested revisiting the ideas of Kropotkin and his work on mutual aid in order to challenge the notion of self-serving human nature and as a critique of capitalism's reliance on that concept. He argues that Kropotkin's work offers an alternative perspective to the "gladiatorial view" of history. Instead, it highlights the legacy of cooperation and mutual support. In the introduction to the 2021 edition of *Mutual Aid: An Illuminated Factor of Evolution*, David Graeber and

access invocations
accessibility
ctivating archives
frofuturism
gency
ging positivity
ltar work
lternative identity
projects
ncestral wisdom
ncestrality
nti-ableism
nti-adultism
nti-racism
nti-racism court
system
rt
rt as/in/of life
rt journaling
rt therapy
rt workers
rt-based group work
rts in medicine
rts-based research
uthentic Movement
utonomous healing
yurveda
eing with
ertha Capen Reynolds
ike and car repair
collectives
lack Panther Party
Free Breakfast
Program
ody as community
ody neutrality
ody positivity
ody Trust
oredom
rave space
reaking the rules
ridge as metaphor
are pods
are-based co-housing
atholic Worker
Movement
entering maintenance
ircular economy
limate cafes
louds as metaphor
oalition
ollaborative
apprenticeship
collective care
common pool resources
commons, the
communing with
animals
community college
community gardens
community newspapers
conjure
constructionist-
design framework, the
consulting your
consultants
contemplative
tradition, the
corn knowledge
credit unions
crip time
critical fabulation
critical hope
critical pedagogy
critical race theory
critical suicide
studies
critical whiteness

Cuestionamos
curiosity
death practices
decolonial
liberatory-based
practices
deep organizing
dérive, the
drumming
embodied expression
embodied knowledge
emergent strategy
empathy
energy work
erasure, avoiding
thereof
esoteric wisdom
traditions
ethnodrama
etymology
existentialism
externalizing
failure
fat positivity
feminism
feminst ethics
of care
fermentation
flâner
food sovereignty
forest bathing
fragments/
fragmentation
freedom
generous systems
gift economies
Grace Lee Boggs
grief as nonlinear
group work
groups
harm reduction
healing circles
healing healers
through the arts
healing justice
healing rituals
Hearing Voices
Network
herbal justice
herbalism
holding space
humanness
humor
illders
improvisation
infinite blackness
intentional
communities
interdisciplinary
cataloging
intergenerational
living
interspecies
organizing
intuitive eating
justice-oriented
counseling
land trusts
land, work
spirit, body
language justice
leaving well
liberatory
education
life cycle
honoring the
liminality
limited-equity
cooperative
housing

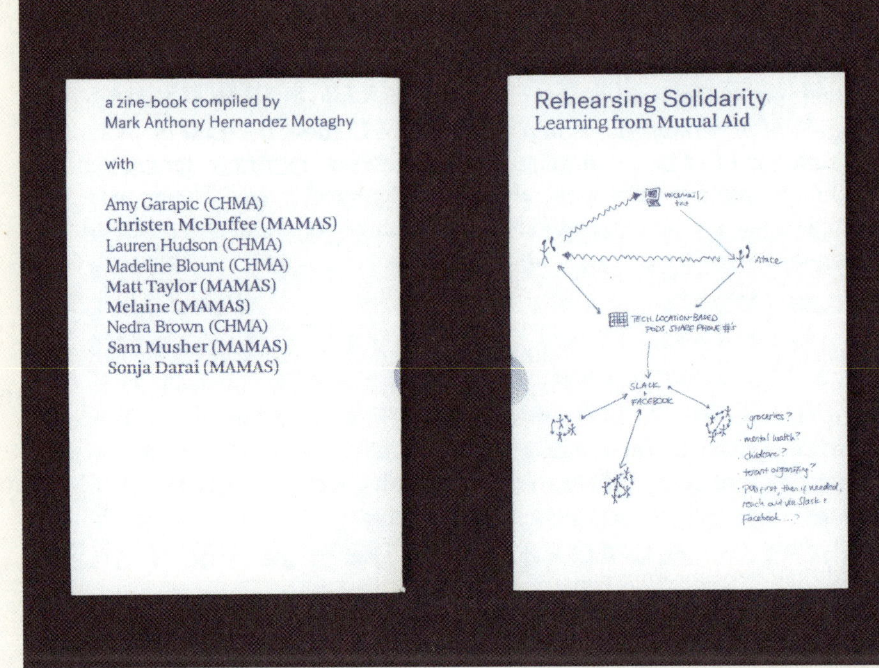

Rehearsing Solidarity: Learning from Mutual Aid, Mark A. Hernandez Motaghy (Thick Press, 2022).

Andrej Grubačić emphasize that this shift in perspective extends beyond anarchist discourse. They state, "It's not just about the nature of government, but the nature of nature—that is, reality—itself."[9]

REHEARSING SOLIDARITY

In 2022, I published the zine-book *Rehearsing Solidarity: Learning from Mutual Aid* with Thick Press. It is an artifact of my mutual aid organizing with Crown Heights Mutual Aid (CHMA) and Mutual Aid Medford and Somerville (MAMAS). The publication archives how these mutual aid groups assembled for COVID-19 and reassembled themselves as groups for the ongoing capitalist crisis. In my experience with mutual aid organizing, I have found that mutual aid is most effective when it is rooted in a political framework. For example, mutual aid can play a crucial role in movements aimed at abolishing the prison-industrial complex or facilitating the solidarity economy.

CHMA began as a large network on Facebook and Slack, with various working groups. As the group grew larger, pods were eventually created to center relationships. Hyperlocal mutual aid groups where participants met their needs through involvement turned out to be the most sustainable. For example, the Crown Heights Food Collective, a project that grew out of the CHMA Pods working group, is a member-led food solidarity collective that cooperates with a nearby farm called Lancaster to meet needs collectively while sharing common values and politics.

In the zine-book, we republished an essay titled "Building Where We Are: The Solidarity-Economy Response to Crisis" by Lauren Hudson, a CHMA member and a scholar of feminist urban geography. We republished this essay because it provided us—fellow CHMA and MAMAS members—the theoretical framework for how mutual aid is integral to the solidarity economy. In the essay, we learn how solidarity economy is a wide-ranging set of cooperative economic practices that include worker, food, financial, and housing cooperatives, community land trusts, and gardens. These practices can be formal, such as with community land trusts, or informal, such as with mutual aid groups. Economic democracy organizing has, in many cases, prioritized the construction of "scalable" institutions, but it often overlooks the importance of mutual aid in fostering solidarity among practitioners and strengthening the infrastructure. The Crown Heights Food Collective is an example of mutual aid operating within the solidarity economy. It brings together a group of neighbors to fulfill their basic food needs, covering the cost of their neighbors when needed and collaborating with an organic farmers' co-op.

Thinkers like David Graeber remind us that the practices of mutuality and solidarity are deeply rooted in history. Conjointly, thinkers like adrienne maree brown emphasize that this work is also a practice of futurity where organizing is like science fiction with the power to shape the future into something entirely new and uncharted. These mutual aid projects, ranging from a simple flyer to an extensive food collective, contribute to the many iterations of a new political economy. Through trial and error, they embody "organizing as a fiction that must be enacted to be believed."[11] ⚙

1 Lauren Hudson, "Building Where We Are: The Solidarity-Economy Response to Crisis."

2 In his book *Mutual Aid: Building Solidarity During This Crisis (and the Next)*, Dean Spade lists the first of three key elements of mutual aid as follows: "Mutual aid projects work to meet survival needs and build a shared understanding of why people do not have what they need."

3 Big Door Brigade, "What is Mutual Aid?"

4 Scahill, "Hope Is a Discipline: Mariame Kaba on Dismantling the Carceral State."

5 See Ariel Aberg-Riger's "'Solidarity, Not Charity': A Visual History of Mutual Aid" for nine illustrated examples of mutual aid networks.

6 For an online version of the zine, visit the Mutual Aid Medford and Somerville website at mutualaidmamas.com.

7 See, for example, the Common Ground Collective's mutual aid response to Hurricane Katrina.

8 Kropotkin, *Mutual Aid: A Factor of Evolution*, "Chapter 1: Mutual Aid Among Animals."

9 Graeber and Grubačić, "Introduction."

10 Hudson, "Building Where We Are: The Solidarity-Economy Response to Crisis."

11 Imarisha, "Introduction," *Social Justice Movements*.

BIO Mark A. Hernandez Motaghy is an artist and cultural worker with a background in architecture.

mycelia as metaphor

SEE: autonomous healing, emergent strategy, gift economies

CONTRIBUTION

MANY FUNGI FORM NETWORKS OF THREADS, or mycelia, which shape the ground below us. Almost all plant roots depend on associations with fungi. Thus, mycelia are radical, in that they literally "grasp at the root." Often "individual" fungi are intimately intertwined with multiple roots, participating in reciprocal exchanges of nutrients and carbon. As they forage through the soil, fungal threads fuse and combine, blurring boundaries between individuals and the collective.

Mycelia are material realities engaged in thorny entanglements in soil; mycelia are also popular presences in metaphors. Thinking belowground alongside mycelia unlocks new ways of envisioning connection, responsibility, community, and being.

*

I move far from home and feel guilty. When no one is looking, I scoop fistfuls of soil spilling across the fence of the botanical garden. I sift through particles of soil and trace routes woven by threads of mycelia. For me, they model how one might always be rooted, yet also always extending, foraging, expanding, fusing. Connections multiplying; exploration without letting go; secretly shaping possibilities aboveground. ❁

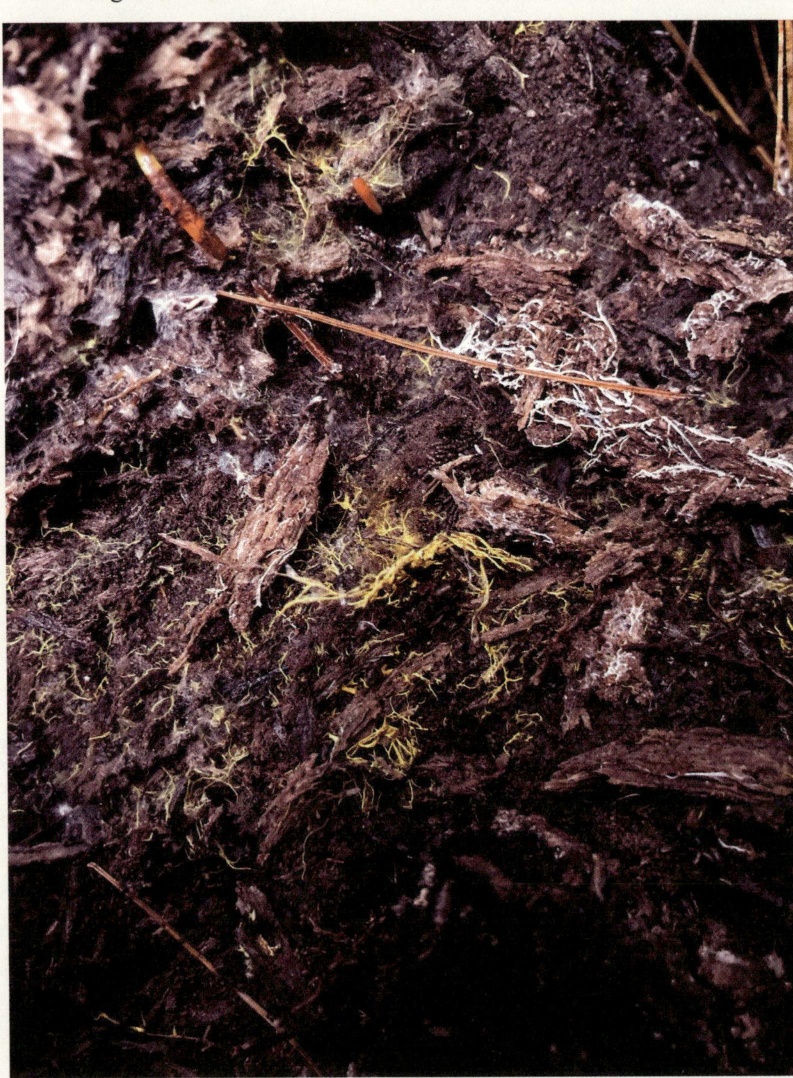

mutual aid

peer-to-peer health network

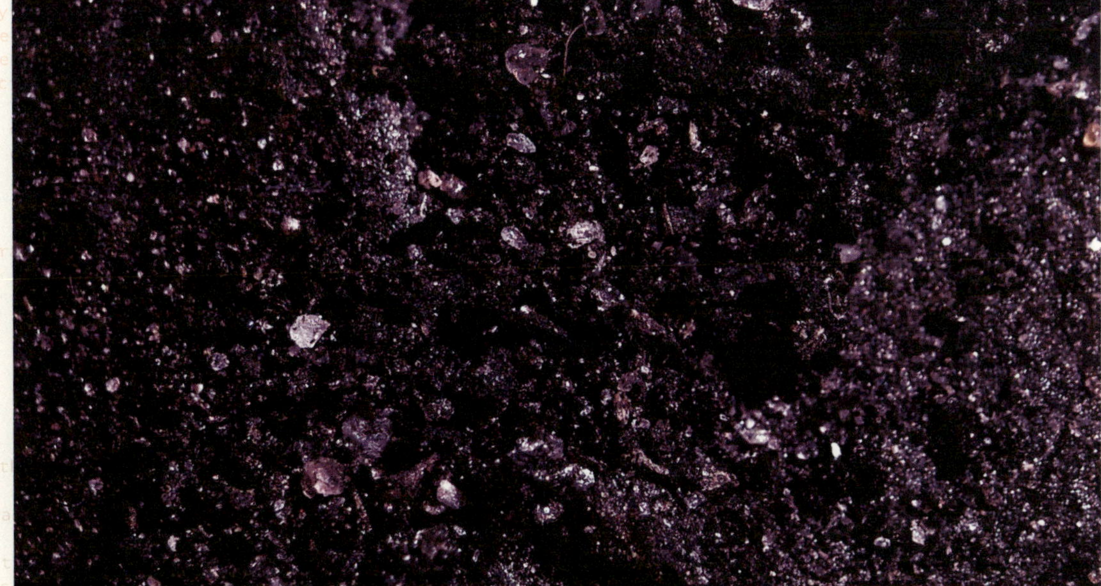

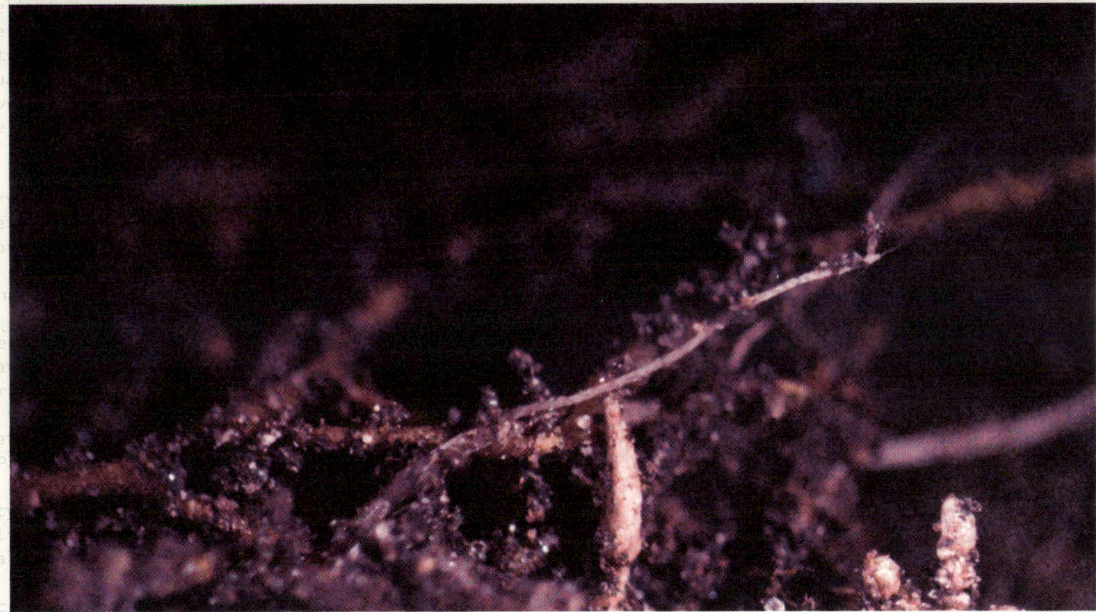

B Mustafa is an ecologist
I who loves exploring
O soil worlds.

narradrama

Authentic Movement
curiosity
ethnodrama
humanness
improvisation

CONTRIBUTION

NARRADRAMA, a term coined in the 1990s by Pam Dunne, a theatre and narrative practitioner, is a drama therapy approach inspired by the work of Michael White. Dunne provides in Narradrama a form of embodied healing practice that can incorporate many types of expressive arts and drama approaches, including Devised Theatre, Theatre of the Oppressed, Improv, and Ethnodrama. By enacting and reauthoring their life narratives as well as discovering new ways to honor their identities, participants learn to express their intersectional identities in a way that may have been silenced or erased. Participants explore, develop, and reflect upon preferred roles through a series of exercises in externalization, sculpting, movements, definitional ceremonies, and witnessing practices. Narradrama has a nine-step process that is non-hierarchical and flexible in nature, meaning that certain steps may happen simultaneously, and certain ones may be revisited or utilized in an order different from the following:

1. Preferred environment and new descriptions of identity
2. Map the influence of the problem
3. Alternative stories, unique outcomes, and pivotal moments
4. Expand personal agency
5. Externalize choices
6. Illuminate values
7. Expand possibility extensions
8. Restory life story
9. Reflect and celebrate.[1]

The nine steps of Narradrama also intersect with the nine core processes of drama therapy, which include: active witnessing, distancing, dramatic play, dramatic projection, embodiment, engagement in dramatic reality, and multi-dimensional relationship.[2]

The most current published research study using Narradrama is with incarcerated students enrolled in a higher education program that explores the transformative impact of narrative therapy and creative arts exercises and performances in helping students reflect upon their interpersonal communication competencies, while also reauthoring their life narratives to develop a new sense of their preferred identities.[3] This work was carried out over a period of four years in a curriculum for a communication studies BA program at a men's prison in Southern California.

Narradrama creates opportunities for the individual's process of transformation to be witnessed and recognized by others. These expressive arts, performance, and narrative methods may benefit mental health professionals and educators in providing embodied experiences that invite perspective-taking, empathy, and expanded use of skills, knowledge, and wisdom. The dramatic distance provided through play with a preferred role invites curiosity, novelty, and the discovery of alternative stories and pivotal moments. ❁

1 Dunne et al., "Narradrama."

2 Mayor & Frydman, "Understanding School-Based Drama Therapy through the Core Processes: An Analysis of Intervention Vignettes."

3 Afary & Malone Alteet, "Narradrama, Intersectionality and Devised Therapeutic Theatre in the Prison Communication Studies Classroom."

BIO Kamran Afary is Associate Professor of Communication Studies at California State University Los Angeles and the co-editor of *Communication Research on Expressive Arts and Narrative as Forms of Healing* (Lexington 2020).

CONTRIBUTION

How would you explain Narrative Medicine?

THE STORY is always about you.

What is happening outside affects us. An entanglement. Our narratives thus need to be more capacious, bolder.

Think about the dissatisfaction we have with medical providers and how we are in fact co-constructing this space with them.

You're not alone. They're not alone.

To be a doctor, nurse, helper requires creativity. You don't have to just memorize what you're told or practice an algorithmic approach in your craft.

Narrative is crucial. A very serious study and engagement with narrative differentiates this discipline from others. It's always a question: What is narrative?

Someone telling someone else that something happened.

The clinical setting ain't hermetically sealed. It's informed by the environment and the people engaged in relationship.

Structural competence. The forces in the room. Not just being frustrated by them but thinking with the patient about them.

The medicine—the relief—is the meeting between two people: the one giving and the one receiving.

Write about a time it wasn't black-and-white. ❁

BIO

Sabrina Tom is a writer and poet whose work has appeared in *Khôra*, *The New Orleans Review*, *Redivider*, and *Hyphen Magazine*. She writes in the space between contradictions; her favorite words are cleave, seeded, lover.

EDITORS' NOTE

If you would like to read more about narrative medicine, Sabrina recommends *The Principles and Practice of Narrative Medicine* by Rita Charon, Sayantani DasGupta, Nellie Hermann, Craig Irvine, Eric R. Marcus, Edgar Rivera Colón, Danielle Spencer, and Maura Spiegel. —ES

narrative therapy

CONTRIBUTION

WHEN I STARTED GRADUATE SCHOOL, if you asked me what kind of therapist I was going to be, I would have told you that I was going to be an existential therapist. A therapist in the tradition of Victor Frankl and Irvin Yalom. I held the belief at the time that meaning making was everything, and I was going to help people make meaning of this chaotic human existence.

After some time in school, and with the help of a mentor, I quickly learned that not everybody is free to make meaning. That for many folks there are constraints to meaning making. These constraints take the form of systemic racism, sexism, heteronormativity and transphobia, and neoliberalism and capitalism just to name a few. These new understandings were destabilizing. Many "truths" I took for granted were turned upside down.

After stabilizing, I found myself wanting to be a different kind of therapist. I did not want to collude with the systems of oppression in my clients' lives, and I wanted to treat those who sought my help with the utmost respect and care. I wanted to center their experience, not mine. I no longer wanted to be an expert but rather a conversational partner. Someone who would walk alongside rather than in front of.

During this experience I discovered narrative therapy. I immediately appreciated how narrative therapy situated me in relationship with those who sought my help. I was also intrigued by the idea that we are all story-making and storytelling creations, and that we organize our inner and outer lives through story. The stories we tell, about ourselves and others, drive our actions, careers, relationships, happiness, health—everything. I wanted to know how to work effectively with these stories that constitute our lives. What to do as a therapist when these stories become problematic? What can be done to access other stories of identity, outside of the problem's reach, that lead to intentions that are more in line with our hopes and dreams?

I also appreciated how narrative therapy decentered me as the expert of people's lives and prioritized clients' local knowledge, skills, and wisdom in the face of problems. It asked what the client's preferences where on how therapy should go. And it had me look at people not as problems to be solved or fixed, but rather as active agents in their own lives, struggling with problems. Ultimately, when I began to adopt narrative practice, I appreciated, and still appreciate, how it brought forth personal agency in those I worked with, and in me.

Constraints to meaning making are still present and strong in contemporary times. However, narrative therapy has provided a lens for me and those I work with to see that in the face of these constraints to meaning making, there can be found acts of resistance grounded in preferences and values, unique outcomes that point to what might be possible, and personal agency that creates movement in who we might be and what we might do, no matter what the constraints or problem/s may be. ❁

BIO

Chris Hoff, PhD, LMFT, is the Founder and Executive Director of California Family Institute and a Liminal Space Tour Guide.

agency
clouds as metaphor
existentialism
externalizing
humanness
liminality

nepantla/nepantleras

CONTRIBUTION

NEPANTLA is rooted in Mexican philosophy, "especially la filosofia de lo mexicano."[1] Queer Chicana writer and Borderlands existential theorist Gloria Anzaldúa described nepantla (Nahuatl: in the middle) as the liminal, ambiguous state of living in between worlds, cultures, ways of thinking, and ways of being. We are often not acutely aware of nepantla until we experience a life event that "turns your world upside down and cracks the walls of your reality, resulting in a great sense of loss, grief, and emptiness, leaving behind dreams, hopes, and goals."[2] Existence is rife with such ruptures, big and small, and these can throw us into a state of shock (*el susto*) and dislocation as we come to realize that we are in nepantla. As distressing and discombobulating as it may be, nepantla is a place of potential for deep transformation, adaptation, change, and connection *en la búsqueda de conocimiento* through the process of "… seeking experiences that'll give you purpose, give your life meaning, give you a sense of belonging."[3] Nepantleras are those who have grown skilled in navigating and negotiating the uncertainty of nepantla for themselves and in community with others for social change. ❁

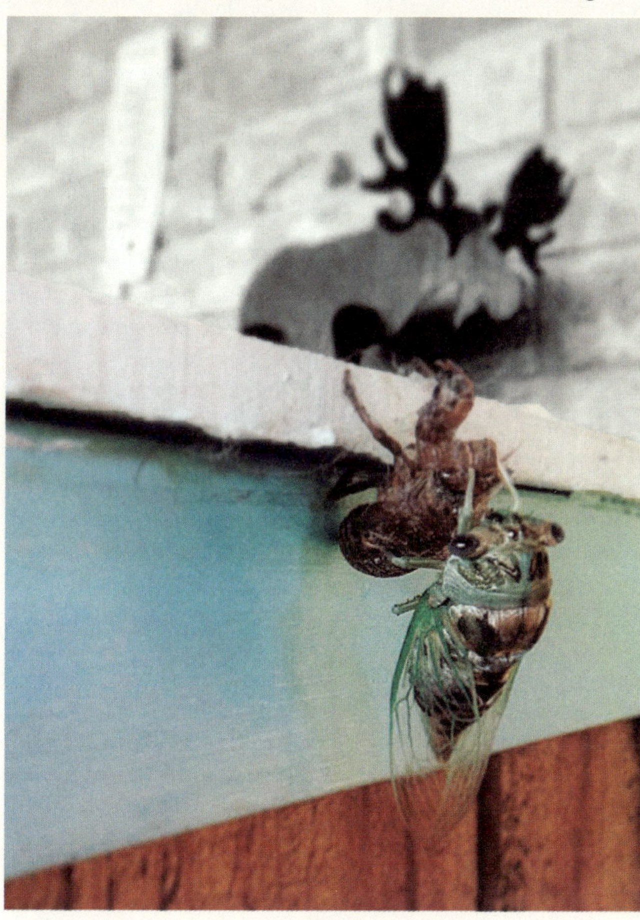

© 2023 Coatlicue Sierra Rose. *Nepantla/La Búsqueda de Conocimiento*

1 Alessandri and Stehn, "Gloria Anzaldúa's Mexican Geneaology: From Pelados and Pachucos to New Mestizas," 12.

2 Anzaldúa, "Now Let us Shift… the Path of Conocimiento… Inner Work, Public Acts," 546.

3 Alessandri and Stehn, "Gloria Anzaldúa's Mexican Geneaology: From Pelados and Pachucos to New Mestizas," 12.

BIO

Dr. Coatlicue S. Rose is a proud queer Xicanx healer, researcher, and policy nerd.

nonviolent communication

SEE: embodied knowledge, empathy, grief as nonlinear group work

CONTRIBUTION

Mourning with NVC

I WAS FACILITATING A CIRCLE OF SIX MEN in a Northern California prison on a Monday afternoon. This was the tenth meeting of our yearlong healing and accountability class. Our group comprised 33 incarcerated students and five facilitators, of whom three were incarcerated. Most of the students had life sentences with an average of 20 years of incarceration. Each meeting was two hours long with a mix of teaching and personal sharing. This Monday, the students were reading a letter from their heart to someone who had died. There were five groups of six to seven students, each spread around the long, rectangular room. In each group, a facilitator was inviting students to take turns reading and connecting with their grief. There is a lot of unprocessed grief in prisons; incarcerated people suffer significant losses, including missing birthdays, funerals, graduations, the loss of dreams, opportunities, health, connection with loved ones, dignity, safety, agency, identity, possessions, and even the loss of life. Groups like ours offer students, who want to heal and transform, a safe space where they can be vulnerable. Few of our students had experienced therapy, meditation, or other healing modalities before they came to prison.

In my group, Joe (not his actual name), a 6-foot-tall white man who I judged to be in his late 60s, with tattoos all over his neck and arms, offered to read his letter first. Joe looked 10 years older than he was, due to a rough life. The tattoo of a pointy-hooded man that looked like a KKK symbol on his arm caught my eye. As a person of color and an immigrant who had encountered xenophobia, I felt uneasy and unsure about holding space for someone with a white power symbol. Joe was quiet and respectful in his demeanor; the black men in my group appeared to be relaxed around him. At that moment, I chose to believe the tattoo was a relic of his past. As a practitioner of Nonviolent Communication (NVC), I knew that I had an "enemy image" of Joe. According to NVC, we hold enemy images when we disconnect from an individual or group's humanity and see them as the "other" in some way. In NVC, we shift out of othering by finding our common humanity. This is one of the reasons I love NVC.

As Joe started to read his letter to his mother, I did my best to give him my undivided attention—to "feel with him" despite my lingering low-level unease with my thoughts about his tattoo. In order to feel with someone, I find it helpful to shift from focusing only on their words to also sensing the vibratory quality or emotional tone of delivery through the tone of voice, intonation, quality of breathing, pauses, eye movement, facial expressions, posture, and gestures. I find that this is similar to broadening my attention from just the visuals in a beautiful space, like a grove of redwood trees, a cathedral, a Zen temple, a garden, etc., to also include their particular vibratory feel. I was also paying attention to the emotional tone of the men who were listening.

In his two-page letter, Joe spoke to his mother, acknowledging the ways he had let her down. His mother never gave up on him despite the different kinds of trouble he got into that eventually landed him in prison. I also heard Joe's regret and pain for her heartbreak when he was sent to prison. The deep sadness, tenderness, and regret in Joe's voice spread through our small group. I could feel and see the heaviness in the shoulders of the men who were listening, some of whom hunched forward. A thick, heavy silence settled on us. It felt like the group was holding their breath. After getting Joe's permission to interrupt, I asked the group if they could feel a deep sadness and heaviness as they heard Joe's letter. There were slow, silent, barely perceptible nods with downcast eyes. We were feeling the sadness together. Joe's sadness created a space wherein each man was touching into his own pool of unshed tears.

In order to resource our nervous systems, I asked the group if they would be willing to take a few deep breaths with me. There were slow nods. I led the group in a few slow, deep inhales and exhales. While we were breathing, I also asked the men to gently push their feet into the ground and then relax their legs a few times. I find this connection with the body and ground to be helpful when feeling intense emotions. In addition to regulating the group, I was slowing us all down to be with the sadness and tenderness that Joe's sharing had brought into our group space.

Once I felt the group was breathing again, I asked Joe to continue reading. As Joe read, I felt his mother's unconditional love and positive regard for Joe. I imagined she may have been the greatest source of love in his life, the one person who never saw him as a monster. In that moment of feeling his mother's love, my enemy image of Joe as a white supremacist dissolved. My fear dissolved and was replaced by warmth and care for Joe. He was no longer the "other" to me. He was just like me in this space of our precious, common humanity. This was the emergence of emotional empathy. I felt Joe relax and soften as I reflected my impression of his mother's unconditional love. Emotional empathy is an act of communion, since we have a shared experience of feelings and thoughts. The sadness and regret were more bearable in this place of human connection. bell hooks says it beautifully: "rarely, if ever, are any of us healed in isolation. Healing is an act of communion."[1]

There was something pure about Joe's sadness and regret. I did not sense significant shame, anger, self-criticism, agitation, judgment, etc. It felt like his feelings were coming from his heart. In NVC, mourning is an organic healing process that emerges when we connect our sadness with the preciousness of what was lost. In NVC lingo, the term "need" represents what's precious or important to us. It felt like Joe's heart was mourning the loss of his connection with his mother where he experienced unconditional love. I asked Joe and the group if they were feeling a quality of love, however subtly, in addition to grief and regret. When they nodded, I led us in a few collective guided breaths to slow us down and make space to feel the love together.

When I checked in with Joe after the breaths, he was connected to the love from which his sadness was emerging. The love did not make the sadness go away. Instead, it changed the quality of sadness, giving it a bittersweet flavor. The pain of loss was tempered by something precious and important to Joe's heart. I could feel a sense of movement as the sadness was being integrated by the connection with love. When Joe confirmed this for me, I knew that the NVC process of mourning was underway. At this stage, there is nothing to do other than to stay present and experience the healing happening in one's body. As I thanked Joe for his courage to be so vulnerable, there were gentle nods and appreciative glances towards him from the other men. I asked Joe to stay present with his internal process as we transitioned away from him. The rest of the group appeared to be integrating the process since they were sitting more upright and making eye contact with me as I spoke.

When we open to the loss of something or someone dear to us, we can feel submerged and lost in an endless ocean of grief, despair, sadness, heaviness, etc. with no way out. NVC's mourning process asks us to connect with the preciousness of what was lost—e.g., our needs. It is like diving for precious pearls within the ocean of grief to unlock an alchemical process of healing. ❁

1 hooks, *All About Love*, 215.

CONTRIBUTOR'S NOTE

To learn NVC, refer to Marshall Rosenberg's book: *Nonviolent Communication: A Language of Life.* Online training: nvcacademy.com. To find a trainer: cnvc.org. –SJ

BIO

Sunil Joseph (he/him) is a certified Mindfulness Teacher facilitating a healing and accountability program in California prisons. Learn more at myempathycoach.com.

ongoingness

SEE: curiosity; t as/in/of life; entering maintenance; freedom

CONTRIBUTION

THE IDEA THAT WE CAN ROOT out oppression like a gardener roots out a pesky weed—it's a neat idea. It's also a tall order—and these days, it feels like tall has morphed into impossible. Julie and I agree that tall expectations overwhelm us, resulting in inaction. Paradoxically, ease often leads to more action; we have observed that we are most effective when we lower our expectations and make room for rest and play punctuated by intense periods of work. When life gets in the way and we find ourselves prioritizing rest over work—well, isn't rest a form of resistance?

That's some of the thinking behind a concept we call ongoingness. For us, emphasizing ongoingness allows us to replace hero narratives with accounts of day-to-day activities performed with others—sometimes feverishly, other times very slowly—in service to liberation, care, and love. Ongoingness is about taking what Mariame Kaba describes as a "long view," in which we understand that "we're just a tiny, little part of a story that already has a huge antecedent and has something that is going to come after that."[1] Ongoingness isn't a new idea: we see strains of it in the writings of women of color poet-theorists from the 1970s; in the folk songs of social movements from all over the world; in the rallying cry *la luta continua*.

The artist Mierle Laderman Ukeles asks, "The sourball of every revolution: after the revolution, who's going to pick up the garbage on Monday morning?"[2] And ongoingness answers something like, "*We* are. Together. But you went to the dump last time, and he doesn't have childcare today, so why don't you two fill the bags and leave them by her back door, and I can pick up the bags and do a dump run in between Zoom calls tomorrow. And next time, we'll take them up on their offer to help. This is becoming a lot for us—and anyway, they told me they've been wanting to see the seagulls at the dump."

Julie and I don't remember when we started using the term ongoingness. It might have been when Ursula Le Guin's *Carrier Bag Theory of Fiction*[3] was circulating around the design department at the school where Julie teaches. Le Guin doesn't use the word "ongoing," but she differentiates between stories of heroes, action, and spears on the one hand, and on the other hand, stories of people and the things they use to carry things like wild oats. This second kind of story, of course, is the one that interests Le Guin, just like it's the one that interests us, particularly with respect to care work and movement work.

When we read Maggie Nelson's *On Freedom: Four Songs of Care and Constraint*,[4] we began to see how *thinking* (and thinking via writing or art-making) can be an ongoing practice of freedom. Nelson is a writer and art critic whose world is fine arts and literature, not the participatory, values-based corner of publishing and art where most of our work lives—which means she isn't really concerned about whether a work of art is *liberatory*. Still, like us, Nelson is interested in exploring how we might understand and experience freedom in ways that account for interconnectedness—characterized by conflict, the compulsion to care, and everything in between. She offers no easy formulas, but circles around some of the places where we, too, have landed: most relevant to ongoingness, the value of divesting from a whole bunch of stuff that's in the air we breathe (our metaphor, not hers). These include progress narratives; the idea that freedom is a momentary act; the American tendency to pit action against thought; the paranoid idea that vigilance prevents bad things from happening; the often well-meaning impulse to police others; and more.

For Nelson, the way to act differently, to find and create *different* stuff in the air, is to act, in the words of David Graeber, "as if one is already free."[5] Nelson does this via the "patient labor" of writing. Interested in what she calls "the knot," she doesn't spend time unknotting freedom from unfreedom by exposing or condemning unfreedom. Instead, she explores, explores, explores. She is very patient and very brilliant and it's very exhausting to read her work—the circles, the associations, the slipperiness. But because she models curiosity and carefulness and a refusal to be seduced by magic bullet theories (without discounting them, either), we find that "staying with the trouble" alongside Maggie Nelson feels like helpful training for our brains. It doesn't feel particularly *good*, but it feels useful, in the unglamorous way we've come to associate with ongoingness.

This piece emerged from Thick Press's ongoing inquiry into care. ❁

1 Kaba, *We Do This 'Til We Free Us: Abolitionist Organizing and Transforming Justice*, 27

2 Ukeles, "Manifesto for Maintenance Art 1969!—Proposal for an Exhibition 'Care,'" 1969/2016.

3 Le Guin, *Carrier Bag Theory of Fiction*.

4 Nelson, *On Freedom: Four Songs of Care and Constraint*.

5 Graeber, quoted in Nelson, *On Freedom: Four Songs of Care and Constraint*.

BIO Thick Press (Erin Segal and Julie Cho) publishes unusual books about care work and the work of care.

love
lunar cycle
Magic School, the
mapping support
marginality (as a site of resistance)
Marxist social work
membership theory in social work
mending
metaphor
mikveh
mobile libraries
movement lawyering
mutual aid
mycelia as metaphor
narradrama
narrative medicine
narrative therapy
nepantla/nepanteras
nonviolent communication
ongoingness
peer counseling
peer-to-peer health network
person-situation perspective
perspective via faith
pleasure
poems/poetry
poetic meter
polarity work
post-oppositionality
postwork imaginaries
poverty-aware social work paradigm, the
power threat meaning (PTM) framework
pre(care)ity
prison abolition
professionalism without performance
progressive education
public benefits
public library, the
Qigong
radical administration
radical care in the arts
radical childcare in movement spaces
radical inclusion
radical papermaking
radical presence
radical social work
Radical Therapist Journal, The
Rank and File Movement (RFM) in social work

rest as resistan
slownes
solidarit
songs/singir
sustaining movemen
therapeutic writin

peer counseling

SEE: care pods, collective care, feminism, group works, groups, harm reduction, holding space

CONTRIBUTION

FIRST, AN OFFICIAL DEFINITION from the Substance Abuse and Mental Health Services administration (SAMSHA):

> Peer support workers are people who have been successful in the recovery process and who help others experiencing similar situations. Through shared understanding, respect, and mutual empowerment, peer support workers help people become and stay engaged in the recovery process, reducing the likelihood of relapse. Peer support services can effectively extend the reach of treatment beyond the clinical setting into the everyday environment of those seeking a successful, sustained recovery process.[1]

It's the "successful, sustained recovery process" that I want to home in on. A peer support worker, also known as a peer counselor, peer specialist, or any other number of things, is different than a friend. A peer counselor has to contend with the professional ethics and boundaries in a way that is similar to the work of a therapist,[2] but with a different scope of care. While a therapist may support a person in processing the past, a peer actually sees a person in recovery in the context of their lived life, within shared communities, helping the client in recovery to remain focused on the present.

Peer counseling is a radical concept. It emphasizes a state of non-hierarchy—that we are vulnerable, that we have our own paths and offer knowledge from the specificity of our experiences.

The client may one day become the counselor; and the counselor understands their own vulnerability and that their recovery process is not finite or taken for granted.

I am excited by the idea of specialist peers. What would it look like for a doctor, a therapist, even a psychiatrist to identify as a peer? What is it like for someone who ends up in a position where they hold power and influence over a patient in a moment of extreme vulnerability to know what it is like to be in that position?

Being a patient is about being vulnerable; being a healer demands accepting authority. But working from the frame of being a peer means that the separation between healer and healed is a cyclical one, and that we all have our own medicine to give and to share. It also holds the idea that continuous learning and practice are important ingredients of transformation and interdependence.

Thank you to the RAMS Division of Peer-Based Services, 2022–2023 peer internship and peer certificate cohorts. Thanks in particular to Ida Poberozovsky, Adisa Stewart, Tim Pursell, and Eva Cisneros. ❁

1 SAHMHSA, "Peer Support Workers for those in Recovery."

2 At present, the state of California has begun implementation of a certification process for peer counselors, which will allow counselors to charge for their services through Medi-Cal. The examination process is similar to therapy licensure examinations, and emphasizes the boundaries of practice and scope of a peer counselor in collaboration with therapists and psychiatrists.

BIO Katherine Agard is a poet based in Northern California. You can learn more about her work at kaa.fyi.

peer-to-peer health networ

CONTRIBUTION

The Hologram

THE HOLOGRAM is a peer-to-peer network for non-expert healthcare. The premise is simple: one person, the "hologram," invites three people that they trust—the "triangle"—to meet online or in person on a regular basis to focus on the physical, mental, and social health of the hologram. You don't need money, space, or time to develop this practice, only a commitment to learning and practicing mutual care. Over time the triangle reflects a multifaceted image of the central person—like a hologram. Eventually the hologram supports each triangle member to become a hologram themselves, and the network expands.

The goal of the project is to create health and stability for all participants so they can survive our capitalist society and be able to build a future without reproducing the systems that make us sick (racism, patriarchy, ableism, ageism, etc.).

The Hologram practice is inspired by the "Integrative Model" developed by the Group for a Different Medicine at the free Social Solidarity Clinic in Thessaloniki, Greece, during the financial and refugee crises beginning in the 2010s. This model attempts to undo some of the hierarchies implicit in medicine, and to provide care no matter who the person is, where they are from, or what kind of resources they have or don't have access to. The model uses the term "incomer" instead of "patient," since the latter term infers that the person is unwell. The Incomer is seen by three caretakers—a doctor, social worker, and a therapist. They ask a broad range of questions about the Incomer's health, including their living, working, eating, and social conditions. After 90 minutes of discussion about all the dimensions of their health, the incomer tells the professionals what kind of support they would like for the next year.

The Hologram does not replace professional medical or psychological care, if you have access to that. Your hologram exists underneath, before, and after institutionalized forms of care. It may help you navigate and advocate for yourself in a traditional medical system. The Hologram recognizes that we are part of a connected social system, and that we need to both give and receive care in order to be healthy. Participating in a hologram should feel good! It should feel very different from other experiences of professional care, or from advice from friends. ❁

BIO

Cassie Thornton is an artist and activist who makes a "safe space" for the unknown, for disobedience, and for unanticipated collectivity. She is also the author of a book that was secretly written with all her friends and published by Pluto Press: *The Hologram: Feminist, Peer-to-Peer Health for a Post-Pandemic Future*.

SEE
narrative medicine
narrative therapy
peer-to-peer health network
pre-(care)ity
storytelling
togetherness
12-step programs

person-situation perspective

CONTRIBUTION

"I am I and my circumstances": *A Person-Situation Perspective in Responding to Trauma*

I FIRST HEARD JOSÉ ORTEGA Y GASSET'S phrase "I am I and my circumstances"[1] during a philosophy class I had taken one winter in Dublin. The words poetically conveyed what I already knew and based my work on since graduating as a social worker some years earlier. Although the person-situation perspective[2] is a foundational principle of social work, hearing Ortega capture the inextricable relationship between the individual and their social world so succinctly prompted me to think about it anew.

At the time, I had just started to work as a social worker in the Emergency Department (E.D.) of a large hospital. I was searching for theories and approaches appropriate to the complexity of human experiences I was encountering in this context. One morning, on my way to meet James and his partner, Helen, I found myself questioning what, if anything, I could say or do that might be a meaningful response to what I imagined they were going through. I knew from the social work referral that James was a thirty-five-year-old man who had tried to end his life the previous night and that his partner, Helen, who had found him, was, according to nursing staff, traumatized. No one theory or approach seemed sufficient to meet the anguish I anticipated. As I walked into a side room where they waited, just off the main E.D. floor, it seemed to make most sense to introduce myself, acknowledge that it had been a really tough night, and then listen carefully and try to understand their experiences. I focused on their feelings, on what was most urgent and significant for each of them, clarifying their needs and how these needs could best be met in the short and medium term. I was mindful that their emotional distress was personal to each of them but was also arising from and affecting their relationship, their individual and shared assumptions, beliefs, and hopes, and was linked to the broader circumstances of their lives. Potential ways forward needed to address all of these dimensions.[3]

Over time I worked with many people referred due to single-incident traumas or other issues such as self-harm or psychosomatic illnesses associated with underlying trauma. Trauma has traditionally been understood within an individualised, psychologised idiom. The "psychiatrization" of trauma as a single disorder—Post-Traumatic Stress Disorder—seemed reductionist in its neglect of the psychosocial and socio- cultural factors that so powerfully shape trauma narratives. I was interested in understanding and responding to the lived experiences of trauma, played out in people's relational worlds and often falling outside the parameters of the PTSD diagnostic category.

This led me to undertake PhD research exploring people's lived experience and their engagement with the social work service of the hospital emergency department.[4] The study further explored the elements of responsive social work in this context and generated a conceptual framework for trauma-informed social work practice. The research was undertaken in collaboration with people who used the service, together with social workers and non–social work emergency department professionals. Semi-structured interviewers and a mini focus group were selected as the approaches to data gathering with a total of 26 participants. Data was analysed using a constructivist grounded theory approach.

The findings indicated that trauma encompasses profound existential feelings including loss, distress, disconnection and disjuncture, a changed sense of self and changed life circumstances, giving rise to experiences of liminality. For many, their trauma experience dominated other aspects of their lives.

Social work was experienced as a relationship-based process that allowed the significance of trauma to be recognised and ways forward [re] viewed and made practicable. Through dialogue, meaning-making, and building on people's strengths, social work intervention was found to have contributed to people's capacity to re-position themselves in relation to the trauma, resulting in reduced levels of distress. This enabled a re-connection with themselves, with other people, and with other aspects of their life, countering the sense of disconnection—a common feature of trauma. Changes in understanding, perception, and self-belief generated hope and promoted a sense of agency that exceeded the transitional space of the social work relationship and positively impacted other relationships and areas of people's lives. The research highlighted the significance of psychosocial and cultural dimensions of trauma and illustrated the value of psychosocial intervention in acute healthcare settings where people often present in the aftermath of traumatic experiences and events.

Through engaging in practice and practice-based research in this context, I came to understand that theories are best used as *sensitising concepts*[5] to help in recognising experiences, accessing information for discussion, deepening understanding, normalising experiences, resisting oppression, expanding worldviews, and generating possibilities and hope. The social work approach emerging from this practice research is inclusive of many ways of understanding experience, allowing people to define and interpret their experience in their own terms, avoiding imposed labels. The focus, echoing Ortega, is the interface of the person and their (now changed) circumstances. ❁

1 Ortega y Gasset, *Obras Completas*, 347–48.

2 Cornell, "Person-in-Situation: History, Theory, and New Directions for Social Work Practice."

3 This paragraph has been adapted from O'Connor, "Relationship-Based Social Work: A 'Thirdspace' in Responding to Trauma."

4 O'Connor, "Relationship-Based Social Work."

5 Blumer, *Symbolic Interactionism: Perspective and Method*.

BIO Erna O'Connor, PhD, is a registered social worker and Assistant Professor in Social Work at Trinity College Dublin, Ireland. Her areas of practice and research are relationship-based social work practice, social work in healthcare, and practice education.

CONTRIBUTION

Perspective

A COMMON PHRASE FOR THOSE WHO WORK in real estate seems to be "location, location, location." For those who follow Jesus out into the troubled and troubling world, it may be "perspective, perspective, perspective."

A pastor told this story about an airplane trip with a seatmate who was both loud and drunk. The pastor was uneasy—probably wishing that he had been assigned another seatmate—and almost certainly glad that the flight would be short. And then, a "God Thing" happened: the annoying seatmate announced that "this is the worst day of my life." And that began something important, a conversation between two travelers, one who had lost a marriage and was still living through the very recent death of his father, and one who just made himself available to really listen. In that exchange, the disturbing seatmate was transformed from a troubling presence into a troubled soul as the pastor's perspective was changed from an annoyed seatmate to a companion who began to listen.

Dr. David Kessler, a grief expert, says in many of his presentations that we need to have our grief witnessed. I would make that a bit broader and say that we all need to have a witness to our pain. And that is exactly what this pastor did and that's what more of us in any community need to do and are called to do. No one should have to experience pain all alone!

We have lots of pain walking the streets and roadways of Jefferson County, West Virginia—and much of that pain goes unwitnessed. But the behaviors that erupt out of that pain, out of some form of trauma from an earlier time, are witnessed, and they're judged as inappropriate ("this is making me feel really uncomfortable"); as non-compliant ("they must do just what we tell them to do"); or as serious enough to call the police. It often seems to us that "Those People" just don't get it.

Every day we see people who don't look like we do, think like we do, act like we do, and, sometimes, don't even smell like we do. Every day we see people from our very own perspectives; we see and, all too often, we judge those differences. When we find it troubling that "those people" are not like us, we miss the soul of the individual. And we miss God and the invitation to help.

Consider some examples:

1. A person labeled as "non-compliant" because helpers didn't listen deeply enough to understand that the "what and how" of their offered help was triggering experiences of being trapped;
2. A person who has been sexually and physically abused for years and remains in poor and declining health is mostly untrusting of offers of help and support;
3. A person who wanders the streets with some purpose known only to themselves and who visits with Vladimir Putin at the American Legion.
4. An adult living with the childhood experience of being given a knife and told by the abused mother to kill the father while he slept.

There are many more. And in almost all cases, adult behaviors have resulted from a problematic childhood, like the last example. These individuals lost their childhood and seem to be losing their adulthood as well. Trauma inflicts deep wounds, leaving individuals feeling hopeless… desperate… and ashamed. But with effective treatment, lives can be reclaimed.

It is true that effective treatment would benefit each of those mentioned above. What is also true is that there is a critical shortage of treatment opportunities—there just aren't enough "treaters."

In his book *Healing*, Dr. Thomas Insel, former director of the National Institute of Mental Health, argues for more "treatment" options for those experiencing mental health issues. He says that good care requires "the three p's"—people, places, and purpose—and introduces Dr. Dixon Chibanda, who, in 2005, was one of 12 psychiatrists in Zimbabwe, a country of 14 million people. Dr. Chibanda created something initially known as a Friendship Bench, or more originally known as the "Granny Bench." He drew on the services of the community grandmothers (a highly respected group in that culture), who received some training in good listening and made themselves available for anyone who just needed some caring company and a witness to their pain.

Here it is: people—the grannies; place—the park bench; purpose—to be with people who perhaps had no one willing or able to just be with them.

People who have been left behind don't have ready access to care, nor are they able to trust most of the rest of us. Far too many of us are either falling or being thrown through that gap; far too many of us either don't see that gap, or do see it and are unable to take action. And here we, who are called to be helpers, stand at the gap because our perspective on so many of the "others" around us is not wide enough to acknowledge their extraordinary needs.

We know that our perspectives are limited and we also know that the only real perspective that matters is Jesus's, and from that perspective, differences melt away. It just doesn't matter where or how we live, what our growing up experiences were, or what hopes we have for our futures.

Maybe it's not that "those people" don't get it—maybe we are the ones who don't get it! ❁

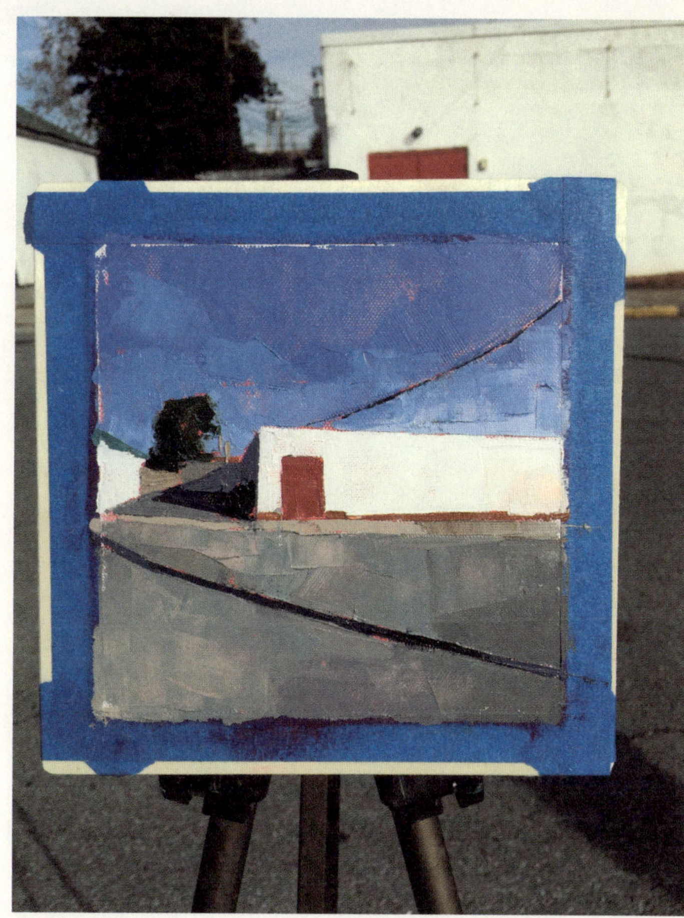

A painting of Jefferson County Community Ministries, where Bob used to serve as the executive director. Kate Fleming, plein air painter, met Bob and made this painting when she and Tom Woodruff passed through West Virginia as part of the 50 States Project.

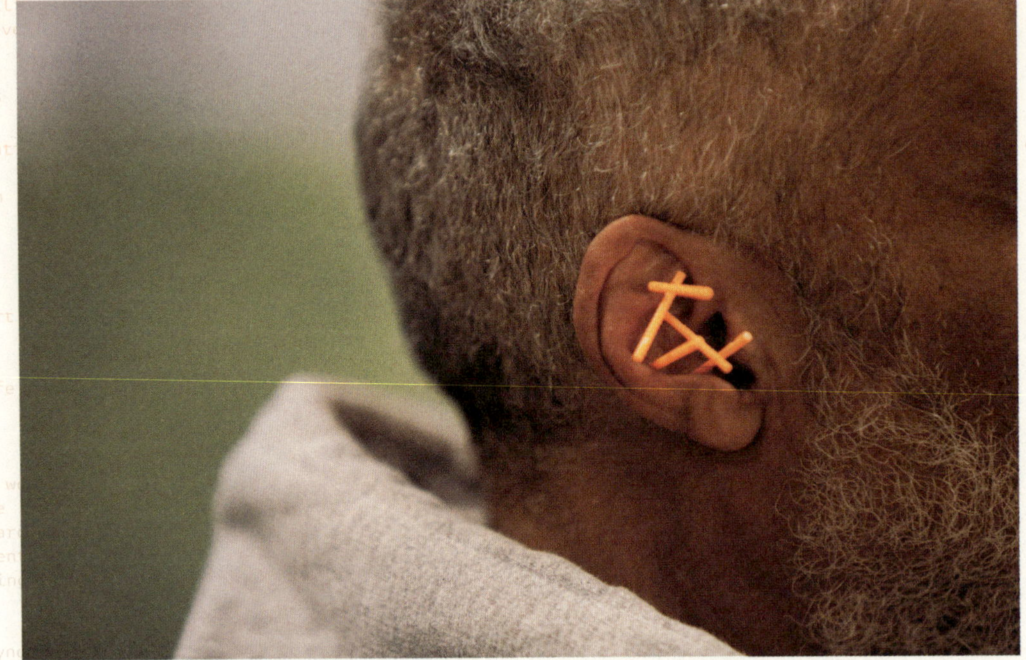

A participant at Jefferson Community Ministries, where Bob used to serve as the executive director, receives auricular acupuncture. Photo by Tom Woodruff, who met Bob and photographed the Ministry while passing through West Virginia with Kate Fleming as part of the 50 States Project.

BIO Bob Shefner is retired from the federal government, has served as a United Methodist pastor, has done clinical and management work in an outpatient mental health clinic, has directed a community ministry, and continues to look for ways to help.

CONTRIBUTOR'S NOTE

PLEASURE ACTIVISM, theorized by adrienne maree brown and supported by works of Black feminists such as Audre Lorde, emphasizes the revolutionary potential of feeling good. Members of marginalized groups (as well as, to a lesser extent, all humans in the society we share) have had their pleasure devalued and demonized. By choosing to prioritize pleasure anyway, one participates in both a radical and restorative act, returning to the individual what is rightfully theirs and giving them the power they'll need for journeys of liberation and creation. This poem invites you to begin, or seeks to keep you company during, your journey toward pleasure and the electric power you will find it brings.—MSM

CONTRIBUTION

Have you considered that your body is on your side? Even in the most
intoxicating of chemical signals?

Have you forgotten that your body will do anything for you? Will
reach for you in pain if it has to?

Unfortunately
The first step is the sweetest
Indulge out of your shame
Find new questions to say yes to
Declare your right to be tempted
Watch yourself survive
I promise
Once you seek to satisfy
One day you will feel satisfied

Any day you are on your own side will produce fruit
When you eat you will feel the nourishment
When you move you will feel the release
When you create you will feel the power
It has been a lifetime of energy expended
I promise
Once you rest
One day you will feel rested

You will lead yourself back even to the painful needs
You will do yourself a favor
And feel some of the next era's pleasure today

BIO

Mia Stone-Molloy (she/her) is a labor organizer and poet with a bachelor's degree in Economics and Political Science from Brown University and a passion for the connection between personal and societal healing.

poems/poetry

SEE: art therapy, arts-based group work

CONTRIBUTION

POEMS use words to make art. Poems ask questions, interrupt assumptions, and mix up ordinary ways of writing, knowing, and being. Poems use rhythm, meter, cadence, and resonant language to enlighten our senses and deepen expression. Reading poems—or writing your own!—can wake us up to new ideas and radical possibility.

Here is a poem I wrote for the radical healers:

Those who work with the suffering suffer themselves because of the work.
—C. R. Figley

our love is powerful love
our energy is powerful energy
our healing is powerful healing
our grief is powerful grief
    lamentation
    lamentation
    lamentation
I carry you in my heart
and my heart is
my heart is.
my heart is
    full up.
    occupied.
    often overflowing.
your radical suffering haunts in the dead of night
makes me crave bourbon and sugar
walking with you in the valley of the shadow of death
I carry you in my heart
I walk beside you
we walk here together
carry me in your heart

❁

BIO

Gioia Chilton, PhD, ATR-BC, CSAC, is an artist, art therapist, researcher, and author who loves her family and art therapy community.

lingering
love
lunar cycle
Magic School, the
mapping support
marginality
(as a site of
resistance)
Marxist social
work
membership theory
in social work
mending
metaphor
mikveh
mobile libraries
movement
lawyering
mutual aid
mycelia as
metaphor
narradrama
narrative
medicine
narrative therapy
nepantla/
nepantleras
nonviolent
communication
ongoingness
peer counseling
peer-to-peer
health network
person-situation
perspective
perspective via
faith
pleasure
poems/poetry
poetic meter
polarity work
post-
oppositionality
postwork
imaginaries
poverty-aware
social work
paradigm, the
power threat
meaning (PTM)
framework
pre(care)ity
prison abolition
professionalism
without
performance
progressive
education
public benefits
public library,
the
Qigong
radical
administration
radical care in
the arts
radical childcare
in movement
spaces
radical
inclusion
radical
papermaking
radical presence
radical
social work
Radical Therapist
Journal, The
Rank and File
Movement (RFM)
in social work

CONTRIBUTION

Meter Magic Spell

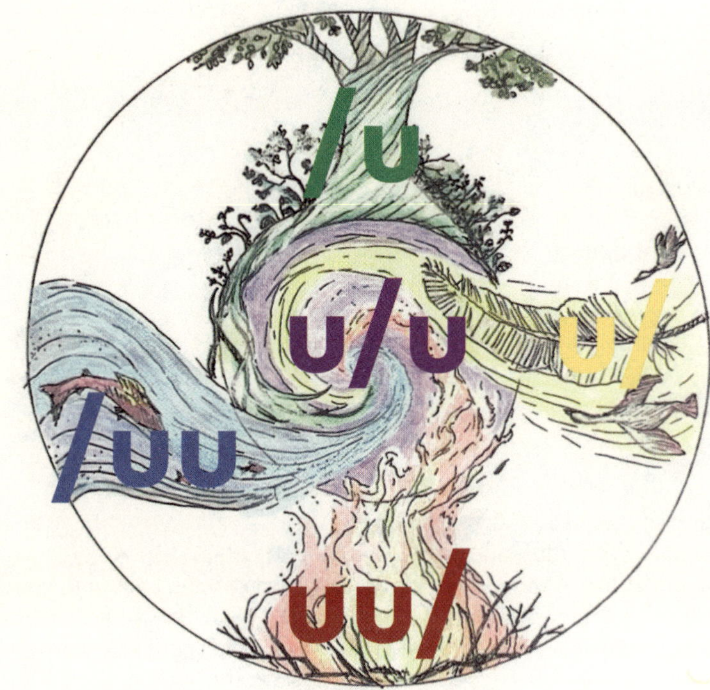

"Element Art" by Ailee Turquette, design by Annie Finch.

METER IS THE PATTERN made by the repeating sounds of words shaped into predictable rhythm, and a meter magic spell is a spell that uses the power of meter to deepen its magic. The most magical cultures in the world—cultures in tune daily with the sacred power of the earth and its cycles—have always used poetic meter as a tool of enchantment. Meter's magic can alter our will, help us remember, unite us together into one experience, change our consciousness, bring us out of ordinary time into sacred time. Long before writing, meter was the secret power of poets, enabling them to remember by heart poems that could take days to recite, poems that carried the precious collective memory of the tribe. From Ghana to Ireland, India to Iceland, Old Europe to North America, these skills gave poets cultural power stronger than that of political rulers.

Today, although we have writing available to us, meter still speaks to our bodies, hearts, and spirits as powerfully as ever. People who pay attention to meter can cast very special spells. Here are some steps you can follow to create your own meter magic spell:

Think of a situation you would like to change in your life; it's best to change your own life rather than someone else's. So for example, if you want someone to love you, then try a spell to make yourself worthy of their love, rather than trying to change them directly! You will end up ahead, either way.

Meditate on the situation and invite some words to come into your mind that feel like good words. Listen closely and see what words come. If no words come, it's okay to make some up.

Write down the words and say them aloud three times, listening closely for their rhythm. Then mark the strong syllables with a wand (/) above the syllable, and the soft syllables with a cup (u). This is called "scanning." ➔

reclaiming selfhood
SE
recognition
redistribution
Reflecting on Justi
reflexivi
Rei
relation
interviewing
relationali
resistan
resisting t
parental los
narrativ
resonan
respectful visiti
respite roo
rest as resistan
reven
revolutiona
mothering
ritu
sanctua
sandplay thera
sau
seed banki
sex positivi
shadow integrati
Sick Woman Theo
slow textil
slowne
social chan
ecosystem framewor
social constructi
social practi
social therapeuti
Social Welfare Acti
Alliance, the
solidari
solidarity econo
somatic heali
songs/singi
sound heali
speculative desi
spel
staying with t
trouble
storytelli
street newspape
strengt
perspective, the
sufficien
sustaining movemen
symb
Taos Institute, t
tar
temporary autonomou
zones
Theatre of t
Oppressed
theories of chang
theosop
therapeutic writi
togetherne
trans practic
transformati
justice
traspati
12-step progra
undercover ant
bullying teams
vigi
wate
wildne
wintering as metapho
wishe
witche
yo
zinemaki

poetic meter

Look for a regular pattern with the wands and cups. If it isn't there yet, change the words until it appears. So if your words are, "I am deliciously ready for happiness," you will discover that you already have a clear repeating pattern:

/ u u / u u / u u / u u
I am deliciously ready for happiness

If your words are:
u / / u u u / u /
I want happiness to show up now

The scanning shows there is no regular pattern, so you can change the words to make them more rhythmical:
u / u / u / u /
Come, happiness, show up for me!

This rhythmical phrase is called a "line." When you have a line you like, then add another line or more in the EXACT SAME PATTERN. This exact repetition of the rhythm is key to the magic: it turns off our conscious mind and invites the universe within and without to step in.

To put yourself in the mood, you can repeat the first line over and over and see if another line comes in the same rhythm. If a new line comes that is not in rhythm, then move the words of the new line around until the scansion (your marking, like a map or musical score, of the scanned syllables) exactly matches the scansion of your first line.

If your ear gets confused, here are a few things you can do:

1. Take a break and come back to the line later.
2. Pretend you are shouting the lines to someone across the room, and the lines' meter will stand out more.
3. Ask someone else to say the line and tell you where they hear the stronger and weaker syllables.

When you have a few lines you like, say them over to yourself and notice if you feel some tingly feelings, maybe in your hands or in your heart area. That's a sure sign of a meter magic spell!

If you want to take it a step further, here are five basic patterns of meter magic you can use and their special magical qualities:

u u / Anapest: Meter of Fire and Passion
u / Iamb: Meter of Air and Clarity
/ u Trochee: meter of Earth and Strength
/ u u Dactyl: Meter of Water and Love
u / u Amphibrach: Meter of Matrix and Magic

Enjoy! ❁

BIO Annie Finch is author of *The Poetry Witch Little Book of Spells* and the founder of Poetry Witch Ritual Theater and PoetryWitchCommunity.org.

When we are stuck in internal conflict
it's so often because we are caught in binary thinking

This mindset, taught to us from birth, makes us believe we have to be either "good" or "bad," "right" or "wrong," "selfless" or "selfish." we push away any parts of ourselves that don't fit our ideal, or suffer because we can't seem to make the undesirable parts of ourselves go away. binary thinking denies the truth that each of us is both good and bad, right and wrong, selfless and selfish. these are unshakable realities of the human experience and their truth forms our existence.

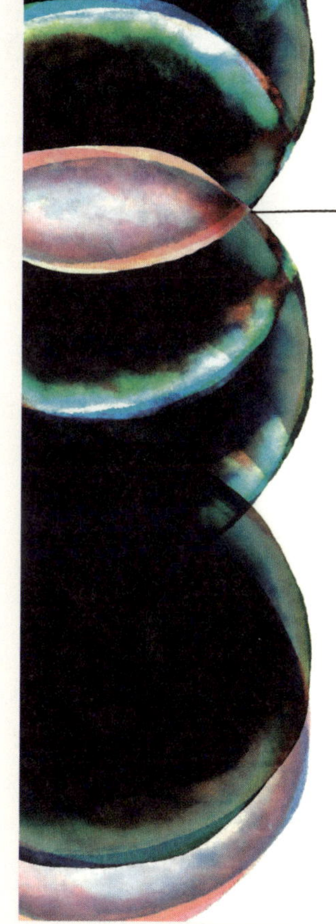

i see binary thinking as a straight line.

we move toward one end, thinking we can escape the other side. we suffer to be together because we are so afraid of being alone. but a funny thing happens when we run away. the more we deny something, the more it seems to shape and motivate our experience, as it does with the socially well-connected person who never feels they have enough friends. as the axiom says, "what we resist, persists." our shadow follows us, no matter how fast we run toward the light.

→

polarity work

to me polarity is a circle

i think replacing binary thinking with a polarity framework can help us reclaim personal and collective wholeness.

Many people see polarity as a magnetic spectrum (again a straight line), but to me, polarity is a circle. we understand that concepts like "good" and "bad," "lonely" and "connected" are actually formed by each other and that we are animated through this dynamic tension.
we start to see the loneliness of always striving for more connection, and how living a life of simplicity can clear more space for connection and joy.

polarity wor

To identify polarity, here's a little guide:

- **Notice** what is upsetting you and give it a name
  (ex: abandonment)
- **See if you can find the opposite** of what you have just named. now you have your polarity!
  (commitment <> abandonment)

Ask yourself what is positive about each end of the polarity. **then ask yourself what is negative** about each end of the polarity. **marvel** at how something you have always labeled as better actually has some pretty real downsides and how something you've always tried to avoid has some real advantages.

one of my favorite parts of polarity is how it flips!

We can be so "good"
that we actually start hurting other people
(purity politics)
and we can be so "bad"
that we actually liberate others
(civil disobedience).

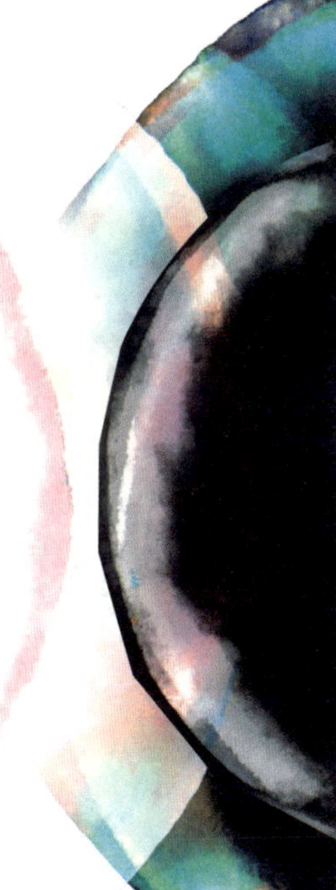

BIOS

Gracy Obuchowicz is a wellness facilitator who is passionate about secondhand fashion, day-to-day meal planning, and connecting the many dots between our personal self-care and collective liberation.

maria habib spends her days in her studio "DesignMa" with her two cats, designing, drawing, and gardening for food and medicine—all the while missing her home, Beirut, Lebanon.

post-oppositionality

E: CONTRIBUTION

TYPICALLY, THOSE OF US RAISED in western cultures and educated within western systems of thought have been trained to define the world in binary-oppositional categories: Me/You. Self/Other. Us/Them. Insider/Outsider. Mind/Body. Spirit/Matter. Right/Wrong. Heaven/Hell. Winners/Losers. Friend/Foe. Normal/Deviant. And the list marches on (*and on and on and on*), normalizing dichotomous ethics and actions: My way or the highway. It's us against them! You're either for us or against us. Pick a side. Choose a team.

These binary-oppositional frameworks are too limited to bring about the radical, progressive change that we so desperately need. While they might facilitate superficial alterations, these minor revisions rely on the same binary logic and thus inadvertently replicate the status quo. Both in my classrooms and in my social justice work more broadly, I've experienced the insidious ways oppositional energies can poison us, despite our best intentions. Repeatedly, I've watched progressive groups break apart, as members use their finely developed oppositional approaches against their allies as well as their foes. We have so thoroughly internalized an oppositional logic that we use it against each other (and often against ourselves). Despite our best intentions and our visionary goals, our over-reliance on oppositional thinking can destroy us from within and inhibit our efforts to address larger unjust systemic issues.

Post-oppositionality—as theory, praxis, and ethics—emerged from my dissatisfaction with this entrenched reliance on oppositional thought. As I searched for alternatives, I was especially drawn to Indigenous philosophies and esoteric wisdom traditions, as well writings by Ralph Waldo Emerson, Paula Gunn Allen, Chela Sandoval, Thich Nhat Hanh, and (especially) Gloria Anzaldúa.[1] These perspectives called out to me. Through intense dialogues with them, I recognized that, in various ways and to varying degrees, they rely on what I call a *metaphysics of radical interconnectedness* that valorizes, justifies, and supports relational worldviews in which everything (and everyone) is intimately interrelated with all that exists. We exist in a reality in which, as Plotinus succinctly attests, "Everything breathes together." Building on this metaphysics of radical interconnectedness, post-oppositionality transforms dichotomous oppositional frameworks into potentially liminal apertures (tiny thresholds, small cracks in the existing oppositional structures) that we can use to develop radical transformation—transformation at the root (e.g., transformation that does not just circulate, in different form, the already-existing structures).

As I define it, post-oppositionality represents an expansive, holistic theory-praxis in which contradictions and apparent opposites co-exist and, through this patient (though tense, challenging, uncomfortable) co-existence, transform each other. I describe this approach as post-oppositional (rather than, say, non-oppositional) to underscore the fact that post-oppositionality includes oppositionality within it: post-oppositionality does not *reject* oppositional consciousness but instead moves through it, borrowing what's useful and *transforming* the rest. (Indeed, to completely reject oppositionality would, itself, be oppositional.) So, for example, a post-oppositional approach does not reject binary, either/or thinking but instead alters it, so that what were previously dichotomous oppositions are viewed relationally. Gloria Anzaldúa's theories of mestiza consciousness and *nepantleras* illustrate two forms this post-oppositional approach can take; Chela Sandoval's theory of oppositional consciousness illustrates another.

Post-oppositionality's implications are immense. I explore several of these many implications in my book, *Transformation Now! Towards a Post-Oppositional Theory and Praxis*, but to briefly mention a few: First,

esoteric wisdom traditions
clouds as metaphor
liminality

post-oppositionality invites us to view differences in relational, rather than oppositional, terms. The binary-oppositional frameworks described previously generally (or perhaps always) define “difference” in hierarchical terms—as deviations from a single unmarked norm. To be different is to be lesser than, to be marked as inferior, abnormal, or in other ways lacking. Post-oppositionality transforms these frameworks into relational networks grounded in interconnectivity. Differences still exist, but when we view these differences relationally, we can look for points of possible connection. Second, this relational approach (with its focus on commonalities) enables us to develop unlikely, highly effective alliances. Third, post-oppositionality facilitates intellectual humility—an open-minded, flexible way of thinking that entails the acknowledgment of our inevitable epistemological limitations; the acceptance of uncertainty and the possibility of error; and intense self-reflection. This intellectual humility fosters creative problem-solving and the invention of fresh ideas, ethics, and actions. In short, post-oppositionality invites us to think more spaciously, to step beyond our conventional rules, to liberate ourselves from the oppositionally-based theories and social justice practices we generally employ. ❁

1 For examples of Indigenous philosophies, see Gregory Cajete and Paula Gunn Allen. Esoteric wisdom traditions cover a broad range of material—including, but not limited to, Taoist teachings, ancient astrology, Renaissance magic, folk magic, conjure, channeled writings, and more.

BIO AnaLouise Keating is a spiritual activist, nepantlerx, author, yoga teacher, and professor of Multicultural Gender & Women's Studies; for information on her work see analouisekeating.com.

postwork imaginaries

SEE: curiosity; generous systems; collaborative apprenticeship

CONTRIBUTION

HYPOTHETICAL JOURNAL PROMPTS for a hypothetical post-capitalist morning:

- When does your body end up sleeping now that it is unrestricted? When does your body want food now that it recognizes that its preferences matter?
- What does quality time mean to you and your loved ones? How else do you prioritize the growth and health of your relationships?
- How do you express your creativity, now that it is no longer valued only for the money it can make?
- What is your relationship with nature like? How will you connect with your world today?
- What ignites your curiosity? What do you learn when you are simply motivated by the joy of learning?
- After you have recovered from a life of work obligations, what responsibilities do you choose to take on? How do you find purpose?
- What feelings can you finally make room to process? ✺

BIO

Mia Stone-Molloy (she/her) is a labor organizer and poet with a bachelor's degree in Economics and Political Science from Brown University and a passion for the connection between personal and societal healing.

EDITORS' NOTE

We first heard the term "postwork imaginaries" in Kathi Weeks's *The Problem with Work: Feminism, Marxism, Antiwork Politics, and Postwork Imaginaries*, an important book that we read as part of Thick Press's "ongoing inquiry into care." —ES & JC

poverty-aware social work paradigm, the

CONTRIBUTION

WHEN I WAS YOUNG, I had this vision that I want to change the way social workers, but also ordinary people in the public, understand people in poverty. I guess this vision was influenced by my mother, who loved to tell us stories about her childhood in poverty in Tel Aviv. The message of her stories was that poverty is something shameful, and that one should distance herself from people in poverty. According to this message, people in poverty were to be blamed for being in poverty, since they did not do the right things to overcome it, like she did. Through marrying up, living in a quiet middle-class community, and working in highly distinguished law firms in Israel, my mother overcame her socio-economic childhood deprivation.

Like a good rebellious adolescent, I reversed her message. My own socio-economic childhood background did not cast a shadow on my identity, as hers did on her. I guess that through my rebellion I wanted to tell her that she had nothing to be ashamed of, that poverty is not shameful, and that people in poverty are not guilty for being in poverty and do not hold sole responsibility for their situation. I thought that poverty is a manifestation of structural violence, a lack of human rights, and not an individual pathology or a personal misbehavior. A sign that one activist held in a demonstration against poverty summarized my perspective: "child forced to shoplift for food—poverty is the crime."

Dedicating my academic career to fighting against poverty through research, teaching, activism, involvement in policymaking, and in social work practice has culminated in the development of the poverty-aware social work paradigm (PAP).[1] The PAP was adopted in 2015 by the welfare ministry in Israel as a leading model for social work practice in the social service departments, bringing about changes in policy and organizational settings, the development of the new role of a *rights social worker*, various new programs, and major transformations in the attitudes and practice of social workers.[2] These, in effect, also had an impact on thousands of service users' lives. Recently, PAP implementation has been extended to the justice, mental health, and education systems.[3]

The PAP is a critical-radical paradigm and constitutes a counter-narrative to the conservative and neoliberal paradigms that have been so dominant in the current professional and public discourse. Its uniqueness lies in its integration of theoretical, ethical, and practical principles. Thus, it aims to give answers to the questions: *What to do in practice?* and *Why to do so?* The PAP is based on the structural paradigm that sees poverty as a problem of unequal societal institutions and arrangements, even as it injects it with the idea of rights and with the addition of micro-level practice methods that focus on relationships and recognition.

The PAP conceptualizes poverty as a violation of human rights in the realms of both structural opportunities (e.g., opportunities for housing, employment, education, and health) and interpersonal relations (e.g., opportunities to receive recognition as an equal human being and to be respected and valued). The second principle of the PAP is its emphasis on the continuing resistance of people to their poverty. People hate to be poor and do everything they can to limit poverty's impact on their lives. Their everyday actions of resistance are seldom recognized as such, since they contradict the hegemonic perception that blames people for their circumstances. According to the third premise, social workers should challenge power relations and learn from people living in poverty by developing close dialogues and relationships with them. Such relationships become possible when social workers adopt an approach of solidarity—the ethical premise of the PAP. Solidarity means that social workers stand by their service users in their struggle instead of encouraging them to adapt to unjust contexts.

According to the PAP, poverty lies at the heart of various situations of human suffering that are often individualized and mistakenly perceived as behavioral problems, such as addiction, violence, school truancy and drop out, and child abuse and neglect. Despite this fact, or maybe because of it, poverty has been brushed aside for many years and treated as a mere background phenomenon in the analysis and treatment of human situations when it should instead serve as a central reference point. Based on a definition of poverty that includes aspects of unequal distribution of both material/social opportunities *and* symbolic-relational ones, the PAP advocates rights-based practices, which are intended to promote economic justice, and practices of recognition, which are intended to promote symbolic-relational justice.[4] In both realms, which in essence are interconnected, specific PAP methods have been developed in line with the critical stance of opposing poverty and standing by the people who experience it. In the realm of rights, these methods include active actualization of rights, material assistance, community development, service development, and policy practice. In the realm of recognition, they include methods from relational psychoanalysis and critical social work such as relationship-based therapy, validation of individuals' trauma and pain, and working through experiences of micro-aggression and powerlessness.[5]

Summarizing the important points of the PAP in a few words, we can say: Poverty is not alright. People living in poverty are not to blame for their poverty. They do not like it. They are doing everything they can to reduce their hardship. They do not succeed because poverty is such a dense web of injustices and oppression that it is beyond the individual to solve. In order for them to succeed, they need our help. Our task is to work alongside them, to become relevant for them, and to find a way to open up possibilities and opportunities for them.

I suggest talking about our commitment and involvement, about caring and solidarity. I propose these words as a platform for practice. ❁

1 Krumer-Nevo, *Radical Hope: Poverty-Aware Practice for Social Work*.

2 Timor-Shlevin, Saar-Heiman, and Krumer-Nevo, "Poverty-Aware Programs in Social Service Departments in Israel: A Rapid Evidence Review of Outcomes for Service Users and Social Work Practice."

3 Krumer-Nevo, "Poverty, Social Work, and Radical Incrementalism: Current Developments of the Poverty-Aware Paradigm."

4 Fraser, "From Redistribution to Recognition? Dilemmas of Justice in a 'Post-Socialist' Age."

5 Krumer-Nevo, *Radical Hope: Poverty-Aware Practice for Social Work*.

B I O
Prof. Michal Krumer-Nevo is the head of the Spitzer Department of Social Work, Ben-Gurion University of the Negev.

power threat meaning (PTM) framework

CONTRIBUTION

AN ALTERNATIVE to the Diagnostic and Statistical Manual (DSM). Unlike the more traditional biopsychosocial model of mental distress, there is no assumption of pathology, and the "biological" is not privileged. The PTM framework[1] takes the position that the challenges folks often face are not fundamentally biological, but experiences of embodied, meaning-based threat responses to the negative effects of power.

Rather than asking, "What is wrong with you?," the PTM framework asks, "What has happened to you?" (How has **Power** operated in your life?) "How did it affect you?" (What kind of **Threats** does this pose?) "What sense did you make of it?"' (What is the **Meaning** of these situations and experiences to you?) "What did you have to do to survive?" (What kinds of **Threat Response** are you using?) ❁

1 Johnstone and Boyle, "The Power Threat Meaning Framework: An Alternative Nondiagnostic Conceptual System."

BIO

Chris Hoff, PhD, LMFT, is the Founder and Executive Director of California Family Institute and a Liminal Space Tour Guide.

pre(care)ity

CONTRIBUTION

Care in Precarity (Or Underclass Love)

1. This idea of pre(care)ity, however brief, however ephemeral, however uprooted, offers a synthesis of two terms, with parentheses holding "care" in the center, signifying something warm, that takes a breath with and for you. Here we connect to a feeling; one grounded in the care-in-precarious-practices that I have witnessed and absorbed within the low-income, multiethnic underclass spaces in which I was nurtured and raised. For to be alive is to be precarious ("a shared condition of human life," as Judith Butler reminds us).[1] Yet this condition is exacerbated within late-stage capitalism by a state-induced, biopolitical experiential force that determines which bodies matter and are deserving of support across various gendered, bodily, classed, and racialized stratifications, in a socio-historical moment increasingly defined by collapsing and highly pressurized social, governmental, economic subsistence-maintenance systems, which were only really provisional for the poor anyway (in the post-war reformist scheme of things).[2]

2. For those of us who live within and beyond statistical extremes of governance, where wages are suppressed to keep inflation down in the name of profit, we find ourselves always coping within the conditions of a-copic imposed on us. As a result of this imperiled status, as outliers of love, of policy, we become the reserve army repository of churning, collateral damage. And whilst experiences of poverty may differ in their impact and effects, indexed by increased mortality rates and complex health determinants across varying contexts, pre(care)ity finds a way to fill in the gaps left by loss, offering a subtle improvisation in the melancholy of the cut and the hurt.

3. Pre(care)ity unfolds within those moments to moments (oftentimes in ways anterior to established welfare or health systems) along shared lives among individuals whom the state has attempted to dislocate and fragment from the Commons. Within pre(care)ity, the ability to be response-able to situations is always challenged, impeded. The answer is we can't always speculate along horizons walled from us; therefore, pre(care)ity is often unplanned, impulsive, and not schemed or anticipated, spiraling out of turbulences of chronic stress and anxiety that affect the brain and nervous systems, making it difficult to envisage the long-term.

4. In other words, pre(care)ious encounters roll with the punches and instability that precarity demands of our modes of living, where phloem-like transport chains grow around the resistant concretions: contact-to-contact; home to home; family to family, famine-to-feast—manifold insulative refrains. Here, we find no bourgeois luxury to separate oneself, forget oneself, actualize oneself in the cleansing-furnace of the Spectacle. Such a modality is impractical when limbs, words, and arteries are bound up and all-knotted, messy, ugly, wounded, open, generating another fatigue among a landscape of fatigue.

5. In this sense, those practicing such forms of class care are oftentimes suffering from the conditions they seek to resolve; a moving mourning. Pre(care)ity thus always goes into the red, into debt, the non-metred, the (un)punctuated. It cannot generate further capital, nor does the gift of a small resource equate to a virtue signal, a contrivance (witness is limited), or a broadcast in advance. Pre(care)ity here is an uncertain ambiance: a type of infrathin. It is the refuge found in the non-spoken or minimally uttered responsibilities, as we ad hoc

and afterward resign softly into node-works of flesh and bone, and dust emanating from old television sets.

6. Never static, never the same, transmutations take place within communities and individuals under spine-curving debt, where labor cannot be outsourced, alienated, or offshored, where the immanence of lack and loss, and strident joy, demands an immediate and bold mode of address, of reckoning: a type of life-dependent hyper-interest in the Other, arising from acute spatio-temporal compressions (we hold these damp walls up). Such models of adaptation are necessary, wherein survival within those more mobile or liquid-modern[3] social contexts does not so much rely on clinging together, as we have had no choice to do. Here we, like Judith Butler, find ourselves refraining: if I lose you, I lose myself.[4]

7. Within pre(care)ity there are no breadwinners, only piece-meals; our under-classes are opaque to the hyper-rationalized ravenousness of markets, where a maternal cultural ethos structures thought, actions, and feeling. In this capacity, care is practiced mostly by those burdened by the feminized stratification of labor, i.e., working-class Women, and Queer folk in so-called "low" skilled, underpaid work. Yet, in the same breath, pre(care)ity also respirates other lines of flight too. For as Power and Hall surmise, "new spaces, relations, networks, and practices of care and caring are emerging in difficult times, in unexpected and unconventional places."[5] Eventually, loss impels us all to become mother at some stage or another.

8. Pre(care)ity, ultimately, announces a refusal to perish as exhausted surplus as a type of minuscule mutualism that sustains and intensifies intra-affective foliage as inflamed bodily response. As such, experience of poverty can heighten the mycelial-like structures of a multitude of bound-sound bodies; wherein the pre(care)ious become vitally vigilant in profound ways. For as the writer Christopher Barnett attests: "Only the poor, the marginalized, the oppressed possess real culture, for what is culture other than 'refined' instinct & only they possess it, invent it, create the new."[6]

9. Pre(care)ity is, at least on the surface, consistent with the conception of mutual aid. Being pre(care)ious is to perform some variation of being poor in the principles (or practices) of ongoing reciprocity, such as those practiced by Australian First Nations communities who share money, food, and housing within extended love-works of families and friends, defying colonial stratification via (un)common code-switchings at the base where the barometer of experience is truly and deeply felt.

10. What we can term as *POOR* (principles of ongoing reciprocity) practices are naturalized over time, pre-modern and post-modern forms of exchange and connection to a particular social role, rather than forced reliance on external systems of provision, which can be found in many impoverished, marginalized, rural, and urban communities around the world in the form of circular sub- or para-economies of exchanges of food, money, clothing, among immigrant, poor, and diaspora communities, having to find other routes, desire paths, or risk being cut off entirely. There are many ways in which POOR practices reveal a type of perpetually provisional necessity of situated-giving-and-living-receiving-giving—reflected in a form of responding without even the precursor of a type of rhetorical asking, i.e., "Can you do this or

that?" Akin to a soft look in the eyes, a subtle acknowledgement. A "yep," and a "no worries," or a head nod, a quick rummaging of the cupboard. A "what have I got and what can I give?" A smoke to lend, help on the tick, little monies forwarded, or redirected at any moment.

11. Care-in-precarity in action is not posed here as a solution or concept but rather a processual understanding of small actions I have viewed, kept afloat within, and been moved by in refractory under- and working-class interactions. Due to our shared interests within pre(care)ity, we seek to converge and coalesce together: of our many mixed storylines, or our loving potentials. Pre(care)ity impels us to meet at a point for that moment, for that time, for that meal, for that caress, for that much-needed and joyous lament. Here, we do not idealize poverty and attempt to negate the failings of the state, the market, or the so-called "conscientious community," but to demonstrate that despite the violent capitalist extraction of those aspects, opportunities, and pathways required for a so-called good life, *nonetheless care in precarity always persists*. ❁

1 Butler, *Frames of War: When Is Life Grievable?*, 13–14.

2 My interpretation here takes inspiration from Butler's statement: "Precarity designates that politically induced condition in which certain populations suffer from failing social and economic networks of support and become differentially exposed to injury, violence, and death." Butler, *Frames of War: When Is Life Grievable?*, 25–6.

3 For an in-depth explanation of this term see: Bauman, *Liquid Modernity*.

4 Butler, *Precarious Life: The Powers of Mourning and Violence*, 22.

5 Power and Hall, "Placing Care in Times of Austerity," 311.

6 Barnett, "Christopher Barnett Public Facebook Page."

BIO James Hazel (jameshazel.net) is a composer, researcher, and artist whose work is concerned with the embodied, poetic, and sonic practices of (extra) ordinary and diverse working-class lives.

CONTRIBUTION

Toward Global Prison Abolition

"What does a *world* without police and prisons look like?"

THE SUMMER UPRISINGS of 2020 brought about a resurgence of outrage over the role that policing, incarceration, and the prison-industrial complex have played in the United States and around the world. Almost overnight, the notion of abolishing police went from a frightening theory to a mainstream slogan. We have seen similar uprisings take place in tropical Africa, Central and South America, Asia, the Middle East, and europe. However, when one begins to research abolition, overwhelmingly the literature and organizations working toward abolition are US-centric. Those of us in the Majority World[1] are all too familiar with the daily extortion and violence enacted by police officers—an experience so common that it has become an expected part of daily life. We also know that prisons do not prevent so-called crime in our communities. Internationalism is core to the movement for abolition, and we must look to paradigms outside the United States if we are to create a world where the needs of the planet and people are met, and prisons are made obsolete.

Prisons and jails have done little to minimize or prevent harm. There is plenty of evidence showing that incarceration deepens individual and collective trauma. Repressive institutions like policing and prisons are neither natural nor necessary. In fact, they are a direct result and function of colonialism, racial capitalism, and imperialism, sustained by fear-based logic, retributive justice, racist drug and migration policy, and manufactured moral panic. Meanwhile most true harms are never addressed. Furthermore, we have come to associate criminality specifically with dark-skinned and queer bodies, even as empirical evidence disproves such myths.

Abolition calls for us to eradicate the root causes of suffering and create systems of accountability and care. It requires that we understand the true motivations of the State, which is and has always been to hoard resources, exploit the labour of the masses, and decimate communities of colour. Abolitionists are not calling for reforms, which only legitimize prisons and the police. Instead, we seek to disrupt carceral logic and dismantle legal systems that frame some lives as more valuable than others.

Around the world, prisons are used to cage political dissidents and those considered socially unsavoury. In May 2023, Ugandan president Yoweri Museveni and his parliament passed the Anti-Homosexuality Act of 2023, criminalizing non-heterosexuals by making queer sex punishable with life in prison and death. This draconian law also discriminates against differently abled people by creating the crime of "aggravated homosexuality" if the "victim" has a disability, effectively denying them the ability to consent to sex. In September 2022, Iran caught fire in protest against the death of Mahsa (aka Jina) Amini, who was killed after being taken into police custody by the Guidance Patrol (the nation's morality police) for how she wore her hijab. In the aftermath over a hundred people were imprisoned for their participation. As of June 2023, the protests are ongoing.

For decades prisoners have pushed back against inhumane living conditions, lack of medical treatment, and violence by prison guards. In recent years, prison protests have occurred across continents and islands including Aotearoa (Waikeria Prison), Burundi (Gitega Prison), Colombia (Tuluá Prison), Thailand (Krabi's main provincial prison), Syria (Sednaya Prison), and Scotland (Cornton Vale Prison). In 2021, six political prisoners in Palestine's Gilboa Zionist Detention Centre pulled off an incredible escape, some having spent more than

20 years behind bars. These feats remind us that when faced with oppression, the people can and will resist.

By far the most common question folks ask when there's talk about abolishing prisons is "where to put all the rapist/murders/etc." People seem to shy away from the abolitionist vision when they don't feel this question is adequately answered, something I have witnessed repeatedly despite the many well-written toolkits and guides that exist in how to respond to this question. Even seasoned organizers in the movement have no doubt asked it. Yet, can we confidently say that all people causing harm are in cages? Absolutely not. There are many legalized actions and entities that actively cause damage to people and the planet, operating without shame or accountability, such as the emerging East African Crude Oil Pipeline (EACOP). Many of us survivors of abuse know that those who harmed us are not in prison, nor would their being there bring us healing or justice.

A key aspect of prison abolition centers around questioning the use of punishment as a means of control. Carceral logic is strong not only in political realms but also in our personal lives. Negative reinforcement to encourage conformity is core to several value systems, especially within industrialized and colonized nations. When children misbehave, they are often beaten or removed from their peers and isolated until they have "learned their lesson." If a hungry person steals food, they are stripped of their agency and prevented from participating in society—essentially isolated until they too have "learned their lesson."

Abolition isn't merely theory; it is a practical means of creating responses to harm that are not carceral and prevent future harms from occurring. As caregivers, social workers, healthcare providers, and others of a helping occupation/profession, we can practice abolition by engaging in campaigns that limit the scope and reach of the prison industrial complex, including campaigns against migrant detention, police in schools, death penalties, life without parole, and the criminalization of transactional sex. Working to abolish the Adoption & Safe Families Act is one way to undo violent legislation that has allowed for the removal of children from black, indigenous, and low/no-income homes. We can also resist mandated reporting and collusion with the police when responding to mental and physical health crises.

It is just as critical to create healthy, equitable communities by uplifting efforts to mediate and/or resolve conflict beyond retribution, provide adequate healthcare and housing, and increase funding for mental health services (not at all to be confused with mental health jails). Though there is variation in the legal structures that allow for public participation, there are examples of resistance and power-building all over the world that we can look to for encouragement for how we take down harmful institutions and build up systems of care. From #endSARS in Nigeria to No New Jails in San Francisco, people's movements have continued to demonstrate that when we fight, we win, and when we care, we thrive.

Abolishing prisons also means abolishing migrant detention centers, courts, and e-carceration (electronic monitoring and surveillance). We do not seek to replace harmful institutions, but to burn them to ash and create ways of living in harmony. It took hundreds of years to develop the present-day prison industrial complex, so we cannot expect solutions to form overnight. There is no single method to undo prisons. It is up to us to experiment and look to those who came before us for a way forward. The Global Prison Abolitionist Coalition,[2] launched in 2020, has been uniting across borders to connect the struggles of political prisoners around the world. Tanzanian scholar Julena Jumbe Gabagambi's Comparative Analysis of Restorative Justice Practices in Africa[3] provides multiple examples of conflict resolution paradigms that bring together survivors, perpetrators, and community members to address harm and disputes. You can access the work of other such scholars through the International Journal of Restorative Justice.[4]

In sharing these few resources, I do not claim that any are flawless. We will stumble and fail along the way but can learn and recover from setbacks. By sharpening our analysis and opening our hearts, we can build compassionate structures of care toward a world that no longer "needs" prisons or police. ❁

1 "Majority World" is a term coined by Bangladeshi activist and photojournalist Shahidul Alam as a decolonial alternative to terms like "global south" and "developing world," which obscure the violence of colonialism. The term highlights the fact that we such people compose the majority of the world's population, and is inclusive of people of color living in western countries.

2 worldwithoutprisons.org/about/.

3 nyulawglobal.org/globalex/Restorative_Justice_Africa1.html.

4 elevenjournals.com/tijdschrift/TIJRJ/detail.

B Onyịnye smiles while
I bathing in the sunlight of
O life // ọchị na anwụ.

professionalism without performance

CONTRIBUTION

DRESS APPROPRIATELY
—> for your personality and sensory needs
RULES ARE RULES
—> to be experimented with and adapted with humility
DEADLINES ARE DEADLINES
—> for those who find them useful and for projects with genuine urgency
DECISIONS ARE DECISIONS
—> made by those who they affect
IF YOU CAN'T MAKE YOUR CRITIQUE POLITELY,
—> don't let it stop you from bringing up an issue
CONSIDER HOW IT AFFECTS THE TEAM
—> when a member neglects themself
DO NOT BRING IN YOUR PERSONAL
—> fear of confronting the realities of other people's lives
THE WORKPLACE IS NOT A PLACE FOR "TALKING POLITICS"
—> for purposes other than trying in good faith to understand and empathize with each other
THERE IS NO ROOM FOR FAILURE
—> to be seen as anything other than an opportunity for growth
DO NOT USE LANGUAGE THAT
—> prevents you from communicating freely and comfortably
TIME IS MONEY
—> (overvalued)
EXPECT TO BE HELD ACCOUNTABLE
—> by those you work with, not just those you work under
RESPECT THE AUTHORITY OF
—> those with lived experience

BIO

Mia Stone-Molloy (she/her) is a labor organizer and poet with a bachelor's degree in Economics and Political Science from Brown University and a passion for the connection between personal and societal healing.

CONTRIBUTION

Dear Society

DEAR SOCIETY,

As a clever, helpful, and dear spider named Charlotte once opened: *Salutations!* The purpose of this introduction is to acquaint you with, or reacquaint you with, progressive education. I think you, Society, will benefit and strengthen from connecting with progressive education.

You might remember the progressive education scholars of the early 20th century in the US, the likes of John Dewey, Caroline Pratt, and Francis Parker. They, along with more recent scholars, will accompany me in this letter. Their thinking, their writing, their *doing* connected to progressive education share a key element: to always think of the individual as an essential part of a group. Communitarianism. (No, not communism, don't freak out.)

Let me, somewhat defensively perhaps, proclaim that communitarianism is an American idea. An American ideal. From one of our great American novels, *The Grapes of Wrath*'s "I to we" message, to quilting circles, to baseball, to barn raisings, to jazz music itself—it is together that we are most powerful. Together we can heal and effect change. Nothing will help you, our society, more than a shift from a competitive, individualistic mindset to an emphasis of the group. We must think of our neighbors, the proximate ones and the ones we don't know.

I believe progressive education is a powerful conduit that invites children to learn how to use their minds and hearts well, becoming adults who know how to use their minds and hearts well—through service to the common good and communitarianism.

More than 10 years ago, progressive educator and sweet man, Tom Little, traveled to dozens and dozens of self-identifying progressive schools across the US (since I was 10, I've loved that "U.S." spells *us*!), seeking to define progressive education. He found 3 common threads among these progressive schools: 1) a focus on democracy and citizenship 2) a focus on the whole child 3) an ardent commitment to social justice.[1]

"What does this look like at a real school?" you might be wondering. Here is the highlight reel at my particular progressive elementary school:

- Children playing! Outside, connected to each other and to nature. (Their most important work is play. It's how they make sense of you, Society, when it gets extra complicated.)
- Children in their classrooms working in committees where they are critically *and* creatively thinking. (Our work together must go beyond criticism.)
- Children block building, painting, hammering, sanding, stitching, singing, sculpting, and dancing. (We are all artists, we are.)
- Children completing math problems by collaborating and cooperating. (Why is learning—learning math in particular—so often an isolating experience?)
- Children earnestly completing their classroom or campus job. ("Don't do for children what they can do for themselves,"[2] Caroline Pratt wrote 75 years ago.)
- Children voting on a classroom issue that is important to them. (Francis Parker said, "A school should be a model home, a complete community, an embryonic democracy.")[3]
- Children struggling! Be it grappling with hard history, repairing a challenging moment with a friend, accounting for a not-great choice they made. (We guide children to do hard so that they can face hard on their own.)
- Parents, guardians, and grandparents sharing their family stories and traditions with their children's classmates through family shares. (Deborah Meier quipped in a talk at the 2017 Progressive Education Network's

Conference in Boston, "If there's one thing children are attuned to, it's how their parents are seen by other people.")

- Children NOT on campus because they are on field trips! They are out in the community making meaning and making connections. (I once heard an early child educator in Reggio Emilia, Italy, assert, "If you want society to care more about children, you have to *show* people in society the work and the culture of children.")
- Children exploring their identity and learning about how they are similar and different from each other, so they can unpack the impact of differences. Children naturally notice what is unfair in their community, so we can support them to take action connected to topics like climate change and food scarcity. (Children have the need to always feel safe. We are obligated to guide them through uncomfortable, however.)
- Children asking questions and grappling with content—while their teacher records the questions and wonderings for future study and pursuit. (Paulo Freire espoused in *Pedagogy of the Oppressed*, "If the structure does not permit dialogue, the structure must be changed.")[4]

Progressive educators Nancy and Theodore Sizer assure us that "the children watch us all the time."[5] They are watching you, they are watching me, they are watching us. I invite us to live out the ideas and values of communitarianism. When these values are centered, they then become internalized. And here's the delightful catch. The learning becomes vital. These values become the *common unity* for the adults guiding the children through their learning and growing up. Thus, children don't just grow, we all grow. We renew our faith in each other. And you, Society! We mustn't just pass on your problems to the next generation.

bell hooks described the limitless possibilities when this type of education occurs. In *Teaching to Transgress*, she wrote: "I entered the classroom with the conviction that it was crucial for me and every other student to be an active participant, not a passive consumer... education as the practice of freedom... education that connects the will to know with the will to become. Learning is a place where paradise can be created."[6] So through progressive education, if we can give ALL children the access to experience the paradise of community and the paradise of freedom, we not only help ourselves, we help you, Society.

And to close with the wise spider Charlotte who greeted you earlier: "By helping you, perhaps I was trying to lift up my life a trifle. Heaven knows anyone's life can stand a little of that."[7]

Yes, let's help each other. We will all get lifted up. Even just a trifle.

Warmly,
Melinda A. Tsapatsaris ❁

1 Little and Ellison, *Loving Learning: How Progressive Education Can Save America's Schools*.

2 I wasn't able to locate the citation for this quote, which is a mantra at my school.

3 Parker, *Progressive Education Vol. 1*, 155.

4 Freire, *Pedagogy of the Oppressed*, 93.

5 Sizer and Sizer, *The Students Are Watching: Schools and the Moral Contract*, xvii.

6 hooks, *Teaching to Transgress*, 12.

7 White, *Charlotte's Web*, 164.

BIO Melinda Tsapatsaris is the Head of School at Westland School in Los Angeles and the mother of three.

public benefit

SEE redistribution

CONTRIBUTION

WHEN I THINK BACK ON OVER TWO DECADES of social work and wonder whether and how I've been helpful to the people I've encountered, I land first on those moments when time slows down and there's an eye-locking sense of presence; some people say this experience arises when we "hold space." It's so very elegant, the idea that healing and possibilities emerge from intersubjective connection. It's also very comforting, because once workers fully grasp the heartbreaking reality that people's needs often go unmet—and, worse, that the extent of unmet needs roughly tracks social factors like race and gender—we need an anchor, something to help us keep on showing up and doing the work.

But here I am, skirting around the form of helpfulness I set out to describe. The *second* piece that comes to mind when I ask myself whether and how I've been helpful has to do with the times when, with a worker's help, people's needs *don't* go unmet. In these situations, resources move toward people—people *catch* resources—because a helper-helpee team is lucky or persistent enough to access an entitlement program or a similar public benefit.

I like the word "entitlement" because it makes people sound dignified and implies that we are all entitled, literally, to care. But dignity is a heavy concept—and learning about entitlement programs and public benefits in general tends to be kind of dull. It reminds me of the first time I ever heard the word "entitlement" in this context. It was my first semester of social work school, and every student was required to watch a 30-minute video of a professor sitting at a desk explaining all the entitlements that every social worker needs to understand: Medicaid, Medicare, SSI, food stamps (now SNAP), welfare (now TANF), and so on.

Years later, I came up with an idea for making public benefits shimmer as shimmeringly as "holding space" and "being with." We could celebrate benefits programs by spelling out their initials in balloons. Balloon-animal acronyms! Or how about fireworks or an ABC-type book with illuminated letters!? That would be so much more captivating than the 30-minute video. When I shared my idea with a colleague, she told me it was offensive. "People really count on these programs," she said.

poverty-aware social work paradigm, the

I guess when something shimmers, people read it as frivolous, unnecessary. I'll give my colleague the benefit of the doubt: I don't think she believes that public benefits—and by extension, the people who receive them—aren't worthy of shimmer. Instead, I think she thought my intervention might devalue the pain involved in resource insecurity, the urgency involved in helping people get their needs met. Perhaps she also worried that my shimmering balloons would feed conservative myths about 1) the fiscal irresponsibilities that accompany bleeding hearts and 2) the shiftiness of racialized "welfare queens."

I've encountered others who reject not necessarily the impulse towards shimmer, but the very *existence* of entitlement programs and other government benefits. They recognize that the government has failed to serve them/us, and therefore they feel a stirring desire for autonomy. Some of these people, like the Martinican theorist Édouard Glissant, believe that government benefits breed complacency and dependency, staving off the revolution. I am grateful for this line of inquiry—but I don't want big ideas to crowd out here-and-now possibilities. Plus, I'm all for resource redistribution, which is what public benefits do, in roundabout ways, despite the hurdles, the shame, and the piddling amounts of most programs (but isn't something better than nothing?).

Childishly, stubbornly, I fantasize that balloons, fireworks, and illuminated letters will help others see that public benefits are worthwhile and it's worthwhile to celebrate them. I also fantasize that shimmer will energize those of us who feel exhausted and avoidant in relation to bureaucracy. So I asked Julie to help me create this flyer. Please copy it; please share it; please attach it to a sea plane and send it to the shoreline. ❁ ➔

1 Glissant and Chamoiseau, *Manifestos*.

SNAP

MEDICAID

1 Gently examine your biases about "dependency" and "government aid," and speak out when you hear others express similar biases. (It might help to educate yourself about the large amount of resources that the government moves toward wealthy individuals and businesses, mostly in the form of tax breaks and subsidies.)

2 Learn about the smorgasbord of programs, vouchers, subsidies, cash support, and other resources that are available in your neck of the woods.

3 Create bulletin boards containing information about accessing resources.

4 Take time out of your helping sessions to help people access and maintain resources.

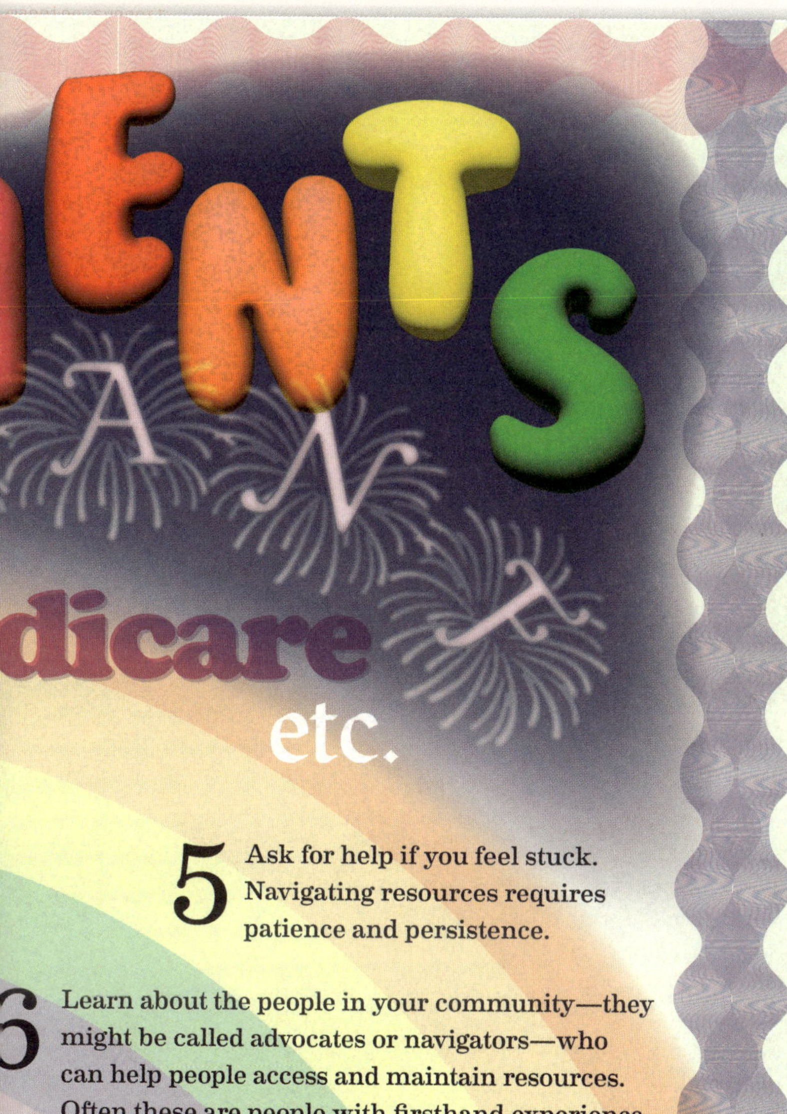

5 Ask for help if you feel stuck. Navigating resources requires patience and persistence.

6 Learn about the people in your community—they might be called advocates or navigators—who can help people access and maintain resources. Often these are people with firsthand experience accessing and maintaining public benefits.

7 Maintain connections with advocates and navigators. They can help you help others navigate benefits; you can help them lobby to maintain and expand programs, vouchers, subsidies, cash support, and other resources.

BIOS

Erin Segal, MSW, PhD, is a middle-aged mother, wife, daughter, and friend who facilitates groups with elders and, along with Julie Cho, publishes unusual books about care.

Julie Cho—graphic designer and design educator who thrives on being in collaboration with others—is one-third of the graphic design studio Omnivore with Alice Chung and Karen Hsu; one-half of Thick Press with Erin Segal; and one-quarter of a family with David, Cleo, and Yoona.

public library, the

CONTRIBUTION

The Future of (Public) Libraries

I'VE BEEN WORKING at a neighborhood branch of a large urban public library for about two years. During that time, one of my former bookstore colleagues launched an independent mutual aid book bike known as The Nonbinarian which, to this day, distributes free queer books in key locations throughout New York. Although we don't live in the same city anymore, this person and I stay in touch and bounce ideas off each other re: libraries, books, information access, mutual aid, etc.

Once, during an Instagram audience Q&A, a follower of The Nonbinarian asked about the future of libraries and my friend hit me up for a reply since I technically work in "the industry." When I got all my thoughts out, though, it was far more than a social media post, so they published an anonymous version of this short piece in their first-ever "Friends of The Nonbinarian" newsletter on Sunday, October 1, 2023.

Between book bikes and book drops, mutual aid and government funding, Instagram communities and fake names, the long-winded story of how this spate of thinking came to be feels representative of how socially and organizationally interconnected the Public Library Question really is. There is a great and dissonant tension between the work of public libraries in theory and the day-to-day reality of the staff who are underpaid to carry out an ever-expanding slew of duties in the buildings that actually say "Public Library." And, spoiler, the future of libraries lies in the fugitive work that happens in between.

SEE: Black Panther Party Free Breakfast Program; community gardens; harm reduction

It's an interesting time for me to be writing about the future of libraries. I work in a large urban public library system. This month, our city's Office of Risk Management hired new staff who are demanding that every community partner we work with produce (oftentimes multiple) certificates of liability insurance as a prerequisite to any official collaboration with the library.

To bring questions of insurance—which I recognize as the professionalized and class-coded sale of the narrative of diminished capital risk—into what is supposed to be a public space feels especially egregious. Who can afford personal liability insurance? Not the casual group of educators who teach basic literacy to Spanish-speaking patrons every Sunday in their free time. Not the mutual aid collective of sex workers with whom I was planning a special story time of *How Mamas Love Their Babies*.

As a librarian lucky enough to clock in with (a majority of) colleagues whose collective philosophy of programming stems from strong relationships with local artists, educators, and mutual aid groups (read: neighbors), this policy change has basically ground our branch and our community life to a halt. *If the public library won't support you, who will?*

The future of libraries is not owned by the government. The public library as it exists today is not the critically immune gold standard for community care as it is often celebrated in popular discourse. Reader: many urban public libraries have their own police force. The behavioral guidelines that these officers enforce are outdated, classist, and ableist. Racist materials stay on the shelves under the argument of "neutrality." Colleagues of color and low income repeatedly hit the ceiling on their upward mobility due to the gatekeeper that is the Master's of Library and Information Science and its ponderous chain of racialized, classed, and cultural baggage. I could keep going, and yet—there's a marketable slogan famously emblazoned upon t-shirts and tote bags that asks: "What's more punk than the public library?"

And yes, public libraries are one of the only places in the US where you can access information and materials for free and are not required to spend money to connect to Wi-Fi or use the bathroom or sit in a chair for hours. But let's not pretend they are the most "punk" initiative out there, because doing so creates a quick and convenient ceiling to our collective imagination.

So, what is more punk than the public library? *If the public library won't support you, who will?* The Nonbinarian Book Bike, aka the reason I'm writing this, for one. Imagine if each major city had a cargo bike pedaling around park to park and slinging the text-based representation that's most actively oppressed in each of their respective communities, connecting folks and organizations along the way. And what I'm really describing here is mobile mutual aid, which happens in many forms that don't have to deal with books or be so visible: the Cajun Navy, the People's Bodega, hot din deliveries, carpools.

Back on the library beat, there's also the Noname Book Club, intentionally built in the memory of community-driven Black bookstores (including that of Noname's mother), which were so often the target of state-based repression during COINTELPRO. Notable about the Noname Book Club is the targeted inclusion of our most marginalized comrades through their robust Prison Program, which brings up the larger project of building carceral libraries, which also is the focus of Reginald Dwayne Betts and Freedom Reads. And have you heard of the Biblioburro that takes books to the Colombian backcountry on a donkey?

You'll notice that something these projects have in common is the question of how to get the most-needed books to people with the least access. How to center our work around our most vulnerable neighbors. And this echoes in the background of the question I always arrive at when banging my head into the wall about libraries: What is public space? Who is it for?

For me, public space is somewhere you won't get thrown out if you fall asleep. The cops aren't there. You aren't required to show papers or ID in order to borrow a book. The collection reflects the community served and features positive and own-voice representation of its most vulnerable members. The water is clean. The computers work. You don't need a prohibitively expensive and professionalized Master's Degree to be taken seriously. There's an active commitment to collective liberation as opposed to "neutrality." A social worker is there all the time and whoa! their labor is appropriately valued. Narcan and test strips and clean needles. Community garden. Free breakfast before school.

Until then, criticism as care. And we take care of us. ❁

B Verity Sturm is a children's
I librarian at a large urban
O public system in the US.

Qigong

Tree Gong

CONTRIBUTION

IN TAOIST PHILOSOPHY, "QI" (pronounced *chee*) is the life-force energy that flows within and without all things. Qi animates and gives vitality to all life.

Qigong is an ancient Taoist health practice and branch of Traditional Chinese Medicine. The word "Qigong" translates to "play with energy." Other branches of Traditional Chinese Medicine include acupuncture and herbalism.

Qigong involves coordinating body postures and movements with controlled breathing and visualization of qi flow. Through these means, activated by the breath, a practitioner is able to attune their mind and body to the subtle flow of qi through their body and between their body and the earth and heavens.

Through years of "playing with energy," an advanced Qigong practitioner may gain remarkable command of qi flow through their system, even directing qi towards injured or upset areas of the body, concentrating qi there to aid healing.

"Tree Gong" is my personal experimental practice that combines forest bathing with Qigong. Tree Gong involves noticing ways in which trees and other natural phenomena interact with qi, then relating these dynamics to particular Qigong exercises. The intention of Tree Gong is primarily to aid the visualization component of the Qigong exercise, and to assist the practitioner in remaining present and connected to their environment. It also helps practitioners remember many Qigong exercises by relating each of them to different observations of nature.

A Tree Gong practitioner's approach may be to act as if their Qigong exercise is emulating the nearby tree's interaction with qi, or even that they are playing with qi *for the tree*. Occasionally, some Tree Gong exercises are accompanied by a short poem, or mantra, that illustrates the natural observation. This poem is recited in the mind, in rhythm with the coordinated breathing, movement, and visualization.

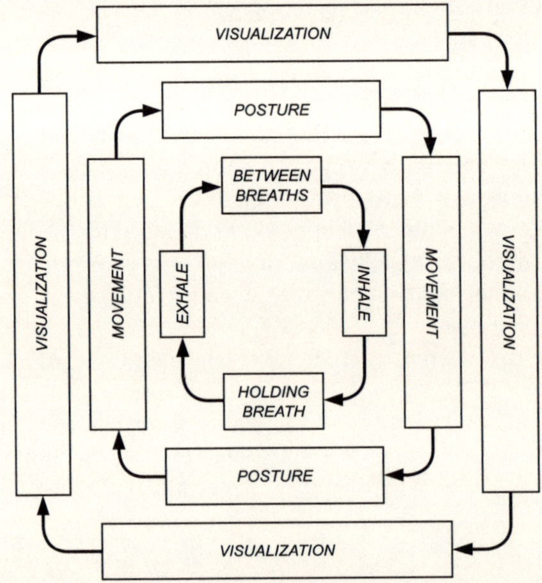

A generic flow chart for visualizing qi flow in coordination with breath, postures, and movement. Specific Qigong exercises may be entered into the POSTURE and MOVEMENT fields. Corresponding natural observations concerning qi flow are entered into the VISUALIZATION field, completing the Tree Gong exercises. It is important to note that it is *your breath* that activates and sets the cadence for your movements and the flow of qi.

Qigong exercises often draw upon nature metaphors and emulate qi dynamics observed in nature, including trees, animals, water, wind, fire, and minerals. Tree Gong did not invent this concept. The distinction between Qigong and Tree Gong lies only in the fact that part of Tree Gong practice is the exploratory act of finding inspiration and new metaphorical connections while forest bathing, which, although relatively common, is not necessarily a significant part of every Qigong practice.

There are a very large number of traditional Qigong exercises and innumerable variations, all of which may be related to any number of qi dynamics observed while practicing Tree Gong. I have made many such connections, including Tree Gong exercises related to:

Leaves, roots, branches, trunks, stumps, thorns, flowers, mushrooms, rocks, waterfalls, water droplets, the water cycle, seasons, mountains, and so on.

Tree Gong practice is no substitute for professional instruction in Qigong, nor are the visualizations borrowed from nature a substitute for actually *feeling* the qi flow through you and feeling your breath *leading* your movements. These feelings come from repeated practice. Tree Gong is a great way to get a Qigong practice started. By walking in the woods, recognizing the presence of qi all around you, anyone can eventually harness that qi for greater health and well-being. ❁

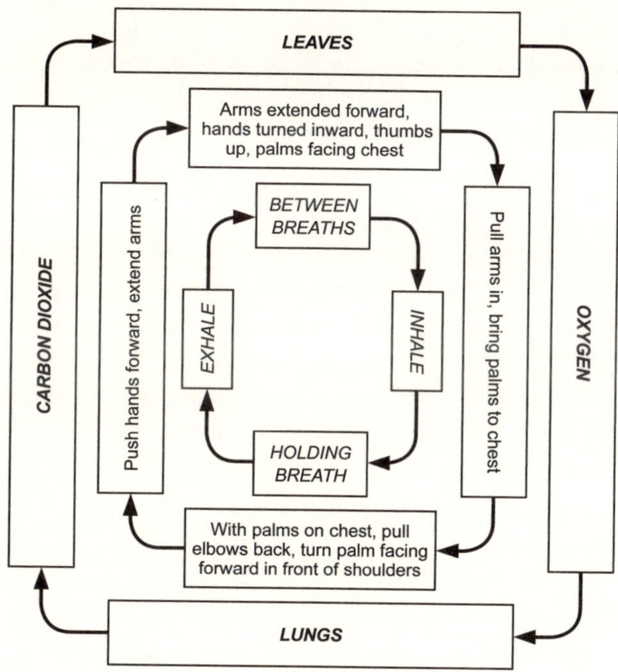

An example chart with a specific exercise plugged in. The Qigong exercise in this chart is for aiding the lungs. The Tree Gong metaphor at work is the relationship between leaves and our breath, the symbiotic exchange of oxygen and carbon dioxide.

B
I
O

Neil Horsky is an artist, educator, musician, writer, and consultant whose creative influences include Fluxus, Dada, Surrealist games, The Situationist International, Taoism, and DIY culture such as zines, house shows, and street art.

adical administration

C
O
N
T
R
I
B
U
T
I
O
N

Against a work environment where labors off-the-desk
are seen as (unrelated) (unequal) (unimportant)
(uninteresting) Radical Administration builds a
structure where currently

25% of <u>**ALL**</u> paid time

is dedicated to off-the-desk work,
defined as each worker wants to define it.
To grocery shop? To organize? To care? To rest? ❁

B
I
O

Sruti Suryanarayanan is a Tamizh American craftsperson and writer, who helps build tools to help people collaboratively question extractive economies.

radical care in the arts

CONTRIBUTION

A manifesto for radical care or how to be a human in the arts

THIS IS A MANIFESTO, a provocation to reimagine ourselves in relation to each other, to work, and the arts. It is a set of principles that I hope will bring radical care into what we do—care that is generative and healing and joyful and unconditional; that contends with past and present injustices.

Radical care means equitable, tangible and sustained improvements to collective well-being—not just for some. It requires a profound redistribution, not just of care work but of power and resources. Radical care is changing the material conditions of work and relationships.

Radical care is an ongoing practice. Structures and systems exist because we collectively allow them to continue. We all need care, we all deserve care, and we are all responsible for manifesting a future of radical care together.

This text is a pool of intentions for you to dip into and take what you need. I hope you may in turn replenish it in your own time.

i. set and respect boundaries

Boundaries are at the forefront of radical care. They send a message to ourselves and to others that we matter, that our experience matters, that our safety matters. Boundaries allow us to rest, process, heal. If we can care for ourselves, we are in an infinitely better place to extend care to others.

When we are squeezed for every ounce of labour, energy, time, and emotional capacity, it becomes hard to prioritise ourselves. What are the situations that leave you feeling off—deep, deep within your body? By setting our limits, we reduce our engagement with life-draining situations and allow energy for the ones that nourish. Such acts can be big or small. Even the most minuscule actions and intentions start to accumulate.

ii. invest in the personal

Radical care is relational and it is personal. We can't give or receive genuine care if we are not in relationship. Every act of care is transmitted through a connection. Even strategies and policies around care are delivered by people.

Relationships are what stay with us once the work or project is over. I don't believe that we are alive to make stuff. I think we're here to form bonds—to think, make, grow, laugh, and cry together. To find joy in each other's company, to console and nurture each other, and to help each other survive.

Radical care requires personal investment. It can mean drawing on personal resources and action when the institution fails or falls short. Consider what is within your personal capacity to do in service of radical care, both in your work and personal life. Exercise this power—it is yours—and resist the urge to deflect to higher authorities. Go slow. Move at the speed of your own intuition.

iii. change can happen within the microcosm

Sometimes thinking about change on a macro scale can be overwhelming; instead, we can bring intention to the things that are within our realm, to the micro. Organisations, projects, individual relationships—these are all microcosms within which we can enact radical care. I don't mean to minimise the macro, but the reality is most of us have little influence at this level. Do what you can within your realm of influence. (Of course, if your microcosm crosses over with macro levels of policy, government, law, multinational corporations, and so forth, then I encourage you to apply these principles at that scale too.)

We can be intentional about where we give care, energy, and resources within our microcosms. Prioritise care of those who need it, not just the ones who are most visible or vocal. Be conscious of the invisible loads that people carry. Consider who might be outside of your care microcosm—how you might bring them in? How might you make space for people to ask for care?

iv. sharing is caring

Sharing is the opposite of hoarding. Sharing ensures power is not accumulated. One of the goals of radical care is decentralising and reducing our reliance on institutions to care for us. This means divesting from them, claiming communal agency and redirecting resources to those who need it most.

Radical care involves transparency, the sharing of information. Radical care requires letting go of control. How can you funnel resources from institutions into communities? What can you do to ensure that care is shared away from power?

Be critical and intentional about who you share with and why. Who gains from your care? Do you tend to share with those in power? Do you expect anything in return—like trust, respect, a returned favour, a reward? The best way to be accountable for the power you possess is to give it away to those with less.

Stop looking to institutions to care for us and start remembering how to care for each other. Think about how you share, with whom, and why. Prioritise sharing with those who have the least. Recognise your own power and privileges, and redistribute outwards. Be critically generous.

v. grow interdependently

Radical care is multidirectional and interdependent. In this ecosystem, care doesn't flow in one direction or even reciprocally but rather gathers where it is needed. It means being able to give and receive care situationally. Interdependence allows us to take care of everyone without exhausting ourselves. It means the burden of care can be shared. It also enables us to receive the full spectrum of care that we need by drawing on different parts of the community.

Everyone deserves care. Who do you hold and who holds you? Who isn't being held? Find and keep close the ones who make giving and receiving care easy. This will make it easier for you to nurture the ones who find it more difficult. Be attuned to those within your orbit who might be in need of care and create ways to bring them into the fold.

If we can practice interdependence to grow communities, and interdependence between communities, we can create vast, interlinked ecosystems of care. Interdependence, combined with sharing outwards (see above), allows us to reduce our reliance on institutions with each and every relationship.

All we have is each other. All we need is each other. We can't do this on our own.

radical care in the art

This is an abridged version of "A manifesto for radical care or how to be a human in the arts" by Tian Zhang. First published by Sydney Review of Books in 2022; see sydneyreviewofbooks.com/essay/a-manifesto-for-radical-care-or-how-to-be-human-in-the-arts/. First print edition published by Lumbung Press during documenta fifteen, 2022. Second print edition published by Agnes Etherington Art Centre on the occasion of An Institute for Curatorial Inquiry, 2022. ❁

BIO Tian Zhang is an independent curator, writer and facilitator, and co-director of Pari, a collective-run gallery on Dharug Country in Parramatta, western Sydney. tian-zhang.com.

Radical Childcare & More Resource List

THE FUTURE GENERATION:

A ZINE-BOOK FOR SUBCULTURE PARENTS, KIDS, FRIENDS + OTHERS, by China Martens (Atomic Book Company 2007; PM Press, 2nd)

An anthology of my zine by the same name that I started in 1990, second edition with an afterword by my grown daughter.

DON'T LEAVE YOUR FRIENDS BEHIND: CONCRETE WAYS to Support Families in Social Justice Movements + Communities

Book compilation of various tips gathered after doing many workshops and zines with the same name. Co-edited with Victoria Law.

REVOLUTIONARY MOTHERING: LOVE ON THE FRONT LINES

by Alexis Pauline Gumbs, China Martens, and Mai'a Williams. Beautiful book gem compiling and archiving mother of color and black queer feminist–centered community wisdom. A gift from and to Revolutionary Mothering everywhere.

RADICAL CHILDCARE: THE KIDZ CITY MODEL

Leaving behind a zine of what we in Kidz City Baltimore learned doing radical childcare collectively. The zine can be accessed and read online as well as printed from the (also now defunct) Intergalactic Conspiracy of Childcare Collectives website. intergalactic-childcare.weebly.com/kids-city-model.html

More Books

Dani McClain of *We Live for the We: The Political Power of Black Motherhood* and Angela Garbes of *Essential Labor: Mothering as Social Change* both give love to Revolutionary Mothering in their books and I see them in the continuing lineage of Revolutionary Mothering writing. Ariel Gore (HipMama) also has a new book, *The Wayward Writer: Summon Your Power to Take Back Your Story, Liberate Yourself from Capitalism, and Publish Like a Superstar*, which is a good resource to help you write your own story.

PM PRESS

The radical press that printed the first three books. You can order the books from pmpress.org. Also, they can be bought from your local or online independent bookstore as well as anywhere else you access books.

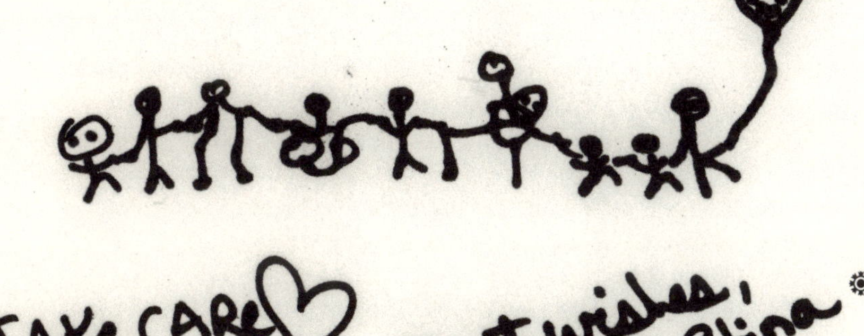

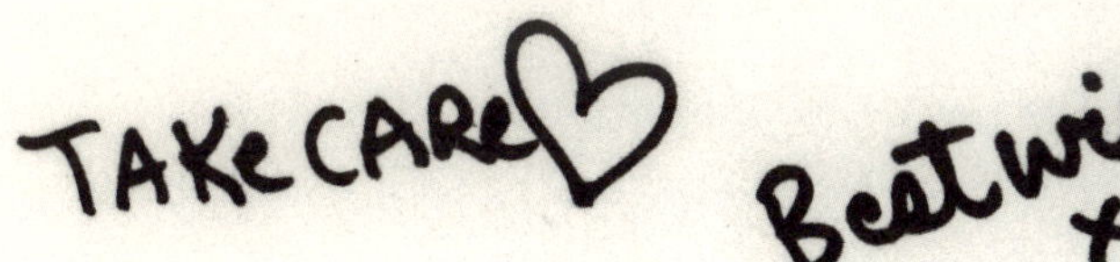

BIO China Martens, author/coeditor of *The Future Generation* (Atomic Book Company 2007; PM Press, 2017), *Don't Leave Your Friends Behind* (PM Press, 2012), and *Revolutionary Mothering* (PM Press, 2016).

EDITORS' NOTE When we invited China Martens to contribute content related to her years-long commitment to supporting parents in social movement spaces, she opted to offer a resource list of work by herself and others. Ever the zinester, China also contributed doodles and titles to be incorporated into the design.
—JC & ES

radical inclusion

SEE: accessibility

freedom

CONTRIBUTION

When a Seat at the Table Ain't Enough

If we begin by putting power at the centre of our understanding of struggle, then we are no longer working on the terms of inclusion but rather what it means to disrupt and dismantle that power that enacts that exclusion in the first place.

—Annette Joseph-Gabriel

in the contemporary western social justice cannon, inclusion has become a somewhat diluted term and aspiration in which justice is considered rendered when all types of people are able to participate in and benefit from capitalism. we celebrate when people from historically and presently oppressed lived experiences (such as but not limited to: black, trans, queer, migrant, working class, etc.) are able to attain the same or greater status as their cis-gender, straight, white peers. americans and followers around the world applauded Obama in 2008 and Kamala in 2020 for their (vice) presidential wins. black women like Lorna Mahlock and Marcia Anderson are celebrated for their high ranks within the various military branches. there are many other examples of those who have been otherized finding (or jostling) their way into typically white, ableist spaces.

one can't help but wonder, is this truly the path to liberation? how exactly do the lives of marginalized people improve when one of us ends up at the proverbial "table"? i haven't the empirical evidence to answer that particular question, but i do know that black, mestizo, asian, and arab folk are still living in deep poverty all over the world, disposed of our ancestral lands and ways of being. trans women are still being killed like it is a sport. wars and conflicts rage on. in what ways has this neoliberal inclusion translated to revolutionary, lasting change for the subaltern? it is a rhetorical question, because it doesn't seem that that has happened.

of course, inclusion in the true meaning of the word is a personal and political aspiration, spanning everything from employment to romantic opportunity. all people, and especially those who have been historically considered undesirable, deserve to be heard and to feel welcome. belonging is a basic animal need, and isolation is often damaging to the social and emotional health of living creatures. while there is still work to be done, it is inspiring to see efforts toward inclusion such as the elimination of first-class seating, employment of the formerly incarcerated, attention to access needs and use of methods like captioning, signing, and translation. this largely depends on the space one is occupying, but can improve how oppressed, divergent, and expansive people move through the world.

yet we must ask ourselves, what spaces do we want to be included in? does our inclusion result in greater liberation for others, or is it merely an opportunity to be tokenized and exploited to make the ruling elite feel better about themselves and look good to the public while they continue on with our erasure?

if you find yourself a person of one or multiple marginalized identities and experiences holding a position of power or proximate to people/institutions with power, it is important to ask yourself: who is benefiting from my being here and in what way? i venture to say that freedom cannot simply be measured by the presence of a marginalized body-mind within or at the helm of an oppressive institution. in fact it may be quite horrifying to know that such a person will be the one signing off on the next airstrike that undoubtedly takes the lives of unsuspecting animals, children, and elders in a faraway land or bailing out corporations while millions starve. this author urges us oppressed to aspire for more than "a seat at the table" and instead create our own uniquely and radically inclusive spaces that compassionately center the unwanted and disposable: the poor, the so-called ugly, the mentally ill, the non-human, the masses of this world. ❁

B Onyịnye smiles while
I bathing in the sunlight of
O life // ọchị na anwụ.

CONTRIBUTION

Radical Papermaking: A Socially Engaged Art Therapy Practice

IN WESTERN CULTURE, there exists a division between the creative practice of art and craft, an ethnocentric bias revealing more about the prejudices of the art historians than the art itself. [1] In the profession of art therapy, this bias exists as well, evidenced by an implicit preference for the use of traditional or fine arts, media, and materials. Art therapy material used in educational training and professional practice has often excluded or minimized the value of non-traditional media and art processes.[2] Students and practitioners benefit from continuing development of "artistic fluency" through ongoing artmaking with various media.[3] In addition, arts-based learning strategies promote increased sensitivity, awareness, and connectedness.[4]

Art therapists are increasingly utilizing papermaking as an art therapy media. Embedded in papermaking processes there lies rich, sensory-based and transformative properties, kinesthetic and sensory experiences that can promote emotional expression, foster self-awareness, or manage recovery, loss, and trauma.[5] The inclusion of this non-traditional media in art therapy practice offers accessibility and cultural resonance to historically marginalized groups. Papermaking supports creative, relational dialogue, a critical element to material use in therapy.[6]

The process begins with concrete steps and ends in the making of meaning, and is valuable in trauma therapy, as these steps provide

1. Blender for pulping

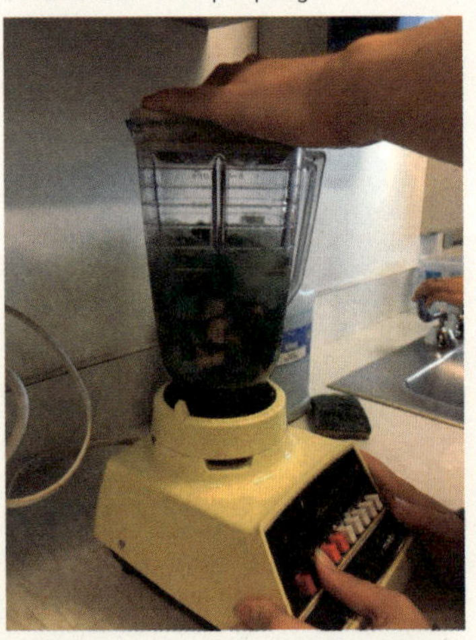

2. Do-it-yourself (DIY) kit for radical papermaking

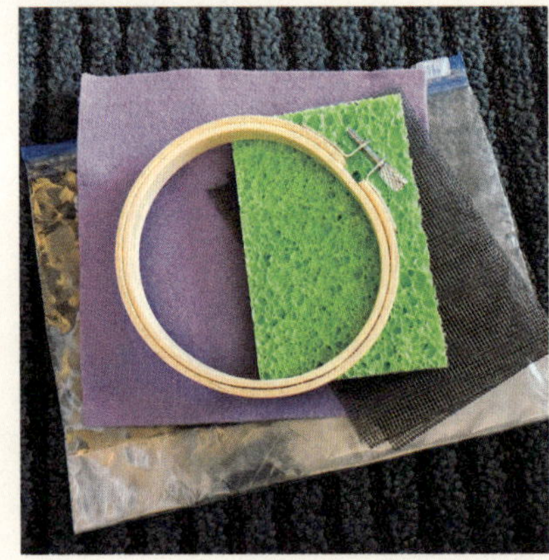

3. DIY papermaking supplies and blender

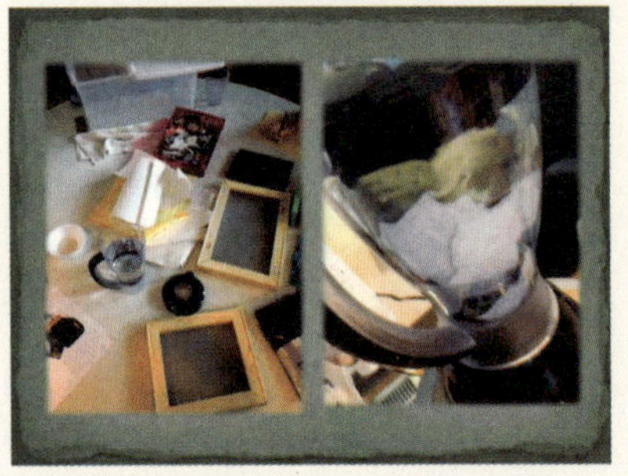

4. Round handmade paper created from DIY kit

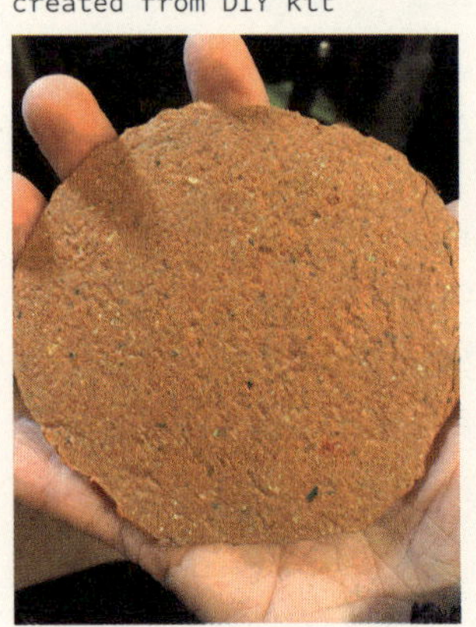

5. Blender pulping action

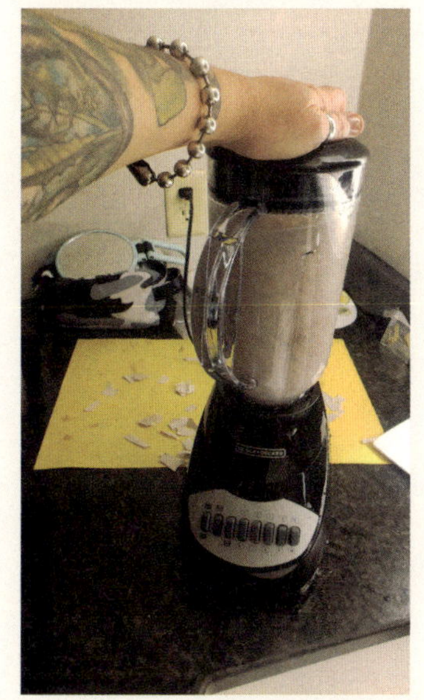

6. Pulp pouring

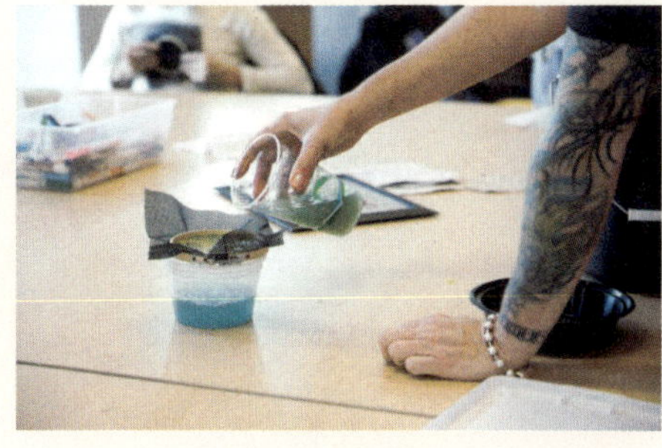

7. Draining pulp through an embroidery hoop

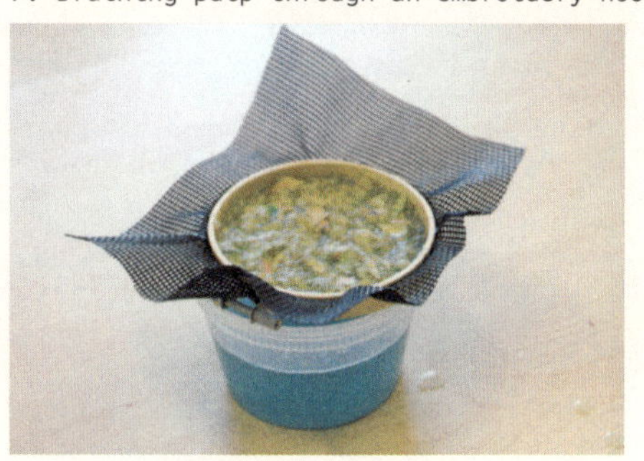

8. Restraint drying on glass

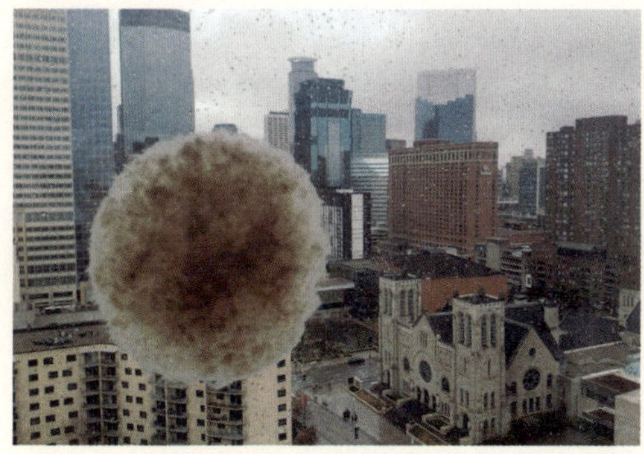

containment, permission to safely share experiences, and opportunities to let go and create new paths towards healing and transformation.[7]

Sequential steps in making paper, from selecting personal fiber, breaking down this material, and then reclaiming the pulp into new sheets or works of art, create ongoing opportunities for meaningful reflection and communication of experiences related to the self, and mirror internal processes of change.

In Matott and Miller's *The Art and Art Therapy of Papermaking*, papermaking is repeatedly identified as an art-based method for social action, community engagement, advocacy, and culturally relevant issues.[8] The process of making paper narrates the reconstruction and expression of personal and communal experiences[9] as well as activates deconstruction and reconstruction, ultimately birthing something new.[10] Lastly, papermaking holds the potential for art therapists to support collective action and social reform.[11] "One of the strengths of the artist," Lerman writes, "is the capacity to reframe—to help people look at their issues and stories from a new perspective and ask, 'what is the bigger story?'"[12] Making paper as an art-based response to an issue, cause, or need can bring awareness and advocacy for injustices, disparities, or challenges individuals, groups, and communities face.➔

adical papermaking

We define radical papermaking as a process that embodies non-traditional media adaptations and material methods to papermaking; promotes papermaking as an accessible, collaborative, community-based, and socially engaged practice; and activates the therapeutic process of papermaking to explore concepts of transformation.[13] Implementing papermaking as a socially informed practice offers opportunities to present non-traditional adaptations and methods to papermaking through didactic and experiential learning. Radical papermaking fosters the opportunity to experience intention and action through the creative process[14] and promotes papermaking as an accessible, collaborative practice that can empower community members through social-action arts practices. ❁

Resources

Slide Presentation & Handouts | www.tinyurl.com/Radical-Papermaking
Peace Paper Project | peacepaperproject.org
People's Paper Co-Op | peoplespaperco-op.weebly.com
The Mobile Mill | themobilemill.tumblr.com
Peace Flags: Peacemaking and Papermaking | youtu.be/LS2v5YF5msI

1 Ivey, "Reshaping the Narrative around People of Color and Craftivism"; Kapitan, "Close to the Heart: Art Therapy's Link to Craft and Art Production."

2 Leone, Craft in *Art Therapy: Diverse Approaches to the Transformative Power of Craft Materials and Methods*; Moon, *Materials & Media in Art Therapy: Critical Understandings of Diverse Artistic Vocabularies*.

3 Wix, "Aesthetic Empathy in Teaching Art to Children: The Work of Friedl Dicker-Brandeis in Terezin."

4 Deaver, "Art-based Learning Strategies in Art Therapy Graduate Education."

5 Matott and Miller, *The Art and Art Therapy of Papermaking: Material, Methods, and Applications*; McMackin, "Hand-papermaking with Student Veterans."

6 Dean, *Using Art Media in Psychotherapy: Bringing the Power of Creativity to Practice*.

7 Peace Paper Project, "Papermaking as Art Therapy."

8 Cochran and Potter, *Social Paper: Hand Papermaking in the Context of Socially Engaged Art*.

9 DeLamater, "Historical, Social, and Artistic Implications of Collaboration in Contemporary Hand Papermaking."

10 Wolf, "Papermaking Reflections: Stories of Change, Growth and Creativity" and "Transformation in Papermaking: When Content Mirrors Process."

11 Leone, *Craft in Art Therapy: Diverse Approaches to the Transformative Power of Craft Materials and Methods*.

12 Lerman, *A Handbook for Artists Working in Community*.

13 Miller and Wolf, "Radical Papermaking: A Socially Engaged Art Therapy Practice."

14 Talwar, "Accessing Traumatic Memory through Art Making."

BIOS

Gretchen M. Miller, MA, ATR-BC, ACTP, is a Registered Board-Certified Art Therapist and Advanced Certified Trauma Practitioner who practices in Northeast Ohio, United States.

Denise R. Wolf, MA, ATR-BC, ATCS, LPC, LPAT, is a Registered Board-Certified Art Therapist, Art Therapy Certified Supervisor, Licensed Professional Counselor and Licensed Professional Art Therapist, and Associate Clinical Professor at Drexel University in the Creative Arts and Counseling Art Therapy Program, who practices and teaches in the Philadelphia area of Pennsylvania, United States.

radical presence

SEE relationali… storytellir…

CONTRIBUTION

RADICAL PRESENCE. Why a term like this? What does it mean? How is it embodied? Several years ago, I found myself discouraged to find that mindfulness—a spiritual practice rooted in Buddhist and Hindu tradition and focused on centering oneself in the present moment without judgement—had been co-opted by the dominant discourse of late capitalism. Ronald Purser writes extensively about this co-optation, referring to it as "McMindfulness," playing on the capitalist franchise we all know so well: McDonald's. I realized that in almost every direction I looked, people were being urged to engage in mindfulness practice. Mindfulness practice—designed to center one amidst a chaotic, complex, and ever-changing world—often takes the form of meditation but can certainly be a focused practice of attention in any present moment. However, as it is taken up, mindfulness appears to be the answer to just about any problem one might confront: disenfranchisement, judgement and evaluation, discrimination, humiliation, competition, poverty, joblessness… the list is long.

The basic message of the contemporary mindfulness movement is that centering oneself amidst social, political, and economic chaos will "cure" the anxiety, depression, and lack of self-confidence brought on by social, political, and economic chaos. In so doing, the person is invited to see himself or herself as the problem. *Why am I not able to cope with discrimination in the workplace? Why am I feeling so anxious about going to work every morning? Why do I let these things bring me down?*[1] If the answer to these questions lies in mindfulness practice—centering oneself in the here and now—then the message is clear: you are the problem. Why? Because others clearly can navigate the complexity of social, political, and economic chaos—but you, evidently, cannot.

Purser claims that:

> …mindfulness has become the perfect coping mechanism for neoliberal capitalism: it privatizes stress and encourages people to locate the root of mental ailments in their own work ethic… it promotes a particular form of revolution, one that takes place within the heads of individuals fixated on self-transformation, rather than as a struggle to overcome collective suffering.[2]

Mindfulness practices have become (yet another) quick fix for large-scale social problems. If you are stressed because you have just been evicted from your home, if you feel insecure because you have lost your job, if you are having a difficult time maintaining relationships, the recommended "cure" is engagement in mindfulness practice. In other words, center yourself, avoid judgement, live in the present, but whatever you do, do not identify the systemic roots of your discomfort. Fix yourself, because our institutions and our cultural practices are either not the problem or are just too complex to fix.

In response to this individualizing and pathologizing discourse—a discourse that fails to address the larger problems we confront in contemporary society—I proposed the idea of radical presence.[3] "Radical" because I wanted to emphasize that, as helping professionals, we must do more than be in conversation with our clients. We need to be hyper-focused and attentive to the unfolding process of relating with our clients (and with each other). Radical presence involves moving from expert voices and unquestioned forms of practice toward an active attentiveness to the processes of relating themselves. It demands that we elevate our attention to processes of relating as opposed to objects or entities or isolated actions. Radical presence is a way of acting in the world, as opposed to a way of observing the world.

So, how might we embody radical presence? It might not be as difficult as we imagine. And, for those who already center unfolding relational processes as the focus of inquiry, embodying radical presence should feel familiar; our

post-oppositionality

curiosity

attention is not on self-contained individuals. When we include multiple voices, for example, we open the space for the complexity and diversity of worldviews. We might do so by engaging in conversations about others who might hold divergent beliefs and values. We might also do this by creating a space where participants feel safe giving voice to their conflicting views.

This raises the question of how we might create such a space. Can we prepare participants to come together not to persuade, but to tell their stories—the very stories that offer credibility and rationality to their beliefs and values? Who are the people, where are the places that gave birth and support to their beliefs? Our stories (i.e., our beliefs) are populated with others. In preparing participants, we might ask each to think about what agreements might be made by all that would allow each to share their beliefs and opinions. This might include agreements such as no interruption, no name calling, no finger pointing. It is amazing to see how stepping out of our desire to persuade others positions us as curious listeners. And that curiosity breeds a sense of mutual respect—if you listen to my story, I might be more interested in listening to yours.

Becoming curious as opposed to being too quick to know (an embodiment of certainty) opens the possibility of being radically present. Listening generously rather than closing conversation and being responsive rather than reactive all are embodiments of radical presence. ✺

1 O'Brien, "How Mindfulness Privatized a Social Problem."

2 Purser, *McMindfulness: How Mindfulness Became the New Capitalist Spirituality*, 6.

3 McNamee, "Radical Presence: Alternatives to the Therapeutic State"; McNamee, "Radical Presence: A Relational Alternative to Mindfulness."

BIO Sheila McNamee, Professor Emerita of Communication at the University of New Hampshire, Founder and Vice President of the Taos Institute.

holding space
humanness

love
lunar cycle
Magic School, the
mapping support
marginality
(as a site of
resistance)
Marxist social
work
membership theory
in social work
mending
metaphor
mikveh
mobile libraries
movement
lawyering
mutual aid
mycelia as
metaphor
narradrama
narrative
medicine
narrative therapy
nepantla/
nepantleras
nonviolent
communication
ongoingness
peer counseling
peer-to-peer
health network
person-situation
perspective
perspective via
faith
pleasure
poems/poetry
poetic meter
polarity work
post-
oppositionality
postwork
imaginaries
poverty-aware
social work
paradigm, the
power threat
meaning (PTM)
framework
pre(care)ity
prison abolition
professionalism
without
performance
progressive
education
public benefits
public library,
the
Qigong
radical
administration
radical care in
the arts
radical childcare
in movement
spaces
radical
inclusion
radical
papermaking
radical presence
radical
social work
Radical Therapist
Journal, The
Rank and File
Movement (RFM)
in social work

SEE
reclaiming selfhood
recognition
redistribution
Reflecting on Justi
reflexivi
Rei
relation
interviewing
relationali
resistanc
resisting th
parental loss
narrative
resonanc
respectful visiti
respite room
rest as resistanc
reveng
revolutionar
mothering
ritua
sanctuar
sandplay therap
saun
seed bankin
sex positivit
shadow integratio
Sick Woman Theor
slow textile
slownes
social chang
ecosystem framework
social constructio
social practic
social therapeutic
Social Welfare Actio
Alliance, the
solidarit
solidarity econom
somatic healin
songs/singin
sound healin
speculative desig
spell
staying with the
trouble
storytellin
street newspape
strengths
perspective, the
sufficienc
sustaining movemen
symbol
Taos Institute, the
taro
temporary autonomous
zones
Theatre of the
Oppressed
theories of change
theosophy
therapeutic writing
togetherness
trans practices
transformative
justice
traspatio
12-step programs
undercover anti-
bullying teams
vigil
water
wildness
wintering as metaphor
wishes
witchery
yoga
zinemaking

CONTRIBUTION

What Is Radical Social Work Practice?

THROUGHOUT THE WORLD, radical social work practice has long included the following elements:

- A structural analysis of the root causes of personal and societal problems
- Recognition of the significance of history, culture, and context
- A synthetic and adaptive rather than rigid ideological perspective
- An understanding of the interconnectedness of issues
- Recognition of the role that race, gender, ethnicity, sexual orientation, class, age, and ability status play in the oppression and marginalization of certain populations
- The establishment and maintenance of broad-based coalitions that cross traditional boundaries of class, race, ethnicity, religion, gender, and even nation
- A belief in collective responsibility for human welfare

Radical social work emerged as a counter-narrative to a professional master narrative that defined social work's mission in terms consistent with the structure of the US political economy, the social roles it generates, and the ideological perspectives that rationalize it. Radical social work critiques the profession for pursuing status enhancement in lieu of being an active participant in the arena of struggle. By contrast, as a counter-narrative, radical social work plays a crucial role in this struggle. As a form of resistance to the dominant culture, it helps validate an alternative reality that embodies social justice goals, egalitarian relationships, and non-hierarchical institutions. It poses fundamental questions, such as: Who benefits from the structural status quo and the various rationales that defend it? Radical social work disrupts these accepted "stories" by postulating a different view of professionalism and redefining the meaning of such basic concepts as social justice, cultural competence, and empowerment. Radical social work challenges prevailing assumptions about the sources of poverty and inequality, white supremacy, sexism, homophobia, and xenophobia. It suggests new, more egalitarian practice roles and pursues new alliances with clients, constituents, and potential allies in the pursuit of social justice. A more egalitarian form of practice would recognize and incorporate the knowledge and skills of the people with whom we work and make them full participants in determining service priorities, shaping the programmatic interventions that affect their lives, and evaluating the effects of these programs.

Radical social workers have long believed that people, individually and collectively, possess the agency to make their own history. A key challenge for radical social workers today and in the future is to forge a new social discourse within which people's alternative stories make sense and are heard. To do this, radical social workers must do more than replace one form of rhetoric or one narrative with another. Radical social work's application of a critical perspective to practice could reorient social work's goals from self-enhancement to the creation of a more egalitarian and just society. A critical perspective questions our longstanding assumptions about human nature, human needs, and human society. It examines the role that history, context, and societal structures play in shaping the practice environment. It analyzes the root causes of people's issues rather than merely assessing the symptoms people exhibit. If there is one overarching lesson from the past which can be applied to a radical social work future, it is that nothing is pre-determined or eternal. ❁

Suggested Reading

Rules for Radicals: A Practical Primer for Realistic Radicals, by Saul Alinsky

"The Radical Voices of Social Workers: Some Lessons for the Future," by Michael Reisch and Janice Andrews, in *Journal of Progressive Human Services*

Anti-Oppressive Social Work Theory and Practice, by Lena Dominelli

Just Practice: A Social Justice Approach to Social Work (4th ed.), by Janet L. Finn

"Radical community organizing," by Michael Reisch, in *The Handbook of Community Practice* (2nd ed.), edited by Marie Weil, Michael Reisch, and Mary L. Ohmer

The Road Not Taken: A History of Radical Social Work in the United States, by Michael Reisch and Janice Andrews

Social Work and Social Justice: Concepts, Challenges, and Strategies, by Michael Reisch & Charles D. Garvin

BIO Michael Reisch is Distinguished Professor of Social Justice Emeritus, University of Maryland, Baltimore.

Radical Therapist Journal, The

The Radical Therapist 1.0

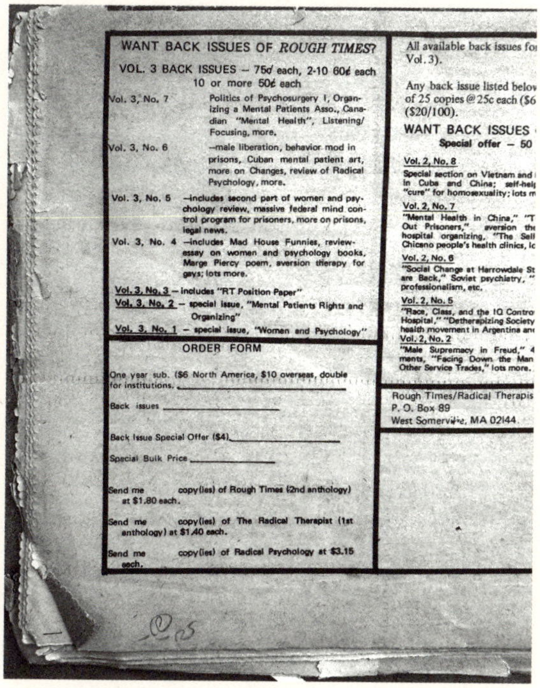

A back page of Vol. 3, No. 8 (1973) of *Rough Times*, formerly known as *The Radical Therapist* and later known as *State and Mind*.

THE RADICAL THERAPIST JOURNAL was first published in 1970. It arose as the voice of then New Left dissident mental health workers (its founders were two Vietnam vet psychiatrists), and people with lived experience as psychiatric patients who felt oppressed by the disrespectful and sometimes barbaric treatments they'd endured. The Anti-Psychiatry movement, as it was called, began to draw connections between the political struggles of the times and the personal experiences that often got labeled and treated as deviant or pathological by the psychiatric establishment. Homosexuality, for example, was considered a psychiatric diagnosis until 1973.

The journal questioned the norms on which behavioral standards were based, norms that often pathologized dissent. An early article exposed the fallacy of the then-standard practice of challenging abused women with the question, "What did you do to provoke him?" From both a diagnostic and a treatment perspective, the magazine sought to critique mainstream practices and to describe alternative ways of thinking about and dealing with emotional and relationship problems. Whether by encouraging equality and women's empowerment in relationships, for example, or considering the often mind-numbing nature of many jobs, *The Radical Therapist* articles sought to expand people's sense of life choices and opportunities beyond the more common therapeutic tenor of the time of helping folk fit in to existing paradigms. The journal's defining slogan was "Therapy means change, not adjustment."

The Radical Therapist was first published in Minot, North Dakota, but within a few years moved its location to Somerville, Mass., near Cambridge, to be in a place where there was more activism. There, the name changed to *Rough Times* to embrace a larger audience: anyone concerned with what we now call the social determinants of health and transforming social structures to be better at promoting psychological well-being for all. By the mid-1970s,

Cuestionamos
decolonial liberatory-based practices
feminism
group work
Hearing Voices Network
Bertha Capen Reynolds

the journal's name had again changed to *State and Mind* (when I became involved in 1976).

No matter what it was called (I'll refer to it as *RT* from now on), it was always collectively run by a non-hierarchical group of writers, editors, and production workers. (Before computers, we literally pasted together the mock-up pages before taking it to the printer). All decisions were made by consensus. The makeup of the group changed some over the years, with notable names like famed social psychologist Nancy Henley participating. Among *RT*'s early contributors were now well-known authors Marge Piercy and Phyllis Chesler, as well as psychiatrist and theorist David Cooper (associate of R.D. Laing).

A large focus of the journal's work during the 1970s was to support the concept of mental patients' rights, informed consent, and the concept of the right to refuse treatment (which did not begin to gain legal traction until the 1980s). Before the massive deinstitutionalization of the Reagan era, there were large state institutions filled with patients involuntarily sedated on massive quantities of psychoactive drugs with debilitating side effects. Many such patients were also given lobotomies and insulin and electroshock therapy, usually against their wills, sometimes at a family's request, because the patients were nonconformists (think *One Flew Over the Cuckoo's Nest*, *The Snake Pit*, and *Frances Farmer*). Leonard Roy Frank was a leader in the SF Bay Area group, Network Against Psychiatric Assault, who worked collaboratively with *RT*, and who published their own journal called *Madness Network News*. Leonard, like many other similarly mistreated individuals, called himself a psychiatric survivor.

RT was distributed both nationally and internationally and was connected with a worldwide movement of Anti-Psychiatry thinkers and activists, including philosophical luminaries like Michel Foucault (author of *Madness and Civilization*) and Felix Guattari (author of *Capitalism and Schizophrenia*). A conference called "International Network: Alternatives to Psychiatry," organized by Franco Basaglia, was held in 1978 in Trieste, Italy, with *RT* participating and reporting, displaying on its cover the conference's banner reading "La Liberta e' Terapeutica."

Members of the *RT* collective worked to develop alternatives to standard treatments, such as mutual support groups and drop-in centers for the many people being let out of large institutions without resources or supports. We participated in professional, even governmental (NAMH) and grassroots trainings and conferences to promote ideas like patient respect, therapy as a partnership, and alternatives to institutionalization, encouraging communities to learn skills (like crisis management) to care for their own, much as the Black Lives Matter movement today encourages alternatives to police involvement in crisis situations, when possible. We promoted social activism and community service as meaningful ways to effect change and heal from the alienation of social oppression. Borrowing words from the Women's Movement that flourished in those years, we believed that the personal is political and vice versa.

By the mid-1980s, *RT* was disappearing from circulation, but had definitely left its mark on the world of mental health. Deinstitutionalization had begun, not in the way envisioned by activists, and for economic not humanitarian reasons, but massive warehousing in state hospitals was no longer an issue. Community mental health was supposed to take its place and, to some degree, in some places has been useful to some people. Over time, the right to refuse treatment and consent laws were enacted. Some states, like

California (with its Mental Health Services Act of 2004), have even included a requirement to employ those who are now called psychiatric consumers as a part of treatment teams. Such laws recognize the value of the mutual aid principles of the Anti-Psychiatry movement, which were themselves borrowed from the 12-step recovery world. Some would say that the pendulum has now swung too far in the other direction and that the homelessness crisis on many city streets today is the result of too little intervention in the lives of people too disturbed to recognize their needs, let alone get them met. But the message of respect for each person's bodily and psychological integrity has become more the norm than not—and we do now recognize, thanks to *RT* and its associates, that what we call mental health has social and political dimensions that need to be addressed for true healing to occur. ❁

BIO

Septuagenarian Sheila Koren has been a social activist, writer, and practicing psychotherapist for many decades, ever including the principles of Radical Therapy in all she does.

Rank and File Movement (RFM) in Social work

CONTRIBUTION

THE RANK AND FILE MOVEMENT (RFM) in social work formed in response to the deteriorating conditions of the Great Depression. The RFM was officially established following Mary van Kleeck's scorching presentation at the 1934 National Conference of Social Work's meeting in Kansas City, MO, whereby she challenged social work to question and challenge New Deal legislation and the legitimacy of the crumbling capitalist system it sought to boost.

Operating between 1934–1942, the RFM was a Socialist-Communist influenced Left-Wing social work organization reflective of the broader labor and social protest movements of the Great Depression. It established the radical journal *Social Work Today* with an estimated circulation of 5,000, spearheaded multiple protests, and took aim at what it considered a bankrupt field ensconced in therapeutic practices and profession-building when social, political, and economic conditions demanded mass-based social action and potentially revolutionary activity.

Movement leaders included the aforementioned economist Mary van Kleeck; Marxist scholar, instructor, and activist Bertha Capen Reynolds; and activist Jacob Fisher among others. At its peak the RFM had local and state chapters and operated in a largely participatory democratic manner complete with a wide array of radical practitioners, community workers, scholars, and activists. Additionally, the RFM was under surveillance by the FBI for much of its existence, and members often found it necessary to hold clandestine meetings and/or to remain anonymous for fear of losing employment or being placed under arrest for their political views.

The RFM flourished until the Nazi-Soviet Nonaggression Pact of 1939. The signing of the pact sent shockwaves throughout the United States and beyond and led to the disillusionment with the Soviet Union amongst many radicals, especially those within the Jewish community.

The RFM, which had a significant radical Jewish membership base, was also rocked by the signing of the pact. While the RFM was not formally associated with the Soviet Union, it was influenced by its existence as the preeminent example of real and existing Communism, and thus, many found it necessary to step back from the organization or reduce their overall involvement. Additionally, the passage of the Social Security Act, federal assistance for social work education and broader social services, and the emerging recovery from the Great Depression diminished interest in the need for a revolutionary style organization.

By 1942, the RFM had declined in size and was nearly out of money. It had to cease publishing its popular journal *Social Work Today*; and the organization faded from view shortly thereafter. Despite its relatively short organizational existence, it remains one of the most important radical social work organizations to have existed in the United States and beyond. It raised important questions and debates in social work, including the legitimacy of mainstream therapeutic approaches in the face of mass social distress and upheaval, the viability of professional status for broader social work that needs to challenge the status quo, and the need to seriously contemplate the legitimacy of capitalism as an organizing ethos in any society interested in genuine equality and social justice. As such, it demonstrated how social, political,

access invitations
SEE:
accessibility
ency
ing positivity
tar work
ternative identity
rojects
cestral wisdom
cestrality
ti-ableism
ti-adultism
ti-racism
ti-racism court
ystem
t
t as/in/of life
t journaling
t therapy
t workers
t-based group work
ts in medicine
ts-based research
thentic Movement
tonomous healing
urveda
ing with
rtha Capen Reynolds
ke and car repair
collectives
ack Panther Party
Free Breakfast
Program
dy as community
dy neutrality
dy positivity
dy Trust
redom
ave space
eaking the rules
idge as metaphor
are pods
are-based co-housing
atholic Worker
Movement
entering maintenance
ircular economy
limate cafes
louds as metaphor
oalition
ollaborative
apprenticeship
ollective care
ommon pool resources
ommons, the
ommuning with
animals
ommunity college
ommunity gardens
ommunity newspapers
onjure
onstructionist-
design framework, the
onsulting your
consultants
ontemplative
tradition, the
orn knowledge
redit unions
rip time
ritical fabulation
ritical hope
ritical pedagogy
ritical race theory
ritical suicide
studies
ritical whiteness

critique
Cuestionamos
curiosity
th practices
decolonial
liberatory-based
practices
deep organizing
dérive, the
drumming
embodied expression
embodied knowledge
emergent strategy
empathy
energy work
erasure, avoiding
thereof
esoteric wisdom
traditions
ethnodrama
etymology
existentialism
externalizing
failure
fat positivity
feminism
feminist ethics
of care
fermentation
flâner
food sovereignty
forest bathing
fragments/
fragmentation
freedom
generous systems
gift economies
Grace Lee Boggs
grief as nonlinear
group work
groups
harm reduction
healing circles
healing healers
through the arts
healing justice
healing rituals
Hearing Voices
Network
herbal justice
herbalism
holding space
humanness
humor
illders
improvisation
infinite blackness
intentional
communities
interdisciplinary
cataloging
intergenerational
living
interspecies
organizing
intuitive eating
justice-oriented
counseling
land trusts
land, work,
spirit, body
language justice
leaving well
liberatory
education
life cycle,
honoring the
liminality
limited-equity
cooperative
housing

and economic conditions along with strong ideas, ideals, and organizing can combine to generate viable left-wing social work activity. Indeed, it helped inspire the radical social workers of the 1960s and 1970s and can do so today. ❁

References and Options for Further Reading

"Technocratic social science and the rise of managed capitalism, 1910–1933," by Guy Alchon.

The Response of Social Work to the Depression, by Jacob Fisher

"Beyond the Rank and File Movement: Mary van Kleeck and Social Work Radicalism in the Great Depression, 1931-1934," by Patrick Selmi and Richard Hunter.

"Our Illusions Regarding Government," by Mary Van Kleeck.

Creative America: Its Resources for Social Security, by Mary Van Kleeck.

BIO Patrick Selmi, PhD, is a faculty member at the University of Windsor with interests in the history of social work and social welfare; radicalism; socialism; social movements; and community organizing.

e-authoring

CONTRIBUTION

Restoring and Re-storying Agency through Conversations about Prescribed Medicines

WE ARE AN INDEPENDENT nurse prescriber (Rob) and a systemic psychotherapist (Helena) from an early intervention in psychosis service in the UK. We work with people and their families who see, hear, sense, or believe things that others do not, and are significantly distressed or adversely affected by these experiences. Sometimes these experiences are referred to as psychosis.

Our contribution to this volume grew out of talking with people about their experiences of, and relationship to, their prescribed medicines such as antipsychotics or antidepressants. The use of medicine in the UK follows us from birth[1] to death[2] and underpins our understanding of health and morbidity. The language of medicine itself, such as "patient," "side effects," "compliance," and "treatment" can render people passive, subjugated, "docile bodies,"[3] lacking in agency and purpose. These medicines can bring about distressing and harmful effects.[4] They can also be considered to be used as a means of social control.[5] The use of medicine can be deemed a sign of failure—for example, by those who advocate for social or psychological approaches, or by those who may view it as passively supporting pharmacological or psychiatric dominance in mental health services.[6] However, medicines can also "have a profound effect in opening up the horizons of people's lives in ways that bring a range of new possibilities for action."[7]

As practitioners, we can also find ourselves caught up between these often-contradictory ideas and practices about medication, which can have limiting effects on our conversations with the people we work with. Here we share some of our experiences of this:

> HELENA: When people have talked to me about the helpful effects of medicine, I have often felt constrained by polarised professional monologues (e.g., psychological "versus" medical models of distress.)[8] I might therefore shy away from such conversations, feeling an implicit expectation to seek out alternative (e.g., social-relational) accounts instead, thus shifting away from the person's subjective experience and risking imposing another ideology in its place.
>
> ROB: For the most part, conversations about medicine focus on their clinical effectiveness; how they might have reduced or improved "symptoms," such as feeling paranoid, having unusual thoughts, or hearing derogatory voices. I think conversations with the people we work with around what can become possible as a result of these changes are not typical in prescribing practice; sometimes it can feel *good enough* to help someone manage or tolerate their experiences better, and perhaps stop there. Although there is an emphasis on collaboration and safe, effective prescribing, and there is a practical and valuable professionally mandated framework[9] that can assist us, this approach can potentially close the door to other avenues where we can better understand people's unique relationship with, and use of, medicine.

ndance
access invocations
E: accessibility
ivating archives
ofuturism
ency
ng positivity
ar work
ernative identity projects
estral wisdom
estrality
i-ableism
i-adultism
i-racism
i-racism court system
as/in/of life
journaling
therapy
workers
-based group work
s in medicine
s-based research
hentic Movement
onomous healing
urveda
ing with
rtha Capen Reynolds
ke and car repair collectives
ack Panther Party
ree Breakfast rogram
dy as community
dy neutrality
dy positivity
dy Trust
redom
ave space
eaking the rules
idge as metaphor
re pods
re-based co-housing
tholic Worker Movement
ntering maintenance
rcular economy
imate cafes
ouds as metaphor
alition
llaborative apprenticeship
llective care
mmon pool resources
mmons, the
mmuning with animals
mmunity college
mmunity gardens
mmunity newspapers
njure
onstructionist-design framework, the
nsulting your consultants
ontemplative tradition, the
rn knowledge
redit unions
rip time
ritical fabulation
ritical hope
ritical pedagogy
ritical race theory
itical suicide studies
ritical whiteness
Critique
Cuestionamos
curiosity
death practices
decolonial liberatory-based practices
deep organizing
dérive, the
drumming
embodied expression
embodied knowledge
emergent strategy
empathy
energy work
erasure, avoiding thereof
esoteric wisdom traditions
ethnodrama
etymology
existentialism
externalizing
failure
fat positivity
feminism
feminst ethics of care
fermentation
fåner
food sovereignty
forest bathing
fragments/ fragmentation
freedom
generous systems
gift economies
Grace Lee Boggs
grief as nonlinear
group work
groups
harm reduction
healing circles
healing healers through the arts
healing justice
healing rituals
Hearing Voices Network
herbal justice
herbalism
holding space
humanness
humor
illders
improvisation
infinite blackness
intentional communities
interdisciplinary cataloging
intergenerational living
interspecies organizing
intuitive eating
justice-oriented counseling
land trusts
land, work, spirit, body
language justice
leaving well
liberatory education
life cycle
honoring the liminality
limited-equity cooperative housing

We found that people had unique responses to both the helpful and adverse effects of medicine based upon their preferences, hopes, values, and commitments. We wondered if assisting people to state a specific purpose or intention, such as re-entering education, might make it more possible for these ideas and initiatives to take hold in their lives. In asking *how* they were "taking advantage of" or "choosing to respond to" helpful effects, such as improved sleep or concentration (e.g., spending time with family, developing new skills), or *why* they specifically wanted to reduce adverse effects such as tiredness or weight gain (e.g., to write music, to attend a daughter's wedding), we explored beyond simply what medicine could reduce or improve and began to see how everyone has their own story around medicine. We were inviting reflections upon people's lives and identities in the process, and therefore becoming engaged in an act of restoring agency through their accounts of their relationship with and use of medicine.

These conversations generated some questions that seemed useful in this process. They are influenced by Michael White's "statement of position" and "re-authoring" maps of narrative practice.[10] They seek to assist the person to experience themselves as someone who is responding to, making the most of, or taking advantage of a helpful effect or change; or minimising or mitigating against an adverse effect or change:

- What is it like taking the medicine(s)?
- Are you noticing any effects (e.g., on your body, emotions, relationships, work, education)? Are they helpful/unhelpful? Do you want more or less of these effects? Why is that?
- What are you doing to take advantage of/minimise these effects?
- How are you responding to this? What are you choosing to do? Did you know that you were doing this? What have other people noticed?
- What does that make possible? Have you chosen to do that or not?

We can then invite reflections upon life and identity, making links to social and relational histories, and then weaving these accounts together to create a richer description and an experience of oneself as an active agent in one's own life and relationships:

- Why would you prefer to have more/less of these effects?
- How and why has taking advantage of/minimising these effects in this way been important to you?
- Has that been important to you for a long time, or more recently? Can you tell me a story that helps us understand why this matters to you?
- Who else knows about what this means to you?
- If they were to see you doing this now, would it fit with how they saw you back then? What would they appreciate about what you are trying to do here?

Developing these questions has opened the door to some unique, surprising, and moving conversations. We are continuing to co-research these practices with those who use medicine, with those who accompany them in this (including family, friends, or professional helpers), and with others who may have an interest in these ideas. We hope that they will assist people in moving from being the objects of medical practice to subjects, actively forming their own lives. ❁

narrative medicine
narrative therapy
power threat meaning (PTM) framework
storytelli
strengt perspective, the

1 Prosen and Krajnc, "Perspectives and Experiences of Healthcare Professionals Regarding the Medicalisation of Pregnancy and Childbirth."

2 Koksvik et al., "Medicalisation, Suffering and Control at the End of Life: The Interplay of Deep Continuous Palliative Sedation and Assisted Dying."

3 Foucault, *Discipline and Punish: The Birth of the Prison.*

4 Whitaker, *Anatomy of an Epidemic: Magic Bullets, Psychiatric Drugs, and the Astonishing Rise of Mental Illness in America.*

5 Conrad, "Types of Medical Social Control."

6 Davidow and Mazel-Carlton, "The Pill Shaming Phenomenon: What's it Really About?"

7 White, *Re-Authoring Lives: Interviews & Essays.*

8 Hart, "Pursuing Choice, Not Truth: Debates around Diagnosis in Mental Health."

9 Royal Pharmaceutical Society, "A Competency Framework for all Prescribers."

10 White, *Maps of Narrative Practice.*

BIOS

Helena Rose is a family therapist, Rob Edwards is a mental health nurse and independent nurse prescriber, and they both work together at Aspire Early Intervention Service in Psychosis in Leeds, UK.

CONTRIBUTION

Self Reclamation: A Practice of TRANSpersonal Alchemy

DO NOT SAY YOU DOUBT YOURSELF. Never declare yourself a lie. There is no space for ambivalence here, only certainty. 1's and 0's. Yet, you were once born your *self,* all perfect and whole. You even bounced in your jellyness and rotundity. You giggled. You slobbered. You teethed. You cast your curious eyes and miniature fingers upon your surroundings while your body grew into semi-rigid form. Pliancy, to compliance. *Did your curiosity stop there, too?* There is a myth in a subset of people that rigidity is the rule. Bodies, once they are formed, can never be undone. They do not change. They do not shift in appearance. They always remain the same. They do not move like particles circulating on an everflowing molecular level. They do not expand. They do not contract. They do not change colour or density. They do not grow or wither or shrink. They do not respond to their environments. No external functions will ever affect form, in their eyes. These individuals do not understand metamorphosis, believing themselves and everyone else to be set in stone for the duration of their life spans. They blanket themselves all the same—can you believe it? Great lengths are pursued to achieve the look of a form they believe themselves to be, despite what their semi-rigid bodies are capable of. 1's and 0's.

Believe it or not, even your bones are made of sponge! Did you know sinew, collagen and helices of keratin can hold the structure of you just as much as your spongy bones?!

The natural world is not static. So how have we come to believe we are rigid? In order to adapt to a life structure of others' rigidities our pliancy can become suffocated. Sometimes we become suffocated in our compliance, too. Many of us were cast in stone from a young age despite our protests. We froze our characteristics and constitutions as we became (mis)recognized as a superficial surface structure by others. An external gaze constructed limitations of our being and becoming. We became mistaken in others' eyes, and in our own eyes too. A mold others gave to us, restricts our internal growth and expansion into more than any of us could possibly dream of. Maybe we could not even begin to dream of our *selves*. Our mercurial natures were muted long before we could expand into our ever growing, ever moving, ever shifting physical forms. *If your sinew goes unnoticed, what happens to YOU?*

What I want you to remember, is that you have always been perfectly imperfect *YOU*. Come to this place where you belong and occupy that which was stolen from you: Your Agency. Release your mind from others> others>others. Let's count together to remember this space is yours. Only you can decide within your personal sovereignty what is yours… and what belongs to give back to others.

Stretch your bones. Shake your muscles. Loosen tendons wired so tightly like ligature. Exhale your breath… s-l-o-w-l-y. Run worn fingers down your limbs and trace back your own lines. E-x-h-a-l-e, again. It is safe to be here and remember what was lost or taken from you without your consent. It is surely a crime against your humanity that your *self* was taken from you? If you doubt where you have disappeared to, or what remains of your knowing spirit relax, we can explore together. My job is a considered study and practice in fostering your needs for safety, always. I exhale with you and on your behalf, when your body and spirit are bound so tightly you fear becoming unbound will collapse you into oblivion. ➔

curiosity
ency
ternative identity projects
erasure, avoiding thereof
atholic Worker Movement
humanness

Parts of ourselves become so invaded by our surroundings we cannot distinguish them from our core. Sometimes we have never been safe to explore. Are we different, the same? Who knows? What matters is you get to decide. What matters is you get to explore, if you wish to. The choice must always be yours.

I want you to remember when you come seeking answers on which way to go… and the doubts, shame, and desire conflate into a state of anxious despair… that *you* are *you* regardless of what decisions you make. Parsing through obligation versus your own breath, cadence, and rhythm is a restorative practice. I invite you to experience your breadth from within yourself, perhaps for the very first time. Building a superstructure of your own choosing takes time. Slow down to be as careful with your needs as you were never allowed to be. Brick, by brick. We will rebuild your scaffolding together, remembering the pieces of you that went missing. Let us bring aspects of yourself that are invisibly obscured back into the shining light of yourself. A matrix underlies your connective tissue and protein matter of ever evolving features—an internalized gradient of rigidity to softness.

Do not say you doubt yourself. Never declare yourself a lie. There is space for ambivalence here. 1's and 0's were never enough to contain you, or your process. You were once born your *self* all perfect and whole. We gather together to fully surface your *self*, once more.

Rigidity was never your sacred rule. You were never meant to be set in stone. Compliance, to pliancy.

B-r-e-a-t-h-e until your spirit remembers itself. ❁

BIO

Sly Sarkisova has spent his life supporting folks surviving structural violence and intergenerational traumas by centering radical emotional honesty, observation, and empathy in his psychotherapy practice, writing, photography, and academic studies.

CONTRIBUTION

WE MAY NOT BE ABLE TO FULLY KNOW ANOTHER (SEE erasure, avoiding thereof), and yet we can recognize each other, and we can feel the gratification of being recognized. We come to know ourselves in the other, seeing a version of ourselves, one of the many reflections we get from those who know us. To be seen, to have a part of me seen that has never been seen before, to be recognized more fully: it brings me more fully into being (SEE erasure, avoiding thereof). How can someone help me if I am not recognized for what and who I am?

Part of seeing is also knowing to look, knowing that there is more to be seen (SEE curiosity). Seeing contains a recognition that what we see is low resolution, or blurry around the edges, or partial rather than complete. Being recognized in this way is to be held but not captured, maintaining the possibility of surprising the other.

We can soothe away the angst of the unknown by prematurely reducing a person to a recognizable quantity. The allure of recognition is that it feels true, it feels like a forgotten thing that is now remembered, or a hidden thing that is now revealed. When it is true enough, or held with the humility of acknowledging its limits, recognition can be generative.

There is a danger to recognition, too: when it goes astray, or when it brings along with it overconfidence and constrains what is possible to be known. False or simplified recognition into a familiar archetype leads to treating a person according to scripts, rather than emergently and in response to the complexity of the other (SEE erasure, avoiding thereof). This is not always terrible. Care is provided in many ways, and sometimes we go for maximizing reach in a way that requires homogenizing others. But it is dangerous if we imagine that our simplified image is accurate just because it feels good to imagine that it is. ❁

BIO

Noriko Martinez works imperfectly as a radical helper by sitting with people, being curious, and loving the world.

edistribution

CONTRIBUTION

REDISTRIBUTION IS A PROMISE; redistribution is a threat. These two opposing perspectives define one of the major fault lines in US social policy. Those who struggle to satisfy their basic human needs often see redistribution as essential to their prospects for a better life. But for those who see redistribution as a threat, any such aid is to be opposed on the grounds that money should never be taken from those who have earned it and given as a reward to those who haven't.

Progressive redistribution—that is, redistribution downward to the needy—is actually a fairly unusual phenomenon in American history. With two major exceptions, it is something that the US federal government has just not done. Instead, the default policy has been to leave outcomes to the marketplace and hope for sufficient trickle-down. Yet because the reverberations from these exceptions persist in the lives of so many Americans, most people do not realize how much of a departure they represent from the long-term patterns of US history and the natural tendency of the marketplace to concentrate income and wealth.

The first exception, Franklin Roosevelt's New Deal of the 1930s, came about because the entire US economy was on the verge of collapse. Prior to the 1930s, the US had certainly experienced severe recessions, but the relationship between goods produced and goods sold eventually returned to a rough equilibrium, and the economy always recovered. Nevertheless, by the 1920s, with the marketplace transitioning from a competitive to a monopoly capitalism, income and wealth became ever more concentrated. As a result, when the stock market crashed in October 1929, the economy plummeted downward, and despite repeated promises, it kept falling: the gross domestic product dropped by 50 percent, and unemployment spiked to 25 percent of the working population. American capitalism was teetering on the brink.

The New Deal emerged from this context. Eager to preempt more radical redistributive schemes, Roosevelt enacted the Social Security Act of 1935, which promised retirement benefits and offered public assistance and unemployment benefits; the Public Housing Act of 1937; and the 1938 Fair Labor Standards Act, which for the first time established a minimum wage. Although a full economic recovery would not occur until the early years of World War II, the New Deal did initiate a redistributive process that finally incorporated poor and working people into the body politic. The results were dramatic, with the income share of the top 1 percent falling from 22 percent in the late 1920s to 11 percent by 1945.[1]

Business elites, however, were concerned about this merest hint of social democracy, and so after World War II, they worked hard to change the trajectory of social policies that came out of the New Deal. This concern provided the impetus for the attack on the Full Employment Act of 1946, which they transformed from a government planning agency that ensured full employment to an advisory Council of Economic Advisors in the President's Executive Office that would, as one wit put it, "give everyone the right to look for a job." It also triggered the McCarthyite anticommunist fevers of the late 1940s and early 1950s, which compressed the range of political possibilities by accusing anyone with remotely liberal principles of harboring communist sympathies.

On racial issues, however, these campaigns came into serious conflict with the post–World War II position of the US as the preeminent national power. Just envision for a moment the following scenario: in the midst of the ideological struggle between American capitalism and Soviet communism, the elites of newly liberated countries in Africa and Asia are posted to the

Washington diplomatic corps, where government officials try to persuade them to ally with the United States. It all sounds very appealing, until they go for a drive on the weekend in the Virginia countryside and encounter "colored-only" drinking fountains. To resolve this dilemma, the aspirations of the United States to international dominance demanded that it finally subordinate the segregationist policies of a fading class of plantation-based conservative Southern Democrats to those of business elites from monopolies in the more powerful industrial sector.

The subsequent anti-poverty, civil rights, and voting legislation of the 1960s (Medicaid, Medicare, and the anti-discrimination provisions of the 1964 Civil Rights Bill) capped the second significant era of redistribution, the period from 1945 to 1970 that is now commonly known as the "Great Compression." Despite the efforts of conservatives to hobble some of the more social democratic initiatives coming out of World War II, strong unions, high taxes on the wealthy, and increased spending on social welfare brought about twenty-five years of steady wage growth, with wages increasing at 2.5 to 3 percent annually, and the income share of the top 1 percent declining still further to 7 percent by the early 1970s. It was the last time in the United States that prosperity was widely shared.

Although an expansion of some social programs such as a children's allowance did briefly reduce poverty in response to the Covid pandemic, redistribution in the United States has mostly functioned to reverse the gains of the 1960s. This trend is emphatically not an aberration of normal market forces; rather, over the last fifty years, this outcome has been the primary goal of conservative policymakers. Conservatives have blamed economic slowdowns on government intervention. They have sought to "liberate capitalism" from regulation by promoting the mobility of large, multinational corporations, who were then free to engage in a race to the bottom that undermined unions and cut wages. By reducing taxes on the affluent, cutting social welfare, and blaming racial minorities for America's social problems, they have been able to secure sufficient support from enough people in the precariously situated middle sector to drive inequality back to the heights it reached in the 1920s. For those who grew up in the last half of the twentieth century, the term "redistribution" retains a progressive aura. But when we speak of redistribution now, we should understand that the only redistribution we have seen over the last fifty years is decisively upward. ❁

1 Cowie, *The Great Exception: The New Deal and the Limits of American Politics*, 12.

BIO Joel Blau is professor emeritus at Stony Brook University School of Social Welfare and the author of numerous books and articles about US social policy.

Reflecting on Justice

CONTRIBUTION

the ethos of reflecting on justice: connectivity in grey.

What started out as
a sneaky little infiltration mission
collided with the magic of co-creation;
a manifestation of usefulness in the synchronicity
and orchestration of justice and resistance.

Toeing the line between creativity and chaos;
using the strategies of mutual aid against capitalism,
Reflecting on Justice attempts to carve out a space
where both truths—
"*the revolution will not be funded*"[1] and that organizing requires funds—
can co-exist together at once.

A new perspective for my natural affinity for logistics;
for the shame I once held for complicity in its harms;
transformed into living the imagination of collective liberation
through accountability and community.

Justice requires accountability and accountability cannot be coerced.
It can, however, be sparked,
kindled,
ignited,
in dignity-filled, radically-loving connection.

So can ideas for change.
And social movements.

And why not therapists?
Therapists, who are uniquely positioned to straddle the crisscrossing lines of
healing + activism.
Therapists, who society sees as experts on mental health.
Therapists, whose "morality privilege" casts a sheen over systemic harms.
Therapists, whose whole profession is to construct the different
through conversation and relationship.

I'm not a thought leader nor a visionary, but I can create community.
And perhaps community is exactly what's useful right now.

After all, despair thrives in isolation.
But hope?
Hope proliferates in community.

And if enough of us shift, the world will shift with us.

PS. The "what" is that we built a community-based unlearning platform. Reflecting on Justice is a mutual aid/wealth redistribution-based membership program for therapists to unlearn and resist systemic oppression, within ourselves and our

SEE: ti-ableism; ti-racism court systems; critical race theory; critical whiteness; decolonial liberatory-based practices; healing circles; justice-oriented counseling profession, through community with other therapists. We occupy the unceded, traditional, and ancestral territories of the xʷməθkʷəy̓əm (Musqueam), Skwxwú7mesh (Squamish), Səlílwətaʔ/Selilwitulh (Tsleil-Waututh), S'ólh Téméxw (Stó:lō), Qayqayt, and kʷikʷəƛ̓əm (Kwikwetlem) peoples. Part of ROJ's commitment to disrupting the colonial project we benefit from and to the duty inherent in our relationship with these lands is to redistribute 50% of our proceeds to Indigenous organizing efforts, independent anti-oppression educators, + mutual aid efforts. As our community grows, the percentage of redistribution will also grow.

Connect with us at reflectingonjustice.com for fiercely unveiled conversations in which we practice decentering ourselves, have our unlearning follow the lead of SDQTBIPOC+ folx, and practice radically loving accountability in community. ❁

Words by Abby, Art by Linda

1 INCITE! Women of Color Against Violence, *The Revolution Will Not Be Funded: Beyond the Non-Profit Industrial Complex.*

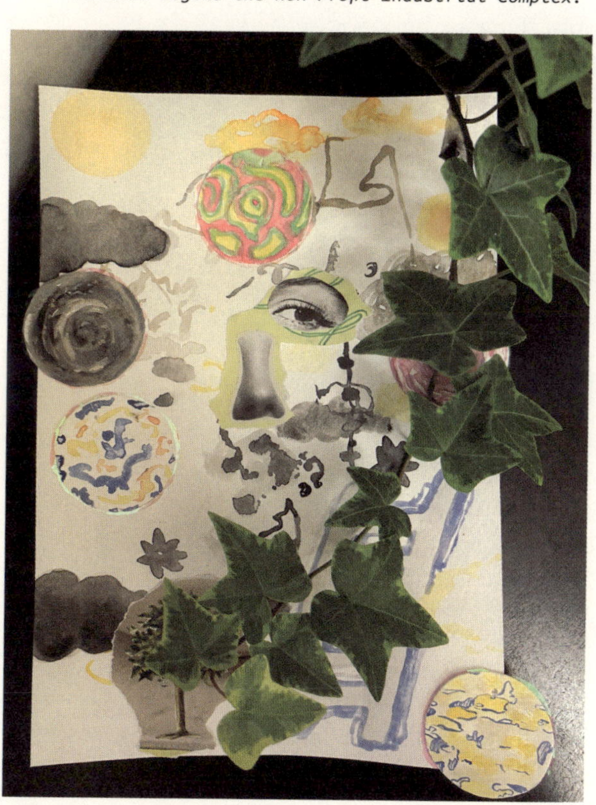

EDITORS'

Sufi poet Jalāl al-Dīn Muḥammad Rūmī has been credited with claiming that the highest form of learning is actually unlearning. Abby, Linda, and their co-conspirators are following through with this encouragement to provide spaces and support for helpers to let go of old ways of thinking and doing that no longer serve our contemporary challenges. Reflecting on Justice and other spaces of unlearning hold much promise in crafting new ways for us to help together. —CH

BIOS

Abby Chow, therapist, writer, and co-conspirator for more radical projects like *Reflecting on Justice, Prospect Counselling + Venturous Counselling*.

Linda Lin, counsellor and art therapist, creative + socials for *Reflecting on Justice*, and founder of *Decipher Counselling*.

eflexivity

SEE: humanness; life cycle honoring the; critical race theory

CONTRIBUTION

LIBERATION BEGINS with an untangling of what is human from what oppresses us.

To take the time to
connect, reflect, release ourselves from the
judgment, binaries, violence,
shoved down our throats
through the systems of
colonization, capitalism, white supremacy.

To reclaim the parts of
our selves, our relating, our knowing
that we hold dear, that we hold sacred.

To resist the perpetuation of
policing, surveillance, othering,
normalized by an oppressive imagination
that keeps us from our divinity.

They tell me that as a therapist, I am my best tool;
that I can only accompany as far as I've gone myself.
I don't know if I believe that to be true, but this I do know:

That connecting as imperfect humans is freedom-making; it is joy; it is liberation.

Self + other is a dichotomy that doesn't actually exist;
they are two sides of the same coin,
two windows into the same house,
two rivers leading to the same ocean.

I don't end where you begin, nor they, nor her, nor him.

Words like redemption are so biblical and contemptuous;
and discovery reminds me of colonization;
so perhaps this untangling, this act of justice,
this reflexivity, this reclamation,
can be called a finding:
a finding that intentionally, rebelliously, creates space for imperfect humanness,
a humanness that sees self + other as one,
a humanness of unfettered generativity, of liberation, of justice.

So,
What are you finding? ❁

BIO

Abby Chow, therapist, writer, and co-conspirator for more radical projects like *Reflecting on Justice, Prospect Counselling + Venturous Counselling*.

EDITOR'S NOTE

Longhofer and Floersch have defined "reflexivity" as the "human capacity to consider ourselves in relation to our contexts; and our contexts in relation to ourselves."[1] A term that originated in qualitative research, reflexivity is now used by therapists and social workers as a way to honor the reciprocity between self, other, and all the material, social, and cultural aspects of the external world that shape and perpetually reshape selves. We can never truly "know" self, other, or the space between, but we can do our best—and, as Abby suggests, perhaps liberation lies in our imperfect attempts at connection. —ES

1 Longhofer and Floersch, "The Coming Crisis in Social Work: Some Thoughts on Social Work and Science," 513.

EDITORS' NOTE

Beyond its energy-focused nature—which differentiates it from many helping modalities taught in the West—Reiki is a good example of a radical helping practice because it is particularly amenable to peer-to-peer healing. Reiki has many masters, as Dani's contribution shows, but it is also possible to practice Reiki on oneself and others after receiving only a little bit of training. When I knew Dani was searching for an illustration for her essay, I asked if I could reach out to Mary Akinadewo, one of the senior citizens who attends a group I facilitate at a Senior Wellness Center. After taking a course in Reiki, another group member, Louise Abercrombie, Mary's friend and neighbor, began practicing Reiki with Center members, including Mary. I invited Mary to create an artwork expressing the out-of-body sense of relaxation she often describes when talking about receiving Reiki from Louise. —ES

CONTRIBUTION

On Reiki

Reiki creates alignment within the body and brings clarity to the mind, moving and transforming blocked emotions, awakening the spirit, and opening the heart.
—Lara Elliott

THE BEST WAY to describe Reiki is to experience it. For me, every session has been a subtle yet profoundly healing experience. After my first *tenohira* (palm healing) treatment with Olivia Burr, an incredible bodywork and energy healer in Topanga, I was deeply moved. I wanted to understand what I had experienced and to share it with people in my life. Olivia led me to Reiki master Lara Elliott. With her, I completed the first two levels of training (*Shoden* and *Okuden*) in the traditional Japanese system of Reiki, created by Zen Buddhist Mikao Usui in the late 1800s.

Reiki is a beautiful healing modality that allows us to clear blockages within our bodies, through the intentional movement of energy. Our being is comprised of five bodies: physical, mental, emotional, energetic, and spiritual. In a training, my teacher Lara said, "Because we are made up of all these different bodies, in the moment of trauma, our physical body doesn't feel safe, and we leave the body. One part of healing is grounding into the body—a mantra you can use for this is: 'It is safe for me to be in my body.'" Reiki brings harmony and healing to our material and metaphysical bodies.

Through somatic meditation, a tenohira treatment draws attention to the places in our bodies that want to open or soften. Your innate, subconscious wisdom will allow you to receive healing wherever you need it. Tenohira is just one aspect of Reiki. The system encompasses breathwork, meditation techniques, symbols, mantras, and more self-healing methods. When you use these tools and practice diligently with loving awareness, Reiki becomes a way of life, and you become Reiki. Reiki feels like coming home to your true nature, your authentic self. Your great, bright, light. ❁

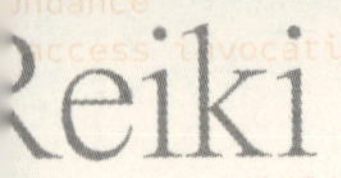

Recommended Reading / Listening

Expanded (podcast) by To Be Magnetic, Ep. 27–"Reiki and Energy Healing," with Lara Elliott

The Japanese Art of Reiki: A Practical Guide to Self-Healing, by Bronwen and Frans Stiene

The Way of Reiki: The Inner Teachings of Mikao Usui, by Frans Stiene

Empowerment through Reiki: The Path to Personal and Global Transformation, by Paula Horan

The Power of Focusing: A Practical Guide to Emotional Self-Healing, by Ann Weiser Cornell

Lara Elliott's website: laraelliotthealing.com

Olivia Burr's website: oliviaburr.life

energy work

healing justice

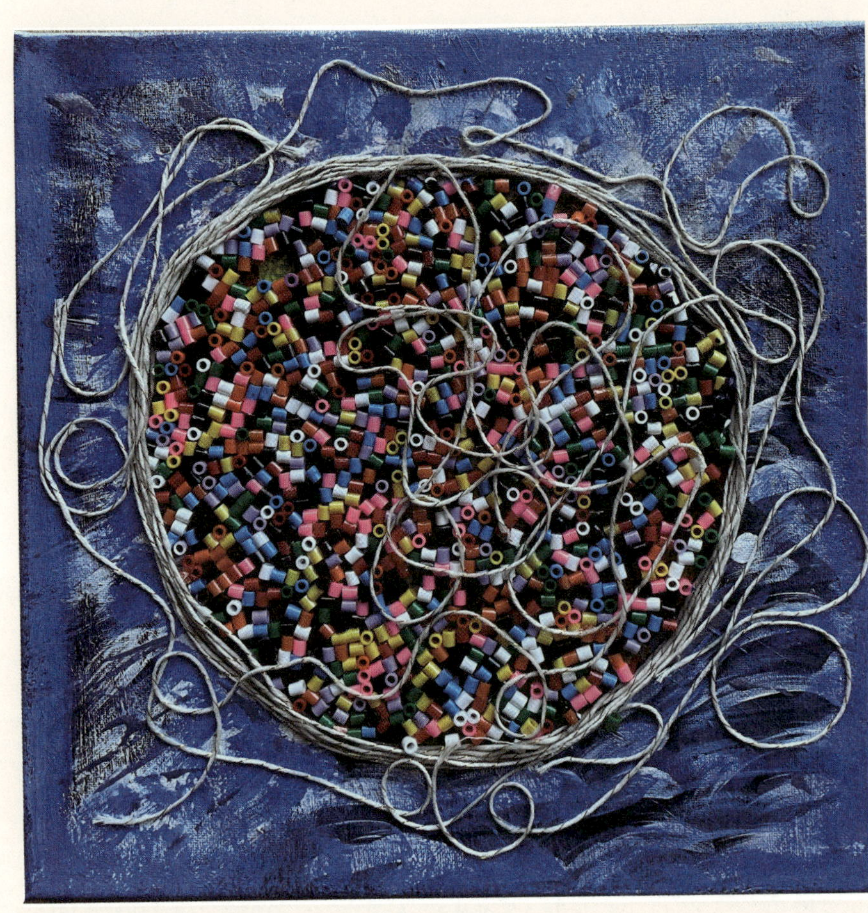

"Peace and Happiness," Mary Akinadewo, 2024.

BIOS

Dani Grossman is a graphic designer and Reiki practitioner from Los Angeles, California

Mary Akinadewo is a retired chef and aspiring artist.

relational interviewing

CONTRIBUTION

I WORK PRIMARILY with couples. I think it is a bit radical these days for a therapist to truly believe that no matter how couples behave, they are fighting *for* their relationship. Even if they look like they are fighting *with* each other, or with me, or quietly drifting apart, they are in my office with a dream of the relationship becoming—or returning to—something that fulfills important purposes and expresses deeply held values in each of their lives. It is radical *not* to see them as examples of familiar pathologies, *not* to see them needing to learn from me, *not* to accept their invitation to mediate. I am not a diagnostician, a teacher, a referee, or most of the other roles that the culture of psychotherapy creates for us. Rather, I think of myself as an enthralled *student* of the purposes they hope their relationship will serve, the values it will express, and the difficulties they encounter when they try to get their relationship to comply with these hopes. My job is to invite a conversation in which these purposes and values spring to life in the room, and thus create paths forward for them.

If I were allowed to ask only three questions, they would be, in this order:

- "What do you want your relationship to *do* for each and both of you, and—while we're at it—for everyone you care about?"
- "What might you have to do *for* your relationship to increase the odds that it might be willing and able to provide these things?" and
- "If your relationship could talk, what would it tell me about what goes wrong when the two of you try?"

Those familiar with narrative therapy will recognize the externalization of "the relationship" that is at the heart of this line of inquiry.

Fortunately, I'm allowed many more questions. Another pass at what might be radical is my purposes in asking *any* questions. I don't ask questions to gather information I would mistakenly feel entitled me to achieve my own understanding of "them." That's a diagnostic approach. And I don't ask questions that are disguised attempts to influence *how* they communicate with each other. That's a didactic approach with the teaching smuggled in. And if I find myself making too many statements and asking too few questions, I've probably slipped out of my student position, my stance of *wonder*. When I catch myself doing these things, I try to return to my avowed purpose: I ask questions that are meant to seed the couple's imagination for how differently things could be going than they are.

Only sufficiently unusual questions can invite imaginative answers. Seeking a balance between not unusual enough and too unusual, a question should stimulate new reflections without inviting people to "defend" themselves or their relationship. If you looked at transcripts of my conversations with couples, much would seem ordinary. But on closer examination you'd find that there are three ways in which a decent percentage of my questions depart from the ordinary. All three of these lines of inquiry take some bravery and much practice, and require that the couple has agreed go down less-familiar roads with me. Reading a transcript, you'd notice…

1. that over time they become comfortable answering questions from *the perspective of their relationship*, rather than from their own perspective.
2. that they also grow accustomed to my asking them to speak speculatively about what they think their partner's experience might be, rather than presenting (and then inevitably defending) their own experience. ➔

3. And that sometimes we have conversations that are structured around the idea of the "embodied other," and I ask them to speak as the other instead of to or about the other.[1]

Why am I avoiding asking them to speak *as themselves*? Again, perhaps it's radical to defy the sacred "I Statement," but I've found that the *least* imaginative and *least different* conversations take the form that their debate is already taking, in which each person presents *and* defends their own perspective while not really taking in the perspective of the other. If you were to ask people to make an I Statement in which their partner can't detect any implicit accusation, they'd discover that it's impossible, and that their partner predictably *will* be defending against that accusation. And if you ask people to repeat what they heard their partner say as proof that they were "hearing" (while they were forming their rebuttal,) well, then you're just training parrots.

Thinking of No. 1 above, I might ask:

LZ: *Jack and Jill,*[2] *if I were to ask your relationship why gathering water is so important, what might it tell me about why it would want you to risk breaking your crown, Jack, or why tumbling after might be worth it, Jill? Who would like to answer first?*

Jill: *Our relationship requires us to gather enough water for all of us, so that none of us go thirsty.*

LZ: *Why is it concerned with your thirst?*

Jill: *It wants us all to survive.*

LZ: *Is your relationship pretty sure that you and Jack have divided up the responsibility for your collective survival in a way that works for both of you, or might it worry that that question is not yet settled?*

Or, No. 2, a series of questions for Jack:

LZ: *What do you think Jill might be feeling as she sees you heading up the hill, knowing the dangers you might face?*

Jack: *She's feeling that it's my job and that I owe it to her.*

LZ: *Is that your best guess about what she might be feeling? To my ear you're describing what she might be believing rather than feeling. So even if you're right about the belief, what do you imagine she's feeling?*

Jack: *Well, certainly not worry about my safety, like your question implied.*

LZ: *Sure, perhaps not. So what instead?*

Jack: *She might be worried about whether my life insurance is paid up.*

LZ: *So she might be feeling some kind of worry or even fear about whether the collective survival we were just speaking of was secure?*

Or, No. 3, an "embodied" interview of each *as* the other, in this example, of Jill as Jack:

> *LZ: Jack (addressed to Jill who has agreed to be interviewed as Jack, while the "real" Jack listens to her "embodied" Jack), what is it like for you to be the one to head up that hill first every time?*
>
> *Jill as Jack: It feels like a lot of responsibility.*
>
> *LZ: Jack, do you feel you chose to take on that responsibility?*
>
> *Jill as Jack: No, not really. It's more like it comes with the territory.*
>
> *LZ: You mean the territory of your gender?*
>
> *Jill as Jack: Yeah, I suppose.*
>
> *LZ: Jack, how well do you think Jill understands what it's like for you to fulfill a role that you might not have entirely chosen of your own accord?*
>
> *Jill as Jack: Not very well.*
>
> *LZ: Jack, do you think she tumbles after you of her own accord, or is her life similarly complicated by what we might say are assigned roles? Might she have preferred a different arrangement than this one?*

Hopefully the three of us are no longer replicating a process where each presents/defends their own experience in endless circles. (And I include myself here.) Here, each might actually listen to the other's answers to more unusual questions about what "the relationship" might want, and to the other's best effort to respond to the more unusual task of presenting their partner's experience rather than their own. Something new might happen.

1 Epston, "Internalized Other Questioning with Couples: The New Zealand Version."

2 This is a reference to the well-known English children's nursery rhyme about Jack and Jill.

BIO
Larry Zucker is a Narrative Therapist living in Los Angeles, California, where he works primarily with couples.

elationality

CONTRIBUTION

Change Is an Ocean: The Meeting of Rivers

AS THERAPISTS WORKING IN INDIA with middle class populations, we have been watching some curious trends. In previously colonized countries, we see a trend where medical and related professionals are really subservient to UK and US models of working, and the psychology/psychotherapy field is no exception. A narrow view of "biology" as the only reality and chemical problems in the brain or internal explanations (thoughts, beliefs, drives and other intra-psychic phenomenon) for mental health issues reigned for a very long time and there is still a sizable number of professionals who cling to it. However, another emerging trend is that of politically aware therapists. While this is an important recognition, what seems to now be happening is that therapy has been reduced to recognizing the intersection of the client (i.e., their caste, class, gender identity, sexual orientation, minority religions status), asking smartly phrased narrative therapy questions (as narrative therapy is a popular model with this group) that make the person feel pumped up with energy, but not really working with their inherent woundedness. What this does is create a sense of imposter syndrome, where we feel a sense of helplessness in front of these huge systems of power.

We feel that both the completely internal and the heavily external explanations tend to miss where change really is: in the relational and intersubjective realm. We think of change as an ocean, a meeting point of two rivers, where we see both the internal and the external as important and harmony between the two (as much as possible) as the goal.

PROJECTION AND BAD PARTS ARE REAL: Neuroscience research supports the psychoanalytic and Jungian psychology concepts of projection and darker parts of the personality. Perhaps allowing the full range of humanness is better than seeing people as all good, simply at the receiving end of oppression. The greyness and nuances of a person are what make them human. If we acknowledge projection (attributing one's own unacceptable urges and feelings to another) and darker sides of the personality as real, fewer behaviours and tendencies will go into our blind spots. For instance, White narrative therapy practitioners have such an all-good idea of narrative therapy that when they work with Indian poor or tribal populations, they are not in touch with the disruption or harm or culture shock that could also be resulting from their intervention.

TRANSFERENCE AS THE HEALING TOOL OF COLLECTIVE INTERDEPENDENCE: Transference (and countertransference) has the potential to be a powerful collective tool of healing, just like coming together and organizing for our rights, if we let it. Transference is subconsciously associating a person in the present with a past relationship. Countertransference is responding to them with all the thoughts and feelings attached to that past relationship. If, just like therapists, we all learn how to work with transference—to hold it gently, not to take it personally, but to help the other work through it to have a fuller understanding of the self and self-in-relationship—then transference can function as successive mirrors or windmills which together create the impact of producing a lot of energy. In that way, then, working with transference in this collective way could be the epitome of interdependence.

FEELING INSTEAD OF THEORIZING: Cognitive, postmodern, and other therapies discuss feelings so much that, quite like academia which dissects feelings but doesn't feel any, we tend to theorize, name, externalise, draw about, reflect on—do everything but actually *feel* our feelings. As Alok Vaid-Menon says, "We do an awful lot to not submit to our feelings, because it makes us remember how common our bodily experience of feelings are. In that way, feelings are equal opportunity, because they can bring the most powerful person to their knees."[1] Perhaps intellectualizing and theorizing retains some of the specialness of the primary narcissism of childhood and is preferred to the authenticity and commonness of feelings.

WE EXPERIENCE SYSTEMS RELATIONALLY: While we can experience systems in abstract ways, we come in touch with them in a real way only in our relationships; for example, when parents enforce gender norms, school teachers impose ideas of ableism, or bosses impose ideas of productivity. We have a lot more agency in these local playing-outs of the systems than we do on the larger systems themselves. And often, we feel that because we cannot do anything about the larger system, we should not even negotiate the impact relationally, because "what's the point?" However, for most of us, if many of our immediate relational environments become less oppressive, our lives will improve significantly.

MOVING FROM RESCUER POSITIONS TO SHARED HUMANITY AND ACKNOWLEDGING LIMITS: Lastly, activism, teaching, therapy, coaching, and other helping professions often fall prey to a rescuer position/tendency. From afar, it feels like we are doing good. However, when we rescue, we center our feelings of being a good person and its gratification and do not center what the help seeker needs. This also makes us want to be thanked and appreciated for our help, and so we then want perfect victims who keep giving us gratitude and who themselves cannot be grey—throwing tantrums, being cranky, etc. Because of this thinking, when we do have an imperfect victim, either we judge them or ourselves. This also prevents us from drawing healthy boundaries that might help us to do the work for longer, sustainably, and creates resentment which then enters our blind spot and makes us be passive aggressive. Lastly, this position does not allow us to give wrathful/cold compassion, as Buddhist psychology would say, when needed, because when we give this type of compassion, we may not be "liked" by the help seeker—but it will nonetheless benefit them in the long term. An alternative to this is to allow imperfections in those we help as a shared humanity and appreciation of everyone's greys, and to work with others within our limits of healthy giving. We are probably going to help more by example if we embody these, rather than trying to be an endless source of help. ❂

1 Vaid-Menon, Goodkind, and Mandelbaum, "The Strength of Feelings."

BIOS

Sadaf Vidha, Therapist and Founder, Guftagu Counselling and Psychotherapy Services.

Aryan Somaiya, Therapist, Gender/sexuality/queer and trans affirmative work trainer, Cofounder of Guftagu Counselling and Psychotherapy Services.

EDITOR'S NOTE

After opening this essay with the concern that narrative techniques and identity-focused political awareness are preventing therapy clients from experiencing real change, Sadaf and Aryan look to relationality as an antidote. Found in both contemporary psychoanalytic thinking and postmodern family therapy/psychology/social work, relationality assumes that the self exists in relation to other selves, arising from affective experiences and symbolic meanings co-constructed between and among individuals and groups. Relationality is philosophically incompatible with the medical model because there exists no essential self to diagnose and treat. Instead, there exist two or more embodied, interrelated persons co-constructing meaning and feeling their feelings together. If you are interested in learning more about relationality from a psychological perspective, check out Ken Gergen's *Relational Being*, or Stephen Mitchell's *Relationality: From Attachment to Intersubjectivity*, or Judith V. Jordan's *Relational-Cultural Therapy*.—ES

esistance

CONTRIBUTION

A MAN RECEIVES AN EVICTION ORDER from his apartment because of big debts he didn't pay; he spends his time in bed, refusing the social worker's offers to help him settle his debts. Another man comes up to his social worker and asks for some money to buy a bus ticket, so he can visit his sick wife at the hospital, although he knows that the social worker has no budget for this kind of help. A woman arrives to the social service department with her three young children and asks the social workers to take the children from her custody because she can't raise them anymore. When the social workers decide to split the children and to send them to different institutions, she attacks the social workers physically.

How can we understand the behaviours of these three service users? Is it a manifestation of their dysfunctional way of doing things? Or a psychological pathology? Or expressions of resistance to unbearable life situations? Should social workers eradicate these behaviours? Or should they support them?

"Resistance" in this context is a concept that captures both service users' agentic power and their limiting and constraining context.[1] The concept of "resistance" enables us to look at the relationship between the people and their context as marked by deep discomfort. It gives us a new lens to understand various behaviours as a response to limiting context instead of seeing them as inherent characteristics of the individual. In fact, it helps us—practitioners of care—to recognize the endless actions people take in order to resist their hardship, no matter if these actions are successful or not.

When the man from the first example was asked why he refused to come out of his bed, he said he understood that he was waiting for the bailiffs to come. "They will have to carry me to the street with my bed," he said, "and then the press will come and only then, when my problem gets to the media, the mayor will solve it." Hearing this plan changed the social worker's interpretation of the man's behaviour. She did not perceive him anymore as only passive and depressed, as a person who ignores his immediate problems, but as an angry man who chose to stay in bed as a protest against injustice. When the man in the second example was asked what brought him to the situation in which he needed help in buying a bus ticket, he showed his social workers that he had filled some bags with little presents for his wife that he got as donations from shop owners in his community. Although he didn't have money to buy presents for her, he didn't want to visit her with empty hands. The bus ticket was the last thing he needed to fulfil his plan—and he couldn't get it by asking the bus driver for a donation. This piece of information—something that the social worker had not imagined—enabled him to shift his interpretation of the man from passive to active, and from dependent to a man who asks for recognition for his efforts. The aggressiveness of the woman from the third example could seem at first as another expression of her pathology. But using the lens of resistance, it can be interpreted as a manifestation of her wounded motherhood, and of her care for her children. Using this lens, the fact that she gave up her custody of the children is seen as a manifestation of her caring for them in a context of extreme loneliness and despair, not of their desertion.

In psychoanalysis, resistance is a psychic configuration of defence against insight. It describes various behaviours of avoidance towards raising unconscious material to the conscious level. Unconsciously, the patient or client avoids revealing impulses, emotions, or memories that threaten the psychic equilibrium. Resistance is evident in all uncooperative behaviour in treatment, whether in the refusal to accept an interpretation, in non-attendance of sessions, in silence or repetitive talk, in late-coming, or in cancellation of sessions. In this context, resistance is a manifestation of being stuck, stagnation, refusal to develop, or an attempt to prevent development.

However, in the critical school of thought that I adopt here, resistance carries fundamentally different meanings. It does not describe a failure "to do the right thing." Rather, it is an active effort by the subordinated to struggle with and to oppose domination. Thus, it acquires political significance. For me, resistance is the struggle of people against hardship. It may be expressed openly, having a normative significance, but it can also be covert and even be manifested in destructive behaviour. It does not even necessarily have to be an action, since it can be expressed as an avoidance from action or as thoughts and emotions that are not realized in action. What makes it resistance is that it is an expression of unwillingness to accept oppression.

Identifying the efforts service users make in the aim of bettering their life is a crucial professional area of expertise for social workers. It is also a source of hope, since it facilitates a fruitful ground for building relationships of trust and partnership. If we accept that people resist their hardship, the role of social workers is not to motivate them to change, but to identify their struggle and to help them make it successful.

This entry is based on the chapter "On minor movements of resistance," in Michal Krumer-Nevo's *Radical Hope: Poverty-Aware Practice for Social Work* (Policy Press, 2020). ❁

1 Lister, *Poverty*.

BIO Prof. Michal Krumer-Nevo is the head of the Spitzer Department of Social Work, Ben-Gurion University of the Negev.

CONTRIBUTION

No One Died: Resisting the Parental Loss Narrative

MANY THERAPISTS WHO EARNESTLY INTEND to support and protect transgender young people may be unwittingly participating in practices that at best lack nuance and sensitivity, and at worst play into anti-trans rhetoric. The discourse of *parental loss* (that is, parents grieving the "loss" of their child when they declare a trans identity)[1] is problematic for many reasons. Yet, therapists lean into this narrative, believing they are doing right by the parents and the young person.

Meanwhile, the anti-trans movement implicitly exploits the notion of parental loss to fuel their claims that transition is dangerous, wrong, self-absorbed, and impetuous. I'm alarmed by therapists' reception of young people's declarations of identity as something to grieve... *like a death*. This renders what should be a celebration of renewal into an elegy for the dead. Implicitly—if not explicitly—this reflects anti-trans rhetoric inasmuch as it 1) denies trans youth author-ity in their lives, 2) centers the experiences of cisgender adults, and 3) insists transition is bad.

The parental loss narrative causes harm to trans youth and creates unnecessary tension in the parent-child relationship. Young people can get recruited into attending to their parents' needs, often at the expense of their own. Some youths avoid or delay sharing their gender with parents in order to protect their parents (as well as themselves) from this grieving. And, as one 10-year-old gender-creative kid said during family therapy, "No one died, Daddy."

DAMN DOMINATING DISCOURSES

Resisting the loss narrative means resisting dominating discourses. **Cisnormativity** and the **gender binary** set up parents to assume cisness. Grieving "the loss" of a child naturalizes the construction of gender and hides these discourses. This is the discursive landscape that fails to make transness a possibility... just like it makes cisness the default. The loss narrative constructed within these discourses specifies and limits identity conclusions. These foreclosed conclusions lead parents to assume cisness. The existence of a trans child explodes this assumption. This leaves parents (and therapists) to conclude that to make meaning within these discourses they must grieve a loss.

There is another powerful discourse operating. **Adultism**—in particular the notion that children are their parents' possessions—sets up parents to feel entitled to grieve a loss of something they don't have rights to. Adultism also dismisses young people's capacity for making decisions; it not only *denies* them agency, adultism also insists young people aren't qualified to be agentic.

These discourses produce *real effects*. Many parents *do* feel grief when their child announces their transness. Parents' experience of despair is very real. When it comes to feelings, it's important to note how discourses of **liberal-humanism** and **individualism** insist that feelings are unquestionable. Emotions are treated not only as sacrosanct, but also as inherent and "true" experiences that exist outside of context.

WHAT TO DO

Taking a queer-theory-informed constructionist stance positions me to view feelings as *products of discourse*, rather than internal states. I have great compassion for parents. I understand that experiencing grief makes perfect sense within the discourses described above. My intention is not to refute their feelings. I am interested in de-naturalizing feelings and situating them in discourse. This makes space for parents to explore alternative ways to make meaning of their child's transition.

I've outlined below what I focus on and offer some examples of how to practice from a queer-theory-informed constructionist stance when addressing the parental loss narrative:

1. **Attend to feelings**: Focus on understanding and validating feelings. Cultivate your compassion for parents. They did not ask for these discourses.

2. **Deconstruct discourses**: Take a both-and approach in which you honor and validate parents' feelings while also asking questions that invite them to examine the influence of discourse. Here are some examples of questions I've asked:[2]
   - *You said, "It's such a big loss... I feel a void..." What's gone missing from your life that filled so much for you when it was there?*
   - *You said, "Nothing prepared us for this..." What were you prepared for? How did you prepare? What helped you prepare?*
   - *In what ways does this "social preparation for a cis kid" contribute to the void of the big loss you're describing?*
3. **Decouple gender**: Invite stories about what parents love, enjoy, admire, value, etc. about their child and decouple these from gender. Their child's achievements, qualities, and ways of being in the world are not *determined by gender*, although some of them may *be gendered*. Help parents construct stories about what they value about their child that holds meaning other than those made around gender. For example:
   - *Do you think "good heartedness" is a feature of Casey's assigned gender, or might it be a value that Casey stands by?*
   - *How have these "gender assumptions" you've identified convinced you that Casey will no longer show up with the "persistence and dedication" you admire now that they're trans?*
4. **Articulate mission**: I often ask parents about their missions as parents. Articulating their mission and the practices that allow them to live into it may help parents: reclaim what's important to them; resist narratives that don't align with their values and their children's best interests; and view normative discourses as barriers to their mission. Here are a few mission questions:[3]
   - *What is your mission as a parent?*
   - *What values or principles inform this mission statement?*
   - *What do you do to live into your mission?*
   - *How does the gender binary support or thwart your mission?*

In summary, I hope to find ways for parents to reposition themselves with gender so that they may live into their missions as parents and join their child in making meaning of transition in ways that give life rather than suggest death. ❁

1 I am specifically and exclusively addressing the notion that parents need to grieve the loss of the child as though they've died or been disappeared. This is not about parents' worry/fear/sadness about having a trans child in a violently anti-trans world.

2 I offer these questions as examples, not as a template. They are disembodied from the actual conversations they emerged within. For a more complete transcript, see Tilsen, *Queering Your Therapy Practice: Queer Theory, Narrative Therapy, and Imagining New Identities*.

3 See Tilsen for more "mission interview" questions.

BIO

Julie Tilsen lives on stolen Dakhóta land, the ancestral and contemporary homeland of the Dakhóta and Ojibwe Native Nations, which was obtained through violent acts of genocide, displacement, forced removal, and broken treaties.

esonance

CONTRIBUTION

Radical Resonances, Social Transformations and Friendship

"*PATA DE PERRO*" IS A TERM used in various parts of Latin America to refer to someone who likes to be away from home or travel a lot. The expression literally translates to "dog's paw" and usually does not have a negative connotation; rather, it is used colloquially to describe someone who likes to wander in search of new destinations. In South America such an attitude can be a recipe for finding trouble, hence you have to be as wily as a stray dog to avoid hassle. When I was growing up in the mountains of central Colombia, family and friends described me several times as a "pata de perro." It wasn't until I was 20 years old that I had the opportunity to leave my hometown to visit a remote destination, Argentina, where an obsession to see remote places ignited in me, which led me to embark on several long, quixotic and penniless trips in which I ended up playing music in the street, hitchhiking, couch surfing and volunteering, among other things, in order to keep on rolling.

He who seeks finds. My comings and goings led me to study sound art in Sweden, where I lived for a few years. It was there that three words that have been fundamental for me began to weave themselves together: resonance, radical and friendship. While experimenting with interactive art in Stockholm, I came to understand how music and sound can be metaphors for understanding social phenomena.

A sound that travels through the air, water, or any other medium fades over time due to the resistance of the medium itself. Sound needs a medium to propagate; this is why there is no sound in a vacuum or in outer space. Such fading out is challenged when one sound meets another synchronous sound, which results in a deeper, prolonged, and more reverberant vibration, i.e., a resonance. From an acoustic point of view this phenomenon represents an energetic amplification and expansion. Sound, as we know it, is just another type of vibration in the midst of the multitude of waves that continuously surround us. Although we associate resonance with sound, it is actually a phenomenon that occurs with all kinds of waves and vibrations, audible or not by our perceptual devices.

All vibrations and waves are the result of motion, which means that there can be no sound without movement. When I first grasped these concepts, I could not help but think that resonance could be understood as a way to make sense of many types of human interactions: everything that moves, including our communication, thinking, relationships, etc., has the potential to create amplifications, which, when it happens, produces more energy than that generated by an isolated emitter.

When an acoustic system resonates, as in the case of two objects vibrating synchronously, they produce an intensification that occurs at specific frequencies, which depends on the degrees of freedom with which an object can oscillate. For instance, pendulums and our knees have only one degree of freedom of movement; our ankles and wrists have two, and our neck and hips have three. Being a mechanical phenomenon, a system can have as many resonance frequencies as it has degrees of freedom, depending on the number of coupled moving parts: hundreds of thousands of resonances in the case of musical instruments and millions in the case of atoms.

Perhaps the most direct metaphor for understanding resonance is music; every musical instrument is a resonator: a device that oscillates at certain frequencies, whose vibrations within it travel as waves, at an approximately constant speed, bouncing back and forth between its sides. In the case of wind instruments, the resonator itself is the narrow cavity through which the air travels; in the case of stringed instruments, it is each taut string that vibrates when stroked; in the case of drums, it is the membrane stretched over a chamber; and so on. All of them produce sound waves in specific tones that have the possibility of coinciding with each other. The reinforcement of the interaction occurs when different instruments sound in the same frequency range and at the same time, increasing and intensifying the energetic result of the system. In contrast, when the objects of a system vibrate at dissimilar frequencies, a dissonance is produced, as when many people talk at the same time without listening to each other. In music, the study of harmony is the study of the possible combinations, progressions, and principles that govern the interaction between sounds to create resonances.

As opposed to resonance, dissonance can also be understood as the tension or clash resulting from the combination of asynchronous vibrations, which causes the waves to interfere and dull each other. When experimenting practically with these concepts, I could not help but think about how dissonance is intentionally orchestrated in the political realm to hinder social transformations. On the other hand, from my individual perspective, I also thought about all the people I have been in contact with throughout my life and how, with many of them, a brief encounter has triggered a lasting and powerful collaboration, in which our respective creative energies found a synchronous vibration. Friendship is a form of resonance of human vibration.

Working with these kinds of ideas led me to found Resonar Lab with a group of radical and "pata de perro" friends who share a common perspective: we believe that through art and participatory practices it is possible to foster constructive social resonances and amplifications. We are a collective of artists and activists from Latin America, Europe and Africa who are committed to collective work and experimentation to generate eco-social transformations. When we use the term "radical," we refer to the etymology of the word, that is, "that which is inherent to the root," and for us this refers to the necessity of work that focuses on the causes of the systemic problems of the reality we live in. Please take a look at our work at resonar.net. ❁

BIO

Ivan Txaparro is a South American artist, musician, designer and educator based in Berlin, deeply motivated by promoting processes of artistic co-creation, storytelling, electroacoustic music and activism.

espectful visiting

SEE: breaking the rules, centering maintenance, community newspapers, curiosity

CONTRIBUTION

WORKING AS A VISITING ARTIST encouraged me to think about the way I arrive in a new community. I was often seeking connections with locals as a way to co-create projects together. There are a lot of important questions to ask when working with a new community: questions around artistic labor, extraction, respect, and intention. Rather than leaning on the overused binaries of local/tourist or insider/outsider, I prefer to think of visiting in terms of a guest/host relationship. I think this leaves more room to regard the power and privilege at play in relationships defined by place, and invites us to consider the responsibilities that we all have when engaging with each other.

A host holds a connection to a place: residence, origin, knowledge, experience. With connection to a place comes the responsibility to understand the place, and act in a way that will sustain it and its ecosystems (social, cultural, ecological). If one chooses to be a host, the role asks them to share, to welcome, and to help guests orient themselves to the social norms of a place.

A guest is seeking a connection to a place. A guest arrives in need of a host. A guest is curious! A guest is humbled by their need for guidance, assistance, and translation. A core responsibility of the guest is to be respectful. A guest must ask questions about the norms of a place, and be self-aware of the impact they might have.

Engaging with a community as a guest requires time, presence, and intention. And the way a place—an established collection of communities—engages with strangers is a defining part of its temperament. The German sociologist Georg Simmel considers "the stranger" an important contributor to any group. He argues that we need newcomers to import conditions into a group. We need newcomers to introduce qualities that do not and cannot stem from the group itself. The stranger brings a necessary outsider viewpoint. I wonder: Can a code of ethics or a community practice framework be an expression of a place's values that helps facilitate meaningful interaction between strangers and established groups? I developed the framework below to formalize my own practice of arriving as a newcomer.

The question of what defines community, and the question of how to be a person in the world—these are tremendous questions. Place, community, identity, connection, relationship: these are some of the biggest and most inexplicable things, and they do not lend themselves to simple answers. As visiting artists and cultural workers, we must instead embrace the complexity and engage with the self-reflection necessary to be good guests.

A POSSIBLE FRAMEWORK FOR VISITING

RECOGNITION of what is there. Think of "place" as a verb, and a process of inquiry, of trying to locate an essence. Can you "place" it? Looking and listening are the action parts, but really seeing and hearing are the hard parts, the heart-parts. The recognition moment takes all of your senses, all of your energy. You must feel a place in your body. You must look first without judgment, and resist having an agenda. Be grateful to others for the energy they share with you. Be humble. Remember, no place is a "blank slate."

REFLECTION on one's own relationship to the place, the context by which you arrive. What does it mean to visit this place? Who is your host? What is their relationship to the community, and what are their expectations for you on your visit? What does it mean for you to have the lodging you have, and what are the economic and social realities that enable you to be there? What is the environmental impact of your presence or practice? What are the power dynamics inherent in your presence, what voice and resources do you have that others in this place may not? How does your socio-economic background shape your position, and what perspectives do you bring with you? What is your intention?

This is the moment to own the reality that no visitor is benign, even (especially not?) a weekend tourist. The reverberations of nuanced impact are real.

RESPECT for what is there. This part requires humility, restraint. This part requires an ongoing unfolding comprehension of the temperature of the place. I've been criticized for hanging back, for acting out of fear or hesitancy, keeping a tight rope on my participation and letting others define my behavior. I've been criticized for censoring creative output and not revealing entire narratives. But I think that there is power in restraint, that there is a way to be actively inactive. Pause is not passivity. The action part necessarily comes later.

RESPONSE to what is there. This is where the visitor becomes a participant and not just an observer. This is the action-moment where I exercise my will, visualize my contributions, and embody my role as a visitor. Artistically, in this phase I'm usually preparing to reflect the narratives of a place into a creative work, and I ask myself, "Which stories are okay to share, and which ones are too sacred? Whose voices are ready to be amplified, and who would prefer to stay quiet?" Remember to speak with people, not at them or for them. The response phase is an important self-check moment: What are the spoken and unspoken social rules of the place that you identified in the "recognition" phase? Are you breaking the rules? Are you blowing up the spot? (Each person will have different impulses to follow or not follow the rules, and it is not necessarily a given that *break the rules = bad / follow the rules = good*. Some social rules are objectively not okay—racist, sexist, ableist, etc.—and need to be broken.) It is simply important for the visitor to become aware of their own behavior and understand how it fits into an established code. Consider the difference between reaction and response.

RECIPROCITY loop. This is the generosity part. What can you give? I think a visitor must give, give, and give before they take. Then they must take, because to be a part of a healthy relationship requires some vulnerability and much gratitude.

REPEAT. Now comes the maintenance. The process of entering a community requires presence and time. Attention. Love. Kindness, patience, willingness to work, and readiness for challenges. Conflict and tension inevitably arise during the maintenance process. It is the deepest feeling of relief to be able to rely, in times of discord and heartache, on the strong lines that have been drawn with respect, reflection, and reciprocity.

This framework was adapted from the essay "Codes and Questions for Anyone Who Goes Anywhere: Towards a Community Framework for Visiting Citizens," first published in *The Changing Times Issue 4: Unincorporated Marin County*, in January 2018. ❁

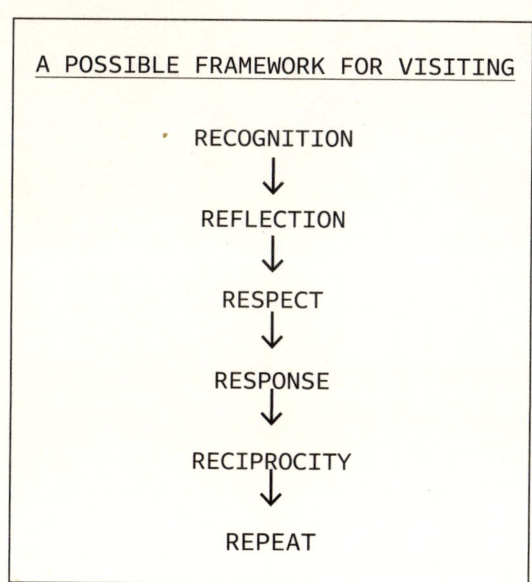

BIO Nicole Lavelle is an artist, writer, and designer whose work addresses place, identity, and community.

undance
access invocations
EE: accessibility
tivating archives
rofuturism
ency
ing positivity
tar work
ternative identity
rojects
cestral wisdom
cestrality
ti-ableism
ti-adultism
ti-racism
ti-racism court
ystem
t
t as/in/of life
t journaling
t therapy
t workers
t-based group work
ts in medicine
ts-based research
thentic Movement
tonomous healing
yurveda
ing with
rtha Capen Reynolds
ike and car repair
collectives
lack Panther Party
Free Breakfast
Program
ody as community
ody neutrality
ody positivity
ody Trust
oredom
rave space
reaking the rules
ridge as metaphor
are pods
are-based co-housing
atholic Worker
Movement
entering maintenance
ircular economy
limate cafes
louds as metaphor
oalition
ollaborative
apprenticeship
ollective care
ommon pool resources
ommons, the
ommuning with
animals
ommunity college
ommunity gardens
ommunity newspapers
onjure
onstructionist-
design framework, the
onsulting your
consultants
contemplative
tradition, the
corn knowledge
credit unions
crip time
critical fabulation
critical hope
critical pedagogy
critical race theory
critical suicide
studies
critical whiteness

critique
Cuestionamos
curiosity
death practices
decolonial
liberatory-based
practices
deep organizing
dérive, the
drumming
embodied expression
embodied knowledge
emergent strategy
empathy
energy work
erasure, avoiding
thereof
esoteric wisdom
traditions
ethnodrama
etymology
existentialism
externalizing
failure
fat positivity
feminism
feminst ethics
of care
fermentation
flâner
food sovereignty
forest bathing
fragments/
fragmentation
freedom
generous systems
gift economies
Grace Lee Boggs
grief as nonlinear
group work
groups
harm reduction
healing circles
healing healers
through the arts
healing justice
healing rituals
Hearing Voices
Network
herbal justice
herbalism
holding space
humanness
humor
illders
improvisation
infinite blackness
intentional
communities
interdisciplinary
cataloging
intergenerational
living
interspecies
organizing
intuitive eating
justice-oriented
counseling
land trusts
land, work,
spirit, body
language justice
leaving wel
liberatory
education
life cycle
honoring the
liminality
limited-equity
cooperative
housing

espite rooms

CONTRIBUTION

The Radical Work of John Roloff, as Experienced thru a Single Object for Nurses, Oracle of a Nightingale

THE ORIGINAL STATUE SEEN FLOATING in this altered photograph was finished in Carrara marble in 1913, made by Francis William Sargant, and can be found in its normal humble sanctuary in the Basilica of Santa Croce in Italy. The sculpture is of Florence Nightingale. Born to a wealthy British family living in Italy, Nightingale became known for her work in the Crimean War, training nurses and caring for soldiers. She is credited with establishing the lifesaving hand-washing practices that we still rely on today. Before her dedication to training nurses in hand hygiene, some 70 percent of soldiers were dying of infections; after her training, only 5 percent succumbed. Her reputation was one of tireless presence. She was known as "the Lady with the Lamp" because she would visit the sick and wounded into the night to check on them, carrying a small lamp to light her way in the wards.

Gifted to the COVID ICU at the UCLA Medical Center in April 2020 for their nurse's respite room, *Oracle of a Nightingale* was created by artist John Roloff for a new group of workers on a front line. It hung in their respite room alongside other artists' beautiful works, like the long line of photos by artist Katrina Umber, moving quotes by social justice leaders, and open sheets of paper for nurses to document their experiences. It bore witness to a lot of private sadness and fear in those early pandemic days.

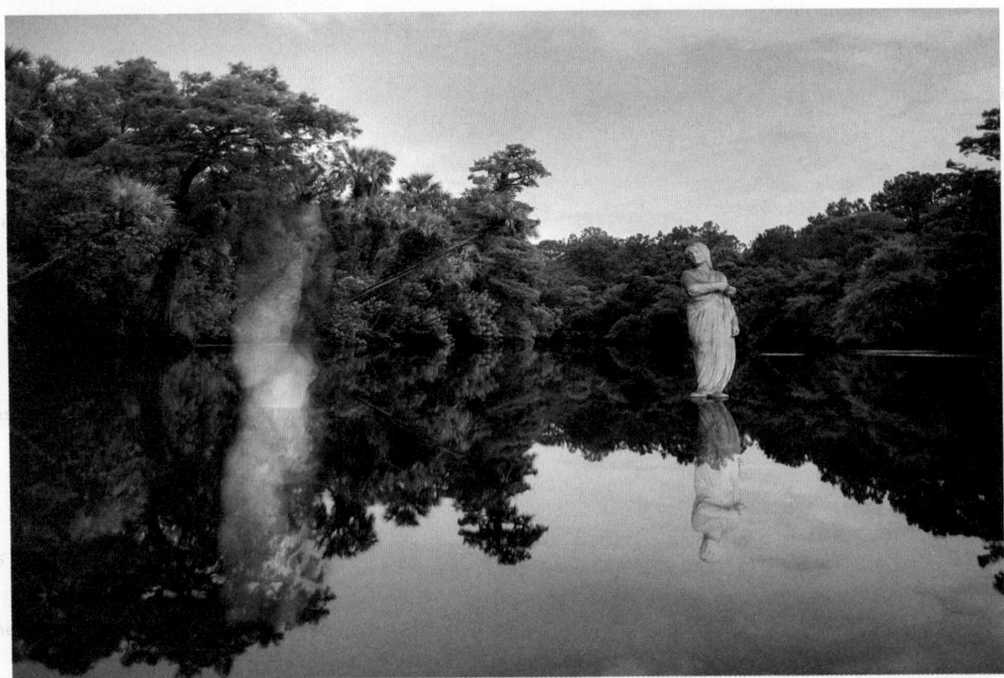

John Roloff, *Oracle of a Nightingale*. Nightingale image adapted from a sculpture by Francis William Sargant, 1913, courtesy of Anglim/Trimble Gallery, San Francisco, CA.

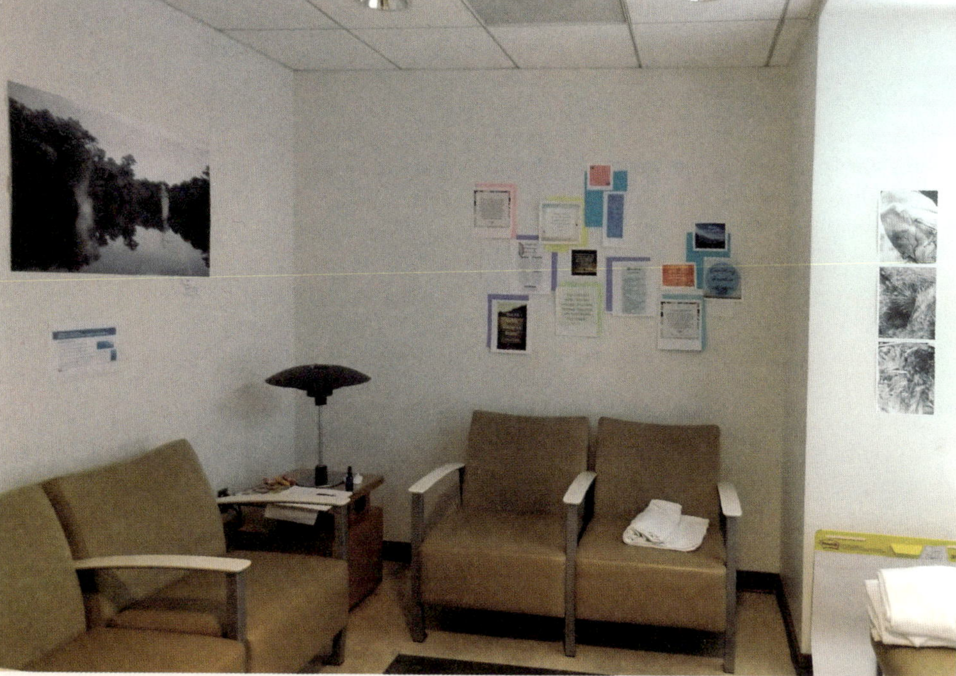

Examining the piece, you see a set of near symmetries playing out. And sitting in front of it over your private, maskless break in this small room meant searching through the image with your mind, and then maybe letting your eyes rest on the perfect water. I always wanted somehow to show how this piece worked for us, but my documentation of our beloved respite room doesn't do either justice. Like Florence, the piece itself was a lamp, tirelessly visiting us in our wounded and reclining time. The respite room is the space of reclining and dorsal rest for a kind of labor that is always up, alert, and inclining, ventrally searching for a sign.

John Roloff is known for a range of works, having worked in sculpture, ceramics, photography, and public installation for 40-plus years. If I were to speak casually about him, I would call him my Art Dad: he was my professor at the San Francisco Art Institute, where I received my MFA. Sadly, during the pandemic, the school closed permanently. After 150 years, and many near-death experiences, the school finally gave its last shuddering heave. Though for me, some upright, ventrally-oriented fire there still burns bright. Just like Florence's lamp and John's influence. ❁

BIO Catherine Fairbanks, an artist and a nurse, practices nursing at UCLA in the Medical ICU, and after receiving her MFA in sculpture from the San Francisco Art Institute, has attended residencies and produced national and international exhibitions.

est as resistance

CONTRIBUTION

Feathers and Wool

Why do we
follow them
like sheep in a flock,
allowing ourselves to be led to the edge
of nowhere,
without thinking
or speaking
or resisting,
even when our backs are breaking
and
our bodies heavy with the burdens of life:
loss, illness, fear, political division, racial injustice, financial hardship, environmental degradation, grief, othering and guilt—
that we carry squarely on our shoulders—
and the expectations
of family, friends, society, peers, colleagues, bosses, and even,
or especially,
of ourselves
hold us in place
conditioned to stand still in a pit of quicksand,
with docility
with obedience
even as our insides writhe in resentment and silent prayers of yearning
to be saved from being pulled under
once and for all.
And still,
we continue to wear our exhaustion
for all to see,
a badge of honor
fixed to the middle of our chest,
puffed out
like sage grouse gathering in the spring
hoping to attract others
to join us
on this hopeless journey
to the edge
of nowhere.

Who are they,
these shepherds
of white supremacy culture
who
control our Time,
and
place
urgency on
quantity over quality
binary thinking
no room for mistakes,
not caring that
our eyes heavy with sleep,

are awakened by bells and buzzers and
alarms that
racialize time
and
tell us
there is no rest for the wicked;
resistance is futile.

Our Time has always
belonged to them.

And so,
we move forward
with eyes open
through the fog
of capitalism
of materialism
not seeing,
simply following
these shepherds of white supremacy culture,
adopting their schedules,
serving their urgency,
willingly handing over
our Time—
ignoring
the value of this precious commodity—
our inherited birthright,
until one day
the fog clears
and our breath catches
as bells toll for our losses
and angry waves of regret
rise in fury and
batter our souls
leaving us to choose:

more of the same?
Or
something different?

What if we
instead of following like sheep,
started counting the sheep
wrapped in blankets of soft wool
nestled into billows of soft feathers,
eyes closed,
breath even,
reclaiming our bodies,
reclaiming our health,
reclaiming our dreams,
reclaiming our Time.
Which hasn't belonged to us for over four hundred years.
And now we

→

est as resistance

resist the old call
to follow and
our chests
puffed out
are trumpets of self-preservation,
announcing a new call
to rest
to dream
to resist
to imagine
a new way of life that
values rest
that values connection
that values our Time
spent in the comfort of feathers and wool.

BIO Dimple D. Dhabalia is the founder of Roots in the Clouds, a global consulting firm working to remove the stigma of workplace mental health and trauma, and author of *Tell Me My Story—Challenging the Narrative of Service Before Self*.

EDITORS' NOTE We included this concept in the initial list after learning about the work of performance artist Tricia Hersey, aka The Nap Minister, author of *Rest Is Resistance: A Manifesto*. Hersey's work has been vulnerable to co-optation, so it is important to locate it in the context of Afrofuturism and Black liberation. Thanks to Dimple for engaging with the concept poetically.
—ES & JC

polarity work
shadow integrati
theories of chang

Care as Revenge, Revenge as Care: Two Riddles

1.

FIRST: Under what conditions could *care* be a form of *revenge*? As we draw to the close of Madison Smartt Bell's magisterial fictionalized trilogy about the Haitian Revolution, we visit the pestilent scene of a makeshift field hospital in 1804. Here, French soldiers, sent by Napoleon to re-enslave the self-liberating Haitian people, lie dying in the thousands from the tropical Yellow Fever to the sound of the Caribbean Sea crashing against the rocks.

As CLR James explains in his classic history *The Black Jacobins*, the visionary Haitian revolutionary leader Toussaint L'Ouverture won that world-shaping struggle for freedom by strategically mobilizing the Caribbean climate and its microbial forms of life as weapons (like the mosquito-borne yellow fever) to help repel the armies of three great European imperial powers.[1]

In Bell's fictionalized account, a weary French doctor speaks to a volunteer nurse, the Creole Mme. Fortier, a character who, throughout the three novels, has suffered every depravity imaginable at the hands of whites. She, like other people of mixed ancestry, is now dangerously caught between the worlds of the revolution. The doctor asks her how she has the stamina to selflessly care for the invading soldiers when "bodies were half decomposed already by the time the doomed man drew his last breath"[2] and when these racist French men verbally abuse her even in their desperate last moments of delirium. Is it in the name of Christian charity and mercy? No, she replies.

"It does content me to watch them die, when I know I have done all I could to save them."[3]

Mme. Fortier's revenge is undertaken through a sacrificial act of care. She does not poison her wards, but nor does she keep them alive to prolong their misery: she has done all that she can for them. And in doing her utmost, in caring fiercely for her enemy, she is content. One bad interpretation of this passage is that her contentment stems from her personal satisfaction at a job well done, or that she has done all she can for another human being in need, in spite of being on the other side of a bloody and cruel war. We want to attribute a pure and ennobling morality to her. But a better interpretation reframes Mme. Fortier as a revolutionary, in an oblique solidarity with the enemies of those for whom she cares, those Haitian guerillas who would perhaps even kill her if they could. There is a wave-like, undulating movement of history, which pushes and pulls both Mme. Fortier, her doomed patients, and the revolutionary soldiers under L'Ouverture. She does all she can and it is not enough, and in doing it Mme. Fortier comes into communion with what (as Phanuel Antwi explains) the Jamaican poet and philosopher Kamau Brathwaite calls *tidalectics*:[4] the folding and folding and folding of history between moon, sea and land.

2.

Next: Under what conditions could *revenge* be a form of *care*? As a young working-class Catholic growing up in the '50s and '60s, Bobby Sands's life in Northern Ireland was plagued by Loyalist abuse and pogroms that forced his family to move several times and cost him his career in a factory.[5] When he joined the Provisional Irish Republican Army at 18, it was out of a sense of desperation: the British government's response to the vicious situation was to deepen the oppression, surveillance and militarization by police. This, in effect, allowed Loyalist thugs, vigilantes and paramilitaries to act with impunity. Five years after joining the IRA, Sands was arrested in the aftermath of the bombing of a furniture showroom and sentenced to 14 years in the infamous Maze Prison.

It was there, in response to petty and draconian new rules calculated to humiliate political prisoners like Sands and break the spirit of the IRA, that Sands and others began a series of non-violent protests. In 1976, they refused to wear clothes. In 1978, they escalated their tactics to refuse to clean their cells or themselves. In 1981, he and others initiated one of the most famous hunger strikes in world history, which would result in his death 66 days later. During that time, the poet Sands, the initiator and charismatic face of the strike, was elected as a member of Parliament to represent Sinn Fein, helping to open the door to a non-violent electoral strategy for the Republican cause. His death was an international scandal with deep ramifications. His funeral was attended by 100,000 mourners in Belfast, where his grave is still venerated. There followed acts and gestures of solidarity around the world. The bloodiest years of The Troubles lay ahead. In spite of the fact that he never renounced or condemned violence, Sands was and is venerated as a non-violent martyr.

The most memorable of Sands's phrases, "Our revenge will be the laughter of our children," can still be seen on murals in Northern Ireland. It echoes an older adage, that "living well is the best revenge," often ascribed (ironically, for Sands) to 17th-century Anglican priest and poet George Herbert, although he himself admits it already existed as a proverb.[6] No matter the attribution, the phrase resonates with an interpretation of Christian scripture in which Jesus instructs his oppressed followers to "turn the other cheek" and lead a virtuous life, trusting to God to right wrongs at Judgment Day.

But Sands's revenge here implicitly and contextually rejects passivity and is resolutely secular. It necessarily evokes the moment of after-care: children laugh when they are safe, nurtured, carefree and perceive themselves to have a future (although much, too, could be said about children's and other people's cruel laughter). While revenge often brings to our imaginations connotations of hot, swift violence, Sands's vision of a care-full revenge is glacially slow and cool, taking generations to form and move. But like a glacier, such care-revenge is not inherently non-violent: it reshapes society, leveling mountains, depositing new earthworks, cutting new paths towards the sea before receding to reveal a new country that, today, cannot exist on any map.[7]

3.

Both these examples might help us move beyond the politically useless and conceptually bankrupt association of care with "good vibes only." If we want a world that cares, we should not sacrifice a consideration of the complexity of violence and destruction on the altar of our narcissistic allergy to discomfort. Clearing space for, then cultivating, then harvesting the fruits of a world that cares, or a caring world, will require a meaningful engagement with what must be destroyed. There are humans and non-humans who benefit from the current order, for example, the corporate CEOs and novel zoonotic viruses that profit from factory animal "farming"; these lifeforms will necessarily be harmed in the making of a better future, and that is a good thing. That harm cannot be separated from a complex form of care. Bringing revenge into proximity with care can help us dwell with these troubling realities, which we would ignore at our grave peril. ❁

1 James, *The Black Jacobins*.

2 Bell, *The Stone That the Builder Refused*, 671.

3 Bell, *The Stone That the Builder Refused*, 672.

4 Antwi, *On Cuddling: Loved to Death in the Racial Embrace*.

5 Yuill, "The Body as Weapon: Bobby Sands and the Republican Hunger Strikes."

6 Herbert, *Outlandish Proverbs*.

7 Haiven, *Revenge Capitalism*.

BIO

Max Haiven is a writer, teacher, editor and Canada Research Chair in the Radical Imagination at Lakehead University.

evolutionary mothering

CONTRIBUTION

I'M NOT SURE HOW MUCH the Zoom room can hold. But it's holding—we're holding. There are four of us here, or three, or sometimes just two—whoever has a minute between feedings, meetings, lunch prep, class prep, writing sessions, meltdowns. We use institutional logins, but right now we are not on the clock. A child's face pops in while we're talking about something serious. A teenager in the background gets indignant when we laugh too loudly.

We are fucking mad at the world, and we are grieving, and we are loving on each other. We're talking about poetry, and organizing, and prison abolition. We're talking about sleep and snacks and society anxiety, sexuality and aging bodies and elder care and depression and breakups and heartbreaks and weaning and gender transition, parent loss and partner loss and climate grief. And pretty much every time we log on, we are asking a version of the same question. Sometimes implicitly, sometimes out loud. *How do we care for children, and each other, in the face of forces that are hostile to our thriving, if not our very survival? How do we sustain each other through the unevenly distributed effects of a climate catastrophe brought on and enabled by the architects of colonialism and global racial capitalism? How do we—through our most intimate practices of caring, which are also political practices—build the world we want to inhabit?*

Revolutionary mothering names practices handed down through generations of radical feminists of color and queer activists committed to resisting interwoven structures of heteropatriarchy, racism, colonialism, and capitalism. It seeks to interrupt the ways in which many of us are habituated into patterns of domination and submission from our earliest moments, in the smallest interactions between parent and child, as well as in the larger systems of power we learn to navigate. *Mothering* as a verb: an ongoing act of nurturance and liberation, not a fixed identity or biological imperative. As Alexis Pauline Gumbs notes in her introduction to the foundational 2016 volume *Revolutionary Mothering: Love on the Front Lines*, mothering is a practice both "older and more futuristic than the category 'woman.'"[1] Revolutionary mothering looks askance at the simultaneously sentimentalized and devalued category of mother, which it knows is a trap, a tool for building an entire economy on unpaid and underpaid labor. In its place, revolutionary mothering offers something queerer and more expansive. My friend Jack calls it "big mom energy": an energetic practice that people of any gender can and do inhabit, whether or not they are parents, though heteropatriarchy ensures that mothering is most often performed by (and demanded of) women and femmes.

Revolutionary mothering resists this frame, while retaining the political and transformative power of care work. The "revolution" in revolutionary mothering helps us name the connection between care work and the practice of freedom—the idea that we might transform society in part by transforming our relationships to children and to one another. That is, if children are how society reproduces itself, our relationships to children are the site where we might transform society. Revolutionary mothering suggests our care for children can help model—and in turn create—practices rooted in radical love and nurturance without manipulation or domination.

Revolutionary mothering is a practice of fostering what June Jordan calls "the creative spirit," the irrepressible but often repressed life-force of children—the breadth of their imagining, the freedom of their visions, the

SEE:
cestrality
ti-adultism
re pods
oalition
llective care
feminism

love
mutual aid
prison abolition
radical childcare in movement spaces
temporary autonomous zones
theories of change

radical openness of their hearts.[2] As anyone who cares for children will recognize, this is exhausting and often soul-stretching work; and in a society that prizes the isolating structure of the nuclear family, it can often seem like parenting and political organizing are materially opposed to one another. But this is what makes the radically collaborative, queer, and horizontal work of revolutionary mothering all the more needful (when Jack arrives at my house at 6:30 a.m. to care for my children while I drive to the local prison for a meeting with collaborators, they're giving big mom energy). We do not, indeed cannot, carry the weight alone.

Working from the acknowledgement that our fates are interconnected (a core tenet of many intersecting justice movements), revolutionary mothering refuses the (white) nuclear family as a unit for the reproduction and accumulation of capital. Instead, it situates care as a political force of mutual recognition and liberation. Under this vision, children are not property—a logic of ownership that underwrote the regime of racial slavery, under which the children of enslaved people were deemed the property of their white enslavers, and the capacity to own property was in turn a racialized signifier of the human.[3] Revolutionary mothering refuses this logic, while insisting on the rights of Black and indigenous and immigrant and poor and queer and disabled mothers to parent their children without fear. And while the US state has practiced family separation as a technique of oppression since its founding—from enslaved and indigenous families, to refugees arriving at the US-Mexico border, to mass incarceration, to police murders of Black children—revolutionary mothering counters with the political force of a love that refuses cages and borders, and that collectively demands their abolition.

In this way, revolutionary mothering insists that the scales of political action, from the smallest acts of care to the largest social movements, are deeply connected. If its enactments are intimate and local, its impacts are global—perhaps immeasurable. As Jordan suggests, empowering children is a political project, as is the search for more loving and less destructive ways to inhabit the planet. "To accomplish such lifesaving alterations of society," she writes, "we will have to deal with power: we will have to make love powerful."[4] Revolutionary mothering means dealing with power, and it means making love powerful. It means we are tasked with caring for each other for our collective survival. So we love, and grieve, and plan, and get shit done, while holding each other's babies, while holding each other. ❁

1 Gumbs, *Revolutionary Mothering*, 9.

2 Jordan, "The Creative Spirit: Children's Literature," 11.

3 See Harris, "Whiteness as Property" and Hortense J. Spillers, "Mama's Baby, Papa's Maybe."

4 Jordan, "The Creative Spirit," 11–12.

B Lindsay Reckson (she/her)
I is a writer, professor, and
O parent.

Rituals: Power for the Young

CONTRIBUTION

EVERY DAY WE RUN THROUGH the self-initiated rituals, series of actions, and behaviors ingrained into our lives that give us a sense of familiarity, comfort, and structure. For some, these rituals are unconscious; for others, they are deliberately created.

For the patients I do art therapy with, their rituals are born out of necessity, a way to fight and survive. A two- or three-year-old might not have the ability to understand why they must be invasively accessed for chemo. In order to cope with the often painful aspects of treatment, they've built rituals that they can control. Rituals for these pediatric patients at my hospital clinic means stacking cups until they fit right on their shelf. It means peeling the backs off stickers, putting them in a designated "trash cup," and then placing them onto her arms. It means scribbling on paper while asking a million questions about the hospital space to establish safety before a medical procedure. It means creating these small rituals to claim a tiny bit of this hospital space for their own, using a ritual created and owned by them, utilizing their autonomy to create an assemblage of control before being placed into an often scary and powerless position.

For the children I work with, building these rituals means creating rhythms of familiarity that feel safe and grounding. Rituals help them endure the day. Together we manage moment by moment, but we always hold space for the rituals. ❁

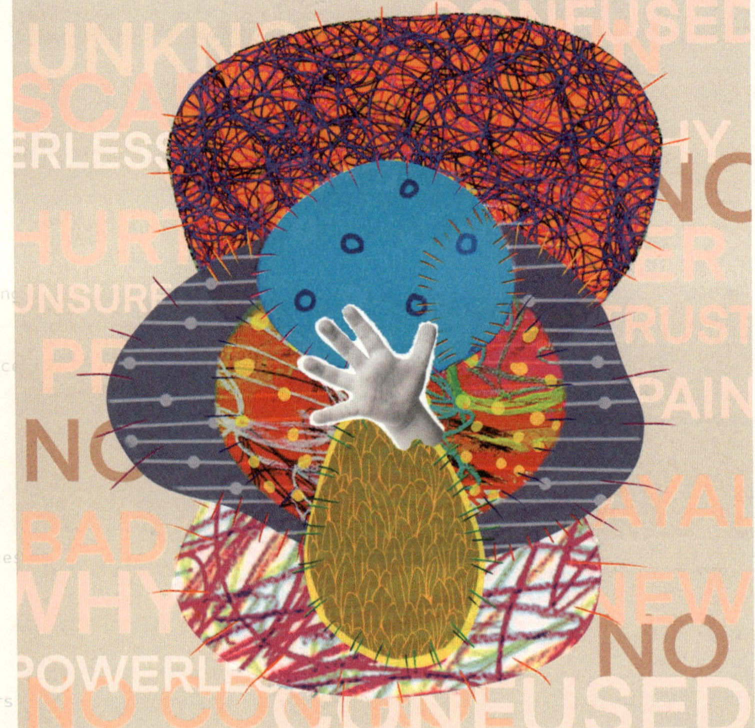

Sara Cantrell, Mixed Media, 2022.

BIO

Sara Cantrell, MA, ATR-P, LGPAT, LGPC, is an Art Therapist for a Pediatric Hematology/Oncology clinic at a Military Hospital who is passionate about using art to create space for voices to be heard, to learn more about oneself, to find opportunities for advocacy, and to foster community.

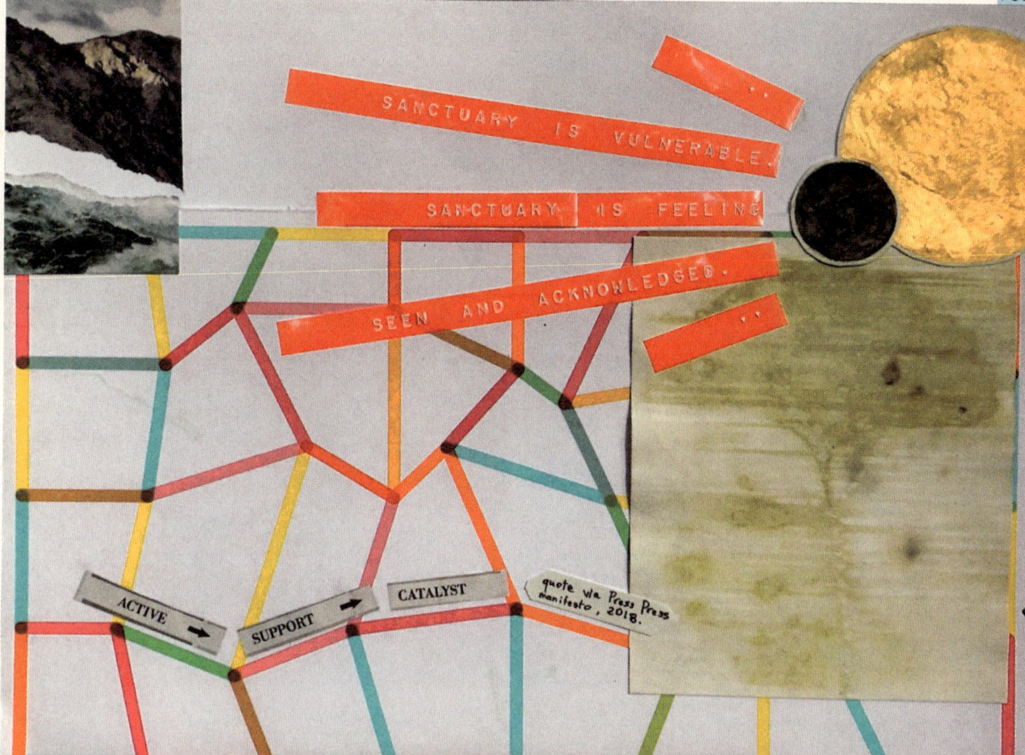

Mixed-media collage, 2023[1]

1 Quotation from Press Press, "Sanctuary: A Manifesto."

BIO Tanya Paperny is a writer, editor, translator, artist, and community builder in Washington, DC—learn more at tpaperny.com.

Sandplay therapy

CONTRIBUTION

Sandplay

Sandplay, 2021. Martín La Roche & Mirthe Berentsen. Wooden sandbox, 4 x 5 metres and 1500 kg of sand. Photos courtesy of the artists.

SANDPLAY is a collaborative artwork between artist Martín La Roche and writer and artist Mirthe Berentsen, who both participated in the artist-in-residence program from the Dutch organization Beautiful Distress at the psychiatric department of the Kings County Hospital in Brooklyn, New York in 2018–2019 and 2017 respectively. In our collaborative works and sessions with clients, therapists, and hospital staff, we were confronted with the limitations of language and the implications these have on care and recovery.

Our journey resulted in the collaborative artwork *Sandplay*. We take the tradition of sandplay therapy, bringing it to an art context by following certain steps, but changing others. For instance, one remarkable change is that we enlarge the sandbox. This is crucial, because the intimate space that this therapy creates in our installation becomes a collective arena where positions are challenged and memories and objects need to be collectively negotiated and resolved by playing. The provisional results of the process are not analyzed, nor are they functional to a medical model. We are thinking of in-between modes of participation, in which you can be part of the artwork/art process, elaborate some object configurations/images/verbal particles, and be part of this collective playing-reshaping—but your engagement is not entirely archived or documented (non-archivable knowledge). Many of the images, objects, configurations, and sentences are part of the process and then erased or exchanged with new configurations in new sandplay sessions.

A diverse repertoire of objects for participants to engage with is an essential component of any *sandplay*. We, the two artists, use our own collections of objects and memories as departure points. La Roche exhibits a part of his extensive collection, with various found objects of different provenances, usually on smaller scales, all stored in a system of boxes. This collection reflects his interest in diverse collection and archival methods, emphasizing the importance of personal narratives in the construction of collective memory. For instance, objects like a folded napkin, a stone figure, and a fan coexist inside a box, waiting to be unfolded.

Berentsen uses her personal memories of clearing out her parental home after their death as a point of departure. She photographed the process of throwing away the domestic residues of a life, all the while questioning the materiality of grief and the value of the objects we choose as companions during life. These pictures serve as models to create replicas of the discarded objects, such as shells, her mother's nightgown, and a spoon. The replicas are crafted in ceramics and felt, materials often used in the context of creative therapy, and presented on a long table where they all have their own outline. During the sandplay, the objects are taken from the table, where the silhouette of the object seems to emphasize that it stems from a memory.

Sandplay deals with the subjective value of memory, questioning the constructability of language and translating memories, texts, and even words into tangible objects. In the exhibition, the personal memories and subjective associations of the artists became part of a collective experience. This translation into the collective domain took place in a sandbox where visitors were welcome to sit down and play with the artworks and objects from the exhibition. This concept draws inspiration from the Jungian sandplay therapy developed by psychoanalyst Dora Kalff in the 1950s. During this therapy objects are freely placed in a sandbox to create new narratives and overcome trauma, especially when it seems impossible to translate emotions into words.

The sandbox in our installation is activated through "I Remember" sessions, during which objects are linked to personal memories and then freely placed in the sand to create new shared narratives. In the sessions, we give workshops based on prompts from Joe Brainard's famous 1975 book of the same title. Using objects from both our collections, but above all the memories of the participants, we write down thoughts and memories, after which the objects are placed in the sandbox. This creates a

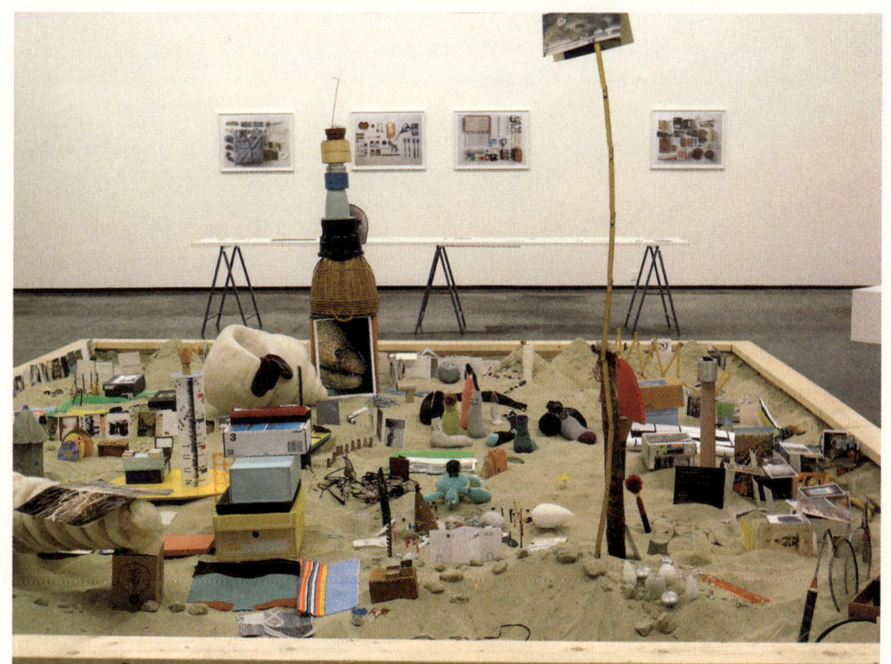

➔

narrative therapy
relationali
social practic
social therapeutic
somatic healin
symbo
wishes

collective experience in which personal memories are activated and transformed into a shared experience and new narratives. In 2021 the collaborative *Sandplay* was first exhibited at the exhibition "I remember" in Amsterdam, the Netherlands, at Beautiful Distress Foundation (2021–2022) and was thereafter presented in Museum Ludwig Koblenz in Germany (2023) and Miriam Gallery in Brooklyn, NYC, USA (2023), among others.

For more information: martinlaroche.nl & mirtheberentsen.com & beautifuldistress.org/blog/i-remember-by-mirthe-berentsen-amp-martin-la-roche-contreras-ykcg8. ❂

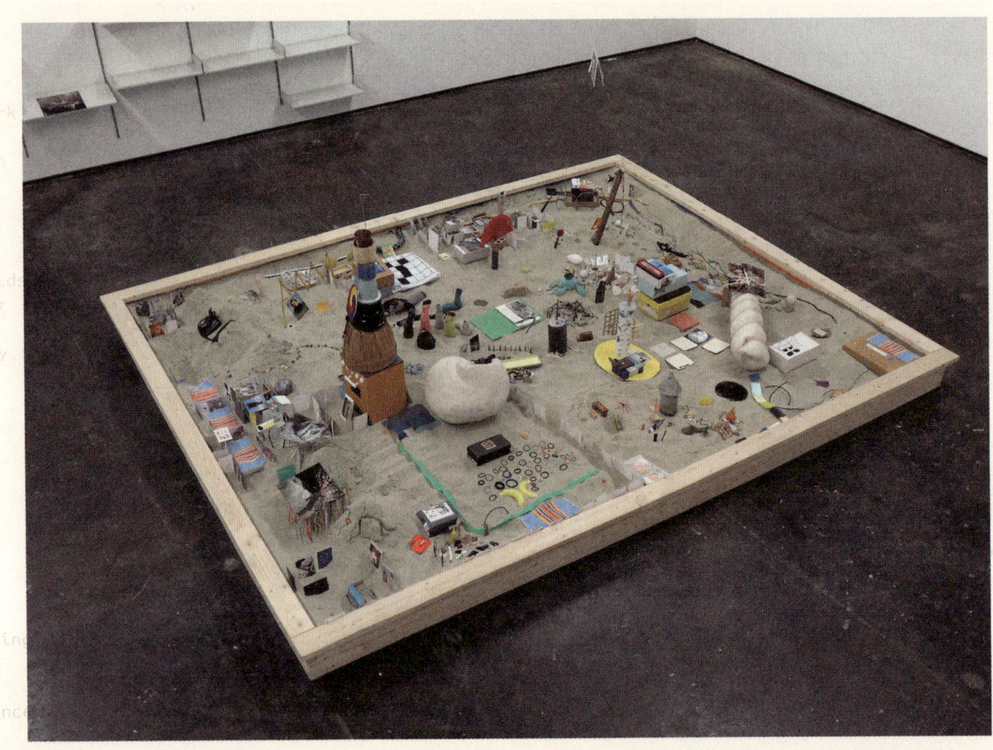

BIOS

Mirthe Berentsen exists in many forms and places.

Martín La Roche lives in Amsterdam and comes back often to Santiago de Chile.

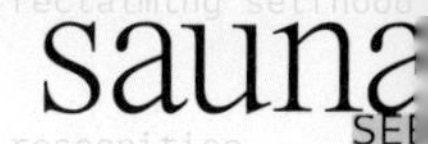

CONTRIBUTORS' NOTE

We know *sauna* as a heated room in which to relax and enjoy warmth. Sauna in Finland has also been the place where babies were born, the sick treated, the dying brought to transition. It has been a place for celebrating milestones and mourning losses, for occasional events and everyday living. To this day, sauna is a place where leaders gather after a meeting, where family members sit in silence or share something vulnerable, where one goes alone to meditate, pray, or just be.

My personal deepening into the medicine of sauna started after experiencing a disorienting shock a few years ago. Along this trauma-healing journey, I was initiated into the mysticism of sauna as an alchemical cauldron where all elements—fire, earth, water, and air—play their part to result in "löyly." Löyly is the term used in contemporary Finnish to speak of heating the sauna by throwing water on hot stones; it has also meant "the spirit of sauna" in the past. Really it is a fifth element in this space that is essentially one of transformation. —AP

CONTRIBUTION

"When I Am Done"

When I'm done getting us undressed
Rinsed, with cool water,
Hydrated, when I've put aside
my phone close enough to check the time
far enough to stay dry
Closed the door
Spread towels over the warm slats
Given my son the anticipated bucket
to play with
filled with water
Fetched the other bucket not anticipated
the one he now says he likes better
When I have made sure he sits on the
  lower bench
on the side farthest from the stove
When I have wiped a few cold splashes
  from my leg
slowed my breath

I deliver my body full length
to flatness
limbs unfolding here and here
angles to lines
Under the thousand eyes of wood spirits
I resume being me
Scrolls of ancient stories rolling
from my insides spreading
over continents
Miniature fetus positions opening
Lava and lava again
There is so much of me
As my organs and bones move
a millionth of a millimetre
and new constellations are born
alignments unexpected
spaces wide and claimed

In the places where I thought life was
laughing at my expense
the worn parts, achy, dull
A timeless laughter I now join
"Look you are here here and here
and forever"
It's hilarious
and expensive
but the currency is everywhere

And here bare under the thousand eyes
of the wood witnesses
the craziest trick one can ever perform
I gather my body into angles and
movement
sit up, take a step
and help my child along the flow of time.

→

"Heat"

The first shhhhh the harsh burst
after the splash of water on stones
shuts the body
eyelids close tight – hands on face – muscles harden –
pores close
don't let it in don't
the sudden intensity
No
But you stay
still
stirred
grows something else
a heat so gentle
surrounding, pervading
opening pores, melting muscles
skin to skin with the tissues of truth
sweating surrender
like the sap of these pine walls
air fire water earth make me digestible
goo
in the oven of time
The heat grows sweet and steady
enveloping, unavoidable
freeing
Yes

"Sauna Sanity"

Grandmother sauna receives me
holds my body in air dense
with silence and heat
Here, fire chases water
pushing out of the body
tears unshed
nameless sorrows
worries and fears unsweated
ground waters,
Here, wood welcomes my weight
pine wisdom singing to my body
braiding its fibres, its resinous scent
to mine,
Here is a place of remembering
in the soothingly dark realm of stillness

With every hush of the hot stones
she fills the space with stories and secrets
Grandmother sauna
She knows our bones and those
of our ancestors
She wrings our core knowing
awakens our marrow

She says that our incarnation is precious,
that some things are contained
so they can expand,
that safety allows the wildness of the heart,
that there is a place of silence within and
how beautiful when it is shared

Here, with every water thrown on the stones
the air transforms
I dissolve
into listening

B I O Anne Paré's work embraces art, healing, and mysticism, steeped in the belief that we can contribute to a sane world by tending to all our relations.

eed banking

CONTRIBUTION

DEAR READER,

Seed banking is both a preparation for the future and an extension of the ways we relate with the plants around us.

When you Google "seed banking," the main articles highlight large and small storage facilities containing catalogues of seed varieties to protect the diversity of plant species. This is increasingly important as the global climate changes and our environments begin to adapt to survive under increasingly warm conditions. What's most exciting is that anyone can seed bank! All it requires is the harvesting and preserving of seeds, which can be done with any organic fruits, vegetables, legumes, etc.

I first came across the process of seed banking in a science fiction short story titled "Deer Dancer" by Kathleen Alcalá in the anthology *New Suns: Original Speculative Fiction by People of Color*. I started reading high volumes of science fiction in the hopes of finding an anchor, or a balm, or any form of true hope to navigate my climate anxiety, as well as all my other anxieties that coalesce around imagining the future. (For those who are also still searching, I *highly* recommend *New Suns* as well as the anthology *Love after the End*). Woven throughout the story are characters with names like Chia, and all characters have an awareness of the flora around them—nettles, salal, salmonberry. The final moments in "Deer Dancer" are of the main character, Tater, finding hope in her history, her culture knowledge, and deciding that if she ever had a daughter, she would name her after the Peruvian indigenous potato Ozette. Under what seems like bleak circumstances, food and seeds represent hope for the future, of more beginnings.

In a world dominated by a country running itself into the ground in the name of capitalism, it is difficult to evaluate and properly identify *value*. Most of my life has revolved around career, success, and celebrity as some of the most valuable currencies. But in imagining a "dystopian" future where survival—food, water, shelter, safety—is the primary focus, notoriety and acclaim quickly lose their value. This short story reoriented the axis on which I measured value. And seeds—seeds are hope; seeds are sustenance; seeds are proof of care. Seeds will always be valuable.

Seed banking is also a way of introducing yourself to a plant. For most gardeners, seed banking is a step that is left to corporations and manufacturers. Having your own seed bank and getting involved in community seed banking efforts allows you to meet the plant in every stage of its life cycle.

The way that I have seed banked looked like going to my local farmers market and buying corn. And when I got home, I boiled all but one of the cobs. The one cob that I did not cook was strung up and left to air dry. After a few weeks and the kernels were completely dry, I harvested them into a container that now sits in my pantry.

I have volunteered at a food forest, where I had the very incredible opportunity to harvest seeds from a variety of Oregon sunflower to preserve for a later season. The work of seed harvesting is simple and repetitive, which on a factory line would be mind-numbing. However, in the company of other people, sitting, harvesting, under the noon sun, caring about this particular plant, a lovely scene forms. The simplicity and repetition of the task, instead of becoming tedious, requires only the barest amounts of focus, which means that you and everyone else with you get to talk and laugh and cry and share wisdom and share silence. Time no longer feels oppressive, the seeds do not know about billable hours or weekdays and weekends or even

-ofuturism
imate cafes
mmons, the
food sovereignty
groups
infinite blackness
life cycle, honoring the

the forsaken invention of seconds. The only time the seeds know are the days, the seasons—and you start to feel that freedom too, sitting there, harvesting seeds for another annum.

Sincerely,
Emma Cooper

P.S. I am no expert, but I largely try to preserve seeds from produce that I can get at a farmer's market or from anywhere where I know that the produce is likely farmed as organically as possible, since that is what will be reproduced. ❁

BIO Emma Cooper lives in Seattle, is currently pursuing an MSW, and loves the rain.

ex positivity

E:
ng positivity
ernative
entity projects
dy positivity
curiosity
fat positivity
feminism
freedom

CONTRIBUTION

SEX POSITIVITY is a non-judgmental, open-minded, and expansive attitude toward sex. With consent—given directly, freely, and knowingly—at its core, sex positivity seeks to normalize the diversity of human sexuality. Sex positivity affirms our human right to pleasure and intimacy and fights back against the ideologies that use sex as a means of shame and control. Sex positivity is about accepting and allowing ourselves and others freedom of sexual thought, identity, orientation, expression, and behavior.

For many, sex positivity means unlearning conscious and unconscious negative beliefs and attitudes toward sexuality and sexual expression. Sex positivity asks us to take out the hierarchy and taboos and approach the full menu of human sexuality and sensuality with open-minded curiosity. Even if not everything is your thing or you just can't understand why someone would do that. For example, I cannot imagine why someone would want to go bungee jumping—and the idea of going on a cruise makes me cringe. But I understand that many people enjoy these activities and find the risks worth it.

In order to move toward accepting the diversity of human sexuality, we can start by questioning our assumptions of who sex is for, what they're allowed to do—and then continue on to the when, how, why, and where of sex. You may already not agree with the statement that "sex should happen only between a man and a woman who are married," but there are likely more assumptions in that statement than we realize. Sex positivity means recognizing and letting go of the patriarchal, heteronormative, monogamy-based hierarchy of sex. Shifting away from these ways of thinking about sex can be uncomfortable, but it helps to remember that just because something is strange, weird, or different does not mean it's bad.

Sex positivity is for everyone and does not discriminate based on race, age, class, culture, and ability. Sex positivity promotes a respect for the diversity of sexual identities, orientations, relationship structures, and behaviors. Whether you're 20 or 80 years old, whether you prefer one partner, many, or just yourself, you deserve to explore desire and intimacy. Sex positivity means de-stigmatizing what might be called deviant and normalizing different sexual thoughts and feelings. And if you have no interest in sex, that's okay too.

With acceptance comes better communication, inclusive information, and accurate education. Sex positivity promotes inclusive health care that supports sexual and reproductive rights. Sex positivity is about letting go of judgment surrounding accessories, products, and services that support sexual pleasure and sexual health. Sex positive education means giving all the information individuals need to make the best decisions for themselves. Looking back over my life I know that my attitudes and beliefs around sex have shifted with more knowledge, exposure, and understanding.

Even with support and education, sometimes things don't go as planned, so sex positivity asks us to take away the shaming of unintended consequences. When we bring in kindness, respect, and acceptance to the conversation about sex, we make space for authenticity. Humans are messy, awkward creatures, and in order to have authentic negotiation and communication around sex we need to create a safe environment for vulnerability.

Sex positivity is about freedom. The freedom to have sex or not have sex. The freedom to have comprehensive sex education. The freedom to communicate about sex without judgment. The freedom to express and explore your sexuality in fantasy and reality. The freedom to let your wants and needs change with time. The freedom to understand and have access to all your sexual health needs. The freedom to ask, "Is this normal?" and seek professional help when you encounter personal obstacles to sexual well-being such as pain and insecurity. It doesn't mean everyone must like and have sex. It means we are all free to say yes or no to sexual exploration, and to be treated with respect and kindness when we do so.

You deserve to find intimacy and connection through sex. You deserve to approach sex from a place of playfulness, curiosity, and joy. And since you deserve the promise of sex positivity, maybe I do too. While you will never find me bungee jumping, maybe one day with the right people and in the right situation, you'll find me enjoying myself on a cruise. ❁

B Maya Druckmann (she/
I her) is a psychotherapist
O in Los Angeles.

CONTRIBUTION

Desire & Don't Like: A Mandorla[1]

To transform opposition into paradox is to allow both sides of an issue, both pairs of opposites, to exist in equal dignity and worth... If I can stay with my conflicting impulses long enough, the two opposing forces will teach each other something and produce an insight that serves them both.[2]

All good stories are mandorlas. They speak of this and that and gradually, through the miracle of story, demonstrate that the opposites overlap and are finally the same. We like to think that a story is based on the triumph of good over evil; but the deeper truth is that good and evil are superseded and the two become one. Since our capacity for synthesis is limited, many stories can only hint at this unity. But any unity, even a hint, is healing.[3]—Robert A. Johnson

I'VE USED the following questions with coaching clients to explore different and opposing parts of themselves. The questions invite "desire" and "don't like" personas to speak to one another, which encourages paradox and play. Below, I've journaled my own answers to each question to provide a model.

Describe the desire and the self you become when this desire is fulfilled. What name would you give this self?

To live on my own in an inspiring environment that is minimal, lean, funky, with lots of space, no clutter, and a pool. I'd feel safe, comfortable, at ease with myself. I'd give myself permission to do nothing but also be creative and therefore spend time making things that inspire me, like crafts with my hands, painting, and writing. I'd have a community of friends who inspire me by how they live their lives. I am relaxed, at ease in my own skin, and with my friends. I balance time alone and with them. I'd be willing to take risks by being honest and vulnerable and allowing for play. The me who lives this life is confident and willing to be uncomfortable to create the life she wants and doesn't act from guilt or shame. She knows what she wants and listens and follows her desires. She is a white-shrouded figure with tendrils of a green plant wrapped around her body. Her name is Green.

Describe the "don't like" and the self you become when experiencing this don't like situation. What name would you give this self?

Afraid. Tentative. Wants approval. Avoids risk. Won't speak up for what she wants. Feels disconnected from her environment and does not feel at home in her space. Is withdrawn a lot of the time. Doesn't trust herself and doesn't often know her own needs as a result. She limits her actions and spends a lot of time blaming others for her unhappiness. She uses past mistakes as ways to shame herself and keep herself frozen. She likes to escape in her head and tell herself stories about what a victim she is. She likes being miserable. She is especially attracted to mistakes and when things go wrong. She likes to replay those experiences because it feels powerful and gives her strength to say so and see it. She's Medusa. All in gray and black. She looks like a black-and-white photo, chalky and dead looking. Snakes wrapped around her body. Smiling in disgust.

What do they have in common?

They are both confident. They both put themselves first. They are both connected to others, but Green wants joyful connection and Medusa wants painful connection. They are both creative and enjoy story and value inspiration. They also long for certainty and like to simplify themselves, their lives, and their relationships. Green has tendrils of plants that coil and grow around her trunk in the same way that Medusa has gray snakes twisting and wrapping around hers. The plants and snakes are moving and circling each of them and that feels potent and essential to their power, serving both as protection and identity.

Get them to talk. What do they want to teach the other? Want *for* the other?

Green to Medusa: You're not as bad as you think you are. In fact, I think you like "being bad" to avoid doing anything other than what you already know and control. I want you to know I don't mind you, though. I enjoy your power. I think you look cool. You're inspiring and kind of badass. If I could teach you something, it would be that you can use your power in ways that don't feel quite so heavy and hard. But it will mean you try something new or see things from a different perspective. I want you to know what it feels like to not know. It's not what you think. It's not empty in the way you imagine. Yes, I want you to see in all your knowing, you still don't know. You know one part and that's good, that's needed. But there's more and it won't hurt you.

Medusa to Green: You're not as pure as you think you are. You don't know everything either. I don't like your smugness and I think you can be greedy and just as self-involved as you think I am. It's not that I don't want the things that you want, but I do want you to see and admit that no actions and desires and pursuits are innocent, that having that life will leave other lives and people behind. Your desires are not without harm or blame. I want you to consider this when you make your decisions, even if you don't change what you want! Yes, you don't have to change the decision, I just want you to consider your impact before doing whatever it is you want to do because it's not always about you.

Although this journal is significantly compressed and edited to address privacy and word count limits, the results continue to surprise me. Yes, I've been surprised by the rich imagery and self-healing that emerges when using this process with clients, but I didn't anticipate such depths on my own. The mandorla itself is surprising: how the unconscious offers such clear and unexpected answers; how it communicates with color, story, and persona; how the frame of similarity between opposites reveals wholeness where there was perceived division. I'm especially surprised to report that months after writing this forgotten entry, I've since moved to a minimal, uncluttered space with a pool. Perhaps less surprising, being "on my own" is "not without harm or blame." Yet, it's comforting to remember Green's and Medusa's compassion for one another. Their conversation and kindness hints at a unity that serves them both. ❁

1

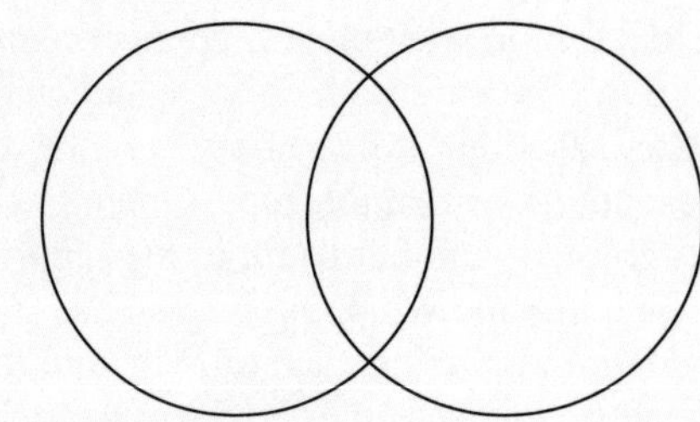

2 Johnson, *Owning Your Own Shadow: Understanding the Dark Side of the Psyche*, 86.

3 Johnson, *Owning Your Own Shadow: Understanding the Dark Side of the Psyche*, 107.

BIO Michelle Jewett is a coach, teacher educator, and rogue scholar currently focused on tarot hermeneutics, edusemiotics, and using mythopoetic inquiry for reflection, integration, and self-healing.

Sick Woman Theory

EDITORS' NOTE

Sick Woman Theory, articulated in a 2016/2020 essay of the same name by Johanna Hedva, politicizes chronic pain and emphasizes vulnerability and precarity. The images and six-word memoir that comprise this encyclopedia entry arrived at Erin's house in March of 2023 in a package from Deb Toscano-Knicos, who sends international and domestic mail art. In an enclosed note, Deb explained that she had never heard of Sick Woman Theory until she discovered our call for *Encyclopedia* entries, and "…became curious and dived in deep, glad and rather astonished at times that I did. I, too, experience life-long health issues that I live with and battle every day. This was perfect how I came to find your open call for contributions. But I have to say I really believe this topic found me. A kind of synchronicity—" —ES & CH, with DK

CONTRIBUTION

SIX-WORD MEMOIR: vulnerable. chronic. but first make visible.

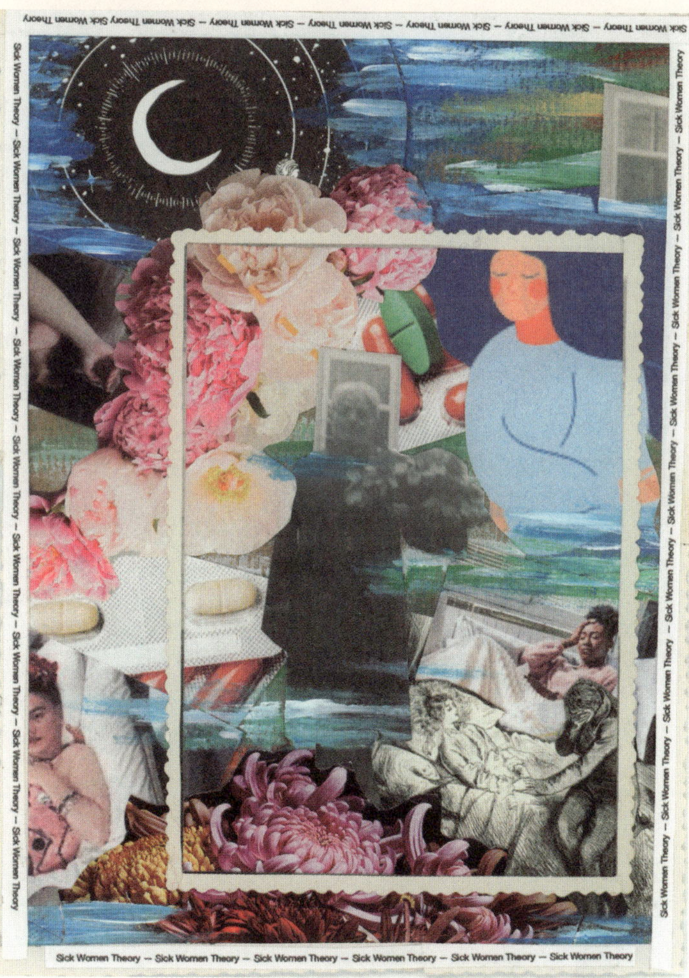

Deb Toscano-Knicos, *Delicate Flower*, March, 2023. Collage. Copy paper, magazine pictures, photographs, acrylic paint, cardboard, glue stick, 5.25 x 7.25 in.

→

Sick Woman Theory

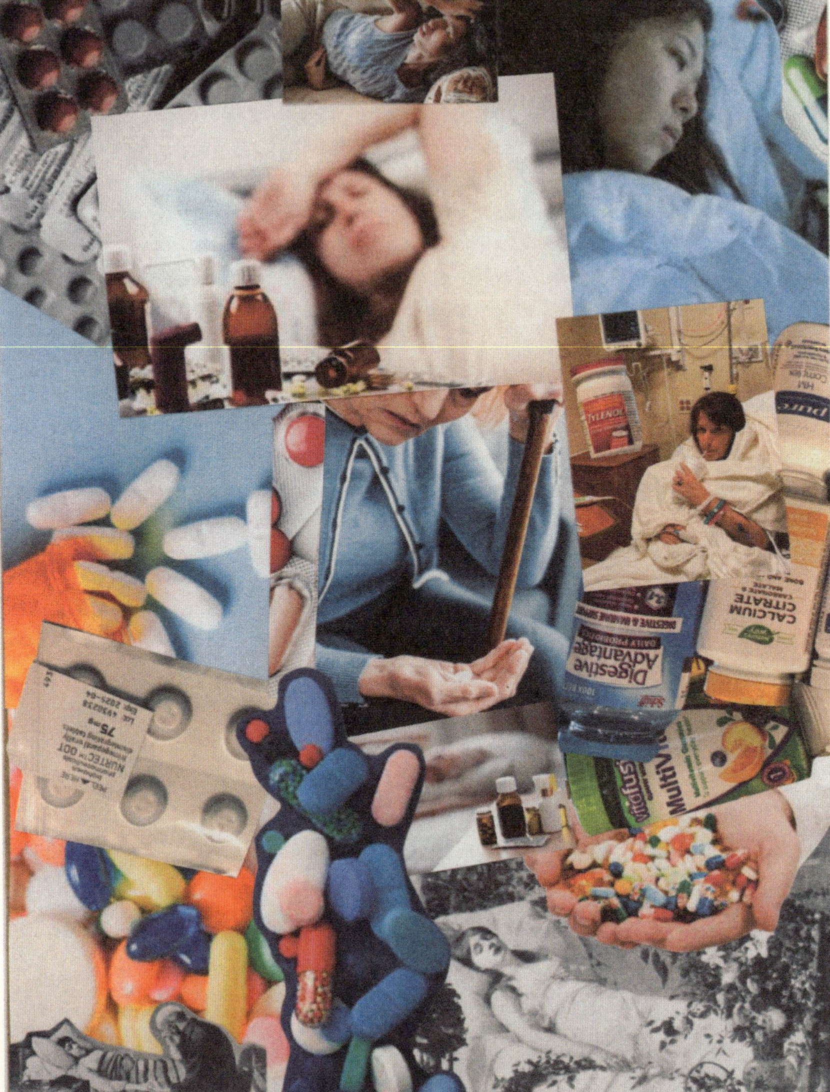

Deb Toscano-Knicos, *Sick Woman Theory Collage #1*, March, 2023. Collage. Copy paper, magazine pictures, photographs, cardboard, glue stick, 6 x 8.5 in.

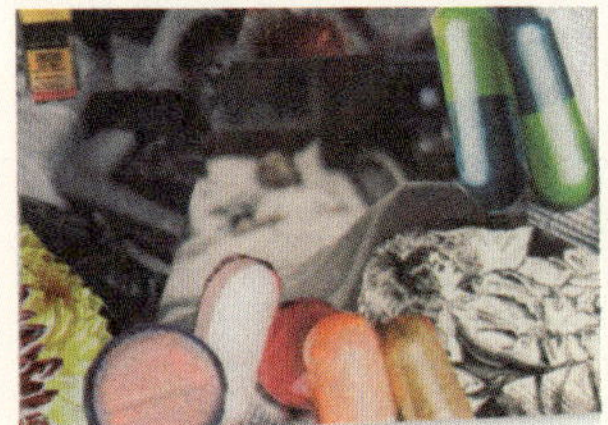

Deb Toscano-Knicos, *Bed*, March, 2023. Collage. Copy paper, magazine pictures, photographs, cardboard, glue stick, 2 x 1.5 in.

B I O

Deb Toscano-Knicos, MA ATR-BC LCAT—Artist—Creative Arts Therapist—Good Human.

love
lunar cycle
Magic School, the
mapping support
marginality (as a site of resistance)
Marxist social work
membership theory in social work
mending
metaphor
mikveh
mobile libraries
movement lawyering
mutual aid
mycelia as metaphor
narradrama
narrative medicine
narrative therapy
nepantla/nepantleras
nonviolent communication
ongoingness
peer counseling
peer-to-peer health network
person-situation perspective
perspective via faith
pleasure
poems/poetry
poetic meter
polarity work
post-oppositionality
postwork imaginaries
poverty-aware social work paradigm, the
power threat meaning (PTM) framework
pre(care)ity
prison abolition
professionalism without performance
progressive education
public benefits
public library, the
Qigong
radical administration
radical care in the arts
radical childcare in movement spaces
radical inclusion
radical papermaking
radical presence
radical social work
Radical Therapist Journal, The
Rank and File Movement (RFM) in social work

C O N T R I B U T I O N

Slow Textiles as a Form of Resistance

ENGAGEMENT IN SLOW TEXTILE PRACTICE acts as an antidote to consumerist attitudes towards textiles in terms of alienation from abstracted labour embedded in undervalued garments in circulation. My restoration of the slower approach to textiles serves as a form of resistance to participating in neoliberal economies and asserts manual stitching as both a method of care for the intergenerational craft-based knowledge and a practice that reclaims time. Furthermore, we assemble an individual sufferer separate from and superior to the non-huMan, with privatized behavioral, emotional, physiological, and cognitive features out of which we can produce needs that will sustain modernity's profitable, practice- or research-outcome-based therapeutic solutions with persuasive or marketable brands of change for consumption. ❁

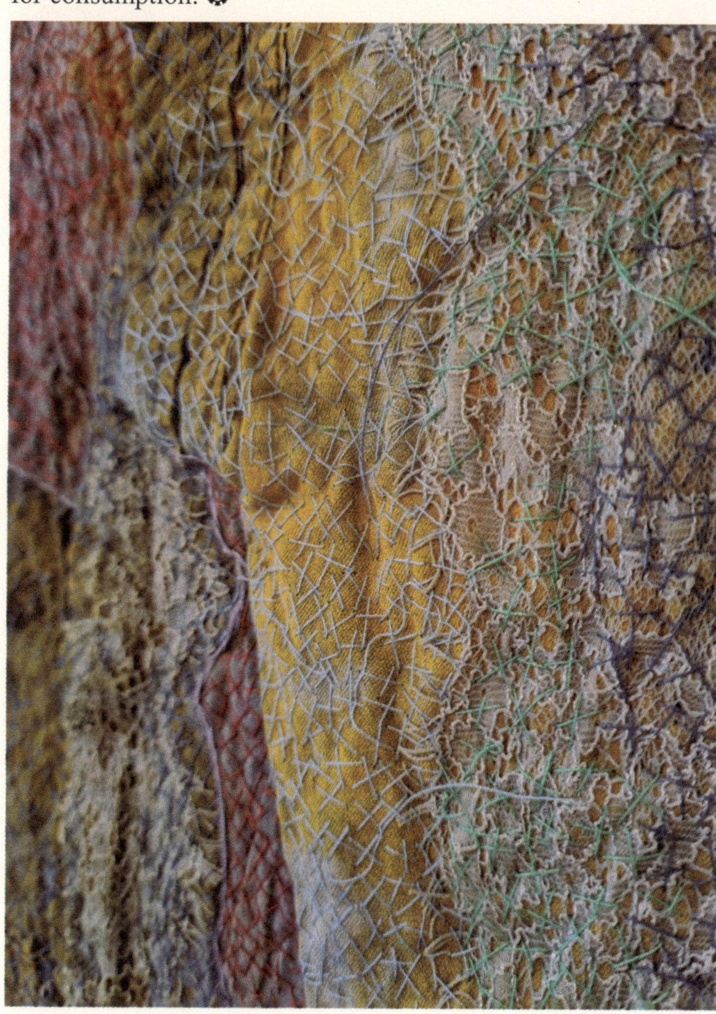

Remediation II, detail, 2021, Turmeric dye, bra lace, and thread on recycled men's shirt, 61 x 44 cm.

B I O Monika Cvitanovic is an artist and a PhD candidate (UNSW, Australia) who uses stitching as a feminist strategy of care encompassing both her lineage of textile-based practices and textiles in circulation.

reclaiming methodo
recognition
redistribution
Reflecting on Justi
reflexivi
Rei
relation
interviewing
relationali
resistan
resisting t
parental loss
narrative
resonan
respectful visiti
respite roo
rest as resistan
reven
revolutiona
mothering
ritu
sanctua
sandplay thera
sam
seed banki
sex positivi
shadow integrati
Sick Woman Theo
slow textil
slowne
social chan
ecosystem framewor
social constructi
social practi
social therapeuti
Social Welfare Acti
Alliance, the
solidarit
solidarity econo
somatic heali
songs/singi
sound heali
speculative desi
spel
staying with the trouble
storytellin
street newspape
strength
perspective, the
sufficienc
sustaining movemen
symbo
Taos Institute, th
targ
temporary autonomou zones
Theatre of th Oppressed
theories of chang
theosoph
therapeutic writin
togetherness
trans practice
transformativ justice
traspati
12-step program
undercover anti bullying teams
vigi
wate
wildnes
wintering as metapho
wishe
witcher
yog
zinemakin

CONTRIBUTION

Rules for Slow Making

RULES FOR SLOW MAKING

1. Start with direction, but make time to wander off course.
2. Remember, the personal can be universal.
3. There is power in the small.
4. Ask if order matters.
5. Think about the standard way [insert form of media] is contained or bound. Try subverting this.
6. Try writing a poem to release yourself from temporal pressure.
7. Keep in mind how the work could emanate.
8. Ask in what ways you can invite.
9. Ask what gifts you can give.
10. Try working with others and let them contaminate[1] your work.
11. If you are lost, keep going.
12. If you are overwhelmed, take a step back.
13. If you are stuck, make up your own rules.

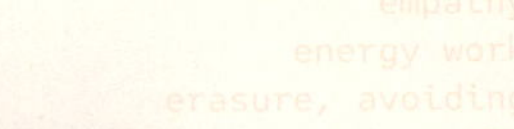

Slowing down is not a function of speed.
It's a function of awareness; a function of presence.
—Báyò Akómoláfé, philosopher, writer, activist

1 Term foraged from Anna Lowenhaupt Tsing, *The Mushroom at the End of the World: On the Possibility of Life in Capitalist Ruins*, Chapter 2: "Contamination as Collaboration."

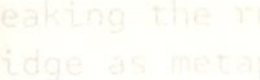

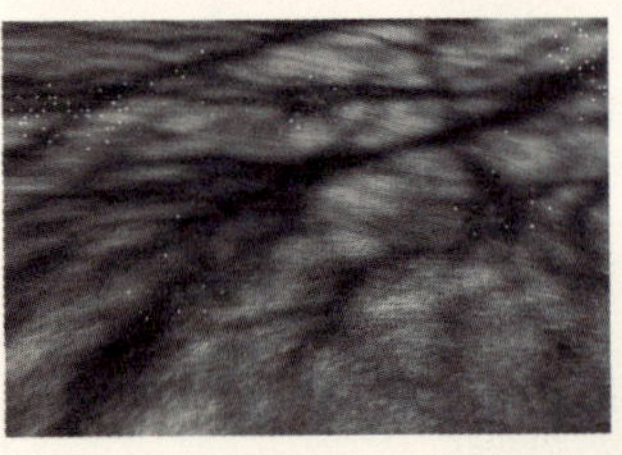

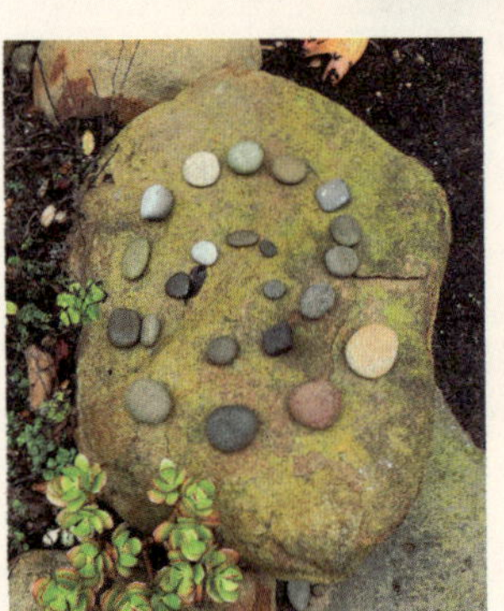

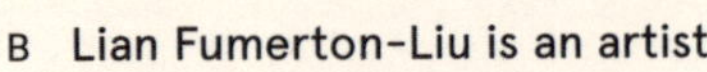

BIO Lian Fumerton-Liu is an artist and designer who finds joy in making time. Her practice explores new pathways and tools that open more accessible routes to approach the world with curiosity and wonder.

ccess invocations
accessibility
ivating archives
ofuturism
ncy
ing positivity
tar work
ernative identity
rojects
estral wisdom
estrality
ti-ableism
ti-adultism
ti-racism
ti-racism court
ystem
t as/in/of life
t journaling
t therapy
t workers
t-based group work
ts in medicine
ts-based research
thentic Movement
tonomous healing
urveda
ing with
rtha Capen Reynolds
ke and car repair
ollectives
ack Panther Party
ree Breakfast
rogram
dy as community
dy neutrality
dy positivity
dy Trust
redom
ave space
eaking the rules
idge as metaphor
re pods
re-based co-housing
atholic Worker
ovement
entering maintenance
ircular economy
imate cafes
ouds as metaphor
alition
ollaborative
apprenticeship
ollective care
ommon pool resources
ommons, the
ommuning with
animals
ommunity college
ommunity gardens
ommunity newspapers
onjure
onstructionist-
design framework, the
onsulting your
consultants
ontemplative
tradition, the
orn knowledge
redit unions
rip time
ritical fabulation
ritical hope
ritical pedagogy
ritical race theory
ritical suicide
studies
ritical whiteness

Cuestionamos
curiosity
death practices
decolonial
liberatory-based
practices
deep organizing
dérive, the
drumming
embodied expression
embodied knowledge
emergent strategy
empathy
energy work
erasure, avoiding
thereof
esoteric wisdom
traditions
ethnodrama
etymology
existentialism
externalizing
failure
fat positivity
feminism
feminist ethics
of care
fermentation
flâner
food sovereignty
forest bathing
fragments/
fragmentation
freedom
generous systems
gift economies
Grace Lee Boggs
grief as nonlinear
group work
groups
harm reduction
healing circles
healing healers
through the arts
healing justice
healing rituals
Hearing Voices
Network
herbal justice
herbalism
holding space
humanness
humor
illders
improvisation
infinite blackness
intentional
communities
interdisciplinary
cataloging
intergenerational
living
interspecies
organizing
intuitive eating
justice-oriented
counseling
land trusts
land, work,
spirit, body
language justice
leaving well
liberatory
education
life cycle,
honoring the
liminality
limited-equity
cooperative
housing

social change ecosystem framewor

CONTRIBUTION

WHAT HAPPENS WHEN YOU WANT TO contribute to social justice efforts but you aren't sure how to plug in or where to start? That's what I experienced in 2014 when I left an executive director job after 10 years. I felt lost and overwhelmed and didn't know where or how I could contribute my skills in the vast landscape of social change movements. That experience sparked a process of reconnecting with my core values and identifying how I could support the ecosystems I cared about in a more intentional manner.

Over the course of the following years, I developed an approach called the social change ecosystem framework, which includes a map of ten roles, from visionary to storyteller to disrupter to experimenter, plus a set of practices designed to strengthen our social change ecosystems and movements. Here is a visual of the social change ecosystem framework.

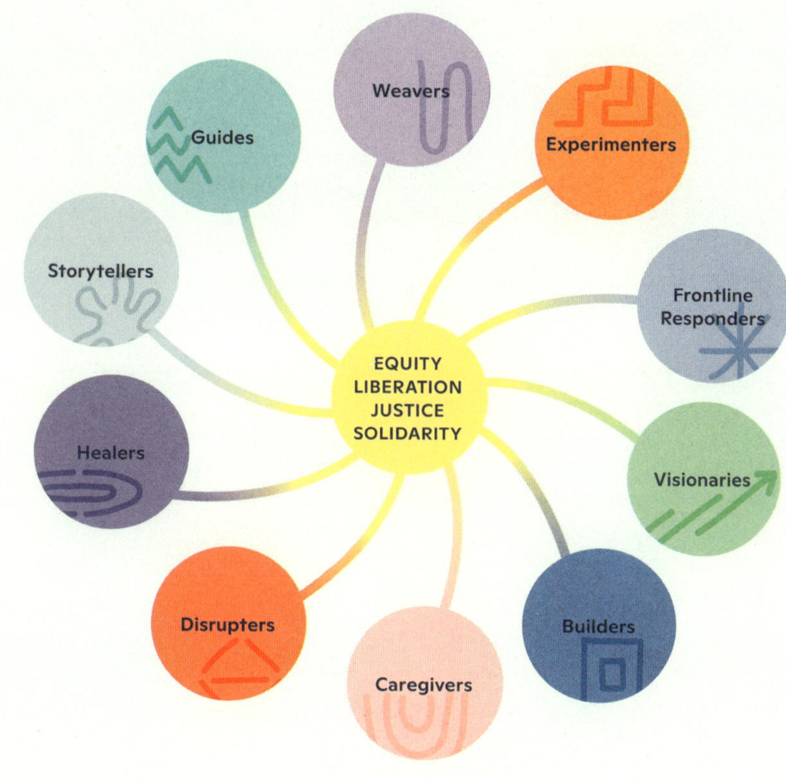

I humbly offer the framework to practitioners and students of social work, counseling, coaching, and other healing modalities. As you review the map, you might immediately resonate with the roles of caregiver and healer. Caregivers nurture and nourish the people around them by creating and sustaining a community of care, joy, and connection. Healers, on the other hand, often have unique knowledge and skills that enable them to provide support to people and groups outside of their immediate circle. Healers often use a variety of modalities, from therapy to somatics to restorative justice practices. They have the capacity to recognize and tend to the generational and current traumas caused by oppressive systems, institutions, policies, and practices. →

In order to use the framework, first articulate your core values, either present or aspirational. Then, identify the roles that you desire to play or already play. This will be based on your skill sets, lived experiences, and knowledge. Finally, identify the ecosystem you wish to support and how you can deepen the connections within it. Note that while being a healer is a natural role for people with your skills and backgrounds, you could also find yourself in the role of a visionary, describing our collective North Star, or a storyteller, interpreting ideas for broader audiences.

Being part of social change is one of the most important ways we can connect with each other at a time when society insists upon compartmentalizing us into silos of identity, thought, political alignment, and geography. When we engage in social change, we resist these silos and choose connection and solidarity. Together, we can change unfair and unjust systems, increase access and opportunity, share knowledge, celebrate and express joy, and create pathways to sharing power. ❁

BIO Deepa Iyer is a South Asian American writer and activist who supports social movements for justice.

social construction

SEE
resisting the parental loss narrative
speculative design
Taos Institute, the

CONTRIBUTION

SOCIAL CONSTRUCTION, a brief introduction
I'll try not to be too abstruse
but it's a challenge to use
old words for what's new
where meaning is found in their use

Social construction, elemental instruction
a guideline for what will ensue
begin with relations
within social situations
no "me" without a "you"

Social construction, how concepts function
is where your attention should lie
seeing language as key
to shaping realities
lessens the urge to reify

Social construction, resists reproduction
of beliefs we would like to transform
such change requires going
into spaces of unknowing
and a critical gaze towards the norm

Social construction, might create a disruption
in the web of beliefs that you hold
but though you might feel unhinged
and your confidence singed
resist coming in from the cold

Social construction, abstains from deduction
understanding comes in degrees
So here's a suggestion
try living your questions
stop insisting on certainty

Social construction, *is* a social construction
it doesn't declare what is True
it's a resource for speaking
understanding and seeking
an invitation to try something new

Social construction, in constant production
a verb more than a noun
you might go to strange places
and create novel spaces
where hope for new futures is found

Welcome!

BIO Stanley L. Witkin (slwitkin@gmail.com), Co-founder, Global Partnership for Transformative Social Work; Professor Emeritus, University of Vermont; Adjunct Professor, University of Pennsylvania; novelist, songwriter, and occasional poet.

EDITOR'S NOTE
If you're interested in learning more about how to apply social construction to professional helping, you might want to check out a volume edited by Stanley, *Social Construction and Social Work Practice: Interpretations and Innovations*. —ES

SEE:
activating archives
art
art as/in/of life
art-based group work
community college
dérive, the
embodied expression
emergent strategy
herbalism

CONTRIBUTION

Social Practice: We Can't Do It Alone

CAROL STAKENAS: Greetings, Mark. I'm excited that we are in conversation about social practice because it's an opportunity to work through a constellation of social relations. You came to this creative practice from your lived experience and through social work. I found my way through liberal arts and studio-based art training. And here's where we meet!

MARK MENJÍVAR: It is exciting! I came to social work out of my own struggles with substance abuse and entanglement with the juvenile justice system when I was a teen. I went to community college for almost two years, and when I discovered the field of social work, I was just lit up by it. I worked in social work for a few years but found it to be too restrictive. I had these other ideas I wanted to pursue. I came to the arts through documentary photography and audio work and I remember a really important shift happening early on: I didn't want to be making work about people; I wanted to be making work with people.

CAROL: As a maker, I am passionate about "materials"—what to use, and why. Along the way, I moved from clay to conversation. Now, I work with networks and systems thinking, which is shaped by conceptual and material intentions.[1] Based on various decisions, social practice can manifest different outcomes, right? This is especially true when socially engaged art intersects with radical helping and "allying efforts to change the status quo."

MARK: Social practice has many different forms. I often think of the Artist Placement Group,[2] which was working in the 1970s, and how they believed that context is half the work. One of the ways that I have begun to embody and live this is to recognize that it's not just *what* you're doing. It's *where* you're doing it that really matters, plus *who you're doing it with*. Are we doing it on a university campus? Is it a community college? Is it an elite university? Are we working in the streets? And then *who* are we working with, right? Are we working with incarcerated individuals and their loved ones? Are we working with students? Community members? Where does the intersectionality of these dynamics begin to stack up? For me, that has been a good grounding point, especially at the beginning of projects, and as a temperature check as projects begin to take shape or change form.

CAROL: Absolutely. With that in mind, I'm curious about your work with Rickey Cummings[3] and his artist book, *Holding Vigil*. I love that he is the author with you contributing the afterword. You flipped it; this is Rickey's work, ideas, and experience with you in a context-building role.

12 P.M.
1 P.M.
2 P.M.
3 P.M.
4 P.M.
5 P.M.
HOLDING VIGIL
RICKEY CUMMINGS
7 P.M.
8 P.M.
9 P.M.
10 P.M.
11 P.M.

MARK: Rickey goes right to the heart of matters in that book, and getting out of the way was the most important thing. We've been building our relationship for the past seven years and he is now one of my closest friends. There was a point where we were discussing, "Do I [Mark] need to add anything at all?" I wanted to recognize our long-term relationship of making work together, while also trying to open doors with the little bit of social capital I've been able to gain over the past 15 years of making art. We talked a lot about how we can leverage that. It's important as artists in doing these projects that we share authorship. And it's also important to be responsible for what you are doing. If something goes wrong or somebody has questions, they need to have a place to go to for accountability.

CAROL: So powerful. Thank you for that. How does uplifting the stories of those with lived experience factor into social practice? I've found that articulating one's commitment and values is needed to center those most impacted and honor their self-determination and get clear on everyone's roles and motivations. *Rosine 2.0*[4] taught me that grassroots communities with radical, liberatory politics make building community power a priority. And for good reason. They're rigorous and protective when defining their relationships with institutions and state structures. They are ready and willing to engage in conflict, even walk away, rather than be co-opted. This is not failure, it's exercising power and holding a long-term vision.

MARK: Yeah, totally.

CAROL: How do we connect with ongoing efforts? The most important part of radical helping is to *really* listen to the folks who are in it for the long haul, setting aside all of the tactics and skills we have as artists until it's clear what is needed.

MARK: It's recognizing what already exists inside of a place and then finding ways for that to move forward or to rise above. Not just creating some kind of object or something that can be easily consumed by the contemporary art world. It's allowing those relationships to guide the form.

CAROL: Especially considering that we can't do it alone.

MARK: Yes! And the process is just as important, if not more important than the final product. And by listening we see that things are often way more complex than they seem. There can be so many possibilities. We can talk about our practices in so many different ways. One primary way of working for me is activating archives. Sometimes that means building archives in collaboration with others. Sometimes I am working with existing archives. I'm trying to find ways for people to have meaningful connections with them. I often think about turning the archive inside out. Instead of waiting for people to come in, how do we bring it out into communities, into different spaces, or into people's homes? How do you approach archives?

CAROL: That's a question and a conversation for a lifetime! When considering the role of archives and storytelling, I want to read aloud the words of Grace Lee Boggs:

> History is not the past. It is the stories we tell about the past, how we tell these stories triumphantly, or self critically, metaphysically, or dialectically, has a lot to do with whether we cut short or advance our evolution as human beings.[5]

Her life and powerful words have crystallized the invitation for social practice to engage archives in a radical way—recognizing the wisdom that emerges from multiple perspectives and deepening critical connections. ❁

1 *What We Want Is Free: Generosity and Exchange in Recent Art*, edited by Ted Purves, strongly influenced my understanding and commitment to systems-based work. In particular, read Jeanne van Heeswijk's chapter, "A Call for Sociality."

2 The Artist Placement Group was founded by Barbara Steveni in 1966 to shift art beyond the gallery by placing artists in governmental and business environments. Check out the APG section in *Byproduct: On the Excess of Embedded Art Practices,* edited by Marisa Jahn, 39–53.

3 Rickey Cummings is a creator who has been fighting for his freedom from Texas's death row for the past 11 years.

4 Rosine 2.0 was a community-driven art project using collective practices to explore harm reduction and healing in Philadelphia (2021–2023). It was led by an interdisciplinary collective of artists, harm reductionists, community archivists, partner organizations, and other community members involved in today's street economies (e.g., sex work and drug use). For more information: rosine2.org.

5 Boggs, *The Next American Revolution: Sustainable Activism for the Twenty-First Century*, 79.

BIOS

Carol Stakenas commissions and produces public art, site-responsive exhibitions, and creative initiatives in service of strengthening social connections and building community power through socially engaged art and transdisciplinary alliances.

Mark Menjívar is an artist and educator whose art practice primarily consists of creating participatory projects while being rooted in photography, oral history, archives, and social action.

ndance
access invocations
accessibility
ivating archives
ofuturism
ncy
ng positivity
ar work
ernative identity
rojects
cestral wisdom
cestrality
ti-ableism
ti-adultism
ti-racism
ti-racism court
ystem
t as/in/of life
t journaling
t therapy
t workers
t-based group work
ts in medicine
ts-based research
thentic Movement
tonomous healing
urveda
ing with
rtha Capen Reynolds
ke and car repair
ollectives
ack Panther Party
ree Breakfast
rogram
dy as community
dy neutrality
dy positivity
dy Trust
redom
ave space
eaking the rules
idge as metaphor
re pods
re-based co-housing
tholic Worker
ovement
ntering maintenance
rcular economy
imate cafes
ouds as metaphor
alition
llaborative
apprenticeship
llective care
mmon pool resources
mmons, the
mmuning with
animals
mmunity college
mmunity gardens
mmunity newspapers
njure
nstructionist-
design framework, the
nsulting your
consultants
ntemplative
tradition, the
rn knowledge
edit unions
ip time
itical fabulation
itical hope
itical pedagogy
itical race theory
itical suicide
studies
itical whiteness

critique
Cuestionamos
curiosity
death practices
decolonial
liberatory-based
practices
deep organizing
derive, the
drumming
embodied expression
embodied knowledge
emergent strategy
empathy
energy work
erasure, avoiding
thereof
esoteric wisdom
traditions
ethnodrama
etymology
existentialism
externalizing
failure
fat positivity
feminism
feminst ethics
of care
fermentation
flâner
food sovereignty
forest bathing
fragments/
fragmentation
freedom
generous systems
gift economies
Grace Lee Boggs
grief as nonlinear
group work
groups
harm reduction
healing circles
healing healers
through the arts
healing justice
healing rituals
Hearing Voices
Network
herbal justice
herbalism
holding space
humanness
humor
illders
improvisation
infinite blackness
intentional
communities
interdisciplinary
cataloging
intergenerational
living
interspecies
organizing
intuitive eating
justice-oriented
counseling
land trusts
land, work,
spirit, body
language justice
leaving well
liberatory
education
life cycle,
honoring the
liminality
limited-equity
cooperative
housing

social therapeutic

CONTRIBUTION

AMONG THE RADICAL THERAPIES EMERGING IN THE LATE 1960S, social therapeutics is a practical-critical, group-based approach to reinitiating the development of persons and communities through activating their capacity to play, perform, philosophize, and create environments in which new ways of seeing and being can emerge. The principles and practice of social therapy originated through the work of Stanford University–trained philosopher and lay psychotherapist, Fred Newman, PhD, and over the next few decades advanced with his East Side Institute co-founder, Lois Holzman, PhD.

Conceived primarily as an activist critique of individuated and pathology-focused psychotherapies, social therapeutics propels the creative, performative activity of participants to positively (and powerfully) create their emotional growth.

Primarily a group approach in which clients learn to create their group-therapeutic environment, social therapy has been practiced in the US and across the globe in diverse therapy settings including clinics, hospitals, schools, community centers, and youth programs. Like narrative, social constructionist, collaborative, and other postmodern therapies, social therapeutics challenges many of psychology's presuppositions about therapy, the therapeutic relationship, illness, cure, and treatment.

Social therapeutics continues to be practiced, advanced, and broadened both at the East Side Institute, which has its headquarters in New York City, and across the globe by hundreds of scholars and activists; psychologists, counselors, social workers, therapists, and coaches; educators and youth workers; doctors and nurses; social justice artists and activists; and community organizers.

SOCIAL THERAPEUTICS 101

- Social therapy is a positive, relational psychotherapy with special focus on emotional development and group creativity.
- This approach is practiced in clinical settings, schools, hospitals, and social service organizations in dozens of countries.
- It draws upon Vygotskian-inspired socio-cultural and activity theoretic views on learning and development.
- The writings of Lev Vygotsky and Ludwig Wittgenstein have helped shape the social therapeutics understanding of people's capacity to change.
- It is a transdisciplinary practice of relating to people of all ages and life circumstances as social performers and creators of their lives.
- It works with an appreciation that people are socially connected and always creating things together.
- The practice is premised on the fact that people have access to creative, emotional, and social resources.
- It is grounded in a psychology of "what is becoming" rather than a psychology of "what is." ❁

BIO

Lois Holzman, PhD, is founder (with Fred Newman) and director of the East Side Institute, a center for social therapeutics and other humanizing approaches to emotional and social development and learning. As a developmental psychologist, activist-scholar and teacher, her work is political-philosophical, community-located and international.

membership theory in social work
narrative therapy
progressive education
relationali
sandplay thera
social constructioni
togethernes

Social Welfare Action Alliance, the

CONTRIBUTION

THE SOCIAL WELFARE ACTION ALLIANCE (SWAA) was founded as the Bertha Capen Reynolds Society in 1985. The name of the group was changed in 1999 because there was debate in the organization around whether people recognized Reynolds, and it became cumbersome to explain. Bertha Capen Reynolds was an early radical social worker, educator, trade unionist, and activist in the United States who was marginalized for her radical practice. She was fired from Smith College of Social Work when she advocated for unionization and racial integration. She thought that pathologizing problems as individual missed the structural issues that led to human suffering.

Reynolds was a member of the Rank and File Movement in social work. The principles that she thought needed to be front and center in social work are principles that SWAA continues to share:

1. "Social work exists to serve people in need."[1] That is, if social work is serving other groups, or classes, it has lost its way.
2. Since social work should focus on people helping themselves, social workers need to support people when they organize themselves for social change and not get in the way.
3. Communication is key. Social workers should listen and learn from those they work with.
4. Social work needs to join together with other liberation movements.
5. Social workers work as partners with people in client status. They need to understand that we are in this together and we all are subject to the same inequalities in a capitalist society.[2]

SWAA promotes radical social work and human services for social change. As an organization, we advocate for practice that addresses the structural causes of human suffering and we work to dismantle those structures that affect us all. This includes addressing how capitalism functions to maintain the status quo and requires that there be poor people in order for the rich to maintain their wealth. Equally important is to understand how capitalism needs racism, homophobia, sexism, and ableism and uses those forms of oppression as a way to separate people and weaken movements for societal liberation. For this reason, SWAA studies the current reality in order to organize and understand how various forces in society affect the work that social workers engage in on a day-to-day basis.

SWAA takes a critical view of the history and professionalization of social work. As founding member Mary Bricker-Jenkins has said: "We were never meant to help." That is, social workers have been part of the larger state apparatus in the US and have been the soft cops, keeping people in their place and serving as a form of social control. With its focus on radical social work, SWAA pushes back against that role imposed upon social workers and educates about how to engage in practice that is radical.

In radical social work, there is "an emphasis on action grounded in an analysis of all social, political, and economic structures that impede the fulfillment of basic human needs, the realization of basic human rights, and the promotion of human capabilities. The scope of analysis spans social work relationships and methods as well as the social welfare institution."[3]

SWAA regularly engages in analysis of the current reality and holds events open to the larger community to discuss issues that affect the work of social workers in society. SWAA begins by looking at the present reality—social, political, economic—at the local, national, and international levels and then discusses how this reality affects the work social workers do, as well as our own lives. Understanding the present reality is critical to effective organizing for social change. And analysis does not exist by itself; we have an ethical imperative to act.[4]

Marxist social work
poverty-aware social work paradigm, the
public benefits
radical social work
Radical Therapist Journal, the
Rank and File Movement (RFM) in social work
solidarit

As an organization, SWAA does not advocate for more social services for people in need. Rather it recognizes that our goal is to create a society where there is no human suffering and where need does not exist. In the case that need does exist, SWAA and like-minded organizations believe that people should not have to capitulate and demean themselves to fulfill their basic human needs and have their human rights respected. SWAA does not agree with "the pathologizing and labeling of behaviors that are functional and adaptive survival mechanisms to oppression, exploitation, and unmet needs."[5]

SWAA is a national organization in the United States, currently with seven chapters. There are chapters that are geographic in nature—Rochester, NY, Buffalo, NY, Connecticut, for example—as well as issue chapters such as Social Workers and Allies Against Solitary Confinement (SWASC) and Social Workers Eliminating Poverty Together (SWEPT). SWAA is a founding member of the Social Work Activist Collective (swactivists.com), which is a collective of a number of social work organizations pushing back against the lack of action by large US social work organizations on issues of social, economic, and environmental justice. SWAA holds webinars, solidarity meetings, and is planning to return to the practice of holding regular conferences or unconferences. We have open membership and encourage anyone who shares our principles to join us at socialwelfareactionalliance.org. SWAA also partners with the *Journal of Progressive Human Services: Radical Thought & Praxis*. ❁

1 Climo, "Review of Bertha Capen Reynolds's *An Uncharted Journey: Fifty Years of Growth in Social Work*," 78.

2 Reynolds, *An Uncharted Journey: Fifty Years of Growth in Social Work*.

3 Bricker-Jenkins, Barbera, and Joseph, "Radical Social Work."

4 Lavalette and Ferguson, "Towards a Social Work of Resistance: International Social Work and the Radical Tradition."

5 Bricker-Jenkins, Barbera, and Joseph, "Radical Social Work."

BIO Rosemary A. Barbera is a social work agitator and educator from Philadelphia, PA.

olidarity

CONTRIBUTION

I USED TO FEEL USELESS AS A THERAPIST. I was taught that empathy was my greatest offering. But when working with SDQTBIPOC[1] in a world where systemic violence is persistent, empathy within the confines of an individualized, commercialized service is not enough. Therapists have tried to offer me empathy while depoliticizing my pain. Their attempts were not only hollow, but sometimes even harmful. Offering empathy while remaining a bystander to the violent systems at the root of the suffering creates an illusion of safety within the relationship and an illusion of moral goodness of the empathizer.

Robin D. G. Kelley critiques the incompleteness of empathy as it requires a recognition of self in the other, whereas "part of solidarity is the people you don't recognize. The people who you don't see yourself in."[2]

Solidarity involves relating with one another through difference. It invites us to co-resist with those we don't see ourselves in, recognizing that our liberations are tied together. Solidarity involves taking political action out in the world, in all aspects of our lives, in the recognition of interconnectedness.[3]

Participate in local mutual aid efforts. Volunteer at tent cities. Offer pro bono services to Indigenous land defenders and local organizers. Mask up in public indoor spaces as disability solidarity in an ongoing pandemic and during flu season for immunocompromised kin. Disrupt cisheteronormativity in your personal relationships. Find alternatives to calling the cops. Center access in your offerings.

I invite professionalized practitioners to expand beyond empathy and explore what solidarity with our marginalized client community members may look like. Unpack the industry-fed narratives of what therapy is and is not, of what therapists should and should not do. Stretch the boundaries. Lean into bell hooks's teachings of love. What would it look like to extend ourselves for the spiritual growth of others? To love and care for one another politically?[4]

May we reimagine the potentialities of our therapeutic roles and relationships. May we disrupt, shift, and co-create alternative, more liberatory worlds in solidarity. ❁

1 SDQTBIPOC stands for Sick, Disabled, Queer, Trans, Black, Indigenous, People of Colour. This is a term I came across through Disability Justice.

2 Black Ink, "'Solidarity Is Not a Market Exchange': An Interview with Robin D. G. Kelley," para. 40.

3 Baik, "Therapists Owe Marginalized Clients More than Empathy."

4 hooks, *All About Love*.

BIO

Ji-Youn Kim (they/she) is a queer, currently non-disabled Corean immigrant and settler, joy-seeker, liberatory dreamer, psych survivor, justice-oriented therapist-ish, and ongoing creation of community.

CONTRIBUTION

WHAT PRACTICES and places can we rely on and strengthen in the years to come?

What might be called an "alternative" economy in the United States is known globally as the solidarity economy. The solidarity economy identifies and unites grassroots practices like lending circles, credit unions, worker cooperatives, community safety initiatives, community media stations, and community land trusts to form a powerful base of political power. The concept emerged in the global South (as *economia solidária*[1])and is now gaining support in the United States under many names, including the community economy, the peace economy, the workers' economy, the social economy, the new economy, the circular economy, the regenerative economy, the local economy, and the cooperative economy.

As many people finally wake up to the reality that white supremacy threatens public health on a daily basis, a wide range of people are educating themselves, assertively dismantling structures of oppression in organizations, and learning to follow the lead of black and brown artists and organizers who have been under siege for centuries and who have always been leaders in the solidarity economy. For more information about the solidarity economy, please visit solidaritynyc.org.

Order a print at unterbahn.com/solidarity
All proceeds go to the Southern Poverty Law Center and the NAACP. →

1 Marco Arruda of the Brazilian Solidarity Economy Network stated at the World Social Forum in 2004: "A solidarity economy does not arise from thinkers or ideas; it is the outcome of the concrete historical struggle of the human being to live and to develop him/herself as an individual and a collective... innovative practices at the micro level can only be viable and structurally effective for social change if they interweave with one another to form always-broader collaborative networks and solidarity chains of production-finance-distribution-consumption-education-communication."

love
lunar cycle
Magic School, the
mapping support
marginality (as a site of resistance)
Marxist social work
membership theory in social work
mending
metaphor
mikveh
mobile libraries
movement lawyering
mutual aid
mycelia as metaphor
narradrama
narrative medicine
narrative therapy
nepantla/nepantleras
nonviolent communication
ongoingness
peer counseling
peer-to-peer health network
person-situation perspective
perspective via faith
pleasure
poems/poetry
poetic meter
polarity work
post-oppositionality
postwork imaginaries
poverty-aware social work paradigm, the
power threat meaning (PTM) framework
pre(care)ity
prison abolition
professionalism without performance
progressive education
public benefits
public library, the
Qigong
radical administration
radical care in the arts
radical childcare in movement spaces
radical inclusion
radical papermaking
radical presence
radical social work
Radical Therapist Journal, The
Rank and File Movement (RFM) in social work

reclaiming selfhoo
recognition
redistribution
Reflecting on Just
reflexivi
Re
relatio
interviewin
relationali
resista
resisting
parental los
narrativ
resona
respectful visiti
respite ro
rest as resista
reve
revolutiona
motherin
ritu
sanctua
sandplay thera
sa
seed bank
sex positivi
shadow integrati
Sick Woman Theo
slow texti
slowne
social cha
ecosystem framewo
social construct
social pract
social therapeut
Social Welfare Act
Alliance, th
solidar
solidarity econo
somatic heal
songs/sing
sound heal
speculative des
spel
staying with t
troubl
storytell
street newspap
strengt
perspective, th
sufficien
sustaining moveme
symb
Taos Institute, t
tar
temporary autonomo
zone
Theatre of t
Oppresse
theories of chan
theosop
therapeutic writi
togethern
trans practic
transformat
justic
traspati
12-step progra
undercover ant
bullying team
vig
wat
wildne
wintering as metaph
wish
witche
yo
zinemaki

olidarity economy

ndance
accessible invitations
accessibility
ctivating archives
rofuturism
ency
ing positivity
lar work
ernative identity
rojects
cestral wisdom
cestrality
ti-ableism
ti-adultism
ti-racism
ti-racism court
ystem
t
t as/in/of life
t journaling
t therapy
t workers
t-based group work
ts in medicine
ts-based research
thentic Movement
tonomous healing
urveda
ing with
rtha Capen Reynolds
ke and car repair
collectives
ack Panther Party
ree Breakfast
Program
dy as community
dy neutrality
dy positivity
dy Trust
redom
ave space
reaking the rules
ridge as metaphor
are pods
are-based co-housing
atholic Worker
Movement
entering maintenance
ircular economy
limate cafes
louds as metaphor
oalition
ollaborative
apprenticeship
ollective care
ommon pool resources
ommons, the
ommuning with
animals
ommunity college
ommunity gardens
ommunity newspapers
onjure
onstructionist-
design framework, the
onsulting your
consultants
ontemplative
tradition, the
orn knowledge
redit unions
rip time
ritical fabulation
ritical hope
ritical pedagogy
ritical race theory
ritical suicide
studies
ritical whiteness

critique
Cuestionamos
curiosity
death practices

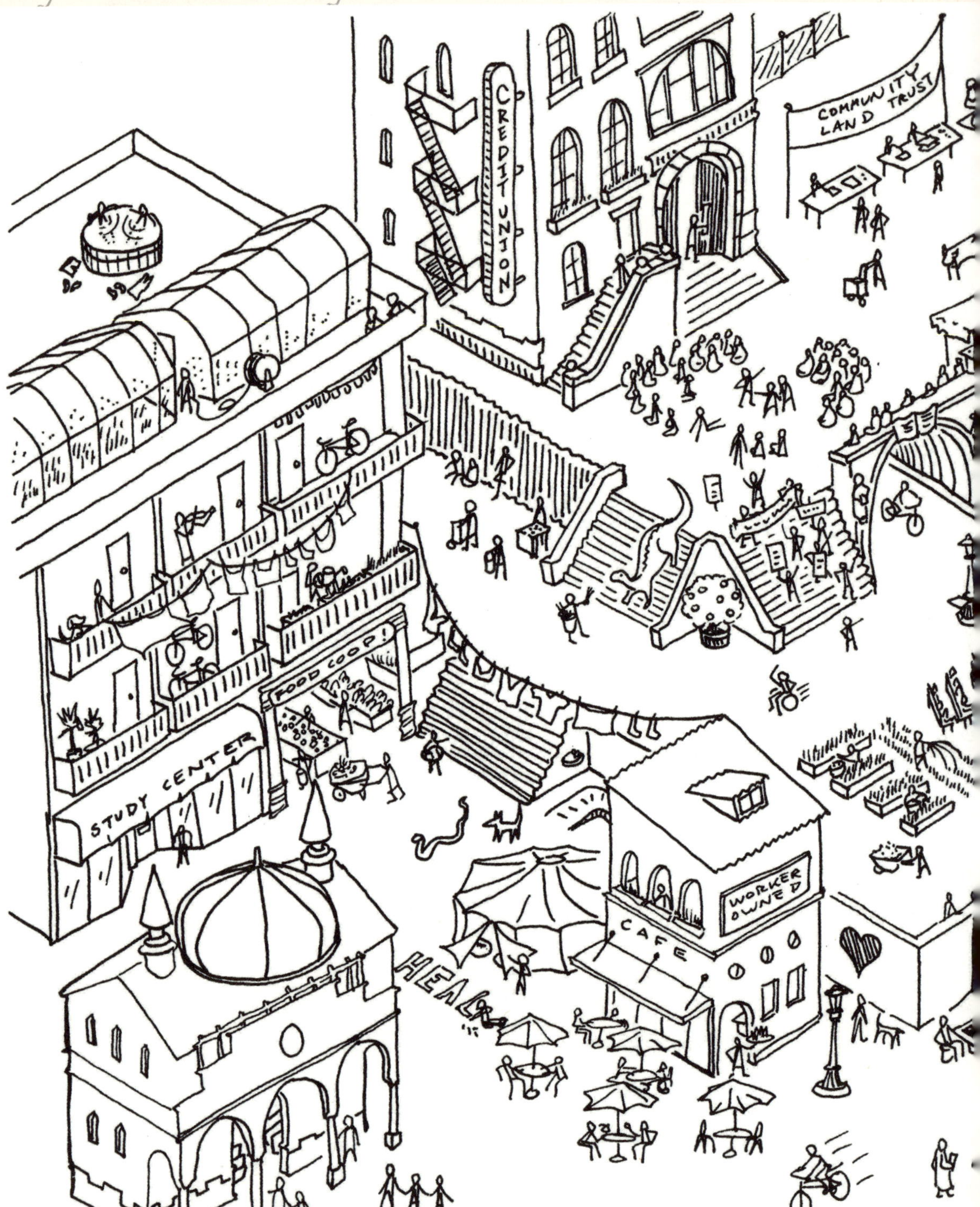

"Solidarity Economy," Jeffrey Yoo Warren and Caroline Woolard, 2016.

land trusts
land, work,
spirit, body
language justice
leaving well
liberatory
education
life cycle,
honoring the
liminality
limited equity
cooperatives
housing

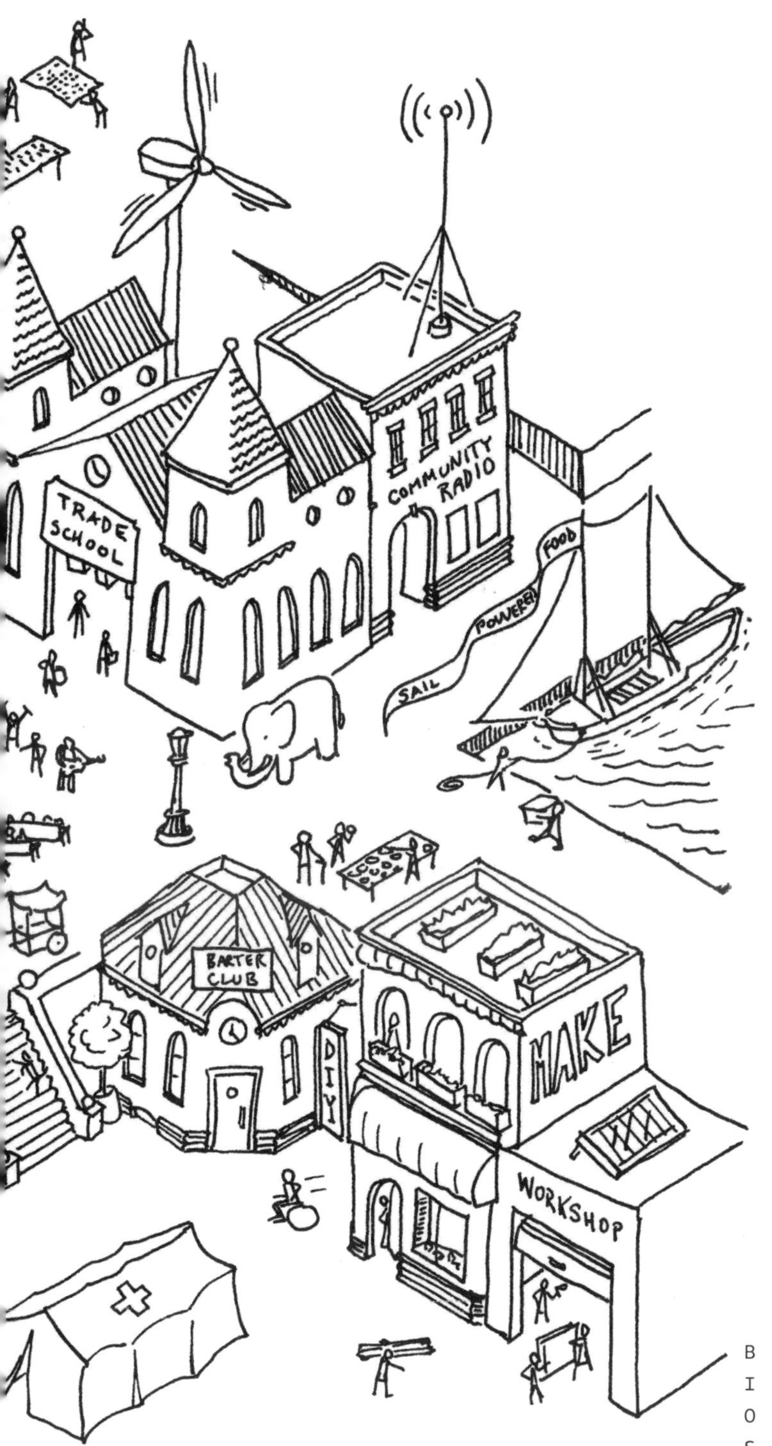

BIOS

Jeffrey Yoo Warren (he/him) is a Korean American artist-educator, community scientist, illustrator, and researcher whose work combines ancestral craft practices and creative work with diasporic memory through virtual collaborative worldbuilding.

Caroline Woolard's life work is to co-create experiences of cooperation.

omatic healing

CONTRIBUTION

IN THE NARROWEST SENSE, somatic healing is a psychological technique, sometimes also called somatic experiencing, that supports a person's mind-body connection in their treatment for post-traumatic stress disorder (PTSD).[1]

In a broader sense, somatic healing is a holistic therapy focused on the "soma," which in Latin translates into "the living body" to unlock the body's wisdom around trauma. The soma, in this model, is an untapped resource within Euro-centric clinical medical models.[2]

In the most expansive sense, somatics is a "path, methodology, and change theory, in which we can embody transformation, individually and collectively,"[3] as expressed by the politicized somatic practice called generative somatics. It is its own radical paradigm that supports the embodiment of change at biological, evolutionary, emotional, social, and psychological levels. Generative somatics views transformations to our individual embodiment as a key part of the practice, but this school of somatics believes that we must practice somatics at systemic and generational scales, and argues that over time we can see impacts on these scales too.

A selected list of somatic therapies include: somatic experiencing, generative somatics, Porges's polyvagal theory, Hakomi, Sensorimotor Psychotherapy, cultural wisdom traditions like ritualistic dance, constellation work, Somatic Abolitionism, children's play therapy, Rolfing, craniosacral, bioenergetics, and a lot more.

1 Salamon, "What is Somatic Therapy?"

2 Erdelyi, "What is Somatic Therapy?"

3 generative somatics, "What Is Politicized Somatics?

BIO

Richael Faithful is a Black trans-southern multi/interdisciplinary healer, culture worker, and attorney.

Authentic Movement
Ayurveda
Body as community
Body positivity
Body Trust
drumming
embodied expression
embodied knowledge
intuitive eating
land, work, spirit, body

songs/singin

CONTRIBUTION

going to shabbat services for the first time in years after the pittsburgh synagogue massacre and realizing that communal singing is healing: the vibrations in the chest, the synchronization across bodies, the hum rising up to the rafters. we will out-sing them. we will outlive them. ❁

BIO

Tanya Paperny is a writer, editor, translator, artist and community builder in Washington, DC—learn more at tpaperny.com.

CONTRIBUTOR'S NOTE

"We will outlive them" is the translation of a Yiddish phrase, *mir veln zey iberlebn*. It originates from Polish Jews using an improvised lyric to resist a German massacre during World War II. I'm a secular Jew, but it felt important to be among other Jews the Saturday after a white nationalist gunman attacked worshippers at Tree of Life Congregation in Pittsburgh, Pennsylvania in October of 2018. Singing together that Shabbat evening reminded me how songs penetrate into your bones and help heal you. —TP

ound healing

CONTRIBUTION:

OF ALL THE FIVE SENSES, sound is a vital way of understanding the world and ourselves. It affects the emotional trajectory of a movie, pumps up a workout class, transforms the ambiance of a restaurant, and so much more. Sound transcends and elevates the human experience but is less acknowledged than its visual counterparts.

Unlike movies and the visual arts, pure sound is a form that requires complete presence and witnessing for true appreciation. It is argued that it is a purer art form than movies for that reason. Sound demands that we truly engage with the world around us and actively listen, not just passively hear.

A book I constantly come back to is *Deep Listening: A Composer's Sound Practice* by Pauline Oliveros. Oliveros, a queer pioneer in electronic music composition, created the practice of Deep Listening in the 1960s by observing how tones can affect your body mentally and physically. By concentrating their attention on a tone, one can change their emotional state.

Because I am someone who emotionally regulates myself through sound, the practice provides a formal structure and deeper engagement for my perceived emotional state. The therapeutic component is evident in deep listening and is the primary purpose of my personal practice, which is conducted through a variety of sonic mediations that can be practiced wherever you are.

Sound healing is a truly accessible form and is everywhere around you. You don't have to spend hundreds of dollars going to a retreat or buy into wellness capitalism to be present in your body and heal with the power of sound.

BIO Camille Nibungco is a designer and ambient musician.

E: accessibility
ivating archives
ofuturism
ncy
ng positivity
ar work
ernative identity
rojects
estral wisdom
estrality
i-ableism
i-adultism
i-racism
i-racism court
ystem
t
t as/in/of life
t journaling
t therapy
t workers
t-based group work
ts in medicine
ts-based research
thentic Movement
tonomous healing
urveda
ing with
rtha Capen Reynolds
ke and car repair
ollectives
ack Panther Party
ree Breakfast
rogram
dy as community
dy neutrality
dy positivity
dy Trust
redom
ave space
eaking the rules
idge as metaphor
re pods
re-based co-housing
atholic Worker
Movement
entering maintenance
ircular economy
limate cafes
louds as metaphor
oalition
ollaborative
apprenticeship
ollective care
ommon pool resources
ommons, the
ommuning with
animals
ommunity college
ommunity gardens
ommunity newspapers
onjure
onstructionist-
design framework, the
onsulting your
consultants
ontemplative
tradition, the
orn knowledge
redit unions
rip time
ritical fabulation
ritical hope
ritical pedagogy
ritical race theory
ritical suicide
studies
ritical whiteness

Cuestionamos
curiosity
death practices
decolonial
liberatory-based
practices
deep organizing
dérive, the
drumming
embodied expression
embodied knowledge
emergent strategy
empathy
energy work
erasure, avoiding
thereof
esoteric wisdom
traditions
ethnodrama
etymology
existentialism
externalizing
failure
fat positivity
feminism
feminst ethics
of care
fermentation
flâneur
food sovereignty
forest bathing
fragments/
fragmentation
freedom
generous systems
gift economies
Grace Lee Boggs
grief as nonlinear
group work
groups
harm reduction
healing circles
healing healers
through the arts
healing justice
healing rituals
Hearing Voices
Network
herbal justice
herbalism
holding space
humanness
humor
illders
improvisation
infinite blackness
intentional
communities
interdisciplinary
cataloging
intergenerational
living
interspecies
organizing
intuitive eating
justice-oriented
counseling
land trusts
land, work,
spirit, body
language justice
leaving well
liberatory
education
life cycle,
honoring the
liminality
limited-equity
cooperative
housing

speculative desig

CONTRIBUTION

SPECULATIVE DESIGN is a means of social dreaming. It asks that we release ourselves, for a moment, from the perceived constraints of reality in order to speculate about what could be—falling somewhere beyond what is probable, towards what is possible, plausible, but stopping just before total fantasy. Then, it asks we put aside any concerns about how to get there for now, and articulate this vision fully using the tools of design.

The term "speculative design" was popularized by Anthony Dunne and Fiona Raby in their book *Speculative Everything*. From their position as industrial designers, Dunne and Raby reflect on the various creative traditions that constitute speculative design's history, articulating the potential of similar approaches for designers and thinkers of today. Their lineage of speculative design can be traced back to radical designers of the '60s and '70s. It is a label often assigned to figures such as Archizoom, Superstudio, Archigram, Ant Farm, Haus-Rucker-Co, and Walter Pichler.[1] But the concept has origins that extend even further back than this. In 1846, in his *Hints to Young Architects*, George Wightwick implored the young designer to "get the wheels of his mind out of the ruts of habitual office practice, and to drive the coursers of his imagination over the free common ground of varied and speculative design."[2] Speculative design is a call to release yourself from habit. It is a way of exercising the imagination.

If "design" sets out to solve problems, "speculative design" proclaims a rejection of the concept of solution. It asks questions, and, in doing so, uncovers more questions. It refuses a diagnose-solve logic. Whilst incommensurable with the logic of healthcare, where a solution to a diagnosis is surely welcomed, there might be some lessons to learn from this refusal. In searching for immediate fixes, the opportunity to think beyond what is readily available risks being overlooked. Speculative design might offer conventional medical discourse something of a methodology in this regard. To offer a simplistic example, I imagine going back in time to a pre-internet, pre-computer era and showing someone a flat rectangular object. Telling them to imagine that this thin screen could conjure up the face of someone, sitting many miles away, that they could speak to about their struggles on a regular basis—the now commonly experienced online therapist's roving presence that listens, understands, supports. Can engaging in speculative design generate ideas for how we might enact therapy and other care work differently in the future?

However, speculative design, in order to be meaningful, must avoid simply dreaming up new worlds resting on the purely technological. Much critical and speculative design, in evading the question of how we might arrive at the new visions it dreams up, avoids committing to any solid program of political action. The leap between what *is* and what *could be* suggests a space in between. This gap is a site of possible action. In order for speculative design to be better connected with critiquing harmful systems and structures of the current era, it might follow the guidance of Ahmed Ansari, speaking at the MIT Media Lab Summit in 2015, and replace *What if?* with *How else?* We should echo his question loudly: "Hell, where are all the colored, the queer, the feminist, the working class people in critical design?"[3]

The global economy functions through speculation. It relies on speculative models of commodities, of equity futures, of insurance. Speculative design shifts the purpose of speculative models away from simple extrapolation in the service of predicting what is likely, and searches an actual space of possibility though proposing more radical futures. This necessitates close observation of the present—a meaning embedded into its linguistic roots. The origins of the word "speculate" come from a Proto-Indo-European root "spek," which means "to observe." It also has links to the Sanskrit *spasati*, which means "sees," the Greek *skopein*, which means to "behold, look, or consider," and the German *spähen*, which means "to spy."[4] In this act of beholding, there lies the potential not only to offer a vision for something else, but to cast a new perspective on what already exists. Particularly when such visions can move beyond the merely abstract, aesthetic, and intellectual towards the active, transformative, and political. Speculative or critical design's provocations cannot be rooted in one narrow ideological imaginary.

Engaging in any kind of speculative design offers the potential to imagine entirely new contexts, scenarios, situations, relationships, and worlds. Ones that might serve us, and the beings we are entangled with, in more generous and fulfilling ways. In *The Utopia of Rules*, the late anthropologist and anarchist David Graeber writes, "The ultimate, hidden truth of the world is that it is something that we make, and could just as easily make differently."[5] The question I ask you is: What is the world that we want to make?

EXERCISE:

- Think carefully about an existing situation, a scenario, an object, a relation. Dream it very differently. Reinvent its form, its gestures, its being. Cast aside, for a moment, the impossibility of materializing this new thing. Describe it fully. Then, reflect. What are the fears, anxieties, desires, imaginaries, and politics lurking within what you have articulated? How has your own class, race, and gender privilege embedded itself into this process of reimagining something anew? What do we want to do away with? What does that tell us of our existing reality? ❁

1 Dunne and Raby, *Speculative Everything: Design, Fiction, and Social Dreaming*, 6.

2 Wightwick, *Hints to Young Architects: Calculated to Facilitate Their Practical Operations*, 41.

3 Ansari, "Design Must Fill Current Human Needs before Imagining New Futures."

4 "*spek-." *Etymology*.

5 Graeber, *The Utopia of Rules: On Technology, Stupidity, and the Secret Joys of Bureaucracy*, 89.

BIO Elise Limon is a designer and educator striving to always ask: *How else?*

spells

SEE poems/poetry, poetic meter, wishes, witchery

CONTRIBUTION

RECITATION OF WORDS to invoke magic or to effect a change. Often associated with witchcraft, new and old. Spells simply must have a force that bends wills, time, and/or events. Beyond Shakespeare's infamous Song of the Witches—"double, double toil and trouble"—examples of other, more recent, and frankly more relevant spells include: *12 Little Spells* by Esperanza Spalding; "radical gratitude spell" by adrienne maree brown; "'No Harm' Protection Spell" by Richael Faithful; and "I Put a Spell on You" by Nina Simone. ❁

BIO

Richael Faithful is a Black trans-southern multi/interdisciplinary healer, culture worker, and attorney.

staying with the trouble

SEE: empathy, fragments/fragmentation, centering maintenance, climate cafes, communing with animals, crip time, liminality

CONTRIBUTION

WE ARE SAID TO BE THE TROUBLEMAKERS with seditious intentions; they say we are the ones destroying the stability and prosperity of our city in their discourses. The law enforcers call us the cockroaches. We are the trouble in their eyes. The state is not dodging the trouble, but solving it by laws. They uphold the belief that putting troublemakers into jail will create a trouble-free world.

Diaspora is our new identity. We left our homeland, departing from our family and friends unwillingly. People in the host countries call us migrants, political migrants, economic migrants, refugees and legal refugees, asylum seekers, or displaced people. No matter where we are geographically, we are staying with the trouble—if we were the troublemakers, as they said. Indeed, we are under the threat of being caught into their jails. This is our trouble because the state said they could do so, and they did.

Staying away from our homeland is a way for us to keep distance from the trouble of being arrested, although it is not absolutely effective. Truth or dare? We are betting on the feasibility of their almighty power of law enforcement. It makes us the outlaws in the state's eyes.

Under their framework, trouble could be solved if we stay in our homeland and obey their laws, pay for it in prison, do and think in the ways they expect. Wait a minute, are we still the troublemakers according to their definition if they need to put so much effort into coping with us? If so, they are just solving the trouble by staying with the troublemakers.

If being concerned about their enforcements of laws, commenting on and criticising their performance, and showing empathy and support to those imprisoned are defined as seditious intentions, then departing from our homeland is creating a space with a certain level of freedom from fear for us to stay with the trouble. ❁

BIO

Heung Gong Yan was born and lived in an ex-British colony in Asia.

EDITORS' NOTE

This well-known phrase is attributed to Donna Haraway, whose book *Staying with the Trouble: Making Kin in the Chthulucene* is on the reading list of Thick Press's "ongoing inquiry into care." We hear people use the phrase when referring to the experience of sitting with all the challenges involved in caring for self and others in a difficult world—an experience that often involves making kin with unexpected, sometimes nonhuman others. It was jarring to read Heung's contribution and see that sometimes "the trouble" is both imminent and life-threatening. We are grateful for Heung's courageous risk-taking. —ES & JC

CONTRIBUTION

The Healing Power of Storytelling: Addressing Moral Injury

narrative medicine
narrative therapy
ongoingness
postwork imaginaries
rest as resistance
slowness
solidarity
therapeutic writing
togetherness

THE LEGACY OF THE INDUSTRIAL REVOLUTION is that we've been conditioned as a society to believe that to be "professional" requires us to compartmentalize different parts of our lives—to prioritize the black and white of profit and productivity while ignoring the gray shades of our feelings, emotions, morals, and values, the parts that are complex and messy.

The parts that make us human.

This sustained effort by those in power to further industrialize our minds and bodies—while insisting that we suppress our emotions because there's no room for them in the workplace—has resulted in toxic workplace cultures that lack empathy and connection. These two elements are key to our ability to flourish. Without empathy and connection, stress settles into our bodies, sitting with its foot on the gas pedal of our nervous system, driving us towards mental and physical exhaustion and dis-ease, a breakdown of our support networks, and in some cases, death.

In our current capitalistic culture, my next sentence may come as a shock to some people: we are not machines—we're living, breathing human beings who have thoughts, are guided by deeply held morals and values, experience emotions, and feel pain. And yet, we make a choice every day to give up our agency and succumb to an expectation, rooted in white supremacy and patriarchy, that we figure out how to turn our humanness on and off like a light switch.

It's this choice to allow others to untether us from our morals, values, beliefs—to untether us from our humanity—that forms the root of moral injury, a wound to our spirit (a facet of our humanity that often feels too messy for many of us and our modern workplaces to acknowledge or care for). We are whole human beings, and in the realm of our whole human experience, there are wounds that cannot be seen but are profoundly felt. This is the essence of moral injury—unseen but profoundly felt. But as anyone who has cut their finger or scraped their knee knows, not caring for our physical wounds doesn't make them go away—it usually makes them worse and often leaves a scar. Wounds to our spirit are no different, except that they're invisible, leaving scars on our minds and in our hearts without us even knowing.

We experience moral injury when we've witnessed or participated in events that violate our moral code. This could include actions taken (or not taken) during armed conflict, emergency responders facing ethical dilemmas, healthcare professionals making difficult decisions, government workers enforcing policies with which they disagree, or any circumstance where we're forced to compromise our own deeply held morals, values, or beliefs. The aftermath of these experiences results in spiritual consequences, including guilt, shame, self-condemnation, anger, and a profound sense of moral dissonance, any one of which has the capacity to impact other facets of our life and well-being.

Despite its impact on our health and well-being, moral injury isn't recognized as a mental health disorder, nor does a validated treatment for it currently exist. Instead, it's often associated with post-traumatic stress disorder (PTSD) and treated with the same fear- and exposure-based approaches. The problem is these approaches often fail to address and process the feelings of shame and guilt that typically arise from moral injury, leaving the people who experience moral injury unable to fully heal. Storytelling, however, has the potential to offer a unique and transformative path towards healing and connection not available through traditional approaches.

As one of our oldest forms of communication, storytelling is how we share what has happened to us, and how we describe our experiences, fears, and dangers. It's an integral part of human culture that helped our prehistoric ancestors navigate survival. We use storytelling every day to express our thoughts, feelings, and experiences in all facets of our personal lives. Imagine what might be possible if we used storytelling to validate and heal moral injury and other occupational traumas in the workplace and created a sense of common humanity and connection with our peers.

Story-*healing* is a form of storytelling rooted in the "healing circles" widely used among Native Americans, First Nations people of Canada, and indigenous peoples. Story-healing circles are a tool to address and heal moral injury through storytelling.

The use of story-healing circles to help individuals in need has grown in recent years and they're now being used in many settings, including neighborhoods, schools, prisons, support groups, families, and marriages to give individuals a safe space to communicate their fears, pain, and traumas. However, story-healing circles are a powerful tool with tremendous potential for addressing occupational traumas and moral injury in the workplace because they not only acknowledge the complexity of workplace trauma, but they also soothe our hardwired need to connect with others, making us feel safe. Through story-healing circles, individuals have opportunities to engage with their experiences, express their emotions, find validation, and ultimately embark on a transformative journey of healing. Story-healing circles foster connection and belonging by using trained facilitators to help individuals work together to create brave, non-judgmental spaces to externalize their internal conflicts, process their emotions, make meaning from their experiences, and initiate the healing process. The act of speaking our story out loud to others is a cathartic experience of releasing suppressed emotions. By recounting the events that led to our moral injury, individuals can express their guilt, shame, and anguish in a safe and non-judgmental space. This emotional release can be profoundly therapeutic, helping to alleviate the burden of moral injury and paving the way for healing.

Having our stories witnessed by others who have experienced similar moral challenges creates a sense of validation and common humanity. Knowing that our struggles aren't unique and that others have faced similar ethical dilemmas can be a comforting reminder that we're not alone. Story-healing circles in the workplace create brave spaces for individuals to find solace, empathy, and understanding from those who can relate to their experiences, reinforcing a sense of belonging and reducing feelings of isolation.

Narrative construction is an essential aspect of how we think and our perceptions of who we are as individuals and as members of a global society. Storytelling enables us to make sense of our moral injury experiences by weaving a narrative thread that connects past events with present understanding. Through this process, we're better resourced to rebuild our personal values, reframe our moral frameworks, and integrate our experiences into a broader narrative of flourishing and growth, bringing about a renewed sense of purpose and contributing to the healing of moral injury.

Story-healing circles also create opportunities for empowering and advocating for change. Sharing our moral injury stories begins to normalize this form of occupational trauma and remove the stigma and shame of being someone who suffers from moral injury or other occupational traumas. It sheds light on the societal or systemic factors that contribute to moral injury and advocates for reforms or interventions that can prevent similar experiences in the future. In this way, story-healing not only aids individual healing, but it also drives broader social awareness and fosters a culture of moral responsibility in our organizations.

Moral injury is a profound wound that requires holistic approaches for healing. Storytelling emerges as a potent tool in this endeavor, allowing us to navigate our emotional landscapes, find validation and connection, make meaning from our experiences, and ultimately transform our pain into pearls of wisdom and growth. Story-healing as a tool for addressing moral injury and other occupational traumas is a compassionate means for facilitating healing and building communities and cultures that uphold the values essential for a more ethical and just world. ❁

BIO Dimple D. Dhabalia is the founder of Roots in the Clouds, a global consulting firm working to remove the stigma of workplace mental health and trauma, and author of *Tell Me My Story—Challenging the Narrative of Service Before Self*.

street newspape

CONTRIBUTION

"STREET NEWSPAPERS (or street papers) are newspapers or magazines sold by homeless or poor individuals and produced mainly to support these populations. Most such newspapers primarily provide coverage about homelessness and poverty-related issues, and seek to strengthen social networks within homeless communities."[1]

This is how the definition of a street newspaper starts in Wikipedia. To activists, artists, and writers, this is rather a minimizing explanation of street newspapers' social, political, and creative potentiality. Thus, what street newspapers meant in the late 19th and early 20th centuries is rather a form of circulation. What they meant in the 1980s, when they started to multiply to the cities as a form of throwing pennies to those affected by the neoliberal rise of accumulation of a speculative market, owned by a ruling class, and not of mutual aid, is being reversed by *Arts of the Working Class (AWC)*.

AWC, the multilingual street newspaper for art and society, wealth and poverty, searches for the softness that disrupts borders, and makes a space for imagining territories of kinship, disobedience as a way of negotiation, and trust as the only element to hold on to, in a rapidly changing global society. In doing so, it seeks to collaborate with established structures that cover a spectrum of society different from other street newspapers—in other words, from working class (non)representative organizations to the ruling class temples, such as museums and institutional and governmental structures. What makes this possible is the growing disconnect between working people's realities and the mindset and interest of the ruling class.

Street newspapers are sold mainly by homeless individuals, but the newspapers vary in how much content is submitted and how much of the coverage pertains to its contributors. While some papers are written and published mainly by homeless or unemployed contributors, others have a professional staff and attempt to emulate mainstream publications. These differences have caused controversy among street newspaper publishers over what type of material should be covered and to what extent the homeless should participate in writing and production. One of the most known street newspapers in the world, *The Big Issue*, has been a focus of this controversy due to its focus on attracting a large readership through coverage of mainstream issues and popular culture, whereas other newspapers emphasize homeless advocacy and social issues and earn less of a profit.

AWC is not exempt from these kinds of controversies, but consciously so. ❁

1 Wikipedia, "Street Newspapers."

BIO

María Inés Plaza Lazo is an art historian, editor, and curator. Together with artist Paul Sochacki, she founded *Arts of the Working Class*, of which she remains its publisher.

ccess invocations
EE: accessibility
tivating archives
rofuturism
ency
ing positivity
tar work
ternative identity
dentity projects
cestral wisdom
cestrality
ti-ableism
ti-adultism
ti-racism
ti-racism court system
t
t as/in/of life
t journaling
t therapy
t workers
t-based group work
ts in medicine
ts-based research
thentic Movement
tonomous healing
urveda
ing with
ertha Capen Reynolds
ke and car repair collectives
lack Panther Party Free Breakfast Program
dy as community
dy neutrality
dy positivity
dy Trust
redom
rave space
reaking the rules
ridge as metaphor
are pods
are-based co-housing
atholic Worker Movement
entering maintenance
ircular economy
limate cafes
louds as metaphor
oalition
ollaborative apprenticeship
ollective care
ommon pool resources
ommons, the
ommuning with animals
ommunity college
ommunity gardens
ommunity newspapers
onjure
onstructionist-design framework, the
onsulting your consultants
ontemplative tradition, the
orn knowledge
redit unions
rip time
ritical fabulation
ritical hope
ritical pedagogy
ritical race theory
ritical suicide studies
ritical whiteness

strengths perspective, the

CONTRIBUTION

THE STRENGTHS PERSPECTIVE FORCES PRACTITIONERS to re-examine their "dictionary of helping."[1] It calls for a strengths lexicon, an em*power*ing vocabulary that energises, enlivens, and elevates … to lift the weight of the problem through affirmation and validation … ❁

wise · unequivocal · understanding · vigourous · visionary · wilful · witty · warm ·
upbeat · thankful · tolerant · understanding · valuable · vibrant · verve ·
thrifty · trustworthy · trouble-shooter · unique · understanding · virtuous · versatile ·
strong · survivor · talented · sociable · task-oriented · unerring ·
successful · self-controlled · strong-willed · self-motivated · tactful ·
self-starter · relational · reserved · resilient · resolute · socially-intelligent ·
reflective · problem-solver · persistent · polite · practical · resourceful ·
playful · original · optimistic · participatory · people-oriented · personable ·
organised · loyal · loving · logical · modest · mindful · motivated · noble ·
keen-to-learn · integrity · idealistic · industrious · inspiring · ingenious · interested ·
intellectual · facilitating · gifted · generous · goal-oriented · good-listener ·
forthright · educated · empowered · enthusiastic · exploratory ·
compassionate · courageous · dependable · dedicated ·
balanced · beautiful · controlled · cheerful · creative · competitive ·
artistic · accurate ·

1 Saleebey, "The Strengths Perspective in Social Work Practice: Extensions and Cautions," 298.

Cuestionamos
curiosity
death practices
decolonial liberatory-based practices
deep organizing
dérive, the
drumming
embodied expression
embodied knowledge
emergent strategy
empathy
energy work
erasure, avoiding thereof
esoteric wisdom traditions
ethnodrama
etymology
existentialism
externalizing
failure
fat positivity
feminism
feminst ethics of care
fermentation
flâner
food sovereignty
forest bathing
fragments/fragmentation
freedom
generous systems
gift economies
Grace Lee Boggs
grief as nonlinear
group work
groups
harm reduction
healing circles
healing healers through the arts
healing justice
healing rituals
Hearing Voices Network
herbal justice
herbalism
holding space
humanness
humor
illders
improvisation
infinite blackness
intentional communities
interdisciplinary cataloging
intergenerational living
interspecies organizing
intuitive eating
justice-oriented counseling
land trusts
land, work, spirit, body
language justice
leaving well
liberatory education
life cycle, honoring the
liminality
limited-equity cooperative housing

strengths perspective, th

· Well-mannered · Xenas (tough, physical, confident woman) · xyresic (razor sharp) · x-factor · youthful · young-at-heart · zesty · building your vocabulary is a form of strength training for social workers and other helping professionals ·

BIOS

Mel Gray (Professor Emeritus at the University of Newcastle, Australia)—photographer and social worker—has a longstanding interest in the art and science of social work practice—its relational-connective and evidence-based aspects that enhance its effectiveness.

Leanne Schubert (PhD)—artist and social worker—has an enduring interest in the relationship between social work and socially engaged art.

ufficiency

CONTRIBUTION

THESE IMAGES are video stills from footage taken during a stay in the ejido El Triunfo II inside the Sepultura Bioreserve in Chiapas, Mexico. This community agreed to be part of a government program to learn and implement MIAF: milpa interspersed with fruit trees. It's an agro-ecological approach to growing maíz in a cropping arrangement that benefits soil health. Fruit trees would provide extra income for the cultivators to sell once harvested. In this region, people are accustomed to living off what is available on their land, due to both campesino/as culture and the lack of accessibility to urban resources. Fulfilling their necessities is an endurance to live within environmental limits—to locate pleasure in continuing the know-how of achieving one's own needs through their surrounding locality. ❂

fermentation
generous systems
ircular economy
ommon pool resources
ommons, the

Moments of daily chores, video stills, courtesy Andrea Macias-Yañez, 2021.

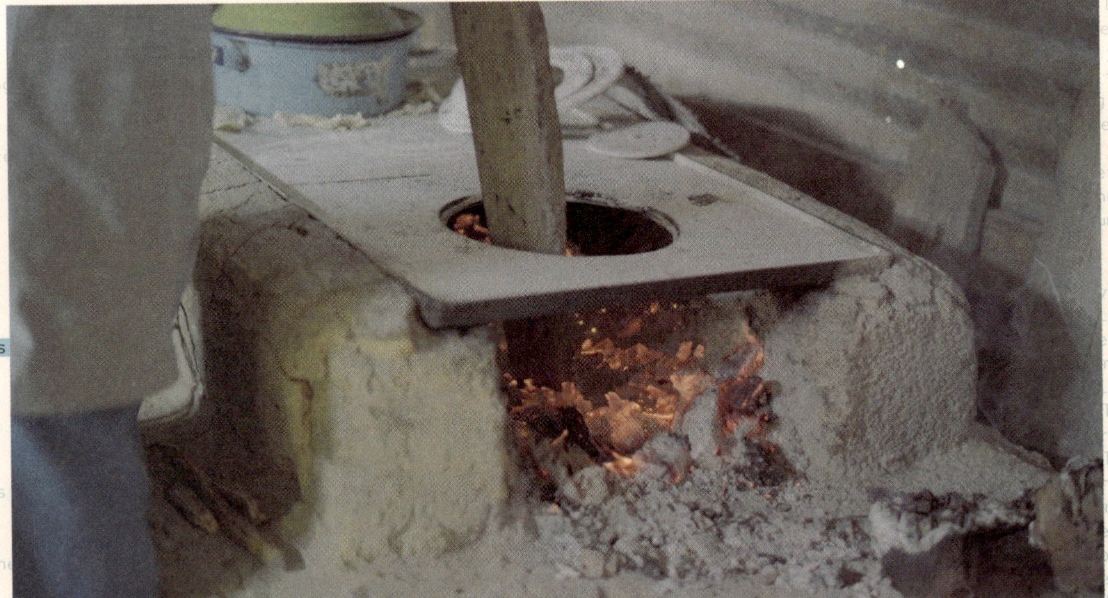

Cooking on adobe stoves made from the ground's clay soil; wood fire collected from the region's oak trees.

Native nanche trees give fruit and Doña Nora goes to harvest the fallen fruit for snacking.

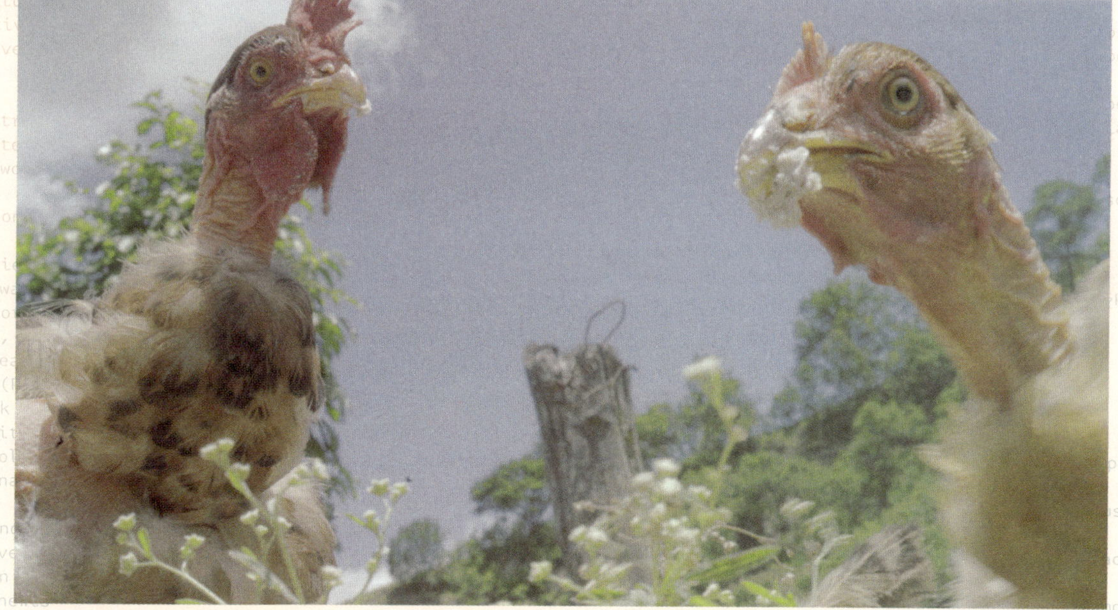

The patio chickens are given sour masa and stale tortillas as food, consuming a portion of the household's "waste."

BIO

Andrea Macias-Yañez is an artist researcher based in Berlin, Germany, working with video and writing to enact forms of environmental remembering, to reveal situated pasts as they exist in the present.

deep organizing
Black Panther Party Free Breakfast Program
healing justice

Chickpea Stew: Steps for Feeding Each Other in This Movement and the Next

MAKES APPROXIMATELY 4 QUARTS

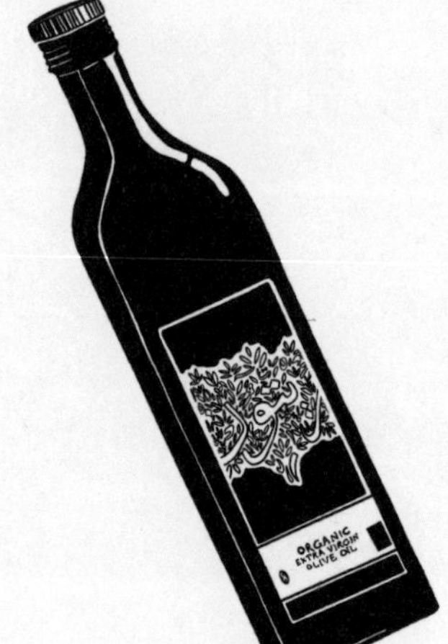

2 tablespoons olive oil
1 teaspoon whole cumin seeds
1 teaspoon whole fennel seeds
1–2 bay leaves
½ teaspoon cayenne pepper powder
Salt, to taste
1 white onion, halved and sliced
4–6 garlic cloves, minced
2 cans diced tomatoes
2 cans chickpeas
32 fluid oz vegetable broth
4 cups water
2 tablespoon white wine vinegar
1 lemon, leave half to garnish
1 tablespoon brown sugar
4–6 oz baby spinach
Bunch of flat-leaf parsley, chopped
Bunch of dill, chopped
Small bunch of mint, finely chopped

1 tablespoon plain Greek yogurt (optional, but highly recommended!)
Half a lemon, to garnish

Mise en place. Look around us. Do we have everything we need?

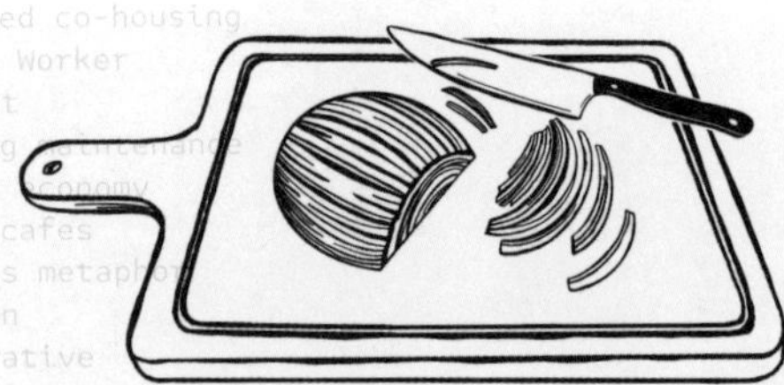

What season is it? Have the barricades fallen? Are the cops still circling with their spy-copters and canisters of tear gas? Are our comrades okay? Are we okay? Are little sprigs of sour grass popping up through the soil, ready to be foraged? Have you eaten yet? No? Let me check the cupboard,
I think I have something in mind.

Step one:
Let's do some prepping! Wash the herbs, rinse the chickpeas, mince the garlic, chop the onion,

oh gosh, my eyes! Quick, grab me some tissues! They're right there on the table. Hey… this sort of reminds me of that one time we got tear-gassed in front of the (pre-burnt) Third Precinct.

Step two:

Hey, can you grab that blue stockpot? Thanks!

Heat up olive oil on medium-high heat until it starts to shimmer and produce little wisps of smoke. Turn heat to low and add whole spices and bay leaves.

Allow the spices to fry in the oil for a few seconds then add onions and sauté, stirring occasionally.

Friend, please, I need to tell you how important it is to bloom your spices! If you don't, it's gonna be bland as fuck.

Next, add garlic and cayenne powder; be mindful, both are fragile and easily scorched. Add tomatoes and cook down.

Step three:

Let's check in. How are we holding ourselves? Avoid sticking, avoid isolation, don't crowd the pan, don't burn out. Speaking of burning out, remember that buddy we met at the Stop Line 3 action? She's been having a tough time. I bet they could use a cup of this stew. Can you drop it off on your way home?

Let stew come to a boil, then turn down heat and add remaining ingredients. Then, let simmer covered for 30 minutes. Simmer uncovered if too watery. Add water if too thick.

Step four:

I know we met during the uprising, but having our friendship continue beyond those actions and that trauma has sustained me in ways I didn't even realize I needed. Without the friendships we've built, I worry I would have just collapsed internally, and I mean, I've done that before. But this time feels different, this moment feels more nourishing. It's hard to bring something back from the verge of ruin. But I feel like that precipice is less dooming when I have you.

Step five:

Give a good stir once or twice while it's simmering.

Are we grabbing bowls or to-go quarts? Bowls, got it. It is curious how hard it can be to feed ourselves and how easy it can be to feed others. If we shared everything we made, we would all have more. Addition becomes multiplication. Some recipes are weird like that. Speaking of weird, can you grab the yogurt? I like it on my stew, it mellows out the spice and makes it all creamy and rich.

Step six:

Serve stew, add a dollop of yogurt (if you're in the know) and a squeeze of lemon. Lemon juice is powerful stuff; be judicious with your acidity.

I struggle with the sourness that builds when we're activated. I feel my body stiffen and get sore with vigilance. I've learned to be more considerate of the way my body interacts in these times, and the way my friendships with you and others have created space for me to ground myself and hold self-compassion. Holding my anger, my fears, and my grief alongside yours has allowed me more room to just be. And being with you is pretty rad.

Step seven:

Take a bite.

Told you, blooming the spices is important!

love
sandplay thera
solidari
somatic heali
storytelli
togethernes
→
wintering as metapho

ustaining movement

To consider together...

The dominant narrative is that after an outburst of militant action, movement work dissipates. The state reports they have stopped us in our tracks, obscuring the cyclical nature of organizing. Revolution has ceased and fallen to the wayside. This narrative falls apart when we emerge again, collaborating towards reimagined actions and initiatives. We know our politics do not exist solely between our boots and the ground. Rises and lulls leave way for experimentation, space for liberatory and relational imaginations.

Who am I eating with? Who am I nourishing? Who is nourishing me? When we're out in the streets, who fosters home? Who lights the candles? Who brews the tea?

How do these friendships built during times of activity sustain us during seasons of repair?

Written with love,

Friends from occupied Dakhóta lands
(also called Minneapolis)
Illustrated by Eva Ngono ❁

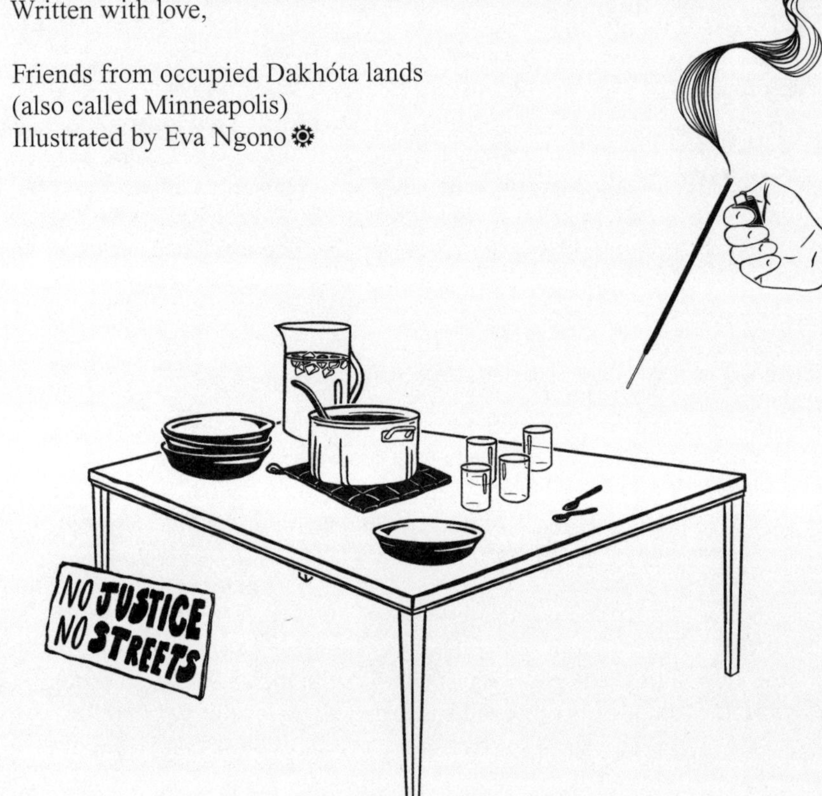

symbo

SE

C O N T R I B U T I O N

A SYMBOL is an idea or object, often represented through visual images, but could be in words or lyrics, which represents multiple other intuitive or mythic ideas that may be condensed or unconscious. Powerful symbols do this well and will have a unique aesthetic quality that makes them meaningful and thought-provoking. Symbols can be archetypal or universal images, found in art, literature, pop culture, and in communication of all kinds. For example, the sun might represent day, warmth, or light, while the moon might mean night, cycles, or change. Symbols can also be understood due to your cultural experiences. Today we might understand an emoji to mean something specific, but people living 50 years ago would not understand it. Symbols sometimes mean something special to you alone, like a kind of butterfly that reminds you of your grandmother. Sometimes by using a symbol, you can express something that you need to say without being explicit, which is helpful when you don't really have the words. Symbolic expression can help us transform and personalize thoughts and feelings, which can be useful in helping us heal. ❁

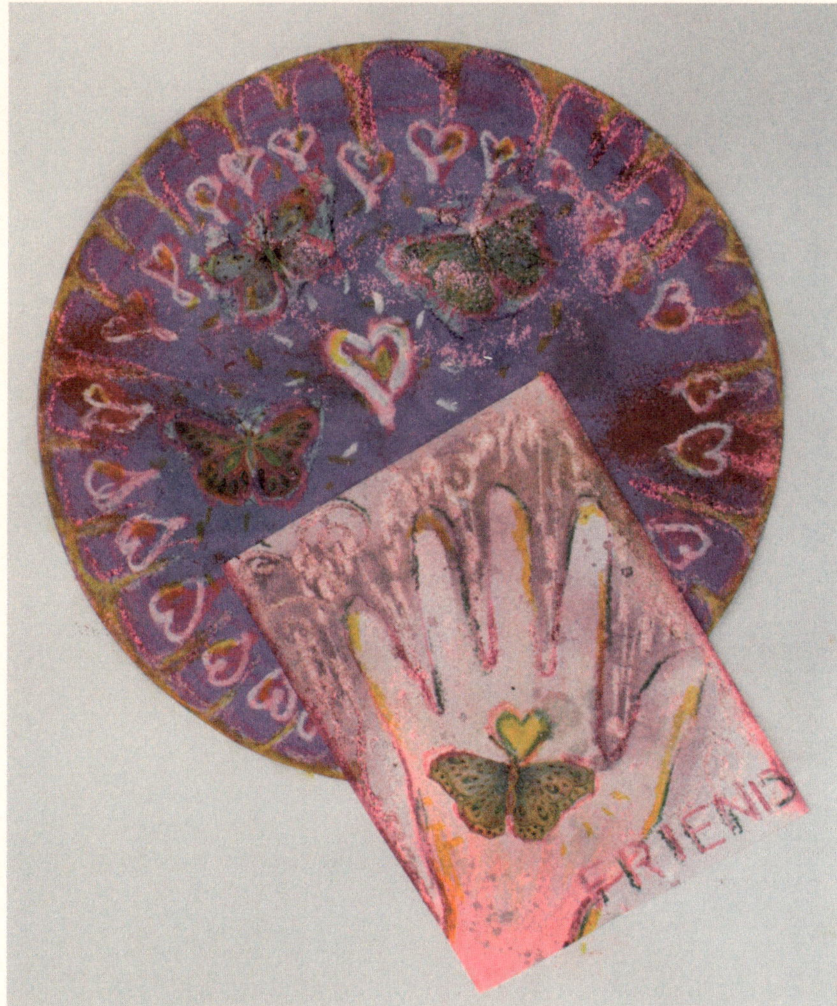

Gioia Chilton, *An Arts-Based Study of the Dynamics of Expressing Positive Emotions within the Intersubjective Art Making Process*, (Doctoral Dissertation, Drexel University).

B I O

Gioia Chilton, PhD, ATR-BC, CSAC, is an artist, art therapist, researcher, and author who loves her family and art therapy community.

Taos Institute, the

CONTRIBUTION

The Taos Institute: Creating Promising Futures One Conversation at a Time

SINCE 1992, the Taos Institute has fostered relationships between scholars, practitioners, students, and change agents from around the world through conferences, courses, workshops, and through the sharing of a wide variety of resources. The Institute promotes social constructionist theory and practice where the source of meaning, value, and action is located within the relational processes of people and environments interacting. The emphasis is relational, collaborative, and appreciative. It is through relational processes that we create more just, inclusive, and diverse worlds in which to live and work.

The Taos Institute offers an online community: *The Taos Institute Commons*. Please join us at taosinstitutecommons.com/spaces/9301489/page ❁

BIO Sheila McNamee, Professor Emerita of Communication at the University of New Hampshire, Founder and Vice President of the Taos Institute.

CONTRIBUTION

WE TURN OVER THE FINAL CARD and there is a ripple of gasps and laughter around the circle: shock, confusion, excitement. A figure dressed in red is blindfolded, her arms tied behind her back. Eight swords pierce the earth in a semi-circle around her. She stands in a shallow puddle of water in the middle of a desolate marshland. In the distance, there is a monolithic castle the colour of concrete. It is a bleak scene of woundedness and humiliation. We ask each other, Who is this figure? What has she done? Is it the people in the castle that have sought to punish her?

*

I ventured deeper into the world of tarot while completing my PhD. I stumbled on a number of artists turning to tarot as a method of forging connections across different crises and contradictions. I often think of a quote from Susan Ballard and Liz Linden, who write on the destabilising effects of anthropogenic climate change and the challenges of representation: "What if the system you seek to capture in your work is *always* bigger than any net of associations you can weave to catch it?"[1] In this sense, tarot offers a method of engaging with complex things without compressing or reducing them into a neat solution. It is a useful tool for thinking across different spatial and temporal scales without erasing one's specific location—a tarot reading always has firm anchors in the present. For me, as a teacher in higher education, a good tarot reading emulates the collaborative and discursive setting of the classroom.

Tarot cards stretch back to the Italian Renaissance, first used as playing cards for entertainment. It was only in the eighteenth and nineteenth centuries that tarot acquired its more recognisable associations with the occult. Classic decks include the Marseille, the Rider-Waite-Smith, and Aleister Crowley's Thoth Tarot. The cards themselves, divided into the Major Arcana and the Minor Arcana, are populated with feudal archetypes, natural elements, gods and goddesses, and so on. Today, there is a vast proliferation of decks that elaborate and reimagine the traditional symbolic language of the tarot. In a typical tarot reading, the querent (or questioner) comes to the reader with a problem for which they are seeking guidance. The reader lays out a spread and interprets the cards, tailoring the reading to the querent's mindset. The spread provides a structure for containing and decoding multiple facets of the problem. The position of each card corresponds to a different factor influencing the querent. A simple three-card tarot spread, for instance, might be divided into past/present/future or situation/obstacle/advice.

To read tarot with a larger group is to come together and invest in a shared problem. When I read with people, I preface the reading with some suggestions about how we go about interpreting the cards. As a form of knowledge production, tarot invites emotional and heuristic responses; it can be cathartic or unsettling. I scaffold the cards with their "official" meanings and explain their position in the spread. However, I try not to exert too much control. I like that tarot opens a space for interpretation and negotiation. I think of tarot reading as akin to Lauren Olamina's Earthseed religion in Octavia Butler's Parable series, set in a post-apocalyptic America filled with gated communities, wildfires, and militias. Earthseed is premised on total impermanence. It offers up a collection of truths that don't cohere into a neat whole. In *Parable of the Talents* (1998), Olamina is reunited with her brother, Marc, a traditional Baptist pastor. He attempts to deliver a sermon to the Earthseed congregation but is met with probing questions. Olamina insists on dialogue as the heart of spiritual practice. Earthseed, like tarot, is pedagogical

ency
esoteric wisdom traditions
groups
ritical pedagogy

and therapeutic. It is not about fixing things into place but working with the irrepressible force of change, or to invoke Olamina's central proverb: God is Change.

*

In December 2022, I facilitate a tarot reading at a conference on "climate emotions" in Sydney. A group of feminist and environmentalist scholars comes together in a small room and we discuss all sorts of things: rage, grief, hope and hopelessness, the ethics of reproduction, migration, plants, fungi, eels, flying foxes, snails, and sniffer dogs. We talk about new practices of ritual and mapmaking. Eventually, we formulate a single question to drive the reading: *What do we need to know right now in this moment as a collective in order to reconnect with ourselves and our bodies?*

We uncover the Four of Swords in the "situation" position; a figure lies flat in a dark chamber. A period of reprieve or rest, a strategic withdrawal in order to heal oneself? Or perhaps a period of mourning? The suit of Swords is often inflected with grief and anger. We talk about catastrophic bushfires, about extinction and politicians who make excuses.

The next card is the Knight of Wands—the "problem" card. A knight on horseback attempts to launch into multiple directions at once. He is eager to move but lacks clarity. We talk about running on the spot in academia, fractured attention spans and the struggle to prioritise. The spread reveals a contradiction: the Four of Swords is a call to return to our bodies while the Knight of Wands shows the extraction of time and labour, spread thin across relationships, projects, and plans.

We sift through the cards, scrutinising and extending their symbols across different contexts. We search each other's interpretations and linger on loose ends. At last, we turn over the Eight of Swords in the "final outcome" position. The figure is alone and blindfolded, standing in the mud, her arms tied behind her back. Her legs, however, are not bound together. The swords do not enclose her. She can walk free if—and only if—she summons the courage to step forward onto treacherous terrain. We tell each other: We must learn how to live without the resources we depend upon the most. We must *disbelieve* in our own helplessness.[2]

Tarot teaches us how to sit with contradictions: the slow and the urgent, the spiritual and material, knowing or not knowing. The point is not to choose one or the other but to plot new movements in the spaces between. There are no big solutions without these messy processes, riddled with fraught questions and unexpected tangents. ❁

1 Ballard and Linden, *Art Writing and Allegory in the Anthropocene*, 105.

2 Pollack, *Seventy-Eight Degrees of Wisdom: A Tarot Journey to Self-Awareness*, 220.

BIO

Anastasia Murney is a writer and teacher living on unceded Gadigal land. She holds a PhD from the University of New South Wales.

temporary autonomous zone

CONTRIBUTION

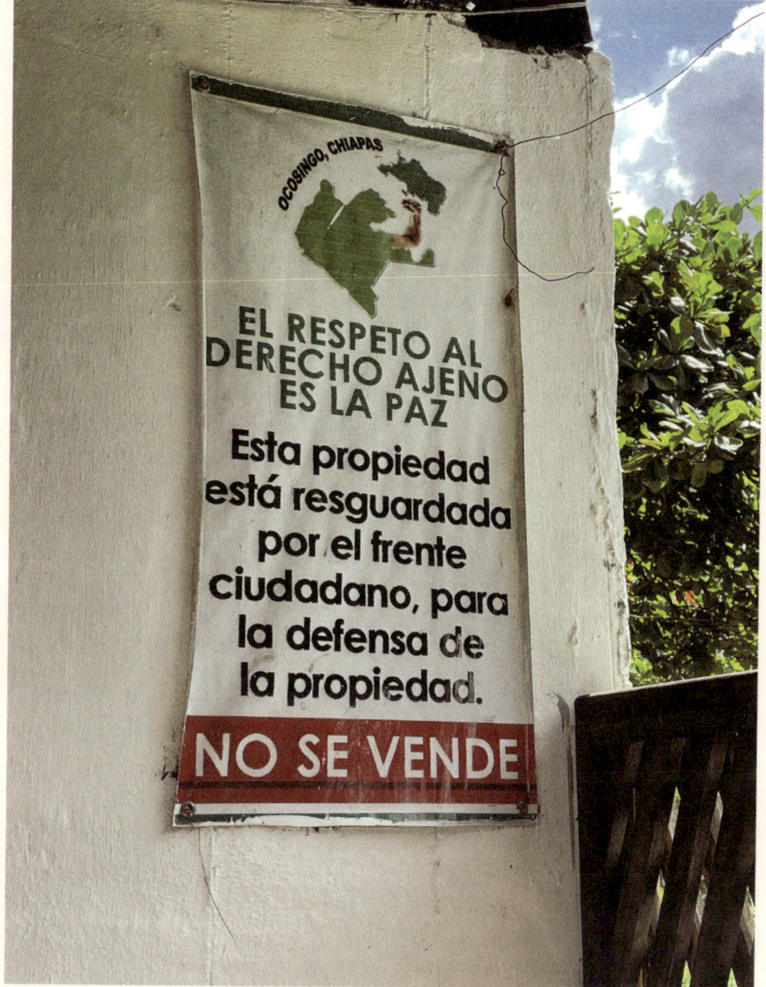

TAZ, sign placed at a home's entrance in Chiapas, Mexico, photo, Andrea Macias-Yañez, 2023.

English translation:

The respect for
the rights of others
is peace.

This property
is protected
by the citizen front,
for the defense of property.

NOT FOR SALE

postwork imaginaries

solidarity econom

togetherness

ONE OF THE DEFINING documents in agrarian governance in Mexico is the Plan de Ayala of 1917 by Emiliano Zapata. This document declared that all land, water, and mineral rights were property of the Mexican people. The slogan "Land & Liberty" grasped the campesino/a's revolutionary call, which eventually led to the creation of Article 27. This marked the legal construction of ejidos: a communal land holding system where the state was meant to expropriate land from large landholders and reassign it to eligible indigenous and campesino/a populations. In this context, "campesino/as" describes the laborers who work and depend on the land for sustenance. Today ejidos make up roughly 30% of Mexican territory and are intended to follow communitarian guidelines set up by the state. This includes having meetings once a month, where every decision, even those of an individual, must be agreed upon within community assemblies. Ejidos came under threat in 1992 due to neoliberal reform in which the first edit to Article 27 was made. It allowed the transformation of ejido land titles into private titles, an opportunity for individuals to surrender their status as communal landowners. The state hoped for ejidos to separate into parcels, making them susceptible to buy-outs by commercial interests.

The legal status of ejidos continues to be a precarious one. This right to land persists symbolically in social memory, a cause to be vocalized—especially in parts of Mexico with high indigenous and campesino/a populations. In this image the sign is placed outside a home of a woman, living inside an ejido, whose family stems from this region for generations. Across her home sits the Mayan archeological site of Tonina. The call for territorial respect grasps the residues of colonial conquest; here ancient spirits are tangible in the land she marks as home. ❁

BIO Andrea Macias-Yañez is an artist researcher based in Berlin, Germany, working with video and writing to enact forms of environmental remembering, to reveal situated pasts as they exist in the present.

lingering
love
lunar cycle
Magic School, the
mapping support
marginality
(as a site of
resistance)
Marxist social
work
membership theory
in social work
mending
metaphor
mikveh
mobile libraries
movement
lawyering
mutual aid
mycelia as
metaphor
narradrama
narrative
medicine
narrative therapy
nepantla/
nepantleras
nonviolent
communication
ongoingness
peer counseling
peer-to-peer
health network
person-situation
perspective
perspective via
faith
pleasure
poems/poetry
poetic meter
polarity work
post-
oppositionality
postwork
imaginaries
poverty-aware
social work
paradigm, the
power threat
meaning (PTM)
framework
pre(care)ity
prison abolition
professionalism
without
performance
progressive
education
public benefits
public library,
the
Qigong
radical
administration
radical care in
the arts
radical childcare
in movement
spaces
radical
inclusion
radical
papermaking
radical presence
radical
social work
Radical Therapist
Journal, The
Rank and File
Movement (RFM)
in social work

Theatre of the Oppresse

EDITOR'S NOTE

The Theater of the Oppressed is a participatory form of theater developed by Brazilian playwright and director Augusto Boal. It aims to engage audiences in interactive, thought-provoking experiences by addressing social and political issues through theatrical techniques, encouraging dialogue, and empowering individuals to explore and challenge oppression in society. Jessie and dizzy's essay, which unfolds like a performance, speaks to Boal's work. —CH

CONTRIBUTION

"bourgeois theater is the finished theater"
or
"reality was & is in transition"
inspired by roland schimmelpfennig

dark as a theater

cluttered as a
theater, an atom
comes on. all
characters provide
their own light

distraction 1:
You are draining me of life like a vacuum cleaner does!
distraction 2:
You don't know me or my story!

A.

photo-romance
web2 social platforms constitute a photo-romance
instagram is a photo-romance
meta is a photo-container
images placed over the eye
a mask as an entry
a mask no longer shuts off access, it opens the wormhole photo-romance is, according to Boal, "sheer trash." here boal taps into the future: the production of 2.01 trillion tonnes of garbage produced annually
trash world, waste planet.

B.

The spect-actor sees me and wants to kill me. The spect-actor carried me and wanted to be me. The spect-actor is me and I am the viewer.

An audience is an archive,
An archive becomes audience.

What I want from theater is everything. What I want from the theater is a hole. The bibliography, the masthead. Teevee screens, lots of ephemera, shoot-outs, duels, musical chairs for neurotic researchers. I am saying: Kiss an actor. You might as well.

C.

An archive can be a graveyard
A graveyard holds an archive
when the audience leaves,
when the ghostlight comes out,
the seats are headstones

→

re-author
reclaiming selfhood
recognition
redistribution
Reflecting on Justi
reflexivi
Rei
relation
interviewin
relationali
resistan
resisting t
parental loss
narrative
resonan
respectful visiti
respite roo
rest as resistan
reven
revolutiona
mothering
ritu
sanctua
sandplay thera
sau
seed banki
sex positivi
shadow integrati
Sick Woman Theo
slow textil
slownes
social chan
ecosystem framewor
social constructio
social practic
social therapeuti
Social Welfare Acti
Alliance, the
solidarit
solidarity econom
somatic heali
songs/singin
sound heali
speculative desig
spell
staying with th
trouble
storytellin
street newspape
strength
perspective, the
sufficienc
sustaining movemen
symbo
Taos Institute, th
taro
temporary autonomou
zones
Theatre of the
Oppressed
theories of change
theosoph
therapeutic writing
togetherness
trans practices
transformative
justice
traspatio
12-step programs
undercover anti-
bullying teams
vigil
water
wildness
wintering as metaphor
wishes
witchery
yoga
zinemaking

Theatre of the Oppressed

D.

myth has faeries & ghosts & titans & banshees. hollering & twinkling & peripherals. faith & doubt are fraternal twins, not enemies. could you hook an audience on a myth? each nonactor, could you make them notice the flecks of light? would mystifying bring about waking from the optimized drudgery?

E.

Nonactor, how do you get a theater to speak?
a body has no mouth a body has no brain
nobody has no brain.
an actor puts on a performance. standing ovation. a play happens in your periphery. a play is a grid & wires & a debt obligation.

an actor runs the program.

F.

Actors will always resent audiences (to some degree). they pull them out of their own suspension in (dis)belief. their presence, who they are, why they are there, their coughs, their awkward laughs, their jewelry, their talking, their heckling, their bright red tomatoes. should actors pull a Latin mass? turn away to face the grand imagined space like a bus driver driving into the foggy night? Some genre may be born to tease this out, but the present encounter allows the possibility of getting it rather than understanding it.

"in theater, any break stimulates"

an atom:
every grain of sand, each moment i wish i could tell you the name and history of all the particles

the coffee cup from above:
but who can blame a single audience member of not knowing where the art begins and the reality sparkles thru?

sixty-year-old steel worker:
forgiveness is an act of maintenance

Hey, do, we are gonna take a moment here to thank our sponsors: Augusto Boal, writer of Theatre of the Oppressed, Urizen Books, the original English publisher, Theatre Communications Group Inc. for the copy we based this production on and viewers like you. Thank you! Thank you! Seriously, thank you.

Commence. ✽

BIOS

Jessie McCarty, cataloger and poet, author of *The Bovine Huff* (Track and Field Studios, 2021).

dizzy turek writes in Chicago, but is originally from Columbus, OH.

theories of change

SEE

C O N T R I B U T I O N

A THEORY OF CHANGE IS AN IDEA that is somewhere between an intuitive hunch and an informed guess about how to get a critical mass of people to change their opinions or take action toward social change. Despite what clueless historians or pompous pundits might believe, social change seldom happens at random or merely because mysterious forces collide to create a set of new conditions or simply because of an Illuminati directive; it often happens due to a kind of social engineering that is done deliberately, over time, through a lot of materials and/or sweat equity in the form of social movements. And social movements are powered by organizers who do their work according to a theory of change. Every organizer or social change project contains a theory of change that articulates (implicitly or explicitly) what they want to change and how that change comes about. A theory of change is distinct from a "strategy," which is *how* a specific group of organizers or project helps contribute to or develop their theory of change.

An example of a powerful theory of change comes from the groundbreaking group, Movement Generation:

> It has become clear we face two distinct possible futures: economic and ecological transition or collapse. If we stay the current course of a globalized industrial economic model, collapse is inevitable. We must, instead, create an intentional pathway—a Just Transition—towards local, living, loving economies. Movement Generation is working hard to build, secure and defend this Just Transition... [1]

Movement Generation's theory of change (which is much longer than excerpted) starts by explaining the political and economic moment we're in, the stakes we face, and makes a proposal about a specific model that will ensure a future for all of us. They share with us a vision of the world that they see, a contrasting vision that they want, and why it's important. A clear theory of change shares a worldview, takes positions with a point of view, and offers solutions that the organizers are a part of. It can be a kind of storytelling about who you are, why you care, and what you believe can be done to improve this tiny, troubled planet. ❁

1 Movement Generation, movement.generation.org/about/.

B I O

Richael Faithful is a Black trans-southern multi/interdisciplinary healer, culture worker, and attorney.

heosophy

CONTRIBUTION

Regarding Theosophy

esoteric wisdom traditions

existentialism

WHEN IT COMES TO questions of religion, philosophy, and theology, an inevitable undercurrent surfaces: tension. But it's hard to do away with our neatly packed systems of understanding the stark, mysterious, ineffable nature of reality. These systems, so dear to us, have long been woven into the fabric of our societies. And despite the fact that there is a myriad of intricate mosaics, sects, and subsects within major belief systems, many schools of thought confidently deem their way the one true way. But this exclusionary system of thinking fosters fragmentation and draws deep divisive lines in the sand.

This way of thinking ultimately lacks a depth of insight that is inclusive of the whole. Consider the intellectual clashes between Aristotle and Socrates, Freud and Jung, or Darwin and Lamarck. Each pairing of thought leaders is fundamentally divided on the nature of the world we live in. The former of each pairing postulates that this material realm is all there is, while the latter acknowledges the existence of an unknown, ineffable realm, one that transcends our material existence. Socrates called it the daemon, Jung named it the collective unconscious, and Lamarck gives credence to the power of intention to direct the way creatures (including us) evolve. These thinkers operate from an understanding that simultaneously acknowledges and involves the analytical material side with the intuitive ineffable side. And while many religions offer navigation to the spiritual realm, they often fall short of including each other. To that end, theosophy gives promise because it acknowledges both truth and shortcoming common to each system of religious approach.

What is theosophy? Etymologically: from the Greek *theos* ("god") and *sophia* ("wisdom"), is generally understood to mean "divine wisdom." It is a spiritual and philosophical system inspired by many religions and spiritualities.

To be a theosophist requires only three things. The three central objects of theosophy:

1. To form a nucleus of the Universal Brotherhood of Humanity, without distinction of race, creed, sex, caste, or color.
2. To encourage the study of comparative religion, philosophy, and science.
3. To investigate unexplained laws of Nature and the powers latent in man.[1]

I'd also like to include here Dr. Annie Besant's primary and secondary meanings for the word theosophy. In her view the primary meaning has to do with the development of the ability to gain a "direct" personal knowledge of the divine. This aspect is present in the mysticism and esotericism of different religions:

> Theosophy is this direct knowledge of God; the search after this is the Mysticism, or Esotericism, common to all religions, thrown by Theosophy into a scientific form, as in Hinduism, Buddhism, Roman Catholic Christianity, and Islamic Sufism. Like these, it teaches in a quite clear and definite way the methods of reaching firsthand knowledge by unfolding the spiritual consciousness, and by evolving the organs through which that consciousness can function on our earth—once more, the methods of meditation and of a discipline of life.[2]

The secondary meaning lies at the level of the basic philosophical and moral teachings shared by different religions:

> Theosophy, in a secondary sense—the above being the primary—is the body of doctrine, obtained by separating the beliefs common to all religions from the peculiarities, specialities, rites, ceremonies, and customs that mark off one religion from another; it presents these common truths as a consensus of world beliefs, forming, in their entirety, the Wisdom-religion, or the Universal Religion, the source from which all separate religions spring, the trunk of the Tree of Life from which they all branch forth.[3]

In my interpretation, theosophy beckons for a more profound exploration and rediscovery of truths inherent in each system. Its explorations delve into the shared essence permeating the world's religions and spiritualities, with a focus on unity. There is an emphasis on universal spiritual wisdom that transcends singular doctrines and schools of thinking. The mission is to cultivate a broader understanding of the nature of our reality and the interconnectedness of all things. That is the very thing I had been culturing and had cultivated in my private world. Like a platonic theosophist, I was approaching the world through philosophical, scholarly, mystical, and religious studies, learning from books on psychology, physics, spirituality, myths, and cross-cultural conversations, syntheses, and parallel comparisons. It is impossible to explain every intricacy and nuance of the pathways I explored to arrive here at this juncture. Nor can I predict the ways my path will continue to unfold and branch onward. But I can say that I am currently enjoying learning to view the world through the lens of theosophy. So for now I will continue to seek and explore timeless spiritual wisdom with the help of the elder sages.

Still, I will state for the record that there is not any one rigid definition of theosophy, save its central tenets. And that is the beauty of it. Perhaps, at the very least, you will be inspired to know there are seekers of arcane knowledge who make a practice creating space for each other, who regularly meet to explore and rediscover the mystery of our reality. After all, we're all just walking each other home. ✺

1 Besant, *Theosophy*, 7.

2 Besant, *Theosophy*, 7.

3 Ransom, *A Short History of the Theosophical Society*.

B Lejla Ćatović is an artist,
I writer, and thoughtworker
O with a penchant for the
mystical.

herapeutic writing

CONTRIBUTION

THERAPEUTIC WRITING is the use of writing as a form of self-communication for healing and well-being. Therapeutic writing is sometimes done in a journal or a diary, or in letters that are not sent to anyone, except yourself. Some forms of therapeutic writing are our efforts to work through past difficult circumstances and traumas. Other times, therapeutic writing is a place to think of new ideas, to set goals, or work out future plans. Some tips for therapeutic writing include keeping your writing private, as it's just for you, not for other people, and not worrying about spelling or grammar or sentence structure—your English teacher will never read your journal! It's a good idea to choose not to write about things that feel overwhelming. If you feel like you're going to freak out about something that you're writing about, don't write about that thing. Wait until another time when you'll be able to handle it; you can always come back to it later. Put the date on what you wrote so that you can remember when you wrote stuff and discover how much you've grown as you look back over your past writing!

Remember to write with self-compassion, being kind to your inner writer. Writing for less than 20 minutes at a time keeps it fresh. It doesn't matter if you write by hand, on a computer, on your phone, or voice to text—whatever you want to do is fine. After you do your writing, take a moment to read it back over and then add a statement at the bottom reflecting on what you wrote. Jot down any questions you have for yourself, or further thoughts, or stuff you're curious about, for next time.

If you can't think of anything to write about, there are lots of books with more prompts. One I liked is called *Journal Therapy for Calming Anxiety* by Kathleen Adams. The internet is a good place to find writing prompts. The benefit of writing is that it helps you work out your thoughts, releasing them from rolling around in your head, ending anxiety and rumination, and adding insight and clarity. Writing is a way of thinking, a way of feeling through things, a way of being. As we write, we discover ourselves. ❁

BIO

Gioia Chilton, PhD, ATR-BC, CSAC, is an artist, art therapist, researcher and author who loves her family and art therapy community.

togethernes

CONTRIBUTION

IN ORDER TO PARTICIPATE fully in togetherness, I have learned the importance of leaving space for pain. Not that this is particularly new, or easy.

It *is* easy to pretend that suffering is somewhere else, somewhere over there and not here. Really it is everywhere. Grief is universally routine.

Instead of being confined like a spider under glass, maybe we can be properly together by acknowledging this squirmy, slippery, consuming thing. A practice of togetherness may involve saying [to others' pain]: "Hi, I'm here. I know you're here too." Not that this statement is a panacea… but pain often stings more in silence.

Maybe you already know this. Maybe it's a little reductive to talk about it in this way. Maybe it's nice that someone said it.

This togetherness is facilitated by an aching that ebbs and flows naturally, purposely un-forgotten. This togetherness feels whole when we remember our pain as a member of the family, and not a ghost.

This togetherness may not fix what has been broken or return what has been lost, but it might make moving forward just that bit easier. ❁

BIO

Deborah Tsogbe is a designer focused on knowing and creating for grief, memory, and comfort.

narrative therapy
poems/poetry
poetic meter
radical presences
solidari
storytelli
zinemakin

rans practices

"I AM NOT TRANS; I PRACTICE TRANS PRACTICES."

Red Tremmel, a queer scholar and activist based in New Orleans, stated this offhandedly as the two of us sat chatting on the grass of Performing Arts Forum, a former-monastery-turned-artist-residency in St. Erme, France. It was 2019, and I was spending the summer in France before beginning a master's program in Choreography and Performance in Germany. I didn't yet identify as trans or nonbinary. But something about what Red said opened a door for my own practice of transness in the years to follow.

In March 2021, I rubbed testosterone gel on my shoulders for the first time. I didn't quite feel "high on T" like Paul B. Preciado (a trans scholar I had come to idolize). Instead, I felt confused, scared, desiring this change yet confronted with biochemical shifts that remained unknown to me. I felt as though I was on the edge of the cliff and choosing to jump off. Sure, I would discover so much below me, but would I like it? Would I want to stay there? Quite literally, the changes wrought by hormone therapy are irreversible, and that sense of finality triggered anxiety in me. At the same time, my intuition felt certain that I would continue to wonder about T if I didn't try it.

To deal with the conflicting emotions inside me, I found myself engaging in practices to stimulate the vagus nerve. I was newly encountering these techniques through a training program in somatic abolitionism with trauma therapist Resmaa Menakem. I hummed while lying on the floor. I danced alone in my bedroom, producing brain chemicals to regulate my nervous system through the catharsis of physical praxis. I also started to furiously do bodyweight and plyometric exercises, looking to build muscle thanks to the boost from T. Throughout all of this, I looked around, hoping to find others dealing with these questions of self-actualization through body modification. I found very few in my immediate vicinity of Giessen, Germany—a grey university town.

That's when the idea of gathering a group of trans people to develop body practices together was born. I had been struck by the level of attention I was giving to my body and its physicality, and I realized that every transgender person—whether engaging in biomedical transition or not—spends an incredible amount of energy considering their bodily presentation and existence. Whether in practices of self-styling, mental health regulation, or social performance, trans people are experts in the performative potential of the body.

I decided to orient my MA performance project set to premiere in Frankfurt in 2022 around this idea. Namely, I wanted to gather a group of trans people—not dancers or performers but simply trans people whose expertise lies in their daily experience of the body—together to explore the question: What are trans practices?

Our four months of monthly rehearsals offered experimental answers to this question rather than stable definitions. In the studio, our group of seven created movement scores out of the daily practices that brought us embodied euphoria; experimented with new pronouns at the beginning of rehearsals; sang improvisational songs exploring the diverse pitches of our voices; and wrote utopian schedules for daily life in the style of Larry Mitchell's *The Faggots and Their Friends Between Revolutions*. On lunch breaks, we discussed challenges to accessing healthcare, the dearth of mixed queer spaces in Frankfurt, and our favorite trans characters on television.

Over time, it became clear that "trans practices" were whatever physical and social practices support bodily autonomy in the self and in others—and that respect the ways we desire to be seen. Trans practices are also dependent on the particular people in a particular room. As gender theorist Judith Butler wrote in *Undoing Gender*, "We are undone by the other. And if we're not, we're missing something."[1] Butler's phrasing implies that we also are "done" by each other; that is, we create the conditions for each other to exist. In my view, trans practices do just this, creating the conditions for humans to move in and out of diverse modes of being, especially in relation to gender presentation and self-definition.

I'll leave the reader with an example of a trans practice that I developed during those four months in Frankfurt and elaborated down the line through further studio research in Berlin. It draws from the practice of Authentic Movement developed by dance therapist Mary Starks Whitehouse and elaborated by dancer Janet Adler; and it pulls from consent-based touch practices developed by sex therapist Betty Martin.

A Trans Practice of Authentic Movement with Consent
drawing on the work of Nancy Starks Whitehouse,
Janet Adler, and Betty Martin

Find a person to pair up with for this practice.
One person is the Mover.
The other person is the Witness.
The Mover's task is to move (whatever that means to you!) without judgement, keeping eyes closed.
The Witness's task is to witness the Mover with a warm, attentive gaze. (Also, offer a guiding hand if they're about to run into a wall!)
Before beginning the tasks, the Witness asks the Mover: "How would you like me to see you?"
The Mover responds from a space of intuition. Any answer is correct, whether it's playful, deep, or scary. For example, "I want you to see me as a bird flying in the sky." Or, "I want you to see me as though I'm your big brother."
The Witness then replies with any questions or clarifications.
Set a timer for 7 minutes.
Begin, with the Mover moving and the Witness witnessing.
When you are finished, immediately trade roles, re-pose the question, and do the practice for another 7 minutes.
Once both partners have practiced both roles, discuss for 3 to 5 minutes about what you felt and observed.

1 Butler, *Undoing Gender*, 23.

BIO elena rose light (they/them), choreographer, performer, writer.

pre(care)ity

somatic heali

ransformative justice

CONTRIBUTION

THERAPEUTIC PRACTICE as transformative justice practice. Therapy as a space to practice different ways of embodying, being, and relating in the world. How can we embody the liberatory worlds that we want to co-create? What do we need to practice? What do we need to process in order to practice differently? How do we navigate harm, violence, rupture, and repair? How do we also lean into pleasure, ease, rest, and joy?

As Mia Mingus says, "If transformative justice teaches us anything, it is that systemic change alone is not enough. There are also many changes that must happen at the community and individual levels as well."[1] And Emergent Strategy teaches us, "Small is good, small is all. (The large is a reflection of the small.)"[2] Shifts in our interpersonal relationships and communities ripple out into society at large.

Therapy can be a space where we unpack the ways that we perpetuate harm in our relationships. It can be a space to practice apology, accountability, and responsibility. We can practice consent, feedback, and mindful emotional expression. We can lean into community care and learn to build care webs that don't rely on harmful institutions of so-called care.

Normative, traditional therapy perpetuates many of the interlocking systems of oppression, and so the first layer requires us practitioners to resist and refuse these harmful practices. Then we are invited to envision and practice alternatives with our client community members. We can re-orient therapeutic practice to one that participates in the co-creating of more liberatory worlds and relationships. The elimination or deconstruction of harmful ways is not enough. The constructive imagining, building, and practicing of alternatives is required for transformation.

What might therapeutic practice look like if we approached it through a transformative justice framework? ❁

1 Mingus, "You Are Not Entitled To Our Deaths," para. 6.

2 brown, *Emergent Strategy: Shaping Change, Changing Worlds*, 4.

BIO

Ji-Youn Kim (they/she) is a queer, currently non-disabled Corean immigrant and settler, joy-seeker, liberatory dreamer, psych survivor, justice-oriented therapist-ish, and ongoing creation of community.

CONTRIBUTION

RUE, BASIL, spearmint, mountain mint, bougainvillea, cilantro, wild cilantro, epazote, white sagebush, guava leaves, black nightshade, Mexican pepperleaf, moringa, fennel, avocado leaves, neem. A backyard, a space tangential or completely surrounding the home. That's where the traspatio lies. Doña Magdalena, Doña Rosenda, Doña Mary Carmen, and Doña Lupe tend to theirs. They cook on thin metal sheets over oak wood. Chickens and maybe turkeys walk around, sometimes cats nap near the adobe stove. Doña Nora shows me the black corn she'll soak tonight. The night before I leave El Triunfo II, Doña Rosenda trims two months' worth of leaves from her malabar bush, so that I may plant it. I'm to make one liter of tea a day, drink it as I do water for one month to soothe my digestion. Back in my family's home, a neighbor recognizes the plant for its medicinal properties for the liver. We pack him a bag full of leaves.

White chili, serrano chili, tepin chili, pomegranate, coconut, jackfruit. Ornamental plants attract pollinators and deflect pests. Herbal gardens provide medicine, particularly convenient when a community is disconnected from urban centers. Together the variety of herbs, vegetables, animals, and trees rooted in the traspatio create dense soils that help prevent erosion. Women share their plants and seeds with each other, making social exchange part of the community's network. These areas reflect the necessities that state infrastructure cannot meet—this is a women's experimental cultivation space. *Red corn, white corn, orchids, dahlias, green avocado, aloe vera.* ❁

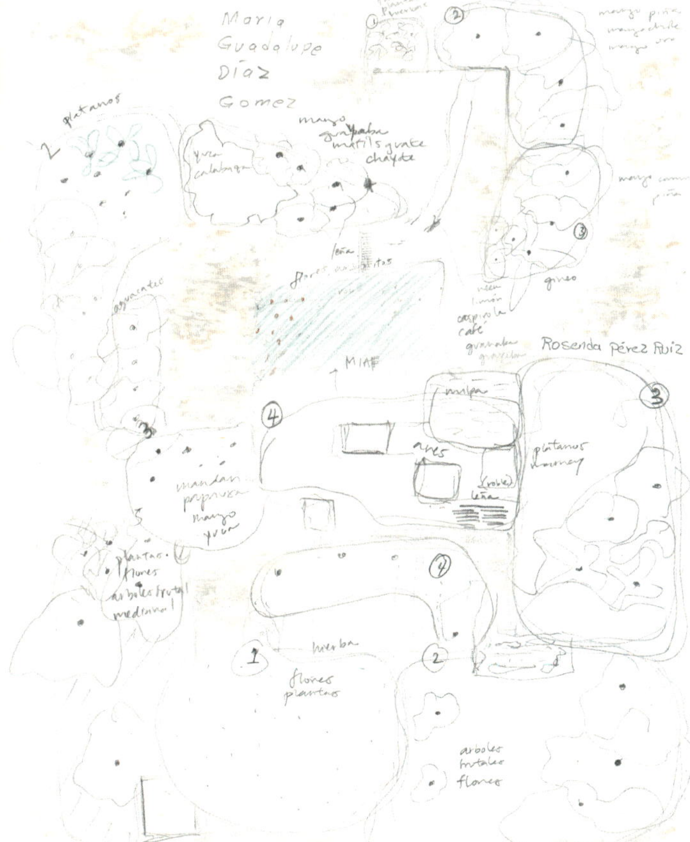

Traspatios belonging to Doña Rosenda, Doña Mary Carmen, Doña Magdalena, and Doña Lupe, living in El Triunfo II inside La Sepultura Bioreserve in Chiapas, Mexico, collage by Andrea Macias-Yañez, 2021.

BIO

Andrea Macias-Yañez is an artist researcher based in Berlin, Germany, working with video and writing to enact forms of environmental remembering, to reveal situated pasts as they exist in the present.

2-step programs

C O N T R I B U T I O N

A Conversation

ERIN: We both have long experiences with 12-step programs, yet it's only at the 11th hour that we've decided to add the concept to our list of radical helping concepts. I can't even remember whether we discussed it at all when we were first generating the list! Why didn't we include it?

CHRIS: Great question. I suppose I didn't think to add it because of some of the more popular critiques of Alcoholics Anonymous and other 12-step programs. These include how the language and literature may not be inclusive or relevant to all individuals, particularly women and people from non-white, non-Christian backgrounds. Plus the focus on abstinence, which many of the harm-reduction folks have had to struggle against. And the 12-step model's dominance in the addiction treatment world and the lack of alternative treatment options. I think it's easy to dismiss AA as a Western modernist approach that is a lot of things other than radical. But after discussing both our histories, it's pretty easy to dive down past the surface and see that 12-step programs can be considered radical in contemporary times due to their stark contrast with the prevailing neoliberal individualism that dominates many aspects of healing practices and self-help culture.

ERIN: Yes, that's exactly it—the collective orientation, the trust in the power of the group, the mutual aid aspects: Those feel so different from individualistic approaches to treatment. You and I have been talking about the longing for "magick" in helping modalities, and I really do think there's something magick-al about how ritualized an AA meeting is, like: "My name is _____, and I'm an alcoholic," "Hi, ___." The Serenity Prayer[1] feels to me like an incantation, a spell. All of the slogans,[2] too! And the idea of anonymity kind of makes AA feel like a secret society, right?

CHRIS: Absolutely, 12-step programs' non-hierarchical structures and commitments to anonymity stand in contrast to the individualistic pursuit of fame, recognition, and social media–driven self-promotion often encouraged by neoliberalism. Members are not required to reveal their identities, titles, or achievements, reinforcing the idea that everyone's recovery journey is equally valuable. You also mentioned the rituals found in AA. Michael White, in his important paper "Challenging the culture of consumption: Rites of passage and communities of acknowledgement," wrote that Alcoholics Anonymous had a profound understanding of the significance of rites of passage and that AA provides a formalization of the stages of separation and reincorporation, which is part and parcel of the journey of recovery. He also wrote how in the ritual of an AA meeting there are opportunities for persons to share about the decisions they have made to break from excessive alcohol consumption, the values and purposes behind these decisions, and to tell and retell the stories of their lives before a group of witnesses, many of whom are veterans of such journeys. Thinking this through has me thinking that many groups looking to bring about change and transformation, or folks trying to build coalitions across difference, could learn a lot from AA. What do you think?

ERIN: Storytelling, narrative, re-storying—however you want to frame it—has been such an important thread running through this Encyclopedia project. Yes, I totally agree that giving testimony in community has incredible transformative potential. But I guess like so many powerful things, that transformative energy could go in a liberatory direction—or it could also result in shame and repression. Or all of the above. It's so complicated.

CHRIS: Indeed, collective endeavors like AA and other similar sorts of communities, especially those with transformative potential, can in fact be messy. The power of storytelling and testimony in these contexts can lead to both liberation and repression, and that tension is precisely what makes them so dynamic and relevant to our uncertain future. It's true that there's no guarantee that communities like AA will always steer in a liberatory direction. However, by acknowledging the potential for both positive and negative outcomes, we can approach them with a sense of responsibility and mindfulness. We can actively work to foster inclusivity, openness, and a commitment to shared values within these communities to maximize their positive impact. In essence, communities like 12-step programs can serve as training grounds for navigating the messy and complex challenges of the future. They remind us that collective action and mutual support can be powerful tools for change, as long as we remain aware of the potential pitfalls and actively work to address them. So, while they may not be perfect, they offer valuable lessons in building solidarity and resilience in an ever-evolving world. ❁

1 Here is The Serenity Prayer:
"God, grant me the serenity to accept the things I cannot change,
the courage to change the things I can,
and the wisdom to know the difference," attributed to Reinhold Niebuhr.

2 Examples of AA maxims include:
Easy does it
One day at a time
This too shall pass
Live and let live
Bottles were only a symbol
First things first
Think, think, think
Let go and let God
Progress, not perfection
Just for today
Nothing changes if nothing changes
HALT: Hungry, angry, lonely, tired

BIOS

Chris Hoff, PhD, LMFT, is the Founder and Executive Director of California Family Institute and a Liminal Space Tour Guide.

Erin Segal, MSW, PhD, is a middle-aged mother, wife, daughter, and friend who facilitates groups with elders and, along with Julie Cho, publishes unusual books about care.

Undercover anti-bullying teams

CONTRIBUTION

ESTABLISHING UNDERCOVER ANTI-BULLYING TEAMS is an example of a practice that breaks new ground for counselors and employs their professional skills in a way that addresses bullying behaviors and transforms relationships without resorting to a punitive approach. It utilizes peer influence to change the experience of the students getting bullied. It can reduce bullying in a school, to the benefit of students' learning, teachers' classroom management, and administrators' workloads. The term "undercover teams" was coined by Bill Hubbard[1] drawing on a "no blame" approach to bullying, after Robinson and Maines.[2]

The intervention draws from a narrative perspective that understands the practice of bullying as a narrative performance. "Perpetrators," "targets," and "bystanders" act out their roles along a known plot trajectory. Each student is a participant in a storyline, rather than a problem person in their essence. We stand on the premise that "The person is not the problem; the problem is the problem."[3] Or in this case, "The bully is not the problem, the bullying is the problem!"

We also do not want to totalize individuals' identities[4] as "bullies" or "victims." Instead, we assume that every person involved in the bullying relationship is also capable of other styles of relationship. No one is a bully or a victim by nature. The bully, the victim, and the bystander are names, not so much of persons as of positions in a narrative. People enter these positions and perform their narrative function, but they can also set the story aside, given an effective invitation to do so. The Undercover Anti-Bullying Team offers an opportunity for each of them to step out of the story of bullying and into another storyline that is incompatible with ongoing bullying. The bullying relationship is more central to the practice of bullying than the personal identity of either the bully or the victim. Hence, it makes sense to target the bullying relationship directly for transformation. The Undercover Anti-Bullying Team approach does just this.

The Undercover Anti-Bullying Team is implemented in five phases.

5-STEP PROCESS:

STEP 1.

- Interview the student getting bullied, by themselves (30 minutes).

  The counselor asks the student who is being targeted to identify six students with the most power, influence, and prestige, which also includes two of the students doing the worst of the bullying.

STEP 2.

- Assemble the undercover team, explain their mission, and complete the five-point plan (30 minutes).
- Inform teachers of the class by e-mail of the existence and purpose of the team.

  The students are then invited to a team to change the experience of the student getting bullied. The counselor reads the story, from the student's perspective, of what is happening to them and how it is affecting them. Then there is a discussion of how they might feel if this were happening to them. The students usually say things such as, "I would not want to be at school," or, "I would be so sad." Together, the team is given an opportunity to create a plan to encourage kindness and respect, and support the student getting bullied. The students usually say things like, "Let's invite her to sit with us at lunch," or, "If we hear something mean, let's tell the kids to stop." Another key element in this approach is to create a sense of an undercover "secret mission." The team is asked to do their work without being too obvious. Many young people enjoy this sense of intrigue and develop elaborate ways to keep the team's work from being revealed.

STEP 3.

- Meet with the student to monitor progress (15–20 minutes).
- Check with the teachers to confirm progress.

The student getting bullied is periodically asked to rate the effectiveness of the team's plan on a scale from 0 to 10, 10 being the worst bullying and 0 being no bullying. The progress monitoring of the intervention continues until the student rates the bullying a 0. The student getting bullied is never required to confront those who are bullying them or even be in the same room at the same time. Instead, the student getting bullied is placed in the powerful position of deciding when the work of the undercover team is complete.

STEP 4.

- Meet with the undercover team to monitor progress and give encouragement (15–20 minutes).

STEP 5.

- When the bullying has stopped, meet the undercover team again to celebrate (15–20 minutes).
- Provide evaluation forms, and plan for the long term.

Once the student rates the problem a 0, the team is disbanded and there is a celebration where the principal acknowledges the work of the team.

For more information, please visit: EliminateBullying.com.

1 Hubbard, "The 'NoBlame' bullying response approach."

2 Robinson and Maines, *Crying for Help: The No Blame Approach to Bullying*.

3 White, *The Externalizing of the Problem and the Re-authoring of Lives and Relationships*, 4.

4 Monk and Winslade, *When Stories Clash: Addressing Conflict with Narrative Mediation*.

BIO Michelle Myers, Program Specialist, Counseling Professor, Restorative Justice Consultant and Trainer.

CONTRIBUTION

THIS IS AN EXCERPT from Rickey Cummings's *Holding Vigil* (2022), a collaboration between Rickey, Mark Menjívar, and Thick Press. Rickey and Mark have been collaborating on artistic projects since 2016.

6 a.m.:

May 19, 2021. 12 hrs. before six.

While I'm not sure what will come of these words, I felt compelled to chronicle my day as I vigil for a man I've gotten cool with over the years here on Texas Death Row. If anything, it's my hope that I'll be able to give them to him sometime in the near future; which would mean that he received a last-minute reprieve from Gov. Greg Abbot. Unfortunately, though, knowing the Governor's record, that doesn't seem likely. If nothing else, though, I'm an optimist. So I'm holding out hope.

Let me back up. Today, May 19, 2021, if the state of Texas has its way, Quintin 'GQ' Jones will be legally, but inhumanely, murdered by the state of Texas by way of lethal injection. Since I arrived on Texas Death Row in November of 2012, I've lost count of how many people have been murdered by the State. It's been so many that one would think I would become numb to seeing men take their last walk off the pod, to & from their last visit with loved ones or loaded onto the transport van so they can be taken to the "death house" in Huntsville, Texas. But I'm not. How could I feel numb when such an inhumane practice is used to end the life of another human being? How can I feel numb when I know that there's a chance that someone I have broken bread, shared stories, and held mutual respect with/for won't be here tomorrow? Nah, the anger, disgust, and pain that I feel won't allow me to feel numb; I do feel helpless, though. Because at the end of the day, there's absolutely nothing I can do to save his life.

What I was able to do, though, was send him a message yesterday letting him know that as he takes his last walk to and from visitation, surrounded by all the administration and ranking officers (the wardens, majors, captains) and the security response team and nurses, I'll be there holding vigil, and the knocking he'll hear on the window will be my way of letting him know that somebody who is FOR him is with him as he takes that walk, so he should do so with his head up & chest out. The gesture is small, but if I was in his shoes, I'd want somebody doing the same for me. If nothing else, it would boost my morale some, and show the guards that my (his) life matters to somebody here.

Normally, I don't look out the window in this cage, which is located about 4 inches from the ceiling and is a horizontal strip that's 3 inches tall & 4 feet wide, because the view is dismal. There's metal barbed wire & electric fences, a concrete building that houses other men, 2 sidewalks, one that leads to the visitation room and 11 Building, the other that leads to 12 Building (which is where Death Row is housed) and other parts of the prison. I also have a view of the back gate, which is where the transport vans & buses arrive. The sidewalk and back gate will be a focal point for the day. ❁

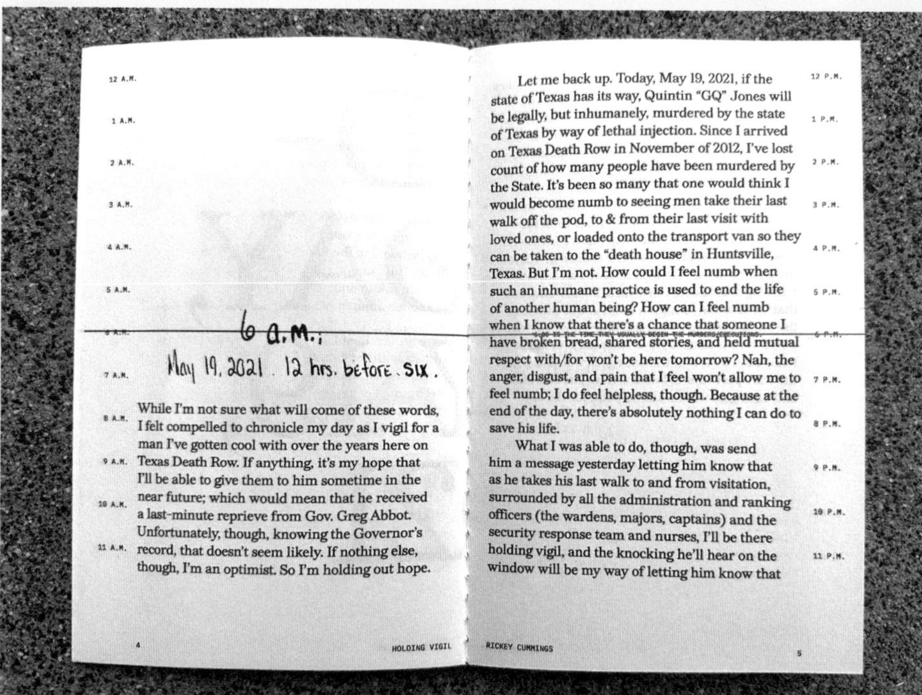
12 A.M.
1 A.M.
2 A.M.
3 A.M.
4 A.M.
5 A.M.
6 A.M.

6 a.m.:

May 19, 2021. 12 hrs. before six.

7 A.M.
8 A.M.
9 A.M.
10 A.M.
11 A.M.

While I'm not sure what will come of these words, I felt compelled to chronicle my day as I vigil for a man I've gotten cool with over the years here on Texas Death Row. If anything, it's my hope that I'll be able to give them to him sometime in the near future; which would mean that he received a last-minute reprieve from Gov. Greg Abbot. Unfortunately, though, knowing the Governor's record, that doesn't seem likely. If nothing else, though, I'm an optimist. So I'm holding out hope.

4 HOLDING VIGIL

Let me back up. Today, May 19, 2021, if the state of Texas has its way, Quintin "GQ" Jones will be legally, but inhumanely, murdered by the state of Texas by way of lethal injection. Since I arrived on Texas Death Row in November of 2012, I've lost count of how many people have been murdered by the State. It's been so many that one would think I would become numb to seeing men take their last walk off the pod, to & from their last visit with loved ones, or loaded onto the transport van so they can be taken to the "death house" in Huntsville, Texas. But I'm not. How could I feel numb when such an inhumane practice is used to end the life of another human being? How can I feel numb when I know that there's a chance that someone I have broken bread, shared stories, and held mutual respect with/for won't be here tomorrow? Nah, the anger, disgust, and pain that I feel won't allow me to feel numb; I do feel helpless, though. Because at the end of the day, there's absolutely nothing I can do to save his life.

What I was able to do, though, was send him a message yesterday letting him know that as he takes his last walk to and from visitation, surrounded by all the administration and ranking officers (the wardens, majors, captains) and the security response team and nurses, I'll be there holding vigil, and the knocking he'll hear on the window will be my way of letting him know that

12 P.M.
1 P.M.
2 P.M.
3 P.M.
4 P.M.
5 P.M.
6 P.M.
7 P.M.
8 P.M.
9 P.M.
10 P.M.
11 P.M.

RICKEY CUMMINGS 5

12 A.M. somebody who is FOR him is with him as he takes that walk, so he should do so with his head up & chest out. The gesture is small, but if I was in his shoes, I'd want somebody doing the same for me. If nothing else, it would boost my morale some, and show the guards that my (his) life matters to somebody here.

Normally, I don't look out the window in this cage, which is located about 4 inches from the ceiling and is a horizontal strip that's 3 inches tall & 4 feet wide, because the view is dismal. There's metal barbed wire & electric fences, a concrete building that houses other men, 2 sidewalks, one that leads to the visitation room and 11 Building, the other that leads to 12 Building (which is where Death Row is housed) and other parts of the prison. I also have a view of the back gate, which is where the transport vans & buses arrive. The sidewalk and back gate will be a focal point for the day.

6 HOLDING VIGIL

RICKEY CUMMINGS 7

B I O S

Rickey Cummings is a creator who has been fighting for his freedom from Texas's death row for the past 11 years.

Mark Menjívar is an artist and educator whose art practice primarily consists of creating participatory projects while being rooted in photography, oral history, archives, and social action.

water

CONTRIBUTORS' NOTE

Water figures in our creative practice, our ways of seeking meaning, our understanding and retelling of unseen histories, and our avenues towards healing. Fid's artwork imagines the pre-colonial waterways and buried creeks that ebbed and flowed freely across what is now DC, evoking a healing relationship with water across deep time. Ama's poem channels water's ambition to render all it encounters supple, able to offer methods for healing.—FT & ABE

CONTRIBUTION

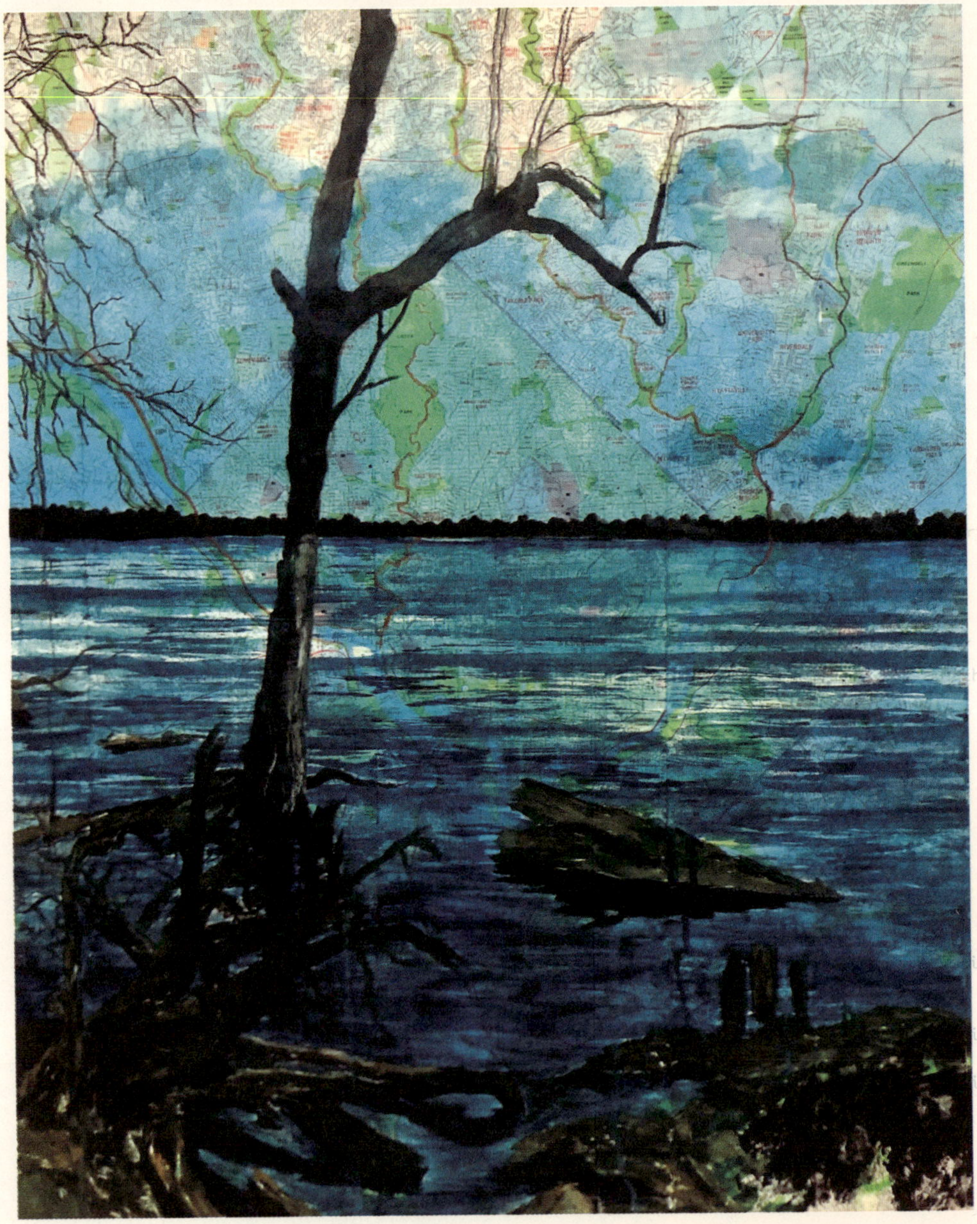

"occasional submergence," 2023, mixed media, 36 x 27 inches

Dive
into the depth of these waters
Cast your gaze on mud beneath the ebb
Reach your fingers down to touch,
and scoop
To unsettle the resting earth,
and make plain the fiction of a sharp,
clean edge.
Squeeze the slurry through fisted fingers,
into clouds of liquid dust and sparkle
Swim in joyful spirals
and stir your body through the brine.

I've never been a strong swimmer. Never grasped the breaststroke, front crawl, or butterfly. In fact, the only stroke I know bears my own name. But, I delight in the water. She is my favorite dance partner—after my Shadow. Our choreography moves the stagnant from my body and prays. No matter the time between our meetings, she always whispers a silken, "Welcome back, I remember you."

Surface
Lay yourself down at the shoals.
To Listen
To wait

I almost drowned once.
I was six, I think. Invited by my expert swimmer, best friend to jump off a diving board. The deep end. The truth was, I was still in floaties. Water and I were nascent in our friendship. But my friend swam like a dolphin, and she promised she'd hold my hand. I was terrified. But, too challenged by my ego to say so. So we did. We jumped.
She held my hand.
And I let go.

Prescription
drip this mud
into potter's hands,
like wax upon itself.

Water is no solitary being. She and Land are partners. Inseparable lovers. Though most of the time, it seems, she takes center stage. She has no reason to be shy. I love this about her.

Fill your lap
Cover your feet
Lather amply across the torso, pelvis,
back, neck and face.
Cup still water
from shadows,
and pour atop your crown.
Trace the course of each
tiny stream,
down your temples,
across the collarbone,
around each breast,
onto memory.

Turn your water logged ear
to the willow bogged earth.
Let the water trickle out.
Send your intentions out
in fainting echoes,
onto the brimming void.

Most times, I reach for the lovers in their meeting place.

I can't resist. I want in on their rendezvous.
I long to experience their union as divine.
And hope not to intrude. In that place,
I slip out a soft, sticky anointing of flesh.
Dripping in mud, I summon a slurry
of sunken remembrances, of us, the
descendants of this love.

Meditation
There, between dust-made flesh
and star-made sea,
hear her drawl and gurgle,
her rush and retreat,
her drawing sighs of relief
in meeting you again.

One morning, I went out to meet a calm, waveless sea. I entered slowly, lay on my back, allowing my body to submit to its own buoyancy. I was always afraid of daydreaming too deeply while floating. Waking up to find myself adrift—past the horizon, never to be found, never to reach ground again. This time, while back floating, my ears beneath the surface, I heard a symphony of squeals. Calls out and gleeful replies.
Whale song. Unseen, undetectable giants in my company, finding me before I was ever lost. ➔

This contact,
the sound of it
is a sacred place,
an aural altar
for the places we siblings gather, and to those
with an impulse to move,
to follow the bends,
to float through narrows,
and take root in the water.

See
that the truth
of the mud
is flux
and flow

Surrender
to this touch,
this chance
to kiss your cheeks
and breathe wet whispers at your nape,
and along the fine edge of
your frame
where liquid and soil coalesce.

Feel
that it is here
where she is
most effervescent,
sodden and tingling.

Skeptics don't believe in water memory.
But I whisper prayers into mine anyway.

Our bodies carve memories
into the brink of these waters
that they were countless
and serpentine
and far too many to map.
There were places
where we bathed
in the clear cool waters.

We adapt to the warming

fractured floes melt
leaving shards in its shallows
slicing with its silver tongues,
letting our blood,
seducing us to stay
still, we take root
in the water
we float on
until ground graces us
I love the Water. Her ways are her own. She
nurtures or swallows us whole. So, we engage
with caution and measure, reverence and
thanks. And pray we have enough grace to

Remember
that we are kin, at once
adrift and ashore,
that we are seedlings here
and hydroponic,
that even in the
quickening sand,
we, too, grow on water.

BIOS

Fid Thompson is a queer writer, gardener, artist, friend and f/allower, in love with all the languages this world has to offer.

Ama BE is an artist who plays with the suppleness of time, materiality, and memory. Drawing on her Ghanaian heritage, she uses organic materials to explore African relationships to land, labor, cosmologies, and migration.

CONTRIBUTION

a parting of speech

wildness (n.)—is landscape is body is water is creatures is total awareness is as ungrasp-able as atmospheres, even as I try to grasp it here in words, the slightwater of it falls through my cupped hands, even as it lives in me, the fire in my belly and water in the sky, it connects each of us with everything else, widestweb, unseen silk ever spinning our homes over and over with invisible belonging.

wild (v.)—to wild; to appeal to that part of us in need of the deepest comfort, the toughest freeing and the greatest re-wilding — by that I mean, tear down the fences between your gardens, invite your neighbours to chew on the tomatoes (yes even the animal ones, even the rats), let the chives pop up where they will, plant a fig tree in a stony shitty place and watch it flourish; put raspberry canes in the earth and let them spread beyond borders; plant enough to share, it's never too late; stop mowing, start allowing; the wild anemone, the bee balm, the plantains and dandelions; allow fellow citizens to grow between your toes and to tall up above you, lilting soft overhead, offering their shade when the sun is strong; accept this gift and give it to someone; be both gifter and receiver, gifted and received; and best of all, lie yourself out on the earth, wherever you are, make the shape of a star, let your limbs go, slack into the ground; to wild is to allow that your senses know things — tickleprickle of grass or smoothwarmth of stone, yellowglow of inner eyelids, a waft (what is more wildness than smellsense?!) of lavender or cumin or za'atar, whirr of a/c unit, warble of tiny brown birds and gurgle of stomach. What flavour is this wildnessing? Can you taste it with your whole body?

wild (adj.)—how wild is our domesticity, our knowing, our pain? how do we describe our truest selves? walked upright and away, as we did, from the heavily forested areas, the woodlands, the places where civilisations of creaturebeings grow up in pleasure and pain and die, the wild terrains of land and self; did you know we can change the information captured? just put a wildness in front of every noun and the scanners are confused, cannot find the category, cannot extract anything from our transmuting target; we make our own wild ways, names, stories, masks, the illogic of meandering; we fathom it into the generations by refusing to call the land empty, by seeing it full and rich and unruly and peopled and creatured and planted and ruined and cycled and tended, by so many.

wildly (adv.)—I definitely sing more wildly in the imagined outdoor shower where trees and squirrels are the only peepers; you screech and run wild-ly whenever you are able, whenever no one at the office is looking; eat with hands, mouths unwiped, licking around lips and fingertips for the full flavour; we eat petroleum in the same way, and all around us piles pile up; we worry about how wildly we consume, how straight the engineering, how and where the pipes are spilling; how we feel so desperately alone; how to learn wildly is to learn together to trust.

wildness/she/they (pronoun)—wildness is just so hungry, wildness wants, wildness feels and beats and breathes with wings in her barbaric chest, wildness is death, turbulence, destruction, as punishing as delivering, wildness is cheeky and clever, winking and wasting, an unruly power, the fighting springfire within us, wildness is gods of all the kinds, as free and savage as anything on this earth. ➔

wildness

wildness (prep.)—think inside and outside, thin skin of us and thin skin of earth, holding all the porous boundaries between; think the in-between of most everything; think ruins, climbing plants covering, sitting atop, growing from and within what was meant to control, fruiting all over it, sticky and sweet the concrete has never tasted this before.

wildness (conj.)—the bothandness of wildness; the trans panness, feral worlds in flux; living in the yesandness of life, in the cycles of endless combinations

wildness (interjection)—you! beautiful! terrible! wildness! destructive and creative! bodybeaming and ephemeral! wow!

wildness (participle)—as in, we are these wilding bodies, in states of composition and decomposition, we are not sure which at any particular point; we see how these wilding bodies (of ours, of others) feed the earth, eat the earth, are the earth; our wilding bodies so often confuse us, made from doing but bathed in being.

wildness (collective n.)—as in, a wildness of queers; a wildness of worth; a wildness of waves, the crest and fall, the drop and rise, the squawking shearwater dipping a wing, the saltspray, the minnows flashing below the surface, the deepest amoebic creature on the ocean floor and the thinning stratus clouds above, all contained within a collective.

wildness (p.o. box)—a home we carry inside us through the homeless landscape of late-stage capitalism, we wild in our awareness, we bellyfire our wildscapes within, we heal our very selves in secretfound spaces, in the home of friendship, in the meeting of our queerest selves, in the beauty of alleyways where life gets out of hand again, bright and big, where allowing, where creatures, where what we call weeds, what we call broken, thrives; a windlashed misty moor, yes, as much as a whippedup ocean or fanged beast; as fictional and fact as anything else; the place of wildness is your own moving address, it sits and waits for you daily.

wildness (PhD)—as in: no test, no fee, no qualification or signed form, no rejection letter, no acceptance letter, no rubber stamp, no border, no status, no military checkpoints, no civilian checkpoints, no Real ID, no ID at all, no corrections, no critiques, no *but*, no uniform, no measurement, no requirement at all, for belonging. ❁

BIO Fid Thompson is a queer writer, gardener, artist, friend and f/allower, in love with all the languages this world has to offer.

love
lunar cycle
Magic School, the
mapping support
marginality (as a site of resistance)
Marxist social work
membership theory in social work
mending
metaphor
mikveh
mobile libraries
movement lawyering
mutual aid
mycelia as metaphor
narradrama
narrative medicine
narrative therapy
nepantla/nepantleras
nonviolent communication
ongoingness
peer counseling
peer-to-peer health network
person-situation perspective
perspective via faith
pleasure
poems/poetry
poetic meter
polarity work
post-oppositionality
postwork imaginaries
poverty-aware social work paradigm, the
power threat meaning (PTM) framework
pre(care)ity
prison abolition
professionalism without performance
progressive education
public benefits
public library, the
Qigong
radical administration
radical care in the arts
radical childcare in movement spaces
radical inclusion
radical papermaking
radical presence
radical social work
Radical Therapist Journal, The
Rank and File Movement (RFM) in social work

wintering as metapho

CONTRIBUTION

A SEASON OF NATURE but also a state of being as described by Katherine May in *Wintering: The Power of Rest and Retreat in Difficult Times*. Viewed by society as a period of humiliation, "wintering" is a fallow period in life when you're cut off from the world, feeling rejected, sidelined, blocked from progress, or cast into the role of an outsider.

Yet these periods can bring about profound insight and wisdom when we allow them. As May writes, "It's a time for reflection and recuperation, for slow replenishment, for putting your house in order. Doing these deeply unfashionable things—slowing down, letting your spare time expand, getting enough sleep, resting—is a radical act now, but it's essential."[1] Rather than push through or ignore the feelings of dejection and alienation, May asks that we bring curiosity and compassion to understand the current state of cold we are inhabiting.

We are told endless summer is the goal in all domains. *How are you? Doing great!* But seasons of perpetual sun don't exist. Possibilities await when we admit and embrace the darkness.

Have you wintered? Did you slow down? Did you rage? Were you overcome with fear? Did you shed a skin? Did you transform? Tell someone about it. We need to know.

Wintering is radical but recounting it may be even more so. Others can learn to welcome the season when it descends.

Our winters can *bind us together* if we let them. ❋ →

1 May, *Wintering: The Power of Rest and Retreat in Difficult Times*, 14.

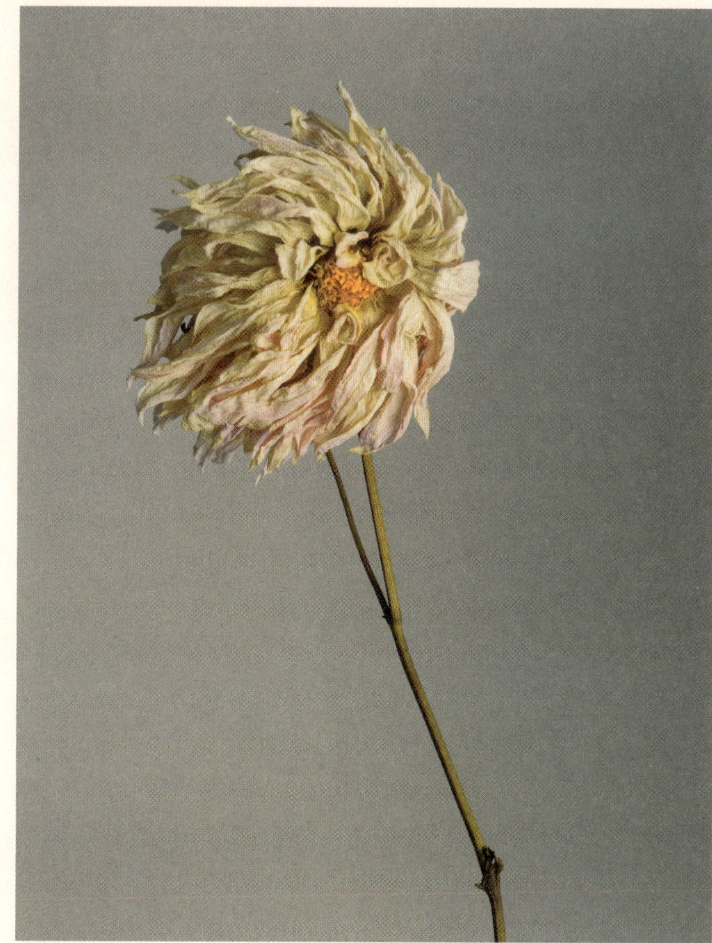

Everlasting, 2022, photograph

reclaiming selfhood
SE
recognition
redistribution
Reflecting on Justi
reflexivi
Rei
relation
interviewin
relationali
resistan
resisting t
parental los
narrativ
resonan
respectful visiti
respite roo
rest
respite roo
rest as resistan
revolutiona
mothering
ritu
sanctua
sandplay thera
sau
seed banki
sex positivi
shadow integrati
Sick Woman Theo
slow textil
slowne
social chan
ecosystem framewor
social constructi
social practi
social therapeuti
Social Welfare Acti
Alliance, the
solidari
solidarity econo
somatic heali
songs/singi
sound heali
speculative desi
spell
staying with th
trouble
storytelli
street newspape
strength
perspective, the
sufficienc
sustaining movemen
symbo
Taos Institute, th
taro
temporary autonomou
zones
Theatre of th
Oppressed
theories of chang
theosoph
therapeutic writin
togethernes
trans practice
transformativ
justice
traspati
12-step program
undercover anti
bullying teams
vigi
wate
wildnes
wintering as metapho
wishe
witcher
yog
zinemakin

vintering as metaphor

December with Barry, 2022, botanical collage

B Tobie Whitman, PhD,
I is the founder of Little
O Acre Flowers.

Magic School, the
narradrama
relation
interviewing
social constructi
strength perspective, the
Theatre of the Oppressed
togetherness

CONTRIBUTION

Wish-Driven

IN MY ARTISTIC AND ACTIVIST PRACTICE I often ask people for their wishes. I prefer a wish-driven practice to processes driven by problems or demands or discourses. However, I never publicly claim to be helping others in this process. Maybe that's because helping others in itself tends to focus on the problems and shortcomings of those being helped. This can be very stigmatizing. Also, problems often present as dead ends of broken, wrongful systems. Focusing on them makes us easily a part of the problem, especially if we try to be part of the solution too hard.

Wishes instead can easily turn into demands, if necessary, and they have lots of discourse around them. Discourse plays a part in generating wishes, while wishes can also counteract discourses. But first and foremost, wishes are desires; they manifest in our bodies, they transgress reason, they possess us, often collectively, and thus have the power to reorganize relations between the one and the many.

How to start a wish-driven process?

Make a wish.

Exactly. That's not easy. Our wish energy has been drained. Wish energy is needed to create consumption. It is also needed for self-governmental discipline: If you wish for that, then you have to do this. Also, wish energy has been deeply frustrated within wrongful binaries like those of child/adult, man/woman, human/animal.

Wish energy has to be reignited.

You can start by asking yourself for your wishes more consistently. Once every day. Do you notice a difference between wishes? Can you try and make stronger and stronger wishes? What inspires you to make a wish?

Do you know, do you have a feeling?

Now make a wish for the people you would like to work with! Maybe they are already knocking on your door?

Who would you like to ask for their wishes? And most importantly, how could you inspire them to make a strong wish?

I, personally, asked hundreds of groups of kids for their wishes and I keep doing that. Recently they wished to feel beautiful—they wished to reclaim beauty beyond race, gender, class, etc. Theatre and performance might have a few spaces and strategies to offer for that.

I also asked refugees from West Africa for their wishes, young adults in Serbia, the cultural workers of Nordrheinwestfalen, female seafarers around the world, and many others.

And then?

What to do with all these wishes?

First and foremost, these wishes should be publicly acknowledged. It is good to have them; they are precious. If you are an artist or activist, you can be the publisher and advocate of these wishes. It is empowering for those who made the wish to witness how they are amplified and taken seriously. To be heard and seen with a desire that goes beyond the given state of things—that strengthens the heart and the back.

On top of that, there is the art of wish-driven processes. To unleash it you might want to look for those wishes which could be fulfilled. Look specifically for the most improbable and most common wish that you, with the help of that specific wishing community, your network, and resources, might be able to fulfill.

If you find that—an improbable wish shared by many, which still could come true eventually—then you found a way, an escape route, a collective research process. To host, facilitate, and organize a process like that is one of the most demanding but also most fulfilling tasks I have ever experienced. Take care of yourself: brace position. Ignition.

How can an improbable collective wish be surprisingly fulfilled?

To do that, superpowers have to be accessed. You might have different superpowers than I do. Mine are these:

Through research & transnational alliances: Like, for example, when impoverished kids in Hamburg, Germany, wished to be so rich they could print their own money. A wish that was answered by members of the alternative Banco Palmas, founded by impoverished people in Brazil, who showed us how we could create the Children's Bank of Hamburg.

By means and resources of art: Like, for example, when we used prime exhibition space in the Museum für Kunst und Gewerbe for the public collection of used items to be shipped to West Africa (as part of the project African Terminal, based on wishes of migrants).

With the emergent quality of togetherness & sharing: Like when the cultural workers of Nordreinwestfalen found new energy to work together on the fulfillment of their wishes, once they shared them publicly.

By the power of the assembly of the many that can be called: Who are the many you would like to call? Be careful how you address them, how you connect to them, how you seat them, how you feed them, how you make them feel. The many can do almost everything, no limits to that. But be ready: to call the many means to call for conflict, too.

By interventions in the binary of reality and fiction: Like when you perform reality in a slightly shifted way, as in looking for ghosts in public buildings, catching them, and inviting everybody for a seance to talk to them. It's called performativity, you might have heard of that.

Disclaimer: Another theory, you might have heard of it, is by Jacques Lacan, Roland Barthes, and other guys from Paris. They are right about one thing: desire is shifting, wishes are rarely ever just fulfilled—instead they move on, they escape to another level. In other words: wish-driven processes are not one-dimensional, they tend to move in several directions. Plus: disappointment is a necessary part of it. In taking disappointment seriously, you will learn the most. Easier said than done, certainly. Which is why I personally prefer to call it research instead of helping. Failure is included. ❁

BIO Sibylle Peters is a performance artist and researcher in love with improbability drives, heterotopian zones, feminist seafaring, social intimacy and collective research (wishfulthinking.eu).

CONTRIBUTION

THE WORD "WITCH" is loaded with connotations, misunderstandings, and anxieties for many people, and since I started using it in public about a decade ago, I have gotten a lot of questions about it. Here are some of the most common.

Why do you call yourself the poetry witch?

I am a spiritual poet whose spirituality is grounded in the earth and in female power. My primary magickal tools are skill in the craft of shaping words into talismans, charms, and spells, and a calling to perform my words in ritual and for healing— and to share them with others who can use them to connect with their own inner Goddess powers.

Are you a witch in real life too?

Yes. I was born on Halloween and have always felt connected spiritually to the earth and to other realities. Since I met my first witch in 1990, I have consciously studied and practiced earth-centered witchcraft alone and with others, using herbs, crystals, symbols, colors, and divination tools in addition to my poetry witch tools of words, chanting, movement, and ritual.

The word "witch" will turn people off. Why not use another word?

I am aware of this, which is why I waited 20 years and considered numerous alternative words before coming out of the broom closet in my 2010 blog, *American Witch*. I made my decision because no other word embodies the combination of reclaimed feminine energy, magic, and power that I needed to express. Since then, I've noticed that a new generation of feminist witches has been making the same choice, and for similar reasons.

Are you a Wiccan?

No, not really. I did start out as a Wiccan, but I find that tradition is too limited, too prescriptive, and too sexist in its roots. I now consider myself a practitioner of folk witchcraft, a broader category that links my beliefs and practices with those of witches across many centuries and continents.

What are those beliefs and practices?

As a witch, I find sacred meaning in the cycles of life and death and the seasons. I believe everything in nature has a spiritual aspect, including our bodies. I like to use spells and ceremonies, some formal and some spontaneous, to shape my own growth and support those I love. I do my best to follow the Witches' Creed: "If it harms no-one, do what you will."

Do you make curses?

No. My spells and magick aim for the best good of everyone involved. Sometimes this may involve "binding" someone dangerous from doing harm, but ideally that happens only after making any personal anger conscious and letting it go. Magic for me is like prayer; I would never want to use it out of anger or violence. If I'm doing magic with people I don't know well, I connect with their most loving self. My poem called "Gulf War and Child: A Curse" is an outraged stand against a system that hurts us all, not directed at any person. I would not call people who aim to hurt—for example, sorcerers I heard about when I visited the Democratic Republic of Congo—"witches" in my sense of the word. "Witch" comes from an old word for "wisdom." There is nothing wiser than the Golden Rule.

Can men be witches too?

Yes. My personal acronym for W.I.T.C.H. is "Women in Touch Coming Home," because I feel witchcraft is connected intimately with feminism and matriarchy and has crucial gifts to offer those of us who identify as women. But today's witchcraft can help bring us home, no matter what our gender, to honor the Divine Feminine inside and around us. A wise witch called Byron Ballard, who comes from an old witchcraft tradition, told me that witchcraft developed in groups of women connected through love and care for society, and that sorcery or witchcraft only got a bad name after men copied the magic for violent purposes. The male witches I know honor the power of the Divine Feminine; they are matriarchal men who know how to center the spiritual power of women together.

Are you part of a coven?

Yes—many layers of them! I have been part of many wonderful women's circles and covens (the difference is that while the circles provide a more general kind of support to women from all spiritual paths, the covens are working groups that actively make magic together). While the circles have had anywhere from three to nine members, the most powerful covens I've been in have been groups of three! I also teach meter in a magic spiral, in an online community called Poetry Witch, that can feel quite coven-like to me. And the more I travel, meeting such wonderful empowered witches and focusing my poetry readings and performances on magic and spells, the more it can feel like the people I encounter are part of a widespread coven that is weaving a healing energetic web around the globe. ❁

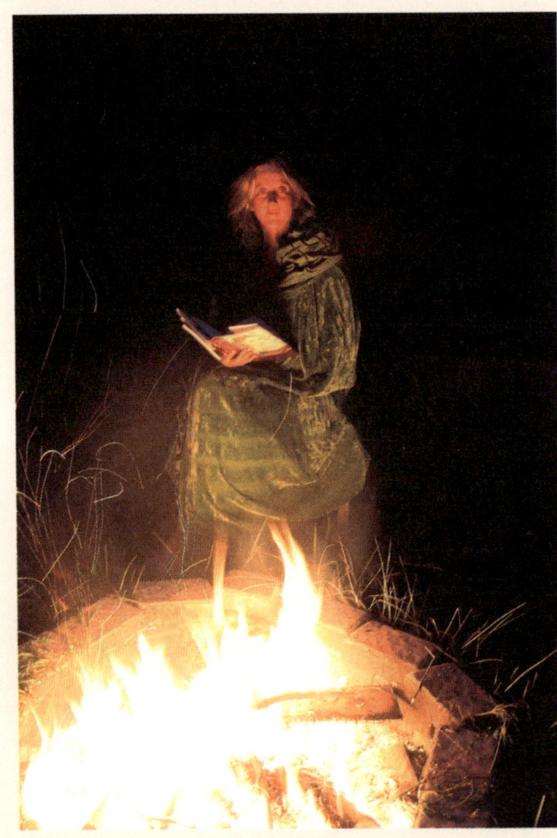

Annie Finch with her book *Spells: New and Selected Poems*. Photo by Karen Middleton.

BIO Annie Finch is author of *The Poetry Witch Little Book of Spells* and the founder of Poetry Witch Ritual Theater and PoetryWitchCommunity.org.

feminism
groups
healing rituals
herbalism
life cycle, honoring the

CONTRIBUTION

Parenting with Yoga

WHEN OUR KIDS BEHAVE "BADLY," we often swoop in to try to change, mold, or manipulate them. We often worry that there is something "wrong" with our children for not being kind enough, self-motivated enough, or pleasant enough. When our children don't meet our expectations, we might become triggered, letting our emotions burst forth uncontrollably. Feeling overwhelmed, we might overreact and lose our cool by yelling, criticizing, nagging, or punishing. Yet when our children are emotional, we tend to try to shut them down, particularly when they seem to react disproportionately to the issue at hand. As a result, we hurry them through their emotions, urging them to return to a happy state, which makes us feel more comfortable. It is easy to be proud of children who don't rock the boat. This is conventional parenting, where we prioritize societal expectations and our unchecked egos rather than considering our children's needs or their long-term mental health.[1]

When we approach parenting from a yoga perspective—embracing all aspects of yoga philosophy, movement, breathing, and meditation—we practice turning inward and focusing on ourselves, which teaches us to pause in highly charged moments. We make some space for ourselves; we think more deeply about our urge to react, yell, punish, and control; and we don't act on it. We recognize that our explosive, emotional reactions are driven by our egos, and they are shaped by childhood traumas or wounds, which resurface when we are triggered in the present. We breathe and find compassion and empathy for ourselves and for all we have been through. We recognize in these reactive moments that our job is to calm ourselves down, to make ourselves feel safe (reminding ourselves that this isn't an emergency), and to regulate ourselves before we decide how to respond to our child. When we create this space and focus internally instead of reacting externally, we are modeling for our children how to calm ourselves instead of transforming our hurt feelings into hostility towards others. This is so much more powerful and effective than lecturing, berating, or punishing. Once calm, our responsible adult self (instead of our reactive ego) can take charge by responding in a calm, compassionate, and patient manner.

Conventional parenting practices often separate us from our children by punishing and isolating them in the midst of their emotional turmoil. In their worst moments, our children are made to feel alone and unworthy of love or understanding. Children often come to view themselves as deserving of this harsh treatment, surmising that there must be something inherently wrong with them for not being able to meet their parents' behavioral expectations. These feelings can have negative consequences for our children's long-term self-esteem and self-acceptance.

Yoga, in contrast, not only helps us to observe and change how we react when we are triggered, but also helps us broaden our perspective in understanding our children's experiences. It encourages us to show up with compassion and curiosity instead of annoyance and anger. It helps us to recognize that life is challenging for our children, too. When our child behaves in a way that is difficult for us to understand, a well-rounded yoga practice encourages us to look below the surface-level behavior to understand the pain and unmet needs driving that behavior. Our aim is to see and validate our children's experiences, so they feel safe, seen, soothed, and secure. When we follow a yogic path of responding with kindness and support, we let our children know that they are loved and worthy, however they behave, and this, ultimately, helps them to develop confidence and self-acceptance. ➔

We show our children we trust them to learn to modify their behavior over time when we approach them with honesty, and when we let them know that we all make mistakes and that they are not alone in their experiences. When we focus on connection and compassion, our kids are more likely to become helpful and thoughtful adults because we are not using fear or pressure to shape their personalities. When we allow them to feel their emotions, however uncomfortable this may be for us, they learn how to release frustration in a healthy way—by letting go of pain and resentment instead of storing it. When we are not perfect parents, we can model honesty and accountability by taking responsibility for our behavior, apologizing sincerely, and finding ways to reconnect and repair. These practices can teach our children how to form healthy relationships built on nonviolence, truthfulness, kindness, and respect.

Our relationships with others are reflections of our relationships with ourselves. Until we can heal and strengthen our connection with—and acceptance of—ourselves, we will struggle to build relationships with others in constructive ways. Once we do the inner work—by regularly scheduling yoga practice, breathing, and meditation, separate from our children—we find the space to get to know, like, and accept our whole selves. In turn, we increase our ability to get to know, like, and accept our children without trying to change or manipulate them. The more we practice these skills, the more we may notice the uniqueness and magic within our children, allowing us to celebrate their inner light instead of dimming it. ❁

1 In yoga, the ego can show up as arrogance or insecurities, formed by wounds and coping strategies from our childhoods. If we felt belittled and unseen in our childhoods, we must consciously resist falling into similar patterns with our children.

BIO Daniella Gould teaches semester-long courses on Parenting with Yoga, is the author of the forthcoming book, *The Metta Parent: Transform Your Parenting with Loving Kindness and Yoga*, and the Owner/Lead Instructor at Santosa Yoga and Health based in San Juan, Puerto Rico.

EDITOR'S NOTE Yoga, a Sanskrit word meaning "union," is a holistic practice with roots extending over 5,000 years in ancient India. It encompasses a wide range of physical postures (asanas), breathing techniques (pranayama), meditation (dhyana), and ethical disciplines (yamas and niyamas) to integrate the body, mind, and spirit. Yoga is traditionally categorized into three main arms: Bhakti (devotion), Jnana (knowledge), and Karma (action). Incorporating yoga into parenting fosters mindfulness, patience, and flexibility, allowing parents to connect deeply with their children and navigate the challenges of child-rearing with grace and balance. –CH

zinemaking

SEE
mobile libraries
mycelia as metaphor
storytelling
sustaining movements
temporary autonomous zones
therapeutic writing

CONTRIBUTION

A SHEET OF PAPER, an implement to write and draw with, perhaps a pair of scissors, a stapler, a glue stick… the basic tools to make a zine are simple. The possibilities for expression and connection held within the pages of a zine, however, are limitless.

You might be wondering: "What is a zine?" The term encompasses printed works of many sizes, shapes, formats, and topics. In general, zines are self-published booklets that have a small distribution compared to, say, a newsstand magazine. Intent also helps define a zine: most are made because the creator feels passionate about their publication's subject, as opposed to seeking financial profit.

Why do people make zines? The reasons are as diverse as zinemakers themselves. Within a zine, you can express yourself; make your voice heard; share your knowledge and skills; spur action and activism; and link your personal story with wider issues and movements. At its very heart, zinemaking is a compelling way to connect with others.

Zines have been around for many decades and have long been deeply tied to cultural, art, and social justice movements, as well as the practice of DIY (Do It Yourself). Zinemaking has endured in print formats, even as our lives move increasingly online, in part because it's an accessible method of creating something, reaching people, and building community. Of course, some zines also are available in digital formats, and zinemakers often use virtual means to find one another and distribute their work. Sharing a zine with others that you made with your own hands, though, still possesses a unique potency.

Like many zinemakers, I discovered zines when I was a teenager. At a riot grrrl show, someone thrust a photocopied booklet into my hands and said, "Here, take one of my zines." I stayed up late that night reading its intensely personal stories and calls to feminist, anti-racist, anti-classist action. By morning, I knew I wanted to create my own zines.

Since then, I've been inspired by the work I see zine folks doing in the arts, social justice, educational, political, and mental health fields. The pages of a zine are a space where the personal can become vibrantly and forcefully political.

Through zines, I've found stories that resonated with my experiences and viewpoints that expanded my perspective. I've learned about ways I can navigate personal challenges, support others, and join efforts to generate positive change. And I've shared my own stories, passions, and knowledge. Just about everyone I've met in the zine community believes, as I do, that making and reading zines has improved their life and enhanced their interpersonal connections.

As a writer, organizer, and social worker, I've integrated zines into my work whenever I can. I've facilitated zinemaking workshops at schools and universities, in group therapy sessions, at community gathering spaces, and around my friends' kitchen tables. Many others are sharing the act of zinemaking just about everywhere you can imagine.

There are two moments that feel particularly powerful to me when people are making zines together. The first moment highlights the act of creation: A hush falls upon the group when everyone is absorbed in their own zinemaking. All you hear is the scratching of markers and pens, the slice of scissors, and the bite of the stapler.

The second moment emphasizes the act of connection: When folks are ready to share the zines they've made, the group's enthusiasm bubbles up into conversation. In this clamor, zinemakers forge relationships, strengthen ties, and sow the seeds for countless future collaborations, in print and beyond. ➔

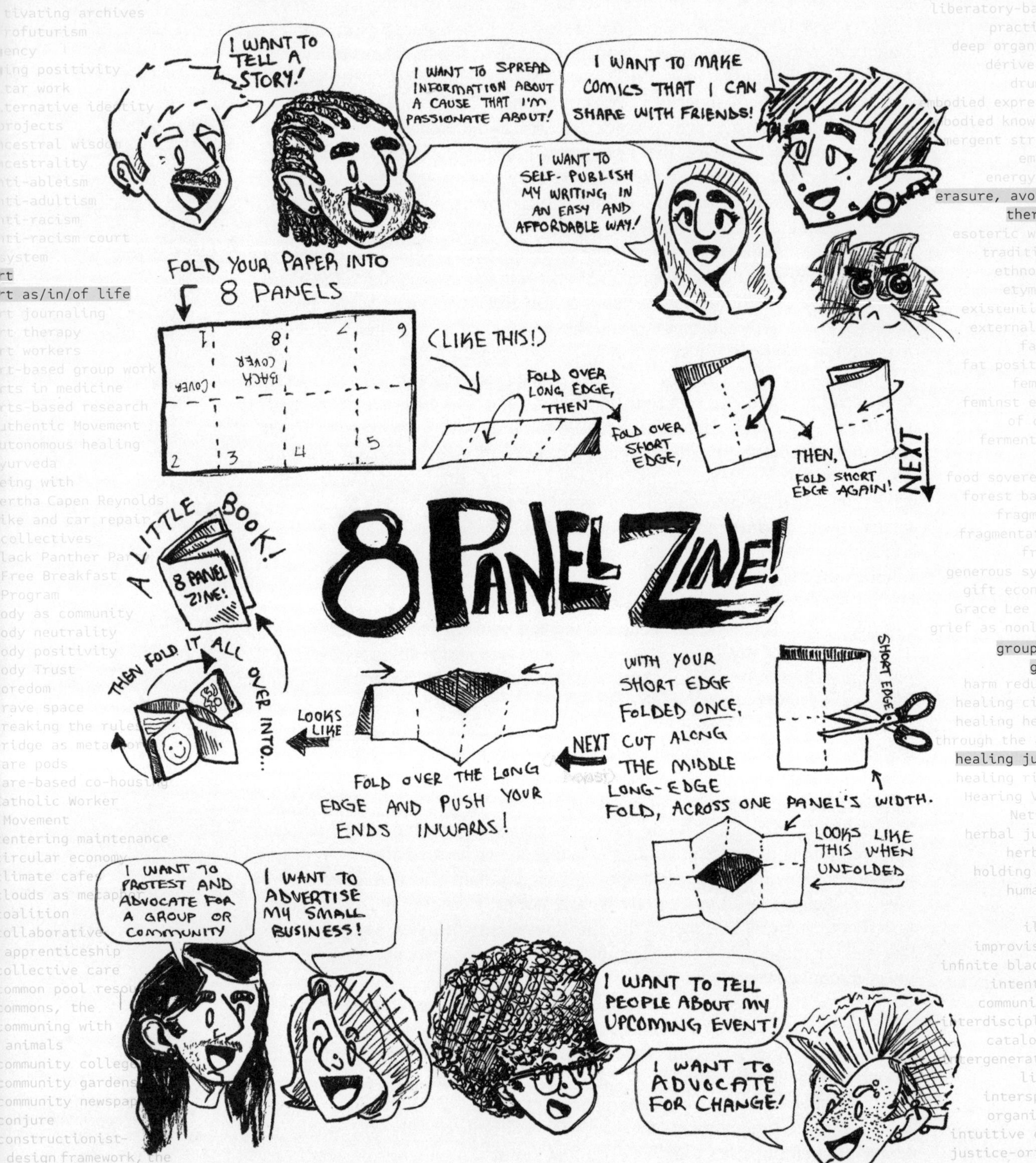

"Zine Community," 2023, digitized ink.

To help facilitate those two types of moments, I began producing a monthly event called Zine Club Chicago in 2018. We get together, in person or online, to discuss and create zines. We've also published collaborative zines, and members have shared their skills at our workshops and zinemaking hangouts. Through the years, our group has become a welcoming, supportive community.

Several members of Zine Club Chicago have gone on to launch zine meetups of their own, as well. Our group is just one example of zine gatherings of all kinds that take place in physical and online spaces across the globe.

Anyone can be a zinemaker, because every single one of us has something to express that will reverberate with someone else. Whenever I envision the person I want to be and the world I want to live in, I know that zinemaking is one of the tools that can help me—and all of us—get there. ❁

BIOS

Cynthia E. Hanifin is a writer, zinemaker, and social worker from the Southwest Side of Chicago.

Jude R. Bettridge is a jack-of-all-trades artist, whose zine work often acts as a tangible comic strip to explore mental health, transgender rights, instructional guides, fantastical storytelling, daily non-happenings, and more.

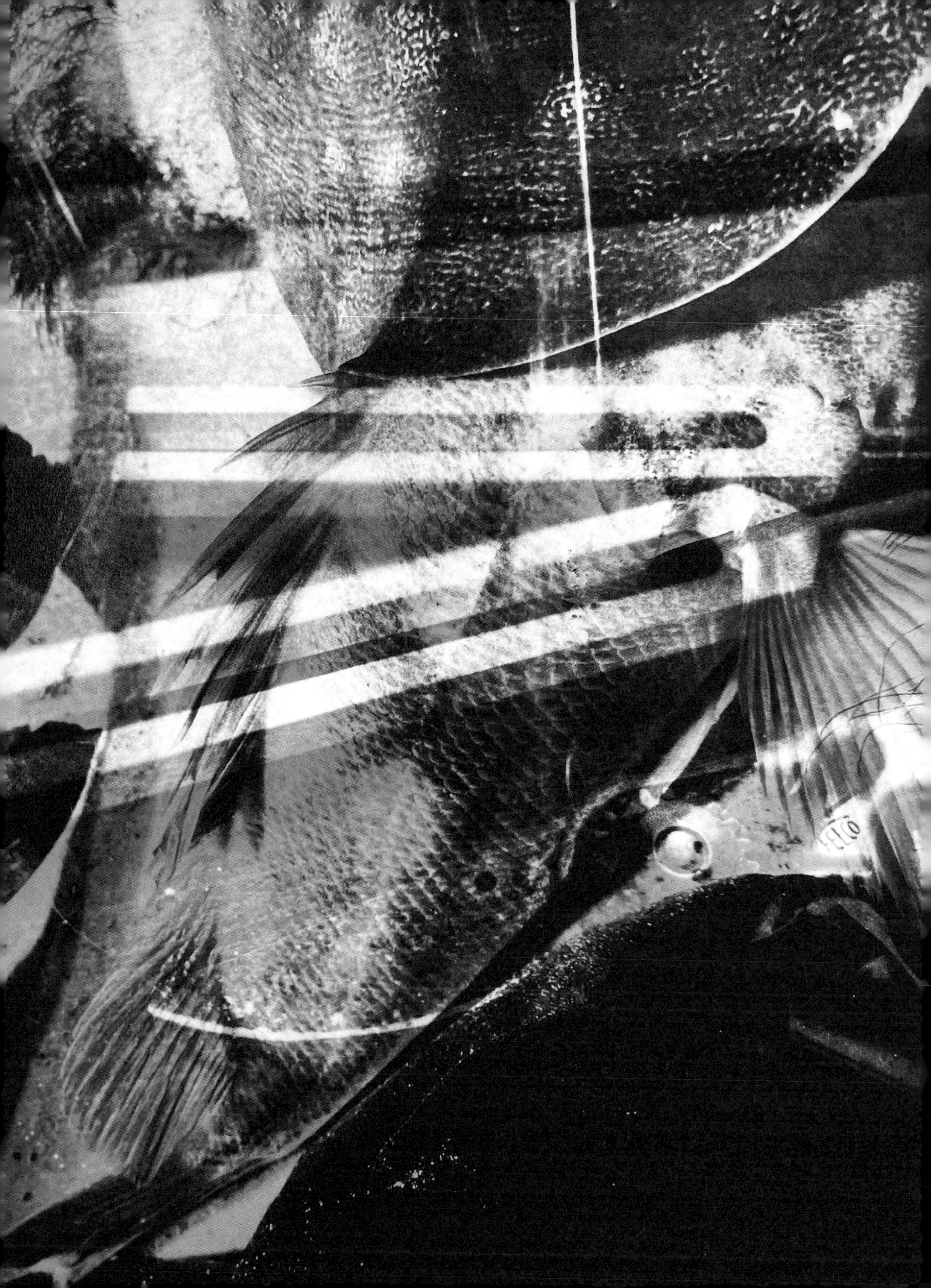

Contributors

Abby Chow
Occupying the unceded and ancestral territories of the xʷməθkʷəy̓əm (Musqueam), Skwxwú7mesh (Squamish), S'ólh Téméxw (Stó:lō), Sə̓lílwətaʔ/Selilwitulh (Tsleil-Waututh), Qayqayt, and kʷikʷəƛ̓əm (Kwikwetlem) peoples.
justice-oriented counseling; Reflecting on Justice; reflexivity

Akin Taiwo
Windsor and London, both metropolitan cities in Ontario, Canada
critique

Alice Chung
New York
forest bathing

Allan Irving
Swarthmore, Pennsylvania (always a Torontonian at heart)
clouds as metaphor; fragments/fragmentation

Alycia Berg (she/her)
Calgary, known as Mohkinstis to the Blackfoot Tribe and original inhabitants of the city
externalizing

Alyssa Smaldino (she/her)
New York City
anti-racism

Ama BE
Ghana/US
water

Amirio Freeman
Washington, DC, a part of the ancestral home of the Piscataway people
food sovereignty

Amy Pekal
Brooklyn, NY, USA
community gardens

AnaLouise Keating
Denton, Texas, USA (Traditional lands of the Comanche, the Wichita, the Tawakani, and the Kiikaapoi)
post-oppositionality

Anastasia Murney
unceded Gadigal land
tarot

Andrea Macias-Yañez
Berlin, Germany
common pool resources; corn knowledge; temporary autonomous zones; sufficiency; traspatio

Anna Stein
lives and works in Los Angeles, CA
generous systems

Anne Paré
Finland, Canada
sauna

Anne Wolf
Richmond, California
embodied expression

Annie Finch
Brooklyn, NY; the woods of northern Maine; anniefinch.com; poetrywitch.org; seeking matriarchal cultures across the globe.
healing rituals; poetic meter; witchery

Anonymous
community college

Antonia
NYC and Mahicantuck Valley
herbal justice

Ariel Gore
Santa Fe, NM & Oakland, CA
Catholic Worker Movement

Arts of the Working Class
The streets of Berlin and the world
art workers

Aryan Somaiya
Mumbai, India
relationality

Ashley Jones MS, LPC, ATR-BC
Dallas-Fort Worth, TX, USA (DFW)
arts in medicine

Ashley M. Lagrange, M.Ed, LPC (They/Them)
Unceded Lenape Land. NYC. Born, raised and residing in Queens.
altar work

Athena Robles
lives and works in Washington, DC
generous systems

Beth Sperber Richie
Silver Spring, Maryland, just outside Washington, DC, on the traditional territory of the Piscataway nation
ancestral wisdom

Bhupie Dulay
Settler who was born and raised on the stolen, unceded ancestral territories of the Semiahmoo, sq̓əc̓iy̓aʔɬ təməxʷ (Katzie), Kwantlen, kʷikʷəƛ̓əm (Kwikwetlem), Qayqayt, and sc̓əwaθenaʔɬ təməxʷ (Tsawwassen) Nations.
justice-oriented counseling

Bob Shefner
Bob, with his wife and dog, lives in a home attached to a backyard ringed with large and awe-inspiring trees that are filled with birds, squirrels, and many sounds and sights of true wonder and peace.
perspective via faith

Dr. Brian Arao (he/him/his)
Sacramento, CA, the historical and contemporary homelands of the Nisenan people.
brave space

Bridget Sumser
Ohlone Land, San Francisco
life cycle, honoring the

Camille Nibungco
Los Angeles, CA/Tongva Land
critical hope; sound healing

Carmen Ostrander
Vancouver, BC, on the Coast Salish Territories.
harm reduction; humor

Carol Stakenas
The ancestral and unceded lands of the Pawtucket and Massachusett, and Naumkeag (Somerville, MA)
activating archives, critical fabulation, social practice

Caroline Woolard
Rhode Island, Berlin, NYC, and Kingston, NY
solidarity economy

Casey Mack
Brooklyn
circular economy; limited-equity cooperative housing

Cassandra Wang, MD
resides in Los Angeles, CA
healing healers through the arts

Cassie Thornton
Lost & Found Department
collective care; peer-to-peer health network

Catherine Fairbanks
LA
respite rooms

Celiane Camargo-Borges, PhD, Celiane Camargo-Borges has been testing her tropical Brazilian blood in the wet and windy weather of Amsterdam for the last 13 years.
constructionist-design framework, the

Charlotte Frost
London
interspecies organizing

Chelsea Call, MA, LPCC, ATR (she/her/they/them)
Chelsea resides in the high desert of O'ghe P'oghe, on Tewa land (Santa Fe, New Mexico).
climate cafes

China Martens
Baltimore, MD
radical childcare in movement spaces

Chris Hoff
Liminality
liminality; narrative therapy; power threat meaning (PTM) framework; 12-step programs

Dr. Coatlicue S. Rose
Turtle Island: Roots in Mexico, heart in the US, body and soul in Canada.
existentialism; nepantla/nepantleras

Connie Sobczak (she/her)
Berkeley, CA
aging positivity; body positivity

Cynthia E. Hanifin
The South Side of Chicago
zinemaking

B I O ←
Katrina Umber is an artist, green witch, mother, folk herbalist, and multidimensional healer.

Contributors

Dana Sturtevant, MS, RD
Portland, OR, the native land of the Multnomah, Kathlamet, Clackamas, Chinook, Kalapuya, and Molalla people
Body Trust

Dani Grossman
Los Angeles, CA
Reiki

Daniella Gould
San Juan, Puerto Rico
yoga

Deb Toscano-Knicos, MA ATR-BC LCAT
Bangor, PA, USA
Sick Woman Theory

Deborah Tsogbe
Massachusetts/LA/Togo
gift economies; togetherness

Deepa Iyer
Washington, DC
social change ecosystem framework

Denise R. Wolf, MA, ATR-BC, ATCS, LPC, LPAT
Elkins Park, Pennsylvania, United States
radical papermaking

Denise Shanté Brown
transnational living throughout Baltimore, México and Colombia lands
grief as nonlinear

Dimitra Stavrou
Athens, Greece
ethnodrama

Dimple D. Dhabalia
Alexandria, VA, USA
rest as resistance; storytelling

dizzy turek
writes in Chicago, but is originally from Columbus, OH.
Theatre of the Oppressed

elena rose light (they/them)
Berlin, Germany
Authentic Movement; critical whiteness; trans practices

Elise Limon
between New Haven, CT, and London, England
speculative design

Emma Cooper
Seattle, WA
seed banking

Erin Segal
Washington, DC
public benefits; 12-step programs

Erna O'Connor PhD
Dublin, Ireland
person-situation perspective

Fid Thompson
Born and grown by a chalky river valley full of old bones in southern UK, still growing on land tended for so long by so many—Piscataway, Nacochtank, Podunks, Poquonook—and on multiple lands across the African continent.
failure; water; wildness

Fiona Hallinan
Cork, Ireland and Brussels, Belgium
death practices

Florence Freitag
Berlin, a constant compost of apples and all places saved in my weather app
empathy

Fran Lassman
Portugal
body as community

Friends
Bde Óta Othúŋwe (also called Minneapolis)
sustaining movement

Gioia Chilton, PhD, ATR-BC, CSAC
Northern Virginia
art journaling; arts-based research; bridge as metaphor; metaphor; poems/poetry; symbol; therapeutic writing

Gracy Obuchowicz
Washington, DC
Ayurveda; holding space; polarity work

Gretchen M. Miller, MA, ATR-BC, ACTP
Cleveland, Ohio, United States
radical papermaking

Hannah Stringer
London, UK
body as community

Harlene Anderson
Houston, Texas, U.S.
humanness

Heather Black-Coyne
Silverado, California
mapping support

Helena Rose
Leeds, Yorkshire, UK
re-authoring

Herban Cura
NYC and Mahicantuck Valley
herbal justice

Heung Gong Yan
United Kingdom, Hong Kong, China
staying with the trouble

Hilary Kinavey, MS, LPC
Portland, OR, the native land of the Multnomah, Kathlamet, Clackamas, Chinook, Kalapuya, and Molalla people
Body Trust

효영 HyoYoung Minna Kim
Coast Salish land, specifically the ancestral land of the Duwamish, Suquamish, Stillaguamish, and Muckleshoot People, colonially known as Seattle, Washington.
care pods

Ivan Txaparro
Germany/Colombia
resonance

James Hazel
So-called Sydney, Australia, on the unceded Gadigal Lands of the Eora Nation.
pre(care)ity

James Mulvale (MSW, PhD, RSW) My workplace is at the Fort Garry campus of the University of Manitoba in Winnipeg, Canada. The university is located on Treaty One territory and on the original lands of Anishinaabeg, Cree, Oji-Cree, Dakota, and Dene peoples, and on the homeland of the Métis Nation. My family home (where I also work much of the time) is located in Caledon East, Ontario. This community is part of the Treaty Lands and Territory of the Mississaugas of the Credit First Nation and is situated on the traditional Territory of the Huron-Wendat, Haudenosaunee Peoples, and the Anishnabek of the Williams Treaties.
Marxist social work

Jamie Stokke, MD
resides in Los Angeles, CA
healing healers through the arts

Jayshree S. Jani, PhD, LCSW-C
Washington, DC, Baltimore, MD USA
critical race theory

Jeffrey Yoo Warren
Providence, RI
solidarity economy

Jen White-Johnson
Baltimore, MD, USA
anti-ableism

Jennifer Brough
Nottingham, United Kingdom
abundance

Jennifer England
Yukon, Canada
contemplative tradition, the

Jennifer McSparron MA, LPC, ATR
Dallas-Fort Worth, TX, USA (DFW)
arts in medicine

Jennifer White
Victoria, BC, Canada which is located on the traditional territory of the ləkʷəŋən peoples
critical suicide studies

Jessica Villegas MPS, ATR-BC, LCAT
Dallas-Fort Worth, TX, USA (DFW)
arts in medicine

Jessie McCarty
Chicago
interdisciplinary cataloging; Theatre of the Oppressed

Ji-Youn Kim (they/she)
unceded Musqueam, Squamish, and Tsleil-Waututh territories in so-called Vancouver, Canada
solidarity; transformative justice

Dr. Jithin Paul Varghese
Namala
Lower Saxony, Germany.
Ayurveda

Joel Blau
Brooklyn/Nova Scotia
redistribution

Jude R. Bettridge
Chicago, IL
zinemaking

Contributors

Jules Rochielle Sievert
Somerville, Massachusetts, traditionally falls on the ancestral lands of the Massachusett people. The Massachusett were a Native American tribe from the region, and their name was eventually adopted by the state of Massachusetts.
movement lawyering

Judge Julie Bernard
Massachusetts
anti-racism court system

Julie Cho
Los Angeles, CA
public benefits

Julie Tilsen
Julie was born and raised and lives super close to Prince's junior high and high school, so the vibes are always purple.
breaking the rules; lingering; resisting the parental loss narrative

K.C.
Naarm
liberatory education

Kamran Afary
West Los Angeles, aka Irangeles, steps away from the Kuruvungna Spring at the site of a former village inhabited by Tongva people.
narradrama

Karlynn BrintzenhofeSzoc, PhD, MSW, FAOSW
I currently live and work in Louisville, Kentucky, but I was born, raised, and started my academic career in Washington, DC.
membership theory in social work

Kassamira Carter-Howard
dreamspace
Afrofuturism

Kate Strain
Wicklow, Ireland
death practices

Katherine Agard
Northern California
peer counseling

Karen Hsu
Pacific Northwest
forest bathing

Katrina Umber
Los Angeles
images on pp 6, 17, 18, and 482

Kelly Waterman
Minneapolis, MN
Hearing Voices Network

Kimi Hanauer
Kimi is based between Lenapehoking, the unceded ancestral land of the Lenape people, and Tovangaar, the unceded ancestral land of the Gabrielino-Tongva people.
coalition

Kirk Shepard
Portland-Pittsburgh—cities with bridges
group work

Kitti Zsiga
Hungary
herbalism

Larry Zucker
I live in Los Angeles, on land originally and still inhabited and cared for by the Tongva, Tataviam, Serrano, Kizh, and Chumash Peoples.
relational interviewing

Lea Joseph
Sheffield, UK.
Hamilton, ON
Black Panther Party Free Breakfast Program

Leanne Schubert
Mulubinba, Awabakal Country (Newcastle), NSW, Australia
art as/in/of life; strengths perspective, the

Lejla Ćatović
Cosmopolitan. Notably: Sarajevo, Munich, Firenze, NYC
theosophy

Lian Fumerton-Liu
Goleta, California—amongst butterfly groves and lagoons
slowness

Libbie Rifkin
Washington, DC
illders

Lili Birk Waehneldt
Germany
herbalism

Lily Luo
New York City
Grace Lee Boggs

Linda Lin
Occupying the unceded and ancestral territories of the Qayqayt, Kwikwetlem, Tsleil-Waututh, Katzie, Semiahmoo, Kwantlen, and Tsawwassen First Nations.
Reflecting on Justice

Lindsay Reckson (she/her)
somewhere between Philadelphia, Los Angeles, and Austin
revolutionary mothering

Dr. Lindsey Hampson
Lancashire, in the North West of England
consulting your consultants; Magic School, the

Lisa Kays
Raytown, Missouri→ Benin, West Africa→Washington, DC→Bethesda, MD
groups; improvisation

Lisa Levine
Oakland, California
embodied expression

Loam
Munsee Lenape territory
mobile libraries

Lois Holzman, PhD
New York, New York
social therapeutics

marcela polanco
Muisca unceded territory (Colombia Nation-State); Kumeyaay unceded territory (US Nation-State)
autonomous healing

Margaret Price
I'm from Ann Arbor, Atlanta, Boston, Columbus, and Honolulu.
access invocations

Margo de Torres, Boston and Puerto Rico
language justice

maria habib
Fairfax, VA, on Manahoac and Piscataway land (and heart in Beirut).
Ayurveda; holding space; polarity work

María Inés Plaza Lazo
Based between Berlin and Düsseldorf, Germany, born and bred in Guayaquil, Ecuador.
street newspaper

Marianna Sachse
Washington, DC, Nacotchtank and Piscataway Lands
mikveh

Marisa Morán Jahn
New York
care-based co-housing

Mark A. Hernandez
Motaghy
Boston
mutual aid

Mark Menjívar
San Antonio, TX
social practice; vigil

Martín La Roche
Martín La Roche lives in Amsterdam and comes back often to Santiago de Chile.
sandplay therapy

Mary Akinadewo
Washington, DC
Reiki

Max Haiven
Berlin (Germany) and Thunder Bay (Canada)
revenge

Maya Druckmann (she/her)
Los Angeles
body neutrality; sex positivity

maya rae oppenheimer (she/her)
Tiohtià:ke/Montreal and London, England
critical pedagogy

Meagan Lyon Leimena
Asheville, North Carolina
life cycle, honoring the

Mel Gray
Eleebana, Awabakal Country (Lake Macquarie), NSW, Australia
art as/in/of life; strengths perspective, the

Melaine Malcolm
Massachusetts
anti-racism court system

Melinda Tsapatsaris
Los Angeles
progressive education

Mia Stone-Molloy (she/her)
Los Angeles
commons, the; credit unions; deep organizing; pleasure; postwork imaginaries; professionalism without performance

Michael Reisch
Baltimore, MD
Bertha Capen Reynolds; radical social work

Contributors

Prof. Michal Krumer-Nevo
Ramat-Gan, Israel
poverty-aware social work paradigm, the; resistance

Michelle Jewett
New Mexico, USA
shadow integration

Michelle Myers
Rancho Cucamonga, California, USA
undercover anti-bullying teams

Miki Nishida Goerdt
Virginia, USA /Land of Monacan, Powhatan, & Manahoac people
art therapy; emergent strategy

Mirthe Berentsen
Mirthe Berentsen exists in many forms and places.
sandplay therapy

Monika Cvitanovic
Gadigal Land/Sydney, Australia
feminst ethics of care; slow textiles

Mustafa
Brooklyn, NY
mycelia as metaphor

Nadia Somers
London, UK
body as community

Naomi Finkelstein
(she/her) Ancestral land of the Council of the Three Fires: the Ojibwe, Odawa, and Potawatomi Nations, currently known as Chicago, IL
fat positivity

Naomi Hattaway
Florida, USA
leaving well

Neil Horsky
Boston & Milwaukee, USA
Qigong

Nicole Lavelle
San Francisco Bay Area (Coast Miwok and Karkin Ohlone).
community newspapers; respectful visiting

Nicole Oxendine
(she/her/hers)
Living with gratitude on the ancestral lands of the Piscataway and Nacotchtank peoples, 300 miles north of Lumbee Tribe of North Carolina current & ancestral homelands, 45 miles south of the Baltimore "Reservation," 330 miles east of Jewel Ridge, Virginia, and 1000+ miles north of Cuba & Miami, 3000+ miles west of Scotland, Ireland & the Canary Islands.
ancestrality

Nina and Sonya
Montenegro
the Midwest
mending

Noriko Martinez
Next to a pond populated with turtles and ducks, frogs and toads, and the occasional egret.
being with; boredom; curiosity; erasure, avoiding thereof; love; recognition

Norma Fabian Newton
Los Angeles, CA/ Tongva land
intergenerational living

Olivia Spring
Belgrade, Maine
crip time

Onyịnye Alheri
somewhere in the Afrotropical realm
infinite blackness; prison abolition; radical inclusion

Owen Smith
Bunorong Country
liberatory education

Patrick Selmi, PhD
Windsor, ON Canada
Rank and File Movement (RFM) in social work

Paula D. Atkinson
Bay Area, CA→San Diego, CA→Washington, DC→ NYC→Washington, DC→ Palm Springs, CA
groups

Paule Potulski
Poland/Germany
herbalism

princex naveed
princex naveed is an uninvited guest on the unceded territory of the Kanien'kehá:ka nation, and frequently resides in central europe.
fermentation

Rachel Gallant, MD, MS
resides in Oklahoma City, OK
healing healers through the arts

Rachel Greenspan
New York
Cuestionamos

Rae Turpin (she/her)
England, UK
agency; dérive, the

Rafi Segal
Boston
care-based co-housing

René Benavides MSW, PPSC, ICF-ACC (they, she)
Ohlone land in San Leandro, California
embodied knowledge

Rhea V. Almeida, MS, PhD, LCSW
Somerset, NJ
decolonial liberatory-based practices; healing circles

Richael Faithful
Washington, DC (colonially known as), Chocolate City (colloquially known as), Nacotchtank Piscataway lands (crucially known as).
conjure; drumming; energy work; healing justice; land trusts; land, work, spirit, body; spells; somatic healing; theories of change

Rickey Cummings
Livingston, TX
vigil

Rob Edwards
Leeds, Yorkshire, UK
re-authoring

Rosemary A. Barbera
from Philadelphia to La Pincoya
Social Welfare Action Alliance, the

Ruth Catlow
London
interspecies organizing

Sabrina Tom
Los Angeles
narrative medicine

Sadaf Vidha
Mumbai, India
relationality

Sam Chavez
The ancestral lands of the Ramaytush Ohlone also known as the San Francisco Bay Area
communing with animals; flâner

Sara Cantrell, MA, ATR-P, LGPAT, LGPC
the Greater DC Area
art; ritual

Sarah Adelaide
Berlin
collective care

Sarah Eggers
Unceded Tongva land aka Los Angeles County/San Gabriel Basin
art-based group work

Sheila Koren
I've been in San Francisco for the past 40 years, originally from NYC.
Radical Therapist Journal, The

Sheila McNamee
Durham, New Hampshire/Portland, Oregon
radical presence; Taos Institute, the

Shelja Sen
New Delhi, India
feminism

Shelley Etkin
USA/Israel-Palestine
herbalism

Shipra Parikh
Mangalore, India, by way of Chicago, Illinois, USA, on unceded Anishinaabe Tribal lands (Ojibwe, Odawa, and Potawatomi, in addition to Ho-Chunk, Kaskaskia, Kickapoo, Mascouten, Menominee, Meskwaki, Myaamia, Peoria, and Sac and Fox)
anti-adultism

Shweta Srinivasan
Aamchi Mumbai, Maharashtra, India. ("Aamchi Mumbai" when translated from Marathi language, means "Our Mumbai." It's a phrase that's often used by Mumbaikars to fondly describe the city.) I'm originally from a small city called Palakkad in the state of Kerala in India. I lived in Dubai for the first 15 years of my life. I have been living in Mumbai, India, for 13 years now.
alternative identity projects

Sibylle Peters
Hamburg, Elbe, North Sea
wishes

Siegmar Zacharias
Romania/Germany
herbalism

Sins Invalid
The San Francisco Bay Area and beyond
accessibility

Sly Sarkisova
Tkaronto (aka Toronto), Canada
reclaiming selfhood

Snack Witch Joni Cheung
(home / knows she wants to die here) — unceded territories of the xʷməθkwəy̓əm, Skwxwú7mesh, Stó:lō, and Səl̓ílwətaʔ/Selilwitulh peoples, colonially known as Vancouver (also home) — Hong Kong (currently home) — unceded territories of the Kanien’kehá:ka peoples, Tiohtiá:ke - Mooniyang - Montréal
intuitive eating

Social-Body Apothecary
Berlin, Germany
herbalism

Sruti Suryanarayanan
Living on the ancestral lands of the Canarsie & Munsee Lenape people and on Lenapehoking
collaborative apprenticeship

Stanley L. Witkin
Maine, USA
social construction

Stella Lawless aka the Good Enough Witch
They currently live cooperatively in Tiohtià:ke/Montréal after fifteen years calling the Ohlone land of San Francisco home.
lunar cycle

Stephanie Marie Cedeño
(she/her)
Berlin, Germany
centering maintenance

Sunil Joseph (he/him)
San Francisco Bay Area
nonviolent communication

Susan Raffo
Mni Sota Makoce, unceded traditional and future homelands of the Dakotah people and within Anishinaabeg territories—Minneapolis, MN/USA
etymology

Tanya Paperny
Washington, DC
marginality (as a site of resistance); sanctuary; songs/singing

Thick Press
DC/LA
ongoingness

Tian Zhang
Western Sydney, Dharug Country, Australia
radical care in the arts

Tim Devin
Somerville, MA
bike and car repair collectives

Tobie Whitman, PhD
Washington, DC
wintering as metaphor

Verity Sturm
US
public library, the

Vero González, Boston and Puerto Rico
language justice

Zach Whitworth
Los Angeles Basin, Southern California
esoteric wisdom traditions; freedom; intentional communities

References

A

A Growing Culture. Instagram post, April 24, 2022. https://www.instagram.com/p/CcvFj42MsAY/?utm_source=substack&utm_medium=email.

Aberg-Riger, Ariel. "'Solidarity, Not Charity': A Visual History of Mutual Aid." Dec. 2020. https://www.arielabergriger.com/mutual-aid.

ACGME Program Requirements for Graduate Medical Education in Pediatrics. 2023. https://www.acgme.org/globalassets/pfassets/reviewandcomment/320_pediatrics_rc_022023.pdf.

Adams, Kathleen. *Journal Therapy for Calming Anxiety: 366 Prompts to Help Reduce Stress and Create Inner Peace* (Volume 1). New York: Union Square & Co., 2020.

Adams, Robert, Lena Dominelli, and Malcolm Payne, ed. *Social Work: Themes, Issues, and Critical Debates*, 3rd ed. London: Red Globe Press, 1998.

Adler, Janet. "Who Is the Witness? A Description of Authentic Movement by Janet Adler." In *Authentic Movement: Essays by Mary Starks Whitehouse, Janet Adler, and Joan Chodorow*, edited by Patrizia Pallaro, 221–22. London: Jessica Kingsley Publishers, 1999.

Adorno, Theodor W. *Aesthetic Theory*. Translated by Robert Hullot-Kentor. London: Athlone, 1997.

Afary, Kamran, and Elizabeth Malone Alteet. "Narradrama, Intersectionality and Devised Therapeutic Theatre in the Prison Communication Studies Classroom." *Drama Therapy Review* 8, no. 1 (April 2022): 23–44.

Akómoláfé, Báyò, and Ayana Young, "On Slowing Down in Urgent Times," *For the Wild* (podcast), January 22, 2020.

Al Jazeera. "Why India's revival of civil militias in Kashmir is raising fears." Al Jazeera, March 13, 2023. https://www.aljazeera.com/news/2023/3/13/why-indias-revival-of-civil-militias-in-kashmir-is-raising-fears.

Alcalá, Kathleen. "Deer Dancer." In *New Suns: Original Speculative Fiction by People of Color*, edited by Nisi Shawl. New York: Solaris Books, 2019.

Alchon, Guy. "Technocratic social science and the rise of managed capitalism, 1910–1933." PhD diss., University of Iowa, 1982.

Alessandri, Mariana. *Night Vision: Seeing Ourselves through Dark Moods*. Princeton, NJ: Princeton University Press, 2023.

Alessandri, Mariana. "Three Existentialist Readings of Gloria Anzaldúa's *Borderlands/La Frontera*." *Cuadernos de ALDEEU* 34 (2020): 117–135.

Alessandri, Mariana, and Alexander Stehn. "Gloria Anzaldúa's Mexican Genealogy: From Pelados and Pachucos to New Mestizas." *Genealogy* 4, no. 1 (2020): 12.

Alexander, Michelle. *The New Jim Crow: Mass Incarceration in the Age of Colorblindness*. New York: The New Press, 2010.

Alinsky, Saul. *Rules for Radicals*. New York: Vintage, 1971.

Allen, Paula Gunn. *The Sacred Hoop: Recovering the Feminine in American Indian Traditions*. Boston: Beacon, 1986.

Almeida, Rhea V. "Creating Collectives of Liberation." In *Feminist Family Therapy: Empowerment in Social Context*, edited by Thelma Jean Goodrich and Louise B. Silverstein, 293–305. Washington DC: American Psychological Association, 2003.

Almeida, Rhea V. (1994) *Expansions of Feminist Family Theory through Diversity*. Reprint, New York: Routledge, 2014.

Almeida, Rhea V. "Hierarchy of Power, Privilege & Oppression Graphic." Somerset, NJ: Institute for Family Services, 2016.

Almeida, Rhea V., Diana Melendez, and José Miguel Paez. "Liberation-based Practice." Published online, December 2015, in *Encyclopedia of Social Work*, edited by Cynthia Franklin, published by National Association of Social Workers and Oxford University Press. https://oxfordre.com/socialwork.

Almeida, Rhea V., Lynn Parker, and Kenneth Dolan-Del Vecchio. *Transformative Family Therapy: Just Families in a Just Society*. Boston: Pearson/Allyn and Bacon, 2007.

American Society of Plastic Surgeons. "American Society of Plastic Surgeons Reveals 2022's Most Sought-After Procedures." September 26, 2023. https://www.plasticsurgery.org/news/press-releases.

Andrews, Janice, and Reisch, Michael. "The Radical Voices of Social Workers: Some Lessons for the Future." *Journal of Progressive Human Services* 13, no. 1 (2002): 5–30.

Anonymous. *The Cloud of Unknowing*, translated by Clifton Wolters. New York: Penguin Books, 1961.

Ansari, Ahmed. "Design Must Fill Current Human Needs before Imagining New Futures." Speech at MIT Media Lab Summit, 2015.

Anthony, C. "Narrative Maps of Practice: Proposals for the Deconstructing Addiction League." *International Journal of Narrative Therapy and Community Work* 2 (2004): 1–9.

Antwi, Phanuel. *On Cuddling: Loved to Death in the Racial Embrace*. London: Pluto, 2023.

Anzaldúa, Gloria. *Borderlands/La Frontera: The New Mestiza*, 2nd ed. (1987) Reprint, San Francisco: Aunt Lute Books, 1999.

Anzaldúa, Gloria. "La Prieta." *This Bridge Called My Back: Writings by Radical Women of Color*, edited by Cherríe Moraga and Gloria Anzaldúa, 198–209. (1981) 4th ed., Albany, NY: SUNY Press, 2021.

Anzaldúa, Gloria. *Light in the Dark/Luz en lo oscuro: Rewriting Identity, Spirituality, Reality*, edited by AnaLouise Keating. Durham, NC: Duke University Press, 2015.

Anzaldúa, Gloria. "Now Let us Shift… the Path of Conocimiento… Inner Work, Public Acts." In *This Bridge We Call Home: Radical Visions for Transformation*, edited by Gloria Anzaldúa and AnaLouise Keating, 540–578. London: Routledge, 2002.

Aoki, Haruka. "An Ode to the Public Library." *The New York Times*, October 21, 2022. https://www.nytimes.com/2022/10/21/arts/new-york-public-library-illustration.html.

Arao, Brian, and Kristi Clemens. "Confronting the Paradox of Safety in Social Justice Education." Conference presentation at the ACPA College Student Educators International Annual Convention, Indianapolis, IN, 2006.

Arao, Brian, and Kristi Clemens. "From Safe Spaces to Brave Spaces." *The Art of Effective Facilitation: Reflections from Social Justice Educators* 135 (2013): 150.

Arao, Brian, and Kristi Clemens. "From Safe Spaces to Brave Spaces: A New Way to Frame Dialogue around Diversity and Social Justice." In *The Art of Effective Facilitation: Reflections from Social Justice Educators*, edited by Lisa M. Landreman, 135–150. New York: Routledge, 2013.

Association for Size Diversity and Health (ASDAH). https://asdah.org/.

Astin, Helen S., and Alexander W. Astin. *A Social Change Model of Leadership Development: Guidebook (Version III)*. Los Angeles: Higher Education Research Institute, University of California, Los Angeles, 1996.

Autistic Hoya. "Autistic Hoya's Brief Abled Privilege Checklist." Updated March, 2016. https://autistichoya.files.wordpress.com/2016/03/brief-abled-privilege-checklist-mar-2016.pdf.

B

Baik, Sun Woo. "Therapists Owe Marginalized Clients More Than Empathy." *Asparagus Magazine*, March 4, 2022. https://www.asparagusmagazine.com/articles/therapists-owe-solidarity-to-marginalized-clients-who-face-racism-oppression-and-violence.

Bailey, Roy, and Mike Brake, eds. *Radical Social Work*. London: Edward Arnold, 1975.

Baines, Donna. "Anti-Oppressive Practice: Roots, Theories, Tensions." In *Doing Anti-Oppressive Practice: Social Justice Social Work*. 3rd Edition. Edited by Donna Baines, 2–29. Fernwood Publishing, 2017.

Baker, Jes. *Things No One Will Tell Fat Girls: A Handbook for Unapologetic Living*. New York: Seal Press, 2015.

Bakhtin, Mikhail M. *The Dialogic Imagination*. Edited by Michael Holquist. Translated by Michael Holquist and Caryl Emerson. Austin: University of Texas Press, 1981.

Baldwin, James. *American Experience*: "The Negro and the American Promise." Interview with James Baldwin. Season 16, aired Jan. 2004. Boston, MA: WGBH Archives. Retrieved from https://www.pbs.org/video/american-experience-james-baldwin-from-the-negro-and-the-american-promise/.

Baldwin, James. *No Name in the Street*. New York: Dial Press, 1972.

Ballard, Susan, and Liz Linden. "Art Writing and Allegory in the Anthropocene," *October* 175 (2021): 88–108.

Barnett, Christopher. "Christopher Barnett Public Facebook Page." Facebook. Last modified July 18, 2023. Accessed September 9, 2023. https://m.facebook.com/profile.php/?id=1485180707.

Baudelaire, Charles. *Flowers of Evil*. Translated by George Dillon and Edna St. Vincent Millay. New York: Washington Square Press, 1962.

Bauman, Zygmunt. *Liquid Modernity*. New York: John Wiley, 2013.

Beckett, Samuel. *Nohow On: Three Novels*. New York: Grove Press, 1996.

Bell, Madison Smartt. *The Stone That the Builder Refused*. New York: Pantheon, 2004.

Besant, Annie, *Theosophy*. London: T. C. & E. C. Jack, 1912.

Bhaskar, Michael. *The Content Machine: Towards a Theory of Publishing from the Printing Press to the Digital Network*. London: Anthem Press, 2013.

Big Door Brigade. "What is Mutual Aid?" bigdoorbrigade.com/what-is-mutual-aid/.

Black Ink, "'Solidarity Is Not a Market Exchange': An Interview with Robin D. G. Kelley," *Black Ink*, January 16, 2020. https://black-ink.info/2020/01/16/solidarity-is-not-a-market-exchange-an-interview-with-robin-d-g-kelley/.

Black Lodge Press. *Growing a Garden Is a Beautiful & Radical Act*, riso print A3. https://blacklodgepress.bigcartel.com/product/gardening-us-a-radical-beautiful-act-riso-print-a3.

Bleger, José. "Theory and Practice in Psychoanalysis: Psychoanalytic Praxis." *The International Journal of Psychoanalysis* 93, no. 4 (2012): 993–1003.

Bloom, Nicholas Dagen, and Matthew Gordon Lasner, eds. *Affordable Housing in New York*. Princeton, NJ: Princeton University Press, 2016.

Blumer, Herbert. *Symbolic Interactionism: Perspective and Method*. Berkeley: University of California Press, 1969.

Boal, Augusto. *Theatre of the Oppressed*. Translated by Charles A. McBride. 1979. Reprint, New York: Theatre Communications Group, 1993.

Boggs, Grace Lee. *American Revolutionary: The Evolution of Grace Lee Boggs*. Directed by Grace Lee Boggs.

Boggs, Grace Lee. *Conversation between Grace Lee Boggs and Angela Davis*. https://www.youtube.com/watch?v=h9IsJwE0B1c.

Boggs, Grace Lee. *Conversation between Grace Lee Boggs and Immanuel Wallerstein*. https://www.youtube.com/watch?v=2CSE0PlsyVk.

Boggs, Grace Lee. (1998) *Living for Change: An Autobiography*. Reprint, Minneapolis: University of Minnesota Press, 2016.

Boggs, Grace Lee, and Scott Kurashige. *The Next American Revolution: Sustainable Activism for the Twenty-First Century*. Berkeley: University of California Press, 2012.

References

Boggs, James, and Grace Lee Boggs. *Revolution and Evolution in the Twentieth Century*. New York: Monthly Review Press, 1974.

Bookchin, Murray. *The Ecology of Freedom: The Emergence and Dissolution of Hierarchy*. Binghamton, New York: PM Press, 2005.

Boudet, Dominique, ed. *New Housing in Zurich: Typologies for a Changing Society*. Zurich: Park Books, 2018.

Boyer, Anne. *A Handbook of Disappointed Fate*. Brooklyn: Ugly Duckling Presse, 2019.

Brainard, Joe. *I Remember*. New York: Granary Books, 2001.

Brandow, Karen, Jim McDonnell, and Vocations for Social Change, *No Bosses Here: A Manual on Working Collectively*. Cambridge, MA: Vocations for Social Change, 1976.

Bricker-Jenkins, Mary, Rosemary Barbera, and Barbara Hunter-Randall Joseph. "Radical Social Work." In *The Encyclopedia of Macro Social Work*, edited by Darlyne Bailey and Terry Mizrahi. National Association of Social Workers Press and Oxford University Press, 2022. https://oxfordre.com/socialwork/page/4007.

brown, adrienne maree. *Emergent Strategy: Shaping Change, Changing Worlds*. Chico, CA: AK Press, 2017.

brown, adrienne maree. *Pleasure Activism: The Politics of Feeling Good*. Chico, CA: AK Press, 2019.

brown, adrienne maree. "radical gratitude spell," https://adriennemareebrown.net/2018/02/20/radical-gratitude-spell/.

Butler, Judith. *Frames of War: When Is Life Grievable?* New York: Verso Books, 2009.

Butler, Judith. *Precarious Life: The Powers of Mourning and Violence*. New York: Verso Book, 2004.

Butler, Judith. *Undoing Gender*. New York: Routledge, 2004.

Butler, Octavia E. *Parable of the Sower*. New York: Seven Stories Press, 1993.

Butler, Octavia. *Parable of the Talents*. New York: Hachette, 1998.

C

Cajete, Gregory. *Look to the Mountain: An Ecology of Indigenous Education*. Skyland, NC: Kivaki Press, 1994.

Cajete, Gregory. *Native Science: Natural Laws of Interdependence*. Santa Fe, NM: Clear Light Publishers, 2000.

Camargo-Borges, Celiane, and Sheila McNamee. *Design Thinking and Social Construction: A Practical Guide to Innovation in Research*. Amsterdam: BIS Publishers, 2022.

Caputo, Nina. *Nahmanides in Medieval Catalonia: History, Community, and Messianism*. Notre Dame, IN: University of Notre Dame Press, 2008.

Carlton, Thomas Owen. *Clinical Social Work in Health Settings: A Guide to Professional Practice with Exemplars*. New York: Springer Publishing Company, 1984.

Carlton, Thomas. *Illustrations of Health Social Work Practice: Lesson from the Membership Theory*. Monograph #5. Virginia Organization of Health Care Social Workers, 1990.

Carlton, Thomas, Hans S. Falck, and Barbara Berkman. "The Use of Theoretical Constructs and Research Data to Establish a Base for Clinical Social Work in Health Settings." *Social Work in Health Care* 10, no. 2 (1985): 27–40.

Catholic Worker Movement. "The Aims and Means of the Catholic Worker." Reprinted from 2019. https://catholicworker.org/aims-and-means/.

Chapman-Hilliard, Collette, and Valerie Adams-Bass. "A Conceptual Framework for Utilizing Black History Knowledge as a Path to Psychological Liberation for Black Youth." *Journal of Black Psychology* 42, no. 6 (2016): 479–507. https://doi.org/10.1177/0095798415597840.

Charon, Rita, and Sayantani DasGupta, Nellie Hermann, Craig Irvine, Eric R. Marcus, Edgar Rivera Colón, Danielle Spencer, Maura Spiegel. *The Principles and Practice of Narrative Medicine*. New York: Oxford University Press, 2017.

Chilton, Gioia. "An Arts-Based Study of the Dynamics of Expressing Positive Emotions within the Intersubjective Art-Making Process." PhD diss., Drexel University, 2014.

Chrystos. "I Walk in the History of My People." In *This Bridge Called My Back: Writings by Radical Women of Color*, edited by Cherrie Moraga and Gloria Anzaldúa, 53. Bloomington, IN: Third Woman Press, 1981; expanded and revised third edition, Berkeley, CA: Third Woman Press, 2002.

Cioran, E. M. *A Short History of Decay*. Translated by Richard Howard. New York: Arcade, 1975.

Circle Keepers. *Circle Keepers Deck and Guidebook*. Philadelphia: Fireball Printing, 2023.

Clifton, Lucille. "i am not done yet." https://www.onlytogrow.com/i-am-not-done-yet.

Climate Psychology Alliance North America. https://www.climatepsychology.us.

Climo, Alison. "Review of Bertha Capen Reynolds's *An Uncharted Journey*." *Reflections* 75 (1995): 77–79.

Cochran, Jessica, and Melissa H. Potter, *Social Paper: Hand Papermaking in the Context of Socially Engaged Art*, 2014. Exhibition, Columbia College Chicago Center for Book and Paper Arts, Chicago.

Coleridge, Samuel Taylor. *Poetical Works*, edited by Ernest Hartley Coleridge. London: Oxford University Press, 1969.

Collins, Patricia Hill. *Black Feminist Thought: Knowledge, Consciousness, and the Politics of Empowerment*. 2nd ed. New York: Routledge, 1999.

Collins, Patricia Hill. *Black Sexual Politics: African Americans, Gender, and the New Racism*. New York: Routledge, 2004.

References

Collins, Patricia Hill. "Foreword: Emerging Intersections—Building Knowledge and Transforming Institutions." In *Emerging Intersections: Race, Class, and Gender in Theory, Policy, and Practice*, edited by Bonnie Thornton Dill & Ruth E. Zambrana, vii–xiii. New Brunswick, NJ: Rutgers University Press, 2009.

Connolly, Nathan Daniel Beau. "Black Panther Party." In *Electronic Encyclopedia of Chicago*, edited by James R. Grossman, Ann Durkin Keating, and Janice L. Reiff, 142. Chicago: Chicago Historical Society, Newberry Library, 2005. http://www.encyclopedia.chicagohistory.org/pages/142.html.

Conrad, Peter. "Types of Medical Social Control." *Sociology of Health and Illness* 1, no. 1 (1979): 1–11.

Contemplative Outreach. "Welcoming Prayer." https://www.contemplativeoutreach.org/welcoming-prayer-method/.

Cope, Suzanne. *Power Hungry: Women of the Black Panther Party and Freedom Summer and Their Fight to Feed a Movement*. Chicago: Chicago Review Press, 2021.

Cornell, Ann Weiser. *The Power of Focusing: A Practical Guide to Emotional Self-Healing*. Oakland, CA: New Harbinger Publications, 1996.

Cornell, Katherine L. "Person-in-Situation: History, Theory, and New Directions for Social Work Practice." *Praxis* 6 (2006): 50–57.

Corrigan, Paul, and Leonard, Peter. *Social Work Practice under Capitalism: A Marxist Approach*. London: Palgrave Macmillan, 1978.

Cowie, Thomas. *The Great Exception: The New Deal and the Limits of American Politics*. Princeton, NJ: Princeton University Press, 2016.

Crenshaw, Kimberlé. "Demarginalizing the Intersection of Race and Sex: A Black Feminist Critique of Antidiscrimination Doctrine, Feminist Theory and Antiracist Politics." *University of Chicago Legal Forum* (1989): 139–167.

Crenshaw, Kimberlé. "Mapping the Margins: Intersectionality, Identity Politics, and Violence Against Women of Color." In *The Public Nature of Private Violence*, edited by Martha Albertson Fineman and Roxanne Mykitiuk, 93–118. New York: Routledge, 1994. See also: *Stanford Law Review* 43, no. 6 (1991): 1241–1299.

Crenshaw, Kimberlé. "Why Intersectionality Can't Wait." *The Washington Post*, September 24, 2015.

D

Dances With Fat (blog). Ragen Chastain. https://danceswithfat.org/.

Daugherty, Tracy. *Hiding Man: A Biography of Donald Barthelme*. New York: St. Martin's Press, 2009.

Davidow, Sera, and Caroline Mazel-Carlton. "The Pill Shaming Phenomenon: What's It Really About?" *Mad in America: Science, Psychiatry and Social Justice*, June 26, 2019. madinamerica.com/2019/06/pill-shaming-phenomenon-whats-it-really-about.

Davids, JD. "The Cranky Queer's Guide to Chronic Illness." *The Body*, April 20, 2018. www.thebody.com/article/the-cranky-queers-guide-to-chronic-illness.

Davids, JD, and Naina Khanna. "Such a Powerful Love: Disabled and Chronically Ill People and Our Long Fight for Justice." In *The Long Covid Survival Guide: How to Take Care of Yourself and What Comes Next*, edited by Fiona Lowenstein, 231–248. New York: The Experiment, 2022.

De Decker, Kris. "How Circular Is the Circular Economy?" Low←Tech Magazine, November 3, 2018. https://www.lowtechmagazine.com/2018/11/how-circular-is-the-circular-economy.html.

Dean, Michelle L. *Using Art Media in Psychotherapy: Bringing the Power of Creativity to Practice*. New York: Routledge, 2016.

Deaver, Sarah. "Art-Based Learning Strategies in Art Therapy Graduate Education." *Art Therapy* 29, no. 4 (December 2012): 158–165. http://doi.org/10.1080/07421656.2012.730029.

Debord, Guy-Ernest (1956), "Theory of the Dérive," translated by Ken Knabb. Reprinted in *Internationale Situationiste* No. 2, 1958.

Decolonial Summer School Middleburg (2017, July 10). Maria Lugones. Self Transformation in Community. Vimeo. https://vimeo.com/225018376.

DeLamater, Katharine Lark. "Historical, Social, and Artistic Implications of Collaboration in Contemporary Hand Papermaking." *Hand Papermaking* 34, no. 1 (Summer 2019): 11–16.

Deleuze, Gilles, and Felix Guattari. *A Thousand Plateaus: Capitalism and Schizophrenia*. Translated by Brian Massumi. Minneapolis: University of Minnesota Press, 1987.

Delz, Sascha, Rainer Hehl, and Patricia Ventura, eds. *Housing the Co-op: A Micro-Political Manifesto*. Berlin: Ruby Press, 2020.

Denborough, David. *Collective Narrative Practice: Responding to Individuals, Groups, and Communities Who Have Experienced Trauma*. Adelaide: Dulwich Centre Publications, 2008.

Despret, Vinciane. *Our Grateful Dead: Stories of Those Left Behind*. Translated by Stephen Muecke. Minneapolis: University of Minnesota Press, 2021.

Diehm, Cade, and Ruth Catlow. Concept paper for *The Treaty of Finsbury Park 2025*. April 10, 2020. New Design Congress, Berlin. https://newdesigncongress.org/en/pub/finsbury-park-2025/.

Dominelli, Lena. *Anti-Oppressive Social Work Theory and Practice*. New York: Palgrave MacMillan, 2002. Reprint, New York: Bloomsbury Publishing, 2017.

Dominelli, Lena, and Eileen McLeod. *Feminist Social Work*. London: Red Globe Press,1989.

Du Bois, W. E. B. *The Souls of Black Folk*. (1903) Reprint, New York: Dover, 1994.

Dulwich Centre. "Narrative Therapy and Research." Retrieved August 10, 2015. https://www.dulwichcentre.com.au/narrative-therapy-and-research.pdf.

References

Dunne, Anthony, and Fiona Raby. *Speculative Everything: Design, Fiction, and Social Dreaming*. Cambridge, MA: MIT Press, 2013.

Dunne, Pamela, Kamran Afary, and Pam Paulson. "Narradrama," In *Current Approaches in Drama Therapy*. 3rd ed. Edited by David Read Johnson & Renée Emunah, 206–249. Springfield, IL: Charles C. Thomas, 2021.

Duschek, Stefan, Lena Nassauer, Casandra I. Montoro Angela Bair, and Pedro Montoya. "Dispositional Empathy Is Associated with Experimental Pain Reduction During Provision of Social Support by Romantic Partners." *Scandinavian Journal of Pain* 20, no. 1 (December 2019): 205–209. https://doi.org/10.1515/sjpain-2019-0025.

Duvall, Jim, and Laura Béres. *Innovations in Narrative Therapy: Connecting Practice, Training,* and Research. New York: W. W. Norton, 2011.

Dyrbye, Liselotte N., Colin P. West, Daniel Satele, Sonja Boone, Litjen Tan, Jeff Sloan, and Tait D. Shanafelt. "Burnout among US Medical Students, Residents, and Early Career Physicians Relative to the General US Population." *Academic Medicine* 89, no. 3 (2014): 443–451.

E

Egan, Elisabeth, and Erica Ackerberg. "A Love Letter to Libraries, Long Overdue." *The New York Times*, February 14, 2023. https://www.nytimes.com/2023/02/14/books/review/library-public-local.html.

Eisendrath, Rachel. *Gallery of Clouds*. New York: *New York Review of Books*, 2021.

Eldridge, Richard. *Leading a Human Life: Wittgenstein, Intentionality, and Romanticism*. Chicago: University of Chicago Press, 1997.

Elliot, Debbie. "5 Decades Later, New Communities Land Trust Still Helps Black Farmers." *Morning Edition*, NPR, October 3, 2019. npr.org/2019/10/03/766706906/5-decades-later-communities-land-trust-still-helps-black-farmers.

Elliot, Lara, and Lacy Phillips. "Reiki and Energy Healing," *Expanded* (podcast) by To Be Magnetic. Ep. 27, February 1, 2019.

Emerson, Ralph Waldo. *Natural History of the Intellect: The Last Lectures of Ralph Waldo Emerson*. Edited by Maurice York and Rick Spaulding. Chicago: Wrightwood Press, 2008.

Emunah, Renée. "Self-Revelatory Performance: A Form of Drama Therapy and Theatre." *Drama Therapy Review* 1, no. 1 (2015):71–85.

Epston, David. "Co-research: The Making of an Alternative Knowledge." Available from Dulwich Centre. First published 1999. https://dulwichcentre.com.au/articles-about-narrative-therapy/co-research-david-epston/.

Epston, David. "The History of the Archives of Resistance: Anti-Anorexia/Anti-Bulimia." Retrieved August 10, 2015. https://narrativeapproaches.com/the-history-of-the-archives-of-resistance-anti-anorexiaanti-bulimia/.

Epston, David. "Internalized Other Questioning with Couples: The New Zealand Version." In *Therapeutic Conversations*, edited by Stephen Gilligan and Reese Price. New York: W. W. Norton, 1993.

Erdelyi, Karina Margit, "What is Somatic Therapy?" Psycom, October 28, 2019. https://www.psycom.net/what-is-somatic-therapy.

Escobar, Arturo. *Autonomía y Diseño: La Realización de lo Comunal*. Buenos Aires: Tinta Limón, 2017.

Ettarh, Fobazi. "Vocational Awe and Librarianship: The Lies We Tell Ourselves." *In the Library with the Lead Pipe*, January 10, 2018. https://www.inthelibrarywiththeleadpipe.org/2018/vocational-awe/.

F

Faithful, Richael. "'No Harm' Protection Spell." https://www.braxtoninstitute.org/blog/2022/8/2/harm-protection-spell.

Falck, Hans S. "Investigations of Membership Theory in Social Work: Their Current State." *Philosophical Issues in Social Work*, Fall/Winter (1992).

Falck, Hans S. *Social Work: The Membership Perspective*, vol. 14. New York: Springer Publishing Company, 1988.

Falck, Hans S. "Social Work and the New Integrative Hospital: A Comment on Disaster," *Social Work in Health Care* 21, no. 3 (1995): 23–25.

Falck, Hans S. "What Is Central in Social Work?" *Health and Social Work* 7, no. 3 (1982): 235.

Falconer, Erin M. "Housing People with Serious Mental Illness in Jails and Prisons: Why Are We Still Criminalizing Mental Illness?" *Behavioral Health News* (Oct. 2017). https://behavioralhealthnews.org/housing-people-with-serious-mental-illness-in-jails-and-prisons-why-are-we-still-criminalizing-mental-illness/.

Fancourt, Daisy, and Saoirse Finn. *What Is the Evidence on the Role of the Arts in Improving Health and Well-Being? A Scoping Review*. Copenhagen: World Health Organization. Regional Office for Europe, 2019.

Fattitude (movie). Directed by Lindsey Averill and Viridiana Lieberman. 2017. https://fattitudethemovie.squarespace.com/about.

Figley, Charles R., ed. *Treating Compassion Fatigue*. New York: Routledge, 2002.

Finkeldey, Jessica G., and Stephen Demuth. "Race/Ethnicity, Perceived Skin Color, and the Likelihood of Adult Arrest." *Race and Justice* 11, no. 4 (2021): 567–591.

Finn, Janet L. *Just Practice: A Social Justice Approach to Social Work*. 4th ed. New York: Oxford University Press, 2021.

Firchow, Peter, trans. *Friedrich Schlegel's* Lucinde *and the Fragments*. Minneapolis: University of Minnesota Press, 1971.

Fisher, Jacob. *The Response of Social Work to the Depression*. Boston: G. K. Hall, 1980.

Fletcher, Adam. *Facing Adultism*. Olympia, WA: Common Action Publishing, 2015.

Food Psych (podcast). Christy Harrison, producer and host. https://christyharrison.com/foodpsych.

Forché, Carolyn. *In the Lateness of the World: Poems*. New York: Penguin Press, 2020.

Foster, John Bellamy. *Marx's Ecology: Materialism and Nature*. New York: Monthly Review Press, 2000.

Foucault, Michel. *Discipline and Punish: The Birth of the Prison*. Translated by Alan Sheridan. New York: Vintage Books, 1975.

Foucault, Michel. *The History of Sexuality*, Vol. 1. (1976) Translated by Robert Hurley. Reprint, New York: Penguin Books, 2020.

Fox, Hugh. "Using Therapeutic Documents: A Review." *International Journal of Narrative Therapy and Community Work* 4 (2003): 26–36.

Frantz, Gilda. "An Approach to the Center: An Interview with Mary Whitehouse by Gilda Frantz." In *Authentic Movement: Essays by Mary Starks Whitehouse, Janet Adler, and Joan Chodorow*, edited by Patrizia Pallaro. London: Jessica Kingsley Publishers, 1999.

Fraser, Nancy. "From Redistribution to Recognition? Dilemmas of Justice in a 'Post-Socialist' Age." In *Theorizing Multiculturalism: A Guide to the Current Debate*, edited by Cynthia Willett, 19–49. Malden, MA: Wiley-Blackwell, 1998.

Fraser, Nancy. "Social-Theoretical Issues: On Class and Status in Capitalist Society." In *Redistribution or Recognition? A Political-Philosophical Exchange*, edited by Nancy Fraser and Axel Honneth, 48–70. London: Verso, 2003.

Freechild Institute for Youth Engagement. "Introduction to Adultism." Retrieved 2023 from https://freechild.org/2021/02/04/introduction-to-adultism/.

Freeman, Jennifer C., David Epston, and Dean Lobovits. *Playful Approaches to Serious Problems: Narrative Therapy with Children and Their Families*. New York: W. W. Norton, 1997.

Freire, Paulo. *Pedagogy of Hope: Reliving Pedagogy of the Oppressed*. (1970) Edited by Ana Maria Arújo Freire and Paulo Freire. Reprint, New York: Continuum, 1994, 2000.

Freire, Paulo. *Pedagogy of the Oppressed*. Translated by Myra Bergman Ramos. New York: Herder and Herder, 1970. Reprint, London: Bloomsbury Academic, 2018.

Friant, Martin Calisto, Walter J. V. Vermeulen, and Roberta Salomone. "A Typology of Circular Economy Discourses: Navigating the Diverse Visions of a Contested Paradigm." *Resources, Conservation and Recycling* 161 (October 2020).

Frye, Northrop. *Fearful Symmetry: A Study of William Blake*. Princeton, NJ: Princeton University Press, 1947.

Furtherfield, *The Treaty of Finsbury Park*. https://treaty.finsburypark.live/

G

Gabagambi, Julena Jumbe. "A Comparative Analysis of Restorative Justice Practices in Africa." Hauser Global Law School Program, September/October 2020. https://www.nyulawglobal.org/globalex/Restorative_Justice_Africa1.html.

Garbes, Angela. *Essential Labor: Mothering as Social Change*. New York: Harper Wave, 2022.

Garrett, Paul Michael. "Social Work and Marxism: A Short Essay on the 200th Anniversary of the Birth of Karl Marx." *Critical and Radical Social Work* 6, no. 2 (2018): 179–196.

generative somatics, "What Is Politicized Somatics?" https://generativesomatics.org/wp-content/uploads/2019/10/Copy-of-What-is-a-politicized-somatics.pdf.

George, Nelson. "Angela Davis Still Believes America Can Change." New York Times, October 19, 2020. https://www.nytimes.com/interactive/2020/10/19/t-magazine/angela-davis.html.

Gergen, Kenneth J. *Relational Being: Beyond Self and Community*. Oxford: Oxford University Press, 2009.

Gibran, Kahlil. *The Prophet*. London, England: Alma Classics. 1923/2020.

Giovanni, Nikki. "Quilting the Black-Eyed Pea (We're Going to Mars)." YouTube video, https://www.youtube.com/watch?v=cMKSSlaqTLE.=.

Givens, Terri E. *Radical Empathy: Finding a Path to Bridging Racial Divides*. Bristol, England: Policy Press, 2022.

Glissant, Édouard, and Patrick Chamoiseau. *Manifestos*. Cambridge, MA: MIT Press, 2022.

Gordon, Aubrey. *What We Don't Talk about When We Talk about Fat*. Boston: Beacon Press, 2021.

Gordon, Lewis R. *Existence in Black: An Anthology of Black Existential Philosophy*. New York: Routledge, 1997.

Gore, Ariel. *The Wayward Writer: Summon Your Power to Take Back Your Story, Liberate Yourself from Capitalism, and Publish Like a Superstar*. Portland, OR: Microcosm Publishing, 2022.

Gottman, John. *The Science of Trust: Emotional Attunement for Couples*. New York: W. W. Norton, 2011.

Graeber, David. *Possibilities: Essays on Hierarchy, Rebellion, and Desire*. Chico, CA: AK Press, 2007.

Graeber, David. *The Utopia of Rules: On Technology, Stupidity, and the Secret Joys of Bureaucracy*. New York: Melville House, 2016.

Graeber, David, and Andrej Grubačić. "Introduction," in *Mutual Aid: An Illuminated Factor of Evolution*, by Peter Kropotkin. Toronto: Between the Lines Books, 2021.

Greenpeace, "Circular Claims Fall Flat Again: 2022 Update." October, 2022. https://www.greenpeace.org/usa/wp-content/uploads/2022/10/GPUS_FinalReport_2022.pdf.

Gumbs, Alexis Pauline. "Introduction." In *Revolutionary Mothering: Love on the Front Lines*, edited by Pauline Alexis Gumbs, China Martens, and Mai'a Williams, 9–10. Binghamton, NY: PM Press.

Gumbs, Alexis Pauline, China Martens, and Mai'a Williams. *Revolutionary Mothering: Love on the Front Lines*. Binghamton, NY: PM Press, 2016.

H

Haiven, Max. *Revenge Capitalism: The Ghosts of Empire, the Demons of Capital, and the Settling of Unpayable Debts*. London: Pluto, 2020.

Halberstam, Jack. *The Queer Art of Failure*. Durham, NC: Duke University Press, 2011.

Halperin, Jennie Rose. "A Contract You Have to Take: Debt, Sacrifice, and the Library Degree." Medium, August 11, 2017. https://little-wow.medium.com/a-contract-you-have-to-take-debt-sacrifice-and-the-library-degree-5dbdfe1f6661.

Hampson, Lindsey. *Jake and the Weather Scare: A Booklet for Health Professionals Working with Children with Fears*. Liverpool: Alder Hey NHS Children's Foundation Trust, 2010.

Hampson, Lindsey. "The League against Upsets after Divorce or Family Change." *The Narrative Forum* 2, 1996.

Hampson, Lindsey. "Lessons Hard Won: An Introduction to the Theory and Applications of 'Consulting Your Consultants.'" *Context: The Magazine for Family Therapy and Systemic Practice*, 2016.

Hankivsky, Olena, and Renee Cormier. "Intersectionality and Public Policy: Some Lessons from Existing Models." *Political Research Quarterly* 64, no. 1 (2011): 217–229.

Hanley, Susan B. *Everyday Things in Premodern Japan: The Hidden Legacy of Material Culture*. Berkeley: University of California Press, 1999.

Haraway, Donna J. *Staying with the Trouble: Making Kin in the Chthulucene*. Durham, NC: Duke University Press, 2016.

Hardin, Garrett. "The Tragedy of the Commons: The Population Problem Has No Technical Solution; It Requires a Fundamental Extension in Morality." *Science* 162, no. 3859 (1968): 1243–1248.

Harding, Sandra. "How Standpoint Methodology Informs Philosophy of Social Science." In *The Blackwell Guide to the Philosophy of the Social Sciences*, edited by Stephen P. Turner and Paul A. Roth, 291–310. Oxford: Blackwell, 2003.

Haringey Council. *Biodiversity Plan*. October, 2009. https://www.haringey.gov.uk/sites/haringeygovuk/files/biodiversity_action_plan_2009-2.pdf.

Harney, Stefano, and Fred Moten, The *Undercommons: Fugitive Planning and Black Study*. Oakland, CA: AK Press, 2013.

Harris, Cheryl I. "Whiteness as Property." *Harvard Law Review* 106, no. 8 (1993): 1701–91.

Hart, Akiko. "Pursuing Choice, Not Truth: Debates around Diagnosis in Mental Health." *Asylum: The Magazine for Democratic Psychiatry* 25, no. 3 (2018): 19–21.

Hart, Kevin. *Postmodernism: A Beginner's Guide*. London: Oneworld Publications, 2004.

Hartman, Ann. "Diagrammatic Assessment of Family Relationships." *Social Casework* 59, no. 8 (1978): 465–476.

Hartman, Saidiya. "Venus in Two Acts." *Small Axe*. Number 26: Vol. 12, no. 2 (2008):1–14.

Hasnaa, Maryam. "Energetic Hygiene." maryamhasnaa.com/energetic-hygiene.

Health at Every Size. HAES Health Sheets. https://haeshealthsheets.com/

Hedva, Johanna. "Sick Woman Theory," 2020. https://www.kunstverein-hildesheim.de/assets/bilder/caring-structures-ausstellung-digital/Johanna-Hedva/cb6ec5c75f/AUSSTELLUNG_1110_Hedva_SWT_e.pdf.

Held, Virginia. *The Ethics of Care: Personal, Political, and Global*. New York: Oxford University Press, 2006.

Hemphill, Prentis. https://www.theembodimentinstitute.org.

Herbert, George. *Outlandish Proverbs*. London: T. Paine, 1651. http://name.umdl.umich.edu/a03057.0001.001.

Hersey, Tricia. *Rest Is Resistance: A Manifesto*. New York: Little, Brown Spark, 2022.

Heynen, Nik. "Bending the Bars of Empire from Every Ghetto for Survival: The Black Panther Party's Radical Antihunger Politics of Social Reproduction and Scale." *Annals of the Association of American Geographers* 99, no. 2 (2009): 406–22. https://doi.org/10.1080/00045600802683767.

Hillier, S. *The Outrageous Adventures and How They Turned Sad Beginnings into Happy Endings*. Liverpool, Australia: Rosebank Publications, 2001.

Hollis, Matthew. *The Waste Land: A Biography of a Poem*. New York: W. W. Norton, 2022.

Holt, John C. *How Children Learn*. Reading, MA: Addison-Wesley Publishing, 1995.

hooks, bell. *All About Love: New Visions*. New York: William Morrow, 2000.

hooks, bell. "Marginality as a Site of Resistance." *Out There: Marginalization and Contemporary Cultures* 4 (1990): 341–343.

hooks, bell. *Teaching Critical Thinking: Practical Wisdom*. New York: Routledge, 2010.

hooks, bell. *Teaching to Transgress: Education as the Practice of Freedom*. New York: Routledge, 1994.

Horan, Paula. *Empowerment through Reiki: The Path to Personal and Global Transformation*. Detroit: Lotus Press, 1998.

Howard, Jane. "Doom and Glory of Knowing Who You Are." *Life Magazine*, May 24, 1963, 81–90.

Hubbard, Bill. "The 'No Blame' Bullying Response Approach: A Restorative Practice Contender?" Unpublished master's thesis, Massey University, Auckland, New Zealand, 2004.

Hudson, Lauren. "Building Where We Are: The Solidarity-Economy Response to Crisis." In *Pandemic and the Crisis of Capitalism: A Rethinking Marxism Dossier*, edited by Vincent Lyon-Callo, Yahya M. Madra, et. al., 172–180. Cambridge, MA: ReMarx Books, 2020. http://www.rethinkingmarxism.org/Dossier2020/18_Hudson.pdf

Hunter, Shona, and Christi van der Westhuizen. "Preface." In *Routledge Handbook of Critical Studies in Whiteness*, edited by Shona Hunter and Christi van der Westhuizen. New York: Routledge, 2022.

Hutson, Wendell. "Afrocentric Bookstore Set to Close Next Month." *The Chicago Defender*, July 8, 2008. https://chicagodefender.com/afrocentric-bookstore-set-to-close-next-month/.

Hyde, Lewis W. *The Gift: Imagination and the Erotic Life of Property*. New York: Random House, 1983.

I

Imarisha, Walidah. "Introduction." In *Octavia's Brood: Science Fiction Stories from Social Justice Movements*, edited by Walidah Imarisha and adrienne maree brown, 2015. Chico, CA: AK Press, 2015.

INCITE! Women of Color Against Violence. *The Revolution Will Not Be Funded: Beyond the Non-Profit Industrial Complex*. Durham, NC: Duke University Press, 2017.

Insel, Thomas. *Healing: Our Path from Mental Illness to Mental Health*. New York: Penguin Press, 2022.

Intergalactic Conspiracy of Childcare Collectives. "Radical Childcare: The Kidz City Model," June 2013. http://intergalactic-childcare.weebly.com/kids-city-model.html.

International Cooperative Alliance. "Cooperative Principles." Accessed August 18, 2023. https://ica.coop/en/whats-co-op/co-operative-identity-values-principles.

IPBES. "The Global Assessment Report on Biodiversity and Ecosystem Services." At Intergovernmental Science-Policy Platform on Biodiversity and Ecosystem Services. Edited by Eduardo Brondizio, Sandra Díaz, Josef Settele, and Hien T. Ngo. May 4, 2019. https://doi.org/10.5281/zenodo.3831673.

Ivey, Diane. "Reshaping the Narrative around People of Color and Craftivism," in *Crafting Dissent: Handicraft as Protest from the American Revolution to the Pussyhats*, edited by Hinda Mandell, 301–318. Lanham, MD: Rowman & Littlefield, 2019.

J

Jahn, Marisa, ed. *Byproduct: On the Excess of Embedded Art Practices*. Toronto: YYZ Books, 2010.

James, C. L. R. *The Black Jacobins: Toussaint L'Ouverture and the San Domingo Revolution*. 2nd ed. New York: Vintage, 1989.

Johnson, Robert A. *Owning Your Own Shadow: Understanding the Dark Side of the Psyche*. San Francisco: HarperSanFrancisco, 1994.

Johnstone, Lucy, and Mary Boyle. "The Power Threat Meaning Framework: An Alternative Nondiagnostic Conceptual System." *Journal of Humanistic Psychology* (Aug. 2018).

Johnstone, Marjorie. "'Don't Take the Social Out of Social Work': The Social Work Career of Bessie Touzel (1904–1997)." *Affilia* 30, no. 3 (2015).

Jordan, Judith V. *Relational-Cultural Therapy*. Washington, DC: American Psychological Society, 2010.

Jordan, June. *Directed by Desire: The Complete Poems of June Jordan*. Edited by Jan Heller Levi and Sara Miles. Port Townsend, WA: Copper Canyon Press, 2007.

Jordan, June. "The Creative Spirit: Children's Literature." In *Revolutionary Mothering: Love on the Front Lines*, edited by Pauline Alexis Gumbs, China Martens, and Mai'a Williams, 11–18. Binghamton, NY: PM Press, 2016.

Joseph, Barbara R. "The Bertha C. Reynolds Centennial Conference June 28–30, 1985: Taking Organizing Back to the People." *Smith College Studies in Social Work* 56, no. 2 (1986): 122–131.

Joshua Whitehead, ed. *Love after the End: An Anthology of Two-Spirit and Indigiqueer Speculative Fiction*. Vancouver: Arsenal Pulp Press, 2020.

K

Kaba, Mariame. *We Do This 'Til We Free Us: Abolitionist Organizing and Transforming Justice*. Chicago: Haymarket Books, 2021.

Kafer, Alison. *Feminist, Queer, Crip*. Bloomington: Indiana University Press, 2013.

Kapitan, Lynn. "Close to the Heart: Art Therapy's Link to Craft and Art Production." *Art Therapy* 28, no. 3 (September 2011): 94–95. http://doi.org/10.1080/07421656.2011.601728.

Kaprow, Allan. *Essays on the Blurring of Art and Life*. Edited by Jeff Kelley. Berkeley: University of California Press, 1993; revised 2003.

Kauder Nalebuff, Rachel. *Stages: On Dying, Working, and Feeling*. Washington, DC: Thick Press, 2020.

Keating, AnaLouise. *Transformation Now! Toward a Post-Oppositional Politics of Change*. Champaign: University of Illinois Press, 2013.

Keating, Thomas. "The Welcoming Prayer." https://www.contemplativeoutreach.org/welcoming-prayer-method.

Keiley, Margaret K. and Fred P. Piercy. "The 'Consulting Your Consultants Interview': A Final Narrative Conversation with Graduating Family Therapy Masters' Students." *Journal of Marital and Family Therapy*, 25 (1999): 461–468.

Kelley, Robin D. G. *Freedom Dreams: The Black Radical Imagination*. Boston: Beacon Press, 2003.

Kinavey, Hilary, and Dana Sturtevant. *Reclaiming Body Trust: A Path to Healing and Liberation*. New York: TarcherPerigee, 2022.

Kindred, kindredsouthernhjcollective.org.

Koksvik, Gitte Hanssen, Naomi Richards, Sheri Mila Gerson, Lars Johan Materstvedt, and David Clark. "Medicalisation, Suffering and Control at the End of Life: The Interplay of Deep Continuous Palliative Sedation and Assisted Dying." *Health* 26, no. 4 (2022): 512–531.

Krey, Kel. "Adults Just Don't Understand: Checking Out Our Everyday Adultism." *Everyday Feminism*, February 7, 2015. https://everydayfeminism.com/2015/02/everyday-adultism/.

Kropotkin, Pyotr. *Mutual Aid: A Factor of Evolution*. New York: McClure Phillips, 1902. https://www.marxists.org/reference/archive/kropotkin-peter/1902/mutual-aid/ch01.htm.

Krumer-Nevo, Michal. "Poverty, Social Work, and Radical Incrementalism: Current Developments of the Poverty-Aware Paradigm." *Social Policy & Administration* 56, no. 7 (Dec. 2022): 1090–1102.

Krumer-Nevo, Michal. *Radical Hope: Poverty-Aware Practice for Social Work*. Bristol, UK: Policy Press, 2020.

L

Lacoue-Labarthe, Francois, and Jean-Luc Nancy. *The Literary Absolute: The Theory of Literature in German Romanticism*. Translated by Philip Barnard and Cheryl Lester. Albany: SUNY Press, 1988.

Lagalisse, Erica. *Occult Features of Anarchism, with Attention to the Conspiracy of Kings and the Conspiracy of the Peoples*. Binghamton, New York: PM Press, 2019.

Lambert, Léopold. "The Black Panthers' Struggle Against the US Politics of Health." Interview with Alondra Nelson. *The Funumbulist Podcast*. Podcast audio. 2014. https://www.librarystack.org/the-funambulist-podcast/.

Lamott, Anne. *Bird by Bird: Some Instructions on Writing and Life*. New York: Pantheon, 1994.

Langer, Marie. "Prólogo." In *Cuestionamos*, edited by Marie Langer, 20–21. Buenos Aires: Granica Editor, 1971.

Latour, Bruno. "An Attempt at a 'Compositionist Manifesto.'" *New Literary History* 41, 3 (2010): 471–490.

Lau, Yuk King. "A Multiple-Family Group with Youngsters Who Refuse to Attend School: Learning and Implications for School-Based Family Counseling." *International Journal for School-Based Family Counseling*, 4 (2012). https://www.researchgate.net/publication/260595403.

Lavalette, Michael, and Iain Ferguson. "Towards a Social Work of Resistance: International Social Work and the Radical Tradition." In *International Social Work and the Radical Tradition*, edited by Michael Lavalette and Iain Ferguson, 1-10. London: Venture Press, 2007.

Law, Victoria, and China Martens. *Don't Leave Your Friends Behind: Concrete Ways to Support Families in Social Justice Movements and Communities*. Binghamton, NY: PM Press, 2012.

Le Guin, Ursula K. *The Carrier Bag Theory of Fiction*. London: Ignota, 1986.

Lee, Poh Lin. "Our Bodies as Multi-Storied Communities: Ethics and Practices." *Journal of Systemic Therapies* 42, no. 2 (2023): 1–21.http://www.narrativeimaginings.com/.

LeFrançois, Brenda A. "Adultism." In *Encyclopedia of Critical Psychology*, edited by Thomas Teo, 47–49. New York: Springer, 2014. https://doi.org/10.1007/978-1-4614-5583-7_6.

Leone, Lauren, ed. *Craft in Art Therapy: Diverse Approaches to the Transformative Power of Craft Materials and Methods*. New York: Routledge, 2020.

Lerman, Liz. *A Handbook for Artists Working in Community*. Fergus Falls/Saint Paul, MN: Springboard for the Arts, 2020. https://springboardexchange.org/artists-working-in-community.

Leung, Sofia Y., and Jorge R. López-McKnight, eds. *Knowledge Justice: Disrupting Library and Information Studies through Critical Race Theory*. Cambridge, MA: MIT Press, 2021.

Light, Ann. "In Dialogue with the More-Than-Human: Affective Prefiguration in Encounters with Others." *Interactions*, July-August, 2023. https://interactions.acm.org/archive/view/july-august-2023/in-dialogue-with-the-more-than-human-affective-prefiguration-in-encounters-with-others.

Lister, Ruth. *Poverty*. 2nd ed. Cambridge: Polity Press, 2021.

Little, Tom, and Katherine Ellison. *Loving Learning: How Progressive Education Can Save America's Schools*. New York: W. W. Norton, 2015.

Longhofer, Jeffrey, and Jerry Floersch. "The Coming Crisis in Social Work: Some Thoughts on Social Work and Science." *Research on Social Work Practice* 22, no. 5 (2012): 499–519.

Lorde, Audre. *Uses of the Erotic: The Erotic as Power*. Brooklyn, NY: Out & Out Books, 1978.

Luna Jimenez Institute for Social Transformation. "Adultism: The Training Ground for All Other Oppression." Dec. 9, 2021. https://ljist.com/how-we-work/adultism-the-training-ground-for-all-other-oppression/.

Lynch, James P., and William Sabol. "Prison Use and Social Control." *Criminal Justice* 3 (2000): 7–44.

Lyotard, Jean-Francois. *The Postmodern Condition: A Report on Knowledge*. Translated by Geoff Bennington and Brian Massumi. Minneapolis: University of Minnesota Press, 1984.

M

MadEcologies.com broadsheet. *Philadelphia Principles: Radical Harm Reduction and the World We Want*. Philadelphia: Fireball Printing, 2023.

Maimonides, Moses, 1135–1204. *The Guide for the Perplexed*. Translated by M. Friedlander. London: Routledge & K. Paul, 1956.

Maintenance Phase (podcast). Michael Hobbes and Aubrey Gordon. https://www.maintenancephase.com/.

Maracle, Lee. *I Am Woman: A Native Perspective of Sociology and Feminism*. (1988) Reprint, Vancouver: Press Gang Publishers, 1996.

Maracle, Lee. *My Conversations with Canadians*. Toronto: Book*hug Press, 2017.

Maria Popova. "Hope, Cynicism, and the Stories We Tell Ourselves." *The Marginalian*. Feb. 9, 2015. https://www.themarginalian.org/2015/02/09/hope-cynicism/.

Marsh, Jaclyn Sanders, and Christine S. Davis. "Ethnodrama and Ethnotheatre," in *The International Encyclopedia of Communication Research Methods*, edited by Jörg Matthes, Christine Davis, and Robert Potter. Hoboken, New Jersey: John Wiley, 2017.

Marsten, David, David Epston, and Lisa Johnson. "Consulting Your Consultants, Revisited." *International Journal of Narrative Therapy and Community Work* 3 (2011): 57–71.

Martens, China. *The Future Generation: A Zine-Book for Subculture Parents, Kids, Friends & Others*. Baltimore: Atomic Book Company, 2007; Reprint, Binghamton, NY: PM Press, 2017.

Martin, Betty, with Robyn Dalzen. *The Art of Receiving and Giving: The Wheel of Consent*. Eugene, OR: Luminare Press, 2021.

Marya, Rupa, and Raj Patel. *Inflamed: Deep Medicine and the Anatomy of Injustice*. London: Penguin, 2021.

Maté, Gabor. *The Myth of Normal: Trauma, Illness, and Healing in a Toxic Culture*. New York: Avery, 2022.

Matott, Drew Luan, and Gretchen Miller. "Papermaking." In *The Routledge Companion to Health Humanities*, edited by Paul Crawford, Brian Brown, and Andrea Charise, 311-316. New York: Routledge, 2020.

May, Katherine. *Wintering: The Power of Rest and Retreat in Difficult Times*. New York: Random House, 2020.

Mayor, Christine, and Jason S. Frydman. "Understanding School-Based Drama Therapy Through the Core Processes: An Analysis of Intervention Vignettes." *The Arts in Psychotherapy* 73 no. 2 (Feb. 2021): 101766.

McAlevey, Jane. *No Shortcuts: Organizing for Power in the New Gilded Age*. New York: Oxford University Press, 2016.

McClain, Dani. *We Live for the We: The Political Power of Black Motherhood*. New York: Bold Type Books, 2019.

McDonough, William, and Michael Braungart. *Cradle to Cradle: Remaking the Way We Make Things*. New York: North Point Press, 2002.

McGoldrick, Monica, and Randy Gerson. *Genograms in Family Assessment*. New York: W. W. Norton, 1985; reprint 2020.

McKillop, Donal, Declan French, Barry Quinn, Anna L. Sobiech, and John O. S. Wilson. "Cooperative Financial Institutions: A Review of the Literature." *International Review of Financial Analysis* 71 (Oct. 2020): 101520.

McKittrick, Katherine. "Yours in the Intellectual Struggle: Sylvia Wynter and the Realization of the Living." In *Sylvia Wynter: On Being Human as Praxis*, edited by Katherine McKittrick, 1–8. Durham, NC: Duke University Press, 2015.

McMackin, Meredith. "Hand-papermaking with Student Veterans," in *Art Therapy with Veterans*, edited by Rachel Mims, 55–57. Philadelphia: Jessica Kingsley Publishers, 2021.

McMichael, Philip. "Food Sovereignty, Social Reproduction, and the Agrarian Question." In *Peasants and Globalization: Political Economy, Rural Transformation and the Agrarian Question*, edited by Haroon Akram-Lodhi & Cristóbal Kay, 288–311. London: Routledge, 2008.

McNamee, Sheila. "Radical Presence: Alternatives to the Therapeutic State," *European Journal of Psychotherapy and Counseling* 17, no. 4 (November 2015): 373–383.

McNamee, Sheila. "Radical Presence: A Relational Alternative to Mindfulness," in *Relational Mindfulness: Fundamentals and Applications*, edited by Roberto Aristegui, Javier Garcia Campayo, and Patricio Barriga, 51–63. New York: Springer, 2021.

Mienczakowski, Jim. "The Theater of Ethnography: The Reconstruction of Ethnography into Theater with Emancipatory Potential." *Qualitive Inquiry* 1, no. 3 (1995): 360–375.

Mignolo, Walter D. "Epistemic Disobedience, Independent Thought and Decolonial Freedom." *Theory, Culture and Society* 26, no. 7–8 (2009): 159–181.

Mignolo, Walter D. "Geopolitics of Sensing and Knowing: On (De)Coloniality, Border Thinking and Epistemic Disobedience." *Postcolonial Studies* 14, no. 3 (2011): 273–283.

Mignolo, Walter D. *The Politics of Decolonial Investigations*. Durham, NC: Duke University Press, 2021.

Miller, Gretchen, and Denise Wolf. "Radical Papermaking: A Socially Engaged Art Therapy Practice." Presentation, 53rd Annual Conference, American Art Therapy Association, Minneapolis, MN, November 11, 2022.

Miller, Scott D., and Mark Hubble. "How Psychotherapy Lost Its Magick: The Art of Healing in an Age of Science." *Psychotherapy Networker* 41, no. 2 (Mar/Apr 2017): 28–37.

Millner, Jacqueline, and Gretchen Coombs, eds. *Care Ethics and Art*. New York: Routledge, 2021.

Millner, Jacqueline, and Moore, Catriona. *Contemporary Art and Feminism*. New York: Routledge, 2021.

Mingus, Mia. "You Are Not Entitled to Our Deaths: COVID, Abled Supremacy & Interdependence," *Leaving Evidence* (blog), January 16, 2022. https://leavingevidence.wordpress.com/2022/01/16/you-are-not-entitled-to-our-deaths-covid-abled-supremacy-interdependence/.

Ministry of the Environment, Government of Japan. "The World in Transition and Japan's Efforts to Establish a Sound Material-Cycle Society." 2008. https://www.env.go.jp/en/wpaper/2008/.

Mitchell, Larry. *The Faggots & Their Friends Between Revolutions*. New York: Calamus, 1977. Reprint, Brooklyn, NY: Nightboat Books, 2019.

Mitchell, Stephen A. *Relationality: From Attachment to Intersubjectivity*. Hillsdale, NJ: Analytic Press, 2000.

Monk, Gerald, and John Winslade, *When Stories Clash: Addressing Conflict with Narrative Mediation*. Taos, NM: Taos Institute, 2013.

Moon, Catherine Hyland, ed. *Materials & Media in Art Therapy: Critical Understandings of Diverse Artistic Vocabularies*. New York: Routledge, 2010.

Morton, Timothy. *Hyperobjects: Philosophy and Ecology after the End of the World*. Minneapolis: University of Minnesota Press, 2013.

Movement Generation. https://movementgeneration.org/about/.

Moyer, Justin Wm. "T-shirt Asking 'What's More Punk Than the Public Library?' Raises 100K for D.C. Branch." *The Washington Post*, September 4, 2021. https://www.washingtonpost.com/dc-md-va/2021/09/04/dc-library-punk-shirt/.

Mullaly, Bob, and Marilyn Dupré. *The New Structural Social Work: Ideology, Theory, and Practice*. 4th ed. Oxford: Oxford University Press, 2018.

Murch, Donna Jean. *Living for the City: Migration, Education, and the Rise of the Black Panther Party in Oakland, California*. Chapel Hill: University of North Carolina Press, 2010.

Mutual Aid Medford and Somerville (MAMAS). *History of Mutual Aid Networks*. https://docs.google.com/document/d/1IcSIKwwGG_7X45mc9bHy7BqJGmFfEE4OOJMOI43K6CY/edit#heading=h.alxyjcump343.

N

National Museum of African American History and Culture, "The Black Panther Party: Challenging Police and Promoting Social Change." August 23, 2020. https://nmaahc.si.edu/explore/stories/black-panther-party-challenging-police-and-promotingsocial-change.

Nelson, Maggie. *On Freedom: Four Songs of Care and Constraint*. Minneapolis: Graywolf Press, 2021.

Nenquimo, Nemonte. "This Is My Message to the Western World—Your Civilization is Killing Life on Earth." *The Guardian*. October 12, 2020. www.theguardian.com/commentisfree/2020/oct/12/western-worldyour-civilisation-killing-life-on-earth-indigenous-amazon-planet/.

Newton, Huey P., and J. Herman Blake. *Revolutionary Suicide*. New York: Harcourt Brace Jovanovich, 1973.

Nhat Hanh, Thich. *Peace Is Every Step: The Path of Mindfulness in Everyday Life*. New York: Bantam Books, 1992.

Nhat Hanh, Thich. *Transformation at the Base: Fifty Verses on the Nature of Consciousness*. Berkeley, CA: Parallax Press, 2001.

Nochlin, Linda. *The Body in Pieces: The Fragment as a Metaphor of Modernity*. New York: Thames & Hudson, 1995.

O

O'Brien, Hettie. "How Mindfulness Privatized a Social Problem." *New Statesman*, July 17, 2019. https://www.newstatesman.com/politics/health/2019/07/how-mindfulness-privatised-social-problem.

O'Connor, Brendan. "How to Build a Global Abolition Movement." *Vice News*, December 7, 2020. https://www.vice.com/en/article/qjpjv7/how-to-build-a-global-movement-to-abolish-prison-police-v27n4.

O'Connor, Erna. "Relationship-Based Social Work: A 'Thirdspace' in Responding to Trauma." PhD diss., Trinity College School of Social Work and Social Policy, 2015.

Obolensky, Nick. *Complex Adaptive Leadership: Embracing Paradox and Uncertainty*. New York: Routledge, 2017.

Oliver Milman. "Anthropomorphism: How Much Humans and Animals Share Is Still Contested." *The Guardian*. January 15, 2016. https://www.theguardian.com/science/2016/jan/15/anthropomorphism-danger-humans-animals-science.

Oliveros, Pauline. *Deep Listening: A Composer's Sound Practice*. Self-published, iUniverse, 2005.

Orr, Andrew R., Nazanin Moghbeli, Amanda Swain, Barbara Bassett, Suzannah Niepold, Adam Rizzo, and Horace M. DeLisser. "The Fostering Resilience through Art in Medical Education (FRAME) Workshop: A Partnership with the Philadelphia Museum of Art." *Advances in Medical Education and Practice* (2019): 361–369.

Ortega y Gasset, José. (1932) *Obras Completas* (VI: 347–48). Madrid: Revista de Occidente.

Ostrom, Elinor. *Governing the Commons: The Evolution of Institutions for Collective Action*. Cambridge: Cambridge University Press, 1990.

Our Consumer Place. "*The MadQuarry Dictionary: A Consumer's Guide to the Language of Mental Health*." Last updated May 2013. https://www.ourcommunity.com.au/files/OCP/MadQuarryDictionary.pdf.

Oved, Yaacov. *Two Hundred Years of American Communes*. New York: Routledge, 1987.

Owen, Robert. *A New View of Society and Other Writings*. (1813) New York: Penguin Classics, 1991.

P

Page, Cara, and Erica Woodland. *Healing Justice Lineages: Dreaming at the Crossroads of Liberation, Collective Care, and Safety*. Berkeley, CA: North Atlantic Books, 2023.

Pallaro, Patrizia, ed. *Authentic Movement: Essays by Mary Starks Whitehouse, Janet Adler, and Joan Chodorow*. London: Jessica Kingsley Publishers, 1999.

Parker, Francis. *Progressive Education, Vol. 1: Or, Considerations on the Course of Life; Observations on the First Four Years of Childhood* (Classic Reprint)

Pavlovskaya, Marianna, Craig Borowiak, Maliha Safri, Stephen Healy, and Robert Eletto. "The Place of Common Bond: Can Credit Unions Make Place for Solidarity Economy?" *Annals of the American Association of Geographers* 110 no. 4 (2020): 1278–1299.

Payne, Malcolm. *Modern Social Work Theory*, 5th ed. London: Oxford University Press, 2021.

Peace Paper Project. "Papermaking as Art Therapy" retrieved June 20, 2023. http://www.peacepaperproject.org/arttherapy.html.

Pendzik, Susana, Renée Emunah, and David Read Johnson. *The Self in Performance: Autobiographical, Self-Revelatory, and Autoethnographic Forms of Therapeutic Theatre*. New York: Palgrave Macmillan, 2016.

Pollack, Rachel. *Seventy-Eight Degrees of Wisdom: A Tarot Journey to Self-Awareness*. Newburyport, MA: Weiser Books, 2019.

Power, Andrew, and Edward Hall. "Placing Care in Times of Austerity." *Social & Cultural Geography* 19, no. 3 (2018): 303–313.

Press Press. "Sanctuary: A Manifesto." (poster) https://www.presspress.info/content/3-document/1-manifesto-for-sanctuary-building-sanctuary-keeping/sanctuary-manifesto-poster.pdf.

Prosen, Mirko, and Marina Tavčar Krajnc. "Perspectives and Experiences of Healthcare Professionals Regarding the Medicalisation of Pregnancy and Childbirth." *Women and Birth* 32, no. 2 (2019): 173–181.

Purser, Ronald. *McMindfulness: How Mindfulness Became the New Capitalist Spirituality*. London: Repeater, 2019.

Purves, Ted, ed. *What We Want Is Free: Generosity and Exchange in Recent Art*. Albany, NY: SUNY Press, 2005.

Q

Quijano, Aníbal. "Coloniality and Modernity/Rationality." *Cultural Studies* 21, no. 2–3 (2007): 168–178.

Quijano, Aníbal. "Coloniality of Power and Eurocentrism in Latin America." *International Sociology* 15, no. 2 (2000): 215–232.

R

Rankine, Claudia, and Beth Loffreda. "On Whiteness and the Racial Imaginary." *Literary Hub*, April 9, 2015. https://lithub.com/on-whiteness-and-the-racial-imaginary/.

Ransom, Josephine. *A Short History of the Theosophical Society*. Adyar, Madras, India: Theosophical Publishing House, 1938.

Redstone, Amanda. "Researching People's Experience of Narrative Therapy: Acknowledging the Contribution of the 'Client' to What Works in Counselling Conversations." *International Journal of Narrative Therapy and Community Work* no. 2 (2004): 1-6.

Reisch, Michael. "Linking Client and Community: The Impact of Bertha Reynolds on Social Work." In *From Vision to Action: Social Workers of the Second Generation*, edited by Janice L. Andrews, 58–74. St. Paul, MN: University of St. Thomas, 1993.

Reisch, Michael. "Radical Community Organizing." In *The Handbook of Community Practice*. 2nd ed. Edited by Marie Weil, Michael Reisch, and Mary L. Ohmer, 361–381. Los Angeles: Sage Publications, 2012. Reprint, New York: NYU Press, 2019.

Reisch, Michael, and Janice L. Andrews. *The Road Not Taken: A History of Radical Social Work in the United States*. New York: Routledge, 2002.

Reisch, Michael, and Charles D. Garvin. *Social Work and Social Justice: Concepts, Challenges, and Strategies*. New York: Oxford University Press, 2016.

Resmaa Menakem, "What Somatic Abolitionism Is." https://www.resmaa.com/movement.

Reynolds, Bertha Capen. *An Uncharted Journey*. Washington, DC: NASW Press, 1963.

Reynolds, Bertha Capen. *Between Client and Community: A Study of Responsibility in Social Casework*. New York: Oriole Press, 1934. (Smith College Studies in Social Work, 5(1), 39–127).

Reynolds, Bertha Capen. *Learning and Teaching in the Practice of Social Work*. New York: Russell & Russell, 1942.

Reynolds, Bertha Capen. *Social Work and Social Living: Explorations in Philosophy and Practice*. Silver Spring, MD: NASW Press, 1975.

Reynolds, Vikki. "An Ethical Stance for Justice-Doing in Community Work and Therapy." *Journal of Systemic Therapies* 31, no. 4 (December 2012): 18–33.

Reynolds, Vikki. "Resisting Burnout with Justice-Doing Part 1: Collective Care and Ethical Pain." Presentation at BC Settlement and Language Service Providers' Provincial Meeting hosted by AMSSA. https://www.youtube.com/watch?v=RHNoFBS5a0g.

Robinson, George, and Barbara Maines, *Crying for Help: The No Blame Approach to Bullying*. Bristol: Lucky Duck Publishing, 1997.

Rosenberg, Marshall B. *Nonviolent Communication: A Language of Life*. 3rd ed. Encinitas, CA: PuddleDancer Press, 2015.

Ross, Alex. "De Minimis," *New Yorker*, April 17, 2023.

Royal Pharmaceutical Society, "A Competency Framework for all Prescribers." Sept. 2021.

S

Saad, Layla F. *Me and White Supremacy: Combat Racism, Change the World, and Become a Good Ancestor*. Naperville, IL: Sourcebooks, 2020.

Sahi, Razia S., Macrina C. Dieffenbach, Siyan Gan, Maya Lee, Laura I. Hazlett, Shannon M. Burns, Matthew D. Lieberman, Simone G. Shamay-Tsoory, Naomi I. Eisenberger. "The Comfort in Touch: Immediate and Lasting Effects of Handholding on Emotional Pain," *PLoS ONE* 16, no. 2 (February 2021): 1–15. https://doi.org/10.1371/journal.pone.0246753.

SAHMHSA. "Peer Support Workers for those in Recovery." https://www.samhsa.gov/brss-tacs/recovery-support-tools/peers.

Sajnani Nisha. "The Implicated Witness: Towards a Relational Aesthetic in Dramatherapy," *Dramatherapy* 34, no. 1 (2012): 6–21.

Salamon, Maureen, "What is Somatic Therapy?" *Harvard Health Publishing*, July 7, 2023. https://www.health.harvard.edu/blog/what-is-somatic-therapy-202307072951.

Saldaña, Johnny, ed. *Ethnodrama: An Anthology of Reality Theatre*. Walnut Creek, CA: AltaMira Press, 2005.

Saldaña, Johnny. "Street Rat: An Ethnodrama." *Journal of Curriculum and Pedagogy* 2, no. 1 (2005): 5–11.

Saleebey, Dennis. "The Strengths Perspective in Social Work Practice: Extensions and Cautions." *Social Work* 41, no. 3 (May 1996): 296–305.

Samuels, Ellen. "Six Ways of Looking at Crip Time." *Disability Studies Quarterly* 37, no. 3, 2017.

References

Sandoval, Chela. "After-Bridges: Technologies of Crossing." *This Bridge We Call Home: Radical Visions for Transformation,* edited by Gloria E. Anzaldúa and AnaLouise Keating, 21–26. New York: Routledge, 2002.

Sandoval, Chela. *Methodology of the Oppressed*. Minneapolis: University of Minnesota Press, 2000.

Sather, Marnie, and David Newman. "Holding Our Heads Up: Sharing Stories Not Stigma after Losing a Loved One to Suicide." Dulwich Centre Foundation. https://dulwichcentre.com.au/Holding-our-heads-up-Sharing-stories-not-stigma-after-losing-a-loved-one-to-suicide-compiled-by-Marnie-Sather-and-David-Newman.pdf.

Scahill, Jeremy. "Hope Is a Discipline: Mariame Kaba on Dismantling the Carceral State." *The Intercept*, March 17, 2021. theintercept.com/2021/03/17/intercepted-mariame-kaba-abolitionist-organizing.

Schelenz, Robyn. "How the Indigenous Practice of 'Good Fire' Can Help Our Forests Thrive." April 6, 2022. https://www.universityofcalifornia.edu/news/how-indigenous-practice-good-fire-can-help-our-forests-thrive.

Schlegel, Friedrich. *Philosophical Fragments*. Translated by Peter Firchow. Minneapolis: University of Minnesota Press, 1991.

Scholem, Gershom. *The Messianic Idea in Judaism: And Other Essays on Jewish Spirituality*. Tel Aviv: Schocken, 1995.

Schwartz, William. "Bertha Reynolds as Educator." *Catalyst* 3, no. 3 (1981): 5–11.

Scott, James C. *Domination and the Arts of Resistance: Hidden Transcripts*. New Haven, CT: Yale University Press, 1990.

Seale, Bobby. *Seize the Time: The Story of the Black Panther Party*. 3rd ed. London: Arrow Books, 1970. Reprint 1996. https://archive.org/details/seizetimestoryof0000seal/page/n1/mode/2up.

Selmi, Patrick, and Richard Hunter. "Beyond the Rank and File Movement: Mary van Kleeck and Social Work Radicalism in the Great Depression, 1931–1934." *The Journal of Sociology and Social Welfare* 28 no. 2 (June 2001) 75–100.

Sen, Shelja. "Just Girls: Conversations on Resistance, Social Justice, and the Mental Health Struggles of Women." *International Journal of Narrative Therapy and Community Work* 1, (2021): 60–69.

Shanafelt, Tait D., Sonja Boone, Litjen Tan, Lotte N. Dyrbye, Wayne Sotile, Daniel Satele, Colin P. West, Jeff Sloan, and Michael R. Oreskovich. "Burnout and Satisfaction with Work-Life Balance among US Physicians Relative to the General US Population." *Archives of Internal Medicine* 172, no. 18 (2012): 1377–1385.

Sharpe, Christina. "Beauty Is a Method." *e-Flux Journal*, 105, December 2019. https://www.e-flux.com/journal/105/303916/beauty-is-a-method/.

Shawl, Nisi, ed. *New Suns: Original Speculative Fiction by People of Color*. New York: Solaris Books, 2019.

She's All Fat (podcast). Sophia Carter-Kahn, creator and host. https://shesallfatpod.com/.

Shotter, John. "Methods for Practitioners in Inquiring into 'the Stuff' of Everyday Life and Its Continuous Co-emergent Development." In *Systemic Inquiry: Innovations in Reflexive Practice Research, edited by* Gail Simon and Alex Chard, 95–123. *Farnhill, UK: Everything is Connected Press, 2014.*

Sills, Renee. "Embodied Astrology." embodiedastrology.com.

Simpson, Leanne Betasamosake. "Land as Pedagogy: Nishnaabeg Intelligence and Rebellious Transformation." *Decolonization: Indigeneity, Education & Society* 3, no. 3 (2014): 1–25.

Sins Invalid. *Skin, Tooth, and Bone: The Basis of Movement Is Our People*. 2nd ed. Berkeley, CA: Sins Invalid, 2019.

Sizer, Nancy Faust, and Theodore Sizer. *The Students Are Watching: Schools and the Moral Contract*. Boston: Beacon Press, 2000.

Snow, Stephen. *Ethno-dramatherapy: Integrating Research, Therapy, Theatre, and Social Activism into One Method*. New York: Routledge, 2022.

Solnit, Rebecca. *The Mother of All Questions: Further Feminisms*. Chicago: Haymarket Books, 2017.

Sorensen, André. *The Making of Urban Japan: Cities and Planning from Edo to the Twenty-First Century*. London: Routledge, 2002.

Southerners on New Ground. Workshop: "The Intersectional Community Map: Land, Body, Work, Spirt." southernersonnewground.org/wp-content/uploads/2019/10/SONG-The-Intersectional-Community-Map-Land-Body-Work-Spirit1.pdf.

Sow, Makoroba. "Black Bookstore Research Guide: The Repression of Black Bookstores." New York Public Library. Last updated January 6, 2023. https://libguides.nypl.org/blackbookstores/repression.

Spade, Dean. *Mutual Aid: Building Solidarity During This Crisis (and the Next)*. New York: Verso, 2020.

Spalding, Esperanza. *12 Little Spells*, studio album. New York: Atomic Sound, 2018.

"*spek-." *Etymology*. Accessed November 29, 2023. https://www.etymonline.com/word/*spek-#etymonline_v_52870.

Spillers, Hortense J. "Mama's Baby, Papa's Maybe: An American Grammar Book." *Diacritics* 17, no. 2 (1987): 65–81.

Stakenas, Carol, Jordan Landes, and Katie L. Price. *Rosine 2.0: Futures and Histories of Collective Care*. Rosine Collective: Swarthmore, PA: Swarthmore College, 2023.

Stavrou, Dimitra. (2020). "Ethnodrama." Interview of Dimitra Stavrou to Kamran Afary about Ethnodrama." [video]. YouTube: https://www.youtube.com/watch?v=qnWVdFZ3OTY, (accessible on 10/08/23).

Stavrou, Dimitra. "Multi-mediations in Therapy and Training." In *The Ultramodern Subject*, edited by K. Navridis and Christakis, 116–126. Athens: Pedio, 2010.

Stiene, Bronwen, and Frans Stiene. *The Japanese Art of Reiki: A Practical Guide to Self-Healing*. New York: O Books/John Hunt Publishing, 2005.

Stiene, Frans. *The Way of Reiki: The Inner Teachings of Mikao Usui*. Winchester, Hampshire: O Books, 2022.

Strings, Sabrina. *Fearing the Black Body: The Racial Origins of Fat Phobia*. New York: NYU Press, 2019.

Sudbury, Julia. "Celling Black Bodies: Black Women in the Global Prison Industrial Complex." *Feminist Review* 80 (2005): 162–179.

T

Talwar, Savneet. "Accessing Traumatic Memory through Art Making: An Art Therapy Trauma Protocol (ATTP)." *The Arts in Psychotherapy* 34, no. 1 (2007): 22–35. https://doi.org/10.1016/j.aip.2006.09.001.

Taylor, Sonya Renee. *The Body Is Not an Apology: The Power of Radical Self-Love*. San Francisco: Berrett-Koehler, 2018.

The Dr. Huey P. Newton Foundation, *The Black Panther Party: Service to the People Programs*, edited by David Hilliard. Albuquerque: New Mexico Press, 2008.

The Salt Lake Tribune. "Nonprofit Playbook: A National Model for Sustaining Local Journalism." https://local.sltrib.com/pdfs/Salt%20Lake%20Tribune%20Nonprofit%20Playbook.pdf.

Tichindeleanu, Ovidiu. "The Struggle for Positive Peace and Pluriversality." Session, 13th edition of the María Lugones Decolonial Summer School, Eindhoven, Netherlands, June 8, 2022.

Tilsen, Julie. *Queering Your Therapy Practice: Queer Theory, Narrative Therapy, and Imagining New Identities*. New York: Routledge, 2021.

Tim Ingold, "On Not Knowing and Paying Attention: How to Walk in a Possible World," *Irish Journal of Sociology* 31, no. 1 (2022). https://doi.org/10.1177/07916035221088546.

Timor-Shlevin, Shachar, Yuval Saar-Heiman, and Michal Krumer-Nevo. "Poverty-Aware Programs in Social Service Departments in Israel: A Rapid Evidence Review of Outcomes for Service Users and Social Work Practice," *International Journal of Environmental Research and Public Health* 20, no. 1 (January 2023): 889.

Tomm, Karl, Sally St. George, Dan Wulff, and Tom Strong, eds. *Patterns in Interpersonal Interactions: Inviting Relational Understandings for Therapeutic Change*. New York: Routledge, 2014.

Tribole, Evelyn, and Elyse Resch. *Intuitive Eating: A Revolutionary Anti-Diet Approach*, 4th ed. New York: St Martin's Press, 2020.

Tronto, Joan, and Berenice Fisher, "Toward a Feminist Theory of Caring," in *Circles of Care*, edited by Emily K. Abel and Margaret K. Nelson, 36–54. Albany: SUNY Press, 1990.

Tronzo, William. *The Fragment: An Incomplete History*. Los Angeles: Getty Research Institute, 2009.

Tsing, Anna Lowenhaupt. *The Mushroom at the End of the World: On the Possibility of Life in Capitalist Ruins*. Princeton, NJ: Princeton University Press, 2015.

Tuck, Eve, and K. Wayne Yang. "Decolonization Is Not a Metaphor." *Decolonization: Indigeneity, Education & Society* 1, no. 1 (2012): 1–40.

U

Ugandan Parliament. "President Assents to Anti-Homosexuality Act." *Parliament of the Republic of Uganda*, May 30, 2023. https://www.parliament.go.ug/news/6737/president-assents-anti-homosexuality-act.

Ukeles, Mierle Laderman. "Manifesto for Maintenance Art, 1969!—Proposal for an Exhibition 'Care,'" In *Mierle Laderman Ukeles: Maintenance Art*, edited by Patricia C. Phillips, 210–211. New York: Prestel Publishing, 2016.

Uncertain Commons, *Speculate This!* Durham, NC: Duke University Press, 2013.

V

Vaid-Menon, Alok, Elisa Goodkind, and Lily Mandelbaum. "The Strength of Feelings," May 31, 2018, in *What's Underneath*, produced by StyleLikeU (podcast).

Video: https://www.youtube.com/watch?v=vS8PWWtd_hM.

Van Kleeck, Mary. *Creative America: Its Resources for Social Security*. New York: Covici Friede Press, 1936.

Van Kleeck, Mary. "Our Illusions Regarding Government." *Proceedings of the National Conference on Social Work*, USA, 1934: 61, 473–486. Chicago: University of Chicago Press.

Varley-Winter, Rebecca. *Reading Fragments and Fragmentation in Modernist Literature*. Brighton, UK: Sussex Academic Press, 2018.

Vázquez, Rolondo. *Vistas of Modernity: Decolonial Aesthetics and the End of the Contemporary*. Prinsenbeek, Netherlands: Jap Sam Books, 2021.

Vermeire, Sabine. "What If... I Were a King?: Playing with Roles and Positions in Narrative Conversations with Children Who Have Experienced Trauma." *International Journal of Narrative Therapy and Community Work* 4 (2017): 50–62.

Verso Books, "Nancy Fraser on Capitalism, Gender Oppression, Marxism, and the Post-Left Populist Moment." July 2023. https://www.youtube.com/watch?v=PNeAvN5eZ0A.

Vickers, Tom. "Marxist Social Work." In *The Routledge Handbook of Critical Social Work*, edited by Stephen A. Webb, 24–34. New York: Routledge, 2019.

Volkas, Armand. "Autobiographical Therapeutic Performance as Individual Therapy." In *The Self in Performance: Autobiographical, Self-Revelatory, and Autoethnographic Forms of Therapeutic Theatre*, edited by Susana Pendzik, Emunah Renée, and David Johnson, 113–127. New York: Palgrave Macmillan, 2016.

References

W

Ward, Stephen M. *In Love and Struggle: The Revolutionary Lives of James and Grace Lee Boggs*. Chapel Hill: University of North Carolina Press, 2020.

Washington Post Editorial Board. "They Clicked Once. Then Came the Dark Prisons." *The Washington Post*, February 13, 2023. https://www.washingtonpost.com/opinions/interactive/2023/political-protest-new-generation-faces/.

Weeks, Kathi. *The Problem with Work: Feminism, Marxism, Antiwork Politics, and Postwork Imaginaries*. Durham, NC: Duke University Press, 2020.

Wenocur, Stanley, and Michael Reisch. *From Charity to Enterprise: The Development of American Social Work in a Market Economy*. Urbana: University of Illinois Press, 1989.

WFHB, "The Strange Life of Work: Kathi Weeks." Audio: PRX. https://beta.prx.org/stories/208925.

Whitaker, Robert. *Anatomy of an Epidemic: Magic Bullets, Psychiatric Drugs, and the Astonishing Rise of Mental Illness in America*. New York: Crown, 2010.

White, E. B. *Charlotte's Web*. (1952) Reprint, New York: HarperCollins, 2012.

White, Michael. "Addressing Personal Failure." *International Journal of Narrative Therapy and Community Work* 3 (2002): 33–76.

White, Michael. "Challenging the Culture of Consumption: Rites of Passage and Communities of Acknowledgement." *Dulwich Centre Newsletter* 2, no. 3 (1997): 38–47.

White, Michael. "The Externalizing of the Problem and the Re-Authoring of Lives and Relationships," *Dulwich Centre Newsletter* (Summer 1988): 3–21.

White, Michael. *Maps of Narrative Practice*. New York: W. W. Norton, 2007.

White, Michael. *Re-Authoring Lives: Interviews & Essays*. Adelaide: Dulwich Centre Publications, 1998.

Wightwick, George. *Hints to Young Architects: Calculated to Facilitate Their Practical Operations*. 1st American ed. New York: Wiley and Putnam, 1847.

Wikipedia, s.v. "Biblioburro." https://en.wikipedia.org/wiki/Biblioburro.

Wikipedia, s.v. "Rochdale Principles." Accessed August 18, 2023. https://en.wikipedia.org/wiki/Rochdale_Principles.

Wikipedia, s.v. "Street Newspaper." https://en.wikipedia.org/wiki/Street_newspaper.

Winslade, John, and Michael Williams, *Safe and Peaceful Schools: Addressing Conflict and Eliminating Violence*. Thousand Oaks, CA: Corwin, 2011.

Witkin, Stanley L., ed. *Social Construction and Social Work Practice: Interpretations and Innovations*. New York: Columbia University Press, 2011.

Wittgenstein, Ludwig. *Culture and Value*, translated by Peter Winch. Oxford: Blackwell, 1980.

Wix, Linney. "Aesthetic Empathy in Teaching Art to Children: The Work of Friedl Dicker-Brandeis in Terezin," *Art Therapy* 26, no. 4 (2009): 152–158. https://doi.org/10.1080/07421656.2009.10129612.

Wolf, Denise. "Papermaking Reflections: Stories of Change, Growth and Creativity" and "Transformation in Papermaking: When Content Mirrors Process." In *The Art and Art Therapy of Papermaking: Material, Methods, and Applications*. Edited by Drew Luan Matott and Gretchen M. Miller. New York: Routledge, 2023.

Woolf, Virginia. *A Room of One's Own*. London: Hogarth Press, 1929. Reprint, New York: Harcourt Brace Jovanovich, 1991.

Wulf, Andrea. *Magnificent Rebels: The First Romantics and the Invention of the Self*. New York: Alfred A. Knopf, 2022.

Y

Yancy, George. "Ableism Enables All Forms of Inequity and Hampers All Liberation Efforts." *Truthout*, January 3, 2023. https://truthout.org/articles/ableism-enables-all-forms-of-inequity-and-hampers-all-liberation-efforts/.

Yang, K. Wayne. "Deep Organizing: To Build the Beloved Community." In *Nexus: Complicating Community and Centering the Self: A 20-Year Retrospective of a College-Based Community Center*, edited by Edwina Welch, Joseph Ruanto-Ramirez, Nancy Magpusao, and Sandra Amon, 9–21. Solana Beach, CA: Cognella Academic Publishing, 2015.

Yuill, Chris. "The Body as Weapon: Bobby Sands and the Republican Hunger Strikes." *Sociological Research Online* 12, no. 2 (March 2007): 111–21. https://doi.org/10.5153/sro.1348.

Z

Zapata, Emiliano. "Plan de Ayala of 1911."

Zazulak, Joyce, May Sanaee, Andrea Frolic, Nicole Knibb, Eve Tesluk, Edward Hughes, and Lawrence E. M. Grierson. "The Art of Medicine: Arts-Based Training in Observation and Mindfulness for Fostering the Empathic Response in Medical Residents." *Medical Humanities* 43, no. 3 (2017): 192–198.

Zeveleva, Olga. "Prison Riots and the Covid-19 Pandemic: A Global Uprising?" *Gulag Echoes*, April 16, 2020. https://blogs.helsinki.fi/gulagechoes/2020/04/15/prison-riots-and-the-covid-19-pandemic-a-global-uprising/.

Zhang, Tian. "A Manifesto for Radical Care or How to Be a Human in the Arts." *Sydney Review of Books*, July 18, 2022. https://sydneyreviewofbooks.com/essay/a-manifesto-for-radical-care-or-how-to-be-a-human-in-the-arts/.

Image Credit

pp. 1–4 and 509–512
Anonymous art book fair attendees in New York, Los Angeles, and Portland, responding to the prompts, "What beyond the Western medical model has helped you?" and "pick a radical helping term, draw or write something inspired by it!"

pp. 6, 17, 18, and 482
Katrina Umber, from her *Pictures of Radical Attunement*

Afrofuturism
Kassamira Carter-Howard

aging positivity
Photos: Collin Morrow

altar work
Ashley M. Lagrange, 2022

anti-ableism
Jen-White Johnson, copyright 2023

art
Sara Cantrell, 2022

art as/in/of life
Leanne Schubert (artworks), Mel Gray (photography), and Fruitful Designs (Barry Jon Gray, graphic design)

art therapy
Miki Nishida Goerdt

art-based group work
Anonymous participant in photography group, printed with permission

arts in medicine
Photos: Arts in Medicine Program at Baylor University Medical Center

arts-based research
Gioia Chilton, 2014

Ayurveda
Maria Habib and Gracy Obuchowicz

Bertha Capen Reynolds
"Bertha Capen Reynolds and friend, July 1939," (cropped), Bertha Capen Reynolds Collection #128 Box 14, Sophia Smith Collection, Smith College, Northampton, MA

bike and car repair collectives
Photo: Shelley Rotner

Black Panther Party Free Breakfast Program
Both photos: © The Regents of the University of California. Courtesy Special Collections, University Library, University of California, Santa Cruz. Ruth Marion Baruch and Pirkle Jones Photographs.

Body Trust
Copyright © 2017 Center for Body Trust, LLC, formerly Be Nourished, LLC

bridge as metaphor
Anonymous, printed with permission

care pods
Screenshot by contributor

care-based co-housing
Carehaus Baltimore, 2020. Architect: Rafi Segal A+U with collaborating artist Marisa Morán Jahn

Catholic Worker Movement
Ariel Gore

circular economy
MeijiShowa/Alamy Stock Photo

climate cafes
Chelsea Call

clouds as metaphor
Farah Markis

common pool resources
Video stills courtesy of Andrea Macias-Yañez, 2021

community college
Thick Press

community gardens
Images: © Amy Pekal; Last image: © Karol Piotrowski

constructionist-design framework, the
Illustration credit: Lara Kensinger; Copyright: Lara Kensinger and Celiane Camargo-Borges

critical whiteness
hannah baer

decolonial liberatory-based practices
Rhea Almeida, 2016

embodied expression
Lisa Levine and Anne Wolf: From the ENOUGH Photo Portrait Series

embodied knowledge
Dorean Raye

emergent strategy
Miki Nishida Goerdt

empathy
© rot.tuna (p. 167); © florence freitag (pp. 168–9)

ethnodrama
Christos Tsakas; Dimitra Stavrou

existentialism
© 2023 Coatlicue Sierra Rose

externalizing
Alycia Berg

feminism
Shelja Sen/Canva for stock images

feminist ethics of care
Monika Cvitanovic

generous systems
Athena Robles and Anna Stein 2009/2022

Grace Lee Boggs
Lily Luo

grief as nonlinear
Denise Shanté Brown, 2023

group work
Kirk Shepard, LPC, CGP

harm reduction
Carmen Ostrander and anonymous participants from the Psychedelic Psycotherapy Forum, Nanaimo, British Columbia, 2022

Hearing Voices Network
© 2023, Kelly Waterman

herbalism
Kitti Zsiga, Lili Birk Waehneldt, and Paule Potulski

holding space
Maria Habib and Gracy Obuchowicz

humor
Carmen Ostrander

illders
JD Davids papers, John J. Wilcox, Jr. LGBT Archives, William Way LGBT Community Center, Philadelphia, PA

infinite blackness
Onyinye Alheri

interdisciplinary cataloging
Jessie McCarty

interspecies organizing
Images courtesy of Furtherfield. Multispecies bullet point icons designed by Cade Diehm

liberatory education
Written by K.C. and Owen Smith; Illustrated by K.C.

limited-equity cooperative housing
Photo courtesy of Rachel Furnari, Graph Books

Magic School
Provided by Lindsey Hampson

mapping support
Heather Black-Coyne

marginality (as a site of resistance)
Tanya Paperny

mending
Nolan Calisch (left); The Far Woods (right)

mobile libraries
Both photos: Aeran Squires

mutual aid organizing
Thick Press with Mark A. Hernandez Motaghy; cover graphic by Madeline Blount

mycelia as metaphor
Mustafa Saifuddin

nepantla/nepantleras
© 2023 Coatlicue Sierra Rose

perspective via faith
Painting: Kate Fleming; Photo: Tom Woodruff

poetic meter
Art: Ailee Turquette; Design: Annie Finch

polarity work
Maria Habib and Gracy Obuchowicz

public benefits
Erin Segal and Julie Cho

Qigong
Neil Horsky

radical childcare in movement spaces
Graphics: China Martens

mage Credits

radical papermaking
Images 1-4: Gretchen M. Miller; images 5-8: Denise R. Wolf

Radical Therapist Journal
Collection of Thick Press; Photo: Julie Cho

Reflecting on Justice
Linda Lin

Reiki
Mary Akinadewo

respectful visiting
Nicole Lavelle

respite rooms
First image: Artist, John Roloff, Nightingale image adapted from a sculpture by Francis William Sargant, 1913, courtesy of Anglim/Trimble Gallery, San Francisco, CA; Second image: Catherine Fairbanks

ritual
Sara Cantrell, 2022

sanctuary
Tanya Paperny

sandplay therapy
Martín La Roche & Mirthe Berentsen, 2021–ongoing. Photos courtesy of the artists.

Sick Woman Theory
Deb Toscano-Knicos, 2023

slow textiles
Monika Cvitanovic

slowness
Lian Fumerton-Liu

social change ecosystem framework
Copyright Deepa Iyer. SM ©2017 Deepa Iyer. All rights reserved. All prior licenses revoked.

social practice
First image: Thick Press (book cover: Thick Press with Mark Menjivar and Rickey Cummings); Second image: Thick Press (book cover: Omnivore Inc. with Rosine Collective)

solidarity economy
© 2016 Jeffrey Yoo Warren and Caroline Woolard. This work is openly licensed via CC-BY-SA.

strengths perspective
Mel Gray and Leanne Schubert

sufficiency
Andrea Macias-Yañez, 2021

sustaining movement
Eva Ngono

symbol
Gioia Chilton

Temporary Autonomous Zones
Andrea Macias-Yañez, 2023

traspatio
Andrea Macias-Yañez, 2021

vigil
Photo of pages from *Holding Vigil*: Julie Cho

water
Fid Thompson

wintering as metaphor
Tobie Whitman

witchery
Photo: Karen Middleton

zinemaking
Jude R. Bettridge

A Note on Proces

MICHAEL BHASKAR'S theoretical model distills the practice of publishing into two elements: filtering and amplification.[1] But for this project, we didn't filter—not really. Instead, we invited contributions by activating our networks: social work (Erin), therapy and family therapy (Chris), design (Julie), and socially engaged art/publishing/solidarity economy (Thick Press, Erin and Julie). Contributors and colleagues brought other contributors into the fold, sharing the call for contributions that we posted on Thick Press's Medium page. We worked gently with contributors to make contributions the best versions of themselves, but we never *required* revisions, only very light copyediting at the end of the process. We included every contribution we received, as long as it spoke to radical helping, defined very broadly.

In copyediting a heterogeneous collection of texts contributed by people writing from different disciplines and different countries, we did not seek consistency across encyclopedia entries, only within each text. The only exception to this was how we handled quotation marks and citations; we thought variation in these cases would be distracting.

We used long notes pasted into emails to offer updates about the projects and communicate with collaborators about the constantly shifting parameters of our process. It is difficult to handle over 200 individuals with the care to which we aspire; these form letters allowed the three of us, working without any administrative support, to communicate transparently and warmly on a larger scale.

Thick Press rarely use contracts in our publishing practice, but because this project has so many contributors, it felt important to have each contributor sign a publishing agreement so that one person's second thoughts or unexpected legal circumstances wouldn't derail the entire project. We also wanted to give Thick Press the freedom to do what we wanted with the book as a whole (while still making sure that each contributor held the copyright to their individual contribution).

The compensation we offered for people's time and hard work was a copy of the book (shipping included, no matter where in the world the book needed to end up). In terms of monetary value, the price of a copy of *An Encyclopedia of Radical Helping* is very small. But no copies of the book would exist without the time, energy, and care that the three of us and 200-plus contributors put into the project. So in some ways, the value of each book, a labor of love, is "priceless" divided by 2500 (the print run)—which still equals "priceless."

Priceless doesn't pay the bills, and we recognized that people have different needs and circumstances, so we invited contributors to ask for honoraria and/or extra books not really as compensation, but as a way to thank them for their work and partially offset their time and trouble. Most people weren't sure what dollar amount to name—and it felt strange for us to ask people to name the amount of a gift—so we began to default to $200 for anybody who said they wanted an honorarium.

Before going to press, we assessed the designed document for accessibility related to color contrast. We chose not to provide image descriptions partly for logistical reason and partly because we didn't want to impose meaning on images. If readers need an audio accessible PDF of the book—or if they have any other access needs that we haven't anticipated—we hope they will reach out to erin@thickpress.org. We will do our best to meet needs and correct oversights in subsequent editions.

The list of encyclopedia concepts that we created—based on Thick Press's "ongoing inquiry into care"; Chris's *Radical Therapist* podcast conversations and reading; suggestions from others; and experiences from our lives—keeps growing. There are currently over 100 unclaimed entries, as you can see from the list of "unclaimed topics" that we've included in this volume. It is our hope that people will step up to fill in these concepts—and suggest new ones, too! Perhaps the new contributions will form an addendum to the book, or new pages in an expanded edition. This project's perpetual work-in-progress-ness fits with the careful focus on emergence that we associate with radical helping.

Up until this point, the three of us have been at the center of all elements of the *Encyclopedia*'s collaborative process. As the book moves into the world, we hope that contributors and readers will begin to connect with one another, creating new rhizomatic networks that will continue extending outwards to other radical helpers. —ES, JC, CH

1 Bhaskar, *The Content Machine: Towards a Theory of Publishing from the Printing Press to the Digital Network.*

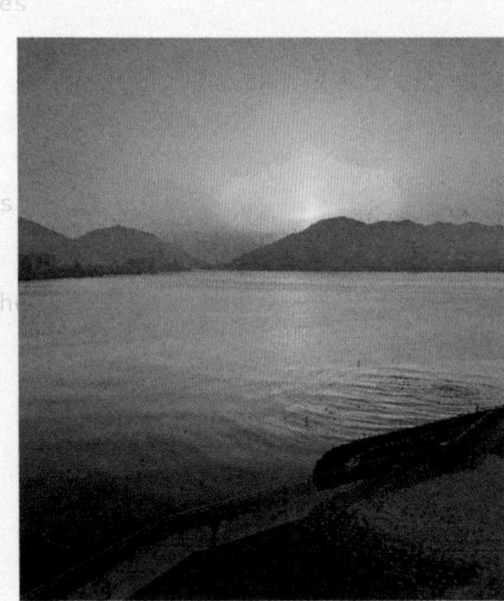

The colors in this book were inspired by an early morning sunrise in Masan, Korea, my mother's hometown. It took a litle while for me to decide on these colors, worrying whether my WHY felt systematic, functional, or interesting enough. And then I just felt my feelings and let myself go. This is the note that I wrote Erin and Chris when I shared this color palette:

> Hi Chris and Erin— sorry it has taken me SO long to get this to you. I am in Korea visiting my mom's hometown in the southernmost tip. I took a photo of the sky the other morning—somewhat hazy and air-polluted but I thought the colors were lovely and felt like *something*. Anyway, the colors aren't precise replicas of that sky, but inspired by...

I am grateful that this *something* found its way into the book. —JC

Thank you

This sprawling project would not have been possible without the loving support—past and present—of our families, our friends, our mentors, and the radical helpers in our own lives. We also want to express our gratitude to Erin's generous and loyal parents, Carl and Cassandra Segal, for financially supporting Thick Press over the years. Many thanks to Peter J. Karol, a brilliant communicator, for pro bono contract preparation and ongoing general orientation to copyright issues. Thanks also to Julie's design studio partners and lifelong friends, Alice Chung and Karen Hsu, for creative feedback and support throughout this process. Thank you, Elias Muhanna for a great conversation about encyclopedias. Many thanks to our copy-editor, Liz Brown, not only for approaching the granular with such careful patience, but also for "getting" this *Encyclopedia* project in such affirming, buoying ways. When we became overwhelmed, longtime Thick Press collaborator Rachel Kauder Nalebuff stepped in to take on a little bit of editing and a lot of moral support; thank you, Rachel! Thick Press also values and appreciates the growing community of Thick Press collaborators who teach us so much about care, helping, trust, collaboration, conflict, and bookmaking. Thanks to all the people (too many to name!) who shared our open call for contributions with others. And most of all, the three of us want to thank each and every radical helper who contributed to this volume. It's been a privilege and a joy to correspond with you, collaborate with you, and learn about the work you do and/or the thoughts you think. Each of you makes these difficult times much more bearable, and for that we are grateful.

—ES, CH, JC

COLOPHON

Published by
Thick Press

thickpress.com

ISBN
978-1-7320666-4-9

Book design:
Omnivore, Inc.

Curating/editing:
Erin Segal, Chris Hoff, Julie Cho

Editing/proofreading:
Thick Press

Typefaces:
Times Now
Attribute Mono
Aperçu

Printing:
Asia Pacific Offset

Any omissions or errors in copyright are inadvertent and will be corrected in subsequent editions.

Second printing

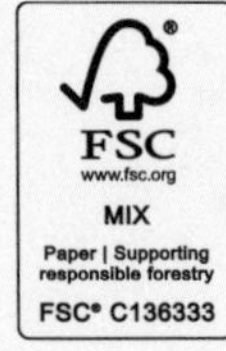

UNCLAIMED TOPICS

PERHAPS NEW contributions based on this list of unclaimed topics (and others, too!) will someday appear in an expanded edition of *An Encyclopedia of Radical Helping*—and/or in an addendum to the volume. Please reach out to erin@thickpress.com if you are interested in contributing text and/or images that speak to one or more of these topics. Please also reach out if you have other ideas for encyclopedia topics, even if you prefer not to be the one to address them. —ES, CH, JC

Afropessimism
allyship
anarchism
anti-capitalist time
appreciative inquiry
auricular acupuncture
barter
boundaries
boycott/divest
Buddhist psychology
buen vivir
capabilities perspective
care/caring
care banking
ceremony
child life
childcare collectives
chorus, the
class suicide
Clearness Committee, the
co-conspiratorship
community bail funds
community choirs
community farms
community fridges
community over everything
community printing presses
"consent not to be a single being"
consent-based touch practices
cooperation
cooperative grocery stores
critical case studies
dance/movement therapy
death positivity
decay
disidentification
domesticated animals
doulaship
dreamwork
eco-psychoanalysis
ecofeminism
ecotherapy
empathic knowing
empowerment tradition in social work
environmental justice
epistemic disobedience
epistemologies of the South
equity
erotic, uses of the
feet, tending to the
fluidity
food justice
fugitivity
games
generosity
Global Partnership for Transformative Social Work
Greek solidarity clinics
healing
honoring creativity
housing justice
human rights
irony
labor unions for care workers
land attribution
laughter
learning from elders
lending circles
liberation theology
Lincoln Hospital, occupation of
listening
mad studies
making kin
Maroon/Marronage
Marxisms
mask-making
memorials
menstrual justice
moneyless exchange
Museum of Care, the
neglect
"nothing about us without us"
other species
people's detox
play
pluri-economies
poverty scholarship
practice
praxis
prayer
public altars
public rituals
queer theory
radical acceptance
radical hospitality
reading rooms
repair cafes
reproductive justice
sober joy
spatial justice
spoken word
structural resilience
study
survival
Sylvia Rivera
Tao Te Ching
tenderness
theory/theorizing
time banking
Transcendentalism
transgression
universal basic income
utopia
Whole Earth Catalog, the
working for free (dugnat, bayanihan, volunteerism, etc.)

empathic knowing

Softness.

pick a radical helping term,
draw or write something inspired by it!

FROM AN ENCYCLOPEDIA OF RADICAL HELPING

What helps is knowledge

Especially slowly working through Science

eco-psychoanalysis

I LOVE MY FAMILY SO MUCH, IT MAKES ME WANT TO CRY.

~~I LOVE ART & DESIGN SO MUCH~~

I THINK ART & BEING CREATIVE IS THE ONLY THING BESIDES THAT MAKES ME FEEL LIKE ME

pick a radical helping term,
draw or write something inspired by it!

FROM AN ENCYCLOPEDIA OF RADICAL HELPING

I've found that the dogs I've fostered have helped me by the very fact that they rely on me (wholly) to get up and care for them, regardless of my mental state. They are a forceful reminder of the fact that it's not all about me.

freedom

pick a radical helping term,
draw or write something inspired by it!

FROM AN ENCYCLOPEDIA OF RADICAL HELPING

What has helped me @ least to concentrait on things is listening to pop music intromentally. I have ADHD so its very hard to focus which has made feel bad about myself.

allyship

agility

pick a radical helping term,
draw or write something inspired by it!

recognition

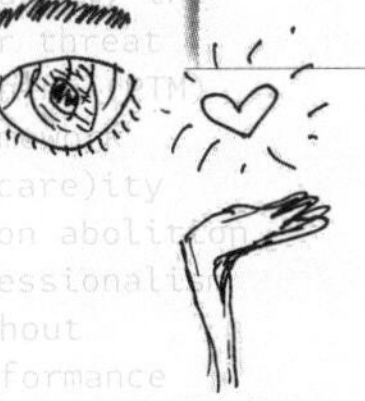

pick a radical helping term,
draw or write something inspired by it!

FROM AN ENCYCLOPEDIA OF RADICAL HELPING

. TALKING. WRITING. GETTING OUT OF MY HEAD. I FIND THAT OFTEN, I KNOW THE ANSWER OR NEXT STEP, BUT IT DOESN'T REVEAL ITSELF UNTIL I TALK IT OUT.

ALSO— SOMEONE ANTICIPATING MY NEEDS. I.E. COOKING ME DINNER AFTER A LONG DAY ♡

deep organizing

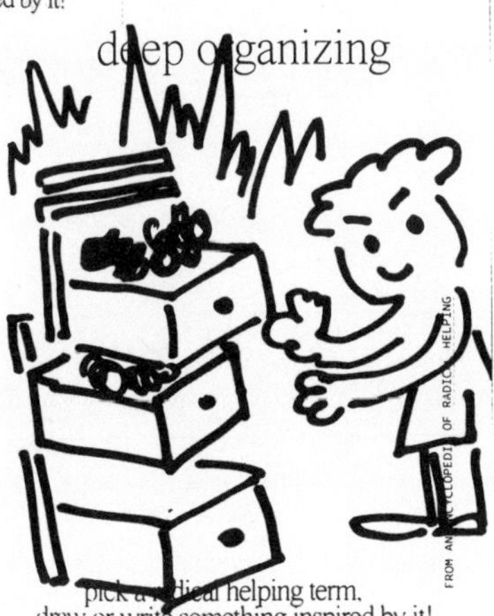

pick a radical helping term,
draw or write something inspired by it!

FROM AN ENCYCLOPEDIA OF RADICAL HELPING

embodied knowledge

intuiton is ancestral knowledge

pick a radical helping term,
draw or write something inspired by it!

FROM AN ENCYCLOPEDIA OF RADICAL HELPING

decolonial/liberatory based-practices

slowing down w/ tactile information as a break from overly saturated media/ doom scrolling. slowness as a practice of listening to our bodies & instict.

pick a radical helping term,
draw or write something inspired by it!

FROM AN ENCYCLOPEDIA OF RADICAL HELPING

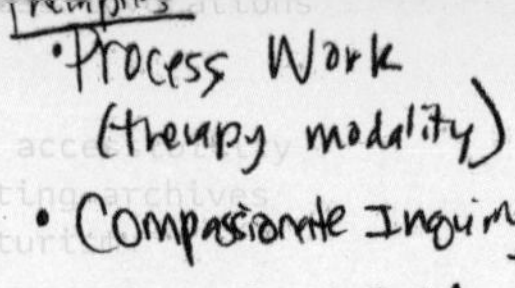

• Compassionate Inquiry

• Psychedelic MDMA therapy

Many movement practices, a dance! 5Rhythms, ecstatic dance, contact improv, ballet, many years on aerial silks

Community living for lot years 5+ people crafting a home together

decolonial/liberatory based-practices

slowing down w/ tactile information as a break from overly saturated media/ doom scrolling. slowness as a practice of listening to our bodies & instict.

pick a radical helping term, draw or write something inspired by it!

FROM AN ENCYCLOPEDIA OF RADICAL HELPING

somatic healing

OUR BODIES. WE ARE OUR BODIES. THERE IS NO SEPARATION THE PAIN IS THAT WE HAVE BEEN DISCONNECTED.

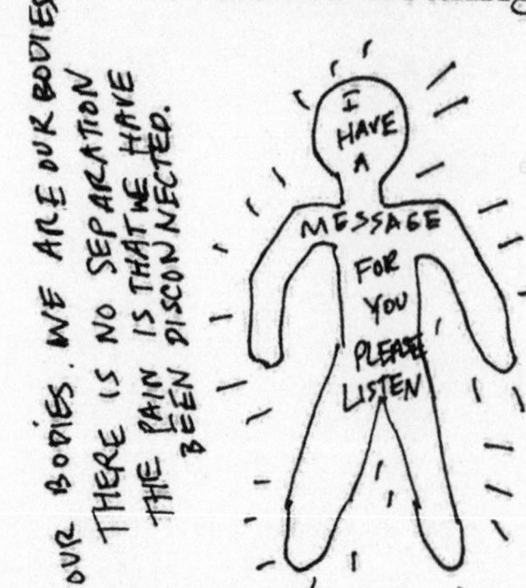

FROM AN ENCYCLOPEDIA OF RADICAL HELPING

sober joy

:)

LIGHT. RENEWAL. FUTURE TO WIN.

DARK TUNNEL.

SHATTERED PIECES OF OLD SELF.

pick a radical helping term, draw or write something inspired by it!

FROM AN ENCYCLOPEDIA OF RADICAL HELPING

ancestrality

My grandmother grew up on a spit of land jutting into the ocean. Now I do too. In winter they brought the cows inside to keep the cottage warm. "It was a lonesome place, but it was a beautiful lonesome place," she said.

My grandfather went as a young man to mine coal in Wales. When he returned,

two years later, he played a trick, or so the story goes. He dressed up as a woman, and was received as a stranger in the family home, before revealing his identity ~~But~~, to great amusement.

I always wondered about this story. Was my grandfather, legendary for his gregariousness, engaging in some gender play? Maybe, and maybe also something else, maybe the ~~[illegible]~~ Irish ~~[illegible]~~ War of Independence ~~[illegible]~~. Never was this discussed,

but the men would gather in rooms and ~~to~~ converse in hushed tones, clamming up when my mother would appear. There was a secrecy and ~~tinders~~ness, decades of exile, and the ~~[illegible]~~ ~~relatives~~ uncles all remember that Granny was involved, maybe in some bombings.

And it turns out that Cork was the center of a major reprisal by British forces during that war. The city center, where my great grandparents were publicans, was burned out.

The truth is that I don't know what my ancestors have given me. I think it is a complicated legacy of historical trauma and upheaval. It is also song and jokes and poetry. ~~[illegible]~~ It's the fucking Church, god help me, and it's a joy in music even when one is unable to carry a tune. But ~~[illegible]~~ it's also a secretive burden that can't be discussed openly, and that is a part of my ancestors I would like to leave behind.

revolutionary mothering

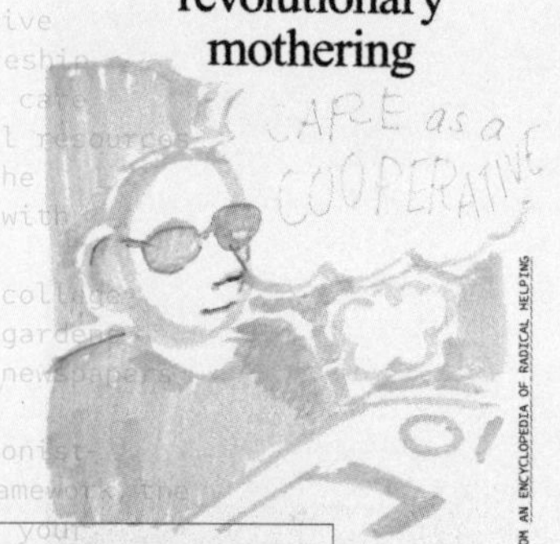

pick a radical helping term, draw or write something inspired by it!

FROM AN ENCYCLOPEDIA OF RADICAL HELPING

sauna

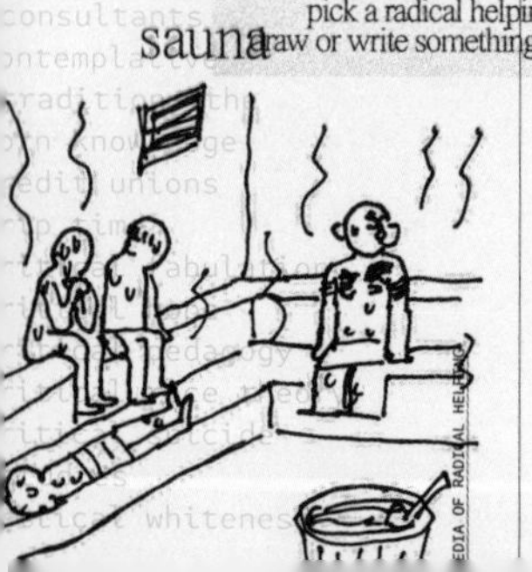

FROM AN ENCYCLOPEDIA OF RADICAL HELPING

love
lunar cycle
Magic School, the
mapping support
marginality
(as a site of
resistance)
Marxist social
work
membership
in social work
mending
metaphor
mikveh
mobile library
movement
lawyering
mutual aid
mycelia as
metaphor
narradrama
narrative
medicine
narrative therapy
nepantla/
nepantleras
nonviolent
communication
onguingness
peer counseling
peer-to-peer
health network
person-situation
perspective
perspective via
faith
pleasure
poems/poetry
poetic meter
polarity work
post-
oppositionality
postwork
imaginaries
poverty-aware
social work
paradigm, the
power threat
meaning (PTM)
framework
pre(care)ity
prison abolition
professionalism
without
performance
progressive
education
public benefits
public library,
the
Qigong
radical
administration
radical care in
the arts
radical childcare
in movement
spaces
radical
inclusion
radical
papermaking
radical presence
radical
social work
Radicalism Journal, The
Rank and File
Movement (RFM)
in social work

land trusts

I think all organizatns who work with land should be in contact & convo w/ local native/indigenous ppls regarding resource/access, and only hire based on the integrity of that relationship, with no regard to academic qualifications or previous work experience whatsoever - be "professionalism" is an arm of white supremacy/colonization and the right connects will have no resume

LAND BACK

pick a radical helping term,
draw or write something inspired by it!

FROM AN ENCYCLOPEDIA OF RADICAL HELPING

dance/movement therapy

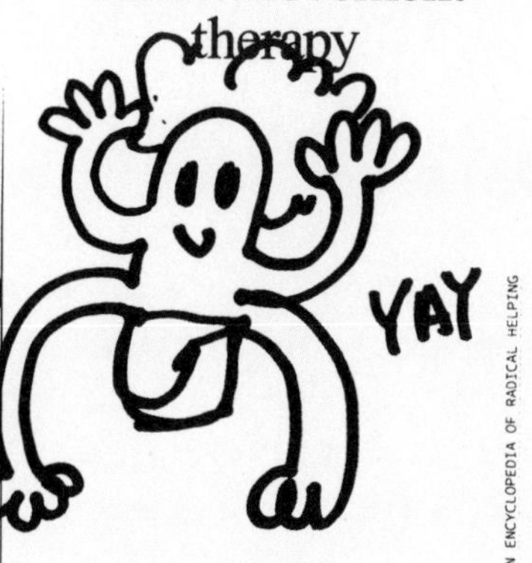

pick a radical helping term,
draw or write something inspired by it!

FROM AN ENCYCLOPEDIA OF RADICAL HELPING

Farming** to heal from orthorexia and bulimia

* specifically WWOOFing on a number of farms representative of our food systems - meat, produce, vegetables, fruit, flowers, and more
* farming as a way to redefine relationships with food & body & care

reclaiming selfhood
recognition
redistribution
Reflecting on Justice
reflexivity
Reiki
relational
interviewing
relationality
resistance
resisting the
parental loss
narrative
resonance
respectful visiting
respite room
rest as resistance
revenge
revolutionary
mothering
ritual
sanctuary
sandplay therapy
sauna
seed banking
sex positivity
shadow integration
Sick Woman Theory
slow textiles
slowness
social change
ecosystem framework
social construction
social practice
social therapeutic
Social Welfare Action
Alliance, the
solidarity
solidarity economy
somatic healing
songs/singing
sound healing
speculative design
spell
staying with the
trouble
storytelling
street newspaper
strength
perspective, the
sufficiency
sustaining movements
symbol
Tao Institute, the
tarot
temporary autonomous
zones
Theatre of the
Oppressed
theory of change
theosophy
therapeutic writing
togetherness
trauma practice
...
justice
translation
12-step programs
... over anti-
bullying teams
vigil
water
wildness
wintering as metaphor
wishes
witchery
yoga
zinemaking

forest bathing

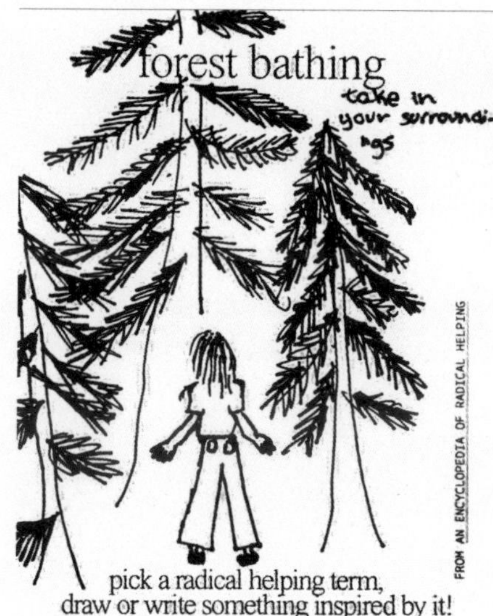

pick a radical helping term,
draw or write something inspired by it!

FROM AN ENCYCLOPEDIA OF RADICAL HELPING

revenge

SOMETIMES THE BEST REVENGE IS LETTING SOMEONE BE EXACTLY WHO THEY ARE

pick a radical helping term,
draw or write something inspired by it!

FROM AN ENCYCLOPEDIA OF RADICAL HELPING

DRAWING PLANTS

IT HELPS ME RELEASE PAIN AND THINK OF NATURE AS A HUMAN BEING

study

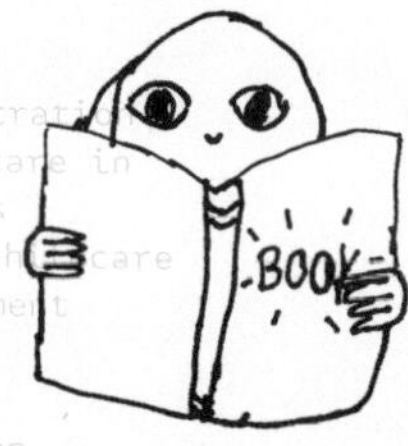

pick a radical helping term,
draw or write something inspired by it!

FROM AN ENCYCLOPEDIA OF RADICAL HELPING

Anonymity

Half baked thought, but: it would be so much easier to use/access the public library if you didn't have to give your data away first. Paperwork & forms are not equally accessible to everyone, & not all people are comfortable + confident leaving copies of their personal information everywhere.

laughter

ENOUGH LAUGHS HERE FOR EVERYONE TO HAVE AT LEAST A FEW!

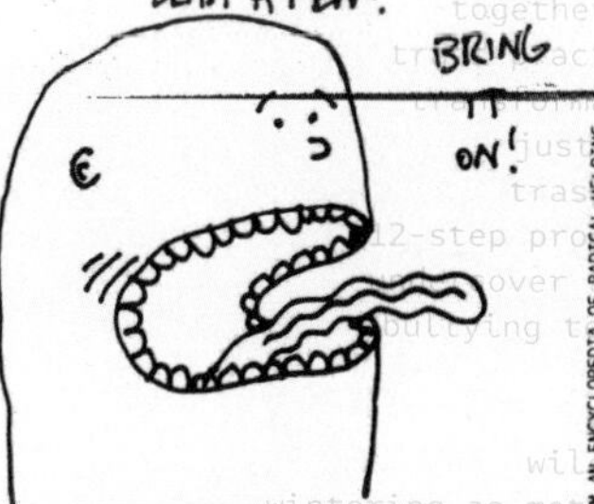

pick a radical helping term,
draw or write something inspired by it!

FROM AN ENCYCLOPEDIA OF RADICAL HELPING

Something that always helps me is when a loved one sits with me when im going through something hard. Usually, just being present with me and allowing me to be in whatever state I'm in and both metaphorically + physically holding me makes me feel loved, seen, heard, and understood. Their connection gives me hope + reminds me that this too will pass.

cove
rumor cycle
Magic School, the
mapping support
marginality
 (as a site of
 resistance)
Marxist social
 work
membership theory
 in social work
mending
metaphor
mikveh
mobile libraries
movement
 lawyering
mutual aid
mycelia as
 metaphor
narradrama
narrative
 medicine
narrative therapy
nepantla/
 nepantleras
nonviolent
 communication
ongoingness
peer counseling
peer-to-peer
 health network
person-situation
 perspective
perspective via
 faith
pleasure
poems/poetry
poetic meter
polarity work
post-
 oppositionality
postwork
 imaginaries
poverty-aware
 social work
paradigm, the
power threat
 meaning (PTM)
 framework
pre(care)ity
prison abolition
professionalism
 without
 performance
progressive
 education
public benefits
public library,
 the
Qigong
radical
 administration
radical care in
 the arts
radical childcare
 in movement
 spaces
radical
 inclusion
radical
 papermaking
radical presence
radical
 social work
Radical Therapist Journal, The
Rank and File
 Movement (RFM)
 in social work

reclaiming selfhood
recognition
redistribution
Reflections on Justi
reflexivi
Rei
relation
interviewing
relationali
resistan
resisting t
parental pos
narrative
resonan
respectful visiti
respite room
rest as resistanc
revenc
revolutiona
mothering
ritua
sanctuar
sandplay therap
saun
seed bankin
sex positivit
shadow integratio
Sick Woman Theor
slow/tactile
slowness
social chang
ecosystem framework
social constructio
social practic
social therapeutic
Social Welfare Actic
Alliance, the
solidarit
solidarity econom
somatic healin
songs/singin
sound healin
speculative desig
spell
staying with the
trouble
storytellin
street newspape
strength
perspective, the
sufficienc
sustaining movemen
symbo
Taos Institute, th
taro
temporary autonomou
zones
Theatre of th
Oppressed
theories of chang
theosoph
therapeutic writin
togetherness
trans practice
transformativ
justice
traspati
12-step program
undercover anti
bullying teams
vigi
wate
wildness
wintering as metapho
wishe
witcher
yoga
zinemakin

decolonial/liberatory based-practices

slowing down w/ tactile information as a break from overly saturated media/ doom scrolling. slowness as a practice of listening to our bodies & instinct.

pick a radical helping term draw or write something

child life

drawing + painting

music

running

prayer

ballet

reading

crocheting

swinging

movies

somatic healing

BODIES. WE ARE OUR BODIES. THERE IS NO SEPARATION. THE PAIN IS THAT WE HAVE BEEN DISCONNECTED.

I HAVE A MESSAGE FOR YOU PLEASE LISTEN

** Farming to heal from orthorexia and bulimia

* specifically WWOOFing on a number of farms representative of our food systems - meat, fruit, vegetables, products, and more

farming as a way to reconnect with nature & care for my body

limited-equity cooperative housing
lingering
love
lunar cycle
Magic School, the
mapping support
marginality (as a site of resistance)
Marxist social work
membership theory in social work
mending
metaphor
mikveh
mobile libraries
movement lawyering
mutual aid
mycelia as metaphor
narradrama
narrative medicine
narrative therapy
nepantla/nepantleras
nonviolent communication
ongoingness
peer counseling
peer-to-peer health network
person-situation perspective
perspective via faith
pleasure
poems/poetry
poetic meter
polarity work
post-oppositionality
postwork imaginaries
poverty-aware social work paradigm, the
power threat meaning (PTM) framework
pre(care)ity
prison abolition
professionalism without performance
progressive education
public benefits
public library, the
Qigong
radical administration
radical care in the arts
radical childcare in movement spaces
radical inclusion
radical papermaking
radical presence
radical social work
Radical Therapist Journal, *The*
Rank and File Movement (RFM) in social work
re-authoring
reclaiming selfhood
recognition
redistribution
Reflecting on Justice
reflexivity
Reiki
relational interviewing